MARIJUANA

Chemistry · Pharmacology · Metabolism and Clinical Effects

Contributors

SUMNER H. BURSTEIN

HABIB EDERY

RAPHAEL MECHOULAM

W. D. M. PATON

R. G. PERTWEE

ELIZABETH TYLDEN

MICHAEL D. WILLINSKY

MARIJUANA

Chemistry · Pharmacology · Metabolism and Clinical Effects

EDITED BY

RAPHAEL MECHOULAM

Laboratory of Natural Products
School of Pharmacy
The Hebrew University
Jerusalem, Israel

ACADEMIC PRESS   New York and London   1973

A Subsidiary of Harcourt Brace Jovanovich, Publishers

ACADEMIC PRESS, INC.
111 Fifth Avenue, New York, New York 10003

United Kingdom Edition published by
ACADEMIC PRESS, INC. (LONDON) LTD.
24/28 Oval Road, London NW1

LIBRARY OF CONGRESS CATALOG CARD NUMBER: 72-77349

PRINTED IN THE UNITED STATES OF AMERICA

If a man declares to you that he has found facts and confirmed them by experience, even though this man is considered most reliable and highly authoritative, be cautious in accepting his opinions and theories . . . For emotion will lead man to irresponsible deeds, particularly in controversy.

MAIMONIDES

Treatise XXV, Aphorism 69 in the "Medical Aphorisms of Moses," by Moshe ben Maimon (Maimonides), ca. end of 12th century. Translation from the Arabic source by J. Schacht and M. Meyerhof.

Contents

List of Contributors xi

Preface xiii

Chapter 1   Cannabinoid Chemistry

Raphael Mechoulam

I.   Introduction 2
II. Historical Overview of the Chemical Research on *Cannabis sativa* 4
III. Isolation and Structural Elucidation of Naturally Occurring Cannabinoids 8
IV. Syntheses of Cannabinoids 31
V.   Cannabinoid Reactions 60
     References 82
     Addendum 88

Chapter 2   Structure–Activity Relationships in the Cannabinoid Series

Raphael Mechoulam and Habib Edery

I.   Introduction 101
II. Assessment of Activity 103
III. Activity of Δ^3-THC Derivatives 107
IV. Activity of the Natural Cannabinoids 115
V.   Activity of Δ^1- and Δ^6-THC Derivatives and Miscellaneous THC Type of Compounds 118
VI. Summary 129
     References 130
     Addendum 133

vii

Chapter 3 Analytical Aspects of Cannabis Chemistry

Michael D. Willinsky

I.	Introduction	137
II.	Noncannabinoid Components	138
III.	Cannabinoid Components	140
IV.	Detection of Cannabinoids in Biological Fluids	153
	References	156
	Addendum	158

Chapter 4 Labeling and Metabolism of the Tetrahydrocannabinols

Sumner H. Burstein

I.	Introduction	167
II.	Preparation of Labeled Tetrahydrocannabinols	168
III.	Metabolism of Labeled Tetrahydrocannabinols	172
IV.	Summary	181
	References	182
	Addendum	183

Chapter 5 The Pharmacology of Cannabis in Animals

W. D. M. Paton and R. G. Pertwee

I.	Introduction	192
II.	Actions of Cannabis	205
III.	Toxicity and Teratogenicity	235
IV.	Metabolism and Fate of Tetrahydrocannabinol in the Body	241
V.	The Active Principles of Cannabis Other Than Δ^1-THC	250
VI.	Cumulation and Tolerance	253
VII.	General Discussion	257
	References	260
	Addendum	265

Chapter 6 The Actions of Cannabis in Man

W. D. M. Paton and R. G. Pertwee

I.	Introduction	288
II.	Effects of Cannabis Involving Perception	291
III.	Perception of Time	297
IV.	Memory	301
V.	Thought Processes	305

VI.	Sense of Unreality and Depersonalization	308
VII.	Feelings of Insight and Significance	309
VIII.	Mood and Emotions	310
IX.	Sleep and Sleepiness, Disinterest, Detachment: The Amotivational Syndrome	312
X.	"Drunkenness" and Light-headedness	314
XI.	Sexual Feeling	314
XII.	Laughter	315
XIII.	General Motor Activity	316
XIV.	Ataxia, Tremor, Reflexes, and Catalepsy	317
XV.	Electroencephalography	320
XVI.	Autonomic and Other Related Effects	320
XVII.	Visceral and Metabolic Effects	324
XVIII.	The Temporal Pattern of Cannabis Action	326
XIX.	Conclusion: Cannabis Action in the Light of Other Psychic Phenomena	326
	References	330

Chapter 7   Clinical Aspects of Cannabis Action

W. D. M. Paton, R. G. Pertwee, and Elizabeth Tylden

I.	Cannabis and Psychiatric Problems	335
II.	Toxicity in Man	357
III.	Therapeutic Potential of Cannabinoids	361
	References	362

Appendix   Formulas of Known Natural Cannabinoids and Metabolites and Some Synthetic Cannabinoids

Raphael Mechoulam

I.	Known Cannabinoids in Cannabis	367
II.	Some THC Metabolites	368
III.	Some Widely Tested Synthetic Cannabinoids	369

Author Index	371
Subject Index	389

List of Contributors.

Numbers in parentheses indicate the pages on which the authors' contributions begin.

SUMNER H. BURSTEIN, Worcester Foundation for Experimental Biology, Shrewsbury, Massachusetts (167)

HABIB EDERY, Israel Institute for Biological Research, Tel Aviv University Medical School, Ness Ziona, Israel (101)

RAPHAEL MECHOULAM, Laboratory of Natural Products, School of Pharmacy, The Hebrew University, Jerusalem, Israel (1, 101, 367)

W. D. M. PATON, Department of Pharmacology, University of Oxford, Oxford, England (191, 287, 335)

R. G. PERTWEE, Department of Pharmacology, University of Oxford, Oxford, England (191, 287, 335)

ELIZABETH TYLDEN,* Psychiatric Department, University College Hospital, London, England (335)

MICHAEL D. WILLINSKY, Department of Pharmacology, University of Toronto, Toronto, Canada (137)

* Present address: 51 Westbourne Terrace, London W2, England.
xi

Preface

Marijuana, hashish, charas, dagga, bhang, and other *Cannabis sativa* L. preparations are estimated to be consumed by 200–300 million people and hence represent the most widely used group of illicit drugs. However, until the late 1950's, the use of cannabis was a minor problem in western society and interest in it was marginal. In recent years the smoking of marijuana by young people in North America and, to a lesser extent, in Western Europe and culturally related countries has assumed epidemic proportions, and public interest in the short- and long-term effects of the drug has become intense. It is a sad truth, however, that until very recently critical scientific evaluations of the different aspects of the problem were few. This lack of pharmacological and clinical data was due, to a large extent, to the fact that the state of our chemical knowledge of cannabis was limited. The use of crude marijuana, or extracts from it, for detailed and reproducible biological work has many disadvantages, the major one being the notorious variability of cannabis preparations. Hence, a firm chemical basis is a prerequisite for quantitative biological work for which pure and well-defined substances are needed. Until 1964 the major active component had not been isolated in pure form and its structure had been known in a general way only. Numerous cannabinoids were known to be present in the plant but only a few had been isolated, and the structure of only one, the psychotomimetically inactive cannabinol, had been fully elucidated.

In the last few years intensive chemical investigations have considerably clarified the chemistry of marijuana. Most natural cannabinoids have been isolated and purified, their structures have been elucidated, syntheses of most of the components have been accomplished, analytical methods have been developed, and metabolic investigations are underway in many laboratories. On this chemical foundation an impressive edifice of pharmacology and experimental psychology has evolved. The number of publications appearing every month on various biological aspects of cannabis action is truly staggering, and the end is nowhere in sight.

The aim of this book is to present the state of the art in cannabis chemistry, in pharmacology, and in the clinic. Although numerous symposia and reviews on cannabis have been published there has not been a book covering all these aspects. I believe that we have answered a need rather than just burdened the library budgets. The chemical chapters, for reasons stated above, present a more complete picture than the metabolic and pharmacological ones. In the latter the gaps in our knowledge are obvious and present a challenge. The most pressing need seems to be for more detailed information on human metabolism and long-term effects of cannabinoids.

Clinical publications differ from laboratory ones: the latter are experimental, the former are frequently just observational. This dichotomy is clearly reflected in the last chapter. Most of the papers cited describe "cases" rather than "experiments." Hence the conclusions drawn may not be accepted as readily by the reader as those of the previous chapters. I believe, however, that in a field so full of contradictions and heated debate the material has been presented objectively.

The contributors have not tried to draw a picture, even if such a picture were possible, from which a clear-cut decision on the social and legal aspects of the problem can be made. To quote Dean Gerald Le Dain, head of the Canadian Royal Commission on the Non-Medical Use of Drugs: "In the end, the decisions in this field are very complex moral decisions based on a number of imponderables and competing values, and in many cases they involve a choice of the lesser of evils. There are few easy choices. There is no way that these kind of decisions can be passed over to experts. In the end, they will have to be handed back to [the public]."

RAPHAEL MECHOULAM

CHAPTER 1

Cannabinoid Chemistry

Raphael Mechoulam

I. Introduction 2
   A. Terms, Scope, and Nomenclature 2
   B. Chemical Literature on *Cannabis sativa* 3
II. Historical Overview of the Chemical Research on *Cannabis sativa* . . 4
III. Isolation and Structural Elucidation of Naturally Occurring Cannabinoids 8
   A. Isolation 8
   B. Chemobotanical Aspects of Cannabinoid Content of *Cannabis sativa* 11
   C. Cannabinol and Cannabivarol 13
   D. Cannabidiol and Cannabidivarol 17
   E. Δ^1-Tetrahydrocannabinol and Δ^1-Tetrahydrocannabivarol . . . 19
   F. Δ^6-Tetrahydrocannabinol 21
   G. Cannabigerol and Monomethyl Cannabigerol 22
   H. Cannabichromene 23
   I. Cannabicyclol 24
   J. Tetrahydrocannabitriol Ester of Cannabidiolic Acid 24
   K. Cannabidiolic Acid 25
   L. Cannabigerolic, Cannabinolic, and Cannabichromenic Acids . . 26
   M. Δ^1-Tetrahydrocannabinolic Acids A and B 26
   N. Cannabielsoic Acids 27
   O. Absolute Configuration of the Cannabinoids 28
   P. Biogenesis 29
IV. Syntheses of Cannabinoids 31
   A. Cannabinol 31
   B. Δ^1-Tetrahydrocannabinol, Δ^6-Tetrahydrocannabinol, Δ^1-Tetrahydrocannabivarol, Cannabidiol, and Cannabidivarol 38
   C. Cannabigerol 50
   D. Cannabichromene and Cannabicyclol 51
   E. Cannabinoid Acids 54
   F. Cannabinoid Metabolites 56

V. Cannabinoid Reactions 60
   A. Acid-Catalyzed Isomerizations and Cyclizations 60
   B. Thermal Reactions 67
   C. Oxidations and Dehydrogenations 71
   D. Photochemical Reactions 75
   E. Additions to Double Bonds 77
   F. Miscellaneous Reactions 80

References 82

Addendum 88

I. Introduction

A. TERMS, SCOPE, AND NOMENCLATURE

In this chapter I propose to review the current status of knowledge on the chemistry of the cannabinoids in a way that will acquaint the nonspecialist chemist with the field.

The term "cannabinoids" has been defined (Mechoulam and Gaoni, 1967b; Mechoulam, 1970) as the group of C_{21} compounds typical of and present in *Cannabis sativa*, their carboxylic acids, analogs, and transformation products. Cannabinoids have not been isolated so far from any other plant or animal species. As the cannabinoids belong to the widely distributed chemical class of natural terpenophenolics, some members of which are chemically very closely related to the cannabinoids, this uniqueness is surprising. In view of the importance of the cannabinoids, this review will concentrate on their particular chemistry; noncannabinoid components of *Cannabis sativa* or its preparations (such as hashish and marijuana) will be discussed briefly, as such *known* constituents are quite unexceptional.

This chapter is an expansion and updating of a review published a few years ago (Mechoulam and Gaoni, 1967b). In the 1967 article a detailed table of physical constants and derivatives of numerous naturally occurring cannabinoids was presented. The infrared spectra of these compounds were also reproduced; hence, they will not be repeated here.

The formulas of the known natural cannabinoids and metabolites as well as those of some synthetic cannabinoids which have been frequently mentioned in the literature are presented in an appendix at the end of this book.

Two numbering systems for the cannabinoids are in use today. In one the formal chemical rules for numbering of pyran type of compounds are used for the tetrahydrocannabinols. For cannabinoids that are not pyrans, this numbering is not applicable; hence, on passing from one compound to another in this series a carbon atom frequently has its number changed. The second nomenclature has a biogenetic basis; the cannabinoids are regarded as substituted monoterpenoids, and the numbering is the accepted one for compounds of this class. It can be used for all cannabinoids; hence, it has the advantage that a carbon atom in the molecule retains the same number in most chemical transformations. As an example, in the following formulas, the major natural tetrahydrocannabinol (THC) and a major inactive component,

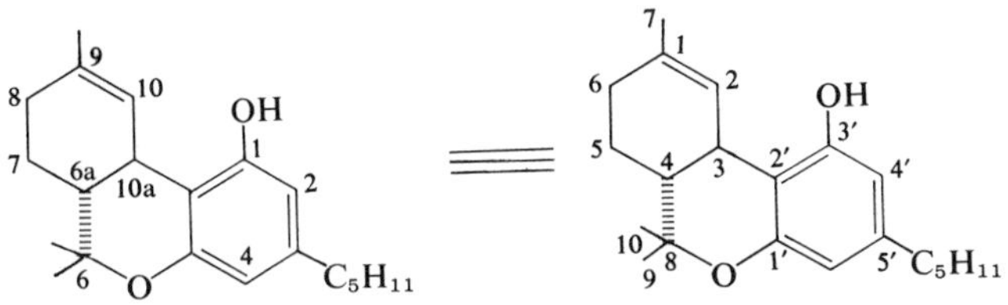

Δ^9-THC Δ^1-THC

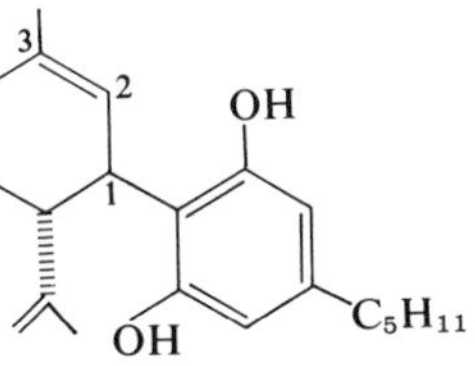

Formal numbering 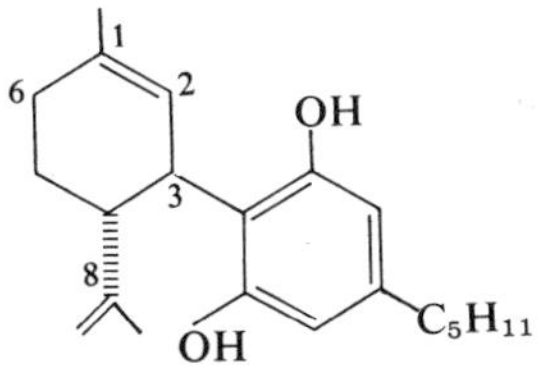   Monoterpenoid numbering
(used in this review)

cannabidiol, are numbered according to both systems. The monoterpenoid numbering only is used throughout this book.*

The full chemical name for Δ^1-THC as used by *Chemical Abstracts* is 3-pentyl-6a,7,8,10a-tetrahydro-6,6,9-trimethyl-6*H*-dibenzo[*b,d*]pyran-1-ol.

B. CHEMICAL LITERATURE ON *Cannabis sativa*

Much of the older work has been critically reviewed by Blatt (1938). Adams (1942) has published a fascinating Harvey Lecture on part of his work. Todd (1946) has presented an overview of the whole field. Schultz (1964), Grlić

---

* Recently *n*-propyl analogs of cannabinoids have been detected in cannabis. The propyl homolog of cannabidiol was named cannabidivarin (Vollner *et al.*, 1969); that of Δ^1-THC was named tetrahydrocannabidivarol (Gill, 1971), tetrahydrocannabivarin (Merkus, 1971; Vree *et al.*, 1971), or propyl-Δ^1-THC (Gill *et al.*, 1970); and the propyl homolog of cannabinol was named cannabidivarol (Gill, 1971) or cannabivarin (Merkus, 1971).

At a recent meeting Merkus and Gill decided that in order to conform with the accepted cannabinoid names, and because these compounds have one or more free phenolic groups, they should be named cannabidivarol, tetrahydrocannabivarol, and cannabivarol. In colloquial usage the names propyl cannabidiol, propyl-THC, and propyl cannabinol will probably continue to be employed.

(1964), and Claussen and Korte (1966b) have published short reviews. The more extensive review by Mechoulam and Gaoni (1967b) has been mentioned. More recently, two summaries have been published (Mechoulam, 1970; Neumeyer and Shagoury, 1971), and the lectures presented at a 1969 symposium on the botany and chemistry of cannabis (Joyce and Curry, 1970) have appeared.

The cannabis field does not suffer from lack of bibliographies. Those mentioned below are not limited to chemical articles alone but cover numerous aspects. The United Nations Commission on Narcotic Drugs (1965) and the *Bulletin on Narcotics* (United Nations Department of Social Affairs, 1951) have published detailed bibliographies. The latter is supplemented every year. Recently the Student Association for the Study of Hallucinogens (STASH) has "dedicated to the Establishment" a very useful and detailed guide to the English-language literature on cannabis (Gamage and Zerkin, 1969). Most articles in this guide are summarized and cross-indexed. Moore (1969) has compiled a bibliography covering the years 1960–1969; Waller and Denny (1971) have published an annotated bibliography of the literature of 1964–1970. It has an extensive subject index, which has been arranged by main topics with "key phrase" subtopics

II. Historical Overview of the Chemical Research on *Cannabis sativa*

A major trend in chemical research throughout the nineteenth century was the quest for active natural products. Numerous alkaloids were isolated in pure form and some of them were partially characterized. Morphine, cocaine, strychnine, and many others were purified and used in medicine. However, most of the major terpenoids were not isolated until the end of the century or even much later, and in many cases their purity was doubtful. The reason behind this disparity is that alkaloids are relatively easy to separate and crystallize, whereas terpenoids are usually present in mixtures whose separation is tedious and in many cases was impossible with the techniques available to the chemist of a hundred years ago. The search for the active component of *Cannabis sativa* is probably one of the best examples. Numerous groups reported initial efforts to obtain an active cannabis component after news of the extensive medical use of its resin in India and the East was widely circulated and the Parisian literary circle around Baudelaire (Walton, 1938) indulged in hedonistic use of Middle Eastern hashish. However, more than a century passed until the major active component, Δ^1-THC, was isolated in pure form and its structure was elucidated.

Tscheepe (1821) seems to have undertaken the first chemical examination of *Cannabis sativa*. His results were unfortunately reported in a thesis only and are unavailable to me for evaluation. Schlesinger (1840) obtained an active extract from the leaves and flowers of hemp; Bohlig (1840) reported a method for the distillation of the fresh plant, which gave a "light yellow oil." Present knowledge suggests that it probably contained mono- and sesquiterpenoids and was not active. Decourtive (1848) described the preparation of an ethanol extract that on evaporation of the solvent gave a dark resin, which he named "cannabin." A resin prepared in a similar manner (called "hashishin") was used by Gastinel (1848) as a drug. Work of closely similar nature was reported by Robertson (1847) and Savory (1843). Smith and Smith (1847, 1848) and Smith (1885) ascribed the physiological action to a resin that they obtained by alcoholic extraction of the dry plant, previously treated with alkali. To the solution "a milk of lime as thick as cream" was added to remove chlorophyll. After filtration and treatment with sulfuric acid the solvent was evaporated. The resin was presumably neutral. This was unusual since most chemists at the time expected the active principle to be, such as those of opium and cinchona, an alkaloid.* The authors record that "two-thirds of a grain of this resin acts upon ourselves as a powerful narcotic, and one grain produces complete intoxication. In this character it is quite analogous to alcohol, but in its hypnotic and soothing effects on the nervous system its resemblance to morphia is very great."

Almost no further progress on the active principle was made for nearly 50 years, although the Pharmaceutical Society of Paris awarded a prize to Personne (1855) for "a good analysis of hemp" (Robiquet, 1857). Personne's volatile oil was shown, however, to be an inactive, impure sesquiterpene (Valente, 1880; Vignolo, 1895).

For some years the possible presence of alkaloids was discussed. Preobraschensky (1876) claimed the presence of nicotine in *Cannabis sativa* resin which he brought with him from China, where he had accompanied an expedition. This was refuted by Kennedy (1886). Jahns (1887) identified choline. Siebold and Bradbury (1881) isolated in a very low yield an oily

---

* It seems that Smith and Smith (1847, 1848) considered their material to be a neutral mixture but never *explicitly* stated that it was not alkaloidal. These articles were curiously misinterpreted and wrongly cited for a century. Wood *et al.* (1896) cite a nonexistent article by T. and H. Smith [*Pharm. J.* 6, 675 (1847)]. Cahn (1931) writes, ". . . it is agreed that the active principle is contained in a high-boiling resin and that it is not alkaloidal, T. and H. Smith, *J. Pharm.* (1857), 21, 47." Todd (1946) states, "In 1857 the brothers T. and H. Smith of Edinburgh showed that the physiologically active principle . . . was not an alkaloid." The reference cited by Todd is T. and H. Smith, *J. Chem. Soc.* 21, 47 (1857). The journal data given by Cahn and Todd, although identical except for the name of the journal, are both incorrect and cannot be traced.

I would like to thank Mr. E. Polacsek of the Documentation Department of the Addiction Research Foundation in Toronto for his kind help in connection with the bibliographic search concerning these papers.

alkaloid, which they named cannabinin. Hay (1883) was able to obtain an alkaloid, tetanocannabin, which possessed strychninelike properties when tested on a frog, while Schulze and Frankfurt (1894) identified trigonellin. Although the balance of evidence was in favor of some alkaloidal substance (in addition to choline and trigonellin) being present in small quantity in Indian hemp, almost no further work along these lines was undertaken. Merz and Bergner (1940) again found that choline and trigonellin were present in hemp, while Obata *et al.* (1960) isolated piperidine. Salemink *et al.* (1965) and Bercht and Salemink (1969) confirmed the presence of choline, trigonellin, and piperidine and suggested the existence of additional bases. Gill *et al.* (1970) showed the presence of unidentified atropinic and muscarinic substances in the watery extract of *Cannabis sativa* as well as the relatively inert trigonellin. Klein *et al.* (1971) have reported the presence of four alkaloids in marijuana, three of which were also found in fresh *Cannabis sativa*. High-resolution mass spectrometry of these alkaloids, named cannabamine A, B, C, and D, suggested the following molecular formulas, respectively: $C_{21}H_{37}N_3O_2$ (or $C_{26}H_{37}N$), $C_{18}H_{21}NO_3$, $C_{14}H_{21}N_3O_3$, and $C_{17}H_{33}N_3O_2$. The total yield of crude alkaloids was 0.02% in dry material and ~0.003% in fresh leaves. Little structural information was presented. The crude alkaloidal mixture caused decreased activity in mice. In view of the low concentration of the alkaloids in the plant it is as yet not possible to determine whether these components are relevant to cannabis activity in man.

At the turn of the century a group in Cambridge (Wood *et al.*, 1896) effected a considerable purification of the components of cannabis by fractional distillation of an ethereal extract from charas. They obtained a terpene, boiling at 160°–180°C (yield 1.5%); a sesquiterpene, boiling at 258°–259°C (yield 2%); a paraffin ($C_{29}H_{60}$?), m.p. 63°–64°C (yield 0.15%); and a high-boiling, viscous oil (yield 33%). The sesquiterpene was apparently identical to that isolated previously by Personne, Valenta, and Vignolo (*vide supra*). The viscous oil ("amber colored when seen in thin layers but ruby red when seen in mass") was assumed to be a single substance, now named cannabinol. The fractions isolated by the Cambridge group were tested by Marshall (1897, 1898). In the Wood *et al.* article (1896) he is quoted as follows:

> The physiological action of the terpenes closely resembles that of the other members of this class, of which ordinary turpentine may be taken as the type. In doses of 0.5 gram they have very little effect and produce none of the characteristic symptoms of cannabis action. The red oil, on the contrary, is extremely active, and taken in doses of 0.05 gram induces decided intoxication followed by sleep. The symptoms produced by it are peculiar to *Cannabis indica*, and as none of the other products appear to possess this action, this substance must be regarded as the active constituent of the plant.

Later Wood *et al.* (1899) and Dunstan and Henry (1898) found that the oil was not homogeneous and isolated from it, after acetylation, a crystalline acetate (25% yield) which could be hydrolyzed to a resinous cryptophenol that analyzed for $C_{21}H_{26}O_2$. To this component they transferred the name cannabinol. Its lack of optical rotation (in contrast to the high negative values of the other major natural cannabinoids known today) and the crystalline acetyl cannabinol and trinitrocannabinol obtained from cannabinol emphasize its purity. Thus, cannabinol represents the first natural cannabinoid to be obtained in pure form. A number of important degradative experiments were carried out with *crude* cannabinol (Wood *et al.*, 1899), but the results remained partially unexplained until the work of Cahn (1930, 1933) in the early thirties. They are discussed more fully in the section dealing with the structure of cannabinol.

It is unfortunate that *pure* cannabinol was not tested at that time for its biological activity. Hence, on the basis of work on crude cannabinol (Marshall, 1898; Fraenkel, 1903) it was wrongly assumed that this component was the active principle of cannabis.

In retrospect it should be pointed out that the isolation of pure cannabinol (via the crystalline cannabinol acetate prepared in a 25% yield from "red oil") had a component of luck. We know today that cannabinol is a minor constituent in fresh cannabis, hashish, or charas and may in fact be an artifact. All the major cannabinoids boil in the same temperature range, and their separation is impossible by distillation. However, in old deteriorated samples the active principle (Δ^1-THC) may have oxidized to cannabinol. The Cambridge group apparently had old charas in which cannabinol represented at least 25% of its red oil.

For over 30 years numerous groups unsuccessfully tried to repeat and expand Wood's findings. As the results were not reproducible with the samples investigated, the work of the Cambridge group was largely ignored. Fraenkel (1903), Czerkis (1907), Casparis and Baur (1927), and Bergel and Wagner (1930) were deceived by the narrow boiling range of the crude active resin into assuming that it was homogeneous cannabinol, to which the formulas $C_{20}H_3O_2$ or $C_{21}H_{30}O_2$ were assigned. The above publications did not help advance the cannabinoid field, although today most of this work can be partially rationalized. Thus, the optical activity of $-150°$ assigned to "cannabinol" by Casparis and Baur (1927) probably shows the presence of considerable amounts of Δ^6-THC ($[\alpha]_D -260°$); the 1.5 hydroxyl groups in the molecule indicate the presence of cannabidiol, etc.

Later developments, starting with Cahn's brilliant reinvestigation of the structure of cannabinol (Cahn, 1930, 1931, 1932, 1933), will be reviewed in the appropriate sections.

III. Isolation and Structural Elucidation of Naturally Occurring Cannabinoids

A. Isolation

The isolation of pure cannabinol by Wood *et al.* (1899) (*vide supra*) could not be repeated until Cahn (1932) reported its preparation from hashish seized from smugglers in Egypt (therefore probably of Eastern Mediterranean origin), as well as from *Cannabis indica* resin of known Indian origin. A portion of the ether extract of hashish boiling at 260°–270°C/25 mm was redistilled and the main fraction of red oil boiling mostly within 4°C was acetylated to give a 28% yield of crystalline acetyl cannabinol, which had a melting point identical with that reported by Wood.

The isolation of cannabinol was later (Work *et al.*, 1939) improved when it was found that its *p*-nitrobenzoate was so sparingly soluble that it precipitated from solution even when present in relatively small amounts in a cannabinoid mixture.

Adams *et al.* (1940a) extracted marijuana with ethanol, removed the lower terpenes by steam distillation, and distilled under high vacuum the residual water-insoluble resin. The red oil thus obtained when treated with 3,5-dinitrobenzoyl chloride in pyridine gave cannabidiol bis-3,5-dinitrobenzoate, m.p. 106°–107°C (47%). We can rationalize today that this extremely high yield reflects the presence of both cannabidiol and cannabidiolic acid. The latter undergoes decarboxylation on distillation to give cannabidiol. In retrospect, it is of some historic interest that the major portion of the component (cannabidiol) which formed the basis of the structural work of Adams was in actuality an artifact of the extraction procedure. The filtrate from the precipitate of the cannabidiol derivative was hydrolyzed and treated with pyridine hydrochloride. The latter reagent destroys cannabidiol. Cannabinol, m.p. 75°–76°C, was obtained, through its urethane, from the residue. Large amounts of both cannabidiol and cannabinol was obtained by the above procedure.

Shortly thereafter Haagen Smit *et al.* (1940) and Powell *et al.* (1941) reported the isolation of active material from "red oil." The component, m.p. 128°–129°C, isolated by Haagen-Smit by distillation and crystallization was named "cannin." A dose of 0.1 mg/kg caused ataxia in a dog. No further work on cannin has been reported, and the experimental details of the isolation procedure are too meager to allow repetition. The active principle isolated by Powell *et al.* was an oil from which a crystalline 3,5-dinitrophenylurethane, m.p. 216°C, was obtained. Hydrolysis of the urethane produced an oily product which was less potent than red oil itself. It is impossible to evaluate these two articles today. One can only surmise that in actuality Haagen-Smit's compound is identical with Δ^2-THC, m.p. 128°C, an artifact isolated many years later by Korte *et al.* (1965c) on distillation of a cannabinoid mixture. Powell's material seems to be cannabinol contaminated with Δ^1-THC.

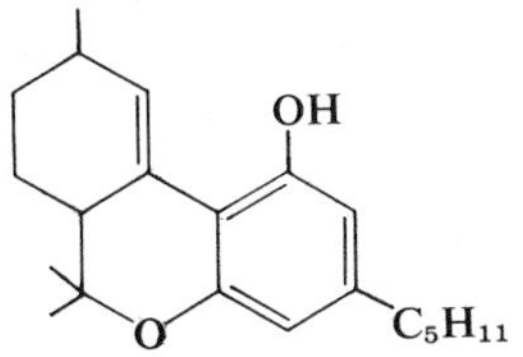

Δ^2-THC

Wollner *et al.* (1942) acetylated the red oil obtained from highly potent charas and the product was purified by molecular distillation. The oily acetate obtained was cleaved by ammonolysis to yield a THC that was not identical with various synthetic or semisynthetic products prepared by Adams (1942). Acetylation of this THC was also reported to give a product different from the acetate from which the THC was originally obtained. This is an indication that at least some isomerization had taken place. Dehydrogenation led to cannabinol. No definite structure was, however, put forward. The rotation reported, $[\alpha]_D -193°$, falls between the values accepted today for Δ^1-THC ($[\alpha]_D -150°$) and Δ^6-THC ($[\alpha]_D -266°$) and it is probable that Wollner's THC was in fact a mixture of these two THC's.

Wollner's work is the last in a long list of attempts to isolate cannabis components by distillation. The use of this technique over many decades was only marginally successful, as most cannabinoids boil within the same temperature range and separation of the constituents by distillation is feasible only if one of the components is present in relatively high concentration. Wollner's report also marks the end of an era of cannabinoid research. Although the active component had not been isolated in pure form and its structure was unknown, this field of investigation was almost completely neglected for the next 20 years.

In the 1950's two groups isolated cannabidiolic acid from the acidic fraction of hemp grown for fiber (Krejči and Šantavý, 1955; Kabelik *et al.*, 1960; Schultz and Haffner, 1958). A chromatographic separation of some cannabinoids was reported by de Ropp (1960) from the Lederle Laboratories. Mexican marijuana was extracted with methanol and the extract was chromatographed on a Florisil column, followed by a partition chromatography on Celite and high-vacuum distillation. Cannabinol and cannabidiol were identified on paper chromatography by comparison with authentic samples from Adams' work 20 years earlier. A third oily component, presumed to be a THC, was also isolated, although there was a marked discrepancy between the analytical values found and those calculated for a THC. The positive ataxia test and the infrared spectrum of this material tend to substantiate the assumption that a THC was obtained. The purity of this material, however, is difficult to determine. No structural work on this component was reported.

The first authenticated case of isolation in a pure form of an active cannabis principle, Δ^1-THC, was reported in 1964 (Gaoni and Mechoulam, 1964a, 1971). A hexane extract of hashish was separated into acidic and neutral fractions. Repeated chromatography of the neutral fraction on Florisil, acid-washed alumina, and alumina containing 12% silver nitrate eluted the following compounds (in order of increasing polarity): (1) a mixture of waxy, noncannabinoid materials, (2) cannabicyclol, (3) cannabidiol, (4) Δ^1-THC, (5) cannabinol, (6) cannabichromene, (7) cannabigerol, and (8) polar constituents and polymers. All cannabinoids were obtained in crystalline form, except Δ^1-THC and cannabichromene, of which crystalline derivatives (Δ^1-THC: 3,5-dinitrophenylurethane, m.p. 115°–116°C; cannabichromene: 3,5-dinitrophenylurethane, m.p. 106°–107°C) were prepared. On hydrolysis pure Δ^1-THC and cannabichromene were obtained. From the acidic fraction, after esterification the methyl esters of cannabinolic acid, cannabidiolic acid, and cannabigerolic acid were obtained by column chromatography (Mechoulam and Gaoni, 1965b). In these isolations THC acid A was not detected, as on separation between acidic and neutral material (by extraction with base) most of this acid remains in the neutral phase or gives a gummy residue. When direct chromatography of the hexane extract of hashish is done on silicic acid, Δ^1-THC acid A, and in some samples Δ^1-THC acid B, can also be isolated (Mechoulam et al., 1969). The cannabielsoic acids are sparingly soluble in petroleum ether or hexane but can be extracted with benzene from the residue remaining after the hexane extraction. They can be purified by column chromatography on silica gel (Shani and Mechoulam, 1970).

The fractions and pure compounds isolated were tested for cannabis-type activity in rhesus monkeys (Mechoulam et al., 1970b). It was shown that except for Δ^1-THC no other major psychotomimetically active compounds were present in hashish.

Recent work in the author's laboratory has indicated that the base separation of acidic and neutral components causes the formation of new, as yet unidentified components (Yagen and Levy, 1970). These can be obtained by base separation at low temperature for a very short period of time; the neutral fraction is then chromatographed on silicic acid.

Korte and Sieper (1960) reported the isolation of crystalline cannabidiol from red oil by countercurrent distribution. The important Δ^1-THC acid A (Korte et al., 1965a) was first isolated by this method. Later cannabichromene (Claussen et al., 1966), cannabicyclol (Claussen et al., 1968a), cannabidivarol (Vollner et al., 1969), and cannabitriol ester of cannabidiolic acid (von

Spulak *et al.*, 1968) were also obtained by this technique. In the initial publications (Korte and Sieper, 1965) the presence of numerous THC's was indicated. Further purification, however, showed the presence of a single THC; the other components assumed to be THC's were found to be isomeric cannabinoids. A certain disadvantage in the countercurrent technique is that the solvent system contains dimethylformamide, which is difficult to remove and frequently contaminates the isolated products. Yamauchi *et al.* (1967) have reported that Δ^1-THC acid A thus obtained contains traces of this high-boiling solvent.

Hively *et al.* (1966) have reported the isolation of Δ^6-THC from a petroleum ether extract of the flowering tops and leaves of *Cannabis sativa* grown in Maryland. By chromatography on silicic acid followed by rechromatography on silver nitrate–silicic acid, cannabinol, Δ^1-THC, Δ^6-THC, and cannabidiol were obtained.

Turk *et al.* (1969) have published a careful study of the isolation of cannabinoids from marijuana; highly purified Δ^1-THC was obtained by chromatography on silicic acid containing silver nitrate. Conditions for preparative gas chromatography of cannabinoids have been reported (Turk *et al.*, 1971). Davis *et al.* (1970) have described the large-scale preparation of cannabinoids.

Reports on the isolation of unidentified cannabinoids have appeared intermittently for a few decades. Cannabol, $C_{21}H_{30}O_2$ (*p*-phenylazobenzoate, m.p. 117°–118°C), was isolated together with cannabidiol by Jacob and Todd (1940a). A crystalline component, m.p. 129°–133°C, was obtained by Covello (1948). It was reported to have a highly inebriating effect on a dog. The melting point and biological activity recall the compound isolated by Haagen-Smit *et al.* (1940) (*vide supra*). Obata and Ishikawa (1966) obtained a Gibbs-positive component (named cannabitriol), m.p. 170°–172°C, from Japanese hemp. Although a noncannabinoid formula, $C_{16}H_{24}O_3$, was attributed to this compound, its infrared spectrum is quite similar to those of most cannabinoids and hence cannabitriol probably belongs to this class of compounds.

Numerous phenolics and sugars (Hegnauer, 1964), terpenoids (Nigam *et al.*, 1965; Bercht *et al.*, 1971; Simonsen and Todd, 1942), and nitrogen bases (see Section II) have been identified in *Cannabis sativa*.

B. CHEMOBOTANICAL ASPECTS OF CANNABINOID CONTENT OF *Cannabis sativa*

It is generally accepted that *Cannabis sativa* grown around the Mediterranean (Greece, Lebanon, North Africa), in Afghanistan, Persia, West Pakistan, parts of India, and Sinkiang yields a product more potent than that from the plant grown in Mexico or the United States. Hemp grown for industrial purposes is assumed to be essentially devoid of psychotomimetic activity (Bouquet, 1950, 1951; Kabelik *et al.*, 1960). A further well-rooted bit of cannabis folklore is that only the female plant yields the active resin.

Investigations into these chemobotanical aspects have been initiated in the last few years. A useful classification has been suggested by Grlić (1962, 1964). Samples in which cannabidiolic acid predominates are considered "unripe"; those with a high THC content are "ripe," and those with a high cannabinol content are "overripe." These terms indicate biogenetic evolution and are not a measure of seasonal variation of chemical content. Grlić has reported that *Cannabis sativa* seeds from a number of countries yield plants whose resins are of varying degrees of "ripeness." Korte and Sieper (1965) have shown that *Cannabis sativa* var. "Indica" and var. "non-Indica" grown in Germany under identical conditions yield resins of different content. In the Indian variety the ratio of cannabidiol to THC was 1:1, while that of the non-Indian variety was 2:1. In a further investigation, Claussen and Korte (1968a) found that German and Swiss hemp contain cannabidiolic acid as their major cannabinoid, while South African and Balkan types (grown in Germany) yield mostly THC acid. Ohlsson *et al.* (1971) have investigated different parts of cannabic plants (both male and female) grown in Sweden from seeds originating from Turkey, Czechoslovakia, Caucasus, Morocco, and Sweden as well as plant samples from Lebanon. Although cannabinoids were found in all parts of the plant, they were most abundant in the flowering tops and the small leaves surrounding the flowers. There was little variation in the relative amounts of cannabidiol and Δ^1-THC; in absolute terms, the concentration of THC was generally higher in plants grown in Lebanon or from Moroccan seeds. Similar results have been reported by Fetterman *et al.* (1971b). These investigations have been interpreted as indicating that the type of cannabinoids produced by the plant is dependent on the inherited properties of the seed and that the influence of the climate is limited. It has further been speculated that, as "good marijuana quality" cannabis seeds can easily be shipped from one country to another, there is no valid base for attempts to correlate the cannabinoid content with geographical source.

Male and female plants on a weight basis produce roughly the same amounts of cannabinoids and show the same degree of activity (Valle *et al.*, 1968; Ohlsson *et al.*, 1971; Fetterman *et al.*, 1971b).

The above conclusions conflict sharply with those of a number of prior investigations. Bouquet (1950, 1951) has reviewed work of his own and others. He claims that plants grown in France from seeds brought from India become after two or three generations completely similar to indigenous plants. The converse also holds good. He also mentions that the Viceroy Mehemet Ali in Egypt attempted to grow hemp for cordage. New seed had to be brought from Europe periodically as the hemp plants soon became incapable of producing good fiber; instead they began to secrete abundant quantities of psychoactive resin. Bouquet's conclusion is that "hemp tends to be similar or different from the characteristic type according to the conditions in which it is grown."

It is possible to reconcile the modern exact analytical data with the older work, apparently produced at a more leisurely pace, if it is assumed that the first generations of cannabis grown from imported seeds do indeed follow largely their genetic character but the environmental influence becomes more apparent after a few generations.

The widely held belief that only female plants contained active resin was probably due to the agricultural practice of eliminating male plants from cannabis plantations in order to prevent fertilization; female plants then apparently produce better resin.

Phillips *et al.* (1970) have reported that the amounts of cannabidiol and Δ^1-THC in fresh plants increase and then decrease a number of times over several months. The THC content was found to be high when cannabidiol content was low and vice versa. This "peaking" phenomenon has not yet been rationalized.

Numerous groups have reported analyses of cannabis preparations. It is frequently difficult to compare these results, as in most cases stored dry material was analyzed. The period of storage is seldom known or indicated, and in the case of confiscated materials the exact origin is uncertain. Some analytical data are presented in Chapter 3. One chemobotanical aspect only will be discussed here. Some samples (and presumably fresh plants) show the presence of considerable amounts of cannabinoids usually absent or found in trace amounts only in most other samples. This seems to be the case with Δ^6-THC (Hively *et al.*, 1966), Δ^1-THC acid B (Mechoulam *et al.*, 1969), tetrahydrocannabivarol (propyl-Δ^1-THC) (Gill *et al.*, 1970), and cannabigerolic acid methyl ether (Shoyama *et al.*, 1970). In the absence of concrete evidence one can speculate that these variations are genetic in character and contribute to the known difference in quality of cannabis batches.

C. CANNABINOL AND CANNABIVAROL

The structure of cannabinol (**1**) was established largely by Cahn (1930, 1931, 1932, 1933) through a reinvestigation of the degradations reported earlier by Wood and some new reactions. The following discussion is a retrospective evaluation of these investigations and does not always follow a chronological order or the structures originally put forward.

By treating a cold acetic acid solution of "crude cannabinol" with fuming nitric acid, Wood *et al.* (1899) obtained a number of amorphous nitro derivatives, which were probably mixtures, and a bright yellow, crystalline trinitrocannabinol, $C_{21}H_{23}O_2(NO_2)_3$ (**2**). Further oxidation of the latter with

Cannabinol (1)

hot nitric acid gave nitrocannabinolactone (**3**). This compound had previously been described as "oxycannabin" by Bolas and Francis (1869). Reduction of **3** with red phosphorus and hydroiodic acid gave the amino derivative **4**, m.p. 120°C, which was converted to the iodo compound **5**, by diazotization with sodium nitrite in hydrochloric acid and iodination with potassium iodide. Reduction of **5** with sodium amalgam in basic solution, followed by acidification, formed cannabinolactone (**6**), which on alkali fusion led to *m*-toluic acid (**7**). Oxidation of **6** with basic potassium permanganate gave cannabinolactonic acid (**8**), m.p. 203°C, which on alkali fusion was converted to isophtalic acid (**9**).

Hydroxycannabinolactone (**10**) was prepared via diazotization and replacement of the amino group of **4**. Alkali fusion of **10** gave 6-hydroxy-*m*-toluic acid (**11**) and acetone.

The structures of cannabinolactone (**6**) and cannabinolactonic acid (**8**) were unequivocally established by synthesis (Bergel and Vögele, 1932) from 4-isopropyl-*m*-toluic acid (**12**). Oxidation of **12** with chromic trioxide in acetic acid/potassium bisulfate gave a mixture of cannabinolactone (**6**) and 4-isopropylisophthalic acid (**13**). Further oxidation of **6** with potassium permanganate led to cannabilactonic acid (**8**), which was identical with a product known in the literature (Bargellini and Forli-Forti, 1910). The structure of **8** was also supported by its conversion to trimellitic acid (**14**) (Cahn, 1932).

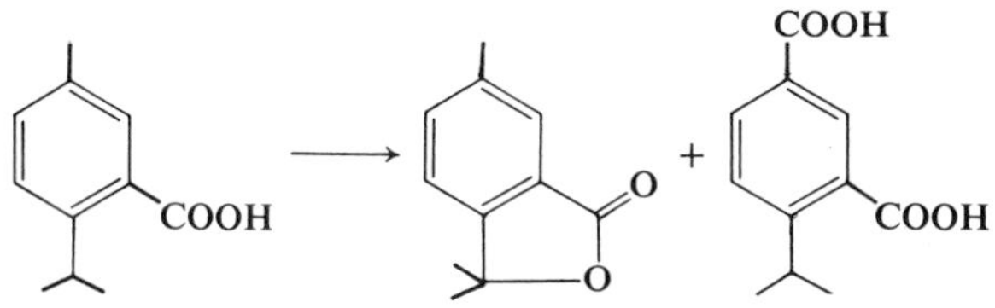

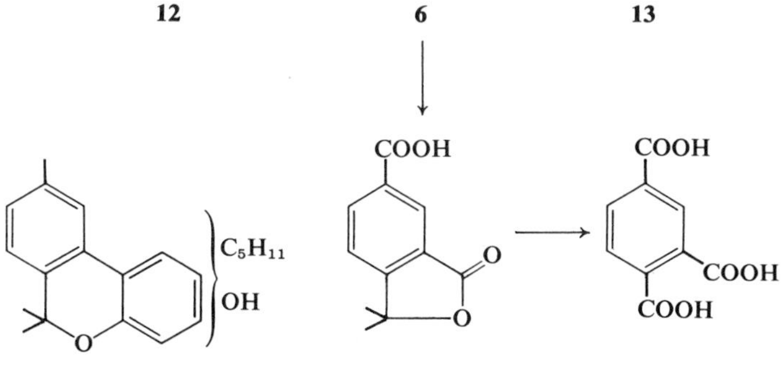

The above-described investigations account for 11 of the 21 carbon atoms in cannabinol. In the rest of the molecule the presence of a free crypto phenolic group and a ring oxygen atom were established by functional group analysis. Since *n*-caproic acid was found among the oxidation products of cannabinol, the existence of an *n*-amyl substituent on the phenolic ring was postulated. These overall results made it possible for Cahn to suggest the partial tentative dibenzopyran formula **15** in which the relative positions of the *n*-amyl and hydroxyl groups were uncertain.

Model syntheses (Cahn, 1933) strongly supported the plausibility of **15**. Anthranilic acid diazonium sulfate and *p*-cresol gave the methyl lactone **16**,

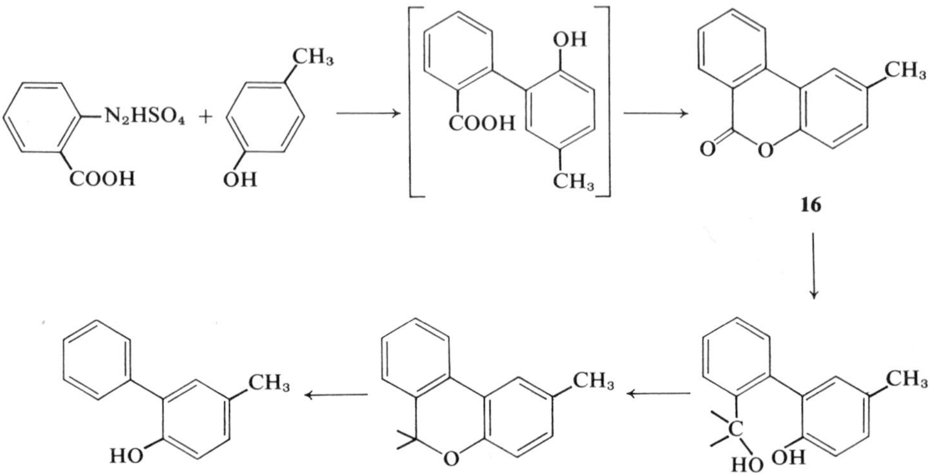

which on addition to an excess of methylmagnesium iodide was converted to the alcohol **17**. Dehydration of the latter gave the pyran **18**. This material is very stable to extreme basic conditions or even to boiling in 50% sulfuric acid. However, concentrated hydrochloric acid at 200°C converted it to the crystalline phenol **19**. This dealkylation takes place also with acetyl cannabinol to give, after hydrolysis, the diphenol **20**, m.p. 61°–62°C. The fact that this reaction took place with both cannabinol and **19** was assumed to indicate that the two compounds were closely related. The structure determinations of these compounds are based on analyses and, in the case of **20**, on oxidation with nitric acid to 6-nitro-*m*-toluic acid (**21**). The diphenol **20** gives a positive

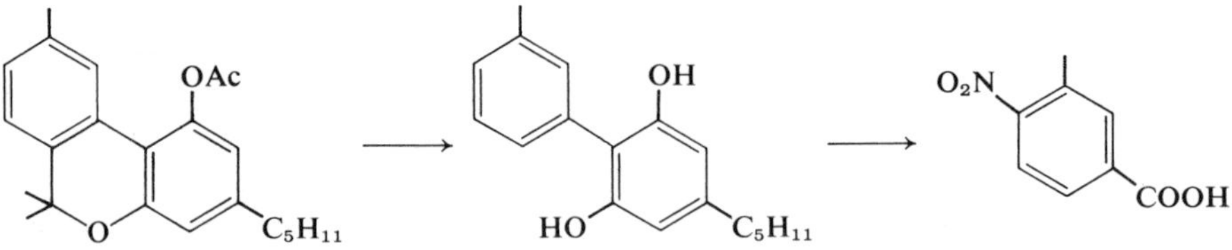

Cannabinol acetate   **20**   **21**

Beam test (purple color in alkaline solution in presence of air), which seems to be typical for 2,5-disubstituted 1,3-diphenols (Mechoulam *et al.*, 1968a). Assuming the validity of the dibenzopyran skeleton, 12 variants of **15** are possible. A strong positive indophenol reaction indicated that the position para to the phenolic hydroxyl was unsubstituted (Jacob and Todd, 1940b); consequently the number of varieties was reduced to four. The ready dinitration of cannabinol required that the free aromatic positions were meta to each other, leaving a choice between **22** and **1**. Structure **1** was ultimately established by total syntheses which will be discussed in the appropriate section.

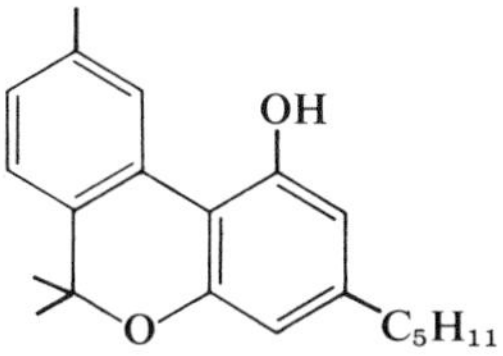

Cannabinol (1) 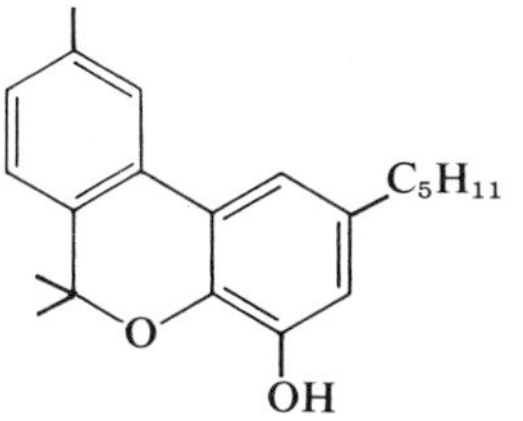   22 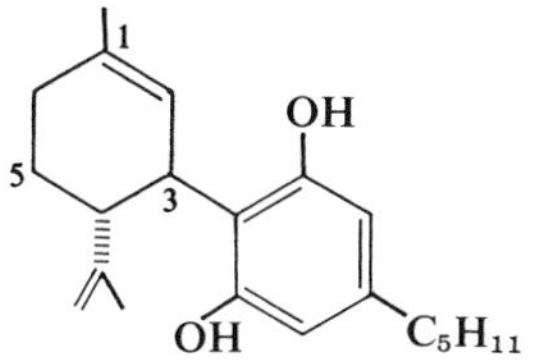   Cannabidiol

Merkus (1971) isolated from Nepalese hashish a new component named cannabivarol. Its physical data [nuclear magnetic resonance (nmr) and mass spectra] correspond to the *n*-propyl homolog of cannabinol. Vree *et al.* (1971) have confirmed this observation.

D. CANNABIDIOL AND CANNABIDIVAROL

Adams *et al.* (1940b) showed that cannabidiol contained two double bonds, one of which was terminal. Hydrogenation produced a tetrahydrocannabidiol (**23**), which could be degraded to a menthanecarboxylic acid (**24**). The latter was correlated with menthol, whose stereochemistry was at the time unknown. Cannabidiol was cleaved by pyridine hydrochloride at a high temperature into the C_{10} and the C_{11} compounds, *p*-cymene and olivetol. The two fragments (C_{10} + C_{11}) contained all the carbons of the natural molecule. Cannabidiol was also correlated with cannabinol by ring closure and dehydrogenation. The above data could be accounted for by partial formula **25**. The position of the ring double bond and the stereochemistry were not determined. Tentatively the double bond was placed at Δ^5. The arguments used for this assignment have not withstood more recent work.

Mechoulam and Shvo (1963) examined the nmr spectrum of cannabidiol. Three olefinic protons were observed: two belonging to the terminal methylene group, and only one on the cyclohexene ring. As the ultraviolet (uv) spectrum eliminated the possibility of conjugation with either the second double bond or the aromatic ring, the cyclohexene double bond had to occupy positions Δ^1 or Δ^6. The later position was eliminated on the basis of the chemical shift of the C-3 proton (at δ3.81), which indicated that it was deshielded by both a double bond and the aromatic ring. An nmr analysis of the chemical shifts of two derivatives, **23** and the epoxy compound **26**, supported this assignment.

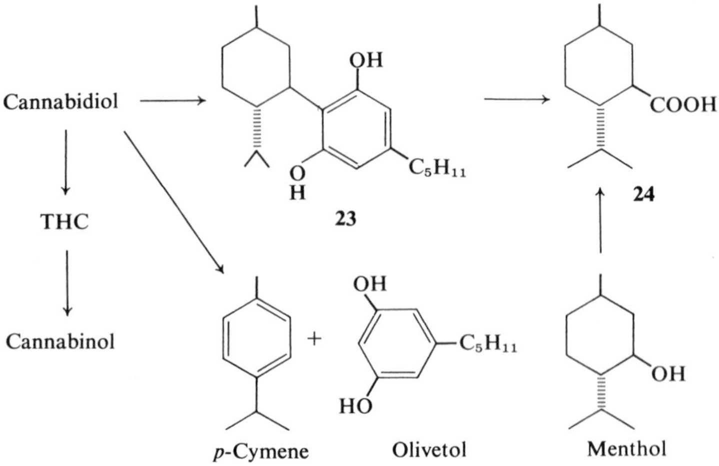

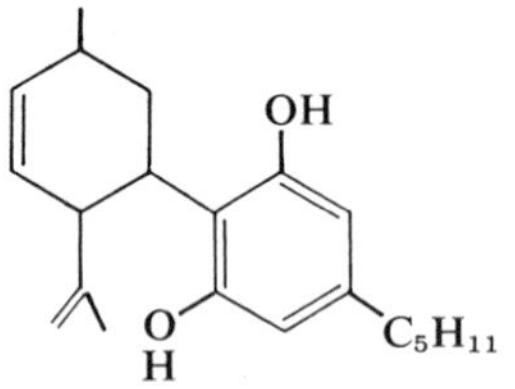

The relative stereochemistry of the two chiral centers was established as trans on the basis of the large coupling constant ($J = 11$ cps) of the protons at these centers. The dihedral angle between these protons was assumed to be 180° to account for this observation. Chemical evidence gave additional support to these conclusions. Menthanecarboxylic acid, a degradation product of cannabidiol, was shown to possess the stereochemistry depicted in structure **24**. Attempted equilibration of the methyl ester of **24** showed that the carbomethoxyl group was equatorial and trans to the isopropyl group. Assuming that the degradation leading to **24** caused no inversion at C-3, the stereochemistry of **24** and cannabidiol should be identical, i.e., trans. The conclusions regarding the position of the double bond and the stereochemistry of the chiral centers were of importance, as it was later shown that most natural cannabinoids follow the same structural and stereochemical pattern.

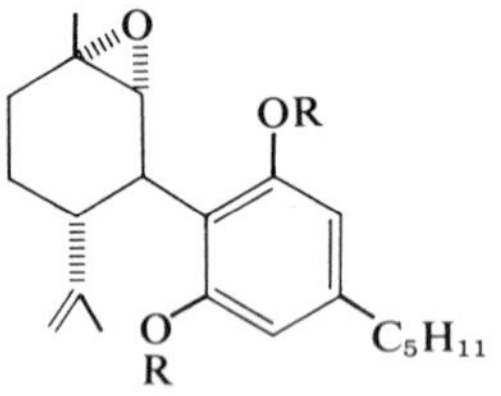

The same conclusions were reached by Šantavý (1964) through analysis of the optical rotation data reported in the older literature. These data, however, are not always reliable owing to uncertainty as to the purity of materials described in the literature in the 1940's.

The minor component cannabidivarol (Vollner *et al.*, 1969; Vree *et al.*, 1971) was shown by mass spectrometry and nmr to be a homolog of cannabidiol. It has a propyl instead of an amyl side chain.

E. Δ^1-Tetrahydrocannabinol and Δ^1-Tetrahydrocannabivarol

The structure of Δ^1-THC was established by spectroscopic measurements and chemical correlations (Gaoni and Mechoulam, 1964a, 1971). The uv spectrum indicates that the double bond is not conjugated with the aromatic ring. The nmr spectrum shows the presence of only one aliphatic methyl group and of three methyl groups, which are either α to an oxygen or are vinylic. These observations place the double bond in the Δ^1 or Δ^6 position. A comparison of the chemical shifts of the C-2 and C-3 protons of Δ^1-THC and cannabidiol provided an insight into the stereochemistry and conformation. The olefinic proton (at $\delta6.35$) in Δ^1-THC is deshielded as compared to that in cannabidiol ($\delta5.59$), while the reverse relationship exists as regards the C-3 protons (3.14 and 3.85, respectively). It was suggested that in cannabidiol the aromatic ring can rotate freely, and in its preferred conformation it is perpendicular to the terpene ring. The C-3 proton is in the plane of the aromatic ring and is deshielded. In Δ^1-THC the additional ring tilts the aromatic ring so that the latter is now nearly in the same plane as the olefinic proton, which is deshielded. Such an effect is possible only if the protons of the two chiral centers are trans and the double bond occupies the Δ^1-position.

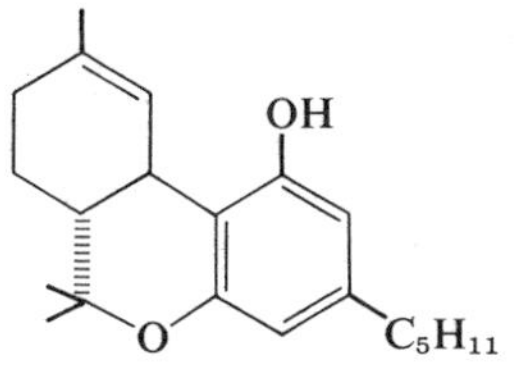

Δ^1-THC 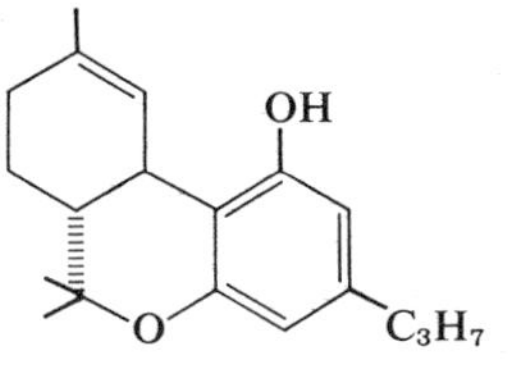 Δ^1-Tetrahydrocannabivarol (propyl-Δ^1-THC) Δ^6-THC

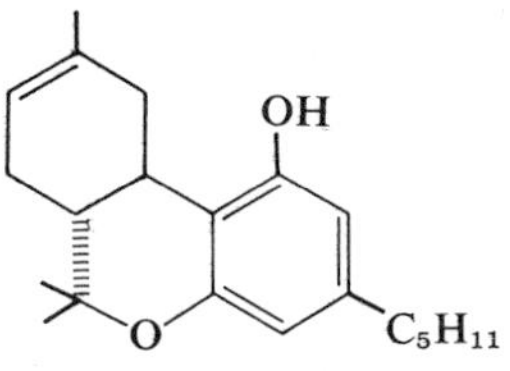

The structure of the carbon skeleton of Δ^1-THC was determined by conversion to cannabinol by dehydrogenation. Later numerous total syntheses (see Section IV) and chemical conversions (see Section V) gave additional support to the proposed structure. When reported in 1964, Δ^1-THC was the first active component whose constitution was fully elucidated.

Archer *et al.* (1970) reported a detailed conformational analysis of Δ^1-THC. From Westheimer and extended Hückel molecular orbital calculation, structures, and energies were obtained. In Fig. 1 the conformation and charge distributions are summarized. Figure 2 depicts the conformation of Δ^1-THC as obtained from a Dreiding model. The distance between one of the C-8

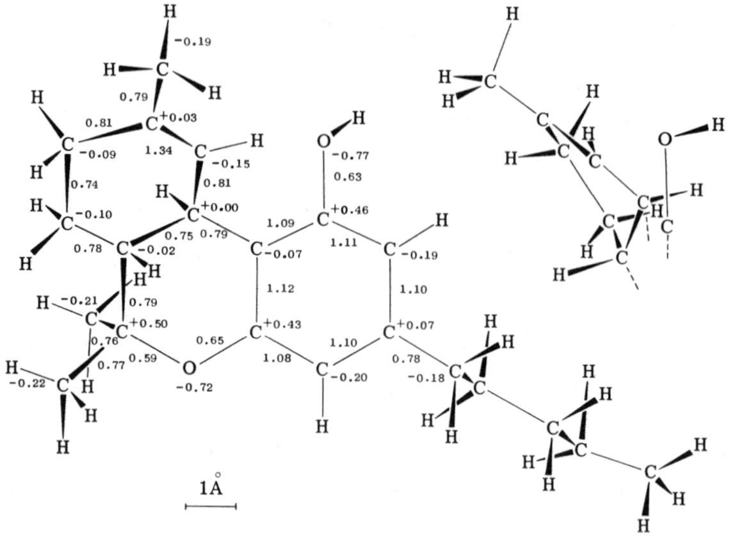

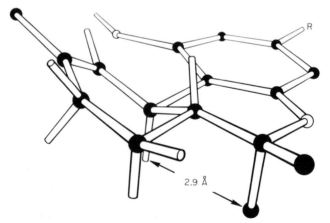

Fig. 1. Conformation and charge distributions of Δ^1-THC. [Archer *et al.* (1970). Reprinted with permission of the authors and the *Journal of the American Chemical Society*.]

methyl groups and the hydrogen on C-3 was derived from Westheimer calculations. It was conclusively shown that ring B adopts a conformation in which the C-8 methyl group is axial and the optimized C-3–C-4–C-8–O dihedral angle is 56°. The cyclohexene ring is expected to exist predominantly in a half-chair conformation. The dihedral angle between rings A and C (C-1′–C-2′–C-3–C-4 dihedral angle) is only 19°. A further interesting con-

Fig. 2. Conformation of Δ^1-THC. [Archer *et al.* (1970). Reprinted with permission of the authors and the *Journal of the American Chemical Society*.]

clusion is that the hydroxyl group, due to steric interaction with the C-2 proton, is bent out of the plane of the benzene ring and the hydroxyl proton optimizes at a position away from ring C. It was also found that Δ^3-THC is considerably more stable than Δ^1-THC, an observation that is in accord with experimental data.

The above theoretical conclusions and the original nmr assignments made 6 years earlier (Gaoni and Mechoulam, 1964a) on a 60 MHz instrument were substantiated and refined by nmr measurements on a 220 MHz spectrometer. Spin-decoupling and nuclear Overhauser effect determinations at 100 MHz and pyridine solvent shifts were employed for defining the three-dimensional identity of the Δ^1-THC system. Thus, irradiation at the high-field methyl singlet (C-8 axial methyl) results in a 17% increase in the intensity of the C-3 proton, while irradiation at the lower-field methyl singlet (C-8 equatorial methyl) causes no effect. These results establish that the two methyl groups are in a different steric relationship to the C-3 proton, a conclusion in accordance with the conformation drawn in Fig. 2. A further example is the exceptionally large pyridine solvent shift of the C-4' aromatic proton ortho to the free phenolic group. It is rationalized that the –OH group in the predominant syn conformation (due to interaction with the C-2 hydrogen) is closer to the C-4' proton than in simpler phenolic systems; hence, the aromatic proton experiences a greater deshielding effect from proximal pyridine molecules coordinated to the OH group.

Tetrahydrocannabivarol has been found in samples of Pakistani and Nepalese hashish by Gill *et al.* (1970) and Merkus (1971), respectively. The structure was established by physical methods and confirmed by synthesis (Gill, 1971). This propyl-Δ^1-THC represented 2% of the crude cannabis tincture base of Pakistani origin as compared to 2.4% of Δ^1-THC. In Nepalese hashish, tetrahydrocannabivarol represented 2.3–5.7% of the total amount of cannabinoids, while Δ^1-THC varied from 3.4 to 11.5%. By contrast, in our analyses of Lebanese hashish by gas chromatography using synthetic tetrahydrocannabivarol as standard, we seldom found more than traces of this material. However, Vree *et al.* (1971) report that all cannabis samples contain at least minor amounts. This observation was made by the use of a new technique combining mass spectrometry and gas-liquid chromatography (glc). Examination of published gas chromatographic analyses of cannabis of various origins indicates that propyl-Δ^1-THC is not a major constituent of most samples.

F. Δ^6-Tetrahydrocannabinol

The cyclization of cannabidiol to Δ^6-THC was first reported by Adams *et al.* (1940f,g), who also converted Δ^6-THC to cannabinol by dehydrogenation, thus establishing the overall carbon skeleton.

The establishment of the stereochemistry of cannabidiol (Mechoulam and Shvo, 1963) determined also that of Δ^6-THC. The structure put forward was later corroborated by physical measurements: mass spectrum (Budzikiewicz et al., 1965) and nmr (Gaoni and Mechoulam, 1966c; Hively et al., 1966). These measurements also established the position of the double bond, whose location was not firmly based in the earlier work. The identification of Δ^6-THC as a minor active constituent prompted a considerable amount of work on the synthesis of this compound (see Section IV,B).

Archer et al. (1970) reported a detailed nmr study of Δ^6-THC, comparable to that described for Δ^1-THC. Exact chemical shifts and coupling constants were established in both deuterochloroform and pyridine-d_5. Of particular interest is the finding that the signal at $\delta 3.22$, previously assigned to the C-3 proton, is in fact that of the equatorial C-2 proton, which is strongly deshielded by the aromatic ring. The C-3 proton signal is at $\delta 2.70$. These assignments are based on spin-decoupling data. Chemical work supports the nmr work. Mechoulam et al. (1972) labeled the C-3 position with deuterium. As expected from the work of Archer et al. the signal at $\delta 3.22$ remains while that at $\delta 2.70$ disappears.

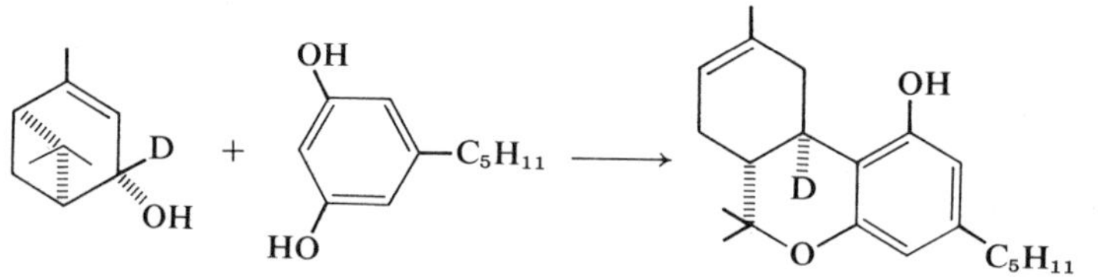

The conformations of ring B and the phenolic hydroxyl group in Δ^6-THC are essentially identical to those in Δ^1-THC (see Fig. 2). This was established (Archer et al., 1970) by an analysis of pyridine solvent shifts and nuclear Overhauser effects.

G. Cannabigerol and Monomethyl Cannabigerol

These minor components are the sole neutral natural cannabinoids whose oxidation level is lower than that of cannabidiol and Δ^1-THC.

The structure of cannabigerol was established by Gaoni and Mechoulam (1964b, 1971). The presence of two double bonds was ascertained by microhydrogenation. The uv spectrum showed that the double bonds are not conjugated. The nmr spectrum indicated that the two aromatic protons are magnetically equivalent, that the protons of the C-8 methylene group are strongly deshielded and split by a single adjacent proton, and that three olefinic methyl groups are present. On the assumption that the C-10 side chain is of the normal monoterpenoid type these findings indicate structure 27. This structure has been supported by syntheses (see Section IV,C). The stereochemistry at the C-6 double bond is supported by its synthesis from geraniol; the isomeric **28** is obtained from nerol.

Cannabigerol monomethyl ether (Yamauchi *et al.*, 1968) has been isolated from a Japanese chemotype of *Cannabis sativa*.

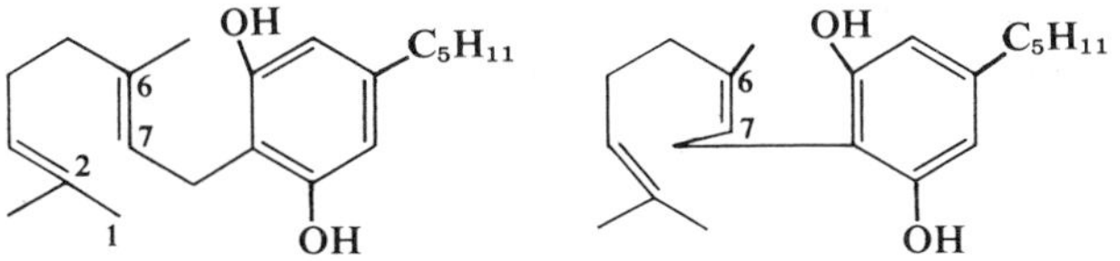

27   28

H. CANNABICHROMENE

Two groups (Claussen *et al.*, 1966; Gaoni and Mechoulam, 1966a, 1971) independently isolated and established the structure of cannabichromene. By a curious coincidence both groups assigned the same name to this material.

The uv spectrum of cannabichromene indicates conjugation of a double bond with the aromatic ring. The nmr spectrum shows that (a) the two aromatic protons are magnetically nonequivalent and that one of the methyl groups on the terpene moiety is α to an oxygen atom, thus determining the point of attachment of the ether oxygen atom, the other oxygen atom being in a free phenolic group, (b) two of the olefinic protons are not flanked by any hydrogen atoms (sharp AB pattern), and (c) the second double bond is in an isopropylidene grouping. These findings are compatible only with structure **29**.

Cannabichromene has been correlated with cannabigerol. Boiling the latter with acid gives a mixture of **30** and **31**. Reduction of **31** produces tetrahydrocannabichromene.

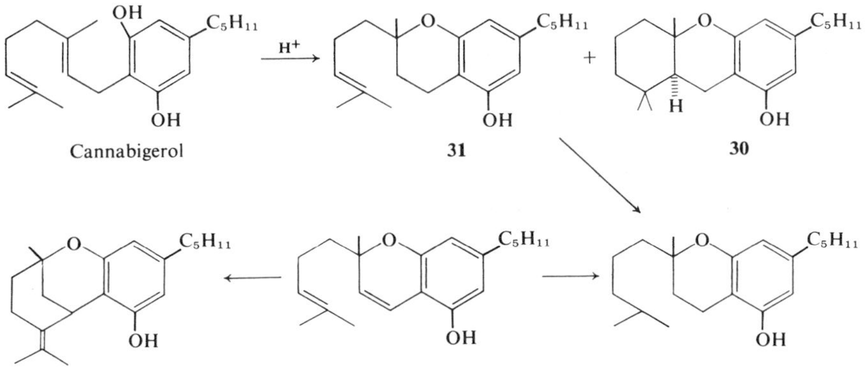

Cannabigerol   31   30

$\Delta^{4(8)}$-iso-THC (**32**)   Cannabichromene (**29**)

Cannabichromene was originally reported to have $[\alpha]_D$ +3.4° or $[\alpha]_D$ −9°. Later work (Gaoni and Mechoulam, 1968) showed that when purified further cannabichromene is optically inactive. The 3,5-dinitrophenylurethane of cannabichromene, m.p. 106°–107°C, has likewise no rotation. Cannabichromene has been correlated with cannabidiol through **32**. The latter compound when obtained from cannabidiol has a rotation of $[\alpha]_D$ −300°, while when prepared from cannabichromene shows no rotation. It seems that natural cannabichromene is indeed racemic and that the rotations recorded were due to impurities.

I. CANNABICYCLOL

This minor, optically inactive, crystalline component was independently isolated by Korte and Sieper (1964) and by Mechoulam and Gaoni (1967b). The latter group suggested the name cannabicyclol and put forward structure **33** as a working hypothesis. The same structure was derived by Claussen *et al.* (1968a), who named the compound cannabipinol. These formulations were based on the uv spectrum, which is typical for the olivetol moiety, and the nmr spectrum, which shows two nonequivalent aromatic protons, four methyl groups, none of which is olefinic but at least one of which is α to an oxygen atom, and no olefinic protons. As cannabicyclol has no double bonds, the elemental composition requires a tetracyclic structure. Crombie and Ponsford (1968b, 1971) showed by a more refined nmr analysis that the benzilic C-3 proton is a doublet (see, however, Kane, 1971) and not a multiplet as required by **33**. The new structure **34** was put forward. This structure has been supported by unequivocal syntheses from cannabichromene (see Section IV,D). Recently, dibromocannabicyclol has been analyzed by X-ray crystallography (Begley *et al.*, 1970). Structure **34** was indeed found to be the correct one. The same structure was deduced from a detailed nmr analysis (Kane, 1971) on a 300 MHz instrument.

J. TETRAHYDROCANNABITRIOL ESTER OF CANNABIDIOLIC ACID

This constituent (**35**) is the first example of a dimeric cannabinoid (von Spulak *et al.*, 1968). On acid treatment **35** is cleaved, dehydrated, and decarboxylated into cannabinol and cannabidiol [on thin-layer chromatographic (tlc) evidence]. A mass spectral analysis of silylated **35** established the molecular weight; the major peaks observed in the spectrum were rationalized on the basis of formula **35**. The nmr spectrum indicates the presence of a cannabidiolic acid moiety in the molecule, as well as a secondary hydroxyl group. Catalytic hydrogenation leads to hexahydro-**35**. In **35** the C-2 proton appears as a singlet while in hexahydro-**35** it is a doublet, indicating that the hydroxyl group is allylic. The chemical shifts, however, seem to be unusual: In **35** the C-2 proton signal is at δ4.35 while in hexahydro-**35** it is at δ4.42. Structure **35** seems to require additional confirmation.

Recent work in the author's laboratory (Yagen and Levy, 1970) indicates the presence of considerable amounts of dimeric cannabinoids. Their behavior under pyrolitic conditions may be of relevance to cannabis smoking.

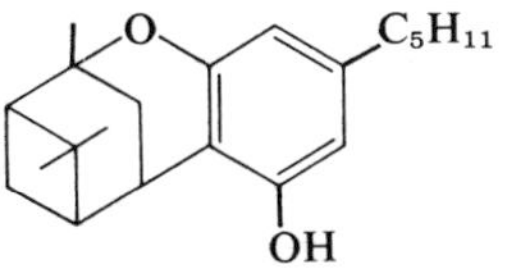

33 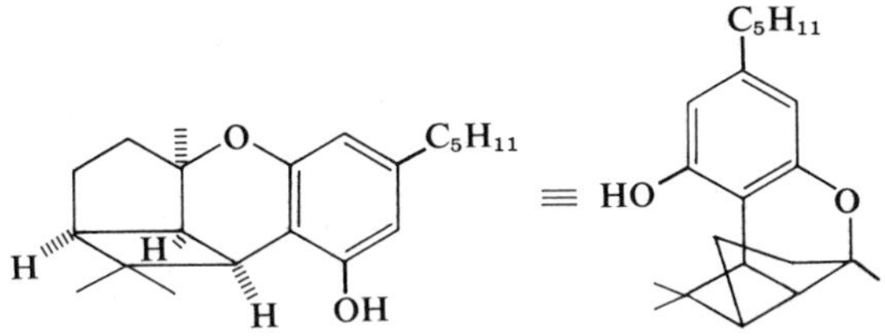   **34**

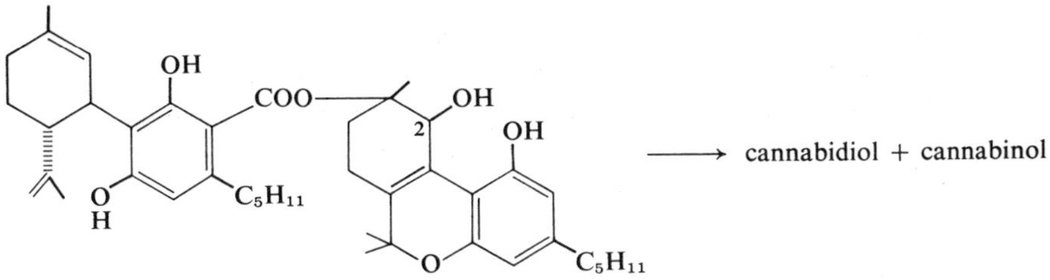

⟶ cannabidiol + cannabinol

35

K. CANNABIDIOLIC ACID

This major cannabis component was first assigned structure **36** on the basis of its conversion on decarboxylation to cannabidiol (Krejči *et al.*, 1958, 1959; Schultz and Haffner, 1958), which at that time was considered to possess structure **26**. The aromatic position of the carboxyl group was established from the strong peak at 1698 cm^{-1} in the infrared spectrum. The modification of the structure of cannabidiol necessitated a parallel revision in the structure of cannabidiolic acid (Mechoulam and Gaoni, 1965b). In the nmr spectrum a signal of one aromatic proton only was observed.

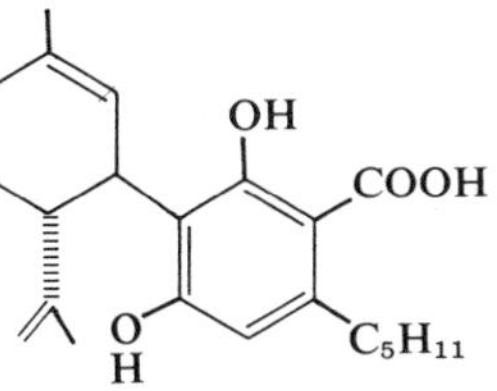

Cannabidiolic acid

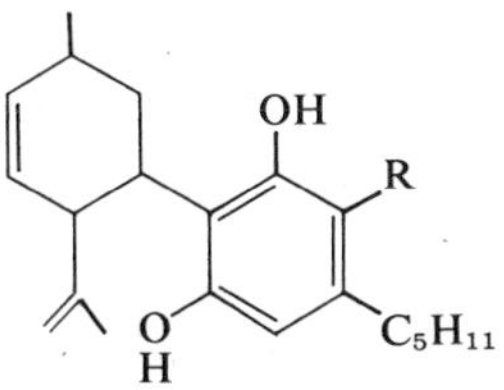

36, R = COOH
26, R = H

L. Cannabigerolic, Cannabinolic, and Cannabichromenic Acids

The structures of cannabigerolic and cannabinolic acids were established by Mechoulam and Gaoni (1965b) by comparison of the nmr spectra of their methyl esters with those of cannabigerol and cannabinol. These spectra are essentially identical except that in the esters one observes a *single* aromatic proton only and an additional methyl signal. The carbomethoxyl group also causes a small deshielding effect on the benzylic methylene protons of the amyl side chain. This effect is also observed in cannabidiolic acid. In cannabinol the two aromatic positions are not equivalent and the existence of two acids is possible. However, only one cannabinolic acid has so far been observed. The carboxyl group is adjacent to the free hydroxyl group. This was established by the strong deshielding of the phenolic proton caused by hydrogen bonding. Cannabigerol and cannabinolic acids are easily converted to cannabigerol and cannabinol. Cannabigerolic acid monomethyl ether has been found in Japanese hemp (Shoyama *et al.*, 1970).

The structure of cannabichromenic acid (Shoyama *et al.*, 1968) was established on the basis of evidence essentially parallel to that employed for the structure elucidation of the above two acids. On decarboxylation cannabichromenic acid is converted to cannabichromene.

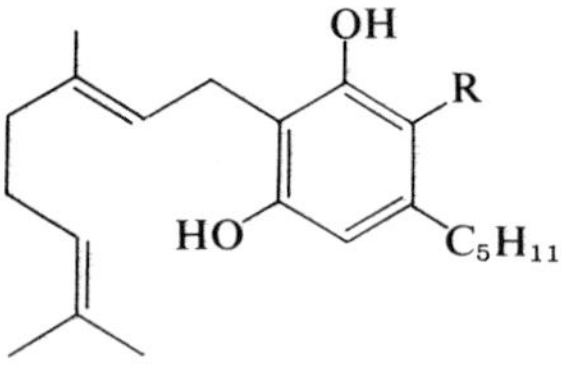

R = H, Cannabigerol
R = COOH, Cannabigerolic acid

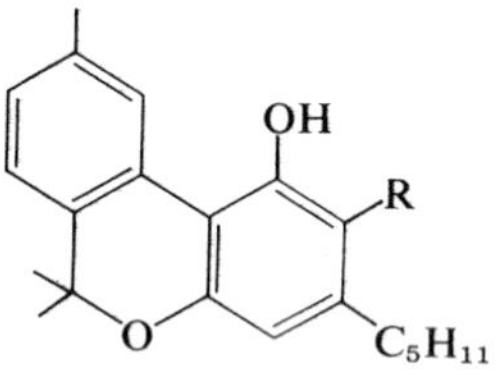

R = H, Cannabinol
R = COOH, Cannabinolic acid

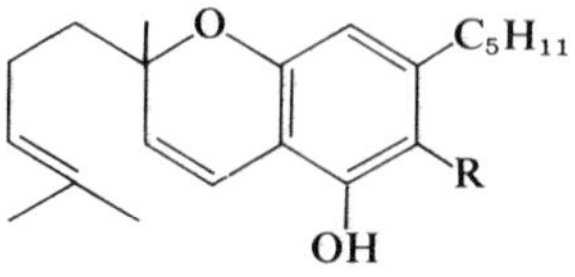

R = H, Cannabichromene
R = COOH, Cannabichromenic acid

M. Δ^1-Tetrahydrocannabinolic Acids A and B

The structure of Δ^1-THC acid A (Korte *et al.*, 1965a) was established on the basis of its nmr spectrum, which corresponds to that of Δ^1-THC. The carboxyl group is adjacent to the phenolic group. Strong hydrogen bonding is observed in both the nmr and infrared spectra.

The spectroscopic properties of Δ^1-THC acid B (Mechoulam *et al.*, 1969) are closely related to those of Δ^1-THC acid A but are by no means identical. Thus, no hydrogen bonding is observed in either the nmr or the infrared spectra. As Δ^1-THC acids A and B are isomeric and are both converted on decarboxylation to Δ^1-THC, the lack of hydrogen bonding in Δ^1-THC acid B places the carboxyl group on a position ortho to the etheric oxygen.

In Δ^1-THC acid B the carboxyl group has lost its coplanarity to the aromatic ring, probably in order to relieve the steric strain caused by the presence of the adjacent groups. In the A series this effect is minimized by hydrogen bonding with the free phenolic group. This conclusion has been drawn from comparison of the infrared and uv spectra of the two THC acids and their methyl esters. Thus, in the B series the carboxyl and carbomethoxy groups absorb between 1710 and 1725 cm^{-1}, while those in the A series absorb at 1615–1650 cm^{-1}.

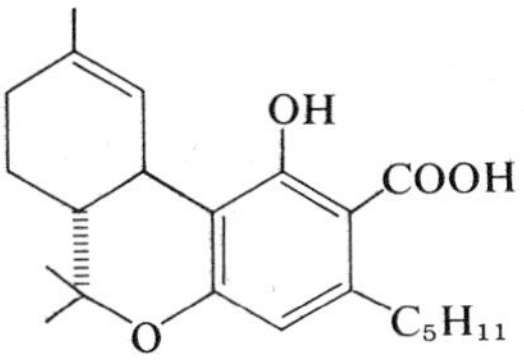

Δ^1-THC acid A 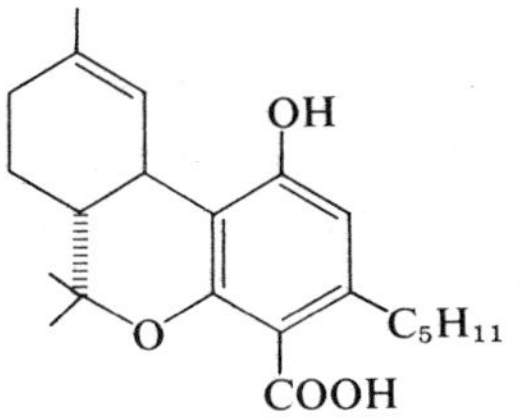 Δ^1-THC acid B

N. CANNABIELSOIC ACIDS

The nmr spectrum of the methyl ester of cannabielsoic acid A (**37**) indicates the presence of one aromatic proton, a terminal methylene group, two methyl groups, one of which is vinylic and the other α to an oxygen, a hydrogen-bonded phenolic group, the C-2 proton at $\delta 4.12$ (a doublet), and the C-3 proton at $\delta 3.38$ (a double doublet). Irradiation of the C-2 proton collapses the signal of the C-3 proton to a doublet; irradiation of the C-3 proton collapses the C-2 proton signal to a singlet.

The aliphatic hydroxyl group does not undergo acetylation. On the basis of these and mass spectral data, structure **37** was put forward (Shani and Mechoulam, 1970). This formulation has been supported by a chemical correlation. Cannabielsoic acid A on reduction, decarboxylation, and dehydration gives the tricyclic **38**. This compound can also be obtained from the olivetyl pinene **39** on irradiation or distillation.

The terpenoid and furanoic rings of the cannabielsoic acids are probably cis. This relationship has been suggested by analogy to related tricyclic dihydrobenzofuran systems formed by radical processes.

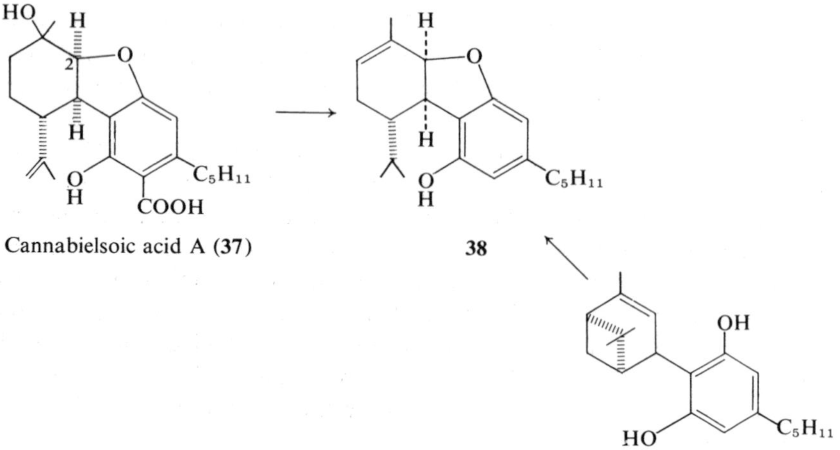

Cannabielsoic acid A (37)　　　　　　　　38

39

In cannabielsoic acid B the carboxyl group is not hydrogen bonded with the phenolic group. The infrared spectra of the carboxyl and carbomethoxy groups of cannabielsoic acids A and B and their methyl esters bear the same relationship as those of the Δ^1-THC acids A and B (*vide supra*).

O. ABSOLUTE CONFIGURATION OF THE CANNABINOIDS

The absolute configuration at both chiral centers (C-3 and C-4) in cannabidiol is (R). As Δ^1-THC, Δ^6-THC, the Δ^1-THC acids, cannabidiolic acid, and cannabielsoic acid A have been correlated with cannabidiol, this determination establishes their absolute configurations as well.

Cannabidiol on reduction gives a mixture of the two C-1 epimers of tetrahydrocannabidiol (Adams *et al.*, 1940b; Mechoulam and Gaoni, 1967a; Gaoni and Mechoulam, 1971). The chromatographically more polar isomer **39** was oxidized with potassium permanganate in acetone to give, after purification and esterification, the methyl ester of menthanecarboxylic acid (**40**), $[\alpha]_D$ −40°. The same ester **40**, $[\alpha]_D$ −40°, was obtained from natural menthol, through the chloride **41**, followed by carboxylation and methylation. Hydrolysis of both methyl esters give an identical menthanecarboxylic acid, m.p. 64°–65°C, $[\alpha]_D$ −44°. The configuration of all chiral centers in menthol is known from interrelation with glyceraldehyde.

The absolute configuration of cannabidiol was confirmed by total syntheses which started from optically active terpenes with known chirality (Petrzilka *et al.*, 1967; Mechoulam *et al.*, 1967, 1972).

The above configuration is not relevant to cannabichromene, cannabicyclol, and cannabichromenic acid, which are optically inactive. It is uncertain whether it applies to the dimeric cannabinoid, cannabitriol ester of

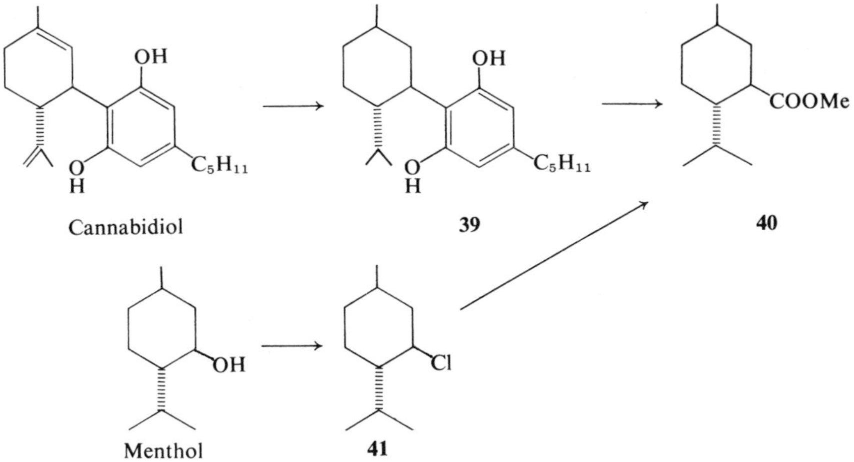

Cannabidiol   39   40

Menthol   41

cannabidiolic acid. The rotation of this compound is $[\alpha]_D +105°$, which contrasts with the strongly negative values obtained for the other optically active cannabinoids.

P. BIOGENESIS

Todd (1946) has suggested that the cannabinoids may be formed initially in the plant by condensation of a menthatriene with olivetol. Schultz and Haffner (1960) examined numerous fresh cannabis plants and reported that cannabidiolic acid is by far more predominant than cannabidiol. They assumed that olivetolic acid, and not olivetol, is the aromatic species involved in the primary condensation.

The isolation of numerous new cannabinoids, in particular cannabigerol and cannabigerolic acid, has made possible a more detailed formulation of the biogenetic process (Mechoulam, 1970). As no experimental work on cannabinoid biogenesis has been published, Scheme 1 should be viewed as a working hypothesis only. The scheme relates mainly to the neutral cannabinoids. The acidic constituents, which may in actuality be the primary products of cannabinoid biogenesis, are formed if olivetolcarboxylic acid is the initial aromatic precursor of the sequence.

Geraniol phosphate, a common biogenetic precursor of terpenoids, may condense with olivetol to form cannabigerol. Oxidation produces 8-hydroxy-cannabigerol (**a**), which for stereochemical reasons cannot be converted directly to cannabidiol. Through allylic rearrangement, however, it can produce the hypothetical intermediate **b**, which can then cyclize to cannabidiol. Alternatively, although less probably, intermediate **a** can form by stereomutation the intermediate **c**, which produces cannabidiol. The latter leads to Δ^1-THC and cannabinol. Cannabidiolic acid on irradiation (or with a radical initiator) in the presence of oxygen gives the cannabielsoic acids. Intermediate **a** can cyclize as such, or through the symmetric species **d**, into cannabichromene, which on irradiation cyclizes to cannabicyclol.

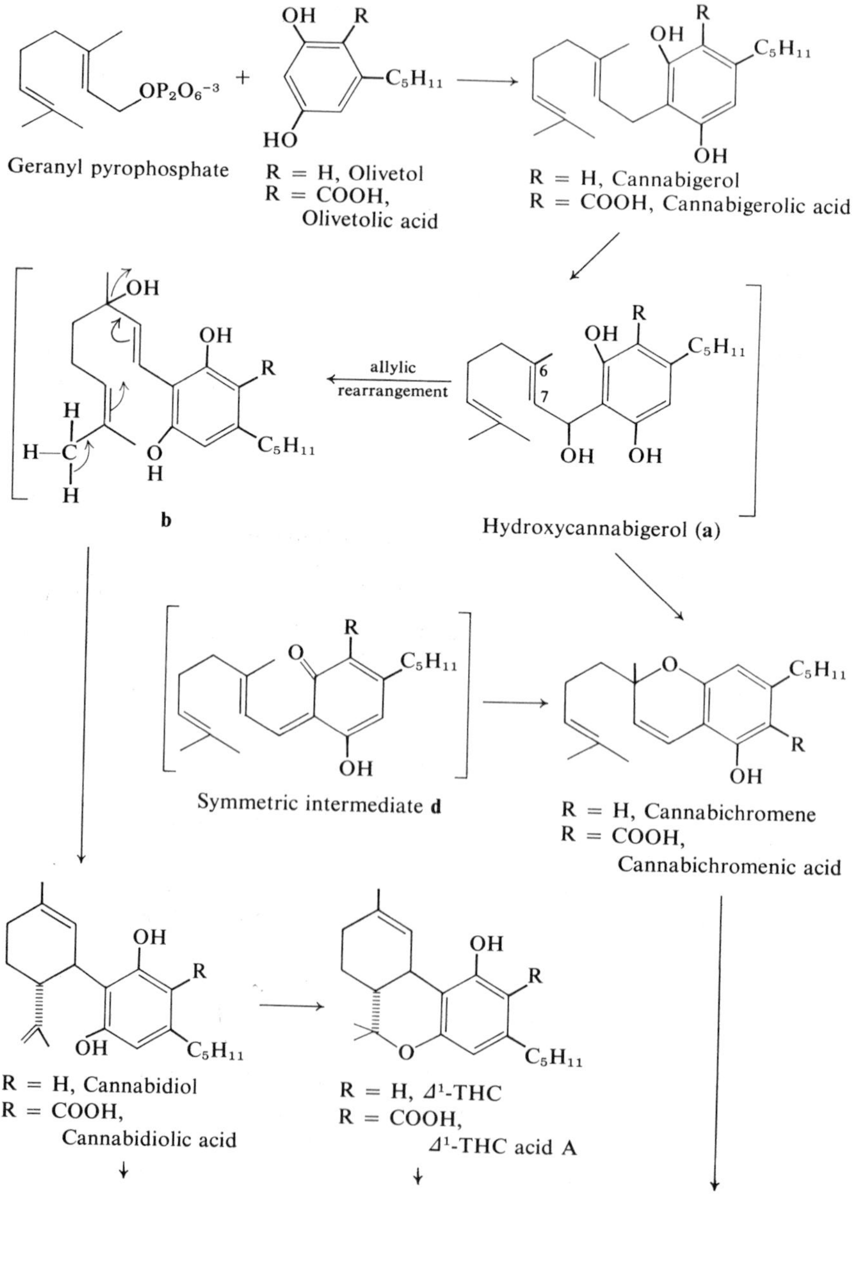

Geranyl pyrophosphate

R = H, Olivetol
R = COOH,
    Olivetolic acid

R = H, Cannabigerol
R = COOH, Cannabigerolic acid

allylic
rearrangement

b

Hydroxycannabigerol (**a**)

Symmetric intermediate **d**

R = H, Cannabichromene
R = COOH,
    Cannabichromenic acid

R = H, Cannabidiol
R = COOH,
    Cannabidiolic acid

R = H, Δ^1-THC
R = COOH,
    Δ^1-THC acid A

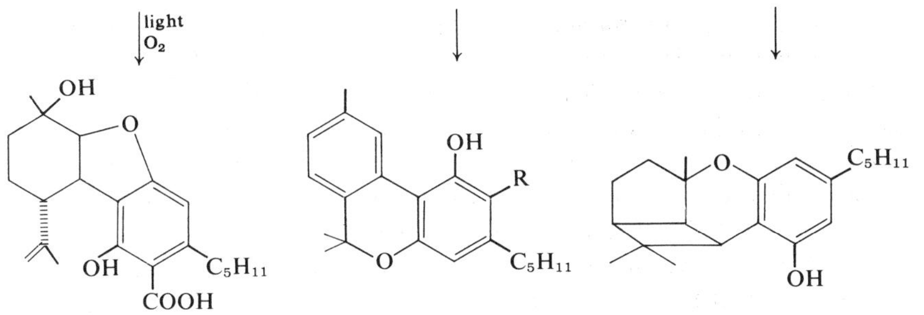

Cannabielsoic acid A   R = H, Cannabinol   Cannabicyclol
                              R = COOH,
                                 Cannabinolic acid

a   c   ⟶ cannabidiol

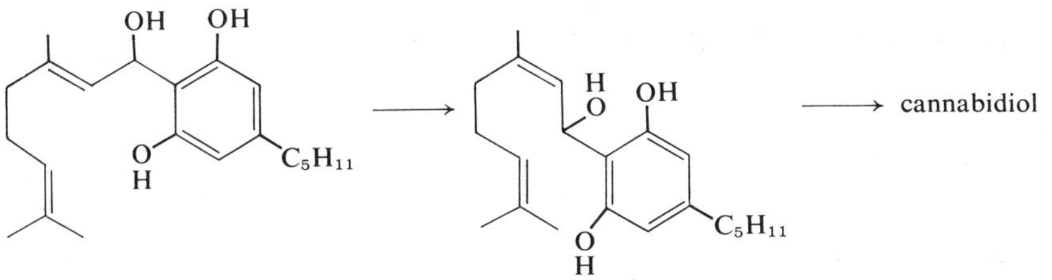

Scheme 1. Proposed biogenesis of the cannabinoids.

The optical inactivity of cannabichromene and cannabicyclol (Gaoni and Mechoulam, 1971) and of cannabichromenic acid (Yamauchi, 1970) makes uncertain their status as natural products. This point needs clarification. If cannabichromene were produced through the symmetric **d**, optical activity would not be expected.

Hydroxycannabigerol (**a**) has not been isolated so far. It is a possible, although not a necessary, intermediate. In the biogenetic sequence it merely serves to indicate that cannabigerol has to be brought to a higher state of oxidation.

Cannabinol and cannabinolic acid are formed with ease *in vitro* from Δ^1-THC and Δ^1-THC acid A, respectively (Levine, 1944; Shoyama *et al.*, 1970). Hence, it is doubtful whether they are true natural products.

IV. Syntheses of Cannabinoids

A. Cannabinol

Cahn's suggestion (1932) that cannabinol was represented by partial formula **42** was taken up by the groups of Todd in England and Adams in the United

States, who initiated a number of synthetic approaches for the preparation
of the various possible isomers.

The synthesis of the cannabinol isomer in which the oxygen groups are
para to each other was achieved by application of the Bamberger reaction
(Ghosh *et al.*, 1940a). 3-Acetamido-4-cyanotoluene (**43**) readily yielded an
unstable nitroso derivative (**44**) on treatment with nitrous fumes, and this
product reacted with 2,5-dimethoxy-*n*-amylbenzene to give **45**. When **45**
was heated with hydrobromic acid, three consecutive reactions took place:
hydrolysis of the nitrile group, demethylation, and lactonization. The
tricyclic **46** was formed; treatment with methyl magnesium iodide led to the
expected product **47**, which was not identical with cannabinol. This result,
although disappointing was not unexpected, as in the meantime a positive
indophenol color reaction (see p. 17) indicated that the two oxygen groups in
cannabinol were not in para position to each other.

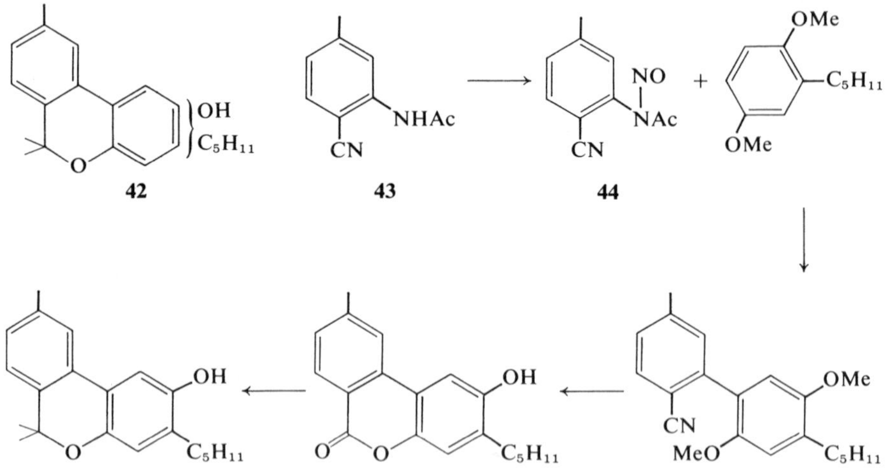

The authors point out that "the precise orientation of these compounds
(from the above synthesis) has not been rigidly proved, but the structures
allotted are, from the mode of synthesis almost certainly correct." Attempts
to extend the above synthesis to derivatives of catechol and resorcinol were
not successful and alternative routes were investigated.

Further cannabinol isomers were synthesized by Adams *et al.* (1940c,d)—
2-bromo-4-methylbenzoic acid (**48**) and olivetol condensed in the presence
of alkali and a copper salt to the lactone **49**, which on treatment with methyl
magnesium iodide gave **50a**. The linkage of the two aromatic rings in **50a** is
ortho to the amyl group. Through the use of the appropriate amylresorcinols,
the cannabinol isomers **50b** and **50c** were prepared.

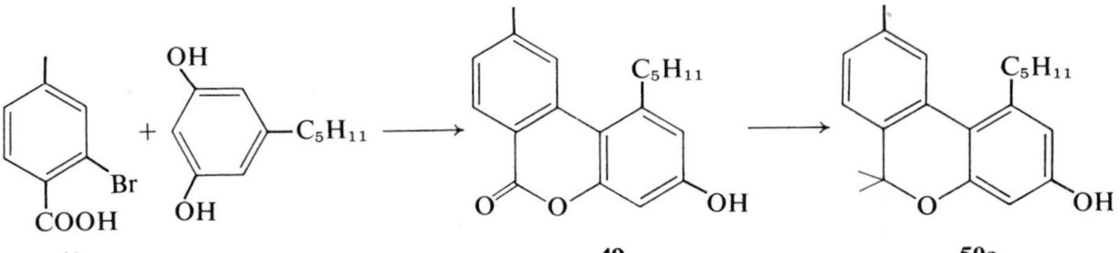

A variation on the above theme led to cannabinol (Adams *et al.*, 1940e). Reaction of **48** with dihydroolivetol under analogous conditions gave the pyrone **51**, which on dehydrogenation formed the dibenzopyrone **52**. Reaction with methyl magnesium iodide introduced the two methyl groups forming cannabinol. The cannabinol isomers **50d** and **50e** were also synthesized by this method, using the appropriate dihydroresorcinol derivatives (Adams and Baker, 1940a).

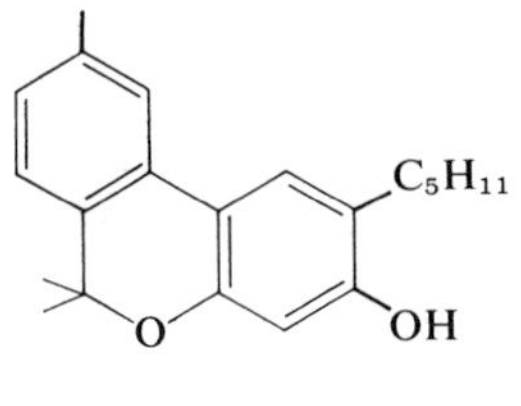

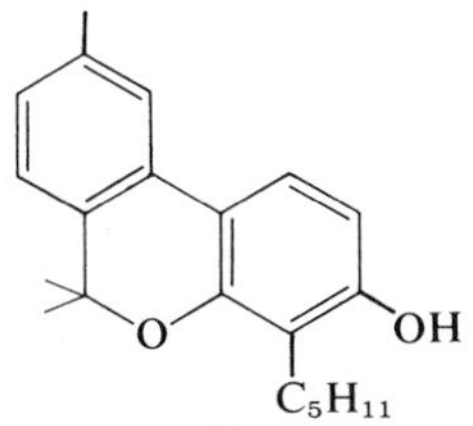

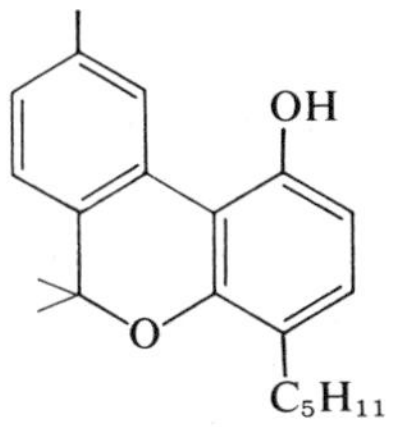

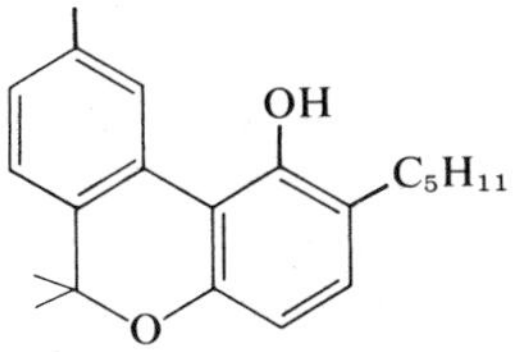

It should be pointed out, however, that in most modern syntheses of THC in which a terpenoid reacts with olivetol (see Section IV,B) the point of attachment of the terpene is seldom *exclusively* in either the 2 or the 4 position of olivetol. Usually a mixture of isomers is obtained. These mixtures are separable only by chromatography. It is quite possible that syntheses achieved in the early forties also gave several isomers, but in most cases only the predominant product was isolated.

Independently, the British and American groups followed a further synthetic route, which fortuitously led to results considerably more important than the synthesis of cannabinol itself (Ghosh *et al.*, 1940b,c; Adams and Baker, 1940b,c). Von Pechmann condensation of olivetol with ethyl 5-methyl-

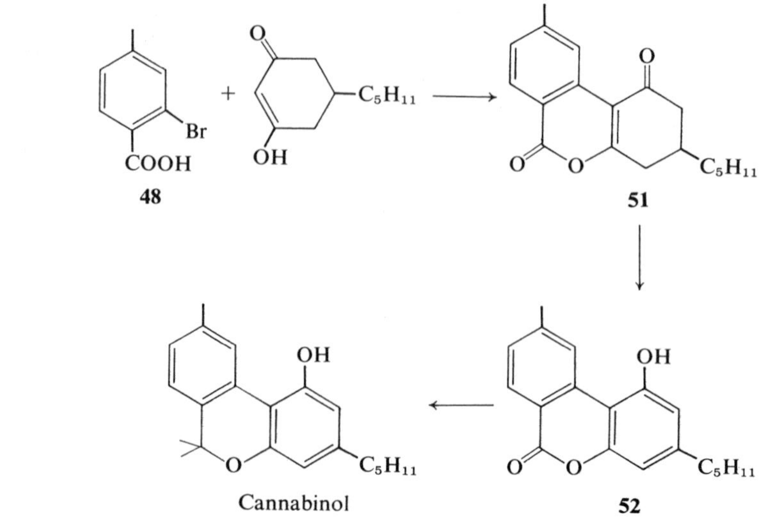

Cannabinol   52

cyclohexanone 2-carboxylate (**53**) with either concentrated sulfuric acid or phosphorus oxychloride led to the tetrahydrodibenzopyrone (**54**), which with excess methyl magnesium iodide gave the oily Δ^3-tetrahydrocannabinol (Δ^3-THC) (**55**). Cannabinol was obtained on dehydrogenation of Δ^3-THC. The intermediate Δ^3-THC was found to cause the characteristic effect of hashish in man and in animals (both dog ataxia and Gayer rabbit blinking tests). As pure natural THC was not available for more than 20 years, Δ^3-THC was used as a standard in most quantitative biological work on

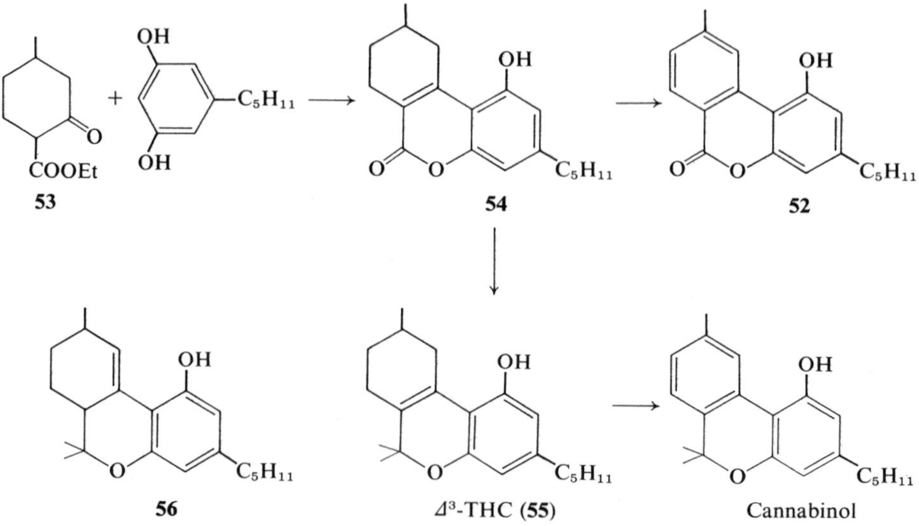

53   54   52

56   Δ^3-THC (**55**)   Cannabinol

cannabis. This method for the synthesis of Δ^3-THC has been extensively employed for the preparation of THC analogs.

Recently the above synthesis was reinvestigated (Claussen and Korte, 1966a; Korte *et al.*, 1965c). The oily impure **55** was purified by countercurrent distribution; three crystalline isomers were identified. The major one (90%), m.p. 62°–63°C, was shown to be **55**. A minor isomer (9%), m.p. 128°C, was Δ^2-THC (**56**). These isomers were identified by nmr methods. The main difference between them is in the chemical shift of the C-2 proton; in **55** it is allylic, while in **56** it is olefinic. A third isomer (0.5%), m.p. 86°–87°C, was not identified. The biological activity of Δ^2-THC, if any, has not been reported.

A further route investigated independently by both Adams *et al.* (1941a) and Todd and associates (Ghosh *et al.*, 1941) was the condensation of pulegone (**57**) and pulegol (**58**) with alkylresorcinols. This route was explored because it was expected that it could lead to optically active products. Initially Todd's group attempted to condense the allylic alcohol pulegol (**58**) with orcinol in the presence of zinc chloride. The oil obtained appeared to consist essentially of **59**, but purification was apparently difficult and no further work along these lines was attempted. It is of some interest that most recent syntheses of THC (Mechoulam and Gaoni, 1965a; Taylor *et al.*, 1966; Petrzilka *et al.*, 1969; Mechoulam *et al.*, 1967) are also based on condensation of monoterpenoid allylic alcohols or aldehydes with olivetol. It is unfortunate that the reaction of pulegol was done with orcinol only. Orcinol is not a good model for cannabinoid syntheses. Frequently, condensations with orcinol occur predominantly on an ortho position to the methyl group, whereas with olivetol the most reactive site is between the two phenolic groups.

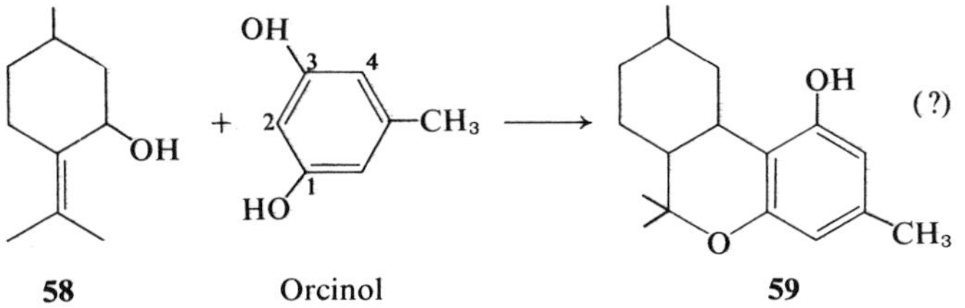

58   Orcinol   **59**

The reaction with pulegone was investigated more thoroughly. Pulegone **57** with olivetol in the presence of phosphorus oxychloride (Adams *et al.*, 1941a) or formic acid (Ghosh *et al.*, 1941; Leaf *et al.*, 1942) gave a product that had the pharmacological properties of a THC. On dehydrogenation, cannabinol was formed in an unspecified yield. It was assumed that in addition to Δ^3-THC the isomeric **60**, **61**, and **62** were also formed.

The Δ^3-THC (**55**) obtained via this sequence is optically active, although some racemization may have occurred in the reaction catalyzed by formic

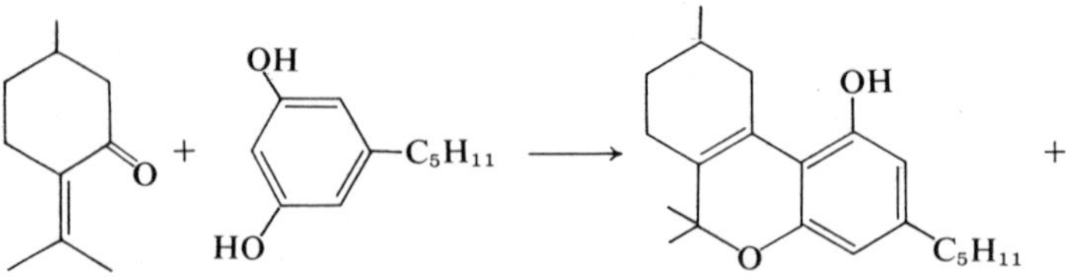

57   **55**

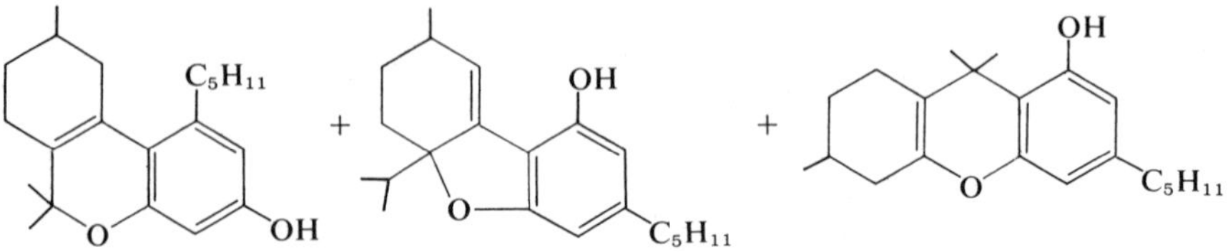

60 (?)   **61 (?)**   **62**

acid. It gave a crystalline menthoxyacetate, m.p. 76°–77°C, $[\alpha]_D$ +52°. An identical (except for optical purity) (+)-Δ^3-THC-menthoxyacetate was obtained via the previously described synthesis employing ethyl 5-methyl-cyclohexanone 2-carboxylate (**53**), which was obtained in an optically active form from (+)-pulegone.

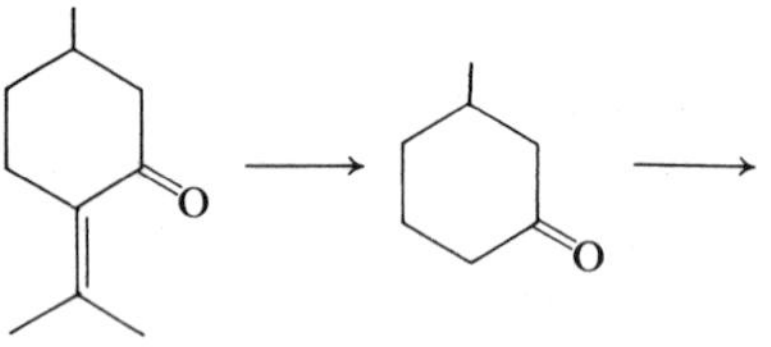

(+)   (+)

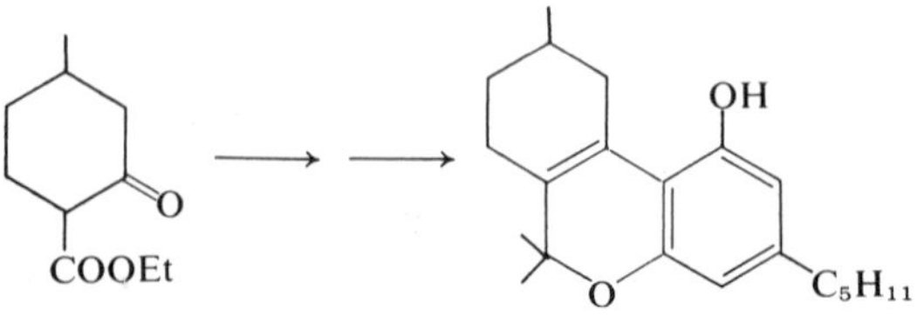

(+) 53   (+)-Δ^3-THC

The (+)-Δ^3-THC-menthoxyacetate, m.p. 76°–77°C, $[\alpha]_D$ +62°, thus obtained from (+)-**53** was hydrolyzed to (+)-Δ^3-THC, $[\alpha]_D$ +118°. It was only $\frac{1}{6}$–$\frac{1}{8}$ as potent in the Gayer test on rabbits as the racemic form. The (−) form was obtained by resolution of (±)-Δ^3-THC. Menthoxyacetylation of (±)-Δ^3-THC gave a crystalline ester, m.p. 56°–57°C, $[\alpha]_D$ −53°.

The olivetol–pulegone condensation has also been reinvestigated. Initially Korte and Sieper (1964) reported that Δ^3-THC was not formed, but later work (Claussen *et al.*, 1968b) established that Δ^3-THC was indeed present in a mixture from which the xanthene **62** could be also isolated.

The parallel pulegone–orcinol condensation was investigated by both Todd and Adams (Ghosh *et al.*, 1941; Leaf *et al.*, 1942; Adams *et al.*, 1941a). When formic acid was used as the condensing agent, a crystalline material (**63**), m.p. 112°C, [α]$_D$ +42°, was obtained. In this case too partial racemization took place. For comparison optically pure **63**, m.p. 104°C, [α]$_D$ +161°, was prepared via the optically active **53**. The nature of this racemization has not been clarified.

Chazan and Ourisson (1968a) have published a detailed second look at this reaction. Condensation with phosphorus oxychloride led to a mixture from which six compounds were isolated and identified.

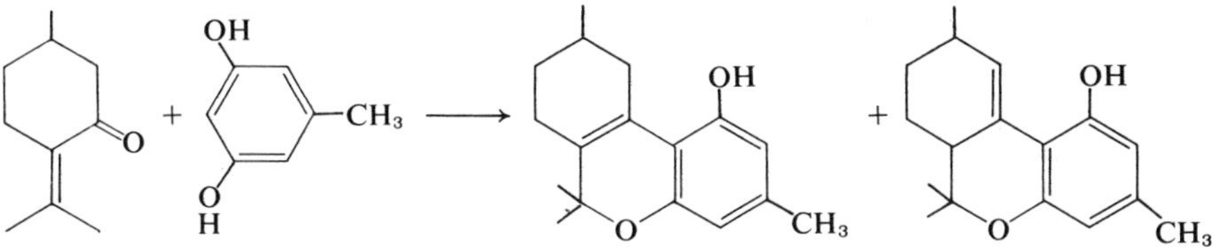

| Pulegone | Orcinol | **63** |

| **64a** | **64b** |

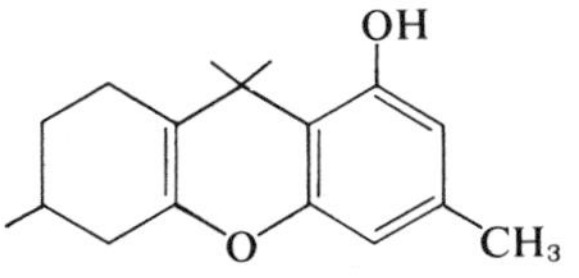

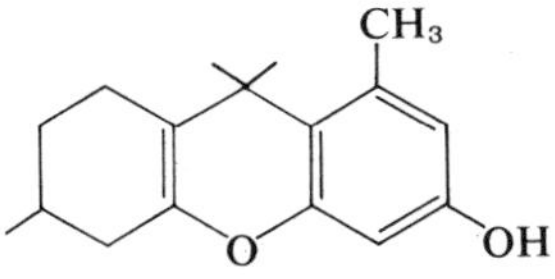

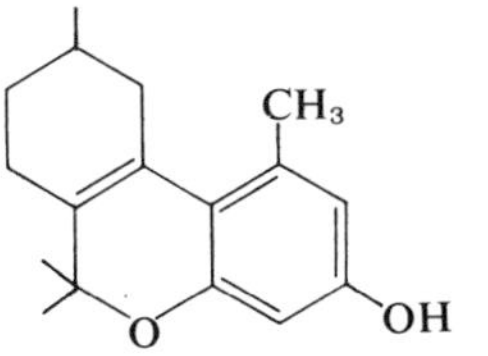

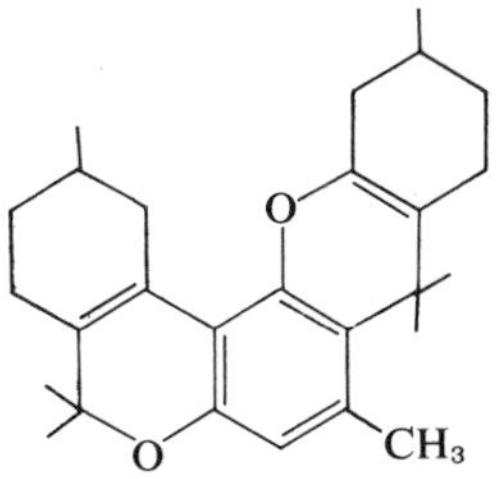

This reaction is another example of the previously mentioned generalization that reactions with orcinol give considerably more complicated mixtures than those with olivetol owing to formation of additional positional isomers.

It is of interest that *thermal* condensation of pulegone with orcinol leads exclusively to the tetrahydroxanthene derivatives **64a** and **64b** (Chazan and Ourisson, 1968b).

B. Δ^1-Tetrahydrocannabinol, Δ^6-Tetrahydrocannabinol, Δ^1-Tetrahydrocannabivarol, Cannabidiol, and Cannabidivarol

Adams (1942) was aware that Δ^3-THC was not a natural product but correctly assumed that the typical marijuana activity manifested by it constituted ponderable evidence that the activity of the plant itself was due to a THC isomer or isomers. He therefore initiated a few synthetic approaches to Δ^6-THC (without defining stereochemistry). Although these investigations were not completed by Adams, his ideas were later taken up and developed with considerable success by other groups (Jen *et al.*, 1967; Taylor and Strojny, 1960).

A facile preparation of Δ^6-THC seemed to be the direct addition of isoprene to an appropriately substituted coumarin (Adams and Carlin, 1943).

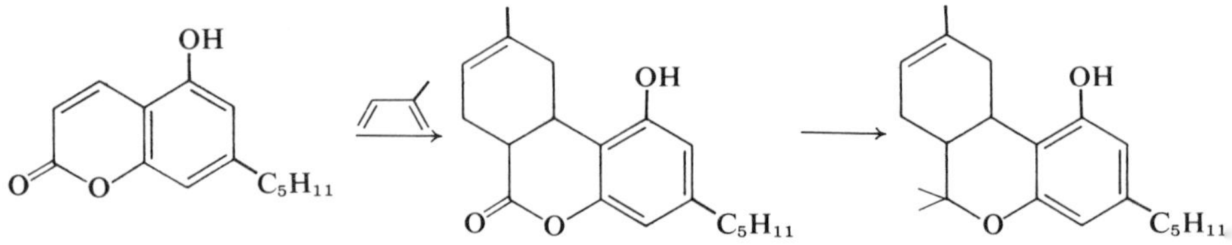

However, model experiments were not successful. Taylor and Strojny (1960) were able to accomplish such a Diels–Alder reaction by the introduction of an electronegative group in conjugation with the double bond of the coumarin, thus increasing its dienophilic activity. 3-Carbethoxycoumarin reacted with isoprene to give **65**. This lactone on hydrolysis apparently underwent ring opening to form the diacid **66**, which on heating gave the new *trans*-lactone **67** and the *cis*-lactone **68**. Both compounds were converted by standard methods to the cis and trans THC type of compounds (**69** and **70**). The cis compound **69** was reported to be a mixture. Later work (Gaoni and Mechoulam, 1968) showed that due to steric proximity related cis compounds cyclize with ease at C-1. It is possible, therefore, that **69** contains **71** or related materials. Taylor's ingenious synthesis, if applicable to the THC's, should be useful for the preparation of derivatives that are otherwise inaccessible.

Following the elucidation of the structure of cannabidiol (**72**) (Mechoulam and Shvo, 1963) and the demonstration that the major active component in hashish is Δ^1-THC (**73**) (Gaoni and Mechoulam, 1964a), numerous groups initiated approaches toward their syntheses. The first report on the successful completion of a synthetic sequence was published within a year (Mechoulam and Gaoni, 1965a). This synthesis is patterned along the suggested biogenetic pathway, which postulates an initial condensation of a monoterpene (geraniol) with olivetol, followed by oxidation and cyclization (see Section III,P). In the synthetic sequence, the oxidation is avoided as the monoterpene employed is already in the higher state of oxidation; citral instead of geraniol is employed. Thus, the reaction of citral (**74**) with the lithium derivative of olivetol dimethyl ether (**75**) afforded a mixture that presumably contained **76**. Tosylation of the mixture led, probably through allylic rearrangement to **77**, to (±)-dimethyl cannabidiol (**78**) in a low yield. As cannabidiol was known to be sensitive to both acidic and strongly basic conditions, neutral demethylation procedures were investigated. The method of choice was found to be the use at high temperature of a dry Grignard reagent. This method was adopted later in other cannabinoid syntheses (Korte *et al.*, 1966; Jen *et al.*, 1967). (±)-Cannabidiol was converted to Δ^1-THC by acid treatment. In view of the known conversion of cannabidiol to Δ^6-THC (**79**), the above route formally represents a synthesis of the racemate of this material. The overall yield was only 2%. The disclosure (Gaoni and Mechoulam, 1971) that the conversion of cannabidiol to Δ^1-THC can be achieved in ~60%

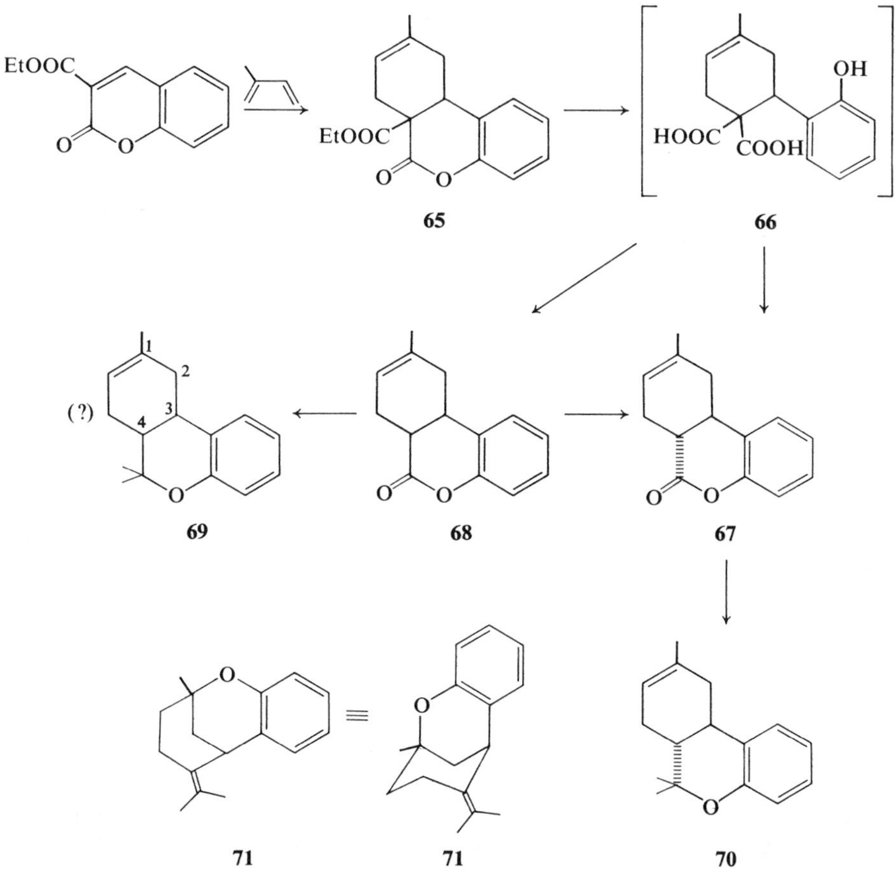

yield by boron trifluoride improves the above reaction. However, in view of later developments this first synthesis of Δ^1-THC is today of chronological interest only.

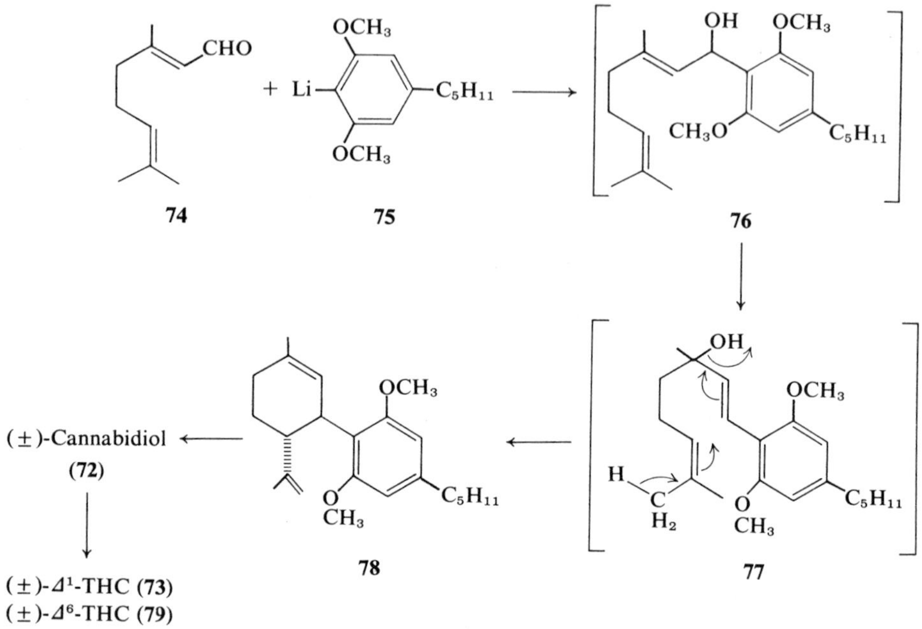

A related, independent synthesis was published within a few months by Taylor et al. (1966). In their approach, olivetol (instead of its dimethyl ether) was used in a reaction that employed 10% boron trifluoride as the condensing agent. The $(\pm)$-Δ^6-THC (**79**) was obtained in 10–20% yield, together with a material that was originally assumed to be Δ^6-cis-THC (**80**) but which was later (Gaoni and Mechoulam, 1966b) shown to be the isocannabinoid **81**. By the use of hydrochloric acid in ethanol, Taylor et al. were also able to obtain the new $(\pm)$-cis-Δ^1-THC (**82**). While the trans isomer **73** was shown to be present in the reaction mixture, it could not be isolated in pure form. A later modification of this synthesis (Mechoulam et al., 1972) which used 1% boron trifluoride in methylene chloride led to $(\pm)$-Δ^1-THC (**73**) in 20% yield. It was accompanied by **82**. The Taylor synthesis and its modification seem to be the most facile preparations of $(\pm)$-Δ^6-THC and $(\pm)$-Δ^1-THC, respectively.

The mechanism of these rather simple syntheses has been discussed but has not yet been completely clarified. It is possible that the intermediate 8-hydroxycannabigerol **a** (with either E or Z geometry) is first rearranged to

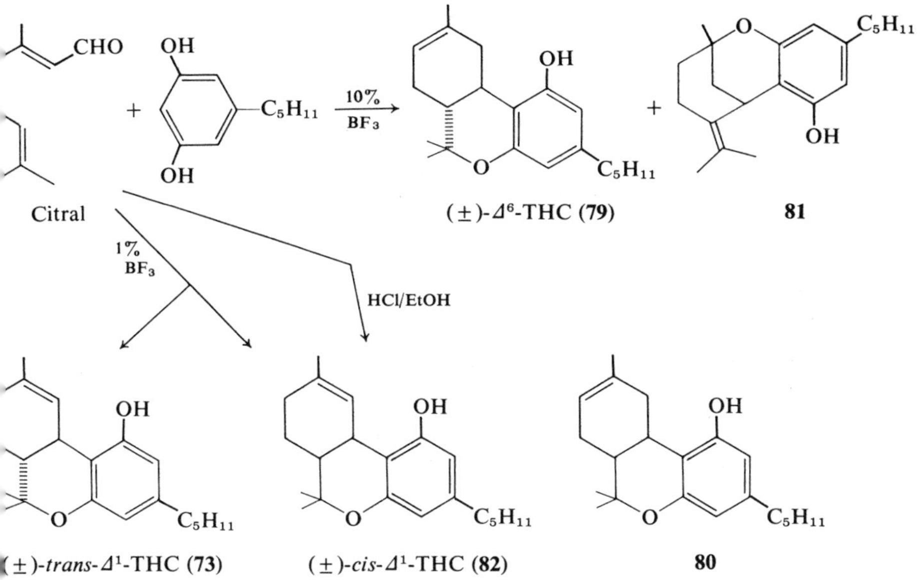

Citral + (reagent) $\xrightarrow[\text{BF}_3]{10\%}$ (±)-Δ^6-THC (**79**) + **81**

(±)-*trans*-Δ^1-THC (**73**)   (±)-*cis*-Δ^1-THC (**82**)   **80**

b, which undergoes cyclization. Crombie and Ponsford (1968c) have assumed that the intermediate **a** reacts in two different conformations (**a₁** and **a₂**) to give the intermediates **c** and **d**, which lead to Δ^1-THC and Δ^1-*cis*-THC, respectively. The transition states leading to **c** and **d** demand Z geometry. It is assumed, however, that due to stereomutation both Z- and E-citral give the same products. This assumption requires confirmation. A third mechanism has been put forward by Kane and Razdan (1969), who assume that the first step is the formation of **e**, which via **f** and **g** leads to *cis*- or *trans*-Δ^1-THC.

A different synthetic approach, based on an idea of Adams (Adams and Carlin, 1943; Adams and Bockstahler, 1952), has been used by a few groups. It employs a Diels–Alder reaction of an appropriately substituted cinnamic acid (or related material) with isoprene. Although *o,o'*-dihydroxycinnamic acid does not react with isoprene, the dimethyl ether of 2,6-dihydroxy-4-amylcinnamic acid (**83**) condenses with ease. The acid **84** thus obtained could not be demethylated and apparently the approach was abandoned. It is of interest to read in Adams' classic review (1942).

> In the chemical field repeated attempts to synthesize a tetrahydrocannabinol with a double bond in the γ,δ-position have failed. Just recently, however, a new approach has appeared and the results have progressed to a point where I am convinced it is merely a matter of time before the goal is reached.

In retrospect, it is amazing to realize that Adams was indeed one easy step away from a total synthesis. Jen *et al.* (1967) reexamined **83** by nmr and showed

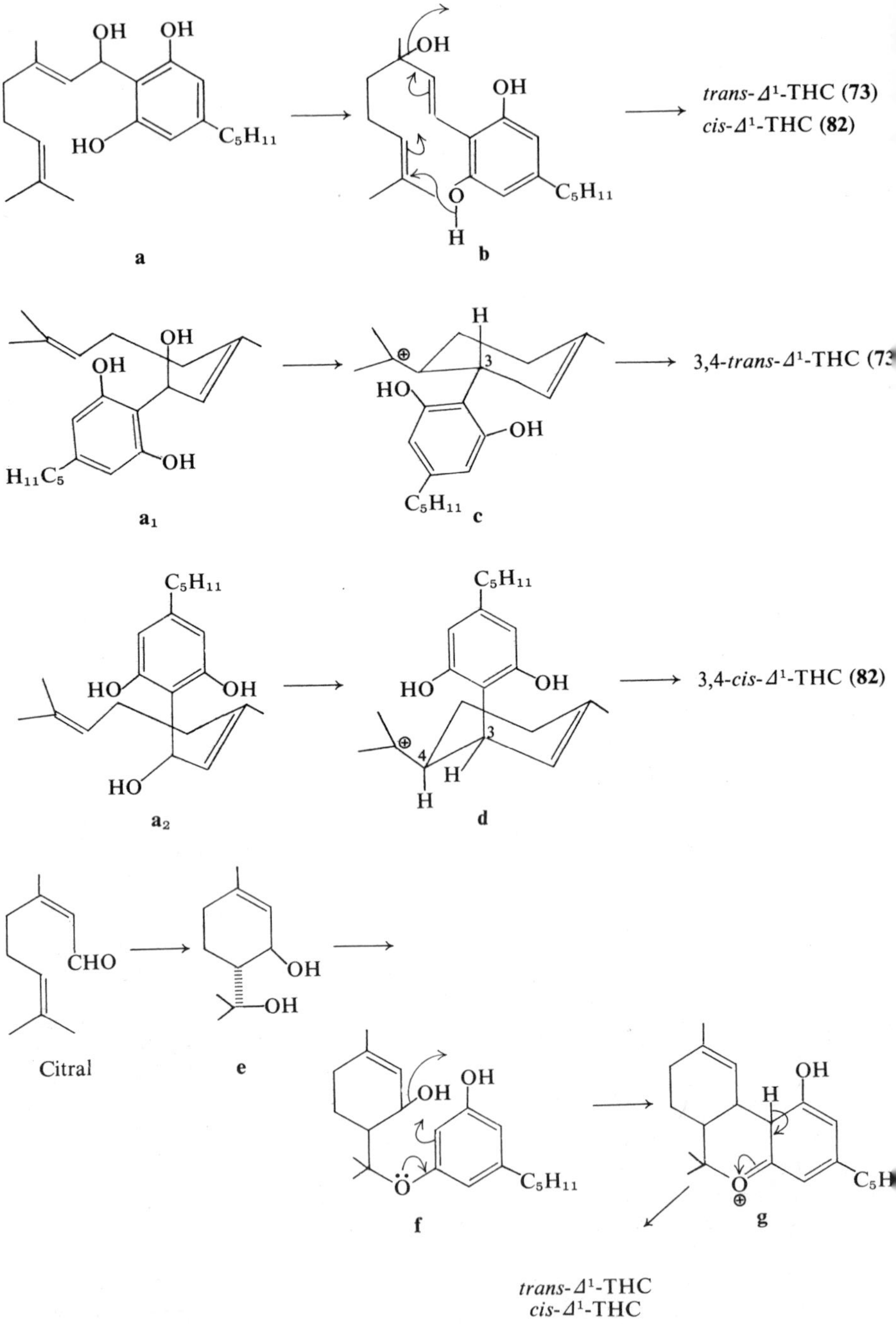

OH
OH
HO
C_5H_{11}
a
OH
OH
O
H
C_5H_{11}
b
trans-Δ^1-THC (**73**)
cis-Δ^1-THC (**82**)
OH
OH
OH
$H_{11}C_5$
a_1
H
3
HO
OH
C_5H_{11}
c
3,4-*trans*-Δ^1-THC (73
C_5H_{11}
HO
OH
HO
a_2
C_5H_{11}
HO
OH
4
3
H
H
d
3,4-*cis*-Δ^1-THC (**82**)
CHO
Citral
OH
OH
e
OH
OH
O
C_5H_{11}
f
OH
H
O
C_5H
g
trans-Δ^1-THC
cis-Δ^1-THC

that it has the trans configuration at the double bond. The Diels–Alder reaction reported earlier hence formed **84**, which had the trans configuration. This conclusion follows from the rule governing the retention of configuration of the dienophile constituents in the Diels–Alder reaction.

The racemic acid **84** was resolved by fractional crystallization of its diastereoisomeric naphthylethylamine salts. Fusion of the resulting (−)-**84** with methyl magnesium iodide demethylated the dimethyoxybenzene ring and converted the carboxyl to a 2-hydroxypropyl group; distillation led to (−)-Δ^6-THC (**38**). The (+)-Δ^6-THC was prepared in the same fashion. Owing to the necessity of optical resolution, this elegant synthesis is probably not practical, except for the preparation of derivatives.

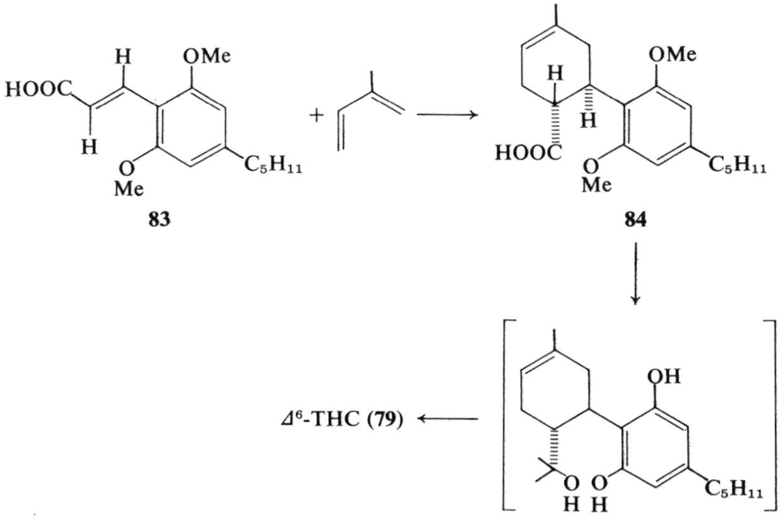

A modified Diels–Alder synthetic approach leading to an isomer of cannabidiol dimethyl ether has been reported by Korte *et al.* (1965b). Lithium dimethyl olivetol was converted to the aromatic aldehyde **85** (Adams and Carlin, 1943), which on aldol condensation with acetone gave the α,β unsaturated ketone **86**. The stereochemistry around the double bond was not determined, but one can assume a trans configuration. A Diels–Alder condensation with isoprene led to the ketone **87**. The stereochemistry at the substituted cyclohexene ring was not investigated. In retrospect, on the basis of the work by Jen *et al.* (1967) discussed above, a trans configuration could be expected. A Wittig reaction with triphenylphosphine–methylene formed the Δ^6 isomer of (±)-cannabidiol dimethyl ether (**88**).

This synthesis was later modified (Korte *et al.*, 1966). The ketone **86** was converted to the diene **89** via a Wittig reaction. A Diels–Alder condensation with methyl vinyl ketone (90) formed the ketone 91, which was converted to cannabidiol dimethyl ether (78), which had previously (Mechoulam and Gaoni, 1965a) been demethylated to cannabidiol. The overall yield was 9.5%.

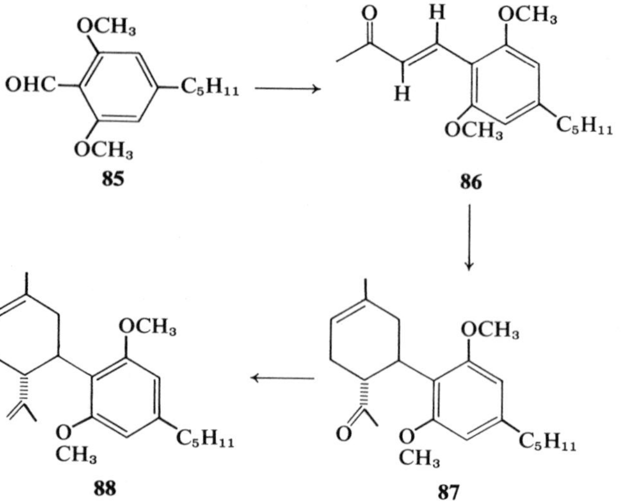

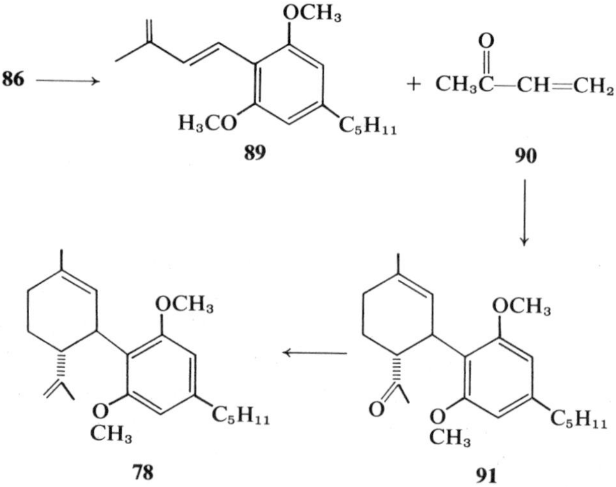

Kochi and Matsui (1967) have independently described an essentially identical synthesis. The only difference is in the preparation of 89, which was accomplished by a Grignard reaction on 86, followed by dehydration.

An original synthesis of racemic Δ^1-THC and Δ^6-THC as well as four of its isomers was reported by Fahrenholtz et al. (1967). The von Pechmann

condensation of olivetol and diethyl α-acetoglutarate (**92**) in the presence of
phosphorus oxychloride gave the coumarin **93**, which in the presence of base
gave the tricyclic **94**. Ketalization followed by reaction with methyl magnesium
iodide and acid hydrolysis led to the α,β-unsaturated ketone **95**. Reduction
with lithium in liquid amonia at −70°C gave a mixture of the cis (**96a**) and
trans (**96b**) isomers. The major product **96b** was converted to (±)-Δ^6-THC
via a Grignard reaction on the acetate of **96b** to give **97** followed by dehydration. The (±)-Δ^1-THC was obtained from **96b** by exchange of the tertiary
hydroxyl group with chlorine on boiling with Lucas reagent. The chlorine in
98 was removed by treatment with sodium hydride in benzene. This reaction
apparently proceeds by formation of phenolate and internal dehydrohalo-
genation. When **98** was treated with potassium hydroxide in ethanol, only

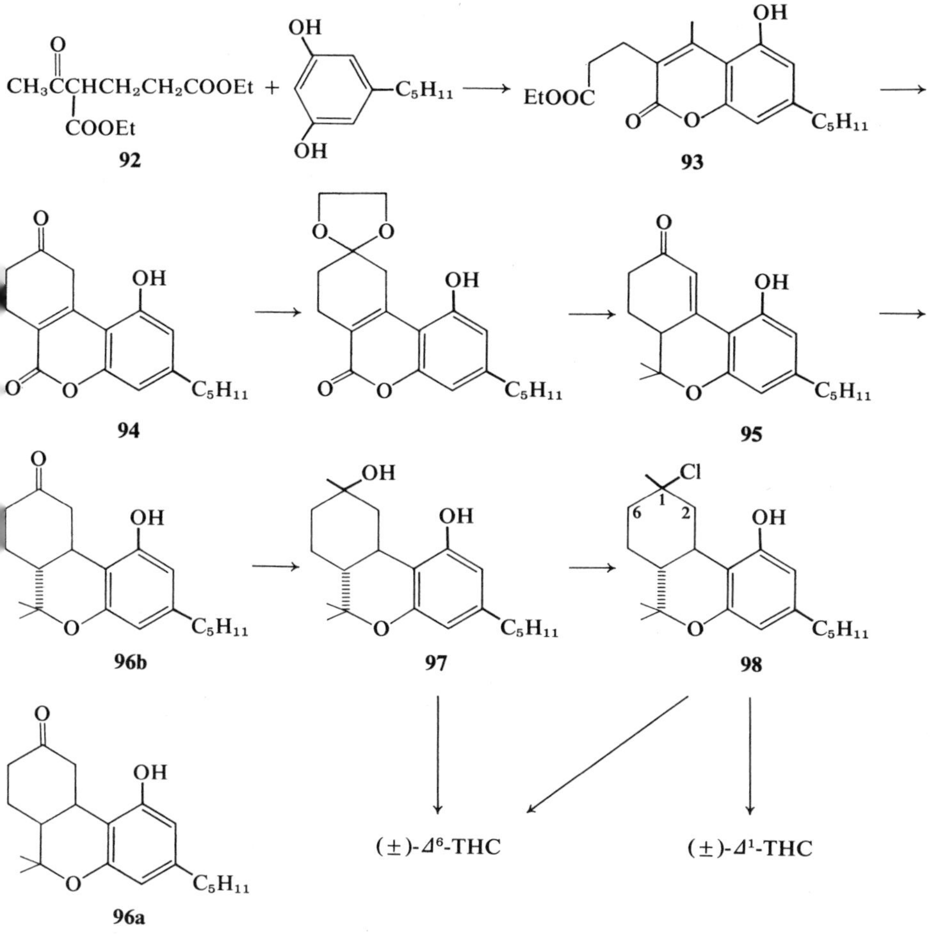

$(\pm)$-Δ^6-THC was obtained. In this case, base attack at the C-6 position, rather than phenolate formation, is preferred.

The ketone **95** was also prepared via a different sequence. The reaction of olivetol with 3-methylcrotonic acid (**99**) in the presence of boron trifluoride led to the isolation of two products, **100** and **101**, the ratio of which depended on the temperature of the reaction. The product **100** was obtained as the major one at high temperature only. Condensation of **100** with ethyl formate gave the hydroxymethylene derivative **102** which on Robinson annelation with methyl vinyl ketone formed **95**.

Three unnatural THC isomers, $(\pm)$-**103**, $(\pm)$-**104**, and $(\pm)$-cis-Δ^1-THC, were prepared by standard routes from various intermediates in the above syntheses.

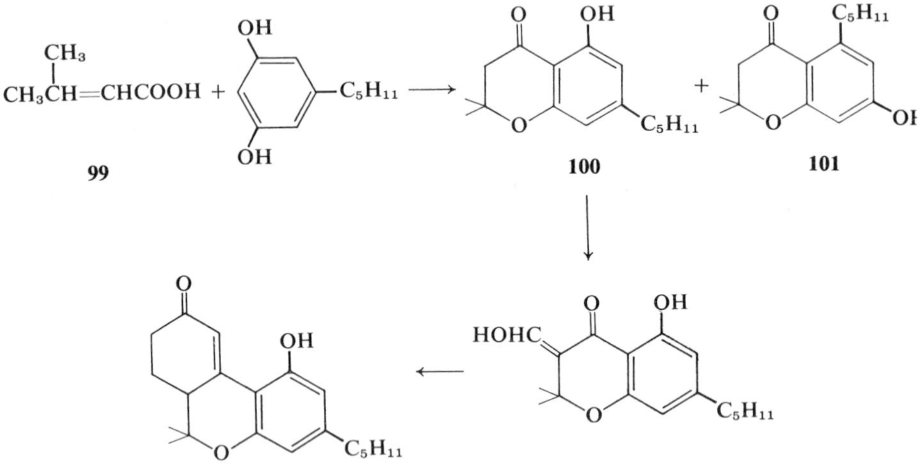

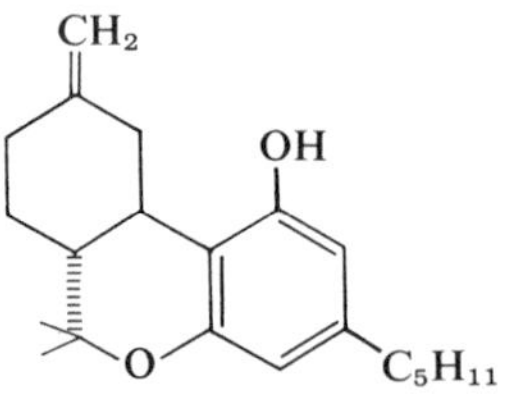

The above elegant, although somewhat elaborate, syntheses by Fahrenholtz *et al.* have been superseded by more facile ones leading to optically active products. However, the intermediate **96a** was used in the first preparation of ^{14}C-labeled Δ^1-THC (Nilsson *et al.*, 1969), as it offers a route for the introduction of the label at a late stage of the synthesis.

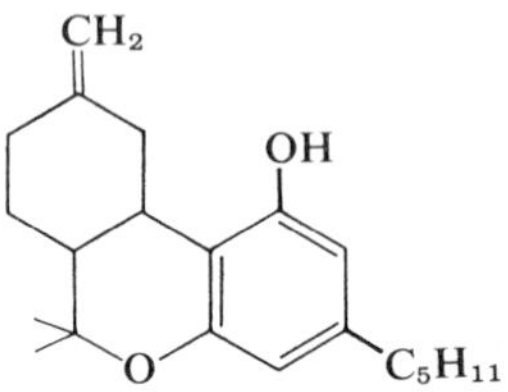

In 1967, two relatively facile syntheses of optically active Δ^1-THC and related cannabinoids were published. Both syntheses are based on the same principle: the condensation of olivetol with optically active monoterpenes. Petrzilka *et al.* (1967) reported the synthesis of (−)-cannabidiol in 25% yield from (+)-*trans*- or (+)-*cis*-p-mentha-2,8-dien-1-ol (**105**) with olivetol in the presence of *N,N*-dimethylformamid–dineopentylacetal, which served as condensing agent. Mild acids such as oxalic acid, zinc chloride, and others were later found to be also suitable. In all cases the isomer **106** was the main product (35%)* (Petrzilka *et al.*, 1969).

Cannabidivarol, the naturally occurring *n*-propyl (instead of pentyl) homolog of cannabidiol (Vollner *et al.*, 1969), has been prepared in the same fashion.

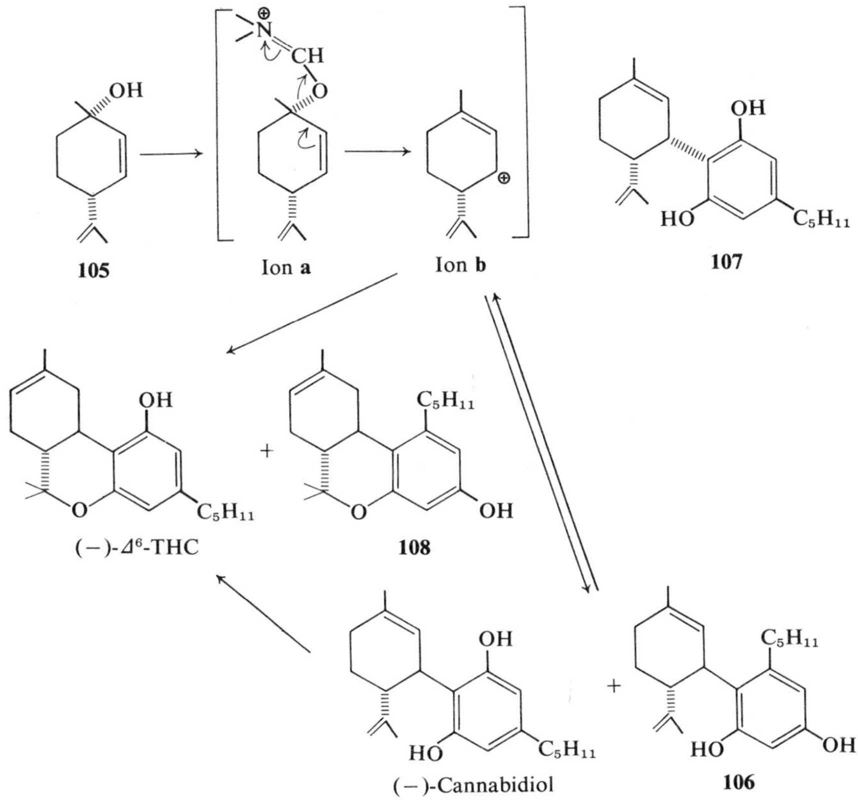

* In the preliminary communication (Petrzilka *et al.*, 1967) it was assumed that *cis*-cannabidiol (**107**) was formed. However, the presumed **107** was shown in the later paper to be **106**.

When the condensation of **105** with olivetol was performed with *p*-toluene-sulfonic acid, the presumed intermediates, cannabidiol and **106** were not isolated but were converted directly to $(-)$-Δ^6-THC (53% yield) and the isomer **108** (13% yield). The gratifying difference in yields between the cannabidiol synthesis and the Δ^6-THC synthesis was explained on the basis of a "retrocondensation" of **106** to "ion **b**." As cannabidiol is known to yield Δ^6-THC in very high yield under these conditions, the recycling process favors its formation. This reaction has been used for the preparation of kilogram amounts of $(-)$-Δ^6-THC by Arthur D. Little Inc., Cambridge, Massachusetts, for the United States government. The starting monoterpenoid mentha-2,8-dien-1-ol (**105**), however, is not readily available.

Mechoulam *et al.* (1967) used a pinene derivative in their synthesis of optically active Δ^1-THC and Δ^6-THC. Pinene is commercially available in $(+)$ and $(-)$ forms, thus allowing an entrance into both the natural $(-)$ and the $(+)$ series. The dimethyl–methylene bridge in pinene was assumed to provide stereochemical control of the condensations; any attack was expected to proceed from the side opposite to the bulky group.

The readily available pinene derivative $(-)$-verbenol was condensed with olivetol in the presence of *p*-toluenesulfonic acid to yield 4-*trans*-(2-olivetyl)-pinene (**109**) in 45% yield, accompanied by the isomeric **110** (20%) and the dipinyl olivetol (**111**) (15%). As expected, all products formed were trans to the dimethyl–methylene bridge in verbenol. Boron trifluoride converted **109** into $(-)$ Δ^6-THC in 85% yield. When the verbenol–olivetol condensation was catalyzed with boron trifluoride, $(-)$-Δ^6-THC was directly isolated in 35% yield. The $(+)$-Δ^6-THC was also synthesized via the above route; $(+)$-verbenol was the starting material. In contrast to the high biological potency of $(-)$-Δ^6-THC, the $(+)$ isomer was found to be devoid of activity.

The above synthetic sequence has been reinvestigated, and by a minor modification in the experimental conditions the yields were increased. Thus, when the olivetol was condensed with *cis*-verbenol, m.p. 67°–69°C, in pure chloroform with *p*-toluenesulfonic acid as catalyst the olivetyl pinene **109** was obtained in 60% yield (Mechoulam *et al.*, 1972).

The first *practical* synthesis of optically active Δ^1-THC was achieved (Mechoulam *et al.*, 1967) by addition of the elements of hydrochloric acid in the presence of zinc chloride across the double bond of $(-)$-Δ^6-THC followed by dehydrochlorination with sodium hydride in tetrahydrofuran. This dehydrochlorination procedure (Fahrenholtz *et al.*, 1967) is based on the intramolecular attack of a thus-formed phenoxide ion. The $(-)$-Δ^1-THC was obtained in 55% yield from $(-)$-Δ^6-THC. The procedure was later improved by Petrzilka *et al.* (1969), who employed potassium *tert*-amylate in the dehydrochlorination reaction. The yield was reported as 100%.

The verbenol–olivetol route for the synthesis of THC's has been used in the preparation of these and related materials in large quantities in the author's laboratory in the last few years. It has also been employed for the synthesis of labeled compounds in these series (Idänpään-Heikkila *et al.*, 1969) and for the preparation of Δ^1-tetrahydrocannabivarol (Gill, 1971).

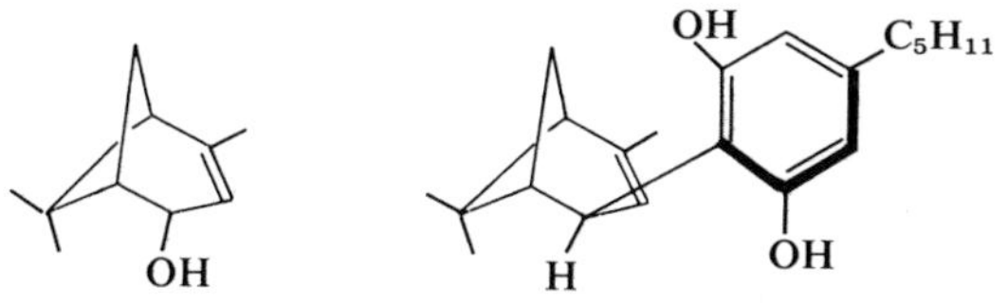

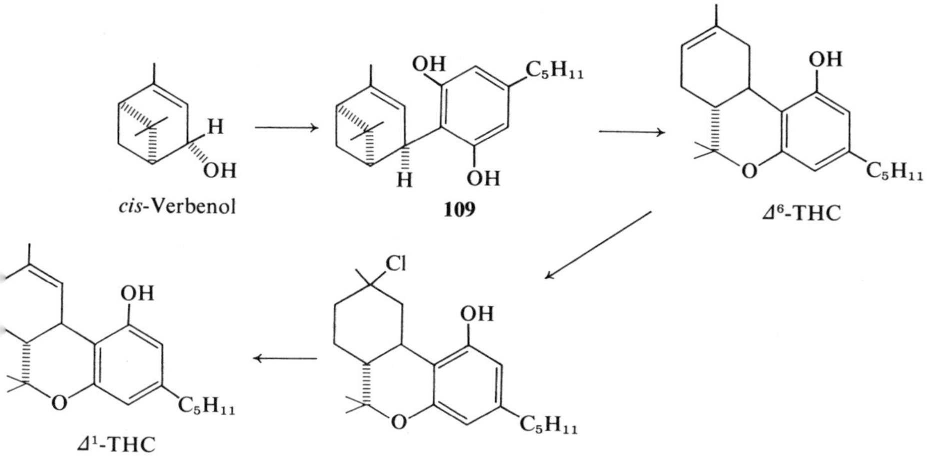

cis-Verbenol   **109** Δ^6-THC

Δ^1-THC

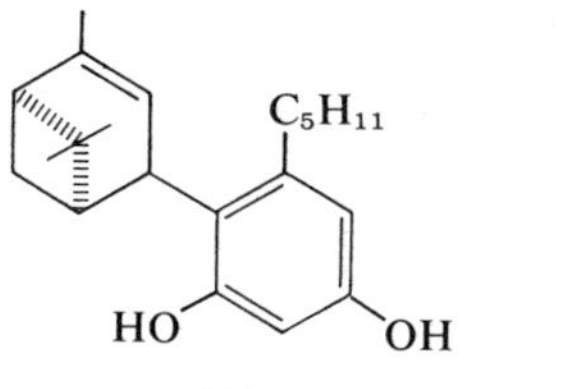

110 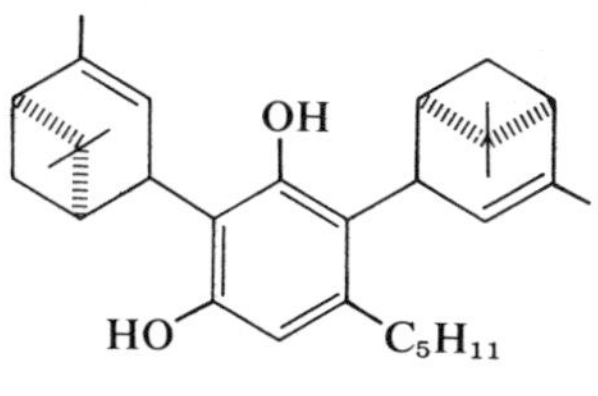   **111**

A further stereospecific synthesis of $(-)$-Δ^6-THC and $(-)$-Δ^1-THC has been reported (Razdan and Handrick, 1970). The reaction of $(+)$-*trans*-2-carene oxide with olivetol in the presence of *p*-toluenesulfonic acid gave $(-)$-Δ^6-THC (23% by glc), $(-)$-Δ^1-THC (7%), and isocannabinoids. When boron trifluoride etherate was used as condensing agent a mixture of Δ^1-THC (28%) and Δ^1-*cis*-THC was obtained. No Δ^6-THC was formed. This mixture was converted to $(-)$-Δ^6-THC (of 80% optical purity) by treatment with *p*-toluene-sulfonic acid. The mechanism of this reaction differs from those described previously.

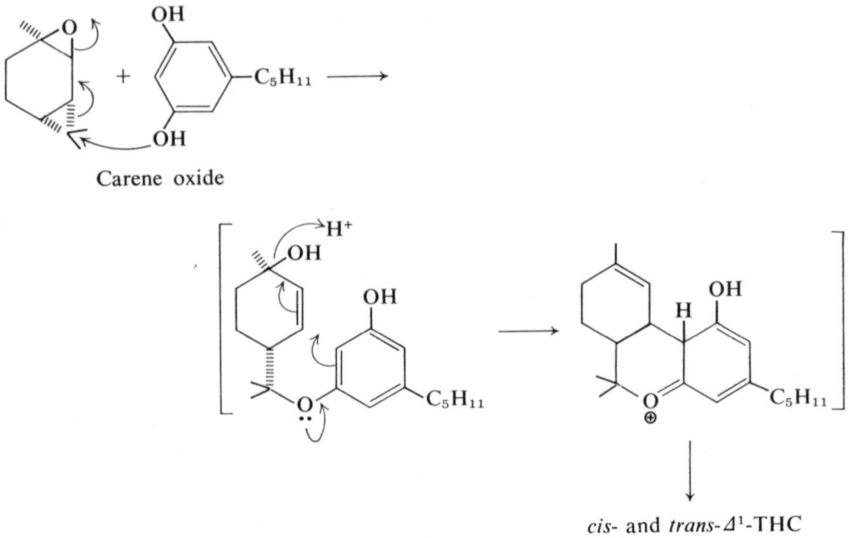

Carene oxide

cis- and trans-Δ^1-THC

C. CANNABIGEROL

Cannabigerol (112) was first prepared by boiling geraniol with olivetol in decalin for 36 hours (Gaoni and Mechoulam, 1964b). The yield was low. More recently, in connection with some mechanistic studies, this synthesis was improved (Mechoulam and Yagen, 1969). Condensation in methylene chloride in the presence of p-toluenesulfonic acid gave 112 (52%), m.p. 49°–50°C. None of the 6-cis isomer 113 was isolated. However, condensation of nerol with olivetol gave 113 (39%) accompanied by 5% cannabigerol.

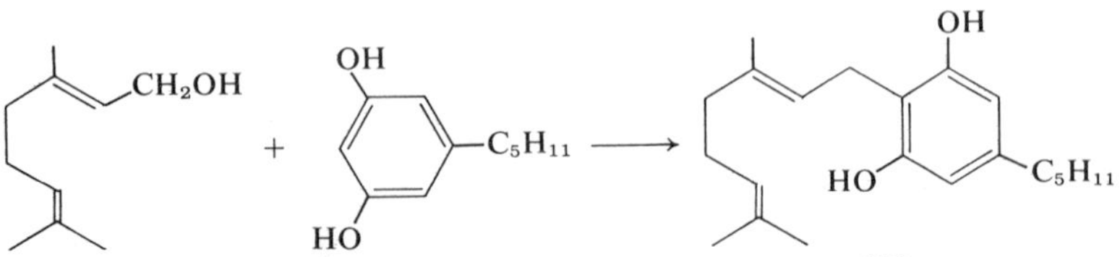

Geraniol

112

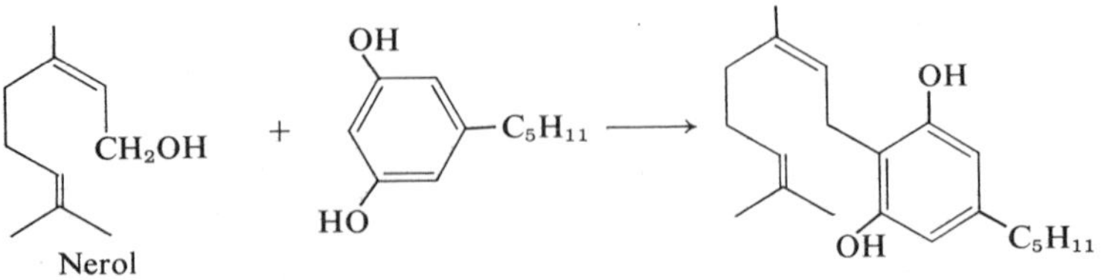

Nerol

113

Cardillo *et al.* (1968) have synthesized the ethyl ester of cannabigerolic acid by alkylation of ethoxycarbonyl olivetol with geranyl bromide. On hydrolysis decarboxylation takes place and cannabigerol is obtained. The overall yield is very low.

D. CANNABICHROMENE AND CANNABICYCLOL

Two different approaches to the synthesis of cannabichromene (114) have been reported. One is based on the dehydrogenation of cannabigerol (112); the other is based on the condensation of citral with olivetol in the presence of pyridine.

Dehydrogenation of 112 with chloranil gave cannabichromene (114) in 45% yield. The tetracyclic 115 was also isolated (Mechoulam *et al.*, 1968b). This unusual diether was later identified as a final product of numerous cannabinoid cyclizations (see Section V). Cardillo *et al.* (1968) obtained cannabichromene by dehydrogenation of cannabigerol with 2,3-dichloro-5,6-dicyanobenzoquinone (DDQ) in an unspecified yield. The mechanism of the dehydrogenation has not been established. It can proceed via either **a** or **b**.

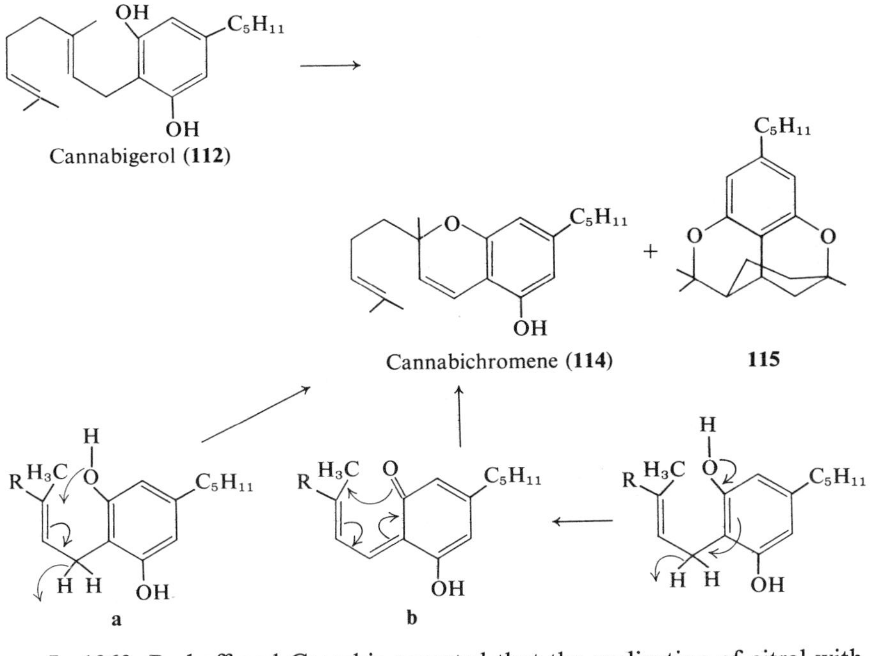

Cannabigerol (112)

Cannabichromene (114)   115

a   b

In 1960, Berkoff and Crombie reported that the cyclization of citral with malonic acid in the presence of pyridine gave "citrylidene malonic acid" (116). On the assumption that some resorcinol derivatives with citral might

116

117

118

behave in an analogous fashion, Crombie and Ponsford (1968a) prepared (±)-deoxybruceol (**117**) from the suitable coumarin **118** and citral. In this reaction a number of related chromenes were also obtained. On this basis the authors rationalized that a "similar reaction with olivetol as the phenol would lead to structures having the correct oxidation level of the major hashish cannabinoids." Indeed, the condensation of olivetol with citral in the presence of pyridine led to a mixture from which cannabichromene (**114**) (15%), the tetracyclic diether **115** (named citrylidene cannabis) (26%), cannabicyclol (**119**) (1%), as well as **120**, **121**, **122a**, and **112b** were isolated (Crombie and Ponsford, 1968b, 1971).

120

121

122a

122b

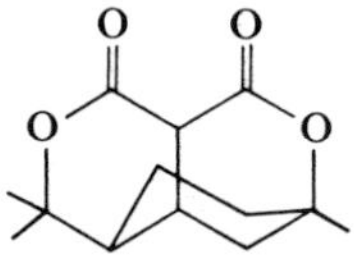

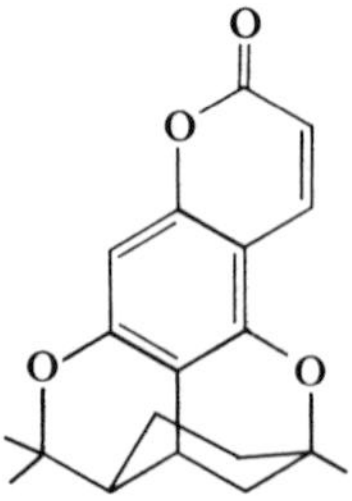

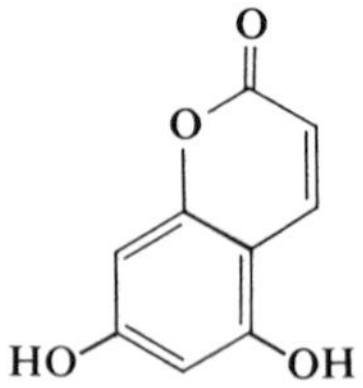

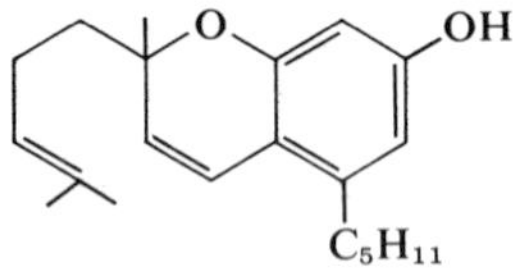

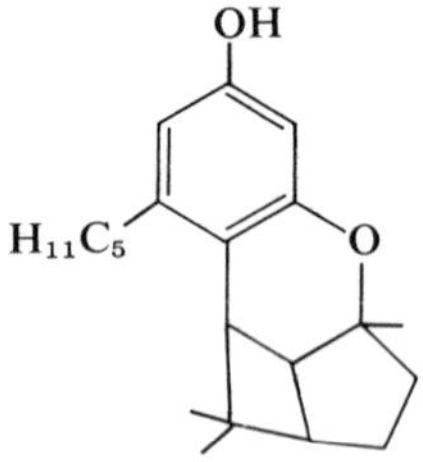

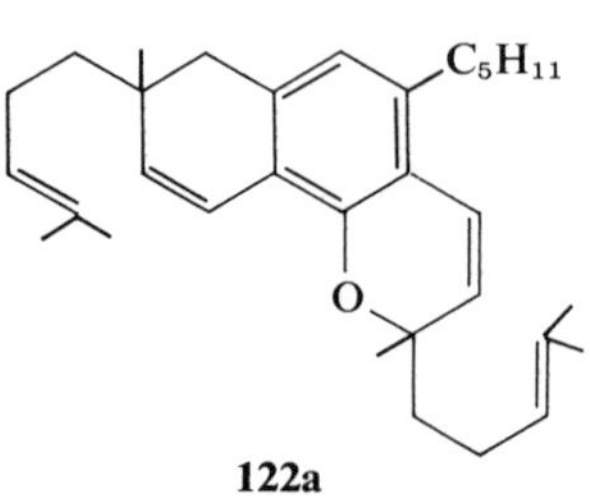

Heating cannabichromene with pyridine led to cannabicyclol (5%) and citrylidene cannabis (34%), suggesting that the chromenes were formed first and then converted to the more complex tetracyclic components.

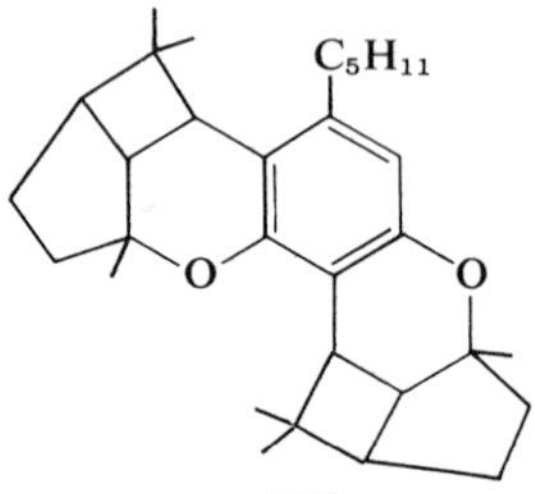

The mechanism of these syntheses can be visualized (Crombie and Ponsford, 1971) to proceed via the intermediate **c**, which can cyclize to cannabichromene. The latter may then form cannabicyclol **(119)** and citrylidene cannabis **(115)**.

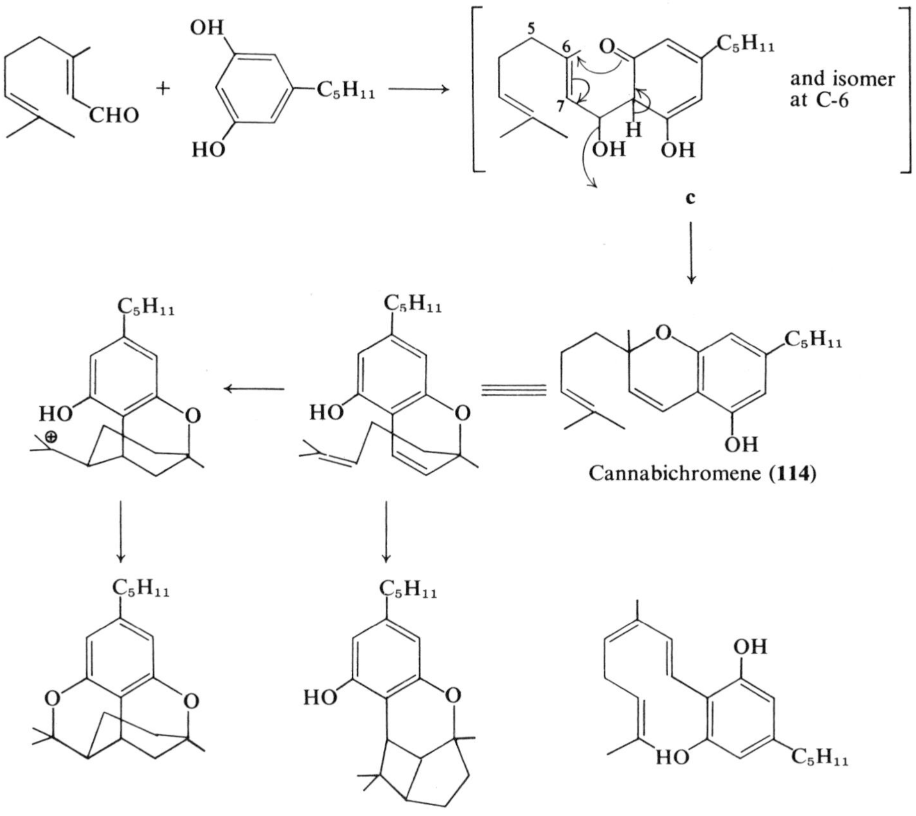

Cannabichromene **(114)**

115   Cannabicyclol **(119)**   d

It is of some interest that the intermediate **c** (in the phenolic form) had earlier been postulated (Mechoulam and Gaoni, 1967b) as a biogenetic precursor of cannabichromene.

Independently, Kane and Razdan (1968) investigated the above synthesis and reported essentially identical results. Cannabichromene (20%), cannabicyclol (5%), and citrylidene cannabis (17%) were isolated. This group has suggested, however, that the triene intermediate **d** formed from **c** is the precursor of cannabichromene (Kane and Razdan, 1969). Recently, further mechanistic possibilities have been put forward (Kane, 1971; Kane and Grayeck, 1971). A highly oxygenated minor component of this reaction has been reported to possess the rather unusual dioxetane cannabinoid structure

123a (Razdan and Kane, 1969). Treatment of 123a with a catalytic amount of
p-toluenesulfonic acid in methanol or with hydrogen with 10% palladium on
charcoal in methanol afforded 123b, m.p. 94°–95°C. The structures 123a and
123b require further confirmation.

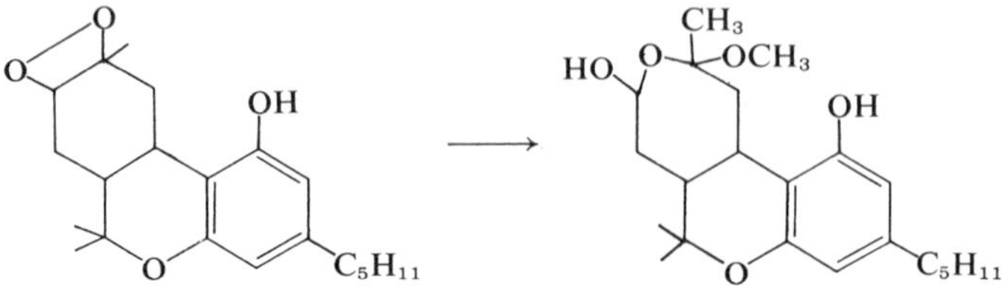

123a   123b

The above syntheses represent a facile route to cannabichromene, but not to
cannabicyclol. The latter compound has been synthesized in a workable yield
(45%) by irradiation of cannabichromene in tert-butanol–acetone with a
450 W lamp (Crombie et al., 1968). Cannabicyclol has also been obtained
(Yagen and Mechoulam, 1969; Crombie and Ponsford, 1971) in practical
yields on treatment of cannabichromene with boron trifluoride etherate.

E. CANNABINOID ACIDS

Phenols are generally carboxylated with ease by the addition of carbon
dioxide to the appropriate phenolate (Kolbe–Schmidt reaction). In the
cannabinoid series a number of variations of this procedure did not lead to the
desired acid. It is probable that, while the carboxylation does take place,
the products are decarboxylated at a fast rate at the high temperature usually
employed in this reaction. A simple solution to this problem was to try to
stabilize the intermediates of the reaction. This was achieved (Mechoulam
and Ben-Zvi, 1969) by a reaction that had previously been used for the
carboxylation of ketones. As resorcinols exchange the hydrogens ortho and
para to the hydroxyl groups with ease (as ketones do), it was assumed that
methyl magnesium carbonate (MMC) would react in an analogous fashion.
Indeed, cannabidiol with MMC, followed by acidification, gave cannabidiolic
acid (124a) in high yield. Cannabigerolic acid was obtained in a similar way
from cannabigerol. Carboxylation of Δ^1-THC led to Δ^1-THC acid A; the
yield was low. The starting material, however, is obtained back and by
recyclization of the reaction the yields can be improved. As expected from the
mechanism of the reaction, Δ^1-THC acid B was not obtained.

As mentioned previously, cannabigerolic acid ethyl ester (125) has been
obtained by alkylation of ethoxycarbonyl olivetol (126) with geranyl bromide.
Hydrolysis of the ester caused decarboxylation of the unstable cannabigerolic
acid (Cardillo et al., 1968).

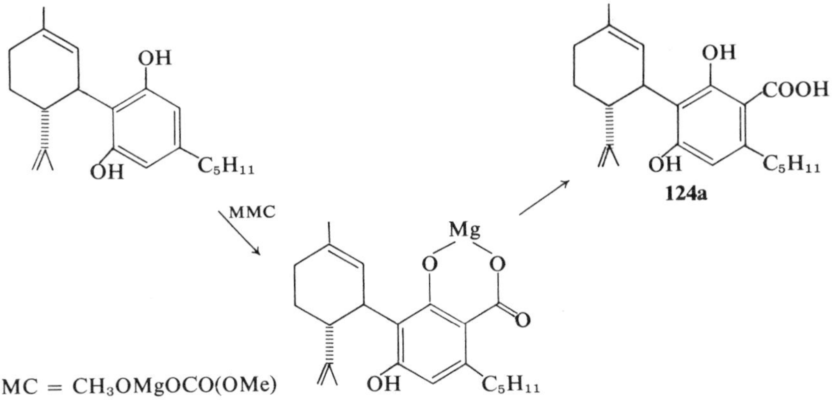

MMC = CH₃OMgOCO(OMe)

Petrzilka *et al.* (1969) have employed their cannabidiol synthesis (see p. 47) for the preparation of cannabidiolic acid ethyl ester (**124b**). The reaction of **126** with (+)-*p*-methadienol (**75**) in the presence of *N,N*-dimethylformamidineopentylacetal or oxalic acid gave the ester **124b**. The acid itself could not be prepared, as hydrolysis led directly to cannabidiol.

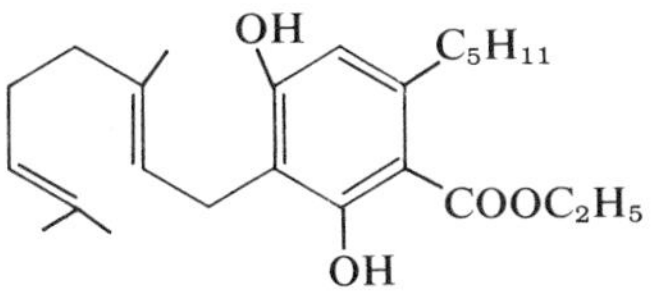

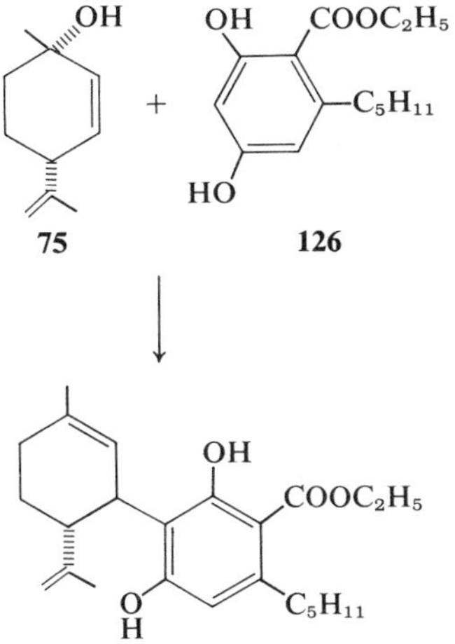

Cannabielsoic acid (**127**) was synthesized by a novel photooxidative cyclization (Shani and Mechoulam, 1970). Irradiation of cannabidiolic acid (**124a**) in the presence of oxygen, followed by reduction of the intermediate hydroperoxides with sodium bisulfite, led directly to a mixture of cannabielsoic acid A and its isomer at C-1. It is of interest that when the reaction mixture was *not* reduced a certain amount of the tertiary alcohols (not only the peroxides) was obtained. In a separate experiment it was shown that the peroxides are indeed reduced to the alcohols on irradiation. The same oxidative cyclization has also been achieved by nonphotochemical means; manganous dioxide and oxygen were used (Shani, 1970). The mechanism of this novel reaction, which was patterned after the supposed biogenetic route, probably involves the formation of a phenolic radical that attacks the double bond, leading to a tertiary radical. The latter forms the peroxides.

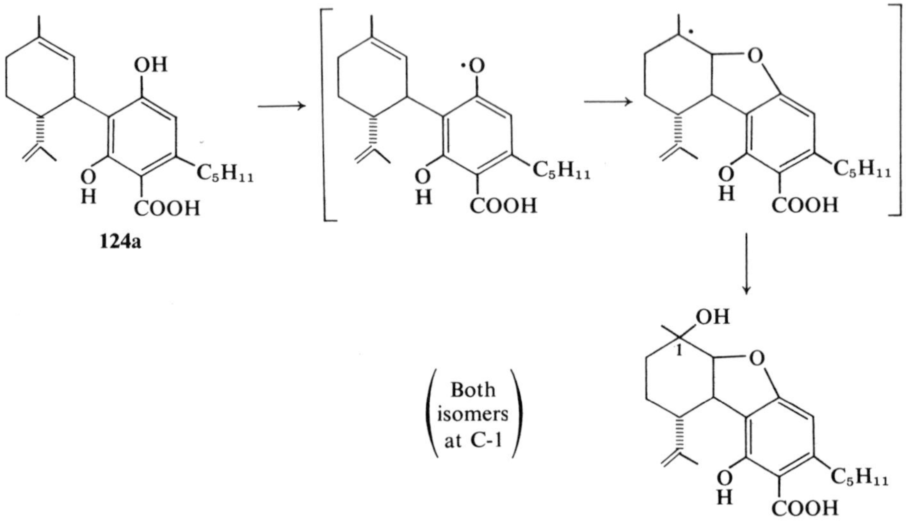

Cannabielsoic acid (127)

A number of naturally occurring furans, such as balfourdine (Rapoport and Holden, 1959), marmesine (Steck et al., 1969), columbianetine (Nielsen and Lemmich, 1964), and others, can probably be synthesized by the above new reaction.

F. CANNABINOID METABOLITES

At a symposium held at the Ciba Foundation in London in April, 1969 (Joyce and Curry, 1970), the isolation of a Δ^6-THC metabolite by Burstein et al. was announced (Mechoulam et al., 1970a), and important advances in the metabolism of labeled Δ^1-THC were presented by Agurell (1970). Reports by these and other groups soon followed (Burstein et al., 1970; Nilsson et al., 1970; Foltz et al., 1970; Wall et al., 1970; for a detailed review, see Chapter 4). The structure of the major identified metabolite of Δ^6-THC was put forward as 7-hydroxy-Δ^6-THC (128) and that of Δ^1-THC as 7-hydroxy-Δ^1-THC (129). In order to fully establish the above structures, as well as to provide material for biological work with these psychotomimetically active materials, synthetic paths to these compounds were explored.

Ben-Zvi *et al.* (1970a) reported the conversion of Δ^6-THC to **128**. Reaction of Δ^6-THC acetate with osmium tetroxide gave 1α,6α-dihydroxyhexahydrocannabinol acetate (**130**), m.p. 75°–76°C, in a good yield. The stereochemistry at the new asymmetric centers was established by nmr analysis of the splitting pattern of the C-6 proton. Acetylation of **130**, followed by dehydration with thionyl chloride in pyridine, gave a mixture of three compounds: the enol acetate **131** and the allylic acetates **132a** and **133**. The allylic alcohol **132b** underwent an allylic rearrangement in the presence of boron trifluoride etherate, forming the desired metabolite **128**. The overall yield was only 2%. The metabolite has not been crystallized; it gives, however, a crystalline bis-3,5-dinitrobenzoate, m.p. 140°–142°C. 7-Hydroxy-Δ^6-THC (**128**) is not stable and is best stored as the diacetate.

The above synthesis has been improved (Ben-Zvi, 1971). The Δ^6-THC acetate with *m*-chloroperbenzoic acid gave 1,6β-epoxyhexahydrocannabinol acetate (**134**), which on treatment with perchloric acid in acetone formed the diol **135a** (80% yield). Dehydration of **135b** with thionyl chloride in pyridin led to a mixture from which 6β-acetoxy-Δ^7-THC (**136a**) was isolated (40%). Allylic rearrangement of **136b** produced the metabolite **128**. The overall yield was 5.7%. It is of interest that the allylic alcohol **136b**, in which the hydroxyl group is pseudoaxial, undergoes the allylic rearrangement in a much better yield (30%) than the epimeric **132b** (10%). A further unusual point is that, in Δ^6-THC, epoxidation and reaction with osmium tetroxide proceed from opposite sides of the molecule.

Two groups have explored the selenium dioxide oxidation of Δ^6-THC. Foltz *et al.* (1970) reported that oxidation in 95% aqueous ethanol, followed by reduction with sodium borohydride, led to a product identical with the natural metabolite, 7-hydroxy-Δ^6-THC. The yield was not specified. Ben-Zvi *et al.* (1970b) oxidized Δ^6-THC acetate and Δ^1-THC acetate with selenium dioxide in ethanol at 50°C. The reaction products were acetylated and chromatographed. 7-Acetoxy-Δ^6-THC acetate was obtained in 15% yield from the reaction with Δ^6-THC acetate.

The reaction mixture from the Δ^1-THC acetate oxidation was purified by column chromatography and two consecutive preparative tlc's. After reduction with lithium aluminum hydride and further chromatographic purification two compounds were obtained, 7-hydroxycannabinol (**137**), m.p. 163°C (18% yield), and 7-hydroxy-Δ^1-THC (**129**), m.p. 133°C (1% yield), identical with the major Δ^1-THC metabolite. The free diol **129** is unstable; it is converted in part to **137**. The diacetate of **129** can be stored for at least a few months. This synthesis represents the first preparation by chemical means of a Δ^1-THC metabolite. The miniscule yield, however, makes this route unsuitable for practical purposes.

After the completion of the above synthesis Widman *et al.* (1971) reported

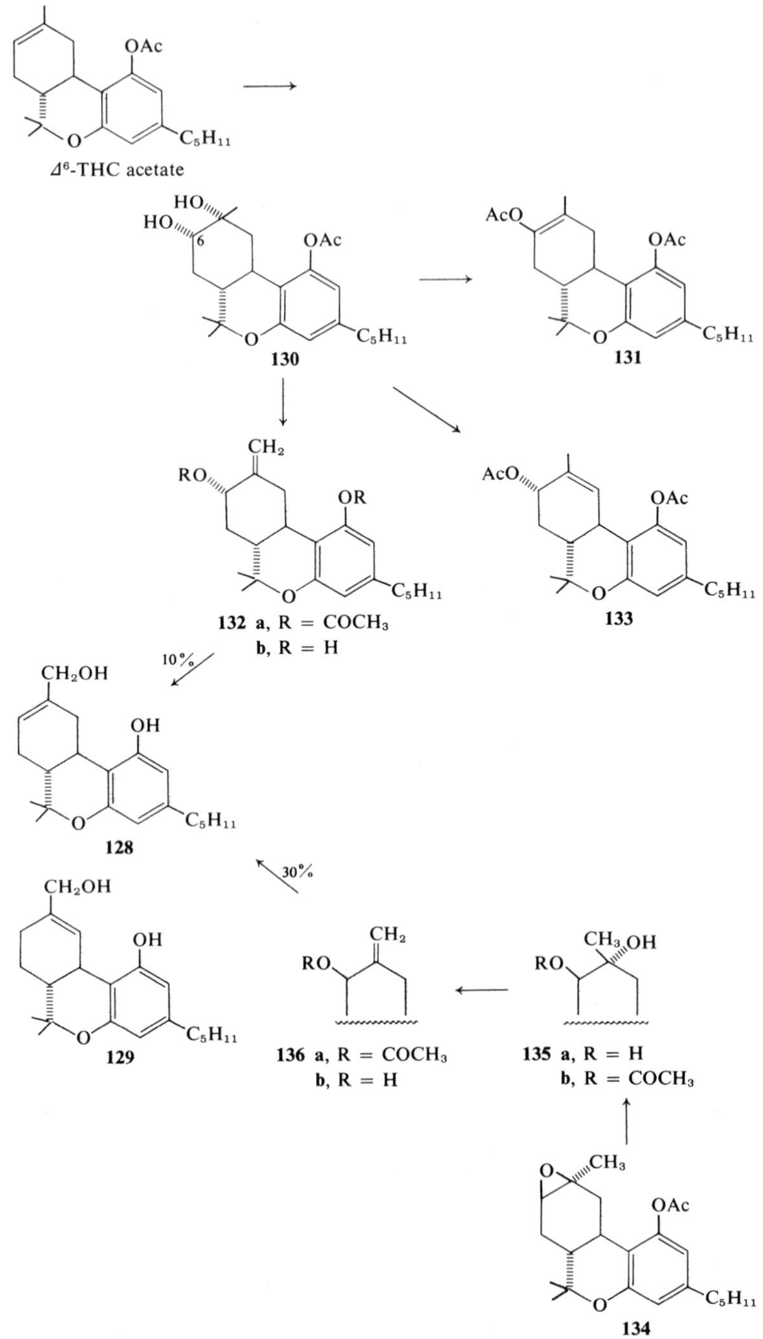
OAc
C_5H_{11}
Δ⁶-THC acetate
HO
HO
6
OAc
C_5H_{11}
130
AcO
OAc
C_5H_{11}
131
CH_2
RO
OR
C_5H_{11}
132 a, R = $COCH_3$
b, R = H
AcO
OAc
C_5H_{11}
133
10%
CH_2OH
OH
C_5H_{11}
128
30%
CH_2OH
OH
C_5H_{11}
129
CH_2
RO
136 a, R = $COCH_3$
b, R = H
CH_3 OH
RO
135 a, R = H
b, R = $COCH_3$
CH_3
OAc
C_5H_{11}
134

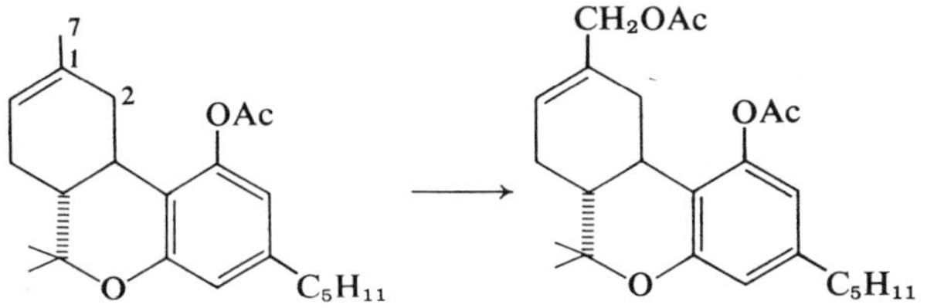

that **137** is the major metabolite of cannabinol; hence, the above preparation represents the first synthesis of this metabolite.

At a 1971 meeting of the New York Academy of Sciences, Wall (1971) reported the isolation of a minor new metabolite, 6β-hydroxy-Δ^1-THC **(138)** from an incubation of Δ^1-THC with rabbit liver homogenate. Its synthesis and biological activity in rhesus monkeys were announced at the

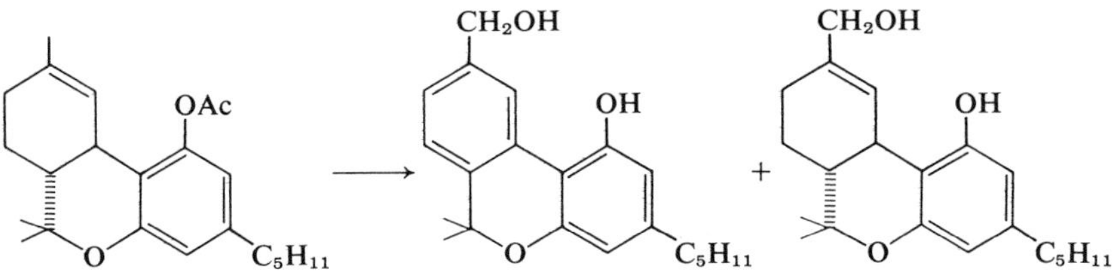

Δ^1-THC acetate   **137**   **129**

same meeting (Edery *et al.*, 1971) and published shortly thereafter (Ben-Zvi *et al.*, 1971). The Δ^6-THC acetate was converted to 6β-acetoxy-1-hydroxy-hexahydrocannabinol acetate **(135b)** via **134** as described before (p. 58). Dehydration of **135b** led to the diacetate of **138**, which on reduction with lithium aluminum hydride gave **138**. This oily compound is transformed into a host of degradation products when kept at room temperature, but it forms a stable, crystalline 1:1 complex with dimethylformamide. 6β-Hydroxy-Δ^1-THC shows cannabis-type activity in the rhesus monkey. If this metabolite is also formed by man it may complicate our understanding of cannabis action; one may have to take into account the presence of several active metabolites which may not have exactly the same type of activity at the molecular level.

Nilsson *et al.* (1971) have reported a further synthesis of 7-hydroxy-Δ^6-THC **(128)**. Photoisomerization of Δ^6-THC furnished Δ^7-THC **(103)**, which was dihydroxylated with osmium tetroxide to **139**. The later was easily converted to **128**.

Wildes *et al.* (1971) have prepared **103** by dehydrochlorination of 1-chloro-hexahydrocannabinol methyl ether **(140)** (obtained by addition of hydrogen chloride to Δ^6-THC methyl ether) with the bulky base, potassium tricyclo-pentylcarbinolate. The etheric blocking group was removed without iso-

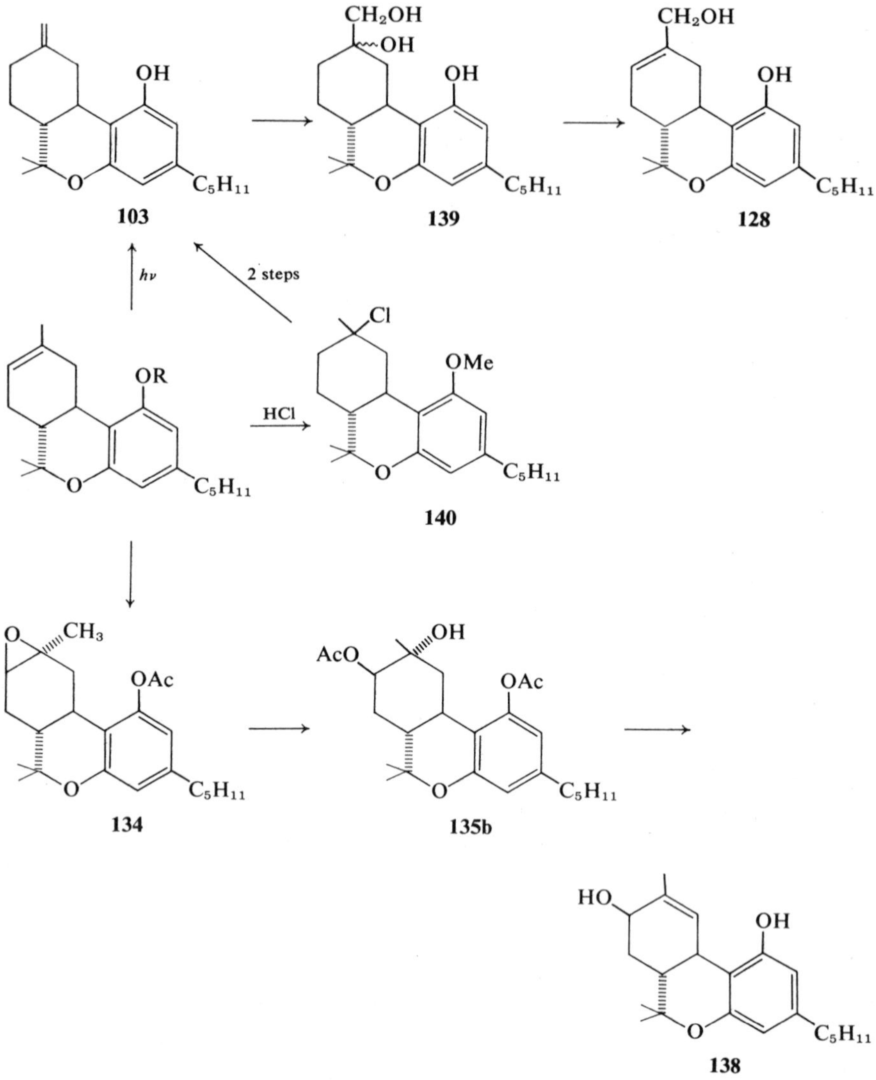

103   **139**   **128**

140

134   **135b**

138

merization of the exocyclic double bond with potassium thiophenoxide in diethylene glycol.

V. Cannabinoid Reactions

A. ACID-CATALYZED ISOMERIZATIONS AND CYCLIZATIONS

The acid-catalyzed migration of the double bond in Δ^1-*trans*-THC (**141a**) to the Δ^6 position takes place with ease (Gaoni and Mechoulam, 1966c;

Taylor *et al.*, 1966; Hively *et al.*, 1966). This reaction has not been observed in the cis series (Gaoni and Mechoulam, 1966b): Δ^1-*cis*-THC acetate (**142a**) is recovered unchanged on boiling with *p*-toluenesulfonic acid (*p*-TSA) in benzene, while Δ^1-*trans*-THC acetate (**141b**) is converted quantitatively to Δ^6-THC acetate (**143a**) under these conditions.

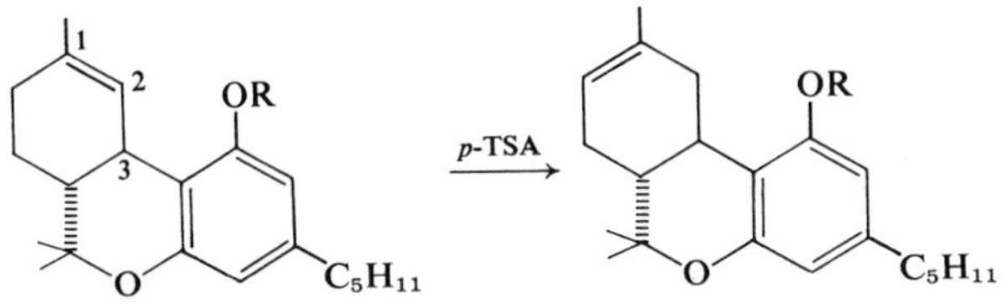

141a, R = H
b, R = COCH₃

143a, R = COCH₃
b, R = H

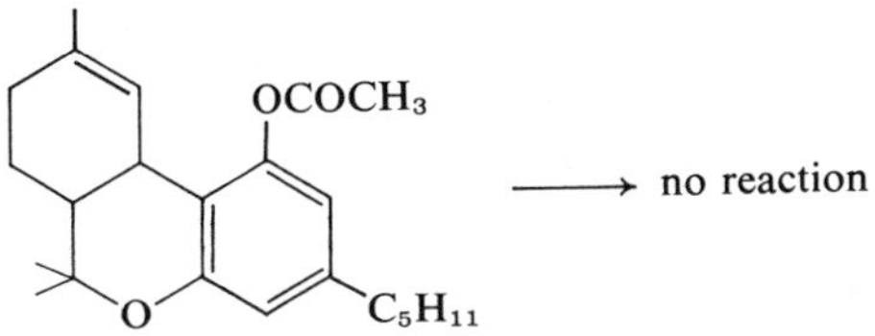

142a

The difference in reactivity may be due to steric strain. In Δ^1-*trans*-THC (**141a**) the olefinic C-2 hydrogen is apparently very close to the free hydroxyl group. The double-bond migration tends to relieve this nonbonded interaction. In the cis series the angle between the aromatic and terpenoid rings is such that there is no driving force for an isomerization.

The isomerization of Δ^1-THC to Δ^6-THC has been observed on gas chromatography on a SE-30 on Diatoport S column (Taylor *et al.*, 1966). On this basis it was suggested that such a process may take place on smoking. However, this isomerization on gas chromatography has not been observed on other columns at the same temperature (Gaoni and Mechoulam, 1966b). It seems that the isomerization reported was due to acid catalysis by the column employed. Several instances of isomerizations of terpenes under these conditions have been reported (Zubyk and Conner, 1960).

Cannabidiol in the presence of boron trifluoride etherate cyclizes to Δ^1-THC (in 60% yield) and to Δ^8-iso-THC (**144**) in 13% yield (Gaoni and Mechoulam, 1971). Boiling cannabidiol with *p*-TSA in benzene gives Δ^6-THC in practically quantitative yield (Adams *et al.*, 1941b; Gaoni and Mechoulam, 1966c). In view of the ready availability of cannabidiol (from cannabidiolic acid) the above reactions make the two active natural THC's easily obtainable.

Adams *et al.* (1941b) reported that dilute ethanolic hydrochloric acid converted cannabidiol to a THC, $(\alpha)_D -130°$. Recent work (Gaoni and

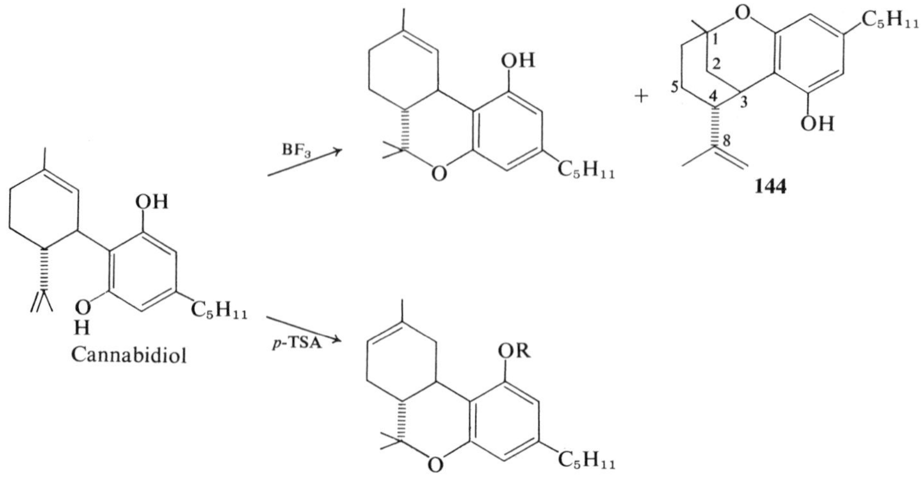

144

Cannabidiol

143a, R = COCH₃
b, R = H

Mechoulam, 1966c, 1968) has shown that the "THC, $(\alpha)_D - 130°$" is in fact a mixture of Δ^1-THC, Δ^6-THC, and two ethoxyhexahydrocannabinols **145** and **146**. On boiling with p-TSA **145** is converted into Δ^6-THC, while **146** gives a mixture of $\Delta^{4(8)}$-iso-THC (**147**) and Δ^4-iso-THC (**148**).

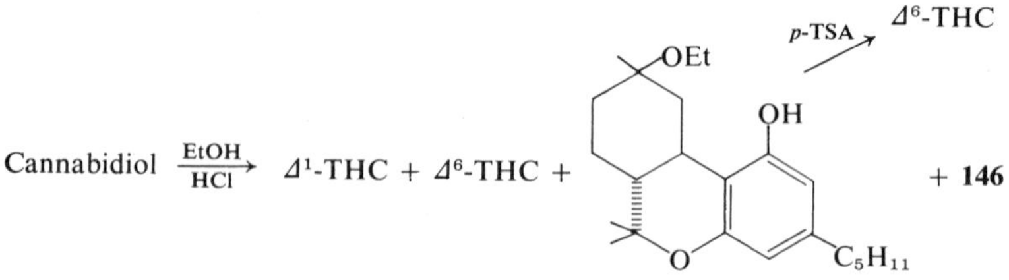

Cannabidiol $\xrightarrow{\text{EtOH}}{\text{HCl}}$ Δ^1-THC + Δ^6-THC + ... + **146**

145

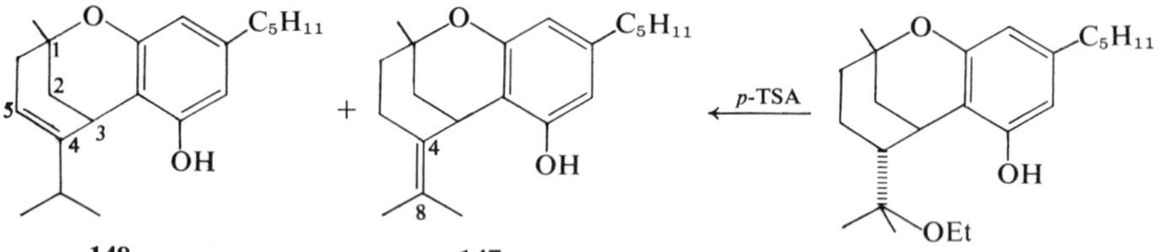

148   147   146

It should be pointed out that Adams' "THC, $(\alpha)_D - 130°$" may also have contained chlorinated cannabinoids, which would not have been observed in the latter work in which purification was done by chromatography. This method is conductive to dehydrochlorination.

On the assumption that the hydrochloric acid cyclization of cannabidiol leads to a single product, Šantavý (1964) suggested that its structure was Δ^1-THC. This conclusion is based on a calculation of the rotation values reported by Adams. Unfortunately, the basic assumption of these calculations has been shown to require revision. Šantavý also considered this "THC" to be identical with the natural material. This conjecture is unsupported.

On boiling with *p*-TSA in benzene Δ^1-*cis*-THC (**142b**) does not give the yet unknown Δ^6-*cis*-THC (**149**) but largely $\Delta^{4(8)}$-iso-THC (**147**) (Gaoni and Mechoulam, 1968). As the acetate of **142b** did not react under these conditions it was suggested that the formation of **147** from **142b** is not a stepwise reaction of a ring cleavage at C-8 followed by cyclization at C-1, but is a concerted reaction. Razdan and Zitko (1969) have examined this reaction in greater detail. They have shown that initially Δ^8-*cis*-iso-THC (**150**) is formed and then is converted mainly to **147**. Treatment of a pure mixture of **150** and **147** under identical conditions formed **142b** and citrylidene cannabis (**151**) in small amounts. They have suggested that **142b** initially forms **151**, which is the equilibrium juncture of Δ^1-*cis*-THC and the iso-THC's. Yagen and Mechoulam (1969) have shown that in boron trifluoride etherate in methylene chloride **147**, **151**, **142b**, **150**, **144**, and **148** equilibrate (presumably through cation **a**) to a mixture in which **147** is the major component. However, Δ^6-THC (**143b**) and cannabicyclol (**152**) are stable and do not participate in this equilibrium. These observations are in accordance with previous reports that **151** gives **147** and/or **150** on acid treatment (Mechoulam *et al.*, 1968b; Crombie and Ponsford, 1968c, 1971).

The acid-catalyzed cyclizations of cannabichromene (**153a**) are closely related (Gaoni and Mechoulam, 1966a, 1968; Crombie and Ponsford, 1968c, 1971; Yagen and Mechoulam, 1969). Cannabichromene with *p*-TSA gives $\Delta^{4(8)}$-iso-THC (**147**); with acetic acid, **150** is formed; with excess 10% boron trifluoride etherate at $-20°C$ the tetracyclic diether **151** (16%) accompanies **150** (67%). These reactions apparently take place with cannabichromene in conformation I through cation **a**.

By contrast cannabichromene acetate (**153b**) with excess boron trifluoride etherate at 4°C gives Δ^1-*cis*-THC acetate (**142a**) (10%), presumably formed through ion **b**.

A minor product of the reaction of cannabichromene acetate with boron trifluoride at 4°C is the reduced cis tricyclic product **154** (Yagen and Mechoulam, 1969). The formation of this material is unusual, as it involves a stereospecific cyclization and a reduction. It has been assumed that the reaction proceeds through conformation II, which allows maximal overlap of π orbitals, and that the cis ring closure is due to the antiparallel nature of the cyclization. The intermediate benzylic cation **c** is then reduced by a hydride ion of uncertain origin. When cannabichromene acetate is cyclized with other

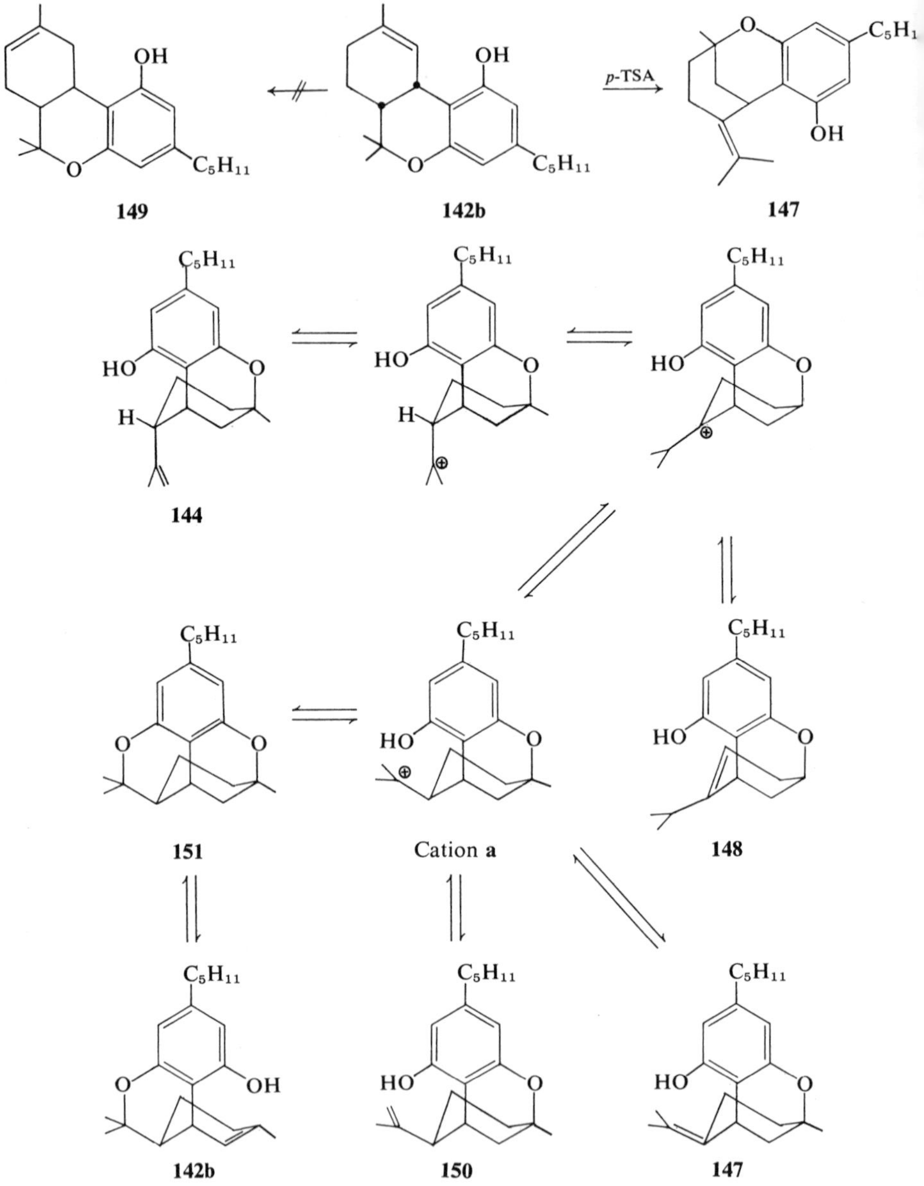

149   142b   147

144

151   Cation a   148

142b   150   147

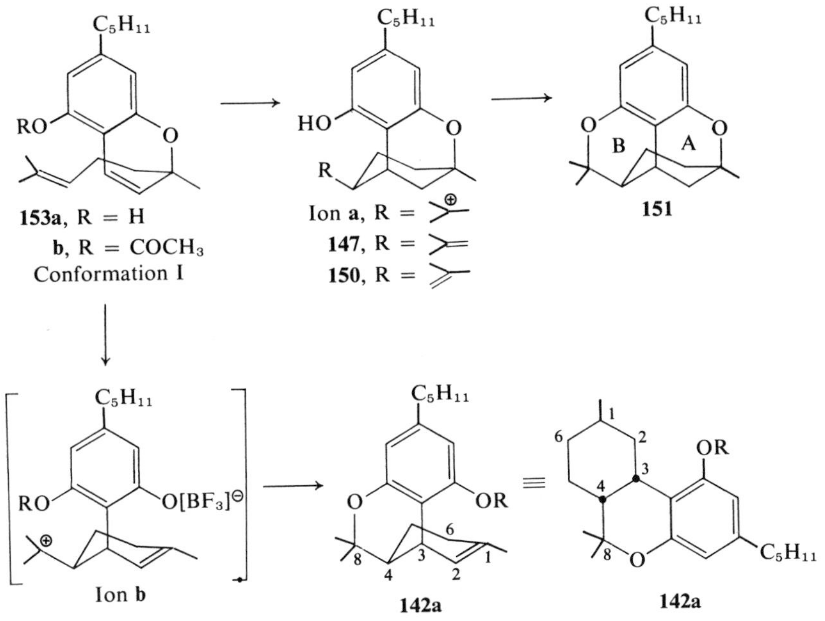

153a, R = H
   b, R = COCH₃
Conformation I

Ion a, R = (cation)
147, R = (group)
150, R = (group)

151

Ion b

142a   **142a**

acids no reduction takes place and the expected tricyclic **155** is obtained. It can be reduced to **154** and its trans isomer.

Cannabichromene with excess 5% boron trifluoride (Yagen and Mechoulam, 1969) gives a different product mixture from which cannabicyclol (**152**) (30%), $\Delta^{4(8)}$-iso-THC (**147**) (56%) and small amounts of Δ^1-*trans*-THC (**141a**), Δ^6-*trans*-THC (**143b**), and Δ^1-*cis*-THC were isolated. The formation of cannabicyclol (**152**) probably proceeds through intermediate **d**.

The production of the *trans*-THC's in the above reaction indicates an opening of the pyran ring in Δ^1-*cis*-THC (**142b**) followed by closure to the thermodynamically more stable trans series. This phenomenon has been independently observed in two other cases. Razdan and Zitko (1969) showed that when Δ^1-*cis*-THC was allowed to react with boron tribromide at $-20°C$ Δ^6-*trans*-THC was formed in 60% yield. Mechoulam *et al.* (1969) have reported that when Δ^1-THC acid B (**156**) and Δ^6-THC acid B methyl ester (**157**) are treated with boron trifluoride they are converted to Δ^6-THC acid A (**158a**) and Δ^6-THC acid A methyl ester (**158b**), respectively. Protonic acids such as *p*-TSA do not cause opening of the pyran ring.

The acid-catalyzed reactions of cannabigerol (**159**) and its cis isomer **160** have been investigated (Gaoni and Mechoulam, 1966a; Mechoulam and Yagen, 1969). It was shown that these 1,5-dienes cyclize at $-30°C$ with 100% sulfuric acid in nitromethane in a highly stereospecific fashion. The trans isomer **159** gives the trans tricyclic product **161**, while the cis **160** produces the

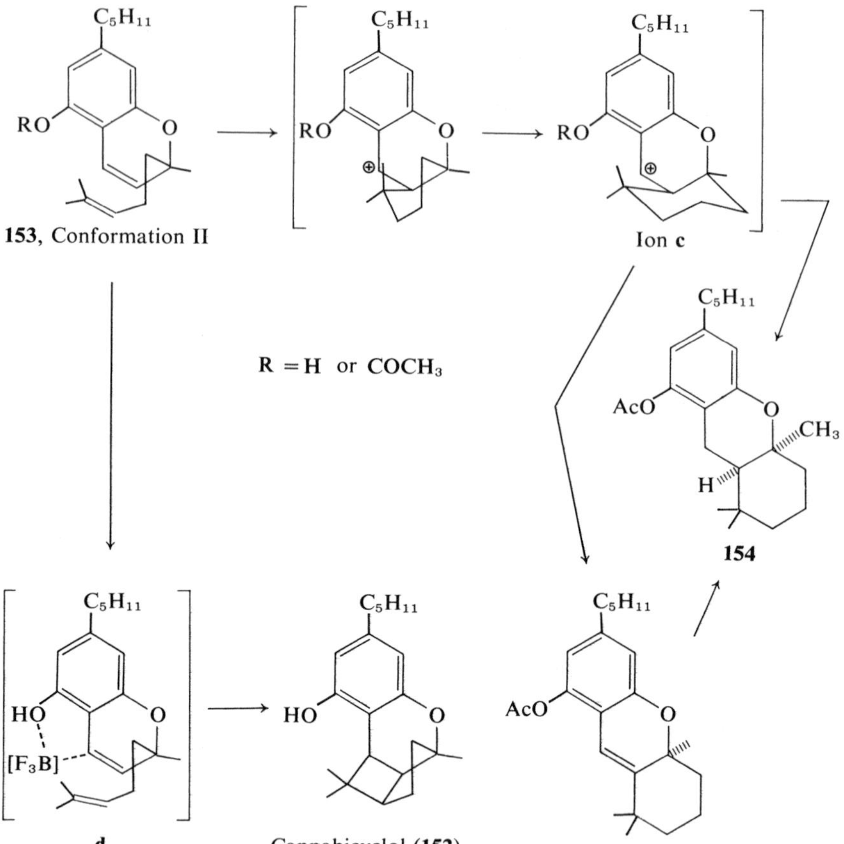

153, Conformation II

Ion c

R = H or COCH₃

154

d

Cannabicyclol (**152**)

155

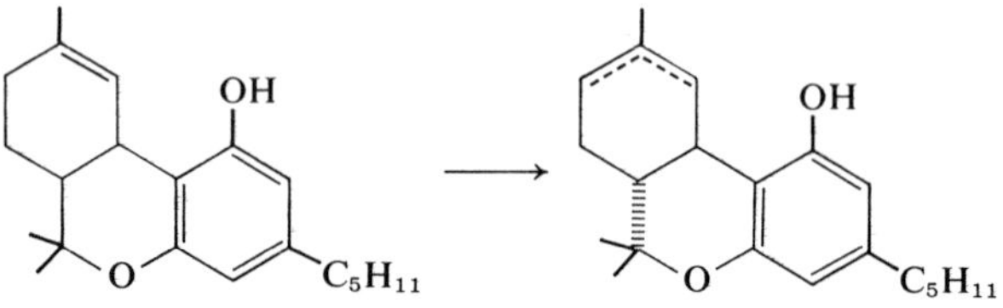

Δ¹-*cis*-THC

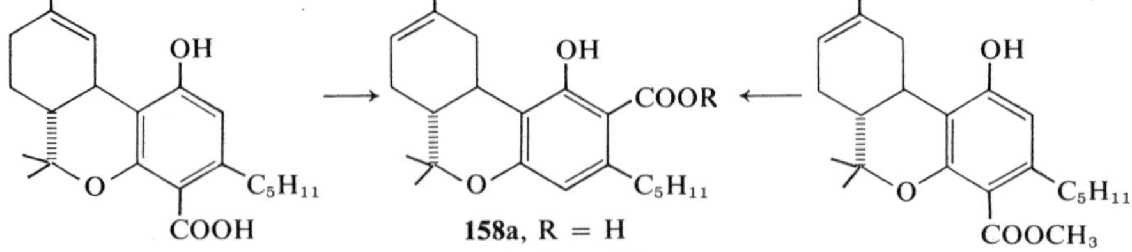

156

158a, R = H
b, R = CH₃

157

cis tricyclic compound **162**. These results have been interpreted as an example of the Stork–Eschenmoser cyclization scheme, which on the basis of conformational considerations assumes the stereospecific formation of polycyclics from 1,5-polyenes. The above cannabinoid examples are one of the few systems in which the cyclization is initiated by a direct protonation of a terminal double bond of the acylic precursor. Most organic–chemical cases described in the literature (Johnson, 1968) deal with suitable sulfonate esters, olefinic acetals, etc. The high stereospecificity of the cannabinoid cyclizations may not be due to concerted processes but to a large extent to the nucleophilicity of the phenolic groups which apparently attack the intermediate cations **f** and **g** *before* the achievement of conformational equilibration.

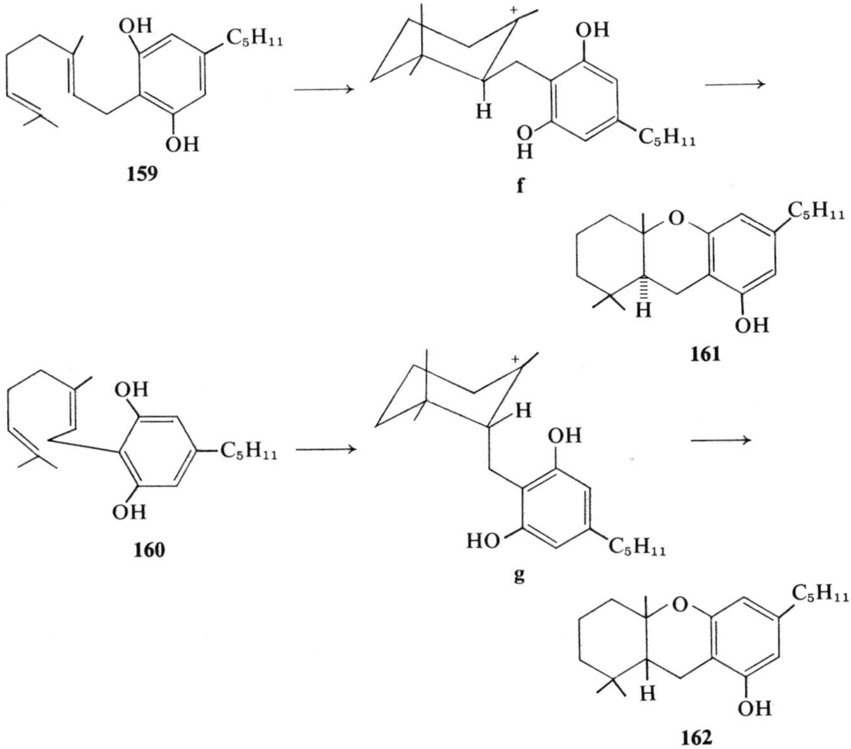

B. THERMAL REACTIONS

The thermal treatment of cannabis preparations is a widely used reaction—although not necessarily always in a laboratory setting. Our understanding of the chemical processes taking place on smoking marijuana is at best fragmentary and contrasts sharply with widespread knowledge of the practical ways and means for the introduction through burning of cannabis components in the human body.

All cannabinoid acids decarboxylate with ease on heating (140°–200°C). On storage at room temperature this process takes place at a much lower rate. Krejči *et al.* (1958) and Schultz and Haffner (1958) reported the high-yield transformation of cannabidiolic acid to cannabidiol. As cannabidiolic acid is a major component of hemp it is conceivable that this acid can be available as an industrial by-product. The inactive cannabidiol obtained on decarboxylation is readily converted on acid treatment to the active Δ^1-THC and Δ^6-THC (see Section V,A). Hence, by these processes cannabidiolic acid can serve as the starting material for the semisynthetic production of THC's. In the author's laboratory, on a bench scale, large quantities of THC's have been prepared via this method in the last few years.

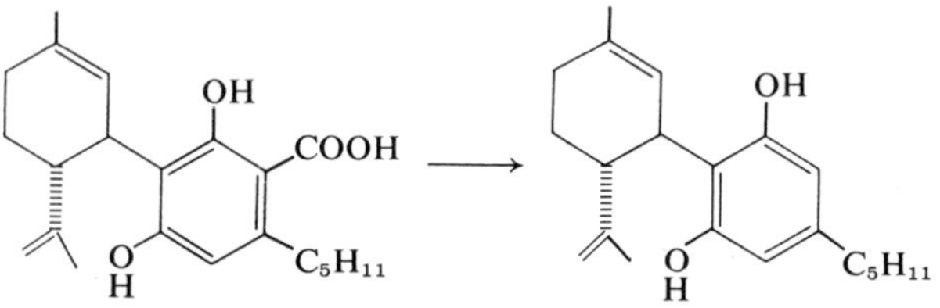

Cannabidiolic acid   Cannabidiol

The parallel decarboxylation of other cannabinoid acids has been reported: Δ^1-THC acids (Mechoulam *et al.*, 1969), cannabichromenic acid (Shoyama *et al.*, 1968), and the cannabielsoic acids (Shani and Mechoulam, 1970). Claussen and Korte (1968b) have reported that on storage, in addition to decarboxylation, cannabidiolic acid and Δ^1-THC acid A isomerize with ease to secondary, as yet unidentified acids.

Of particular importance is the decarboxylation of the THC acids, especially Δ^1-THC acid A, which is a major component of apparently all psychotomimetically active chemotypes of *Cannabis sativa* as well as cannabis preparations. In stored cannabis, Δ^1-THC acid A is probably slowly converted to Δ^1-THC, which is, in turn, oxidized to cannabinol. It is possible that the THC acids thus constantly replenish the dwindling amounts of Δ^1-THC in stored hashish.

The formation of Δ^1-THC from the Δ^1-THC acids undoubtedly takes place during the crude production of marijuana, hashish, and charas from fresh cannabis. Although no critical chemical investigation on this point seems to have been reported, the descriptions of the production itself leave no doubt on the qualitative aspect of the process. Lys (1932) described in detail the large-scale preparation of hashish in Lebanese villages: The female plants are cut during August to November and left for a week on an open terrace "pour prendre l'humidité de la nuit." The drying process is then continued in the shade. The production of hashish lasts during the entire winter. The dried flowering tops (or the whole plant) are shaken and then gently beaten several times over a cloth. The powder is then sieved. The material obtained after the first shaking or beating is considered to be of the highest quality ("hashish zahra"). The powder is collected in small cloth bags, which are then exposed to steam. The powder is thus partially resinified and glued together, and the cloth bags are pressed into "soles."* Numerous authors have described the preparation and handling of various other cannabis preparations: marijuana and others (Walton, 1938), Greek hashish (Rosenthaler, 1911), and Belouchistan charas (Hooper, 1908). Marshall (1902) observed the collecting of Indian charas. Bouquet (1950, 1951) has described the various methods for the production of hashish as well as the numerous culinary and smoking styles of Middle Eastern habitués. Decarboxylations of the cannabinoid acids undoubtedly occur during the above-described elaborate manipulations of the crude materials.

The chemistry of cannabis smoking has been investigated by several groups but is still only partially understood. Most investigators have found no conversion of cannabidiol or its acid to THC (Claussen and Korte, 1968a; Agurell and Leander, 1971; Coutselinis and Miras, 1970; Shoyama *et al.*, 1969). However, Mikeš and Waser (1971) have noted that the ratio of Δ^1-THC to cannabidiol increases in the smoke as compared to the starting material and have proposed that a partial cyclization does indeed take place. It was also suggested that this could explain the observed activity in human smokers of marijuana with a low content of Δ^1-THC. This suggestion is difficult to reconcile with the view generally held (but not documented) that European industrial hemp, which has a high content of cannabidiolic acid, is totally inactive. In any case this important observation should be further experimentally clarified.

A certain conversion of Δ^1-THC to cannabinol takes place on smoking (Claussen and Korte, 1968a; Mikeš and Waser, 1971; Shoyama *et al.*, 1969; Coutselinis and Miras, 1970). The exact percentage of cannabinol formed is difficult to estimate, as this requires a precise knowledge of the rate of destruction through burning of both cannabinoids. However, Shoyama *et al.* (1969) have estimated that $\sim 10\%$ of the Δ^1-THC is thus transformed into cannabinol. Petcoff *et al.* (1971) reported that the smoke condensate of a machine-smoked sample of Δ^1-THC contained 60% Δ^1-THC and 40% cannabinol. The analysis was performed by the novel technique of centrifugal chromatography. Manno *et al.* (1970) have indicated that some of the THC is

* The term "hashish sole" is widely used in the Middle East. It originates from the fact that the pressed bags containing hashish used to be smuggled inside the shoes of traffickers.

converted to both cannabinol and cannabidiol (on gas chromatographic evidence). The latter reaction is unusual and has not been observed by other groups. It needs further documentation. The dehydrogenation of cannabinoids is further discussed in the next section.

Many investigators (Claussen and Korte, 1968a; Miras *et al.*, 1964; Agurell and Leander, 1971; Shoyama *et al.*, 1969) have reported that the cannabinoid acids are completely decarboxylated on smoking to the respective neutral components. This reaction is of considerable importance, as the content of THC acids in marijuana and hashish is frequently considerable.

Cannabigerol, cannabinol, and Δ^6-THC are not transformed into other cannabinoids on smoking (Agurell and Leander, 1971; Shoyama *et al.*, 1969). As discussed in the previous section the possible conversion of Δ^1-THC to Δ^6-THC on smoking has been suggested. Under normal smoking experimental conditions this reaction is not observed (Claussen and Korte, 1968a; Shoyama *et al.*, 1969; Mikeš and Waser, 1971; Agurell and Leander, 1971; Manno *et al.*, 1970). However, heating Δ^1-THC under argon at 230°C (in a steel or copper vessel) for 2 hours caused a partial double-bond isomerization (Claussen and Korte, 1968a). The authors consider the time factor the cause of this difference. It is difficult to accept this rationalization without further experimentation in view of the generally established rate/temperature relationships of chemical processes. A cationic reaction cannot be discounted. Complete isomerization of Δ^1-THC to Δ^6-THC was observed on smoking "artificial" hashish made from extracted hemp straw and Δ^1-THC. This artificial hashish is reported to burn very poorly and not uniformly. While the prolonged time of smoking (unfortunately unspecified) can be the isomerization factor, the possibility that organic acids in the straw catalyze the process has not been discounted. The experimental evidence seems to suggest that the Δ^1- to Δ^6-THC isomerization is of little importance in the smoking of marijuana or hashish cigarettes. However, it should be taken into account when the material or the smoke has had the chance to be in contact with acidic substances or metal surfaces.

The above-described results point out that except for decarboxylation of the cannabinoid acids there is little difference between the major cannabinoids of the smoke and those in the drug itself. However, at the high temperature of the smoking process some (or most) of the cannabinoids are destroyed and hence only part of the active THC reaches the lungs. On this point the experimental results differ widely, as they clearly depend on the experimental conditions. Claussen and Korte (1968a) have reported that 98–99% of the THC in tobacco cigarettes containing Δ^1-THC is destroyed on smoking. An unknown, nonpolar compound is formed. If these results are relevant to non-experimental smoking they can be interpreted to mean that Δ^1-THC when delivered through the lungs is active at doses (~ 0.5 μg/kg) that are comparable to those required for LSD activity. This follows from the observation by

Isbell *et al.* (1967) that cigarettes containing 50 μg Δ^1-THC/kg of body weight are active. Kiplinger *et al.* (1971) have reported that even doses about 5 times lower cause changes in motor and mental performance.

Manno *et al.* (1970) and Coutselinis and Miras (1970) reported that after being smoked on a machine imitating the normal technique for smoking, approximately 50% of the Δ^1-THC originally in the cigarette was delivered in the smoke. In an additional experiment Manno *et al.* showed that in the smoke expired after inhalation by the subject less than 0.1% of the THC in the cigarette could be recovered and less than 5% remained in the butt. Mikeš and Waser (1971) found that the amount of unpyrolized components (Δ^1-THC and cannabidiol) in the smoke from a smoking machine ranged between 21 and 23% of the amount present in the cigarette. Agurell and Leander (1971) reached similar results: 14–20% of the cannabinoid constituents of hashish cigarettes were transferred to the respiratory system on smoking. The corresponding figures for pipe smoking were ~45%. Over 80% of the inhaled cannabinoids from a hashish–tobacco cigarette were retained in the lungs if the smoke was not immediately exhaled. More precise determinations were not possible using hashish cigarettes due to the considerable background interference from the admixed tobacco in the gas chromatographic determination. Smoking of marijuana cigarettes allowed very high retention of the cannabinoids when the smoking was by the deep inhalation technique practiced by cannabis smokers. Apparently the cannabis smoking technique of experienced habitués has now been experimentally justified.

The experimental methods used by the various groups differ to such an extent that it is very difficult to form an opinion regarding the exact percentage of THC delivered from a cigarette to the lung. It seems to this author that the results of the Swedish and Swiss groups are best relevant to human consumption. Calculation based on their data (~80% destruction of THC on smoking) and those of Kiplinger *et al.* (1971) cited above indicates that the lowest active dose (for the parameters measured) of THC delivered and absorbed in the lungs is ~2.5 μg/kg body weight. For a discussion of the smoking process from a pharmacological viewpoint see Chapter 5, Section I,A.

On gas chromatography the cannabinoid acids are completely decarboxylated. This may be an advantage in a routine analysis, for this reaction parallels the smoking process. All the THC available to a smoker in a given sample can thus be determined. When an exact determination of the content is required, decarboxylation can be prevented by esterification (Lerner, 1963) or by silylation (Fetterman *et al.*, 1971a).

C. Oxidations and Dehydrogenations

The deterioration of cannabis preparations with time has been known in the hashish trade for centuries. Marshall (1909) showed experimentally that this loss of potency is due to oxidation. He passed oxygen through "active cannabinol" (red oil) kept fluid by immerson in a bath at 150°–160°C. After passing oxygen for 6 hours the activity was found to be considerably lowered. Carbon dioxide passed in the same way had almost no effect. A sample of "active cannabinol" patiently kept in a sealed tube for 10 years exhibited no loss in activity. Charas exposed to air for the same length of time lost 90% of its potency.

Levine (1944) examined a 100 lb lump of charas at the beginning and the end of a 3-year period. He found that the potency of the interior portion was unchanged. The activity of the outer crust had fallen, however, to one-twentieth of its former value. The crusty material yielded a considerable amount of cannabinol. No cannabinol was found in the inner part of the lump, whose content of "THC" remained constant. It was concluded that "THC" was dehydrogenated spontaneously to cannabinol.

The loss of potency in old samples of cannabis preparations, although a well-known phenomenon, has not been fully investigated from a chemical viewpoint. The dehydrogenation of Δ^1-THC to cannabinol is undoubtedly the major process. However, under certain conditions, di- or polymerization may be expected to occur. Hashish contains considerable amounts of polyphenolic materials which have not been examined. As phenols are notorious for their facile self-condensations, it can be surmised that some of the polyphenols in cannabis are produced from cannabinoids.

In order to prevent the decomposition of Δ^1-THC it should be stored under nitrogen or in a sealed tube, preferably in an inert solvent (carbon tetrachloride of petroleum ether) at 0°–5°C. In this manner Δ^1-THC has been kept unchanged in the author's laboratory for many years. Similar conditions have been suggested by Turk et al. (1971).

The dehydrogenation of Δ^3-THC, Δ^6-THC, and related compounds to cannabinol with sulfur or selenium was reported by the groups of Adams and Todd (see Sections III,F and IV,A). Wollner et al. (1942) found that their natural "THC" was easily converted to cannabinol by the above dehydrogenation reagents or by boiling with chloranil in benzene. This conversion was later confirmed with pure Δ^1-THC (Gaoni and Mechoulam, 1964a). Recently Shoyama et al. (1970) showed that cannabinolic acid was formed on storage, apparently from Δ^1-THC acid A.

The driving force for the formation of cannabinol appears to be considerable. The isocannabinoids **144, 147,** and **148** are easily converted to cannabinol on sulfur dehydrogenation (Gaoni and Mechoulam, 1968). On mechanistic grounds this reaction is not exceptional.

The mechanism of the chloranil dehydrogenation of cannabinoids has been discussed in some detail (Mechoulam et al., 1968b). It was found that in contrast to Δ^1-THC, Δ^1-cis-THC and Δ^6-THC are not converted to canna-

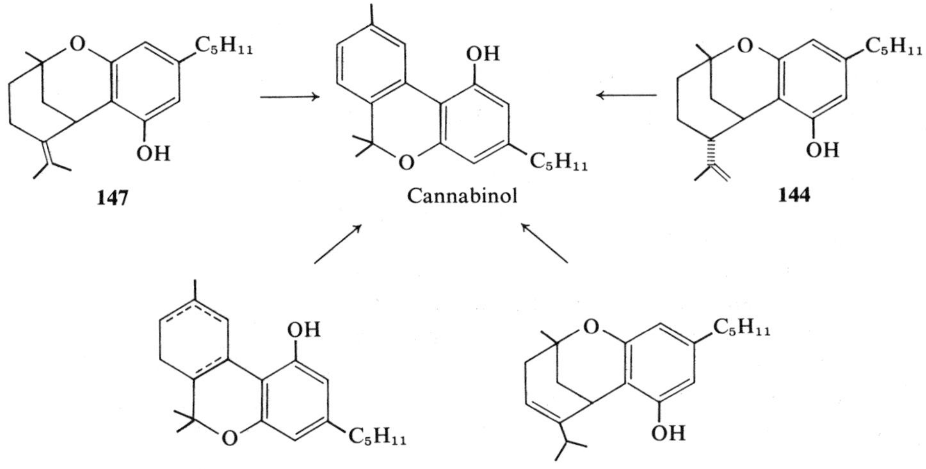

147 Cannabinol **144**

Various THC's **148**

binol and that cannabidiol does not undergo any change on boiling with chloranil in benzene. This dichotomy has been attributed to stereoelectronic factors. The difference in reactivity between Δ^1-THC and Δ^6-THC is due to the absence of allylic activation on the C-3 benzylic hydrogen in the latter compound. This also explains the greater stability of Δ^6-THC in oxidation in general as compared to Δ^1-THC. The difference between the other cannabinoids is more subtle. In Δ^1-THC, the C-3–H during abstraction as the hydride will remain in constant overlap with the π electrons of both the double bond and the aromatic ring, thus lowering the energy of the transition state. In cannabidiol the terpenoid and aromatic rings are perpendicular to each

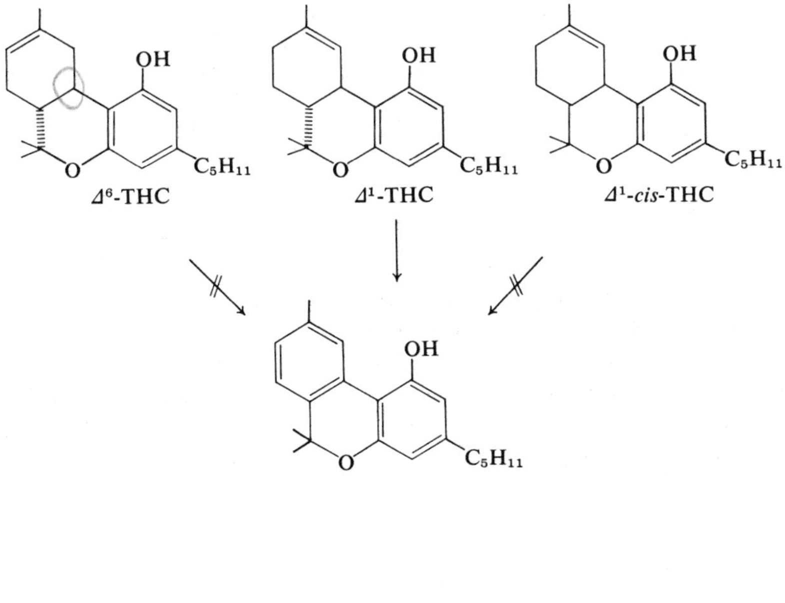

Δ^6-THC Δ^1-THC Δ^1-*cis*-THC

other, and therefore overlap is possible with the π electrons of the double bond only. The C-2–H in the preferred conformation of Δ^1-*cis*-THC is at a dihedral angle of $\sim 35°$ with the C-3–H, and σ–π overlap in the transition state is limited to the phenolic ring only, with which C-3–H forms an angle of $\sim 80°$.

The dehydrogenation of cannabigerol to cannabichromene with chloranil and DDQ has been described (see Section IV,D).

The air oxidation of cannabidiol in the presence of potassium hydroxide is the basis of the Beam test for identification of cannabis. Under these conditions cannabinoids in which both phenolic groups are free and have at least one unsubstituted aromatic position are oxidized to a mixture of quinones (Mechoulam *et al.*, 1968a). In the case of cannabidiol the main products are **163** and the dimeric **164**. The anions of these two compounds are violet and are responsible for the Beam color test.

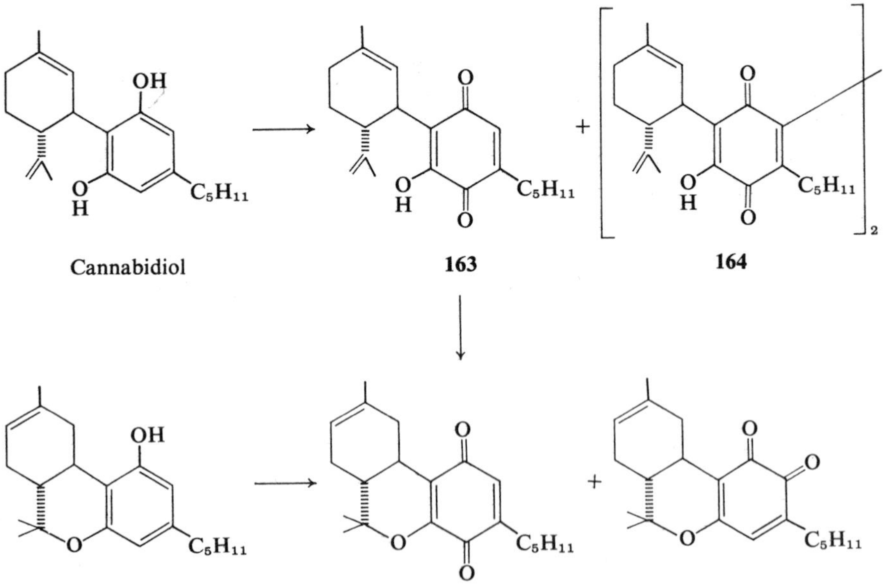

Cannabidiol   163   164

Δ^6-THC   165   166

The *p*-quinone **163** has been correlated with Δ^6-THC. The latter, on oxidation with *m*-chloroperbenzoic acid, gives a mixture of **165** and **166**. The quinone **163** on acid treatment gives **165**.

The selenium dioxide oxidations of Δ^1-THC and Δ^6-THC are discussed in Section IV,F dealing with metabolite syntheses. The oxidation of Δ^6-THC acetate with *tert*-butyl chromate gives 5-keto-Δ^6-THC acetate (**167**), which on reduction yields two allylic alcohols (Varconi, 1970).

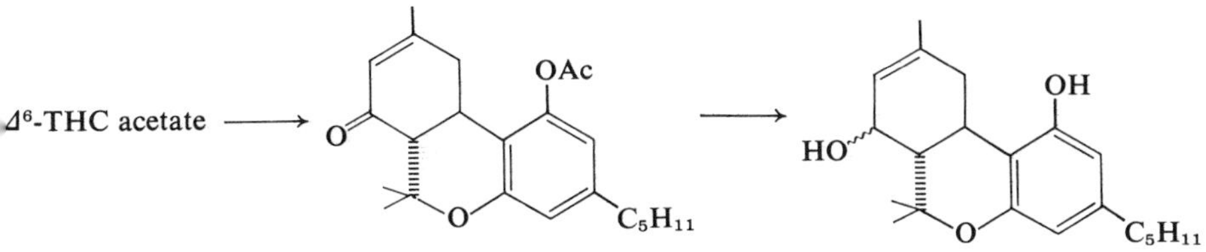

Δ^6-THC acetate ⟶

(167)

D. Photochemical Reactions

The photochemical syntheses of cannabicyclol from cannabichromene (Crombie *et al.*, 1968) and of cannabielsoic acid A from cannabidiolic acid in the presence of oxygen (Shani and Mechoulam, 1970) have been described (see Sections IV,D and IV,E respectively).

A related reaction is the conversion of olivetyl pinene (**168**) to a tetrahydrodibenzofuran (**169**), which takes place on irradiation in methanol (Shani and Mechoulam, 1970). This reaction is apparently initiated by a phenolic radical attack. It is of interest that the same reaction is observed on distillation of **168**.

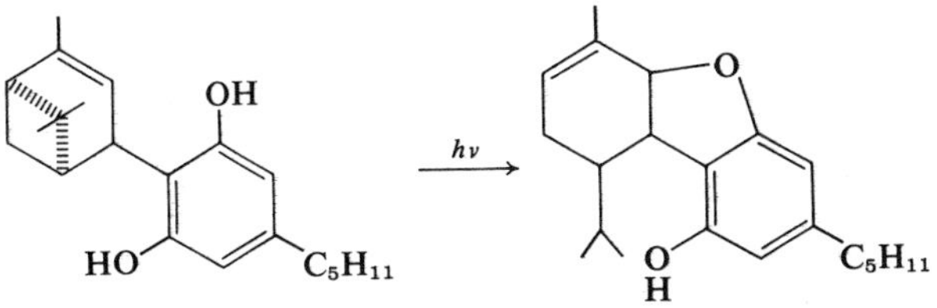

168   **169**

The chemical behavior of cannabidiol on irradiation has been cursorily mentioned a number of times in the literature. Loewe (1950), in a review of the pharmacological work of his group, mentions that on ultraviolet irradiation cannabidiol gives a mixture that on the basis of a dog ataxia test contains ~2% active material. Korte and Sieper (1965) exposed cannabidiol to lights of different energies. An unidentified compound was the major product; it had no psychotomimetic activity. Hively (1966), in a thesis, reported that cannabidiolic acid diacetate on irradiation gave Δ^6-THC. This unusual transformation has not been confirmed (Shani and Mechoulam, 1971).

Recently, the photoreactivity of cannabidiol has been reinvestigated (Shani and Mechoulam, 1971). Irradiation in methanol gave mainly 1-methoxydihydrocannabidiol (**170**). Both C-1 isomers were obtained. Irradiation of cannabidiol in cyclohexane produced a complicated mixture from which Δ^1-THC, Δ^8-iso-THC (**144**), 8-dihydrocannabidiol (**171**), and 3'-

cyclohexylcannabidiol (172) were isolated. The biological activity of the irradiated mixture correlated well with its Δ^1-THC content. The formation of Δ^1-THC and Δ^8-iso-THC has precedence in related intramolecular Markovnikoff-type additions of phenols to double bonds.

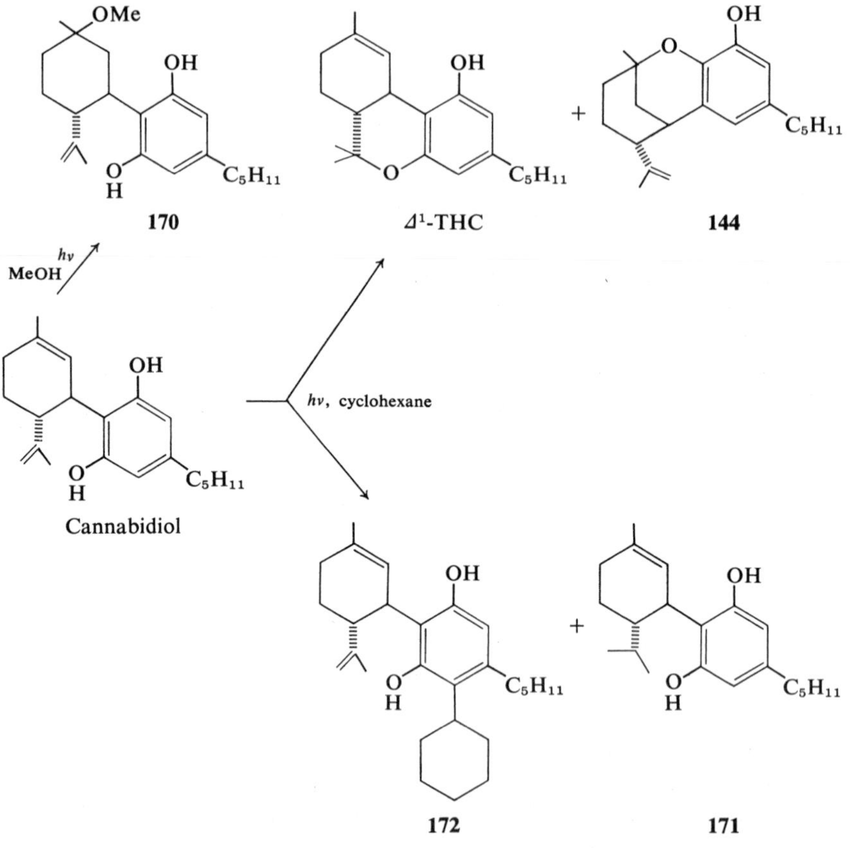

It is doubtful that any Δ^1-THC found in nature, or produced during the clandestine manufacture of cannabis preparations, is formed through a photochemical sequence. The Δ^8-iso-THC in the reaction is formed in a yield equal to that of Δ^1-THC. However, no iso-THC's have ever been isolated or observed in hashish.

The photolability of the double bond in Δ^6-THC (Nilsson et al., 1971) is described in Section IV,F.

The photo-Fries rearrangement of cannabidiol esters has been observed (Shani, 1970). Cannabidiol diacetate on irradiation gives a mixture of cannabidiol, acetyl cannabidiol acetate (173), and acetyl cannabidiol (174).

The ester **175** on irradiation forms the ketone **176**, which is easily converted to isocannabichromene (**177**).

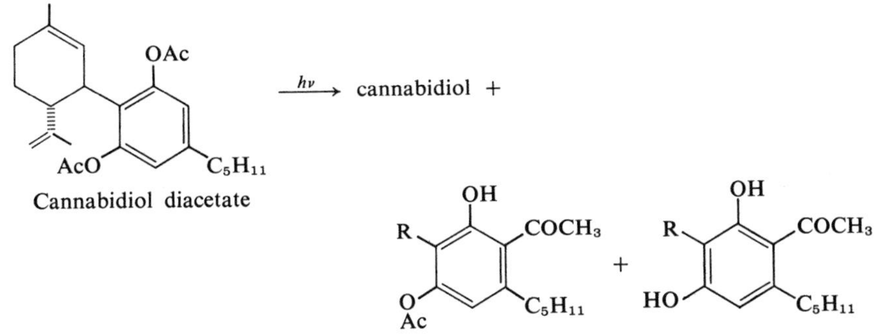

Cannabidiol diacetate

$\xrightarrow{h\nu}$ cannabidiol +

173 + **174**

R = Terpene moiety

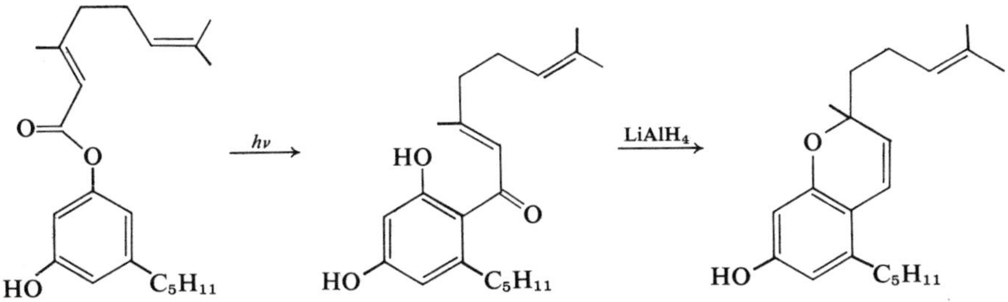

175 $\xrightarrow{h\nu}$ **176** $\xrightarrow{\text{LiAlH}_4}$ **177**

Shoyama *et al.* (1970) have described the photochemical conversion (in the presence of air) of Δ^1-THC acid A to cannabinolic acid.

E. ADDITIONS TO DOUBLE BONDS

The Δ^8-double bond in cannabidiol can be hydrogenated over platinum oxide in preference to the Δ^1 double bond (Gaoni and Mechoulam, 1968). This selectivity is probably due to the greater steric accessibility of the isopropylidene side chain as compared to that of the cyclohexene ring. Further hydrogenation takes place at a lower rate and leads predominantly to the tetrahydrocannabidiol **178**, in which the methyl group is equatorial (Mechoulam and Gaoni, 1967a).

Epoxidation of cannabidiol bisdinitrobenzoate takes place on the ring double bond. This is due to the electrophilic nature of the reaction (Mechoulam and Shvo, 1963). The epoxide ring thus formed is α, i.e., trans, to the

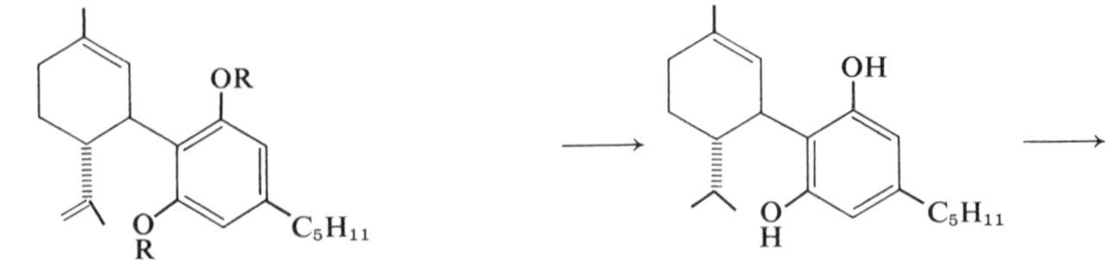

Cannabidiol, R = H
Cannabidiol
bisdinitrobenzoate, R = COC$_6$H$_3$(NO$_2$)$_2$

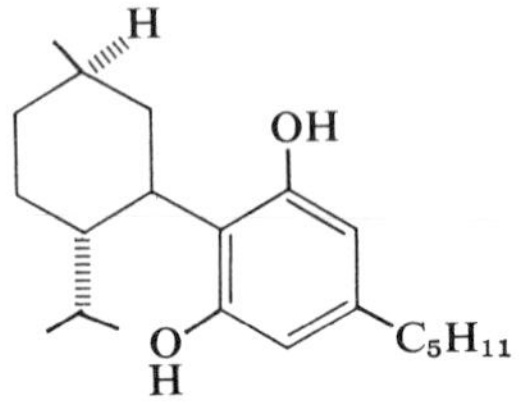

178

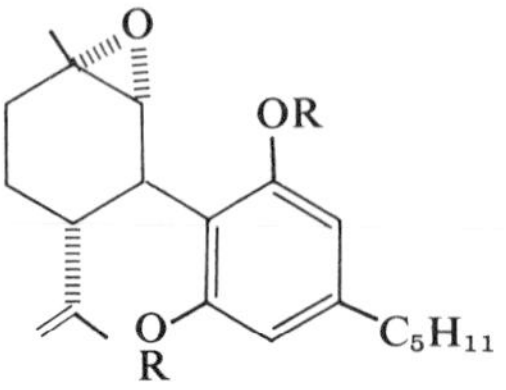

phenyl ring. The stereochemistry of this reaction is in accordance with the empirical rule that hydrogenation and epoxidation occur from the same side of the molecule.

Hydrogenation of Δ^6-THC over platinum oxide gives the isomers **179a** and **179b** in a 3:1 ratio (Gaoni and Mechoulam, 1966c; Archer *et al.*, 1970), while that of Δ^1-THC leads to a predominant α attack; the ratio of the isomers in this case is 1:2. The stereochemistry of **179a** at C-1 has been determined by a detailed nmr analysis, including nuclear Overhauser effect observations. The axial C-1 methyl group in **179a** causes a significant deshielding of the C-3 proton signal, whereas the corresponding equatorial methyl in **179b** has no effect. It was also shown that irradiation at the signals of the axial C-8 methyl and axial C-1 methyl resulted in an integrated intensity increase of the C-3 proton of 25%. Irradiation of the C-8 methyls only (in related compounds) led to a much lower intensity increase. This indicates the proximity of the C-1 methyl to the C-3-H and establishes its position as axial (α).

Epoxidation of Δ^6-THC acetate leads predominantly to the β-epoxide, which by stereospecific rearrangement with boron trifluoride gives the ketone **180**. Rearrangements of this type are known to proceed with inversion. Ketone **180** is stable on basic treatment, thus establishing the equatorial nature of the C-1 methyl. Wolf–Kishner reduction of **180** leads to **179b** (Ben-Zvi, 1971). The epoxidation in Δ^6-THC proceeds therefore in the same stereochemical direction as hydrogenation.

Epoxidation of Δ^1-THC acetate takes place, as expected, by predominant α attack, forming **181** (Ben-Zvi, 1971; Varconi, 1970). This was established

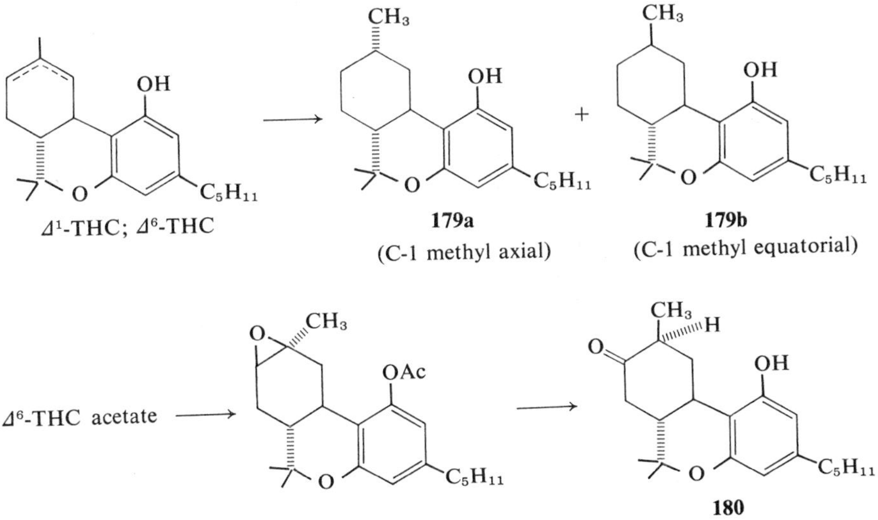

Δ¹-THC; Δ⁶-THC → 179a (C-1 methyl axial) + 179b (C-1 methyl equatorial)

Δ⁶-THC acetate → ... → 180

by a rearrangement to the corresponding ketone **182**. Equilibration of the ketone with base leads to the more stable isomer **183**, in which the C-1 methyl is equatorial. Lithium aluminum hydride reduction of **182** gives **184**.

Hydroboration of Δ¹-THC acetate leads to a mixture from which the two possible isomers **184** and **185** were isolated in ~12% yield each. Owing to the low yields, no conclusions can be drawn as to the stereochemical preference of the reaction. The diol **184** melts at 240°C, an exceptionally high melting point for a cannabinoid. This may be due to a strong hydrogen bond between

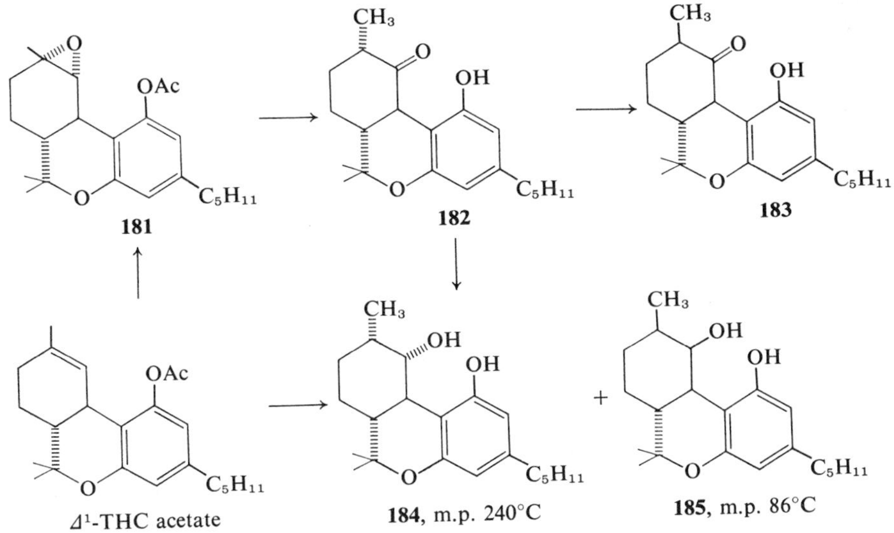

181 → 182 → 183

Δ¹-THC acetate → 184, m.p. 240°C + 185, m.p. 86°C

the two alcohol groups; the molecule acquires the characteristics of a poly-cyclic molecule. It may be a coincidence that the only natural cannabinoid that crystallizes with ease is the tetracyclic cannabicyclol (152).

Hydroboration of Δ^6-THC gives a mixture of the two 6-hydroxyhexahydro-cannabinols 186 and 187. Each was obtained in 20–25% yields. The structures of these compounds were determined by conversion to the respective tosylates, and through lithium aluminum hydride reduction, to the corresponding hexahydrocannabinols 179a and 179b.

The tosylate of 186 can be converted to the hitherto unknown Δ^5-THC (188) by treatment with potassium *tert*-butylate in benzene (Varconi, 1970).

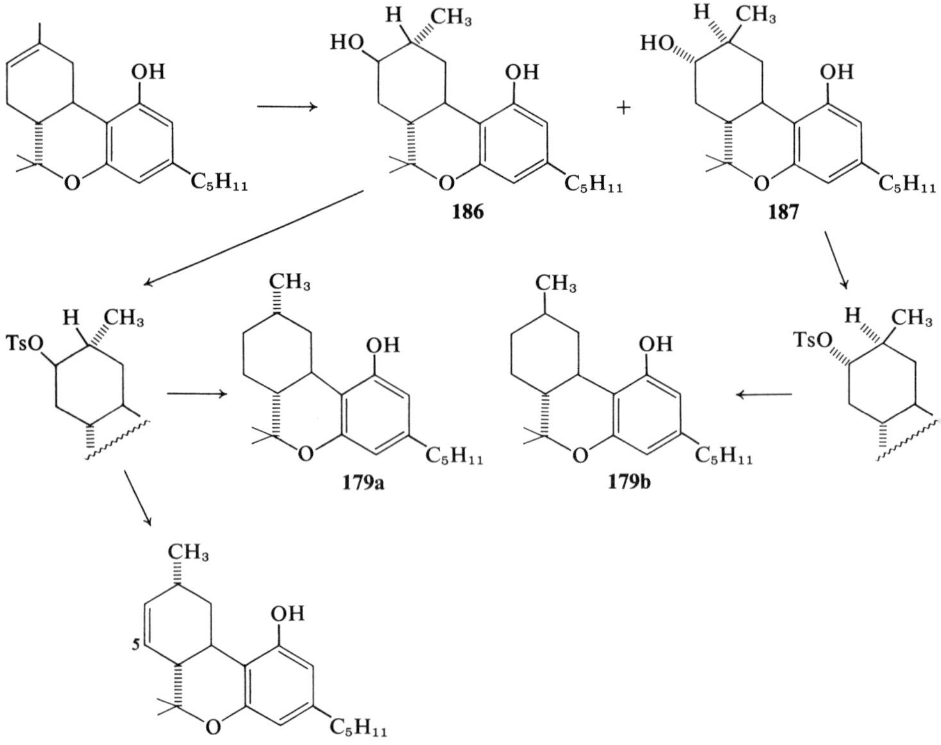

The reaction of Δ^6-THC acetate with osmium tetroxide (Section IV,F) and the acid-catalyzed (Section V,A) and photochemical additions (Section V,D) of alcohols to double bonds in the cannabinoid series have been discussed.

F. MISCELLANEOUS REACTIONS

Cannabidiol is split into olivetol and *p*-cymene by pyridine hydrochloride at 220°C (Adams *et al.*, 1940b). Dihydrocannabidiol dimethyl ether (189) undergoes a similar cleavage: On boiling in benzene with *p*-toluene-sulfonic acid, olivetol dimethyl ether is isolated (Adams *et al.*, 1941b). These cleavages can be viewed as reversed Friedel-Crafts reactions.

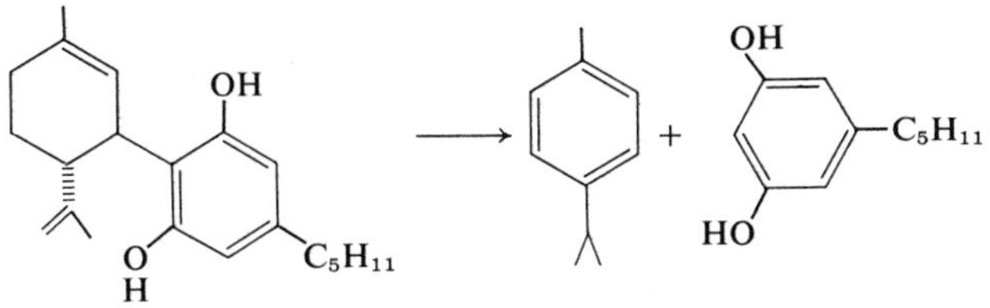

Cannabidiol

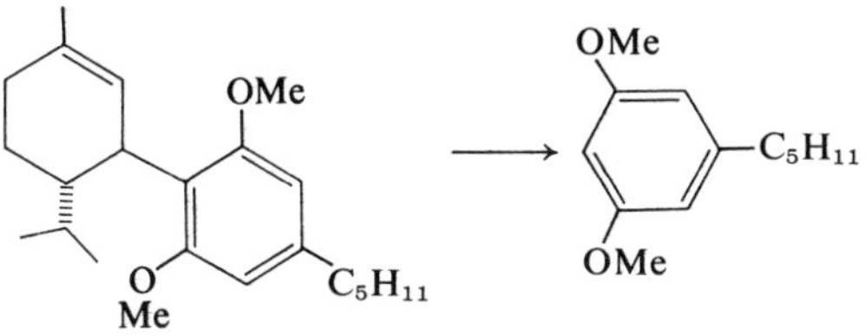

189

It has been pointed out (Section IV,E) that cannabidiol easily undergoes aromatic carboxylation with methyl magnesium carbonate. This reaction does not occur with monophenols and is typical for resorcinols. It is an expression of the high reactivity of the aromatic positions ortho to the free phenolic group. A further aromatic substitution due to this reactivity is the formation of the amide **190** (in addition to the expected urethane) from the reaction between Δ^1-THC and 3,5-dinitrophenyl isocyanate (Gaoni and Mechoulam, 1971). This substitution seems to be the first case of a comparable reaction of a phenol.

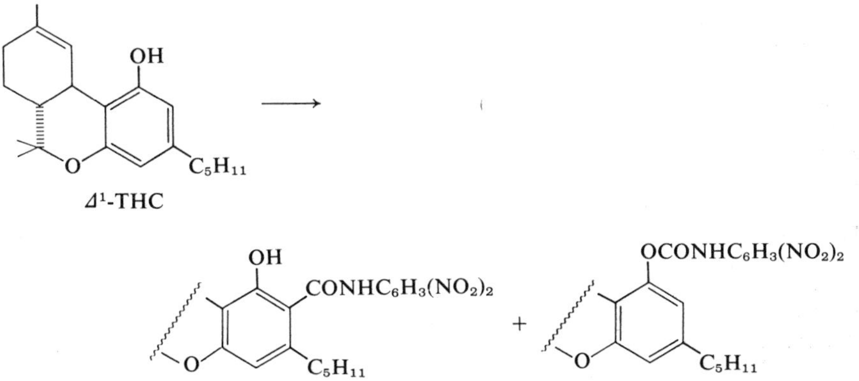

Δ^1-THC

190 Δ^1-THC-3,5-dinitrophenylurethane

Cannabinoid acids and esters are reduced on lithium aluminum hydride treatment directly to the corresponding alkyl derivatives. Thus, Δ^6-THC acid methyl ester gives 4′-methyl-Δ^6-THC (191) (Ben-Zvi, 1971). This new type of THC derivative is biologically active, although less than the parent Δ^6-THC.

191

References

Adams, R. (1942). *Bull. N.Y. Acad. Med.* **18**, 705.

Adams, R., and Baker, B. R. (1940a). *J. Amer. Chem. Soc.* **62**, 2208.

Adams, R., and Baker, B. R. (1940b). *J. Amer. Chem. Soc.* **62**, 2401.

Adams, R., and Baker, B. R. (1940c). *J. Amer. Chem. Soc.* **62**, 2405.

Adams, R., and Bockstahler, T. E. (1952). *J. Amer. Chem. Soc.* **74**, 5436.

Adams, R., and Carlin, R. B. (1943). *J. Amer. Chem. Soc.* **65**, 360.

Adams, R., Hunt, M., and Clark, J. H. (1940a). *J. Amer. Chem. Soc.* **62**, 196.

Adams, R., Hunt, M., and Clark, J. H. (1940b). *J. Amer. Chem. Soc.* **62**, 735.

Adams, R., Pease, D. C., Clark, J. H., and Baker, B. R. (1940c). *J. Amer. Chem. Soc.* **62**, 2197.

Adams, R., Cain, C. K., and Baker, B. R. (1940d). *J. Amer. Chem. Soc.* **62**, 2201.

Adams, R., Baker, B. R., and Wearn, R. B. (1940e). *J. Amer. Chem. Soc.* **62**, 2204.

Adams, R., Pease, D. C., Cain, C. K., Baker, B. R., Clark, J. H., Wolff, H., and Wearn, R. B. (1940f). *J. Amer. Chem. Soc.* **62**, 2245.

Adams, R., Pease, D. C., Cain, C. K., and Clark, J. H. (1940g). *J. Amer. Chem. Soc.* **62**, 2402.

Adams, R., Smith, C. M., and Loewe, S. (1941a). *J. Amer. Chem. Soc.* **63**, 1973.

Adams, R., Cain, C. K., McPhee, W. D., and Wearn, R. B. (1941b). *J. Amer. Chem. Soc.* **63**, 2209.

Agurell, S. (1970). *In* "The Botany and Chemistry of Cannabis" (C. R. B. Joyce, and S. H. Curry, eds.), pp. 175–191. Churchill, London.

Agurell, S., and Leander, K. (1971). *Acta Pharm. Suecica* **8**, 391.

Archer, R. A., Boyd, D. B., Demarco, P. V., Tyminski, I. J., and Allinger, N. L. (1970). *J. Amer. Chem. Soc.* **92**, 5200.

Bargellini, G., and Forli-Forti, G. (1910). *Gazz. Chim. Ital.* **40**, 74.

Begley, M. J., Clarke, D. G., Crombie, L., and Whiting, D. A. (1970). *Chem. Commun.* 1547.

Ben-Zvi, Z. (1971). Ph.D. thesis, Hebrew Univ., Jerusalem.

Ben-Zvi, Z., Mechoulam, R., and Burstein, S. (1970a). *J. Amer. Chem. Soc.* **92**, 3468.

Ben-Zvi, Z., Mechoulam, R., and Burstein, S. (1970b). *Tetrahedron Lett.* 4495.

Ben-Zvi, Z., Mechoulam, R., Edery, H., and Porath, G. (1971). *Science* **174**, 951.

Bercht, C. A. L., and Salemink, C. A. (1969). U.N. Secretariat Document ST/SOA/ SER.S/21.
Bercht, C. A. L., Küppers, F. J. E. M., Lousberg, R. J. J. Ch., Salemink, C. A., Svendsen, A. B., and Karlsen, J. (1971). U.N. Secretariat Document ST/SOA/SER.S/29.
Bergel, F., and Vögele, K. (1932). *Ann. Chem.* **493**, 250.
Bergel, F., and Wagner, R. (1930). *Ann. Chem.* **482**, 55.
Berkoff, C. E., and Crombie, L. (1960). *J. Chem. Soc.* 3734.
Blatt, A. H. (1938). *J. Wash. Acad. Sci.* **28**, 465.
Bohlig, J. F. (1840). *Jahrb. Prakt. Pharm.* 1.
Bolas, T., and Francis, E. E. H. (1869). *J. Chem. Soc.* **22**, 417.
Bouquet, J. (1950). *Bull. Narcotics* **2**, No. 4, 14.
Bouquet, J. (1951). *Bull. Narcotics* **3**, No. 1, 22.
Budzikiewicz, H., Aplin, R. T., Lightner, D. A., Djerassi, C., Mechoulam, R., and Gaoni, Y. (1965). *Tetrahedron* **21**, 1881.
Burstein, S. H., Menezes, F., Williamson, E., and Mechoulam, R. (1970). *Nature (London)* **225**, 87.
Cahn, R. S. (1930). *J. Chem. Soc.* 986.
Cahn, R. S. (1931). *J. Chem. Soc.* 630.
Cahn, R. S. (1932). *J. Chem. Soc.* 1342.
Cahn, R. S. (1933). *J. Chem. Soc.* 1400.
Cardillo, G., Cricchio, R., and Merlini, L. (1968). *Tetrahedron* **24**, 4825.
Casparis, P., and Baur, E. (1927). *Pharm. Acta Helv.* **2**, 108.
Chazan, J.-B., and Ourisson, G. (1968a). *Bull. Soc. Chim. France* 1374.
Chazan, J.-B., and Ourisson, G. (1968b). *Bull. Soc. Chim. France* 1384.
Claussen, U., and Korte, F. (1966a). *Naturforscher* **21b**, 594.
Claussen, U., and Korte, F. (1966b). *Naturwissenschaften* **53**, 541.
Claussen, U., and Korte, F. (1968a). *Ann. Chem.* **713**, 162.
Claussen, U., and Korte, F. (1968b). *Ann. Chem.* **713**, 166.
Claussen, U., von Spulak, F., and Korte, F. (1966). *Tetrahedron* **22**, 1477.
Claussen, U., von Spulak, F., and Korte, F. (1968a). *Tetrahedron* **24**, 1021.
Claussen, U., Mummenhoff, P., and Korte, F. (1968b). *Tetrahedron* **24**, 2897.
Coutselinis, A. S., and Miras, C. J. (1970). U.N. Secretariat Document ST/SOA/ SER.S/23.
Covello, M. (1948). *Farmaco* **3**, 8.
Crombie, L., and Ponsford, R. (1968a). *Chem. Commun.* 368.
Crombie, L., and Ponsford, R. (1968b). *Chem. Commun.* 894.
Crombie, L., and Ponsford, R. (1968c). *Tetrahedron Lett.* 4557.
Crombie, L., and Ponsford, R. (1971). *J. Chem. Soc. C* 796.
Crombie, L., Ponsford, R., Shani, A., Yagnitinsky, B., and Mechoulam, R. (1968). *Tetrahedron Lett.* 5771.
Czerkis, M. (1907). *Ann. Chem.* **351**, 467.
Davis, K. H., Martin, N. H., Pitt, C. G., Wildes, J. W., and Wall, M. E. (1970). *Lloydia* **33**, 453.
Decourtive, E. (1848). *C. R. Acad. Sci.* **26**, 509.
de Ropp, R. S. (1960). *J. Amer. Pharm. Ass.* **49**, 756.
Dunstan, W. R., and Henry, T. A. (1898). *Proc. Chem. Soc. London* **14**, 44.
Edery, H., Grunfeld, Y., Ben-Zvi, Z., and Mechoulam, R. (1971). *Ann. N.Y. Acad. Sci.* **191**, 40.
Fahrenholtz, K. E., Lurie, M., and Kierstead, R. W. (1972). *J. Amer. Chem. Soc.* **89**, 5934.

Fetterman, P. S., Doorenbos, N. J., Keith, E. S., and Quimby, M. W. (1971a). *Experientia* **27**, 988.

Fetterman, P. S., Keith, E. S., Waller, C. W., Guerrero, O., Doorenbos, N. J., and Quimby, M. W. (1971b). *J. Pharm. Sci.* **60**, 1246.

Foltz, R. L., Fentiman, A. F., Leighty, E. G., Walter, J. L., Drewes, H. R., Schwartz, W. E., Page, T. F., and Truitt, E. B. (1970). *Science* **168**, 844.

Fraenkel, S. (1903). *Arch. Exp. Pathol. Pharmakol.* **49**, 266.

Gamage, J. R., and Zerkin, E. L. (1969). "A Comprehensive Guide to the English Language Literature on Cannabis (Marihuana)." STASH Press, Beloit, Wisconsin.

Gaoni, Y., and Mechoulam, R. (1964a). *J. Amer. Chem. Soc.* **86**, 1646.

Gaoni, Y., and Mechoulam, R. (1964b). *Proc. Chem. Soc. London* 82.

Gaoni, Y., and Mechoulam, R. (1966a). *Chem. Commun.* 20.

Gaoni, Y., and Mechoulam, R. (1966b). *J. Amer. Chem. Soc.* **88**, 5673.

Gaoni, Y., and Mechoulam, R. (1966c). *Tetrahedron* **22**, 1481.

Gaoni, Y., and Mechoulam, R. (1968). *Isr. J. Chem.* **6**, 679.

Gaoni, Y., and Mechoulam, R. (1971). *J. Amer. Chem. Soc.* **93**, 217.

Gastinel, J. B. (1848). *Bull. Acad. Roy. Med. Belg.* **13**, 675, 827, 1386.

Ghosh, R., Pascall, D. C. S., and Todd, A. R. (1940a). *J. Chem. Soc.* 1118.

Ghosh, R., Todd, A. R., and Wilkinson, S. (1940b). *J. Chem. Soc.* 1121.

Ghosh, R., Todd, A. R., and Wilkinson, S. (1940c). *J. Chem. Soc.* 1393.

Ghosh, R., Todd, A. R., and Wright, D. C. (1941). *J. Chem. Soc.* 137.

Gill, E. W. (1971). *J. Chem. Soc. C* 579.

Gill, E. W., Paton, W. D. M., and Pertwee, R. G. (1970). *Nature (London)* **228**, 134.

Grlić, Lj. (1962). *Bull. Narcotics* **14**, No. 3, 37.

Grlić, Lj. (1964). *Bull. Narcotics* **16**, No. 4, 29.

Haagen-Smit, A. J., Wawra, C. Z., Koepfli, J. B., Alles, G. A., Feigen, G. A., and Prater, A. N. (1940). *Science* **91**, 602.

Hay, M. (1883). *Pharm. J.* **42**, 998.

Hegnauer, R. (1964). "Chemotaxonomie der Pflanzen," Vol. 3, p. 350. Birkhaeuser, Basel.

Hively, R. L. (1966). Ph.D. thesis, Univ. of Delaware, Newark.

Hively, R. L., Mosher, W. A., and Hoffmann, F. W. (1966). *J. Amer. Chem. Soc.* **88**, 1832.

Hooper, D. (1908). *Pharm. J.* **81**, 347.

Idänpään-Heikkila, J., Fritchie, G. E., Englert, L. F., Ho, B. T., and McIsaac, W. M. (1969). *N. Engl. J. Med.* **281**, 330.

Isbell, H., Gorodetzky, C. W., Jasinski, D., Claussen, U., von Spulak, F., and Korte, F. (1967). *Psychopharmacologia* **11**, 184.

Jacob, A., and Todd, A. R. (1940a). *Nature (London)* **145**, 350.

Jacob, A., and Todd, A. R. (1940b). *J. Chem. Soc.* 649.

Jahns, E. (1887). *Arch. Pharm. (Weinheim)* **25**, 479.

Jen, T. Y., Hughes, G. A., and Smith, H. (1967). *J. Amer. Chem. Soc.* **89**, 4551.

Johnson, W. S. (1968). *Accounts Chem. Res.* **1**, 1.

Joyce, C. R. B., and Curry, S. H., eds. (1970). "The Botany and Chemistry of Cannabis." Churchill, London.

Kabelik, J., Krejči Z., and Šantavy, F. (1960). *Bull. Narcotics* **12**, No. 3, 5.

Kane, V. V. (1971). *Tetrahedron Lett.* 4101.

Kane, V. V., and Grayeck, T. L. (1971). *Tetrahedron Lett.* 3991.

Kane, V. V., and Razdan, R. K. (1968). *J. Amer. Chem. Soc.* **90**, 6551.

Kane, V. V., and Razdan, R. K. (1969). *Tetrahedron Lett.* 591.

Kennedy, G. W. (1886). *Pharm. J.* **46**, 453.

Kiplinger, G. F., Manno, J. E., Rodda, B. E., and Forney, R. B. (1971). *Clin. Pharmacol. Ther.* **12**, 650.

Klein, F. K., Rapoport, H., and Elliot, H. W. (1971). *Nature (London)* **232**, 258.

Kochi, H., and Matsui, M. (1967). *Agr. Biol. Chem.* **31**, 625.

Korte, F., and Sieper, H. (1960). *Ann. Chem.* **630**, 71.

Korte, F., and Sieper, H. (1964). *J. Chromatogr.* **13**, 90.

Korte, F., and Sieper, H. (1965). *In* "Hashish. Its Chemistry and Pharmacology" (G. E. W. Wolstenholme and J. Knight, eds.), pp. 15–30. Churchill, London.

Korte, F., Haag, M., and Claussen, U. (1965a). *Angew. Chem. Int. Ed. Engl.* **4**, 872.

Korte, F., Hackel, E., and Sieper, H. (1965b). *Ann. Chem.* **685**, 122.

Korte. F., Sieper, H., and Tira, S. (1965c). *Bull. Narcotics* **17**, No. 1, 35.

Korte, F., Dlugosch, E., and Claussen, U. (1966). *Ann. Chem.* **693**, 165.

Krejči, Z., and Santavý, F. (1955). *Acta Univ. Palacki. Olomuc.* **6**, 59.

Krejči, Z., Horák, M., and Šantavý, F. (1958). *Acta Univ. Palacki. Olomuc.* **16**, 9.

Krejči, Z., Horák, M., and Šantavý, F. (1959). *Pharmazie* **14**, 349.

Leaf, G., Todd, A. R., and Wilkinson, S. (1942). *J. Chem. Soc.* 185.

Lerner, M. (1963). *Science* **140**, 175.

Levine, J. (1944). *J. Amer. Chem. Soc.* **66**, 1868.

Loewe, S. (1950). Arch. Exp. Pathol. Pharmakol. **211**, 175.

Lys, P. (1932). *Ann. Fac. Med. Pharm. Beyrouth* **1**, 333.

Manno, J. E., Kiplinger, G. F., Bennett, I. F., Haine, S., and Forney, R. B. (1970). *Clin. Pharmacol. Ther.* **11**, 808.

Marshall, C. R. (1897). *Proc. Cambridge Phil. Soc.* **9**, 149.

Marshall, C. R. (1898). *J. Amer. Med. Ass.* **31**, 882.

Marshall, C. R. (1902). *Pharm. J.* **69**, 263.

Marshall, C. R. (1909). *Pharm. J.* **82**, 418.

Mechoulam, R. (1970). *Science* **168**, 1159.

Mechoulam, R., and Ben-Zvi, Z. (1969). *Chem. Commun.* 343.

Mechoulam, R., and Gaoni, Y. (1965a). *J. Amer. Chem. Soc.* **87**, 3273.

Mechoulam, R., and Gaoni, Y. (1965b). *Tetrahedron* **21**, 1223.

Mechoulam, R., and Gaoni, Y. (1967a). *Tetrahedron Lett.* 1109.

Mechoulam, R., and Gaoni, Y. (1967b). *Fortschr. Chem. Org. Naturst.* **25**, 175.

Mechoulam, R., and Shvo, Y. (1963). *Tetrahedron* **19**, 2073.

Mechoulam, R., and Yagen, B. (1969). *Tetrahedron Lett.* 5349.

Mechoulam, R., Braun, P., and Gaoni, Y. (1967). *J. Amer. Chem. Soc.* **89**, 4552.

Mechoulam, R., Braun, P., and Gaoni, Y. (1972). *J. Amer. Chem. Soc.* **94**, 6159.

Mechoulam, R., Ben-Zvi, Z., and Gaoni, Y. (1968a). *Tetrahedron* **24**, 5615.

Mechoulam, R., Yagnitinsky, B., and Gaoni, Y. (1968b). *J. Amer. Chem. Soc.* **90**, 2418.

Mechoulam, R., Ben-Zvi, Z., Yagnitinsky, B., and Shani, A. (1969). *Tetrahedron Lett.* 2339.

Mechoulam, R., Shani, A., Yagnitinsky, B., Ben-Zvi, Z., Braun, P., and Gaoni. Y. (1970a). *In* "The Botany and Chemistry of Cannabis" (C. R. B. Joyce and S. H. Curry, eds.), pp. 93–117. Churchill, London.

Mechoulam, R., Shani, A., Edery, H., and Grunfeld, Y. (1970b). *Science* **169**, 611.

Merkus, F. W. H. M. (1971). *Nature (London)* **232**, 579.

Merz, K. W., and Bergner, K. G. (1940). *Arch Pharm. (Weinheim)* **278**, 49, 97.

Mikeš, F., and Waser, P. G. (1971). *Science* **172**, 1158.

Miras, C. J., Simos, S., and Kiburis, J. (1964). *Bull. Narcotics* **16**, No. 1, 13.

Moore, L. A. (1969). "Marijuana (Cannabis) Bibliography," 55 pp. Bruin Humanist Forum, Los Angeles, California.

86

RAPHAEL MECHOULAM

Neumeyer, J. L., and Shagoury, R. A. (1971). *J. Pharm. Sci.* **60**, 1433.
Nielsen, B. E., and Lemmich, J. (1964). *Acta Chem. Scand.* **18**, 2111.
Nigam, M. C., Handa, K. L., Nigam, I. C., and Levi, L. (1965). *Can. J. Chem.* **43**, 3372.
Nilsson, I. M., Agurell, S., Nilsson, J. L. G., Ohlsson, A., Sandberg, F., and Wahlqvist, M. (1970). *Science* **168**, 1228.
Nilsson, J. L. G., Nilsson, I. M., and Agurell, S. (1969). *Acta Chem. Scand.* **23**, 2207.
Nilsson, J. L. G., Nilsson, I. M., Agurell, S., Akermark, B., and Lagerlund, I. (1971). *Acta Chem. Scand.* **25**, 768.
Obata, Y., and Ishikawa, Y. (1966). *Agr. Biol. Chem.* **30**, 619.
Obata, Y., Ishikawa, Y., and Kitazawa, R. (1960). *Bull. Agr. Chem. Soc. Jap.* **24**, 670.
Ohlsson, A., Abou-Chaar, C. I., Agurell, S., Nilsson, I. M., Olofsson, K., and Sandberg, F. (1971). *Bull. Narcotics* **23**, No. 1, 29.
Personne, J. (1855). *J. Phar. Chim.* **28**, 461.
Petcoff, D. G., Strain, S. M., Brown, W. R., and Ribi, E. (1971). *Science* **173**, 824.
Petrzilka, T., Haefliger, W., Sikemeier, C., Ohloff, G., and Eschenmoser, A. (1967). *Helv. Chim. Acta* **50**, 719.
Petrzilka, T., Haefliger, W., Sikemeier, C. (1969). *Helv. Chim. Acta* **52**, 1102.
Phillips, R., Turk, R., Manno, J., Jain, N., Crim, D., and Forney, R. (1970). *J. Forensic Sci.* **15**, 191.
Powell, G., Salmon, M., Bembry, T. H., and Walton, R. P. (1941). *Science* **93**, 522.
Preobraschensky, B. (1876). *Pharm. Z. Russ.* 705.
Rapoport, H., and Holden, K. G. (1959). *J. Amer. Chem. Soc.* **81**, 3738.
Razdan, R. K., and Handrick, G. R. (1970). *J. Amer. Chem. Soc.* **92**, 6061.
Razdan, R. K., and Kane, V. V. (1969). *J. Amer. Chem. Soc.* **91**, 5190.
Razdan, R. K., and Zitko, B. A. (1969). *Tetrahedron Lett.* 4947.
Robertson, A. (1847). *Pharm. J.* **6**, 70.
Robiquet, E. (1857). *J. Pharm. Chim.* **31**, 46.
Rosenthaler, L. (1911). *J. Pharm. Elsass-Lothringen* **38**, 232.
Salemink, C. A., Veen, E., and De Kloet, W. A. (1965). *Planta Med.* **13**, 211.
Šantavý, F. (1964). *Acta Univ. Palacki. Olomuc.* **35**, 5.
Savory (1843). *Pharm. J.* **3**, 80.
Schlesinger, S. (1840). *Repertorium Pharm.* 190.
Schultz, O. E. (1964). *Planta Med.* **12**, 371.
Schultz, O. E., and Haffner, G. (1958). *Arch. Pharm.* (*Weinheim*) **291**, 391.
Schultz, O. E., and Haffner, G. (1960). *Arch. Pharm.* (*Weinheim*) **293**, 1.
Schultze, E., and Frankfurt, S. (1894). *Chem. Ber.* **27**, 769.
Shani, A. (1970). Unpublished results.
Shani, A., and Mechoulam, R. (1970). *Chem. Commun.* 273.
Shani, A., and Mechoulam, R. (1971). *Tetrahedron* **27**, 601.
Shoyama, Y., Fujita, T., Yamauchi, T., and Nishioka, I. (1968). *Chem. Pharm. Bull.* **16**, 1157.
Shoyama, Y., Yamaguchi, A., Sato, T., Yamauchi, T., and Nishioka, I. (1969). *Yakagaku Zasshi* **89**, 842.
Shoyama, Y., Yamauchi, T., and Nishioka, I. (1970). *Chem. Pharm. Bull.* **18**, 1327.
Siebold, L., and Bradbury, T. (1881). *Pharm. J.* **41**, 326.
Simonsen, J. L., and Todd, A. R. (1942). *J. Chem. Soc.* 188.
Smith, T. (1885). *Pharm. J.* **44**, 853.
Smith, T., and Smith, H. (1847). *Pharm. J.* **6**, 171.
Smith, T., and Smith, H. (1848). *Pharm. J.* **8**, 36.

Steck, W., El-Dakhakhny, M., and Brown, S. A. (1969). *Tetrahedron Lett.* 4805.

Taylor, E. C., and Strojny, E. J. (1960). *J. Amer. Chem. Soc.* **82**, 5198.

Taylor, E. C., Lenard, K., and Shvo, Y. (1966). *J. Amer. Chem. Soc.* **88**, 367.

Todd, A. R. (1946). *Experientia* **2**, 55.

Tscheepe (1821). Thesis, Tübingen, Germany. Cited by United Nations Commission on Narcotic Drugs (1965).

Turk, R. F., Forney, R. B., King, L. J., and Ramachandran, S. (1969). *J. Forensic Sci.* **14**, 385.

Turk, R. F., Manno, J. E., Jain, N. C., and Forney, R. B. (1971). *J. Pharm. Pharmacol.* **23**, 190.

United Nations Commission on Narcotic Drugs (1965). "The Question of Cannabis. Cannabis Bibliography," Document E-CN 7-479, 250 pp. U.N. Econ. Soc. Council, New York.

United Nations Department of Social Affairs (1951). *Bull. Narcotics* **3**, No. 1, 59; No. 2, 42.

Valente, L. (1880). *Gazz. Chim. Ital.* 479.

Valle, J. R., Lapa, A. J., and Barros, G. G. (1968). *J. Pharm. Pharmacol.* **20**, 798.

Varconi, H. (1970). M.Sc. thesis, Hebrew Univ., Jerusalem.

Vignolo, G. (1895). *Gazz. Chim. Ital.* 262.

Vollner, L., Bieniek, D., and Korte, F. (1969). *Tetrahedron Lett.* 145.

von Spulak, F., Claussen, U., Fehlhaber, H. W., and Korte, F. (1968). *Tetrahedron* **24**, 5379.

Vree, T. B., Breimer, D. D., van Ginneken, C. A. M., van Rossum, J. M., de Zeeuw, R. A., and Witte, A. H. (1971). *Clin. Chim. Acta* **34**, 365.

Wall, M. E. (1971). *Ann. N.Y. Acad. Sci.* **191**, 23.

Wall, M. E., Brine, D. R., Brine, G. A., Pitt, C. G., Freudenthal, R. I., and Christensen, H. D. (1970). *J. Amer. Chem. Soc.* **92**, 3466.

Waller, C. W., and Denny, J. J. (1971). "Annotated Bibliography of Marihuana (*Cannabis sativa* L.) 1964–1970." The Research Institute of Pharmaceutical Sciences, Univ. of Mississippi, University.

Walton, R. P. (1938). "Marihuana. America's New Drug Problem," 223 pp. Lippincott, Philadelphia, Pennsylvania.

Widman, M., Nilsson, I. M., Nilsson, J. L. G., Agurell, S., and Leander, K. (1971). *Life Sci.* **10**, 157.

Wildes, J. W., Martin, N. H., Pitt, C. G., and Wall, M. E. (1971). *J. Org. Chem.* **36**, 721.

Wollner, H. J., Matchett, J. R., Levine, J., and Loewe, S. (1942). *J. Amer. Chem. Soc.* **64**, 26.

Wood, T. B., Spivey, W. T. N., and Easterfield, T. H. (1896). *J. Chem. Soc.* **69**, 539.

Wood, T. B., Spivey, W. T. N., and Easterfield, T. H. (1899). *J. Chem. Soc.* **75**, 20.

Work, T. S., Bergel, F., and Todd, A. R. (1939). *Biochem. J.* **33**, 123.

Yagen, B., and Mechoulam, R. (1969). *Tetrahedron Lett.* 5353.

Yagen, B., and Levy, S. (1970). Unpublished results.

Yamauchi, T. (1970). Personal communication.

Yamauchi, T., Shoyama, Y., Aramaki, H., Azuma, T., and Nishioka, I. (1967). *Chem. Pharm. Bull.* **15**, 1075.

Yamauchi, T., Shoyama, Y., Matsuo, Y., and Nishioka, I. (1968). *Chem. Pharm. Bull.* **16**, 1164.

Zubyk, W. J., and Conner, A. Z. (1960). *Anal. Chem.* **32**, 912.

Addendum

Cannabis Literature

A bibliography covering more than 3000 titles has been prepared (Polaczek, 1973). Most of the papers cited are available in the library of the Alcoholism and Drug Addiction Research Foundation in Toronto.

Natural Cannabinoids—Isolation and Identification

Vree et al. (1972) have identified, by combined gas chromatography and mass spectrometry at different electron voltages, a new series of cannabinoid homologs in which the side chain is a methyl (instead of a pentyl) group. These constituents, named cannabidiorcol, Δ^1-tetrahydrocannabiorcol, and cannabiorcol, were found in very small amounts in some samples from Brazil and Lebanon. On the basis of structure–activity studies summarized in Chapter 2 it can be assumed that these homologs have no psychotomimetic activity.

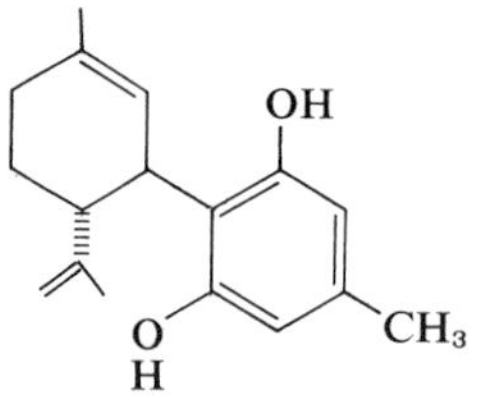

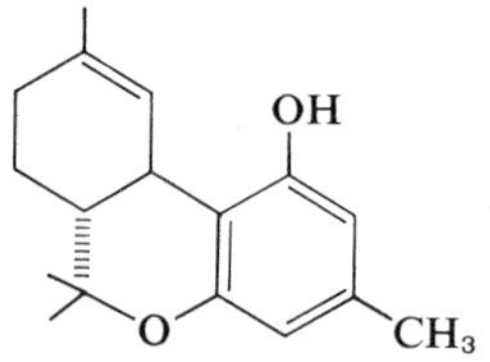

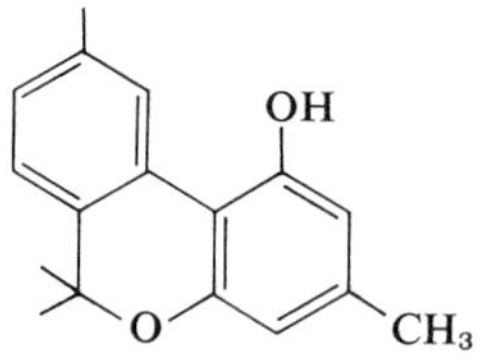

Cannabiorcol

De Zeeuw et al. (1972b) have published details of the isolation, identification, and occurrence in cannabis of propyl cannabinoids. The same group (De Zeeuw et al., 1972a) has confirmed that Δ^1-THC acid is an important component in the evaluation of cannabis products. Paris and Elmounaj (1972) have reported the isolation of cannabidiolic and THC acids from *Cannabis sativa* by preparative thin-layer chromatography.

There are further reports on the presence of alkaloids in cannabis (Aguar, 1971; Samrah et al., 1972). On the basis of preliminary data these alkaloids have been tentatively assigned an indole grouping. However, a positive identification has not been put forward.

The identification of new metabolites is discussed in Chapter 4.

Variations in Cannabinoid Content of Cannabis Plant Material*

Reports continue to appear with data showing the extreme variability of cannabinoid content of cannabis samples. Fairbairn et al. (1971a) found that leaves of cannabis plants grown in England from South African seeds

* See also Section III,B of this chapter and Section III,B of Chapter 3.

possessed 8.54 mg THC per gram of fresh plant material. In the flower tops
the amount of THC was 10.15 mg/gm. Nepalese strains had 7.63 mg/gm
in the leaves and 3.40 mg/gm in the flower tops. Other strains also showed
considerable variations. The main conclusion drawn was that cannabinoids
are probably formed in many parts of the plant but are stored mainly in the
glandular hairs of the floral parts or in the sessile glands (Fairbairn *et al.*,
1971b).

Kimura and Okamoto (1970) have reported that THC acid shows a
different distribution pattern in the various sections of the plant body
depending on the season. A remarkable increase in the bractlet was observed.
This increase paralleled the ripening of the seeds. The top leaf content of
THC acid, however, decreased during the same period. The authors concluded that THC acid is contained in the parts of active growth.

Haney and Kutscheid (1973) have reported that production of Δ^6-THC,
Δ^1-THC, cannabinol, and cannabidiol is determined, to a large extent, by
environmental conditions of the site where plants are grown (in a relatively
homogeneous genetic population). Δ^1-Tetrahydrocannabinol is under the
strongest environmental control. In general, content of these compounds is
higher in marijuana from stands where plants are stressed. Two types of
stress were suggested by the data, nutrient deficiency and inadequate moisture.
Competition from other plants enhances the content of cannabinoids, and
this relationship strengthens the stress hypothesis.

Turner and Hadley (1973) have confirmed a previous report by de Faubert-
Maunder (1970) that cannabidiol is not present in some South African
cannabis (dagga) samples.

CANNABINOID SYNTHESES

Cardillo *et al.* (1972) have investigated the condensation of terpenoid
allylic alcohols with olivetol in an acidic aqueous medium. The following
reactions were reported:

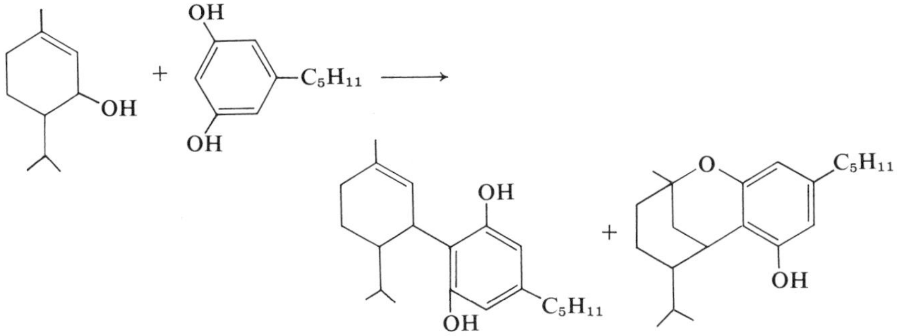

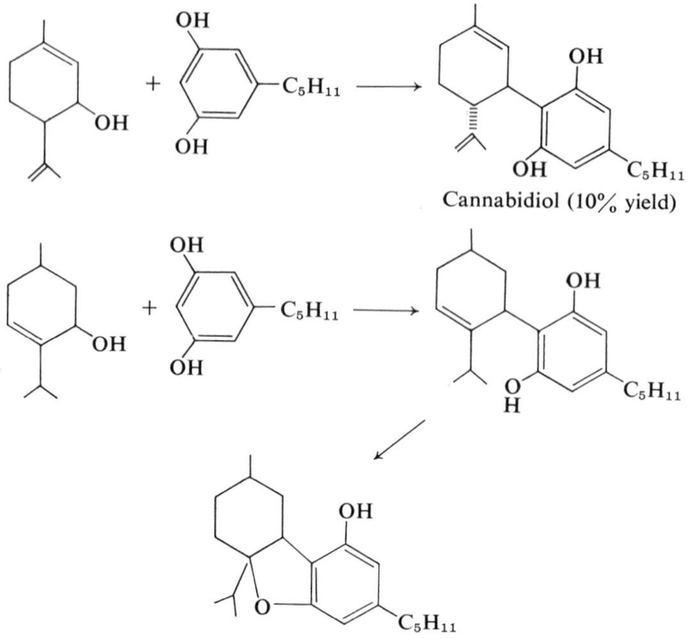

Cannabidiol (10% yield)

Of particular interest in the above reactions is the new synthesis of cannabidiol. However, the low yield and difficulty of preparing isopiperitenol make this route at present unattractive.

Bailey and Verner (1972b) have reported that a major by-product of the synthesis of Δ^6-THC from menthadienol and olivetol (see Section IV,A) is the following positional isomer:

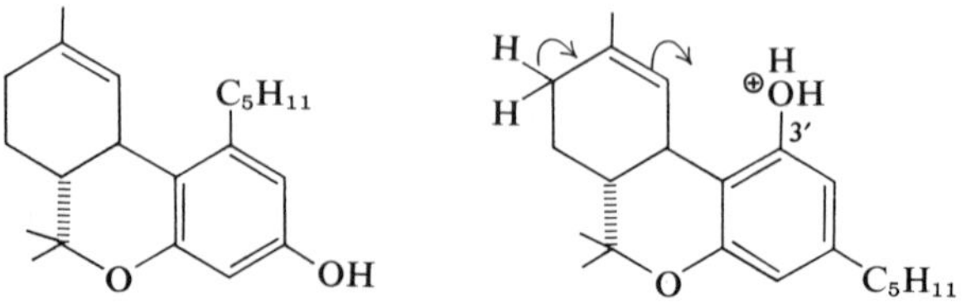

The formation of this isomer in the strongly acidic medium of the reaction rather than the Δ^6 isomer was explained on the basis of the nonexistence of the low-energy transition state shown above, which is obviously possible only for compounds that possess an oxygen-containing substituent at C-3'.

Manners *et al.* (1972) have reported biogenetic-type syntheses of isoprenoid and diisoprenoid derivatives of orcinol. The compounds obtained (from acyclic allylic alcohols, like geraniol and nerol, with orcinol) are rather similar to those reported for the parallel reactions with olivetol (see Sections IV,C and V,A). However, in the orcinol case, attachment of the terpenoid to the aromatic species can, and does, occur with equal ease at both the C-2 position and the C-4 position, leading to complicated mixtures.

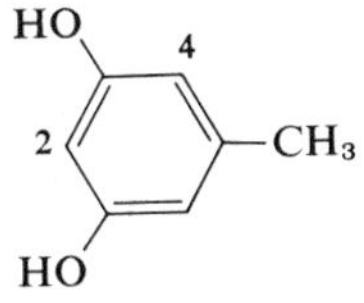

Combes *et al.* (1972) have investigated the syntheses and reactions of analogs of cannabichromene derived from phloracetophenone. Most of the numerous cyclization products obtained parallel those in the cannabinoid series (see Section V,A).

Mechoulam *et al.* (1972b) have published the details of their syntheses of ($\pm$)-cannabidiol, ($\pm$)-Δ^6-THC, and ($\pm$)-Δ^1-THC (from geraniol and olivetol) as well as that of ($-$)-Δ^6-THC and ($-$)-Δ^1-THC (from verbenol and olivetol) (see Section IV,B). Improved yields are reported.

Greb *et al.* (1972) have reported the synthesis of a novel group of aza-cannabinoids:

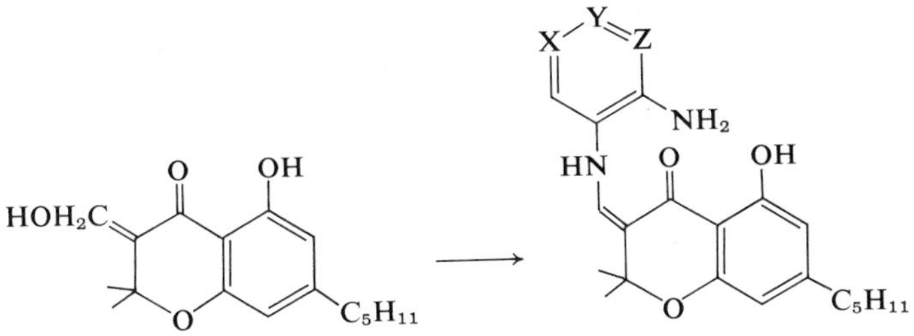

	X	Y	Z
a	CH	CH	CH
b	CH	C—CH₃	CH
c	CH	CH	C—CH₃
d	N	CH	CH

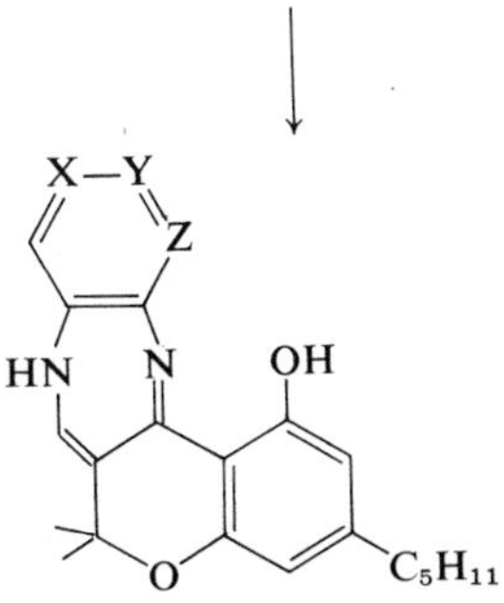

SYNTHESES OF CANNABINOID METABOLITES

Two additional syntheses of 7-hydroxy-Δ^6-THC have been described. Petrzilka et al. (1971) have used the following procedure:

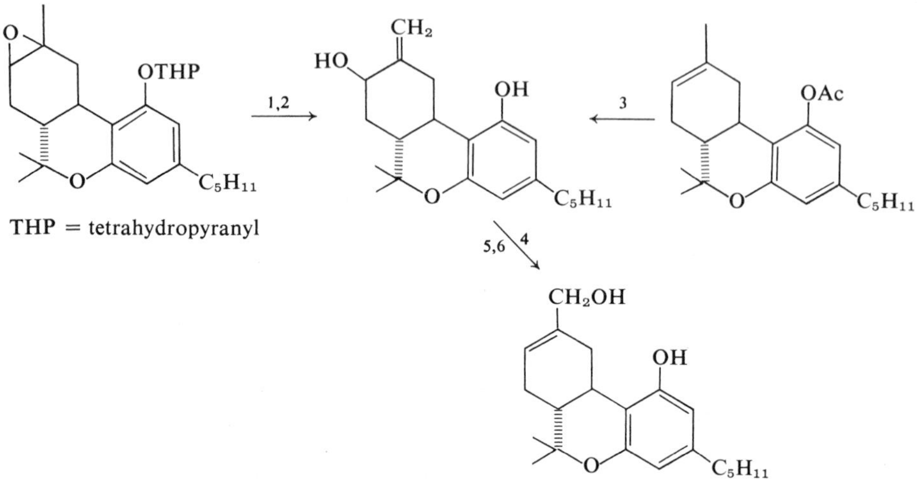

THP = tetrahydropyranyl

Reagents: 1, butyl lithium; 2, H$^+$; 3, irradiation, O$_2$-sensitizer, followed by NaBH$_4$; 4, Ac$_2$O/Py; 5, temp., 290°C; 6, LiAlH$_4$.

Weinhardt et al. (1971) have used $\Delta^{1(7)}$-THC, available as a minor by-product from a Δ^6-THC synthesis (Petrzilka's route, see Section IV,B), to obtain 7-hydroxy-Δ^6-THC:

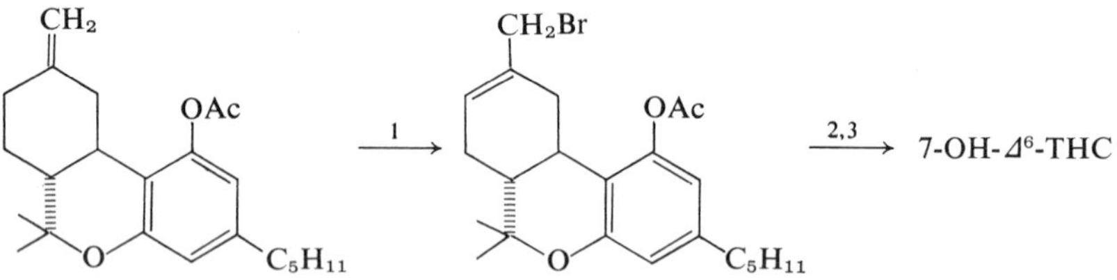

Reagents: 1, CH$_3$CONHBr; 2, silver acetate, AcOH; 3, NaOH.

A new approach to the preparation of 7-hydroxy-Δ'-THC has been taken by Lander et al. (1973):

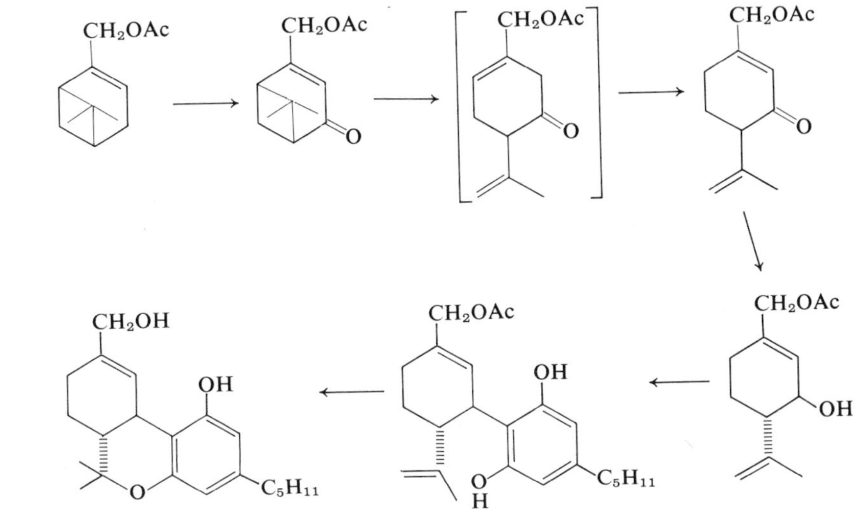

7-OH-Δ^1-THC

The bottleneck of this total synthesis is the preparation of the monoterpenoid intermediates. The overall yield is low.

Gurny *et al.* (1972) have described the isolation and the structures of five new THC metabolites produced from *in vitro* incubation with a microsomal supernatant liver fraction of a squirrel monkey. Δ^1-Tetrahydrocannabinol was metabolized to Δ^1-THC-6-one and 1,2-epoxyhexahydrocannabinol; Δ^6-THC gave Δ^6-THC-5-one and the C-5 isomers of Δ^6-THC-5-ol. These five metabolites were synthesized as follows (Mechoulam *et al.*, 1972c):

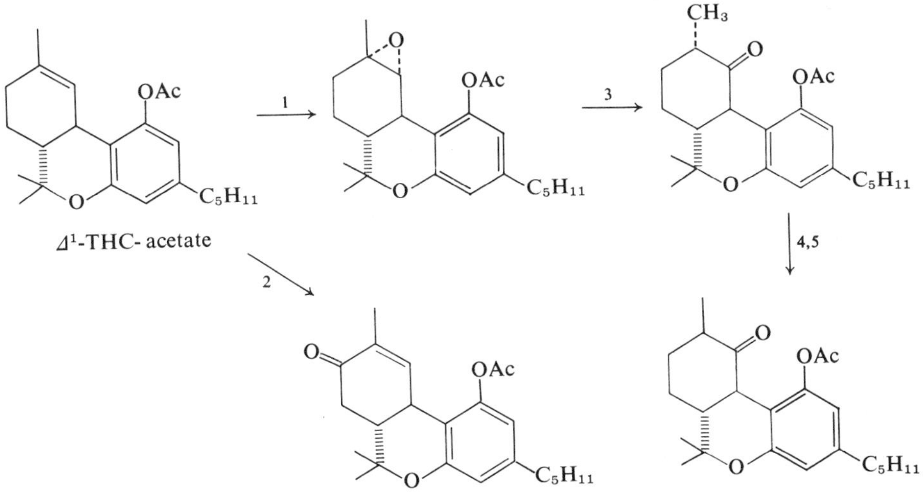

Δ^1-THC- acetate

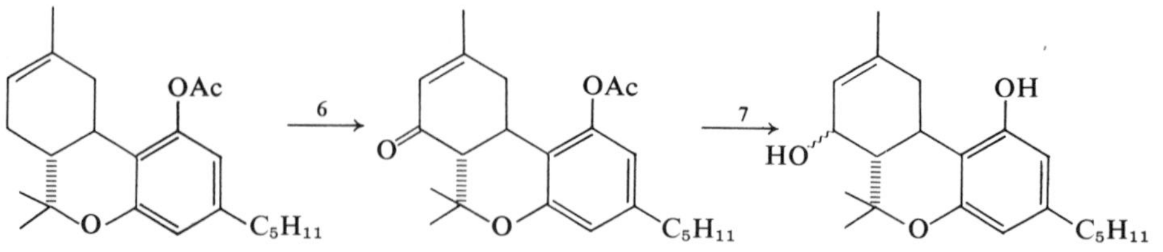

Δ^6-THC-acetate

Reagents: 1, m-chloroperbenzoic acid; 2, SeO_2; 3, BF_3; 4, base; 5, Ac_2O/Py; 6, *tert*-butyl chromate; 7, $LiAlH_4$.

The epoxide was synthesized in the same fashion by Gurny *et al.* (1972). The stereochemistry of the epoxide was elucidated (Mechoulam *et al.* 1972c) by stereospecific opening with boron trifluoride to the thermodynamically unstable hexahydrocannabinol-2-one (C-1 methyl axial), which on equilibration with base gave the stable isomer, hexahydrocannabinol-2-one (C-1 methyl equatorial).

Except for Δ^1-THC-6-one the above metabolites are active in monkeys at minimal doses between 0.5 and 2 mg/kg. These findings led the authors to comment as follows:

> The plethora of metabolites of Δ^9-THC isolated from *in vivo* or *in vitro* studies with different animal species or animal organ homogenates makes it imperative to determine the *human* metabolic pathways *in vivo* before any conclusions as regards the molecular basis of marihuana activity in humans can be made. However the fact that many of the THC metabolites so far isolated are active in psychobiological tests in animals and in humans supports the tentative suggestions that the effects of cannabis are caused (in part at least) by metabolites.

Maynard *et al.* (1971) have described the isolation of two new Δ^6-THC metabolites: 1″-hydroxy- and 3″-hydroxy-Δ^6-THC. Fahrenholz (1972) reported the syntheses of these compounds. He was unable to achieve a direct coupling of 1″- or 3″-hydroxyolivetol or 1″- or 3″-oxoolivetol with methadienol. However, the suitable thioketals produced the expected products:

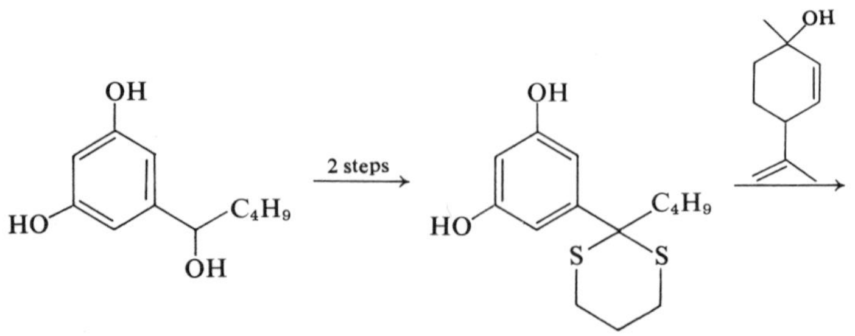

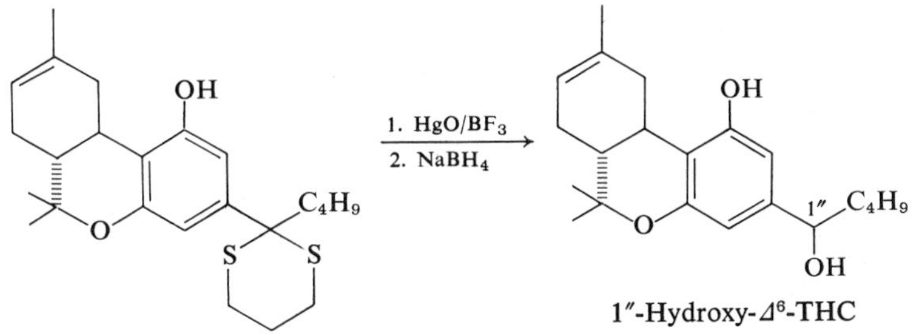

1″-Hydroxy-Δ⁶-THC

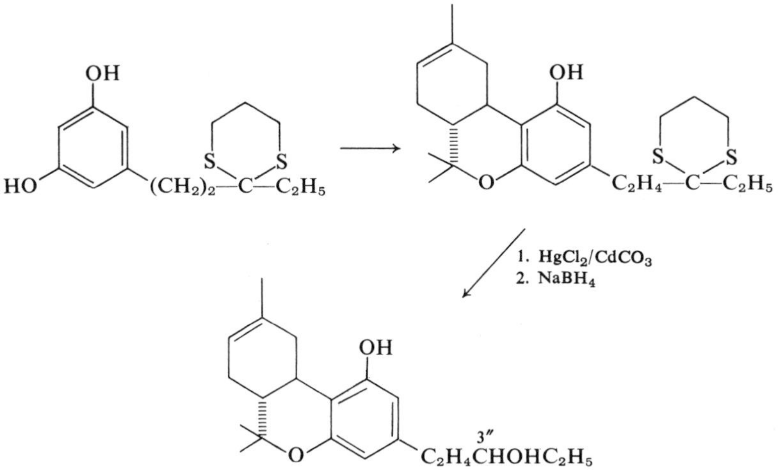

3″-Hydroxy-Δ⁶-THC

1″-Hydroxy-Δ^6-THC has also been synthesized by Mechoulam *et al.* (1972a) in one step as follows:

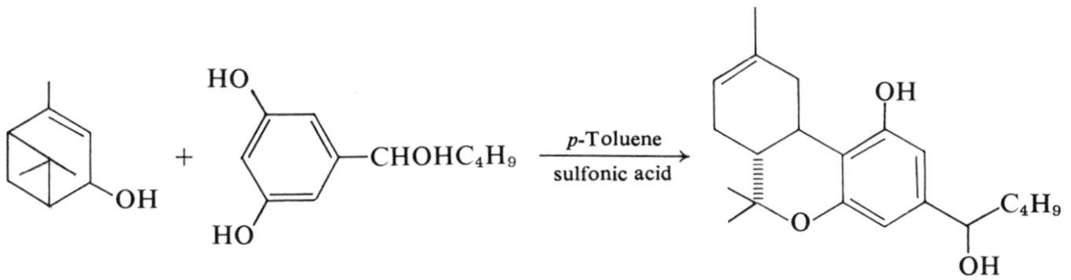

1″-Hydroxy-Δ^6-THC thus synthesized was inactive when tested iv in rhesus monkeys (Mechoulam *et al.*, 1972a).

As a result of a collaboration between the Shrewsbury group (Burstein and collaborators), the Swedish group (Agurell, Nilsson, and collaborators), and the Jerusalem group (Mechoulam and collaborators) the early indications in Shrewsbury and Stockholm that acids are the final cannabinoid metabolites led the Swedish and Jerusalem groups to initiate a synthetic approach toward possible THC acids. When Burstein *et al.* (1972) finally elucidated the structures of these major metabolites as THC-7-oic acids hydroxylated on the side chain (see addendum, Chapter 4) some synthetic materials were already available.

The Δ^6-THC acid methyl ether was synthesized as follows (Nilsson *et al.*, 1972):

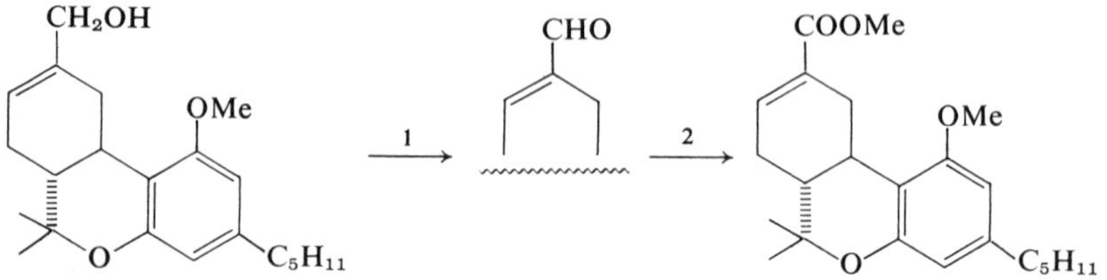

Reagents: 1, CrO_3/Py or $MnO_2/NaCN/AcOH$; 2, $MnO_2/NaCN/MeOH/AcOH$.

The free, nonmethoxylated Δ^6-THC-7-oic acid has been obtained in a similar manner (Mechoulam *et al.*, 1972a):

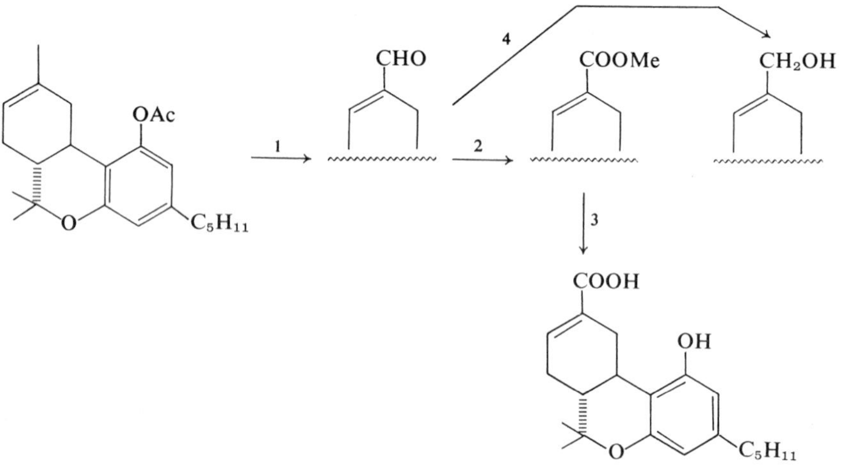

Reagents: 1, SeO_2; 2, $MnO_2/NaCN/MeOH$; 3, hydrolysis; 4, $LiAlH_4$.

Although this acid has not yet been identified as a Δ^6-THC metabolite, preliminary observations suggest that it is a metabolite of 7-hydroxy-Δ^6-THC (Agurell, 1972). The above synthesis also represents the best route (in 30% yield) to 7-hydroxy-Δ^6-THC.

The $\varDelta^6$-THC-7-oic acid (Mechoulam *et al.*, 1972a) is inactive in rhesus monkeys up to 10 mg/kg, and this observation suggests that the Burstein metabolites ($\varDelta^1$-THC-7-oic acids hydroxylated on the side chain) are also inactive. This assumption is supported by the above-mentioned inactivity of 1″-hydroxy-$\varDelta^6$-THC.

The research summarized above and in Chapter 4 points in a definite direction: THC is metabolized to numerous monooxygenated species, some of which are active and probably represent the active species in the body. On further oxidation, inactive acids, and possibly polyhydroxylated THC's, are formed.

NEW CANNABINOID PHYSICAL DATA*

Wenkert *et al.* (1972) have published the first ^{13}C nuclear magnetic resonance spectra of cannabinoids ($\varDelta^1$-THC, $\varDelta^6$-THC, and "$\varDelta^6$-3,4-*cis*-THC"). The last-mentioned substance is in actuality probably the THC isomer **108** shown on page 47 (Wenkert, 1972).

NEW CANNABINOID REACTIONS

Bailey and Verner (1972a) have observed that the reaction of $\varDelta^6$-THC with α- or β-glucose pentaacetate in benzene in the presence of boron trifluoride leads to *C*-glucosidation rather than *O*-glucosidation. For a discussion of related observations see Section V,f.

Razdan *et al.* (1972) have been able to trap as a Diels-Alder product a diene intermediate in the dehydrogenation of $\varDelta^1$-THC to cannabinol.

THC STABILITY*

Razdan *et al.* (1972) have published details of their studies on the stability of $\varDelta^1$-THC. Samples spread on filter paper were completely converted to cannabinol on heating in an oven at 80°C for 7 days. At 25°C, however, only 10% was lost after 1 month and 75% after 10 months. In ethanol, $\varDelta^1$-THC remained unchanged after 75 days at room temperature; in hexane or carbon tetrachloride some loss was observed. As expected, $\varDelta^6$-THC was stable under all the above conditions.

Kubena *et al.* (1972) found, on the basis of glc, tlc, and behavioral work, that a 43-year-old alcohol extract of cannabis had broken down very little over the years.

Chemical archeology (in storeroom sites) has also been reported by Marderosian and Murthy (1973), who analyzed *Cannabis sativa* L. leaf samples ranging in age from 7 to 90 years and observed the presence of

* See also Chapter 3.

cannabinol, cannabidiol, and tetrahydrocannabinol in varying concentrations. Analysis methods included both tlc and glc.

Fairbairn et al. (1971b) observed that pure Δ^1-THC in petroleum spirit was stable in the dark at 4°C (no measurable loss after 7 months) and at room temperature. However, in bright light total destruction occurred after 6 days. Carefully dried herb, in which the glands were intact, showed no decrease of THC content even when exposed to light.

PHARMACEUTICAL PREPARATIONS*

Rosenkranz et al. (1972) have reviewed the published oral and parenteral formulations of cannabinoids. Moreton and Davis (1972) have reported a simple method for the preparation of injectables of THC's and cannabis extracts. These authors use an Arlacel-20/Tween-65 suspension, which is claimed to be suitable when concentrations greater than a few milligrams per milliliter are desired.

Zitko et al. (1972) have reported the preparation of water-soluble THC morpholino- or piperidinobutyric acid esters, whose activity is identical to that of THC. It is yet to be determined whether these water-soluble derivatives can replace the lipid-soluble cannabinoids in pharmacological research.

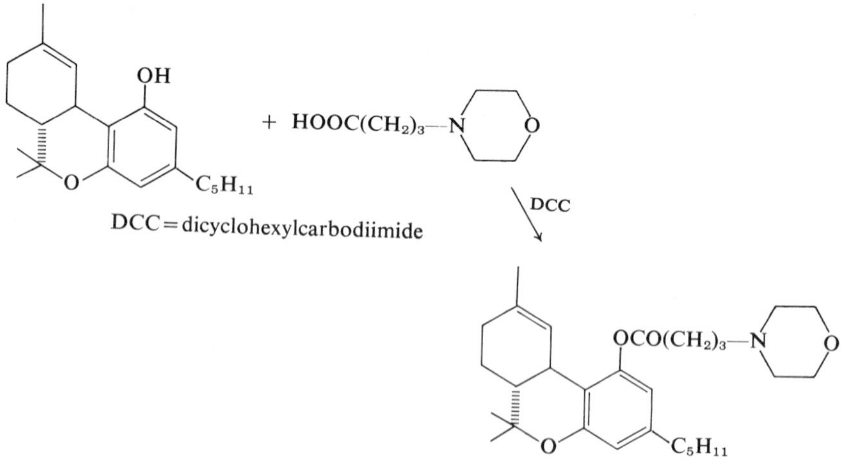

DCC = dicyclohexylcarbodiimide

References

Aguar, O. (1971). U.N. Document ST/SOA/Ser. S/27.
Agurell, S. (1972). Private communication.
Bailey, K., and Verner, D. (1972a). Chem. Commun. 89.
Bailey, K., and Verner, D. (1972b). Can. J. Pharm. Sci. 7, 51.
Burstein, S. H., Rosenfeld, J., and Wittstruck, T. (1972). Science 177, 62.

* See also Chapter 5, Section I,A.

Cardillo, B., Merlini, L., and Servi, S. (1972). *Tetrahedron Lett.* 945.

Combes, G., Montero, J. L., and Winternitz, F. (1972). *C. R. Acad. Sci. Ser. C* **274**, 1313.

De Faubert-Maunder, M. J. (1970). *J. Ass. Publ. Anal.* **8**, 42.

De Zeeuw, R. A., Malingré, T. M., and Merkus, F. W. H. M. (1972a). *J. Pharm. Pharmacol.* **24**, 1.

De Zeeuw, R. A., Wijsbeek, J., Breimer, D. D., Vree, T. B., van Ginneken, C. A. M., and van Rossum, J. M. (1972b). *Science* **175**, 778.

Fahrenholz, K. E. (1972). *J. Org. Chem.* **37**, 2204.

Fairbairn, J. W., Liebmann, J. A., and Simic, S. (1971a). *J. Pharm. Pharmacol.* **23**, 558.

Fairbairn, J. W., Liebmann, J. A., and Simic, S. (1971b). *Acta Pharm. Suecica* **8**, 679.

Greb, W., Bieniek, D., and Korte, F. (1972). *Tetrahedron Lett.* 545.

Gurny, O., Maynard, D. E., Pitcher, R. G., and Kierstead, R. W. (1972). *J. Amer. Chem. Soc.* **94**, 7928.

Haney, A., and Kutscheid, B. B. (1973). *J. Econ. Bot.* (in press).

Kimura, M., and Okamoto, K. (1970). *Experientia* **26**, 819.

Kubena, R. K., Barry, H., Segelman, A. B., Theiner, M., and Farnsworth, N. R. (1972). *J. Pharm. Sci.* **61**, 144.

Lander, N., Ben-Zvi, Z., and Mechoulam, R. (1973). In preparation.

Manners, G., Jurd, L., and Stevens, K. (1972). *Tetrahedron* **28**, 2949.

Marderosian, A. H. D., and Murthy, S. N. S. (1973). *J. Pharm. Sci.* (in press).

Maynard, D. E., Gurny, O., Pitcher, R. G., and Kierstead, R. W. (1971). *Experientia* **27**, 1154.

Mechoulam, R., Ben-Zvi, Z., Shani, A., Zemler, H., Levy, S., Edery, H., and Grunfeld, Y. (1972a). In "Cannabis and its Derivatives: Pharmacology and Experimental Psychology" (W. D. M. Paton and J. Crown, eds.). Oxford Univ. Press, London and New York.

Mechoulam, R., Brown, P., and Gaoni, Y. (1972b). *J. Amer. Chem. Soc.* **94**, 6159.

Mechoulam, R., Varconi, H., Ben-Zvi, Z., Edery, H., and Grunfeld, Y. (1972c). *J. Amer. Chem. Soc.* **94**, 7930.

Moreton, J. E., and Davis, W. M. (1972). *J. Pharm. Pharmacol.* **24**, 176.

Nilsson, J. L. G., Nilsson, I. M., Agurell, S., Ben-Zvi, Z., and Mechoulam, R., (1972). *Acta Pharm. Suecica* **9**, 215.

Paris, M., and Elmounaj, D. (1972). *Ann. Pharm. Fr.* **30**, 322.

Petrzilka, T., Demuth, M., and Lusuardi, W. (1971). *Acta Pharm. Suecica* **8**, 679.

Polaczek, E. (1973). "Cannabis Bibliography." Alcoholism and Drug Addiction Foundation, Toronto, Canada (in press).

Razdan, R. K., Puttick, A. J., Zitko, B. A., and Handrick, G. R. (1972). *Experientia* **28**, 121.

Rosenkranz, H., Thompson, G. R., and Braude, M. C. (1972). *J. Pharm. Sci.* **61**, 1106.

Samrah, H., Lousberg, R. J. J. Ch., Bercht, C. A. L., and Salemink, C. A. (1972). U.N. Document ST/SOA/SER. S/34.

Turner, C. E., and Hadley, K. (1973). *J. Pharm. Sci.* (in press).

Vree, T. B., Breimer, D. D., van Ginneken, C. A. M., van Rossum, J. M., De Zeeuw, R. A., Witte, A. H. (1972). *J. Pharm. Pharmacol.* **24**, 7.

Weinhardt, K. K., Razdan, R. K., and Dalzell, H. C. (1971). *Tetrahedron Lett.* 4827.

Wenkert, E. (1972). Private communication.

Wenkert, E., Cochran, D. W., Schell, F. M., Archer, R. A., and Matsumboto, K. (1972). *Experientia* **28**, 250.

Zitko, B. A., Howes, J. F., Razdan, R. K., Dalzell, B. C., Dalzell, H. C., Sheehan, J. C., Pars, H. G., Dewey, W. L., and Harris, L. S. (1972). *Science* **177**, 442.

CHAPTER 2

Structure–Activity Relationships in the Cannabinoid Series

Raphael Mechoulam and Habib Edery

I. Introduction 101
II. Assessment of Activity 103
III. Activity of Δ^3-THC Derivatives. 107
    A. Syntheses 107
    B. Structure–Activity Relationships 107
IV. Activity of the Natural Cannabinoids 115
V. Activity of Δ^1- and Δ^6-THC Derivatives and Miscellaneous THC Type of Compounds 118
VI. Summary 129
    References 130
    Addendum 133

I. Introduction

The accidental discovery that the unnatural Δ^3-tetrahydrocannabinol (Δ^3-THC) (1) caused ataxia in dogs and corneal areflexia in rabbits (Adams and Baker, 1940; Ghosh *et al.*, 1941)—tests that were accepted to parallel marijuana activity in man—led in the 1940's to the synthesis of numerous related compounds. Most of the compounds prepared by Adams' group at the University of Illinois were tested by Loewe, whose work is summarized in detailed reviews (Loewe, 1944, 1950). The cannabinoids synthesized by Todd, Bergel, and their co-workers in England were examined by Macdonald at the University of Manchester (Todd, 1946). The practical outcome of the work of these groups was the introduction around 1950 of the hexyl analog of Δ^3-THC (2) (named synhexyl in the United States and pyrahexyl in the United Kingdom) as a new antidepressant drug. However, with the discovery

101

of the major tranquilizers and other psychopharmacological agents interest in this area waned before its potentialities were fully explored. The pre-occupation of pharmacologists with the exciting new areas of psychobiology was undoubtedly one of the reasons for the complete neglect of the canna-binoid field in the 1950's. Contributing factors were as follows. (a) The natural active principle had not been isolated in pure form, its structure was unknown, and it was unavailable for sophisticated investigations; (b) the biological tests used by the pioneers in the field did not seem to be relevant to human use, both in dose levels and in effects; and (c) clinical work was hampered by the scientifically illogical, legal ties of the opiates with cannabis.

The last 5–6 years have witnessed a renewed interest in the cannabinoid field. The advances in chemistry and pharmacology are reviewed in the appropriate chapters in this book. The identification of Δ^1-THC (3) as the major active cannabis principle (Gaoni and Mechoulam, 1964) and the successful use of monkeys as test animals (Scheckel et al., 1968; Grunfeld and Edery, 1969; Mechoulam et al., 1970a; Kubena and Barry, 1970) have opened new approaches to structure–activity relationships (SAR). This interest has yet to express itself fully. A limited amount of work has already been published. It is a fair guess, however, that in view of the interest of a number of pharmaceutical firms in this type of compound, as evidenced by scattered publications, we can assume that a considerable amount of un-published knowledge in this field has accumulated.

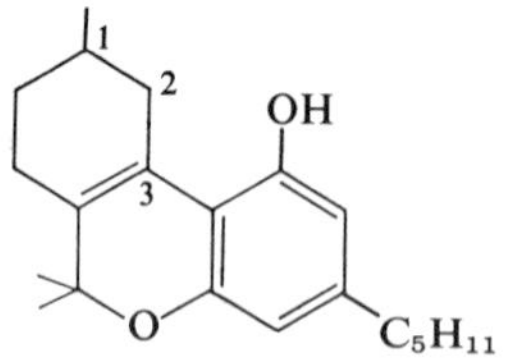

Δ^3-THC (1) 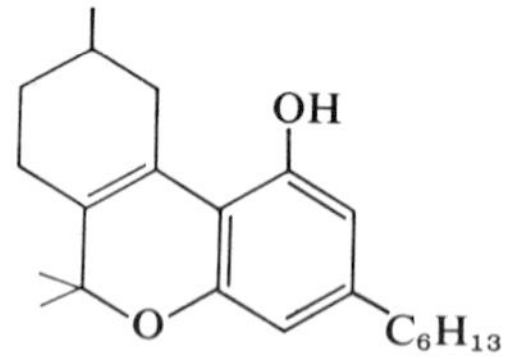   2 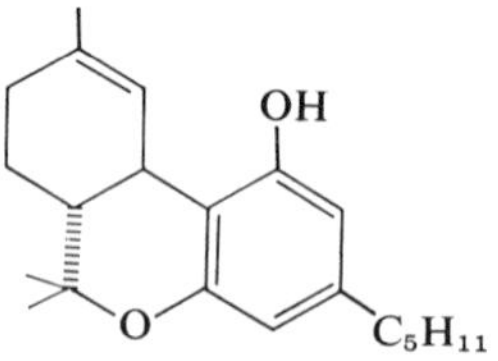 Δ^1-THC (3)

We have attempted to subdivide the published material into three major, interrelated parts. The first deals mostly with work reported in the 1940's regarding the activity of Δ^3-THC derivatives, the second with that of the natural constituents, and the last with the activity of Δ^1-THC and Δ^6-THC derivatives and of miscellaneous THC type of materials. The division is arbitrary and cannot be justified on a fully rational basis.

It should be emphasized that most of the early work, as well as some of the more recent studies, should be evaluated with an appropriate degree of sophistication. The cannabinoids are nearly always high-boiling oils. Their purification is a difficult undertaking, even with the advanced techniques available today. Most of the synthetic materials reported in the 1940's were racemic and, in many cases, a mixture of isomers was synthesized and administered. Although this is obvious from the chemical papers, it is not indicated (or even realized) in the pharmacological reports. The synthetic work of Adams and Todd and their associates has to be accepted with the necessary caution which is to be applied to all comparable work of three decades ago.

The cannabinoids are labile substances (see Chapter 1, Section V). It is seldom indicated in most publications whether a substance was reanalyzed just prior to administration. Hence isolated experiments may be misleading.

The testing of psychopharmacological agents has so radically changed since the 1940's that one intuitively feels that most of the old work is probably useless. In the cannabinoid field this conjecture does not seem to be valid. Although undoubtedly dated, most of the tests reported by the groups of Loewe and Macdonald seem to be of value today. However, in view of the paucity in this field of data on man, one can really only surmise their relevancy to actual human use. This is especially poignant since in many cases low doses of marijuana (or Δ^1-THC) cause in habitués or volunteers no effects that can be detected by pharmacological, psychological, or chemical tests, and the only way to know whether such a person is "high" is through his personal admission.

II. Assessment of Activity*

Dog ataxia (Liautaud, 1844; Fraenkel, 1903; Walton et al., 1938; Loewe, 1950; Bose et al., 1964; Garriott et al., 1968; Grunfeld and Edery, 1969) and suppression of rabbit corneal reflex (Gayer, 1928; Todd, 1946) have frequently been employed to assess the psychotropic activity of cannabis extracts and of synthetic or naturally occurring cannabinoids on the assumption that the activity in these tests correlates with the psychotomimetic effects observed in man. However, well-controlled parallel experiments in support of this assumption are lacking. Opinions are divided regarding the usefulness of rabbit corneal areflexia. It was found to be satisfactory by some workers (Bose et al., 1964; Valle et al., 1966; Carlini et al., 1970), but most agree that this test is unreliable (Loewe, 1946; Joachimoglu, 1965; Lipparini et al., 1969).

Other animal tests less frequently used include ichthyotoxicity (Duquénois, 1939; Valle et al., 1967); cataleptoid reaction in mice (Loewe, 1946; Gill et al., 1970; Carlini et al., 1970) and rats (Grunfeld and Edery, 1969; Carlini et al., 1970); suppression of isolation-induced aggressiveness in mice (Garattini, 1965; Carlini et al., 1970), their fighting behavior (Santos et al., 1966), motor activity (Joachimoglu, 1965; Bicher and Mechoulam, 1968; Kubena and

* For a detailed discussion, see Chapter 5.

Barry, 1970; Dewey *et al.*, 1970; Carlini *et al.*, 1970), and performance in rotarod (Grunfeld and Edery, 1969); gross behavior of rats and mice scored to a predetermined scale (Garattini, 1965; Foltz *et al.*, 1970; Razdan and Pars, 1970); and gerbil digging activity (Grunfeld and Edery, 1969). Recently, cannabinoids were examined with a variety of operant condition techniques in rats (Boyd *et al.*, 1963; Abel and Schiff, 1969; Grunfeld and Edery, 1969; Silva *et al.*, 1969; Kubena and Barry, 1970; Webster *et al.*, 1971), pigeons (Siegel, 1969; McMillan *et al.*, 1970), gerbils (Walters and Abel, 1970), and squirrel monkeys (Scheckel *et al.*, 1968; Kubena and Barry, 1970).

The value of animal testing to assess the activity of cannabinoids has been questioned (Weil, 1969), although apparently only dogs and rabbits were considered. Undoubtedly, there is an inherent difficulty in equating effects of psychotropic drugs in man with those observed in animals (regardless of how phylogenetically close to man they may be). This difficulty represents a serious (although not insurmountable) drawback in the evaluation of cannabinoids.

Experience with several animal species (Grunfeld and Edery, 1969) led us to consider the rhesus monkey as a suitable model. The use of Norton's (1957) sheet permits a thorough monitoring of rhesus behavioral patterns, many items of which can be severely affected by active cannabinoids. Table I compares the major effects of Δ^1-THC in man and monkey. Symptoms elicited by Δ^1-THC, such as redness of conjunctivas as well as pseudoptosis, decline of aggression, and indifference to the environment, could be readily observed in rhesus monkeys (Figs. 1 and 2). These symptoms seemed specific for primates. Furthermore, rhesus monkeys administered active cannabinoids adopted peculiar postures closely resembling those taken by some hashish smokers. On the other hand, euphoria and hallucinations reported to occur in man under the influence of Δ^1-THC (Hollister *et al.*, 1968; Weil *et al.*, 1968; Weil, 1969) could not be ascertained in rhesus monkeys. A hallucinatory-like state, however, has been described in squirrel monkeys administered high doses of the compound (Scheckel *et al.*, 1968).

Practice has shown that adult rhesus monkeys of the active, alert, and aggressive type are the most sensitive and suitable for cannabinoid testing. Usually two to four animals were maintained in a spacious cage kept in either a quiet room or an open noiseless space. A similar number of experimental animals and controls was injected with the test compound and solvent, respectively. Because of the fact that cannabinoids are practically insoluble in water, organic solvents such as propylene glycol, polyethylene glycol, dimethylformamide, or dimethyl sulfoxide were used. Fortunately, these solvents at workable doses did not cause visible changes in control animals, even when injected intravenously. Two independent observers, unaware of the material being injected, recorded on appropriate printed sheets the behavioral and somatic changes in the monkey. Usually the

Fig. 1. The monkey on the right was administered intravenously 0.1 mg/kg of Δ^1-THC, whereas the animal on the left (control) received 0.2 ml of propylene glycol. Picture taken 1½ hours after injection.

Fig. 2. Monkey injected with 0.25 mg/kg of Δ^1-THC. Picture taken 1 hour after injection.

105

TABLE I

COMPARISON OF MAJOR EFFECTS ELICITED BY Δ^1-TETRAHYDROCANNA-
BINOL IN MAN[a] AND MONKEY[b]

Effect	Man	Monkey
Somatic		
Threshold effective dose (50 μg/kg)[c]	+	+
Dose-dependent effects	+	+
Impairment of motor coordination	+	+
Redness of conjunctivas	+	+
Pseudoptosis	+	+
No increase in pupil size	+	+
Loss of muscle strength	+	+
Heart rate increase	+	+
Slow movements	+	+
Behavioral		
Indifference to environment	+	+
Euphoria	+	?
Uncontrollable laughter	+	−
Decline of aggression	+	+
Sleepy state	+	+
Impairment of performance	+	+
Hallucinatory state	+	?

[a] Isbell et al., 1967; Hollister et al., 1968; Weil et al., 1968; Manno et al., 1970; Hollister and Gillespie, 1970.
[b] Scheckel et al., 1968; Grunfeld and Edery, 1969.
[c] Rough comparison of intravenous administration in monkeys to oral administration in man.

observation period extended for ½ hour before and for 5 hours after the administration of compounds. When assessing the relative activities of different cannabinoids (Grunfeld and Edery, 1969; Mechoulam et al., 1970b; Edery et al., 1971, 1972) it was convenient to first check the sensitivity of the animals with a standard dose of Δ^1-THC or Δ^6-THC. Graded doses of these compounds elicited a satisfactorily reproducible pattern of changes which could be scored in accordance with the severity of the symptoms. After about a week a new cannabinoid could be tested in the same animals, and the effects compared. No signs of tolerance were noted with this injection schedule.

In view of previous results (Grunfeld and Edery, 1969) it seems that rhesus monkeys can also be advantageously used in the development of antidotes against psychotomimetic cannabinoids.

III. Activity of Δ^3-THC Derivatives

A. SYNTHESES

The synthesis of Δ^3-THC (1, R = C_5H_{11}) was achieved independently by the groups of Adams and Todd (for a detailed discussion, see Chapter 1, Section IV). The most facile route is the one outlined below.

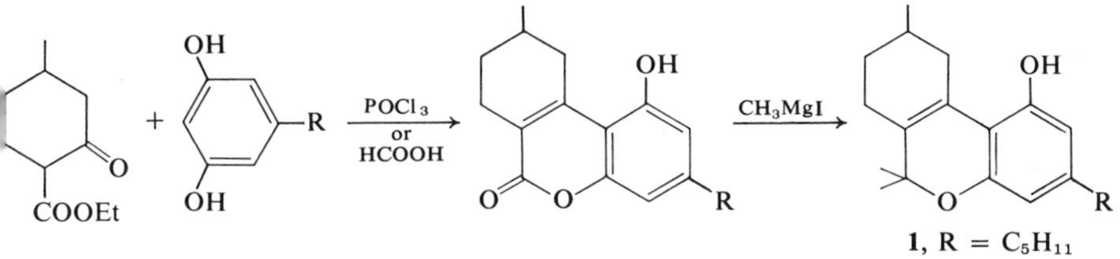

1, R = C_5H_{11}

The required 5-alkylresorcinols are prepared by conventional means. An old synthesis and some recent syntheses of a typical compound, olivetol, are outlined in Scheme 1. A different preparation of 5-(1', 2'-dimethylheptyl)-resorcinol has been described in a patent (Dever, 1962). Aaron and Ferguson (1968) were able to synthesize the isomers of this compound.

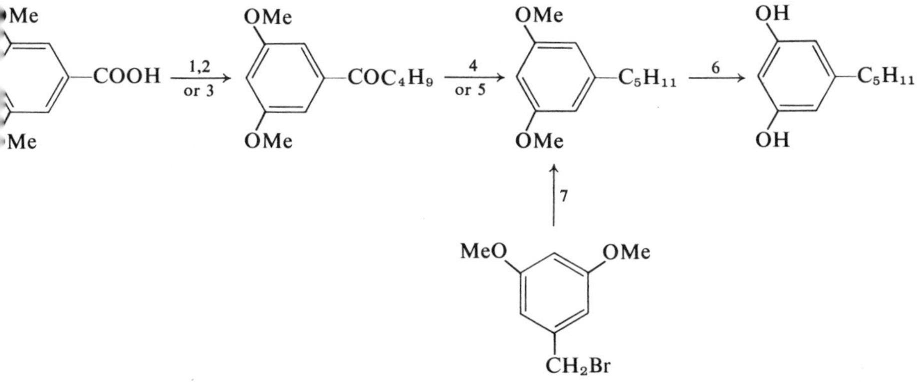

Scheme 1. Syntheses of olivetol: (a) by Suter and Weston (1939)–reagents: (1) thionyl chloride, (2) butyl cadmium, (4) Wolf–Kischner reagent, (6) hydroiodic acid; (b) by Baeckström and Sundström (1970)–reagents: (3) butyl lithium, (5) palladium on carbon, (6) hydroiodic acid; and (c) by Petrzilka *et al.* (1969)–reagents: (7) cuprous chloride and butyl lithium, (6) hydroiodic acid.

B. STRUCTURE–ACTIVITY RELATIONSHIPS

The SAR and literature data for the reported Δ^3-THC derivatives are presented in Tables II and III. This compilation has been greatly facilitated by a detailed list of cannabinoids and their biological activities prepared by Isbell (1968) for a meeting of the Committee on Drug Dependence.

Most of the data compiled concern Δ^3-THC analogs with a modified side chain. The dog ataxia tests (DA) and the corneal areflexia tests in rabbits (CA) show that on passing from a methyl side chain to a longer nonbranched side chain (ethyl, propyl, etc.) the activity increases. It reaches a maximum when the side chain is hexyl and slowly drops again. Branching of the side chain may result in a spectacular increase in activity. Thus, addition of a single methyl group on the amyl side chain results in an approximately threefold increase both in DA and in CA activity; the 1-methylhexyl side chain analog is about 5 times more active than Δ^3-THC; the 1-methylheptyl analog is 16 times as active in the DA test and more than 500 times as active in the CA test. The 1,2-dimethyl analogs cause an even more striking DA change. The dimethylhexyl homolog is 39 times as active as Δ^3-THC, whereas the dimethylheptyl homolog 4 (DMHP) is as much as 500 times more active. However, a sample of the same compound from a different synthetic batch was only about 60 times as active. In view of the three chiral centers in the molecule, it is possible that these variations were due to different proportions of isomers in the batches tested (Loewe, 1950). More recently, the eight possible isomers have been obtained in optically pure form (Aaron and Ferguson, 1968). The SAR of the isomers has not been published, although the activity of the mixture in animals and in man has been described (see Table II). Sim (1970) reported that the acetate of 1″,2″-dimethylheptyl

TABLE II
ACTIVITY OF SIDE CHAIN HOMOLOGS AND ANALOGS OF Δ^3-THC[a]

Compound tested[b]		

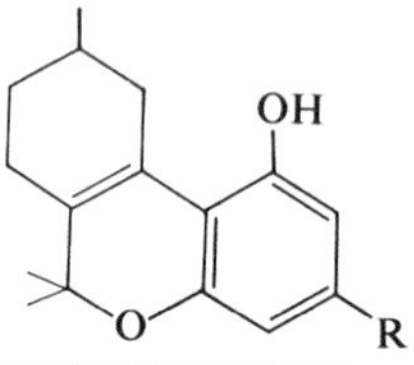

	Biological test[a]	Reference
R = C_5H_{11}	DA: ED_{50} (high activity) 3.65 mg/kg (used as reference unit, 1.00) Rhesus monkey: see Table V	Loewe (1944, 1950), Adams and Baker (1940)
	CA: 1.0 mg/kg 4.6 mg/kg	Russell et al. (1941a) Carlini et al. (1970)
	H (oral): 120 mg dose is active	Adams (1942), Allentuck and Bowman (1942)
	H (smoking): inactive at 0.4 mg/kg	Isbell et al. (1967)

TABLE II (*Continued*)

Compound tested[b]		

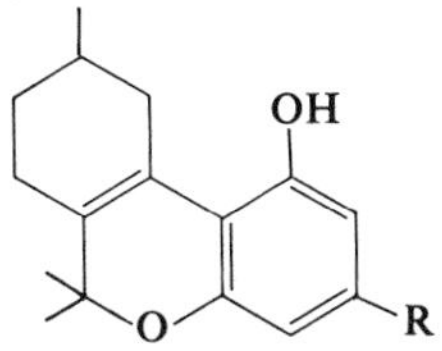	Biological test[a]	Reference
	H (smoking): active at 15 mg (total dose)	Hollister (1970)
(−), R = C_5H_{11}	DA: 1.66	Loewe (1944), Adams et al. (1942c)
	CA: 11–15 times more active than (+) form	Leaf et al. (1942)
(+), R = C_5H_{11}	DA: 0.38	Adams et al. (1942c)
	CA: active at 6–8 mg/kg	Leaf et al. (1942)
R = CH_3	DA: 0.16	Adams et al. (1941a), Russell et al. (1941b)
	CA: inactive at 20 mg/kg	
R = C_2H_5	CA: inactive at 15 mg/kg	Russell et al. (1941b)
R = $C_3H_7(n)$	DA: 0.40	Adams et al. (1941a)
	CA: inactive at 20 mg/kg	Loewe (1944)
R = $C_4H_9(n)$	DA: 0.37	Adams et al. (1941a), Loewe (1944)
	CA: 1 mg/kg	Russell et al. (1941b)
R = $C_6H_{13}(n)$ (synhexyl, pyrahexyl)	DA: 1.82	Adams et al. (1941a)
	CA: 0.1 mg/kg; 0.03 mg/kg	Avison et al. (1949), Russell et al. (1941b)
	H (oral): dose of 60 mg is active	Adams (1942), Williams et al. (1946)
	H (smoking): effect at 15 mg total dose	Hollister (1970)
	H (oral): 1/3 as active as Δ^1-THC	Hollister et al. (1968)
R = —$C_7H_{15}(n)$	DA: 1.05	Adams et al. (1941a)
	CA: 0.1 mg/kg	Russell et al. (1941b)
R = —$C_8H_{17}(n)$	DA: 0.66	Adams et al. (1941a)
	CA: 1 mg/kg	Russell et al. (1941b)
R = —$CH(CH_3)C_3H_7$	DA: 1.84	Adams et al. (1945)
R = —$CH(C_2H_5)C_3H_7$	DA: 1.67	Adams et al. (1945)
R = —$CH(C_3H_7)C_4H_9$	DA: 3.17	Adams et al. (1945)
R = —$CH(CH_3)C_4H_9$	DA: 3.65; 3.17	Adams et al. (1948a)
	CA: 0.3 mg/kg	Avison et al. (1949)
R = —$CH(CH_3)C_5H_{11}$	DA: 4.85	Adams et al. (1945)
R = —$CH(CH_3)C_6H_{13}$	DA: 16.4	Adams et al. (1948a)
	CA: 0.0025 mg/kg	Avison et al. (1949)
R = —$CH(CH_3)C_7H_{15}$	DA: 32.6	Adams et al. (1948a)
R = —$CH(CH_3)C_8H_{17}$	DA: 2.08	Adams et al. (1948a)

TABLE II (*Continued*)

Compound tested[b]

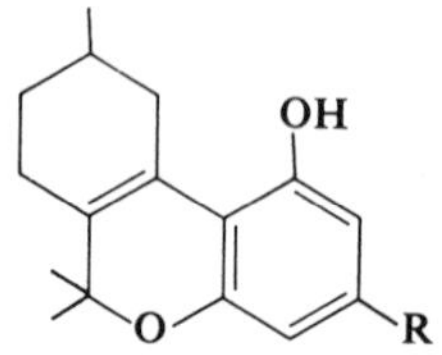	Biological test[a]	Reference
R = —$C_2H_4CH(CH_3)C_2H_5$	DA: 1.26	Adams *et al.* (1948a)
R = —$C_3H_6CH(CH_3)_2$	DA: 1.14	Adams *et al.* (1948a)
R = —$CH_2CH(CH_3)C_3H_7$	DA: 1.58	Adams *et al.* (1948a)
R = —$C(CH_3)_2C_3H_7$	DA: 4.18	Adams *et al.* (1948b)
R = —$C(CH_3)_2C_6H_{13}$	DA: 21.8	Adams *et al.* (1948b)
R = —$CH(CH_3)CH(CH_3)C_2H_5$	DA: 3.80	Adams *et al.* (1948b)
R = —$CH(C_2H_5)CH(CH_3)CH_3$	DA: 3.40	Adams *et al.* (1948b)
R = —$CH(CH_3)CH(CH_3)C_5H_{11}$	DA: 512	Adams *et al.* (1949)
	60	Loewe (1950)
	H: marijuana-like effects; postural hypotension at 1.0–5.0 mg (total dose)	Isbell (1968)
	H: 10–20 µg/kg (see text)	Sim (1970)
R = —$CH(CH_3)CH(CH_3)C_4H_9$	DA: 39	Adams *et al.* (1949)
R = —$CH(CH_3)CH(CH_3)C_6H_{13}$	DA: 19	Adams *et al.* (1949)
R = —$CH(CH_3)CH(CH_3)$-—$CH_2CH(CH_3)C_2H_5$	DA: 39	Adams *et al.* (1949)
R = —OH	CA: inactive at doses of 15 mg/kg	Russell *et al.* (1941b)
R = alkoxy group (*n*-butoxy to *n*-heptoxy)	CA: inactive	Bergel *et al.* (1943)
Δ^3-THC acetate	CA: as active as Δ^3-THC; action slow in developing but prolonged	Leaf *et al.* (1942)
Δ^3-THC, disodium phosphate	CA: inactive	Bergel *et al.* (1943)

[a] Expressed as (1) relative activity in the dog ataxia (DA) test when compared with Δ^3-THC taken as 1.0, (2) ED_{50} of corneal areflexia (CA) in rabbits; human testing is indicated by H. The activity in DA units in the original papers is given with a high degree of accuracy, such as 1.67 ± 0.33, for example. We doubt whether the purity of the compounds justifies such a treatment. We have indicated in the above case 1.67 only. This number means that the compound is 1.67 as active as Δ^3-THC.

[b] All compounds with a single chiral center are racemic, except when otherwise indicated. Those with numerous such centers are mixtures.

homolog of Δ^3-THC (**4**) (DMHP) when administered to humans at 10–20 μg/kg caused mydriasis, thirst, headache, tachycardia, some increase in blood pressure, and colored visual hallucinations. At higher doses, marked postural hypotension, weakness, giddiness, blurred vision, marked psychomotor retardation, and a decrease in body temperature of as much as 3°F were observed.

Changes in the terpenoid or pyranic ring of Δ^3-THC (see Table III) cause a drop in activity. However, few modifications have been made, and as the compounds retain some potency it may be worthwhile to test a wider range of compounds in this series.

TABLE III
ACTIVITY OF MISCELLANEOUS Δ^3-THC DERIVATIVES[a]

Compound tested	Biological test	Reference
(structure: OH, O, C$_5$H$_{11}$)	DA: 0.137 CA: inactive at 20 mg/kg	Adams *et al.* (1941b) Russell *et al.* (1941b)
(structure)	DA: 0.25 CA: 1 mg/kg	Adams *et al.* (1941b) Russell *et al.* (1941b)
(structure)	DA: 0.75	Adams *et al.* (1942b)
(structure)	DA: 0.11	Adams *et al.* (1942b)
(structure)	DA: 0.10	Adams *et al.* (1942b)

TABLE III (*Continued*)

Compound tested	Biological test	Reference
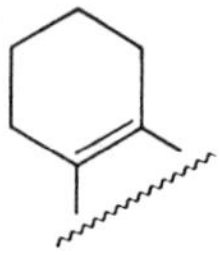	DA: 0.13 CA: 5 mg/kg	Adams *et al.* (1941b) Russell *et al.* (1941a)
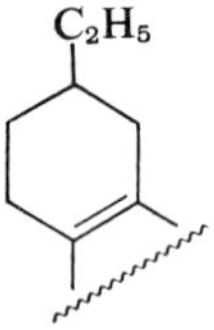	DA: 0.22	Adams *et al.* (1942b)
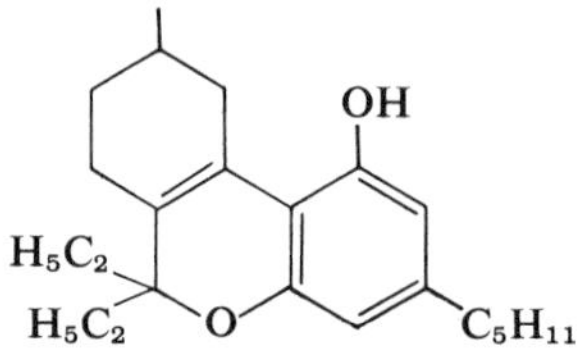	DA: 0.12 CA: inactive at 20 mg/kg	Adams *et al.* (1941b) Russell *et al.* (1941b)
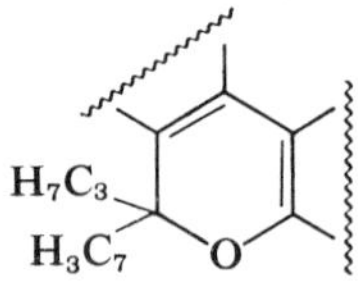	DA: 0.04	Adams *et al.* (1941b)
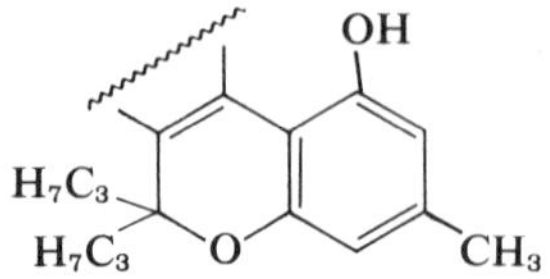	CA: inactive at 15 mg/kg	Russell *et al.* (1941b)
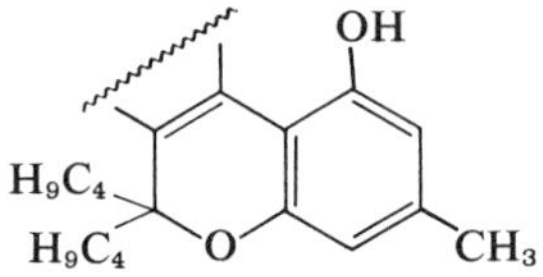	CA: inactive at 20 mg/kg	Russell *et al.* (1941b)
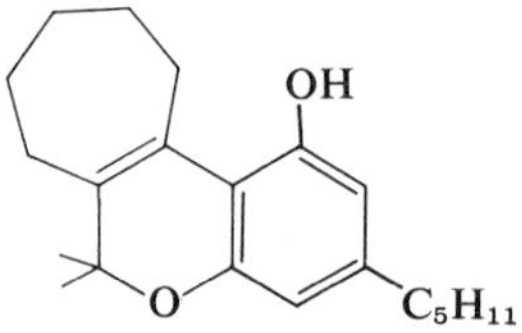	DA: 0.2	Adams *et al.* (1942b)

TABLE III (*Continued*)

Compound tested	Biological test	Reference
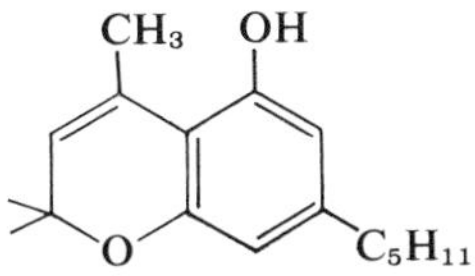	DA: 0.03 CA: inactive at 15 mg/kg	Adams *et al.* (1941c) Russell *et al.* (1941a)
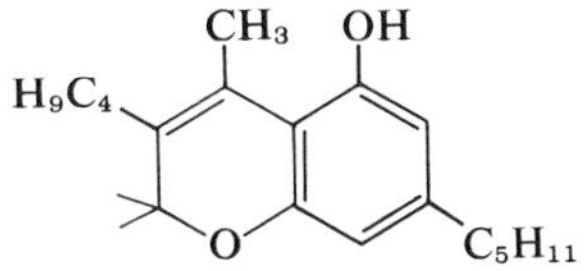	DA: 0.04 CA: inactive at 10 mg/kg	Adams *et al.* (1941c) Russell *et al.* (1941b)
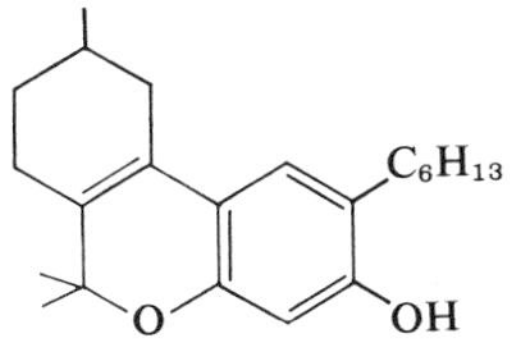	CA: 0.125 mg/kg LD_{50}, mice: 490 mg/kg	Avison *et al.* (1949)
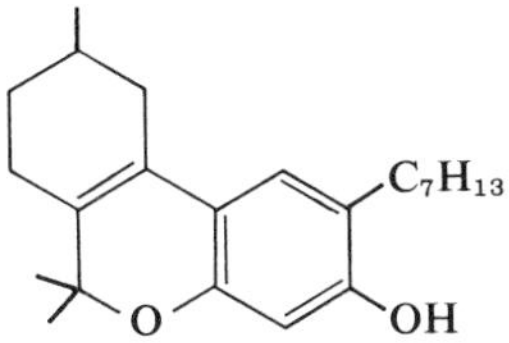	CA: 0.06 mg/kg LD_{50}, mice: 188 mg/kg	Avison *et al.* (1949)
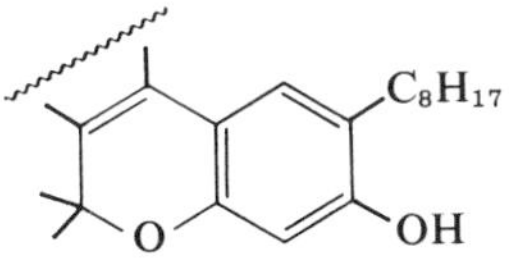	CA: 0.044 mg/kg LD_{50}, mice: ~400 mg/kg	Avison *et al.* (1949)
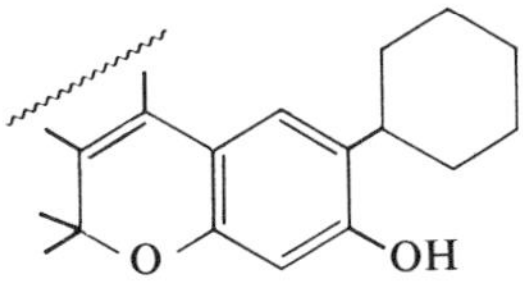	CA: 0.04 mg/kg LD_{50}, mice: 60 mg/kg	Avison *et al.* (1949)
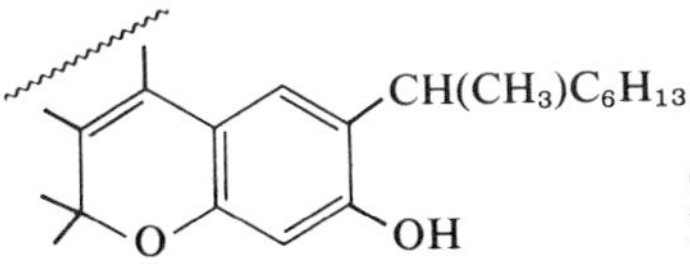	CA: 0.07 mg/kg LD_{50}, mice: ~400 mg/kg	Avison *et al.* (1949)

TABLE III (Continued)

Compound tested	Biological test	Reference

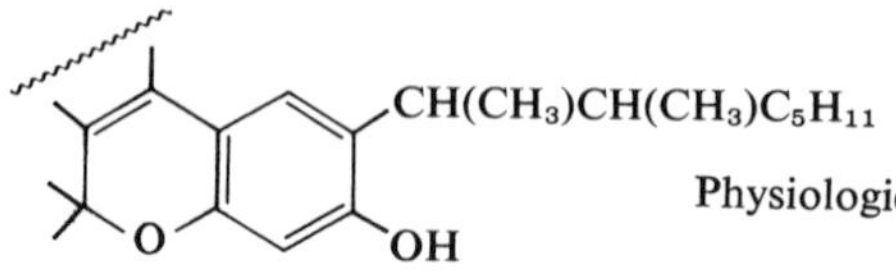

Physiologically inactive   Taylor *et al.* (1967)

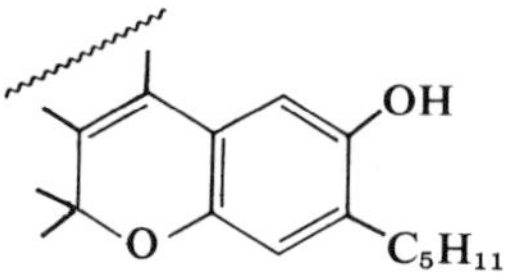

CA: not active at 20 mg/kg   Russell *et al.* (1941a)

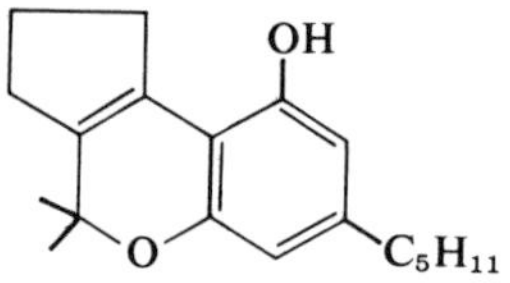

CA: not active at 30 mg/kg   Russell *et al.* (1941a)

a See footnote *a* to Table II.

Of some interest are the positional isomers of type **5**. It has been reported (Avison *et al.*, 1949) that in a few compounds of this type a certain analgesic activity was observed. In view of the increase of potency associated with the dimethylheptyl side chain in Δ^3-THC, the corresponding analog (**5a**) was prepared by Taylor *et al.* (1967). The complete inactivity of this compound casts some doubt as to the activity of the previously reported compounds.

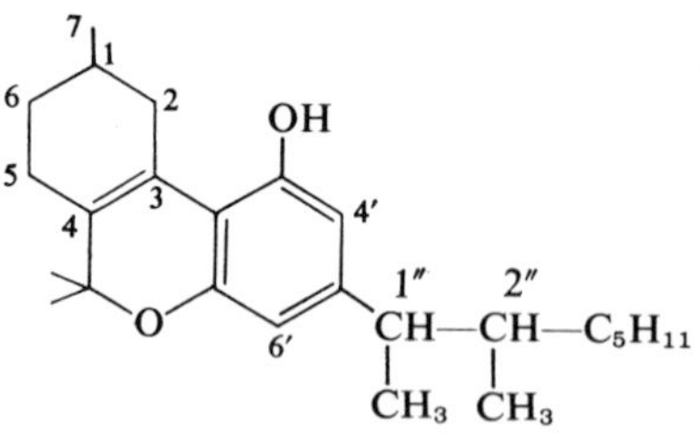

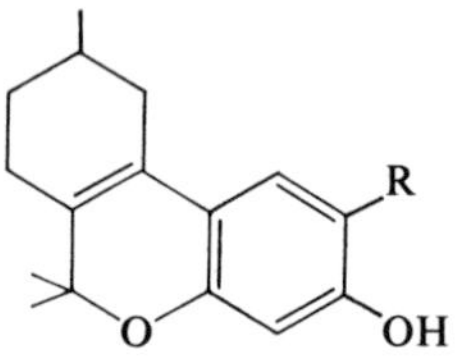

5a, R = CH(CH$_3$)CH(CH$_3$)C$_5$H$_{11}$

The replacement of the side chain in Δ^3-THC with a hydroxyl or an alkoxyl group eliminates the activity.

IV. Activity of the Natural Cannabinoids

In this section we will not attempt to examine and discuss the entire literature on the subject. We shall try to present the picture as seen today from a SAR viewpoint only.

From the end of the last century (Wood *et al.*, 1896) until Cahn's work in the early thirties (Todd, 1946) cannabinol was considered the active cannabis constituent. With the purification and synthesis of cannabinol it became obvious that the original positive tests (dog ataxia and Gayer's rabbit areflexia test) had actually indicated the presence of impurities in cannabinol (Loewe, 1944, 1950). Cannabidiol, which was isolated in the early 1940's (see Chapter 1), was shown to be inactive, but the products of its acid-catalyzed cyclization were highly potent in the dog ataxia test (Loewe, 1944, 1950). The nature of these cyclization products has been clarified (Gaoni and Mechoulam, 1966, 1968) (see Chapter 1, Section V,A). The only pure material obtained originally seems to have been Δ^6-THC, which was produced by treatment of cannabidiol with *p*-toluenesulfonic acid in benzene. All the remaining semisynthetic THC's discussed by Loewe in his papers on SAR were in fact very complicated mixtures, the biological activity of which was due to varying amounts of Δ^6-THC and Δ^1-THC.

In 1942, Wollner *et al.* isolated a fairly purified THC (or rather a THC mixture). The activity (dog ataxia) of this THC was ~14 times higher than that of the standard, synthetic Δ^3-THC. It seems that the amounts of Wollner's THC were quite limited and very little further work was undertaken with this material.

In the 1950's cannabidiolic acid was isolated and shown to possess antibiotic properties (Schultz and Haffner, 1958; Kabelik *et al.*, 1960). A sedative effect was also observed. We have been unable to confirm such an effect in the rhesus monkey (Mechoulam *et al.*, 1970b). A considerable amount of work on the potential human and veterinary use of cannabidiolic acid as antibiotic has been reported. As this chapter deals with the SAR in relation to psychotomimetic activity these studies will not be discussed here. The interested reader is referred to the review by Kabelik *et al.* (1960) and the more recent paper by Krejči (1970).

In 1964 the isolation of Δ^1-THC from hashish was reported (Gaoni and Mechoulam, 1964). It was tested in the dog ataxia test and found to be active (H. Edery, cited by Mechoulam and Gaoni, 1964; Grunfeld and Edery, 1969). Tests on volunteers showed that Δ^1-THC is active in man at a dose level of 3–5 mg (Mechoulam and Gaoni, 1967; Mechoulam *et al.*, 1970a). The extensive pharmacological work on Δ^1-THC in animals and man is discussed in Chapters 5 and 6. Numerous other components were isolated (for references see Chapter 1). A systematic chemical analysis of a hashish sample monitored by tests in rhesus monkeys was undertaken to establish whether Δ^1-THC is the only (or major) active component (Mechoulam et al., 1970b). A hashish sample was extracted consecutively with petroleum ether, benzene, and methanol. When tested intravenously in monkeys only the petroleum ether fraction was active. This material was further fractionated. Cannabinol, cannabidiol, cannabichromene, cannabigerol, and cannabicyclol as well as the cannabinoid acids and the combined polar, noncannabinoid fractions when administered by intravenous injection in doses up to 10 mg/kg caused no behavioral changes in rhesus monkeys. The only active component isolated was Δ^1-THC.

Two additional active components are present in some cannabis samples: Δ^6-THC (Hively et al., 1966) and the propyl homolog of Δ^1-THC (Gill et al., 1970). Recently, two types of active metabolites of the natural THC's were identified: 7-hydroxy-Δ^1-THC, 7-hydroxy-Δ^6-THC, and 6β-hydroxy-Δ^1-THC (for a detailed discussion see Chapter 4).

The natural cannabinoids represent a wide variety of structural types of terpenophenolics. The terpene moiety can be acyclic (as in cannabigerol), monocyclic (as in cannabidiol), or bicyclic (as in cannabicyclol). The terpene and resorcinol moieties can form furans (as in the cannabielsoic acids), chromenes (as in cannabichromene), or pyrans (as in Δ^1-THC). And yet, the only natural cannabinoids that show significant marijuana type of activity are some of those possessing a pyran moiety: Δ^1-THC, Δ^6-THC, propyl-THC, and the above-mentioned metabolites. Cannabinol, however, which is a dibenzopyran, is not active. The cannabinoid acids including Δ^1-THC acid A and Δ^1-THC acid B are inactive. Two important conclusions regarding structure–activity relationships can be drawn from these results. (a) A pyran ring is apparently a definite requirement but does not by itself confer activity, and (b) a carboxyl group on either the 4' of the 6' aromatic position eliminates the activity of the THC molecule. The activity of natural cannabinoids is summarized in Table IV.

TABLE IV
ACTIVITY OF NATURAL CANNABINOIDS

Cannabinoid[a]	Test	Reference
Cannabinol	Dog ataxia, no activity	Loewe (1944, 1950)
	Corneal areflexia, no activity	Todd (1946)
	Human (smoking), no activity up to 2 mg/kg; caused headache and nausea	Isbell et al. (1967)
	Rhesus monkey, no activity	Mechoulam et al. (1970b)
Cannabidiol	Rhesus monkey, no activity	Mechoulam et al. (1970b)
	Dog ataxia, no activity	Loewe (1944, 1950)

TABLE IV (*Continued*)

Cannabinoid[a]	Test	Reference
	Synergistic hypnotic activity to barbiturates	Loewe (1944)
	Antibiotic (gram-positive bacteria)	Schultz and Haffner (1958), Kabelik *et al.* (1960)
Cannabigerol	Antibiotic (gram-positive bacteria)	Mechoulam and Gaoni (1965)
	Rhesus monkey, no activity	Mechoulam *et al.* (1970b), Grunfeld and Edery (1969)
Cannabichromene	Human (smoking), no activity	Isbell *et al.* (1967)
	Rhesus monkey, no activity	Mechoulam *et al.* (1970b)
	Mice, at 10 mg/kg, passive, slight loss of muscular coordination; at 15–30 mg/kg, cyanosis, urination increased	Razdan and Pars (1970)
Cannabicyclol	Rhesus monkey, no activity	Mechoulam *et al.* (1970b)
	Mice, at 10 mg/kg, irritable when touched, pilo erection, increased respiration	Razdan and Pars (1970)
Δ^1-THC	Major psychotomimetic principle	See Chapters 1 (for chemistry), 5 and 6 (for pharmacology)
Δ^6-THC	Minor psychotomimetic principle	See Table V for data on rhesus monkeys
Δ^1-Tetrahydro-cannabivarol	Minor psychotomimetic principle	Gill *et al.* (1970)
Cannabidiolic acid	Sedative, antibiotic	Kabelik *et al.* (1960), Schultz and Haffner (1958)
	No sedative activity in monkeys	Mechoulam *et al.* (1970b)
Δ^1-THC acid A, Δ^1-THC acid B	Inactive in rhesus monkey	Mechoulam *et al.* (1969), Edery *et al.* (1972)
Cannabielsoic acid	Inactive in rhesus monkey	Shani and Mechoulam (1970)
7-Hydroxy-Δ^1-THC, 7-Hydroxy-Δ^6-THC, 6β-Hydroxy-Δ^1-THC	Parallel Δ^1-THC and Δ^6-THC activity	Ben-Zvi *et al.* (1970), Wall *et al.* (1970), Foltz *et al.* (1970), Nilsson *et al.* (1970), Ben-Zvi *et al.* (1971), Christensen *et al.* (1971)

[a] The structures of the natural cannabinoids are presented in an appendix at the end of the book.

V. Activity of Δ¹- and Δ⁶-THC Derivatives and Miscellaneous THC Type of Compounds*

With the development of syntheses of Δ^1-THC and Δ^6-THC, modifications have been made on these substances. The changes reported so far involve most parts of the molecule, but only a few modifications of each type have so far been accomplished. In view of the frequently made statement that the activity of cannabis is due to a mixture of double-bond and stereoisomers of THC, it is of considerable interest that such changes in most cases eliminate the activity. Thus $(+)$-Δ^1-THC, $(+)$-Δ^6-THC, $(-)$-Δ^5-THC, Δ^7-THC, and $(\pm)$-*cis*-Δ^1-THC are inactive in monkeys. The inactivity of the $(+)$ series indicates that cannabis action apparently has a strict biochemical–enzymatic basis.

Changes in the side chain may cause increase in activity in rhesus monkeys (Table V). These variations in activity were expected in view of the SAR in

TABLE V

ACTIVITY OF Δ^1- AND Δ^6-THC DERIVATIVES AND RELATED MATERIALS[a]

Compound	Structure	Dose (mg/kg)	Activity
$(-)$-Δ^1-THC		0.05	+ (activity lasts 1 hour)
		0.1	+ +
		0.25	+ +
		0.5	+ + + (activity lasts 4.5 hours)
$(+)$-Δ^1-THC		0.5	−
		1.0	−
$(-)$-Δ^6-THC		0.1	±
		0.25	+
		0.5–0.9	+ +
		1.0–2.0	+ + + (activity lasts ~4 hours)
$(+)$-Δ^6-THC		1.0	−

* In this section few details and references are presented in the text. These are given in Tables V, VI, and VII. The pharmacology of Δ^1-THC and Δ^6-THC is discussed in detail in Chapters 5 and 6. The data concerning these compounds in Table V are for comparison purposes only.

TABLE V *(Continued)*

Compound	Structure	Dose (mg/kg)	Activity
$(\pm)$-Δ^3-THC		0.5 1.0 5.0 10.0 20.0	— + + + + + + + +
$(-)$-Δ^5-THC		5.0 10.0	— —
$(\pm)$-3,4-*cis*-Δ^1-THC		1.0 1.5	— —
$(\pm)$-Δ^7-THC			Not active in a monkey test[b]
Δ^1-THC methyl ether		10.0	—
Δ^6-THC methyl ether		10.0	—
Δ^1-THC acetate		0.2 0.5 1.0	± + + +
Δ^6-THC acetate		0.2 0.5 1.0 5.0	— + + + + + +
Hexyl homolog of Δ^6-THC		0.05 0.1	+ + +
1″-Methylpentyl homolog of Δ^6-THC		0.1 0.2 1.0	— + + + +

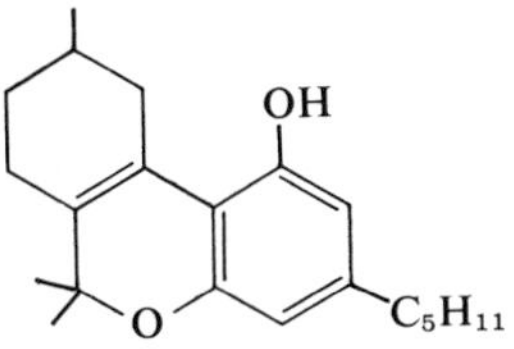

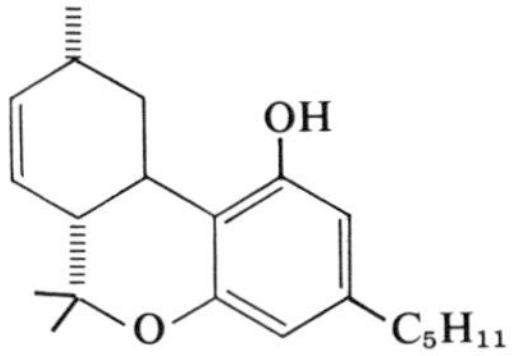

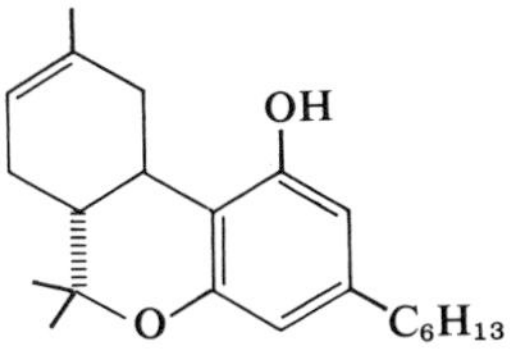

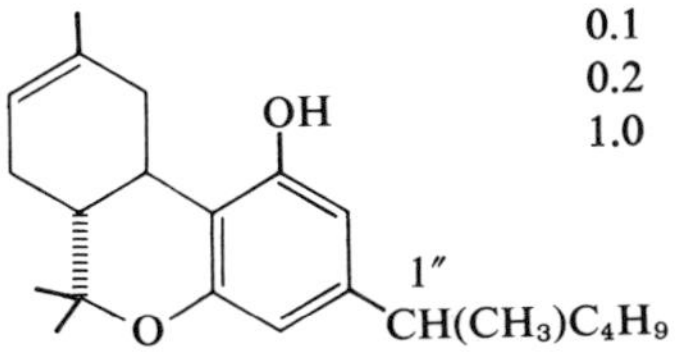

TABLE V (*Continued*)

Compound	Structure	Dose (mg/kg)	Activity
1″,2″-Dimethylpentyl homolog of Δ^6-THC	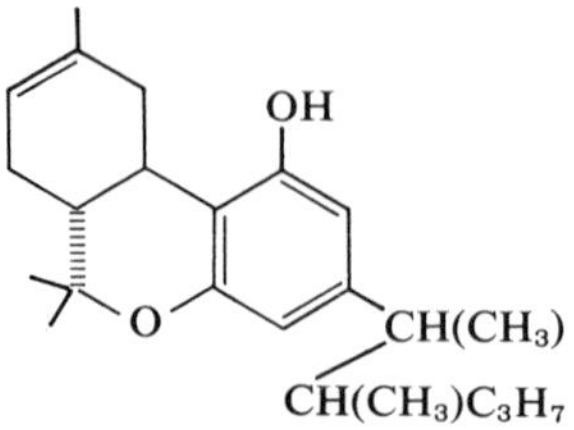	0.025 0.05 1.0	− + + + + + (activity lasts for approx 30 hours)
1″,2″-Dimethylheptyl homolog of Δ^6-THC	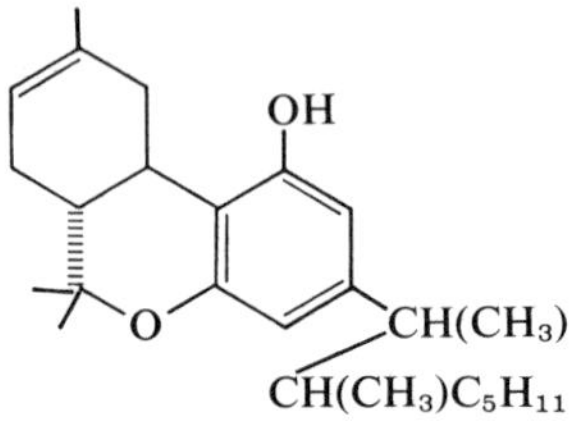	0.025 0.05 0.1 1.0	− + + + + + (activity lasts 7 hours) + + + (activity lasts 48 hours)
Hexyl homolog of Δ^1-THC	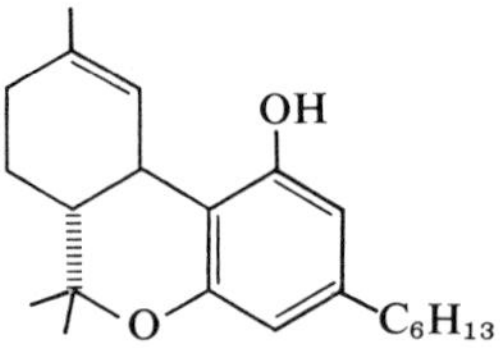	0.05 0.1 0.5	− + + + +
1″-Methylpentyl homolog of Δ^1-THC	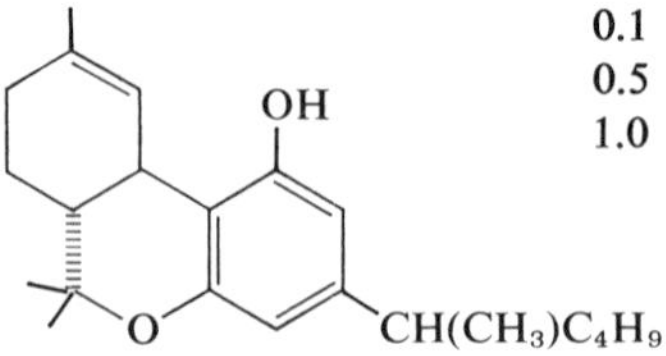	0.1 0.5 1.0	− − + +
1″,2″-Dimethylheptyl homolog of Δ^1-THC	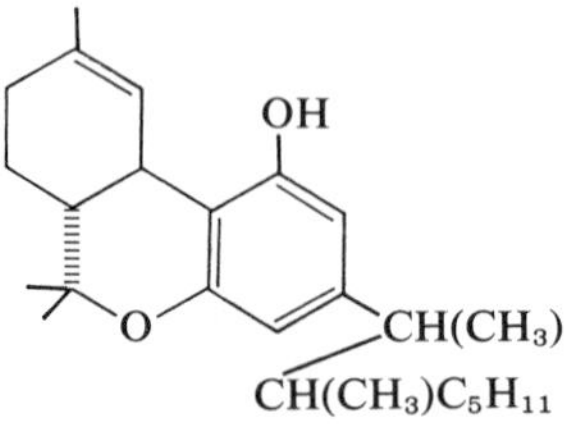	0.05 0.1 0.5	± + + + + (activity lasts 24 hours)
4′-Carbomethoxy-Δ^6-THC	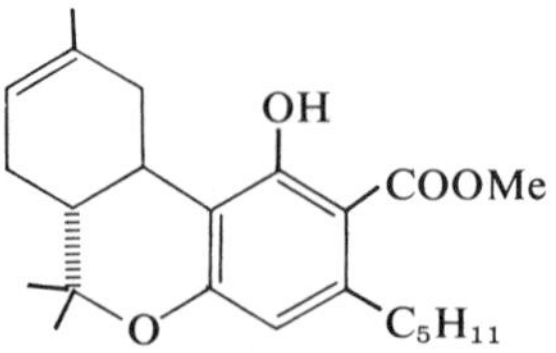	10.0	−

TABLE V (Continued)

Compound	Structure	Dose (mg/kg)	Activity
6'-Carbomethoxy-Δ^6-THC	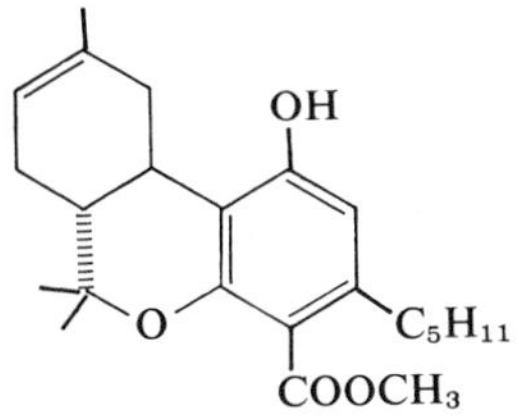	5.0	−
4'-Acetyl-Δ^6-THC	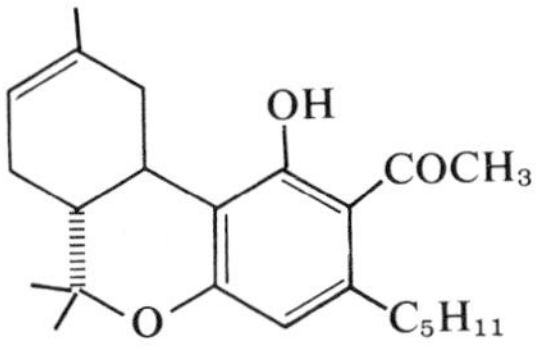	10.0	−
Δ^6-THC quinone	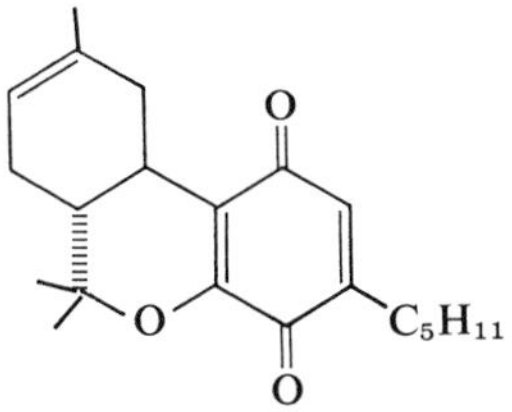	5.0 10.0	− −
4'-Methyl-Δ^6-THC	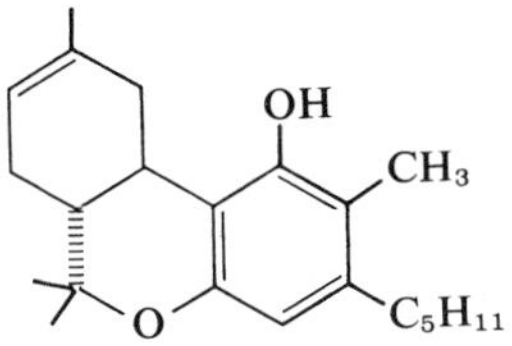	1.0 5.0	+ + + +
4'-Ethyl-Δ^6-THC	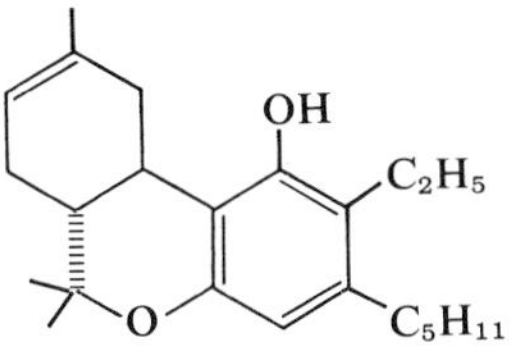	1.5	+ +
4'-Methyl-Δ^1-THC	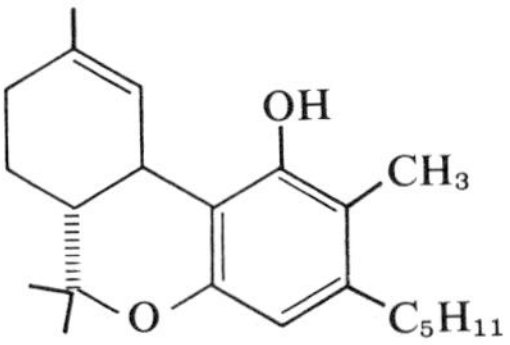	0.1 0.5 1.0	± + + + + +

TABLE V (*Continued*)

Compound	Structure	Dose (mg/kg)	Activity
4'-Ethyl-Δ^1-THC	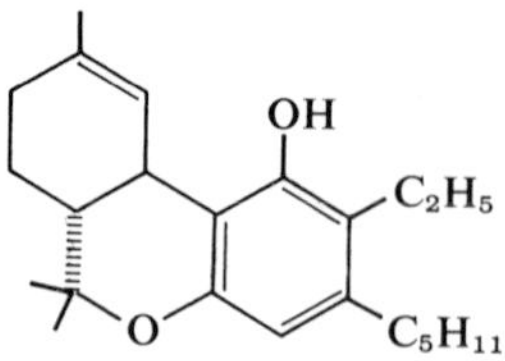	0.2 0.5 1.5	± + + + +
6'-Ethyl-Δ^6-THC	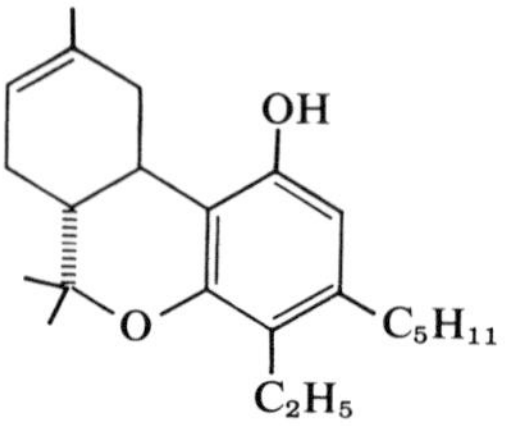	10.0	−
6'-Methyl-Δ^6-THC	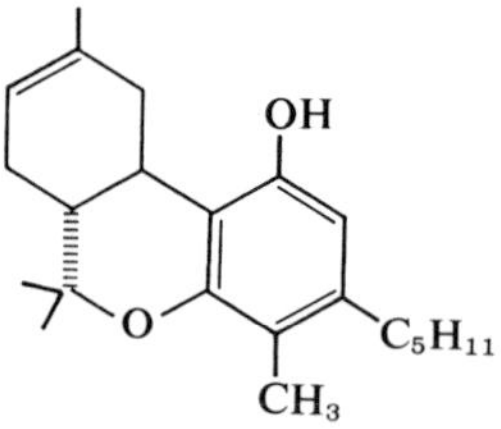	5.0 10.0	− −
6'-Acetoxy-Δ^6-THC acetate	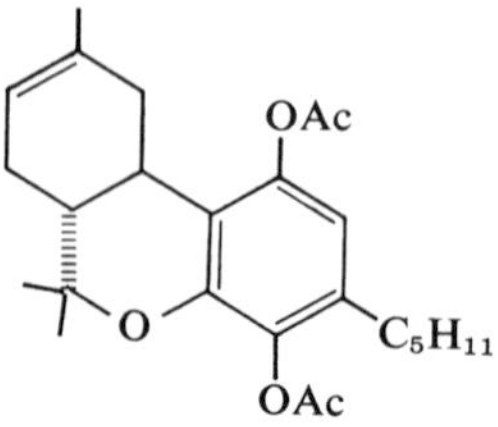	5.0 10.0	− −
2β-Hydroxy-Δ^6-THC	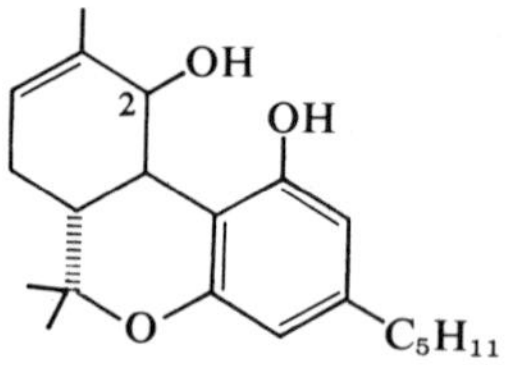	1.0 2.0 2.5 10.0	− + + + + +
2α-Hydroxy-Δ^6-THC		0.1 0.2 0.5	+ + + + + +

TABLE V (*Continued*)

Compound	Structure	Dose (mg/kg)	Activity
Hexahydrocannabinol (mixture of isomers)		Dog ataxia, 0.5–3.30 as active as Δ^3-THC[c] Corneal areflexia, active at 2.5 mg/kg[d]	
Hexahydrocannabinol (C-1 CH$_3$ equatorial)	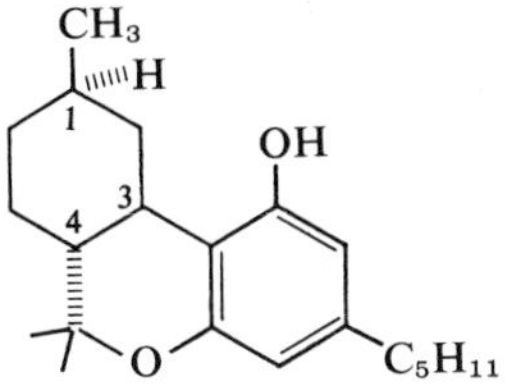	0.1 0.5 1	± + + + + +
Hexahydrocannabinol (C-1 CH$_3$ axial)	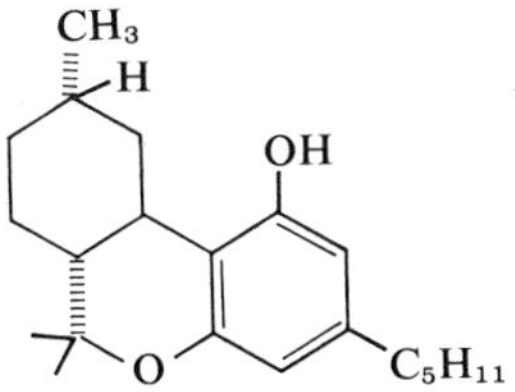	1.0 2.0 5.0	− + + +
1α,2α-Dihydroxyhexa-hydrocannabinol	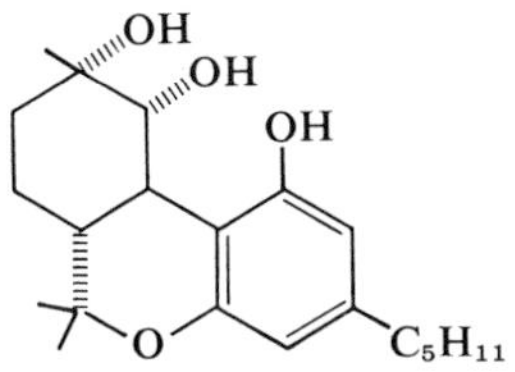	5.0 10.0	− −
6α-Hydroxy-Δ^1-THC	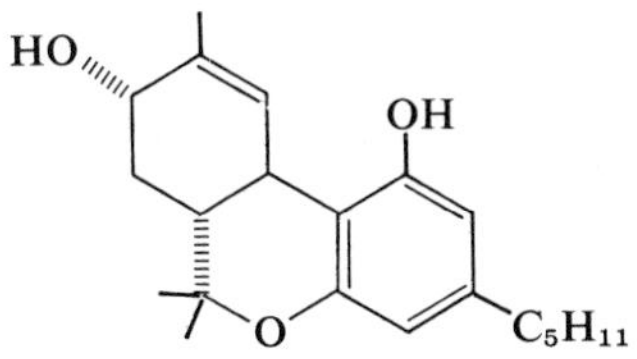	0.5 2.0	− + +
6β-Hydroxy-Δ^7-THC	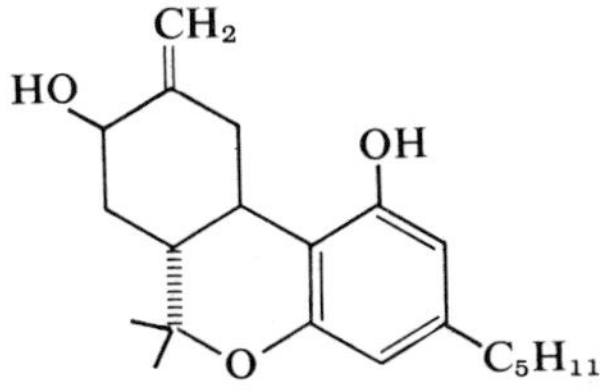	5.0 10.0	+ +

TABLE V (*Continued*)

Compound	Structure	Dose (mg/kg)	Activity
6α-Hydroxy-Δ^7-THC		5.0	−
		10.0	+

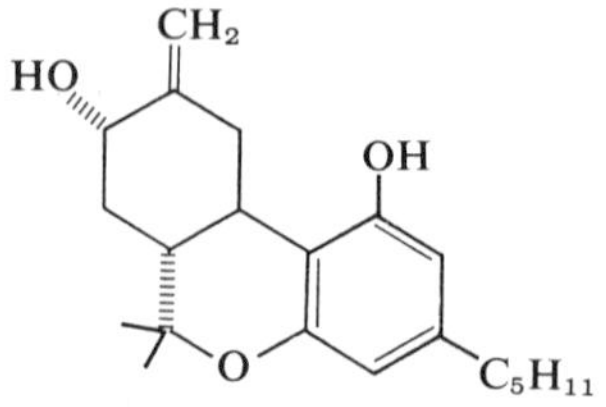

[a] The data in this table are for rhesus monkeys (unless otherwise indicated); they are taken from Mechoulam *et al.* (1967), Grunfeld and Edery (1969), Edery *et al.* (1971), Edery *et al.* (1972) and from nonpublished results. They were rated in accordance with the effects of Δ^6-THC taken as reference. The compounds were intravenously injected into rhesus monkeys: − indicates no changes; ±, tranquility; +, drowsiness, decreased motor activity, occasional partial ptosis, occasional head drop; + +, stupor, ataxia, full ptosis, suppression of motor activity, typical crouched position ("thinker position") for up to 3 hours, presence of reaction to external sensorial stimuli; + + +, severe stupor and ataxia, full ptosis, immobility, "thinker position" lasting for more than 3 hours, and absence of reaction to external stimuli.
[b] Farenholtz (1970).
[c] Loewe (1944), Adams *et al.* (1942a).
[d] Russell *et al.* (1941a).

the Δ^3-THC series discussed in Section III, B. Thus, in comparison to Δ^6-THC the threshold activity dose is somewhat lowered in the hexyl and 1″,2″-dimethylheptyl analogs. The most striking effect, however, is the prolongation of activity. Whereas the effects of Δ^6-THC last ~4 hours (for 1.0–2.0 mg/kg dose), those of 1″,2″-dimethylheptyl analog last 48 hours (at the same dose level). In the Δ^1-THC series we observed no lowering of the threshold dose and only with the 1″,2″-dimethylheptyl analog was a persistent effect observed. It is of interest that in the dog the structure–activity relationships are different than in the rhesus monkey. Thus, in the dog Δ^1-THC causes ataxia at 250–500 μg/kg, whereas the 1″,2″-dimethylheptyl homolog of Δ^1-THC is active at 40 μg/kg. As mentioned above, in the monkey the threshold dose is lower (~50 μg/kg) but is not noticeably influenced by the side chain variation.

Blocking the free hydroxyl group as an ether abolishes the activity, whereas acetylation seems to cause a slight diminution (Table V).

Substitution of a hydrogen on the aromatic ring of Δ^1-THC or Δ^6-THC with a carboxyl, a carbomethoxy, an acetyl, or an acetoxyl group eliminates (or drastically reduces) the activity. Alkyl substitution at C-4′ on the aromatic ring leads to compounds that are still active. Alkyl substitution at C-6′ eliminates activity. It seems that while the changes produced by the carbonyl-containing groups are electronic in character those of the alkyl groups are of a different kind. Possibly, alkyl substitution on C-6′ blocks a molecular position required for activity, whereas a parallel reaction on C-4′ is of no major consequence.

The terpenoid ring has a number of attractive sites for structure modification, although few have been explored so far. A mixture of the two hexahydrocannabinols is active (dog ataxia) (Table V). More recently it was found that the axial isomer is considerably less active in monkeys than the equatorial isomer (Table V). Considerable activity was found in 2α-hydroxy-Δ^6-THC, in which the hydroxyl group is equatorial. The axial isomer was much less potent. Although these examples are too limited to allow definite conclusions it seems that substituents on C-1 or C-2 of the terpenoid ring which "stick out" of the ring tend to reduce the activity. This may be of particular importance as regards the methyl group on C-1, as activity may be associated with functionalization of this group (Edery *et al.*, 1971). It is conceivable that the free phenolic group (on C-3′) and the hydroxymethyl group (on C-1) are needed for attachment to an active site. This could be possible as long as they are almost coplanar, which is indeed the case in Δ^1-THC, Δ^6-THC, or hexahydrocannabinol, in which the C-1 methyl is equatorial. If the methyl group (or the corresponding hydroxymethyl group) is axial such an interaction could become less facile. The above assumptions are as yet in the realm of speculation.

A few heterocyclic analogs of THC isomers have been tested (Table VI). The aza-Δ^3-THC (**6**) was inactive; apparently so was the isomeric **7**. However,

TABLE VI
HETEROCYCLIC ANALOGS OF THC's

Compound	Biological test	Reference
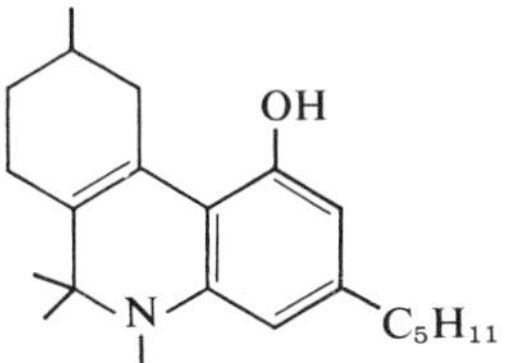 **6**	Inactive in unspecified tests	Hoops *et al.* (1968), Biel (1970)
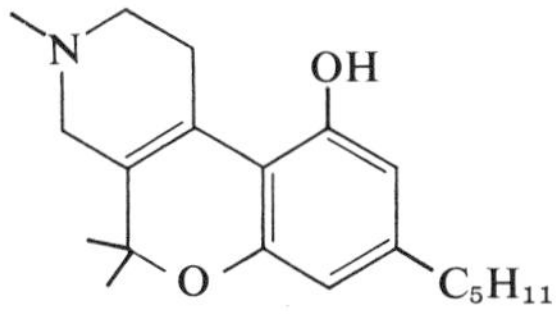 **7** and dihydro derivative	No analgesic activity	Anker and Cook (1946)

TABLE VI (Continued)

Compound	Biological test	Reference

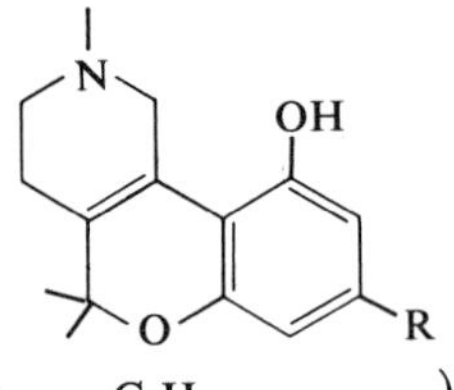

8, R = —C$_5$H$_{11}$
9, R = —CH(CH$_3$)C$_5$H$_{11}$
10, R = —CH(CH$_3$)C$_{12}$H$_{25}$
11, R = —CH(CH$_3$)CH(CH$_3$)C$_5$H$_{11}$
and dihydro derivatives

Parallel THC activity
THC-like activity

Pars *et al.* (1966)
Dewey *et al.* (1970)

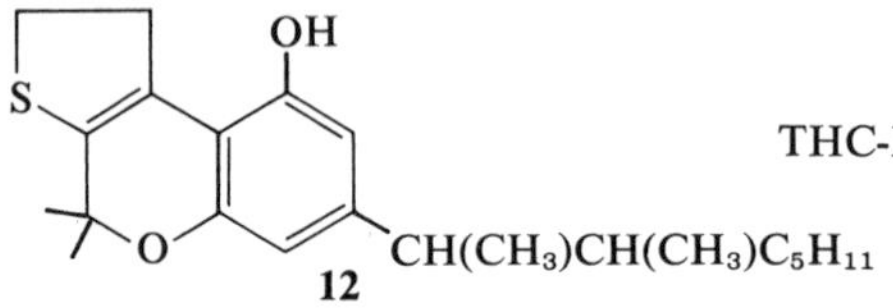

12

THC-like activity

Dewey *et al.* (1970)

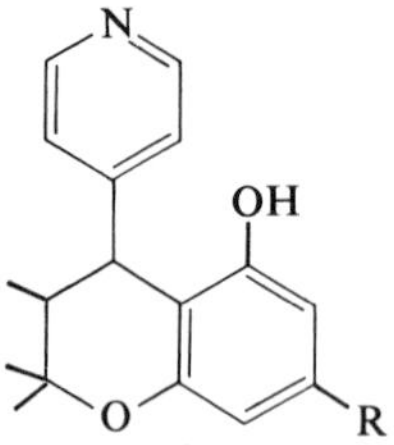

13   **14**

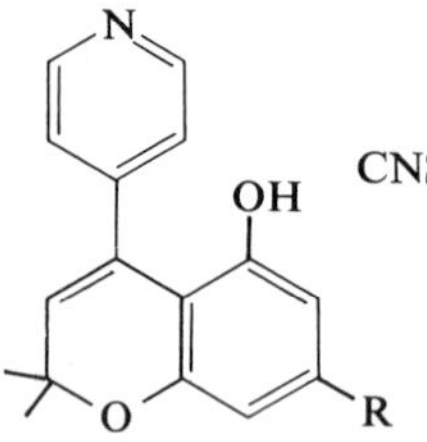

CNS activity

Harris *et al.* (1967),
Razdan and Pars
(1970), Razdan *et al.*
(1967)

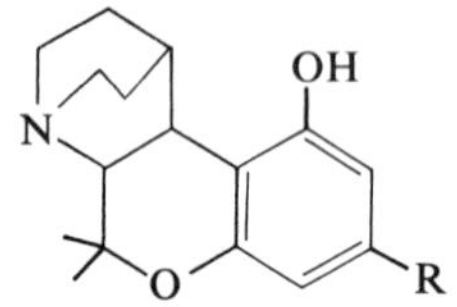

CNS activity

Razdan and Pars (1970)

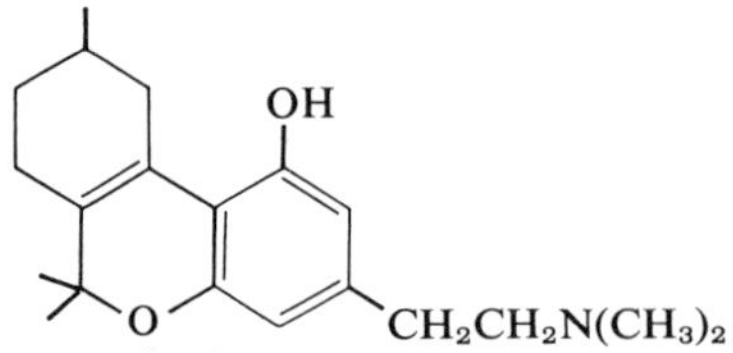

CNS activity

Razdan and Pars (1970)

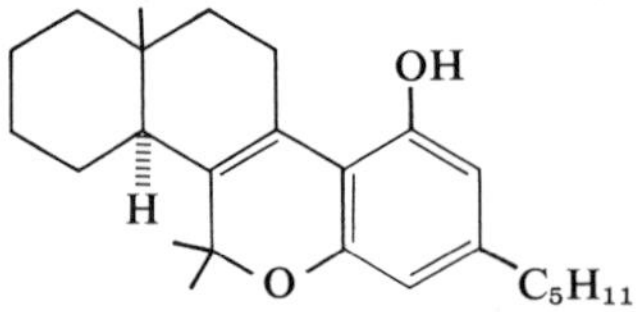

No CNS activity

Razdan *et al.* (1968)

8 has been reported to parallel the natural THC's in activity. Homologs in which the side chain varied (**9, 10**) were also active. Recently, **11** and the sulfur analog of $\varDelta^3$-THC (**12**) were examined in greater detail. They seem to parallel $\varDelta^1$-THC and $\varDelta^6$-THC in potentiation of epinephrine and norepinephrine, reduction of spontaneous activity in mice, and analgesic activity. A group of related compounds (**13** and **14**) with CNS activity has been described.

Major changes in the molecule seem to cause a steep reduction of activity. A representative of the iso-THC's (Table VII) was inactive. Minor or no activity was observed in a number of compounds in which either the aromatic or the terpenoid part was radically changed (Table VII).

TABLE VII
ACTIVITY OF MISCELLANEOUS CANNABINOIDS

Compound	Test	Activity	Reference
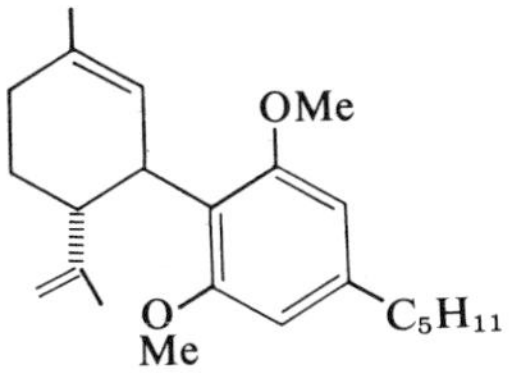 Cannabidiol dimethyl ether	Human smoking	Inactive up to 0.4 mg/kg	Isbell *et al.* (1967)
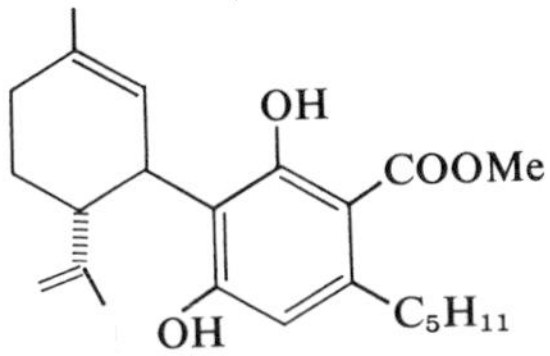	Rhesus monkey	Inactive at 5 mg/kg	Edery *et al.* (1972)
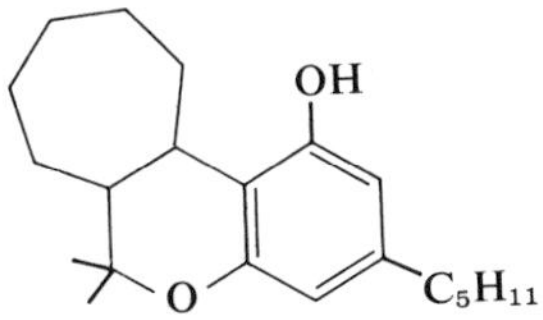	Dog ataxia	0.2 as active as $\varDelta^3$-THC	Loewe (1944)
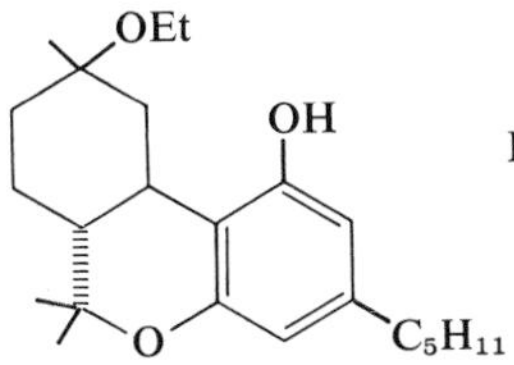 1-Ethoxyhexahydrocannabinol	Rhesus monkey	Inactive up to 7 mg/kg	Gaoni and Mechoulam (1968), Grunfeld and Edery (1969)

TABLE VII (*Continued*)

Compound	Test	Activity	Reference
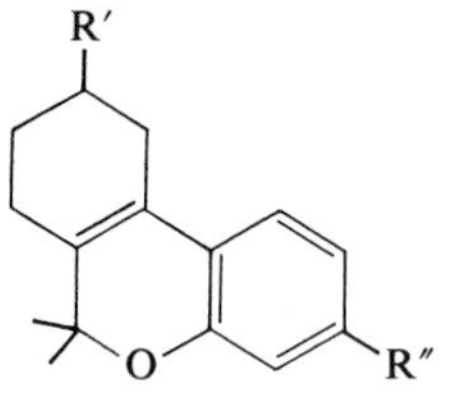 R′ = H or CH₃ R″ = OH, OAc, OCOC₃H₇ = OEt, OBu = CH₃, C₅H₁₁	Dog ataxia Corneal areflexia	Inactive Inactive	Alles *et al.* (1942) Ghosh *et al.* (1940)
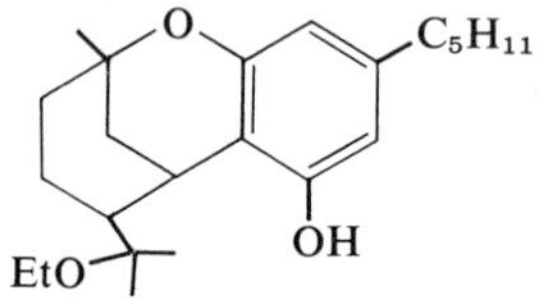 8-Ethoxy*iso* hexahydrocannabinol	Rhesus monkey	Inactive up to 7 mg/kg	Gaoni and Mechoulam (1968), Grunfeld and Edery (1969)
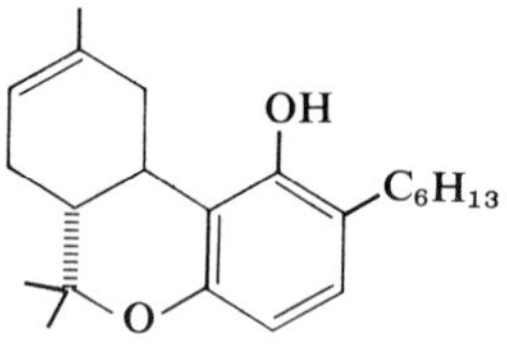	Rhesus monkey	Inactive up to 7 mg/kg	Grunfeld and Edery (1969)
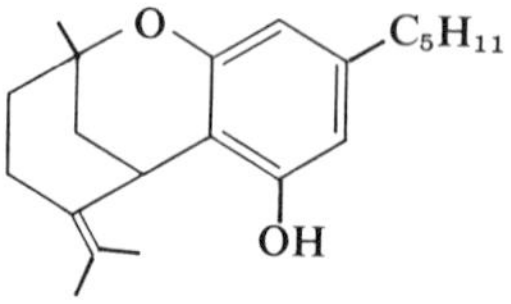 $\Delta^{4(8)}$-iso-THC	CNS activity in mice	Not active	Mechoulam (1970)
Iso-THC (isomer not specified)	CNS activity in mice	At 10 mg/kg, aggressiveness	Razdan and Pars (1970)
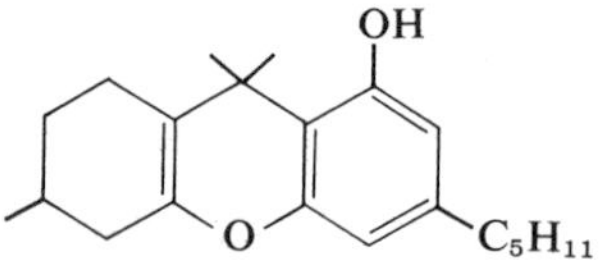	Motor activity (mice) Corneal areflexia (rabbits) Catatonia (mice) Aggressiveness (mice)	Inactive Inactive Inactive ~ ⅓ as active as Δ^1-THC	Carlini *et al.* (1970)

TABLE VII (*Continued*)

Compound	Test	Activity	Reference

| 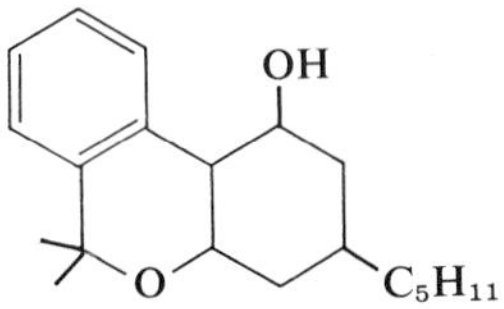 | Tests of previous compound | Inactive | Carlini *et al.* (1970) |

| 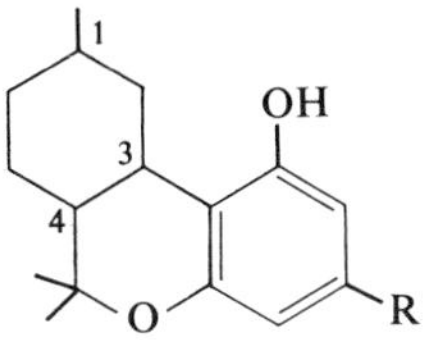 | Dog ataxia | Varies from 0.24 to 1.86 of activity of Δ^3-THC | Adams *et al.* (1942a) |
| | Corneal areflexia | Active at 5 mg/kg | Russell *et al.* (1941a) |

Stereochemistry at C-1, C-3, C-4 not known
R = C_3H_7, C_4H_9, C_6H_{13}, C_7H_{15}

VI. Summary

The data presented in the tables in this chapter allow the drawing of some conclusions regarding SAR in this series. As usual in this type of empirical work the conclusions are tentative at best. The following points seem to be relevant to cannabinoid SAR.

1. A benzopyran type of structure with a hydroxyl group at the 3′ aromatic position and an alkyl group on the 5′ aromatic position seems to be a requirement. Opening of the pyran ring leads to complete loss of activity.

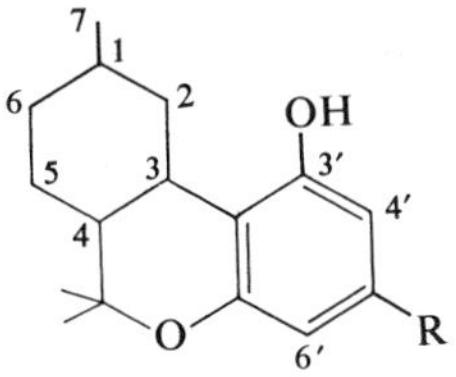

2. The aromatic hydroxyl group has to be free or esterified. Blocking of the hydroxyl group as an ether inactivates the molecule.

3. When alkyl groups are substituted on the phenolic ring at C-4′, activity is retained. Substitution at C-6′ eliminates activity. Electronegative groups such as carboxyl, carbomethoxy, and acetyl at either C-4′ or C-6′ eliminate activity.

4. A certain length of the aromatic side chain is a requirement for activity. Branching of the side chain may lead to considerable increase in potency. The 1,2-dimethylheptyl side chain seems to be optimal.

5. The terpenoid ring may apparently be amended considerably. It seems that substituents on C-1 and C-2 have to be in the plane of the ring (i.e., equatorial) in order that high activity be retained. A double bond in the terpenoid ring is not a requirement.

6. With introduction of a hydroxyl group on the C-1 methyl group, activity is retained. Both 6-hydroxy-Δ^1-THC's are active; Δ^1- and Δ^6-THC are active in the 3R, 4R series only; Δ^5-THC and Δ^7-THC are inactive; Δ^3-THC is active; Δ^1-3,4-cis-THC is inactive.

7. The terpenoid ring may be exchanged by some heterocyclic systems. The scope of this major modification is unknown.

8. Some activity is shown by compounds whose structure does not follow the above rules (for example, cannabicyclol). This is observed only when the compounds are administered in very high doses in mice.

Points 1–6 in the above list have been established in rhesus monkeys and in some cases in other animals. Points 7 and 8 are based on work with mice only. The relevancy of the above observations to activity in man has not been ascertained, although scattered experiments tend to support the view that they are indeed pertinent. We have, however, reservations concerning the relevancy of point 8.

References

Aaron, H. S., and Ferguson, C. P. (1968). *J. Org. Chem.* **33**, 684.

Abel, E. L., and Schiff, B. B. (1969). *Psychonom. Sci.* **16**, 38.

Adams, R. (1942). *Harvey Lect.* **37**, 168.

Adams, R., and Baker, B. R. (1940). *J. Amer. Chem. Soc.* **62**, 2405.

Adams, R., Loewe, S., Jellinek, C., and Wolff, H. (1941a). *J. Amer. Chem. Soc.* **63**, 1971.

Adams, R., Smith, C. M., and Loewe, S. (1941b). *J. Amer. Chem. Soc.* **63**, 1973.

Adams, R., Cain, C. K., and Loewe, S. (1941c). *J. Amer. Chem. Soc.* **63**, 1977.

Adams, R., Loewe, S., Smith, C. M., and McPhee, W. D. (1942a). *J. Amer. Chem. Soc.* **64**, 694.

Adams, R., Loewe, S., Theobald, C. W., and Smith, C. M. (1942b). *J. Amer. Chem. Soc.* **64**, 2653.

Adams, R., Smith, C. M., and Loewe, S. (1942c). *J. Amer. Chem. Soc.* **64**, 2087.

Adams, R., Chen, K. H., and Loewe, S. (1945). *J. Amer. Chem. Soc.* **67**, 1534.

Adams, R., Aycock, B. F., and Loewe, S. (1948a). *J. Amer. Chem. Soc.* **70**, 662.

Adams, R., MacKenzie, S., Jr., and Loewe, S. (1948b). *J. Amer. Chem. Soc.* **70**, 664.

Adams, R., Harfenist, M., and Loewe, S. (1949). *J. Amer. Chem. Soc.* **71**, 1624.

Allentuck, S., and Bowman, K. M. (1942). *Amer. J. Psychiat.* **99**, 248.

Alles, G. A., Icke, R. N., and Feigen, G. (1942). *J. Amer. Chem. Soc.* **64**, 2031.

Anker, R. M., and Cook, A. H. (1946). *J. Chem. Soc.* 58.

Avison, A. W. D., Morison, A. L., Parkes, M. W. (1949). *J. Chem. Soc.* 952.

Baeckström, P., and Sundström, G. (1970). *Acta Chem. Scand.* **24**, 716.
Ben-Zvi, Z., Mechoulam, R., and Burstein, S. (1970). *J. Amer. Chem. Soc.* **92**, 3468.
Ben-Zvi, Z., Mechoulam, R., Edery, H., and Porath, G. (1971). *Science* **174**, 951.
Bergel, F., Morrison, A. L., Rinderknecht, H., Todd, A. R., Macdonald, A. D., and Woolfe, G. (1943). *J. Chem. Soc.* 286.
Bicher, H. I., and Mechoulam, R. (1968). *Arch. Int. Pharmacodyn.* **172**, 24.
Biel, J. H. (1970). *In* "Psychotomimetic Drugs" (D. H. Efron, ed.), p. 336. Raven, New York.
Bose, B. C., Saifi, A. Q., and Bhagwat, A. W. (1964). *Arch. Int. Pharmacodyn.* **147**, 285.
Boyd, E. S., Hutchinson, E. D., Gardner, L. C., and Meritt, D. A. (1963). *Arch. Int. Pharmacodyn.* **144**, 533.
Carlini, E. A., Santos, M., Claussen, U., Bienek, D., and Korte, F. (1970). *Psychopharmacologia* **18**, 82.
Christensen, H. D., Freudenthal, R. I., Gidley, J. T., Rosenfeld, R., Boegli, G., Testino, L., Brine, D. R., Pitt, C. G., and Wall, M. E. (1971). *Science* **172**, 165.
Dever, J. L. (1962). U.S. Patent 3,278,606. (1966). *Chem. Abstr.* **65**, 20062.
Dewey, W. L., Harris, L. S., Howes, J. F., Kennedy, J. S., Granchelli, F. E., Pars, H. G., and Razdan, R. K. (1970). *Nature* **226**, 1265.
Duquénois, P. (1939). *Bull. Sci. Pharmacol.* **46**, 222.
Edery, H., Grunfeld, Y., Ben-Zvi, Z., and Mechoulam, R. (1971). *Ann. N.Y. Acad. Sci.* **191**, 40.
Edery, H., Grunfeld, Y., Porath, G., Ben-Zvi, Z., Shani, A., and Mechoulam, R. (1972). *Arzneim.-Forsch.* **22**, 1995.
Farenholtz, K. E. (1970). Private communication.
Foltz, R. L., Fentiman, A. F., Leighty, E. G., Walter, J. L., Drewes, H. R., Schwartz, W. E., Page, T. F., and Truitt, E. B. (1970). *Science* **168**, 844.
Fraenkel, S. (1903). *Arch. Exp. Pathol. Pharmakol.* **49**, 266.
Gaoni, Y., and Mechoulam, R. (1964). *J. Amer. Chem. Soc.* **86**, 1646.
Gaoni, Y., and Mechoulam, R. (1966). *Tetrahedron* **22**, 1481.
Gaoni, Y., and Mechoulam, R. (1968). *Isr. J. Chem.* **6**, 679.
Garattini, S. (1965). *In* "Hashish. Its Chemistry and Pharmacology" (G. E. W. Wolstenholme and J. Knight, eds.), pp. 70–78. Churchill, London.
Garriott, J. C., Forney, R. B., Hughes, F. W., and Richards, A. B. (1968). *Arch. Int. Pharmacodyn.* **171**, 425.
Gayer, H. (1928). *Arch. Exp. Pathol. Pharmakol.* **129**, 312.
Ghosh, R., Todd, A. R., and Wilkinson, S. (1940). *J. Chem. Soc.* 1121.
Ghosh, R., Todd, A. R., and Wright, D. C. (1941). *J. Chem. Soc.* 137.
Gill, E. W., Paton, W. D. M., and Pertwee, R. G. (1970). *Nature (London)* **228**, 134.
Grunfeld, Y., and Edery, H. (1969). *Psychopharmacologia* **14**, 200.
Harris, L. S., Razdan, R. K., Dewey, W. L., and Pars, H. G. (1967). *In* "Summary of Lectures, Troisième Rencontre Chimie Thérapie (France)," p. 167.
Hively, R. L., Mosher, W. A., and Hoffmann, F. W. (1966). *J. Amer. Chem. Soc.* **88**, 1832.
Hollister, L. E. (1970). *Nature (London)* **227**, 968.
Hollister, L. E., and Gillespie, H. K. (1970). *Arch. Gen. Psychiat.* **23**, 199.
Hollister, L. E., Richards, R. K., and Gillespie, H. K. (1968). *Clin. Pharmacol. Ther.* **9**, 783.
Hoops, J. F., Bader, H., Biel, J. H. (1968). *J. Org. Chem.* **33**, 2995.
Isbell, H. (1968). *In* "Proceedings of the Meeting of the Committee on the Problems of Drug Dependence," Addendum 1. Nat. Acad. Sci. Washington, D.C.

Isbell, H., Gorodetzsky, C. W., Jasinski, D., Claussen, U., von Spulak, F., and Korte, F. (1967). *Psychopharmacologia* **11**, 184.
Joachimoglu, G. (1965). *In* "Hashish. Its Chemistry and Pharmacology" (G. E. W. Wolstenholme and J. Knight, eds.), pp. 2–11. Churchill, London.
Kabelik, J., Krejči, Z., and Šantavý, F. (1960). *Bull. Narcotics* **12**, No. 3, 5.
Krejči, Z. (1970). *In* "The Botany and Chemistry of Cannabis" (C. R. B. Joyce and S. H. Curry, eds.), pp. 49–55. Churchill, London.
Kubena, R. K., and Barry, H. (1970). *J. Pharmacol. Exp. Ther.* **173**, 94.
Leaf, G., Todd, A. R., and Wilkinson, S. (1942). *J. Chem. Soc.* 185.
Liautaud, R. (1844). *C. R. Acad. Sci. Ser. D.* **18**, 149.
Lipparini, F., de Carolis, A. S., and Longo, V. G. (1969). *Physiol. Behav.* **4**, 527.
Loewe, S. (1944). *In* "The Marihuana Problem in the City of New York" (Mayor's Committee on Marihuana), pp. 149–212. Jacques Cattell Press, Lancaster, Pennsylvania.
Loewe, S. (1946). *J. Pharmacol. Exp. Ther.* **88**, 154.
Loewe, S. (1950). *Arch. Exp. Pathol. Pharmakol.* **211**, 175.
McMillan, D. E., Harris, L. S., Frankenheim, J. M., and Kennedy, J. S. (1970). *Science* **169**, 501.
Manno, J. E., Kliplinger, G. F., Bennett, I. F., Haine, S. E., and Forney, R. B. (1970). *Clin. Pharmacol. Ther.* **11**, 808.
Mechoulam, R. (1970). *Science* **168**, 1159.
Mechoulam, R., and Gaoni, Y. (1965). *Tetrahedron* **21**, 1223.
Mechoulam, R., and Gaoni, Y. (1967). *Fortschr. Chem. Org. Naturst.* **25**, 175.
Mechoulam, R., Braun, P., and Gaoni, Y. (1967). *J. Amer. Chem. Soc.* **89**, 4552.
Mechoulam, R., Ben-Zvi, Z., Yagnitinsky, B., and Shani, A. (1969). *Tetrahedron Lett.* 2339.
Mechoulam, R., Shani, A., Yagnitinsky, B., Ben-Zvi, Z., Braun, P., and Gaoni, Y. (1970a). *In* "The Botany and Chemistry of Cannabis" (C. R. B. Joyce and S. H. Curry eds.), pp. 93–117. Churchill, London.
Mechoulam, R., Shani, A., Edery, H., and Grunfeld, Y. (1970b). *Science* **169**, 611.
Nilsson, I. M., Agurell, S., Nilsson, J. L. G., Ohlsson, A., Sandberg, F., and Wahlqvist, M. (1970). *Science* **168**, 1228.
Norton, S. (1957). *In* "Psychotropic Drugs" (S. Garattini, and V. Ghetti, eds.), pp. 73–82. Elsevier, Amsterdam.
Pars, H. G., Granchelli, F. E., Keller, J. K., and Razdan, R. K. (1966). *J. Amer. Chem. Soc.* **88**, 3664.
Petrzilka, T., Haefliger, W., and Sikemeier, C. (1969). *Helv. Chim. Acta* **52**, 1102.
Razdan, R. K., and Pars, H. G. (1970). *In* "The Botany and Chemistry of Cannabis" (C. R. B. Joyce and S. H. Curry, eds.), pp. 137–149. Churchill, London.
Razdan, R. K., Thompson, W. R., Pars, H. G., and Granchelli, F. E. (1967). *Tetrahedron Lett.* 3405.
Razdan, R. K., Pars, H. G., Granchelli, F. E., and Harris, L. S. (1968). *J. Med. Chem.* **11**, 377.
Russell, P. B., Todd, A. R., Wilkinson, S., Macdonald, A. D., and Woolfe, G. (1941a). *J. Chem. Soc.* 169.
Russell, P. B., Todd, A. R., Wilkinson, S., Macdonald, A. D., and Woolfe, G. (1941b). *J. Chem. Soc.* 826.
Santos, M., Sampaio, M. R. P., Fernandes, N. S., and Carlini, E. A. (1966). *Psychopharmacologia* **8**, 437.
Scheckel, C. L., Boff, E., Dahlen, P., and Smart, T. (1968). *Science* **160**, 1467.

Schultz, O. E., and Haffner, G. (1958). *Arch. Pharm.* (*Weinheim*) **291**, 391.
Shani, A., and Mechoulam, R. (1970). *Chem. Commun.* 273.
Siegel, R. K. (1969). *Psychopharmacologia* **15**, 1.
Silva, M. T. A., Carlini, E. A., Claussen, U., and Korte, F. (1969). *Psychopharmacologia* **13**, 332.
Sim, V. (1970). *In* "Psychotomimetic Drugs (D. H. Efron, ed.), pp. 332–338. Raven, New York.
Suter, C. M., and Weston, A. W. (1939). *J. Amer. Chem. Soc.* **61**, 232.
Taylor, E. C., Lenard, K., and Loev, B. (1967). *Tetrahedron* **23**, 77.
Todd, A. R. (1946). *Experientia* **2**, 55.
Valle, J. R., Souza, J. A., and Hypolitto, N. (1966). *J. Pharm. Pharmacol.* **18**, 476.
Valle, J. R., Baratella, M. R., Tangary, M. R., and de Silva, T. N. (1967). *Ann. Acad. Brasil. Cienc.* **39**, 445.
Walters, G. C., and Abel, E. L. (1970). *J. Pharm. Pharmacol.* **22**, 310.
Walton, R. P., Martin, L. F., and Keller, J. H. (1938). *J. Pharmacol. Exp. Ther.* **62**, 239.
Wall, M. E., Brine, D. R., Brine, G. A., Pitt, C. G., Freudenthal, R. I., and Christensen, H. D. (1970). *J. Amer. Chem. Soc.* **92**, 3466.
Webster, C. D., Willinsky, M. D., Herring, B. S., and Walters, G. C. (1971). *Nature* (*London*) **232**, 498.
Weil, A. T. (1969). *Sci. J.* **5**, 36.
Weil, A. T., Zinberg, N. E., and Nelsen, J. M. (1968). *Science* **162**, 1234.
Williams, E. G., Himmelsbach, C. K., Wikler, A., Ruble, D. C., and Lloyd, B. J., Jr. (1946). *Pub. Health Rep.* **61**, 1059.
Wollner, H. J., Matchett, J. R., Levine, J., and Loewe, S. (1942). *J. Amer. Chem. Soc.* **64**, 26.
Wood, T. B., Spivey, W. T. N., and Easterfield, T. H. (1896). *J. Chem. Soc.* **69**, 539.

Addendum

The isolation, synthesis, and biological testing of THC metabolites (see addenda, Chapters 1 and 4) have thrown additional light on the relationships between structure and activity in the cannabinoid series. New observations are summarized in the Table A-I (see also Table IV in this chapter).

Some of the results reported here are unexpected. The activity of 1α,2α-epoxyhexahydrocannabinol and of 5-keto-Δ^6-THC opens new possibilities for SAR investigations. The differences in effectiveness between 5α-hydroxy- and 5β-hydroxy-Δ^6-THC emphasize the importance of stereochemistry for activity in this series. However, at present it is impossible to define the SAR requirements regarding the terpenoid ring in THC.

Hardman *et al.* (1971) have reported that the dimethylheptyl homolog of Δ^3-THC is 100–200 times more potent than Δ^3-THC in its ability to cause behavioral and respiratory changes, cardiovascular effects, and hypothermic responses. The methyl homolog was inactive; the 1-methyloctyl homolog was almost as active as the dimethylheptyl homolog. The dimethyl carbamate of Δ^3-THC was equipotent to Δ^3-THC, probably due to hydrolysis of the ester

TABLE A-I

ACTIVITY OF SOME NEW METABOLITES AND RELATED CANNABINOIDS IN RHESUS MONKEYS[a]

Cannabinoid	Dose (mg/kg)	Activity[b]
	0.1 0.5 1.0	− + and + + + + +
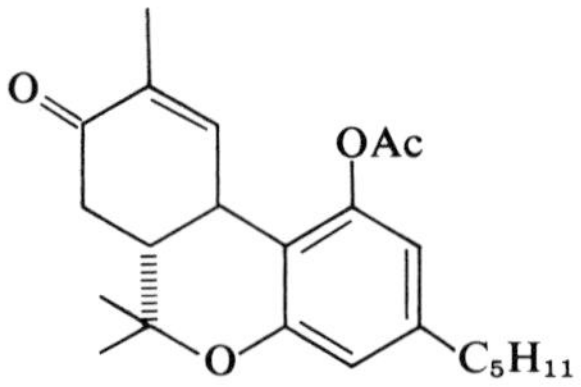	5.0	−
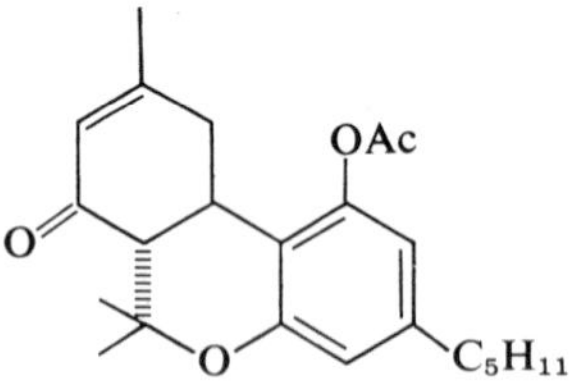	0.5 1.0	± and + + +
	0.25 0.50 1.0	± + and + + + +
	1.0 2.0 5.0	− + + +

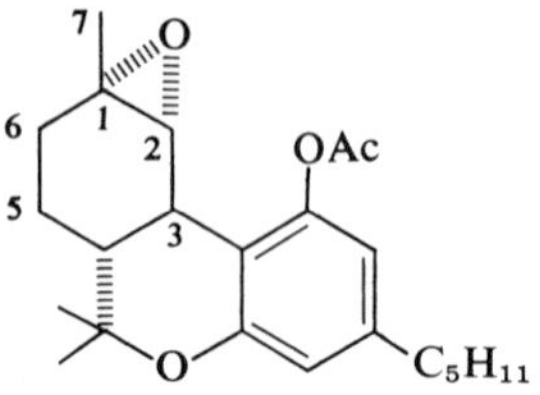

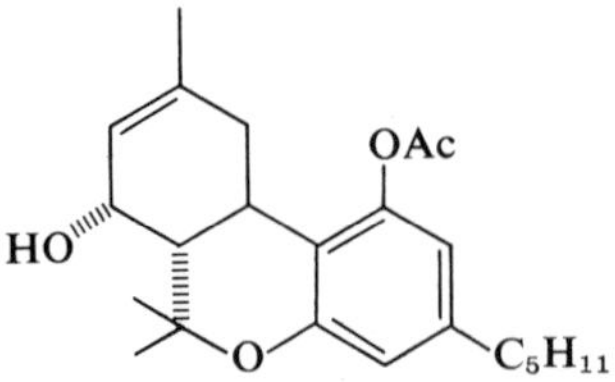

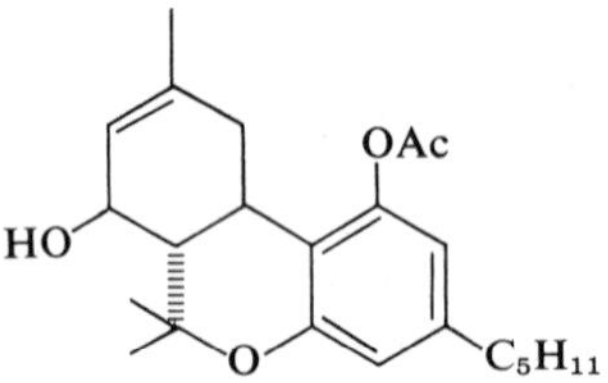

TABLE A-I (*Continued*)

Cannabinoid	Dose (mg/kg)	Activity[b]

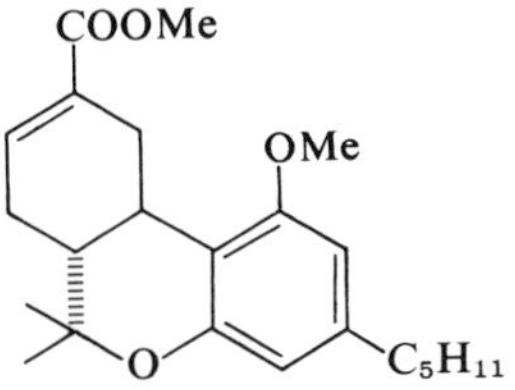

COOMe

OMe

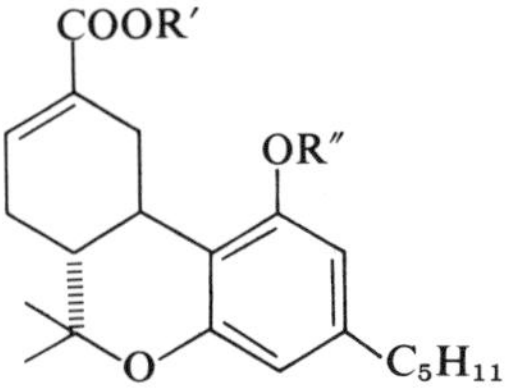

C5H11

5.0   −

COOR′

OR″

C5H11

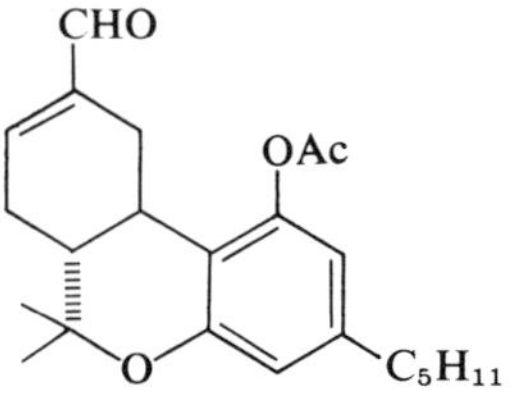

5.0   −

R′ = H or CH₃
R″ = H or COCH₃

CHO

OAc

C5H11

1.0   +

OAc

C4H9

OH

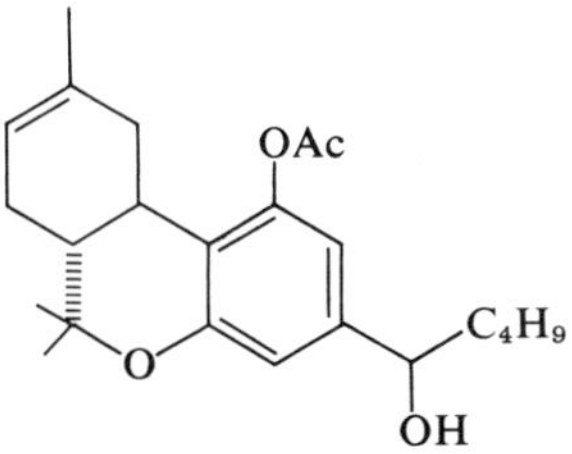

5.0   −

[a] The compounds were administered as described by Edery *et al.* (1971). The data are from Mechoulam *et al.* (1972a,b) and from unpublished results.

[b] Notation is as follows: (−) no changes; (±) tranquility; (+) drowsiness, decreased motor activity, occasional partial ptosis, occasional head drop; (++) stupor, ataxia, full ptosis, suppression of motor activity, typical crouched position ("thinker position") for up to 3 hours, presence of reaction to external sensorial stimuli; (+++) severe stupor and ataxia, full ptosis, immobility, "thinker position" lasting for more than 3 hours, and absence of reaction to external stimuli.

linkage. Surprisingly, the Δ^3-THC analog in which the etheric oxygen was exchanged with a secondary amino group retained activity (dog ataxia). However, the doses used were unusually high (10 mg/kg). The N-methyl derivative of this compound has been found to be inactive by another group (see Table VI).

References

Edery, H., Grunfeld, Y., Ben-Zvi, Z., and Mechoulam (1971). *Ann. N.Y. Acad. Sci.* **191**, 40.

Hardman, H. F., Domino, E. F., and Seevers, M. H. (1971). *Proc. West. Pharmacol. Soc.* **14**, 14.

Mechoulam, R., Ben-Zvi, Z., Shani, A., Zemler, H., Levy, S., Edery, H., and Grunfeld, Y. (1972a). *In* "Cannabis and its Derivatives: Pharmacology and Experimental Psychology" (W. D. M. Paton and J. Crown, eds.). Oxford Univ. Press, London and New York.

Mechoulam, R., Varconi, H., Ben-Zvi, Z., Edery, H., and Grunfeld, Y. (1972b). *J. Amer. Chem. Soc.* **94**, 7930.

CHAPTER 3

Analytical Aspects of Cannabis Chemistry

Michael D. Willinsky

I. Introduction 137
II. Noncannabinoid Components 138
   A. Alkaloids 138
   B. Waxes 138
   C. Essential Oils 139
III. Cannabinoid Components 140
   A. Extraction and Isolation 140
   B. Variation in Cannabinoid Content 141
   C. Colorimetric Tests 142
   D. Thin-Layer Chromatography 144
   E. Gas-Liquid Chromatography 146
   F. Ultraviolet Spectroscopy 149
   G. Infrared Spectroscopy 150
   H. Stability of Cannabinoids 150
   I. Extraction Methods and Chromatography of Cannabinoid
     Metabolites 152
IV. Detection of Cannabinoids in Biological Fluids 153
   A. Radioactive Tracer Label 153
   B. Fluorescence Assay of Δ^1-THC 154
   C. Thin-Layer Assay of Cannabinoids in Urine 154
   D. Radioimmune and Spin-Label (esr) Immunoassay Methods . . 154
   References 156
   Addendum 158

I. Introduction *

The purpose of this review is to discuss the currently important methods and techniques being used for the analysis of cannabis and its constituents.

* The following abbreviations are used: THC, tetrahydrocannabinol; CBD, cannabidiol; CBN, cannabinol; CBDA, cannabidiolic acid.

The earlier analytical chemistry of marijuana was well reviewed by Blatt (1938), Farmilo and Genest (1959), and Grlić (1964, 1968). Considerable progress has been made in the last few years in the chemistry and quantitative assay of the components of cannabis. Consequently, this review is focused primarily on newer methods with a cursory discussion of earlier work. This review covers the following areas of cannabinoid chemistry: extraction methods, colorimetric tests, thin-layer chromatography, gas-liquid chromatography, ultraviolet and infrared spectroscopy, stability of cannabinoids, extraction and tentative identification of cannabinoid metabolites, and new methods for the detection of cannabinoids in biological fluids by radioactive tracer labeling, fluorescence assay, radioimmunoassay, and spin-label [electron spin resonance (esr)] immunoassay.

II. Noncannabinoid Components

The analytical chemistry of cannabis is concerned mainly with the identification of cannabinoids; however, in addition to these compounds there are the following extractable fractions: (A) water-soluble, nitrogen-containing compounds (alkaloids), (B) soluble waxes, and (C) essential oils. Some methods are available for the study of these noncannabinoid components.

A. ALKALOIDS

The suggested presence of nitrogen-containing compounds in cannabis is reviewed in Chapter 1. If a petroleum ether extract of cannabis is shaken several times with a dilute acid solution, these nitrogen-containing compounds are partitioned out of the petroleum ether solution (Farmilo, 1955). Alcohols have been reported to extract nitrogen-containing compounds from cannabis that has been previously extracted with petroleum ether (Obata and Ishikawa, 1960a). The known alkaloids include trigonelline, piperidine, and choline. Several authors (Salemink et al., 1965; Gill et al., 1970; Klein et al., 1971) have reported the presence of alkaloids with physiological activity in cannabis extracts. Owing to the uncertain state of our knowledge of their chemistry, these alkaloids have not yet been employed in analytical tests for cannabis.

B. WAXES

Alcohols (methanol or ethanol) are often used to extract hashish or marijuana. They successfully solubilize the cannabinoids. However, plant waxes, chlorophyll, piperidine, and other unidentified compounds are also extracted from the sample simultaneously (Obata and Ishikawa, 1960a). The composition of the wax extracted from cannabis is complex and contains numerous paraffinic materials (Mechoulam, 1971).

One of the major plant waxes extracted from cannabis leaf with methanol is *n*-nonecosane (Wood *et al.*, 1896). Nonecosane, m.p. 63°–64°C, is physiologically inactive. In a petroleum ether extract of cannabis, a portion of the extracted waxes precipitates at room temperature and can be filtered off. Cooling of this same solution to −4°C precipitates still further waxes.

Chlorophyll is readily extracted from cannabis plant material by methanol. It can be removed from the methanolic solution by chromatography on a Florisil column, eluting the cannabinoids with 9:1 pentane:ether.

The active cannabinoid(s) are found in the petroleum ether extract of hashish. Once hashish is extracted with petroleum ether, subsequent extractions with methanol or benzene yield only small amounts of inactive cannabinoids. For this reason, and because of the apparently greater selectivity of petroleum ether for cannabinoids, this is the solvent of choice for extraction of cannabis for cannabinoids (Gaoni and Mechoulam, 1971).

C. ESSENTIAL OILS

Studies to determine the geographical and botanical origin of marijuana samples, by analyzing the plant's essential oils, have yielded considerable information about the oils of cannabis (Martin *et al.*, 1961; Nigam *et al.*, 1965). The essential oil of cannabis is obtained by steam distilling marijuana. This crude oily mixture is then fractionated, under reduced pressure in a Towers column, to yield five fractions. These fractions are then chromatographed by gas chromatography to determine their composition. The physicochemical constants and gas chromatograms for oils from either the male or female plant are virtually identical (Nigam *et al.*, 1965). The essential oil of *Cannabis sativa* is a complex mixture, as can be seen in Table I.

Cannabis plant material and resin have a characteristic smell at room temperature; burning marijuana has a resinous petrol odor, somewhat similar to the smell of burning leaves. The active components of the plant, the cannabinoids, do not produce the characteristic smell of marijuana smoke when they are burned. Several volatile odoriferous oils that contribute to the odor of marijuana have been identified.

The low boiling point terpene fraction consists mainly of myrcene (Nigam *et al.*, 1965), *p*-cymene, and possible other methylisopropylbenzenes (Simonsen and Todd, 1942). Obata and Ishikawa (1960a,b) identified eugenol, guajacol, and piperdine in hemp leaves and flowering tops. Some of the odoriferous principles that contribute to the smell of the plant are caryophyllene, β-farnesene, α-selinene, β-phellandrene, limonene, and piperidine (Meresz, 1971).

TABLE I

COMPOSITION OF *Cannabis sativa* OIL

Constituent	Yield (%)[a]
α-Pinene	1.3
Camphene	0.1
β-Pinene	0.8
Myrcene	1.3
α-Terpinene	0.1
Limonene	2.8
β-Phellandrene	2.7
γ-Terpinene	1.3
p-Cymene	0.4
Alcohol A	0.2
Linalool oxide	0.8
Linalool	0.2
Sabinene hydrate	0.4
α-Bergamotene	5.0
Terpinen-4-ol	0.4
Caryophyllene	45.7
β-Farnesene	5.1
α-Terpineol	0.6
β-Humulene	16.0
α-Selinene	8.6
Curcumene	1.4
α,β-Unsaturated ketone	0.2
Alcohol B	1.6
Caryophyllene oxide	1.7
Unidentified	1.5

[a] Percent yield as determined by gas-liquid chromatography using 10% Reoplex 400 on acid–base-washed Chromosorb W (Nigam *et al.*, 1965).

III. Cannabinoid Components

A. EXTRACTION AND ISOLATION

Various authorities (Adams *et al.*, 1941; Todd, 1946; Mechoulam and Gaoni, 1965) have stated that the tetrahydrocannabinols are the main psychoactive ingredients in a petroleum ether extract of cannabis. More recently, Mechoulam *et al.* (1970a) have claimed that the Δ^1-THC isomer is the only major active component in cannabis. The other cannabinoids and their corresponding acids are much less active or totally inactive; however, they may be capable of adding to or detracting from the pharmacological effect of THC. One must reserve final judgment on this matter because of a number of technical limitations in the work done to date. They include lack of parallelism between pharmacological activities of some ingredients in monkeys and man, possible presence of minor active ingredients, the possibility of chemical change during combustion of hashish versus injection of purified components, and difference in the time of onset of pharmacological effects after administration via the different routes used.

Cannabinoids have been isolated from marijuana by several methods. Steam distillation, derivative formation, and adsorption chromatography on alumina were used by Wollner et al. (1942). Others (de Ropp, 1960; Gaoni and Mechoulam, 1971; Garriott et al., 1967; Grlić, 1968) have used solvent extraction and chromatographic separation to isolate the cannabinoid fractions from cannabis. The following method has been used with good success in this laboratory. Twenty grams of "manicured"* plant material is extracted with two 150 ml portions of petroleum ether (b.p. 50°–60°C). The two extracts are pooled and refrigerated overnight at 4°C to remove plant waxes, then filtered cold, and evaporated at 40°C *in vacuo*. For column chromatography the residue is redissolved in 10 ml of petroleum ether, and Florisil (100–120 mesh) is added and mixed by swirling until all the residue appears to be adsorbed to it. The Florisil plus extracted residue is placed in a (3 × 40 cm) column packed with 260 gm Florisil (100–120 mesh) in a pentane slurry and eluted with increasing proportions of ether in pentane. Fractions of 100 ml each are collected using a device to prevent the column from running dry (Meresz, 1965).

Six crude fractions may be isolated by this chromatographic method. Repeated chromatography yields pure fractions. Table II shows the percent yield of cannabinoids following extraction and chromatography of marijuana and hashish. For additional details on the isolation and separation of cannabinoids from cannabis see Chapter 1.

B. VARIATION IN CANNABINOID CONTENT

A number of authors (Davis et al., 1963; Toffoli et al., 1968; Davis et al., 1970; Gill, 1971; Fairbairn et al., 1971) have reported differences in the cannabinoid content of different samples of cannabis. Fetterman et al. (1971a) reported variation in the cannabinoid content of different strains of marijuana grown under similar conditions. These authors found wide variations in the range of concentrations of the three major components, cannabidiol, tetrahydrocannabinol, and cannabinol, as shown in Table III.

---

* Manicured marijuana is marijuana from which all seeds and stalks have been removed by sieving. Crude marijuana yields approximately one-third of its weight in manicured material.

TABLE II

YIELD OF CANNABINOIDS FROM MARIJUANA AND HASHISH

Compound	Marijuana[a] Neutral and acid cannabinoids (% dry weight)	Hashish[b] Neutral cannabinoids (% dry weight)	Acid cannabinoids (% dry weight)
Cannabicyclol (CBC)	0.09	0.11	
Cannabidiol (CBD)	0.04 (0.07)[c]	3.74 (1.4) (2.5)	3.5
Δ^6-Tetrahydrocannabinol (Δ^6-THC)	Not detected	Not detected	
Δ^1-Tetrahydrocannabinol (Δ^1-THC)	0.72 (1.1)	3.30 (1.4) (3.4)	2.1
Cannabinol (CBN)	0.26 (0.52)	1.30 (0.3) (1.2)	0.2
Cannabichromene	Not detected	0.19	
Cannabigerol	0.11	0.30	0.2

[a] As percentage of marijuana (street sample of unknown origin) by glc analysis of total cannabinoid content (neutral plus acid cannabinoids) (Willinsky, 1971).

[b] As percentage of hashish (Lebanese, 1 year old, confiscated) by glc analysis of neutral cannabinoids (Gaoni and Mechoulam, 1971) and acid cannabinoids (Mechoulam, 1971).

[c] Parentheses indicate partial analysis of a sample.

TABLE III

VARIATION IN THE TOTAL CANNABINOID CONTENT OF DIFFERENT STRAINS OF MARIJUANA GROWN UNDER SIMILAR CONDITIONS[a]

Country of origin of seeds	CBD (%)	THC (%)	CBN (%)
Mexico	0.05–0.80	0.01–3.7	0.002–0.59
Turkey	0.03–1.7	0.007–0.37	0.02–0.08
Minnesota, U.S.	0.77–1.3	0.04–0.07	0.003–0.02
Thailand	0.11–0.16	1.3–2.2	Trace only

[a] Analysis by glc; 2% OV-17 on 100–120 mesh Gas-Chrom Q (Fetterman et al., 1971b).

C. COLORIMETRIC TESTS

Since extensive reviews of the colorimetric tests for cannabis have previously appeared (Blatt, 1938; Grlić, 1964), this review will not cover these methods in great detail.

Three colorimetric tests are commonly used for the forensic identification of cannabis, the Beam (Beam, 1911), the Duquénois (Duquénois and Negm, 1938) and the Ghamrawy (Ghamrawy, 1937) tests. These microcolor reactions are all based on empirical observations that an extract of marijuana or hashish can be positively identified by the production of characteristic colors with the reagents used. The tests were intended to be specific for cannabis; however, functional groups associated with other molecules may give false positive tests. The specificity of these tests has been investigated by Grlić (1964). The Beam test—a purple color with 5% ethanolic potassium hydroxide—is relatively specific. Out of 120 plant species examined, only two, *Rosmarinus officinalis* and *Salvia officinalis*, give a weakly positive reaction; out of 48 pure substances of vegetable origin (monoterpenes, sesquiterpenes, and aromatic compounds), only one, the quinone juglone, develops a color close to that of the Beam test. The Duquénois–Negm reaction—a purple color with vanillin, acetaldehyde, and ethanol in hydrochloric acid—although less specific than the Beam test is more sensitive. The extended Duquénois test (Butler, 1966) greatly enhances the discriminating value of this test for cannabinoids and is described below.

About 5 mg of cannabis are extracted with 2 ml of petroleum ether (b.p. 40°–60°C) and the extract is evaporated to dryness. The residue is taken up in a few drops of Duquénois reagent [vanillin 0.4 gm, acetaldehyde 5 drops, ethanol (95%) to 20 ml] and twice the volume of concentrated HCl is added and mixed. If a violet color develops within 5–10 minutes, this solution is shaken with an equal volume of chloroform. With cannabis most of the violet color transfers to the chloroform layer. By decreasing the volume of reagents used, as little as 0.2 mg of cannabis can be identified. The compounds that may give a positive Duquénois color reaction are some terpene alcohols and aldehydes, and aromatic phenolic compounds (Nelson and May, 1969). It has been reported that some brands of coffee also give a positive reaction (Focht-man and Winek, 1971). This finding may have legal implications.

The chemical basis of the Duquénois test is not yet clear. Mechoulam and Zemler (1971) have found that compounds of type A indicated below are

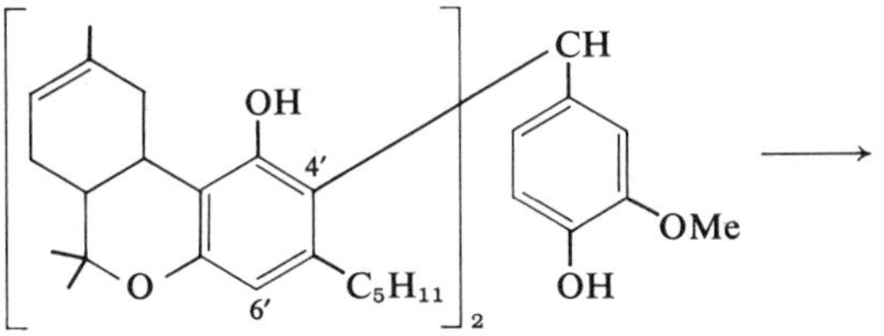

A

The attachment can
also be on the 6' position

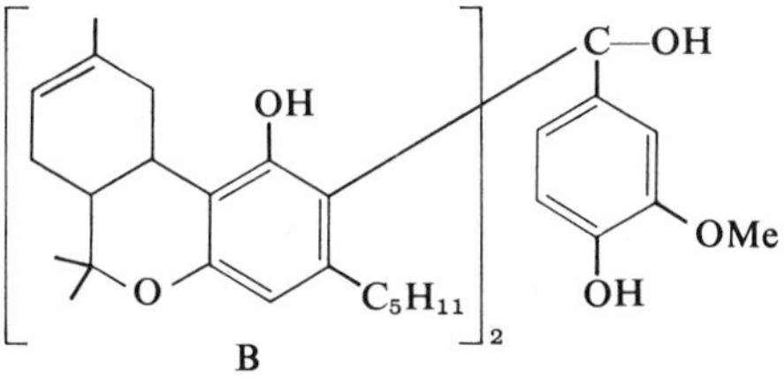

B

formed. These on oxidation can produce tertiary alcohols (B), which in the presence of acids can lead to colored species. It is not certain whether these account for the total intensity of the color.

The above-mentioned colored species are extractable in chloroform. Resorcinol gives the same color, but it is not extractable in chloroform and hence gives a negative reaction in the Butler modification of the Duquénois test.

The chemical basis of the Beam test, the oxidation of CBD, cannabigerol, and their corresponding acids to hydroxyquinones, has been elucidated by Mechoulam *et al.* (1968) (see Chapter 1). All these color reactions provide a rapid, simple, and inexpensive method of tentatively identifying cannabis. When employed in parallel they offer a high probability for a positive identification. They are frequently accompanied by microscopic and thin-layer chromatography as further confirmatory tests.

D. THIN-LAYER CHROMATOGRAPHY

Further identification of cannabinoids may be accomplished by thin-layer chromatography (tlc). Many different thin-layer systems have been employed for the analytical separation and identification of cannabis constituents.

A partition chromatography system using Kiesel-gel chromoplates impregnated with dimethylformamide and developed with cyclohexane was suggested by Korte and Sieper (1964a). Aramaki *et al.* (1968) and Nelson and May (1969) have reported variability in the R_f values for the cannabinoids with the Korte and Sieper method. This is presumably due to variation in the amount of dimethylformamide on the tlc plate. Impregnation of the plate with methylformamide: carbon tetrachloride 40:60 provides an equally good separation and better reproducibility of R_f values of the cannabinoids (Willinsky, 1971).

Adsorption chromatographic methods have also been employed: silica gel plates developed in either petroleum ether (b.p. 40°–60°C) plus ether in a ratio of 4:1 (Machata, 1969) or 88:12 pentane: ether (Gaoni and Mechoulam, 1971). Acetone: hexane 7:10 with silica gel plates provides good separation and avoids the oxidative degradation of labile cannabinoids which could be caused by peroxide-contaminated ethyl ether. This is an important consideration in chromatographing cannabinoid metabolites. Further tlc methods have been described by Betts and Holloway (1967), Caddy and Fish (1967), Aramaki *et al.* (1968), and de Faubert-Maunder (1969).

Detection of the separated cannabinoids can be accomplished by iodine vapor, $KMnO_4$ in a saturated solution of cupric acetate (Gaoni and Mechoulam, 1971), or a freshly prepared solution of di-*o*-anisidine tetrazolium chloride (Fast Blue Salt B, Merck) in cold 0.1 N NaOH (Korte and Sieper,

1964a). The latter detection method provides both great sensitivity (detectable level 50 ng for THC and CBD) and a distinct color differentiation for the major components: CBD, orange; THC, scarlet; CBN, violet. Table IV gives R_f values for the cannabinoids developed on both a partition and absorption system.

TABLE IV

THIN-LAYER CHROMATOGRAPHIC R_f VALUES FOR PETROLEUM ETHER
EXTRACT OF HASHISH

Compound	R_f (partition system)[a]	R_f (absorption system)[b]
Cannabicyclol	0.87	0.52
Cannabichromene	0.80	0.43
Δ^1-THC	0.61	0.51
CBN	0.35	0.47
CBD	0.26	0.58
Cannabivarol[c]	0.18	—
Cannabigerol	0.12	0.42
Δ^1-THC acids	0.0	0.0

[a] Silica gel chromoplates impregnated with dimethylformamide:carbon tetrachloride 40:60, developed in cyclohexane saturated with dimethylformamide according to Korte and Sieper (1964a).
[b] Silica gel chromoplates, developed in pentane-ethyl ether 88:12. Data from Gaoni and Mechoulam (1971).
[c] The R_f value for cannabivarol from Merkus (1971b).

Korte and Sieper (1964b) reported a quantitative thin-layer chromatographic method utilizing a tetrazolium salt as detector. Each color zone was eluted from the chromatogram, and the absorption maxima were measured spectrophotometrically. This method requires careful attention to detail, since the color reaction with Fast Blue Salt is dependent on several variables, temperature, pH of detector solution, concentration of cannabinoid on plate, amount of detector applied to plate, and time between development of plate and elution for spectrophotometry (Willinsky, 1971).

Quantitative thin-layer chromatography by densitometric scanning of the chromoplate, after the developed plate is sprayed with light mineral oil to reduce background interference, is both faster and easier than elution and measurement of absorption maxima. However, considerable variability in results may occur. Thin-layer chromatography is an excellent method for qualitative identification of cannabinoids and successfully separates these compounds from a large number of chemically unrelated substances occasionally found mixed with marijuana (tobacco, labiate herbs). The practical threshold of sensitivity for identification of Δ^1-THC by these methods is approximately 100 ng, since smaller amounts produce spots with Fast Blue Salt B which fade rapidly. This level of sensitivity tends to reduce the usefulness of tlc for quantitative estimation of the minor cannabinoids, since large amounts of an extract have to be spotted on the thin-layer plate to allow quantitation of the minor cannabinoids. Such large concentrations of major components reduce the resolution of the chromatoplate. Grlić (1970a,b, 1971) reported two highly sensitive thin-layer techniques using precoated silica gel sheets (Eastman 6060). In one system the sheets were first dipped in an ethanolic solution of silver nitrate and then developed in toluene. Spots were visualized by spraying with 1% solution of freshly prepared Fast Blue Salt in 70% ethanol. This system, with 1–4 cm of solvent run, is more sensitive (limit 1–5 ng) and more rapid than other reported tlc methods for the cannabinoids. In the second system reported by Grlić (1970b), Eastman 6060 precoated sheets are dipped in diethylamine for 2–3 seconds, then developed in toluene with 4 cm of solvent run. The detectable limit for CBD and THC is over 50 ng and for CBN over 20 ng. As mentioned previously, at such low concentrations of cannabinoids, the color that develops with Fast Blue Salt B fades. A comparison of a number of tlc methods for cannabis constituents by Merkus (1971a) gives a more detailed account of the different thin-layer methods.

Paper chromatographic methods for separating cannabinoids have also been reported by de Ropp (1960), Korte and Sieper (1960), Kolšek et al. (1962), and Patterson and Stevens (1970). The latter authors used paper strips impregnated with silver nitrate. Sensitivity limits for this method were not stated.

E. GAS-LIQUID CHROMATOGRAPHY

The method of choice for rapid qualitative and quantitative identification of all cannabinoids is gas-liquid vapor-phase chromatography (glc). Farmilo and Davis (1961) and Davis et al. (1963) employed this method using an SE-30 column. Since that time, many systems have been tried using columns of QF-1 (Fujita et al., 1967), OV-7 (Willinsky, 1971), OV-17 (Lerner, 1969), or XE-60 (Caddy et al., 1967). All these methods provide adequate separation of the major cannabinoids, cannabidiol, Δ^1-tetrahydrocannabinol, and cannabinol. However, separation of the two isomers of tetrahydrocannabinol Δ^1-THC and Δ^6-THC, is more difficult to achieve. Trimethylsilyl ether derivatives of the neutral cannabinoids increase the separation of Δ^1-THC and Δ^6-THC (Claussen et al., 1966). The cannabinoids are evaporated to dryness in vacuo at 40°C and reacted with 0.5 ml N,O-bis(trimethylsilyl)acetamide dissolved in anhydrous pyridine (BSA) available from Pierce Chemical Co.) and heated to 60°C for 10 minutes.

For a routine analysis of naturally occurring cannabinoids, increased separation of the isomers of THC may not be very important since the major naturally occurring THC is Δ^1-THC (see Chapter 1).

A gas-liquid chromatograph of a petroleum ether extract of hashish is shown in Fig. 1.

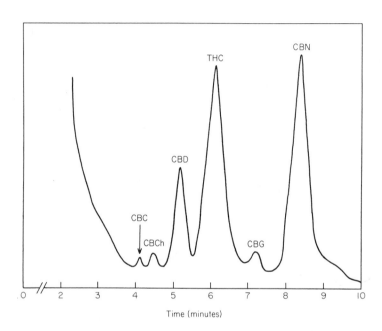

Time (minutes)

Fig. 1. Analysis of total cannabinoids (neutral plus carboxy acids) by glc. Varian 2100, 6 ft × 1/8 in. glass column packed with 3% OV-17 on Gas-Chrom Q, 100–120 mesh; Attenuation 10^{12} × 1024; column temperature 235°C, injector temperature 250°C, detector temperature 250°C; 1 μl of a petroleum ether extract made up to 2 mg/ml was injected on column. Petroleum ether was used as solvent for injection. Cannabidiol, Δ^1-THC, and CBN were identified by a comparison of the retention time of known pure standards. Cannabicyclol (CBC), cannabichromene (CBCh), and cannabigerol (CBG) were identified from published data (Mechoulam and Gaoni, 1967).

In fresh marijuana over 95% of Δ^1-tetrahydrocannabinol and cannabidiol has been reported to exist as the corresponding acids: Δ^1-THC acid A, Δ^1-THC acid B, and cannabidiolic acid (CBDA), respectively (Fetterman et al., 1971b). The positions of the carboxy acid moiety on these acidic cannabinoids are shown in Fig. 2.

Several authors have reported that the cannabinoid acids are quickly converted to their respective neutral cannabinoids on heating and more

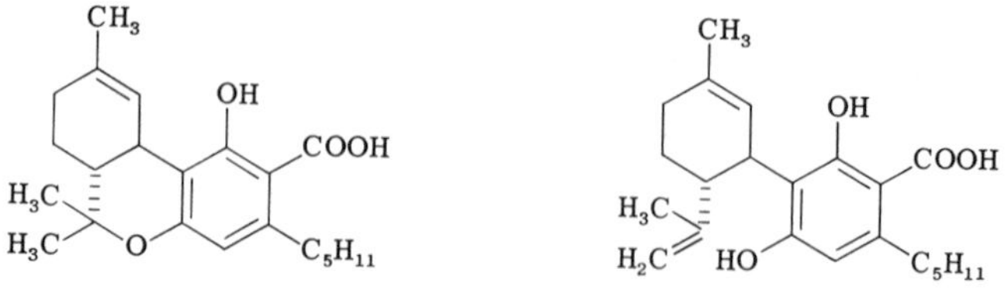

Δ'-THC acid A

Cannabidiolic acid (CBDA)

Fig. 2. Structures of the major cannabinoid acids naturally occurring in *Cannabis sativa.*

slowly on storage (Claussen and Korte, 1968; Doorenbos *et al.*, 1971). According to Lerner (1963), after 1 year, marijuana contains less than 50% of the cannabinoids in their acid form. Marijuana can be decarboxylated to less than 5% cannabinoid acids by heating the plant sample to 100°C for 75 minutes in a nitrogen atmosphere. Little decarboxylation occurs during this same period at temperatures lower than 80°C (Doorenbos *et al.*, 1971). This is important to the analyst, because the recorded gas chromatographic peaks for the neutral cannabinoids will be increased by decarboxylation of their corresponding cannabinoid acids. Decarboxylation readily occurs during injection of the sample extract due to the high temperatures (185°–250°C) used for the glc analysis.

Most of the natural cannabinoid acids can be removed from a petroleum ether extract of cannabis by partitioning the petroleum ether solution with 1.0 *N* sodium hydroxide. Use of other bases (Na₂CO₃) does not provide adequate removal of the acids from the plant extract (Willinsky, 1971). Decarboxylation of the acids can be prevented by methyl ester formation (Lerner, 1963) or by silylation (Fetterman *et al.*, 1971a). The silyl ether derivatives are chromatographed under the same conditions as the neutral cannabinoids, but at lower column temperatures.

Quantitative determination of the cannabinoids by glc presents some specific problems. The use of pure cannabinoid external standards is unsatisfactory for glc quantitation, owing to the high relative error (5–8%) inherent in this method. This large error arises from technical difficulties in reproducing exact injection volumes, column absorption and destruction, and variation in detector responses. The internal standard method decreases the error of the determination to 1–2%. Methadone (Lerner, 1969), *n*-eicosane (Betts and Holloway, 1967), methyl stearate (Fujita *et al.*, 1967), cholestane (Willinsky, 1971), and 4-androstene-3,17-dione (Fetterman *et al.*, 1971b) have all been used as internal standards. Only an internal standard whose peak appears after the cannabinoids, i.e., cholestane or 4-androstene-3,17-dione, should be used to ensure that the internal standard peak does not interfere with the cannabinoid peaks.

Since injection of an equal amount of cannabidiol, cannabinol, or Δ^1-tetrahydrocannabinol does not produce a gas chromatographic peak of equal area, it is important to utilize a separate calibration curve for each cannabinoid component being analyzed to derive accurate quantitative data for the different cannabinoids present in an extract of cannabis. By using an internal standard and the above glc method it is possible to detect as little as 2 ng of Δ^1-THC from a pure standard solution.

Considerable difficulty has been encountered in using glc to quantitate levels of cannabinoids in biological fluids. This difficulty is in part due to the low circulating levels of Δ^1-THC found in man shortly after smoking ^{14}C-Δ^1-THC (Lemberger *et al.*, 1970) and to the lack of specificity of existing extraction methods. Detectable amounts of ^{14}C-labeled metabolites remain in the plasma of man for many days (Lemberger *et al.*, 1970), but these levels are too low to be estimated by present extraction, purification, and gas-liquid chromatography techniques.

F. ULTRAVIOLET SPECTROSCOPY

Grlić (1968) reported that ultraviolet and infrared spectral data from plant extracts are useful in classifying cannabis plant material into various ripeness groups using a ratio (THC + CBN)/(CBD + CBDA). The individual uv maxima for the cannabinoids are shown in Table V.

TABLE V
ULTRAVIOLET ABSORPTION OF SOME CANNABINOIDS [a]

Compound	Absorption maxima (millimicrons)
Petroleum ether extract of marijuana	218, 272
Δ^1-THC	277 (1,640), 282 (1,550)
Δ^6-THC	275 (1,260), 282 (1,320)
CBD	212 (37,150), 273 (1,110), 280 (1,050)
THC acid A	221 (26,500), 260 (7,900), 303 (4,100)
CBN	220 (35,600), 285 (18,000)
Cannabichromene	228 (25,100), 280 (8,900)
Cannabicyclol	275 (1,240), 282 (1,270)
Cannabigerol	272 (1,100), 280 (1,050)
7-Hydroxy-Δ^1-THC	276 (1,250), 283 (1,280)
6,7-Dihydroxy-Δ^1-THC	276 (1,250), 283 (1,280)

[a] All uv spectra recorded in ethanol; values in parentheses are extinction coefficients. Values for Δ^1-THC, Δ^6-THC, CBD, CBN, cannabichromene, cannabicyclol, and cannabigerol are from Mechoulam and Gaoni (1967). Values for 7-hydroxy-Δ^1-THC and 6,7-dihydroxy-Δ^1-THC are from Wall *et al.* (1970). Value for THC acid A is from Mechoulam *et al.* (1969).

The low extinction coefficient of Δ^1-THC makes uv spectroscopy a relatively insensitive method for the estimation of these components. On the other hand, it is possible to oxidize THC to cannabinol by dehydrogenation in the presence of sulfur (Gaoni and Mechoulam, 1971). This may be useful, since cannabinol has a tenfold increase in extinction coefficient at the 285 nm wavelength maximum. The shorter-wavelength maximum (220 nm) for Δ^1-THC and CBN is not useful since it is not always reproducible (Mechoulam, 1971).

Bawd *et al.* (1971) reported that trace amounts of cannabinoids may be detected by means of the intense fluorescence emission peaks that develop on ultraviolet irradiation of these compounds. In addition to identification of cannabinoids this technique affords additional parameters for the characterization of the cannabinoids. The ultraviolet absorption data of the derivatives of the cannabinoids as well as the nuclear magnetic resonance spectra (nmr) of both the cannabinoids and their derivatives were reported by Mechoulam and Gaoni (1967).

G. Infrared Spectroscopy

Infrared (ir) spectroscopy is an excellent method for the identification of isolated pure components. In contrast to ultraviolet absorption spectra, in which organic compounds generally have one or two absorption maxima, the many absorption bands in the infrared region give more complete information with regard to functional groups present in the molecule.

The fingerprint region is especially useful for the identification of unknown compounds against pure standards, the ir spectra of some of which have been published (Mechoulam and Gaoni, 1967). These comparisons can be done with little experience in spectroscopy. Unfortunately, reference spectra recorded under identical conditions are not always available for all cannabinoids. For this reason Fig. 3 was compiled to allow the reader a convenient overview of characteristic cannabinoid absorptions. Although not clearly indicated in this figure, the broadness of the ir peaks seen in a petroleum ether extract of marijuana indicates the presence of a mixture of compounds. In spite of this, ir spectra of extracts of cannabis have been used as a method of estimating the variations in the composition of different samples of cannabis (Grlić, 1964).

H. Stability of Cannabinoids

Razdan (1970) reported that Δ^1-THC oxidizes to cannabinol at a rate of 10% per month when spotted on filter paper and kept at room temperature. At higher temperatures (80°C) over 50% of the Δ^1-THC is converted to CBN

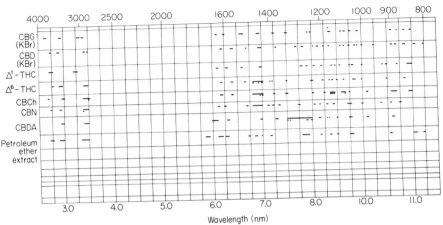

Fig. 3. A comparison of the characteristic positions of infrared absorption maxima for the cannabinoids. Linewidths indicate the intensity of absorption bands. Composite lines (lines with dots below) indicate fine structure of a broad absorption band. All spectra were recorded in CCl_4 solution unless otherwise indicated. The spectral data were either compiled from published material (Mechoulam and Gaoni, 1967) or obtained with a Perkin Elmer 137 spectrophotometer.

in 4 days, whereas Δ^6-THC is reported to be quite stable under these conditions with little change occurring. Lerner (1963) reported that the concentraction of Δ^1-THC in marijuana decreases at a rate of 3–5% per month when stored at a room temperature of 24°C. This rate of oxidation of Δ^1-THC in marijuana requires further examination since "street users" of marijuana state that they do not detect noticeable changes in the potency of marijuana stored at room temperature for periods up to 1 year.

As mentioned earlier, over 95% of the major cannabinoids occur in nature as their corresponding acid forms. These acids are unstable and decarboxylate on storage to yield the neutral cannabinoids. (For a more detailed discussion, see Chapter 1, Section V,B.)

Since very little cannabinol (CBN) is found in fresh marijuana (Korte and Sieper, 1960) the presence of high concentrations of CBN probably indicates that the hashish or marijuana sample has been stored for some time prior to analysis. Therefore, it is of considerable importance to know the age of the material to be analyzed if one is interested in classifying samples into "drug type" or "fiber type," since major shifts in the concentration of Δ^1-THC to CBN can occur.

Another product of the degradation of Δ^1-THC in its pure form is a violet-brown compound, which rapidly appears in Δ^1-THC on storage in the presence of oxygen. The chromatographic behavior of this compound suggests that it may be a polymer of Δ^1-THC.

To decrease these degrative changes Δ^1-THC should be stored in an inert solution, preferably not chloroform or ether but in any dilute alcohol or hydrocarbon solvent under nitrogen. The samples should be refrigerated but not frozen. This method of storage reduces the rate of oxidative degradation of Δ^1-THC to cannabinol, and also decreases the rate of possible polymer formation, since polymerization is more likely to occur in dry Δ^1-THC than in Δ^1-THC in solution.

I. Extraction Methods and Chromatography of Cannabinoid Metabolites*

Extraction methods and chromatography of Δ^1-THC, Δ^6-THC, CBN, and their corresponding major metabolites 7-hydroxy-Δ^1-THC, 6,7-dihydroxy-Δ^1-THC, 7-hydroxy-Δ^6-THC, 5,7-dihydroxy-Δ^6-THC, and 7-hydroxy-cannabinol have been reported by several groups (Burstein et al., 1970; Nilsson et al., 1970; Foltz et al., 1970; Wall et al., 1970). The cannabinoids and metabolites can be extracted from a whole liver homogenate with hexane or petroleum ether followed by further extraction with ethyl ether. Either of the first two solvents extracts unchanged Δ^1-THC; the ether extracts the more polar metabolites (Nilsson et al., 1970). Ethyl acetate alone has also been used to extract THC and its metabolites from whole liver homogenerates and liver microsomal incubates (Wall et al., 1970). Table VI gives the R_f values and other physical data for some metabolites. Several other thin-layer chromatographic systems reported to separate THC and its major metabolites are included in Table VII.

TABLE VI
The R_f Values and Physical Characteristics of Products of in vitro Metabolism of Δ^1-THC^a

Compound	R_f	Physical characteristics
Δ^1-THC	0.76	Light-yellow oil
7-OH-Δ^1-THC	0.39	Crystalline, m.p. 136.5°–138°C
6,7-diOH-Δ^1-THC	0.07	Crystalline, m.p. 139°–140.5°C

^{a} Chromatographic system—silica gel G; 1:4 acetone:chloroform (Wall et al., 1970).

Wall et al. (1970) reported that silylation of the extract of a CBN rat liver incubate improved the gas chromatographic separation of CBN and its metabolites. The relative retention times for the silyl derivatives of CBN metabolites are given in Table VIII.

* See Chapter 4 for a detailed discussion of these metabolites.

TABLE VII
THE R_f VALUES FOR Δ^1-THC METABOLITES IN THREE SOLVENT SYSTEMS[a]

System	R_f (7-OH-Δ^1-THC)	R_f (6,7-diOH-Δ^1-THC)
Hexane:acetone 3:1	0.28	0.10
2% Ethanol in chloroform	0.22	0.03
20% Ethanol in chloroform	0.53	0.37

[a] Eastman Silica Gel Chromatogram Sheets. Data from Lemberger *et al.* (1971).

TABLE VIII
RELATIVE RETENTION TIMES OF SILYL DERIVATIVES OF CANNABINOL
in vitro METABOLITES[a]

Derivative	Relative retention time
Silyl-CBN (I)	1
Silyl-7-OH-CBN (II)	2.5
Silyl-7-(side chain)-diOH-CBN (III)	1.7
Silyl-(side chain)-OH-CBN (IV)	3.3

[a] System: 6 ft column OV-17 1.4% on Chromasorb W-Hp; column temperature 180°C; $N = 35$ ml/minute. Metabolites with hydroxylation of the pentyl side chain (III and IV) have been tentatively identified by mass spectral data (Wall, 1971).

IV. Detection of Cannabinoids in Biological Fluids

A. RADIOACTIVE TRACER LABEL *

As a result of the recent availability of tritium-labeled Δ^1- or Δ^6-THC (Burstein and Mechoulam, 1968; Agurell *et al.*, 1969) and ^{14}C-labeled Δ^1- or Δ^6-THC (Liebman *et al.*, 1971), *in vitro* and *in vivo* studies on the metabolism and distribution of labeled THC have been undertaken in animals (Burstein *et al.*, 1970; Agurell *et al.*, 1969; Ho *et al.*, 1970; Klausner and Dingell, 1971; Truitt and Anderson, 1971; Willinsky, 1971) and in man (Lemberger *et al.*, 1970). The majority of the administered THC is metabolized to more polar compounds in all species tried so far (mice, rats, rabbits, monkeys, and man) and excreted via urine and feces. The proportion of metabolite excreted via kidney or feces varies with the species.

Quantitation of the tritium- or carbon-labeled material has been accomplished by radioscanning thin-layer plates (Wall, 1971), direct liquid scintillation spectroscopy (Lemberger *et al.*, 1970), or oxygen combustion and liquid scintillation spectroscopy (Willinsky, 1971).

* For a detailed discussion of metabolism, see Chapter 4.

To date, radiolabel tracer techniques remain the most sensitive method of tracing the absorption, biotransformation, and excretion of Δ^1-THC and its metabolites, since by this method it is possible to detect subpicogram quantities of the native THC or its metabolites.

B. Fluorescence Assay of Δ^1-THC

King and Forney (1967) and Bullock et al. (1970) have reported the use of fluorescent analysis for the determination of THC. The first authors pretreated rats with Δ^1-THC, collected bile and feces, and extracted for THC metabolites. The extract was reacted with 2,6-dichloroquinone–N-chloroimine and assayed fluorometrically. Large polar fluorescent tags such as 2,6-dichloroquinone–N-chloroimine tend to mask the differentiation between polar and nonpolar metabolites and therefore limit the usefulness of this method. Bullock et al. (1970) reported a fluorescent analysis for cannabinoids and their metabolites with a threshold sensitivity of 600 ng. The cannabinoids and their metabolites are condensed with maleic acid in the presence of polyphosphoric acid to form highly fluorescent derivatives. These compounds are then quantitated fluorometrically. The authors claim that it is possible to distinguish between the parent cannabinoids and their respective metabolites. This method has been used to follow THC levels in dogs and is now being examined to determine its usefulness in man.

C. Thin-Layer Assay of Cannabinoids in Urine

Mørkholdt Andersen et al. (1971) have reported a method for the detection of cannabis intake by thin-layer chromatography of a urine extract. The urine is washed with petroleum ether, then extracted with peroxide-free ethyl ether at pH 3.8. The ethyl ether extract is dried, evaporated at 37°C, and this residue is boiled in benzene containing p-toluenesulfonic acid. This solution is then washed, filtered, evaporated to dryness, and chromatographed. A positive result is indicated by two spots, one corresponding to the R_f for cannabinol, the other for THC. The compound with an R_f value corresponding to THC has been shown to be neither Δ^1- nor Δ^6-THC (Mechoulam, 1971). Previous to refluxing with p-toluenesulfonic acid, the ethyl ether extract of the urine does not give a positive color test when sprayed with Fast Blue Salt as detector. The suggestion to react urinary metabolites of THC with p-toluenesulfonic acid was first suggested by Mechoulam et al. (1970b).

D. Radioimmune and Spin-Label (esr) Immunoassay Methods

Several groups of investigators (Burstein and Caldwell, 1971; Hsia, 1971) are presently developing an immunoassay method for Δ^1-THC and its metabolites from plasma and urine of human subjects.

Immunoassay of small molecular weight compounds such as steroids (Peron and Caldwell, 1970), morphine (Spector and Parker, 1970), and dinitrophenol (Hsia, 1967) has been accomplished by covalently linking the nonantigenic drug molecule to larger antigenic compounds such as bovine serum albumin. The production of antibodies to large molecular weight substances is also directed against the small hapten groups (drug molecules) that "stick out" from the surface of the drug–protein conjugate. For this reason, the drug nucleus which is bound to the bovine serum albumin becomes an important site for antibody formation. Burstein and Caldwell (1971) have induced the production of antibodies against Δ^1-THC in rabbits and are presently attempting the development of a radioimmunoassay of Δ^1-THC for the routine estimation of nanogram levels in peripheral blood samples. This method could also be applied to the measurement of the metabolites of Δ^1-THC in biological fluids.

Hsia (1971) is preparing a spin-label immunoassay with the aim of developing a one-step method for determining nanogram quantities of Δ^1-THC and its metabolites in body fluids and laboratory animal tissue extracts with electron spin resonance (esr) spectroscopy. The principle of spin-label immunoassay is identical to that of radioimmunoassay. However, the unpaired electron or spin label, instead of the radioactive element, is used as the probe. Δ^6-THC acid a has been covalently bound to a stable free radical, which forms a complex with purified anti-THC antibodies produced in rabbits. The tumbling rate of the THC-SL–antibody complex is slow on the esr time scale (see Fig. 4) which results in a broadening of the peaks in the

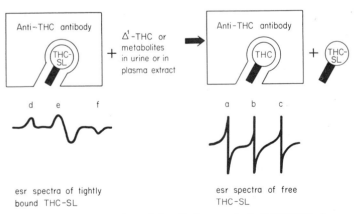

esr spectra of tightly
bound THC-SL

esr spectra of free
THC-SL

Fig. 4. Schematic representation of the displacement of Δ^1-THC-SL from antibody active site by free Δ^1-THC. Quantitation of free spin-labeled THC is accomplished by measurement of peak height of peak c. Peaks a, b, and c gradually reduce in height until all the THC-SL in solution is bound to the antibody. In this condition a new spectrum with peaks d, e, and f is seen. This spectrum indicates that the THC-SL is tightly bound, greatly reducing the spin frequency in the spin label (Hsia, 1971).

esr spectrum. When THC in biological fluids is added to THC-SL–antibody complex, the free THC causes displacement of THC-SL from the antibody. The displaced THC-SL tumbles freely in solution, resulting in an esr spectrum with the sharp peaks. The difference in peak height is a direct measure of THC concentration. This method is presently being extended to urinary metabolites of THC.

The advantage of spin-label immunoassay over radioimmune assay is the simplification of assay procedure with reliable results at concentrations of 1×10^{-7} M. Another advantage is that the time for a complete determination is less than 5 minutes with a sample volume of 20 μl.

Acknowledgment

I thank Mr. Eric Polaschek (Archives Department, Addiction Research Foundation of Ontario) and Dr. O. J. Kalant for their assistance in obtaining certain references, and Dr. H. Kalant, Dr. O. Meresz, and Dr. J. C. Hsia for their discussion and comments.

References

Adams, R., Loewe, S., Jelinek, C., and Wolff, H. (1941). *J. Amer. Chem. Soc.* **63**, 1971.
Agurell, S., Nilsson, I. M., Ohlsson, A., and Sandberg, F. (1969). *Biochem. Pharmacol.* **18**, 1195.
Aramaki, H., Tomiyasu, N., Yoshimura, H., and Tsukamoto, H. (1968). *Chem. Pharm. Bull.* **16**, 822.
Bawd, A., Byrom, P., Hudson, J. B., and Turnbull, J. H. (1971). *Talanta* **18**, 697.
Beam, W. (1911). "Fourth Report of the Wellcome Tropical Research Laboratories," Vol. B, p. 25. Gordon Memorial College, Khartoum.
Betts, T. J., and Holloway, P. J. (1967). *J. Pharm. Pharmacol.* **19** (Suppl.), 97S.
Blatt, A. H. (1938). *J. Wash. Acad. Sci.* **28**, 465.
Bullock, F. J., Bruni, R. J., and Werner, E. (1970). Abstract of paper presented at the 160th Nat. Amer. Chem. Soc. Meeting, Chicago, Illinois.
Burstein, S., and Caldwell, B. V. (1971). Personal communication.
Burstein, S., and Mechoulam, R. (1968). *J. Amer. Chem. Soc.* **90**, 2420.
Burstein, S. H., Menezes, F., Williamson, E., and Mechoulam, R. (1970). *Nature (London)* **225**, 87.
Butler, W. P. (1966). Publication 341 (Rev. 12), p. 105. Washington, D.C. Internal Revenue Service.
Caddy, B., and Fish, F. (1967). *J. Chromatogr.* **31**, 584.
Caddy, B., Fish, F., and Wilson, W. D. C. (1967). *J. Pharm. Pharmacol.* **19**, 851.
Claussen, U., and Korte, F. (1968). *Ann. Chem.* **713**, 162.
Claussen, U., Borger, W., and Korte, F. (1966). *Ann. Chem.* **693**, 158.
Davis, K. H., Martin, N. H., Pitt, C. G., Wildes, J. W., and Wall, M. E. (1970). *Lloydia* **33**, 453.

Davis, T. W. M., Farmilo, C. G., and Osadchuk, M. (1963). *Anal. Chem.* **35**, 751.

de Faubert-Maunder, M. J. (1969). *J. Pharm. Pharmacol.* **21**, 334.

de Ropp, R. S. (1960). *J. Amer. Pharm. Ass.* **49**, 756.

Doorenbos, N. J., Fetterman, P. S., Quimby, M. W., and Turner, C. E. (1971). *Ann. N.Y. Acad. Sci.* **191**, 3.

Duquénois, P., and Negm, H. (1938). *Ann. Med. Leg.* **18**, 485.

Fairbairn, J. W., Liebmann, J. A., and Simic, S. (1971). *J. Pharm. Pharmacol.* **23**, 558.

Farmilo, C. G. (1955). U.N. Document E/CN. 7/304.

Farmilo, C. G., and Davis, T. W. M. (1961). *J. Pharm. Pharmacol.* **13** (Suppl.), 767.

Farmilo, C. G., and Genest, K. (1959). U.N. Document E/CN. 7/373.

Fetterman, P. S., Doorenbos, N. J., Keith, E. S., and Quimby, M. W. (1971a). *Experientia* **27**, 988.

Fetterman, P. S., Keith, E. S., Waller, C. N., Guerrero, O., Doorenbos, N. J., and Quimby, M. W. (1971b). *J. Pharm. Sci.* **60**, 1246.

Fochtman, F. W., and Winek, C. L. (1971). *Clin. Toxicol.* **4**, 287.

Foltz, R. L., Fentiman, F., Leighty, E. G., Walter, J. L., Drewes, H. R., Schwartz, W. E., Page, T. F., and Truitt, E. B. (1970). *Science* **168**, 844.

Fujita, M., Shimomura, H., Kuriyama, E., Schigehiro, M., and Akasu, M. (1967). *Shoyakugaku Zasshi* **21**, 57.

Gaoni, Y., and Mechoulam, R. (1971). *J. Amer. Chem. Soc.* **93**, 217.

Garriott, J. C., King, L. J., Forney, R. B., and Hughes, F. W. (1967). *Life Sci.* **6**, 2119.

Ghamrawy, M. A. (1937). *J. Egypt. Med. Ass.* **20**, 193.

Gill, E. W. (1971). *J. Chem. Soc.* 579.

Gill, E. W., Paton, W. D. M., and Pertwee, R. G. (1970). *Nature (London)* **228**, 134.

Grlić, L. J. (1964). *Bull. Narcotics* **16**, No. 4, 29.

Grlić, L. (1968). *Bull. Narcotics* **20**, No. 3, 25.

Grlić, L. (1970a). *Acta Pharm. Jugoslav.* **20**, 19, 35.

Grlić, L. (1970b). *J. Chromatogr.* **48**, 562.

Grlić, L. (1971). *Eur. J. Toxicol.* **4**, 43.

Ho, B. T., Fritchie, G. E., Kralik, P. M., Englert, L. F., McIsaac, W. M., and Idänpään-Heikkilä, J. (1970). *J. Pharm. Pharmacol.* **22**, 538.

Hsia, J. C. (1967). Ph.D. dissertation, Univ. of Hawaii, Honolulu.

Hsia, J. C. (1971). Personal communication.

King, L. J., and Forney, R. B. (1967). *Fed. Proc. Fed. Amer. Soc. Acad. Sci.* **26**, 540.

Klausner, H. A., and Dingell, J. V. (1971). *Life Sci.* **10**, 49.

Klein, F. K., Rapoport, H., and Elliot, H. W. (1971). *Nature (London)* **232**, 258.

Kolšek, J., Maticic, M., and Repič, R. (1962). *Arch. Pharm. (Weinheim)* **292**, 151.

Korte, F., and Sieper, H. (1960). *Tetrahedron* **10**, 153.

Korte, F., and Sieper, H. (1964a). *J. Chromatogr.* **13**, 90.

Korte, F., and Sieper, H. (1964b). *J. Chromatogr.* **14**, 178.

Lemberger, L., Silberstein, S. D., Axelrod, J., and Kopin, I. J. (1970). *Science* **170**, 1320.

Lemberger, L., Tamarkin, N. R., Axelrod, J., and Kopin, I. J. (1971). *Science* **173**, 72.

Lerner, N. (1963). *Science* **140**, 175.

Lerner, P. (1969). *Bull. Narcotics* **21**, No. 3, 39.

Liebman, A. A., Malareck, D. H., Dorsky, A. M., and Kaegi, H. H. (1971). *J. Label. Compounds* **7**, 241.

Machata, G. (1969). *Arch. Toxikol.* **25**, 19.

Martin, L., Smith, D. M., and Farmilo, C. G. (1961). *Nature (London)* **191**, 774.

Mechoulam, R. (1971). Personal communication.

Mechoulam, R., and Gaoni, Y. (1965). *Tetrahedron* **21**, 1223.

Mechoulam, R., and Gaoni, Y. (1967). *Fortschr. Chem. Org. Naturst.* **25**, 175.

Mechoulam, R., and Zemler, H. (1971). Unpublished results.

Mechoulam, R., Ben-Zvi, Z., and Gaoni, Y. (1968). *Tetrahedron* **24**, 5615.

Mechoulam, R., Ben-Zvi, Z., Yagnitinsky, B., and Shani, A. (1969). *Tetrahedron Lett.* 2339.

Mechoulam, R., Shani, A., Edery, H., and Grunfeld, Y. (1970a). *Science* **169**, 611.

Mechoulam, R., Shani, A., Yagnitinsky, B., Ben-Zvi, Z., Braun, P., and Gaoni, Y. (1970b). *In* "The Botany and Chemistry of Cannabis" (C. R. B. Joyce and S. H. Curry, eds.). Churchill, London.

Meresz, O. (1965). *Chem. Ind. (London)* **852**, 44.

Meresz, O. (1971). Personal communication.

Merkus, F. W. H. M. (1971a). *Nature (London)* **232**, 579.

Merkus, F. W. H. M. (1971b). *Pharm. Weekbl.* **106**, 49.

Mørkholdt Andersen, J., Nielsen, E., Schou, J., Steentoft, A., and Worm, K. (1971). *Acta Pharmacol. Toxicol.* **29**, 111.

Nelson, D. F., and May, A, V. (1969). U.N. document ST/SOA/SER. S/19.

Nigam, M. C., Handa, K. L., Nigam, I. C., and Levi, L. (1965). *Can. J. Chem.* **43**, 3372.

Nilsson, I. M., Agurell, S., Nillson, J. L. G., Ohlsson, A., Sandberg, F., and Wahlqvist, M. (1970). *Science* **168**, 1228.

Obata, Y., and Ishikawa, Y. (1960a). *Bull. Agr. Chem. Soc. Jap.* **24**, 660.

Obata, Y., and Ishikawa, Y. (1960b). *Bull. Agr. Chem. Soc. Jap.* **24**, 667.

Patterson, D. A., and Stevens, H. M. (1970). *J. Pharm. Pharmacol.* **22**, 391.

Peron, F. G., and Caldwell, B. V., eds. (1970). "Immunologic Methods in Steroid Determination." Appleton, New York.

Razdan, R. K. (1970). *In* "Proceedings of the National Academy of Science Committee on Problems of Drug Dependence," 32nd Meeting, Feb. 17–20, Toronto.

Salemink, C. A., Veen, E., and De Kloet, W. A. (1965). *Planta Med.* **13**, 211.

Simonsen, J. L., and Todd, A. R. (1942). *J. Chem. Soc.* 189.

Spector, S., and Parker, C. W. (1970). *Science* **168**, 1347.

Todd, A. R. (1946). *Experientia* **2**, 55.

Toffoli, F., Avico, U., and Cirrani, E. S. (1968). *Bull. Narcotics* **20**, No. 1, 55.

Truitt, E. B., and Anderson, S. M. (1971). *Ann. N.Y. Acad. Sci.* **191**, 68.

Wall, M. E. (1971). *Ann. N.Y. Acad. Sci.* **191**, 23.

Wall, M. E., Brine, D. R., Brine, G. A., Pitt, C. G., Freudenthal, R. I., and Christensen, H. D. (1970). *J. Amer. Chem. Soc.* **92**, 3466.

Willinsky, M. D. (1971). Ph.D. dissertation, Univ. of Toronto.

Wollner, H. J., Matchett, J. R., Levine, J., and Loewe, S. (1942). *J. Amer. Chem. Soc.* **64**, 26.

Wood, T. B., Spivey, W. T. N., and Easterfield, T. H. (1896). *J. Chem. Soc.* **69**, 539.

Addendum

Since the completion of this chapter, a number of pertinent reports have been published. The purpose of this addendum is to bring the chapter as up to date as possible. The brevity of this section has necessitated the omission of many important technical details in the methods cited. I refer the reader to the original reports for this information.

CANNABINOID COMPONENTS

Colorimetric Tests

An additional color test for cannabis, the furfural test, which was developed in the 1940's following observations on the acid beam test, has been published by its originator (Fulton, 1970). A petroleum ether extract of cannabis is decolorized with activated charcoal, and 3–4 ml of methanol, 0.2–0.3 ml furfural in ethanol (1%), and 0.2–0.3 ml concentrated hydrochloric acid are added. This mixture is then evaporated to dryness on a steambath. A small amount of sulfuric acid:absolute ethanol 55:45 is added to the dry, green residue and a very strong purplish color is produced. The author states that this is a simple, reliable color test for cannabis.

A colorimetric breath test for cannabis users (McCarthy and Van Zyl, 1972) is based on the color change of Fast Blue Salt B in the presence of cannabinoids. The authors reported that, following cannabis smoking, cannabinoids can be detected by blowing into a filter paper or tissue bag freshly dampened with an aqueous solution of Fast Blue Salt B 1% w/v. An orange-pink to deep orange-pink color is obtained up to 15 minutes after smoking, and a color is obtainable up to 2 hours after smoking, although its formation is not always instantaneous. The authors reported that certain brands of roasted cigarette tobaccos may give a similar color reaction. The rate and intensity of color development and the sensitivity of the reaction can be enhanced by using a Fast Blue Salt B solution prepared with 0.1 N sodium hydroxide. However, the nonspecificity of this color reaction and the lack of quantitative information about the dose absorbed or the degree of the subject's intoxication limit the general application of the method.

Gas-Liquid Chromatography

Hoffman and Yang (1972) reported a comparative study on quantitative glc of cannabinoids using a variety of silicone columns. They also examined the possible chromatographic benefits to be derived from trimethylsilyl or trifluoroacetyl esters of Δ^1-THC. They concluded that derivative formation had no chromatographic advantage over native THC. All the columns tested (OV-1, OV-17, OV-210, OV-225, and Dexsil-300 GC) yielded linear standard curves for THC, with intercepts near zero, the 3% liquid phase columns showing greater variation than the 5% columns. Their reported limit for detection of Δ^1-THC was 50 ng.

In spite of the wide use of gas chromatography for the study of canna-binoids, quantitative results remain unreliable. In a recent survey ("Cannabis, A Report of the Commission of Inquiry into the Non-Medical Use of Drugs," 1972) two samples, one marijuana and the other a hexane-extracted alfalfa impregnated with Δ^1-THC, were submitted for analysis of the cannabinoids present to five government-licensed analytical laboratories in Canada and the United States. All the laboratories identified the cannabinoids correctly, but their quantitative results varied over several hundred percent. Domino (1970) also reported large discrepancies in Δ^1-THC content in a single marijuana sample analyzed by three different laboratories over a short period of time. Such variations in quantitation of the cannabinoids limit the interpretation of present pharmacological studies.

A glc method with good reproducibility for quantitation of Δ^1-THC, CBD, and CBN in plant samples has been reported by Willinsky and Di Simone (1972). A 100-mg sample is powdered in a mortar and pestle and extracted five times with 1 ml of petroleum ether (b.p. 40°–60°C) containing 0.70 mg/ml of cholestane as an internal standard. The combined extracts are pipetted into a 10-ml Luer Lok syringe and expressed through a Millipore filter (0.45 pore size) attached to the syringe. Two microliters of the clear, nearly colorless extract, free of all particulate matter, is injected into a gas chromatograph (conditions for gas chromatography given in the legend of Fig. A-1).

To quantitate neutral cannabinoids, the petroleum ether extract was first partitioned twice with 5 ml of 0.1 N sodium hydroxide to remove the acidic components and dried with 50 mg of anhydrous sodium sulfate; a 2-μl sample was then injected into the chromatograph. The cannabinoid content of a sample may be read directly from the individual calibration curves for THC, CBD, and CBN after calculating the ratio of peak areas according to area cannabinoid peak/area cholestane peak. The difference in the standard curves for the major cannabinoids (Fig. 1) clearly demonstrates that the detector response for CBD and CBN is greater than that for Δ^1-THC. The error in using a THC calibration curve to quantitate CBD and CBN is variable and assumes larger values as the concentration of cannabinoids increases. On repeated double-blind analysis by two operators, the experimental error of this method was $\pm 6\%$.

Stability of Cannabinoids

A study of the proteolytic properties of about 40 minor components of hashish and the behavior of some 50 minor components of marijuana following smoking on a smoking machine were reported by Strömberg (1971) using temperature-programmed gas chromatography to monitor any changes in the compounds. The results indicate that chromatography of hashish extracts at injection port temperatures between 150° and 300°C produced little change in these compounds. At the lowest temperature, in spite of some asymmetry of the CBN peak, all the minor components were present in the chromatogram, indicating that they are not artifacts formed by the high temperatures of the injection port of the chromatograph. The stability of the minor components of marijuana was demonstrated by comparing the

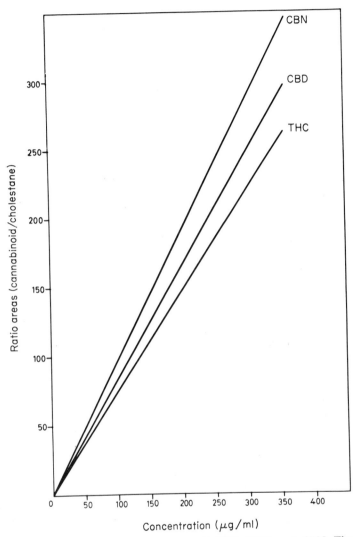

Concentration (μg/ml)

Fig. A-1. Combined calibration curves for Δ^1-THC, CBD, and CBN. The detector responses for CBN and CBD are both greater than that for Δ^1-THC. In practice, individual curves were used with percent dry weight of the cannabinoid written on the right-hand ordinate. The conditions for chromatography were as follows: Perkin Elmer gas chromatograph, series 900, equipped with dual flame ionization detectors; glass columns, 1.8 × 2 mm, packed with 3% OV-7 on silinized Gas Chrom P 80/120 mesh; column temp, 235°C; injector temp, 250°C; detector temp, 250°C.

chromatograms of unsmoked marijuana extract and smoke condensate. The heavier components, including the cannabinoids, remained essentially unchanged; however, some of the light components seem to have decomposed, giving rise to some 20 new compounds, possibly cracking products. Unfortunately, the author did not give details of the smoking procedure he used. This is important because the rate of burning of the cigarette and the temperature reached during combustion markedly effect the products remaining in the smoke condensate. In order to make smoking apparatus tests relevant, the smoking conditions must approximate the normal rate of burning of marijuana or hashish under conditions of social usage.

DETECTION OF CANNABINOIDS IN BIOLOGICAL FLUIDS

Extraction of Cannabinoids from Urine

Burstein et al. (1971) have reported a method for the extraction of both the conjugated and free metabolites of ^{14}C-labeled Δ^1-THC in the urine of rabbits and man. The urine is acidified to pH 3.5 and chromatographed on an XAD-2 resin column to extract the cannabinoids. The cannabinoids are then eluted from the resin and partitioned with water/chloroform. The organic phase is rechromatographed several times and the major peaks are methylated and thin-layer chromatographed, resulting in two barely separated zones. The water-soluble metabolites are hydrolyzed by refluxing for 2 hours in methanol plus 0.2 N sodium hydroxide, acidified to pH 3.5, and then extracted with chloroform. This extract is partitioned with dilute sodium bicarbonate and the bicarbonate fraction is reacidified, extracted with chloroform, methylated, and thin-layer chromatographed. This yields two barely separable zones, which is similar to the results for the unconjugated compounds. Nuclear magnetic resonance and mass spectral data suggest that the two isolated compounds are 7-carboxy-Δ^1-THC's with an additional hydroxy group on the C-1, C-2, or C-3 carbon of the side chain.

A large part of the cannabinoids in the urine are found as conjugates. This fraction may be sufficiently rich in metabolites to follow the extraction and clean-up method through only for the water-soluble metabolites, after initial acidification and concentration by the XAD-2 resin. Such a simplified method could provide a quantitative measure of THC intake, by identification of the side-chain-hydroxylated 7-carboxy-THC metabolites, that is practical outside the research laboratory.

Fluorescent Assay

Preliminary reports of a fluorescent labeling technique for cannabinoids (Forrest et al., 1971) suggest another possible method for identification of urinary metabolites of the cannabinoids. Nine different cannabinoids were converted to their 1-dimethylaminonaphthalene 5-sulfonate derivatives, and mixtures of the derivatives were separated by thin-layer chromatography and identified by simple viewing under a black ray uv light source at 0.5 ng per spot. A study is in progress to assess the effectiveness of this method for urinary metabolites.

Thin-layer Methods

The results of the Mørkholdt Andersen *et al.* (1971) urinary assay for cannabinoids in which the urine is refluxed with *p*-toluenesulfonic acid in benzene are now in question following a paper by Schou *et al.* (1971). These authors stated that the chloroacetyl derivative of the thin-layer spot from the urine extract, which corresponded in R_f value to CBN, had the same retention time by gas chromatography as authentic chloroacetyl-CBN. However, the derivative of the thin-layer spot, which corresponded closely to Δ^1-THC, did not have the same retention time as chloroacetyl-Δ^1-THC.

Kanter *et al.* (1971), using the procedure of Christiansen and Raphaelsen (1969) for the detection of cannabis metabolites in human urine, also reported conflicting results. Urines of subjects who received Δ^1-THC per os were consistently negative for cannabinoids, whereas some but not all the urines of subjects who received natural cannabis preparations per os were positive for CBD, CBN, and occasionally THC. These last results indicate that published thin-layer methods for tentative identification of urinary metabolites of THC or cannabis are not presently reliable.

A review of the tlc methods used for cannabinoids has been published (Parker and Fiske, 1972).

Immunofluorescent Assay

Another type of THC assay in biological fluids is based on some earlier work by Gross *et al.* (1968) with estrogen assays. The estrogen assay research established that diazobenzoic acid, under appropriate conditions, may enter the steroid ring structure, yielding estrogen azobenzoic acid derivatives. These compounds can be coupled to proteins and the drug–azobenzoyl–protein conjugate used to elicit antibodies in rabbits. The drug–azobenzoic acid derivative is then reduced to the hydrazo derivative, the drug molecule thereby being fluorescently labeled without introduction of a foreign fluorescent marker molecule. A quantitative competitive displacement of fluorescent hydrazo–drug from the antibody by nonfluorescent free drug exists. By plotting fluorescence quenching inhibition against drug concentration, one can obtain a calibration curve in the low nanogram range. Applying this technique to THC resulted in an elegant immunofluorescent assay in the

10^{-11}–10^{-13} mole/ml range (Grant *et al.* 1972). The water solubility of the azobenzoyl- and hydrazo-THC derivatives, and the probability that the haptenic THC moiety retains all the native determinants chemically and sterically necessary for its specific recognition, make the method a simple, reliable physical–chemical assay for THC. Extension of this method to the 7-carboxy-THC metabolites, and a further examination of the specificity of the immune recognition mechanism, suggest that a practical assay for marijuana metabolites in biological fluids is near at hand.

Gas Chromatography/Mass Spectrometry Assay

In a preliminary study Skinner (1972) has extended the combination of gas chromatography and mass spectrometry to the monitoring of THC and its metabolites in the urine of marijuana smokers and the blood and urine of rats receiving low doses of Δ^1-THC intraperitoneally. The urine or blood sample was titrated to pH 5.5, diluted with phosphate buffer, and incubated overnight with glucuronidase. Petroleum ether:isoamyl alcohol and diethyl ether were then used in succession to extract the urine. The extracts were pooled and evaporated under nitrogen, and an aliquot was injected into a gas chromatograph interfaced to a mass spectrometer. Best results were obtained by monitoring *m/e* 299, where THC and 7-hydroxy-Δ^1-THC could be detected at the 200 pg level. This method may have future widespread use in the research laboratory because of its certainty and high sensitivity. However, a different *m/e* peak may have to be chosen, as the side-chain-hydroxylated Δ^1-THC-7-oic acids, which seem to be the major urinary components, probably do not have a *m/e* 299 peak.

References

Burstein, S., Rosenfeld, J., and Wittstruck, T. (1971). *Science* **76**, 422.
"Cannabis, A Report of the Commission of Inquiry into the Non-Medical Use of Drugs" (1972). Catalogue No. H21-5370/4, Information Canada.
Christiansen, J., and Raphaelsen, O. J. (1969). *Psychopharmacologia* **15**, 60.
Domino, E. F. (1970). *Electroencephalogr. Clin. Neurophysiol.* **29**, 321.
Forrest, I. S., Green, D. E., Rose, S. D., Skinner, G. C., and Torres, D. M. (1971). *Res. Commun. Chem. Pathol. Pharmacol.* **2**, 787.
Fulton, C. C. (1970). *Bull. Narcotics* No. 2, **22**, 33.
Grant, J. D., Gross, S. J., Lomax, P., Wong, R. (1972). *Nature (London)* **236**, 216.
Gross, S. J., Campbell, D. H., and Weetall, H. H. (1968). *Immunochemistry* **5**, 55.
Hoffman, N. E., and Yang, R. K. (1972). *Anal. Lett.* **5**, 7.
Kanter, S. L., Hollister, L. E., Moore, F., and Green, D. E. (1971). *Clin. Chem.* **17**, 636
McCarthy, T. J., and Van Zyl, J. D. (1972). *J. Pharm. Pharmacol.* **24**, 489.
Mørkholdt Andersen, J., Nielsen, E., Schou, J., Steenhoft, A., and Worm, K. (1971). *Acta Pharmacol. Toxicol.* **29**, 111.
Parker, J. M., and Fiske, H. L. (1972). *J. Ass. Offic. Anal. Chem.* **55**, 876.

Schou, J., Steenhoft, A., Worm, K., Mørkholdt Andersen, J., and Nielsen, E. (1971). *Acta Pharmacol. Toxicol.* **30**, 480.
Skinner, R. F. (1972). *Proc. West. Pharmacol. Soc.* **15**, 136.
Strömberg, L. E. (1971). *J. Chromatogr.* **63**, 391.
Willinsky, M. D., and Di Simone, L. (1972). Paper presented at the Fifth Int. Congress on Pharmacology, San Francisco, July.

CHAPTER 4

Labeling and Metabolism of the Tetrahydrocannabinols

Sumner H. Burstein

I. Introduction 167
II. Preparation of Labeled Tetrahydrocannabinols 168
   A. Biosynthetically ^{14}C-Labeled THC 168
   B. Tritium-Labeled THC 169
   C. ^{14}C-Labeled THC. 171
III. Metabolism of Labeled Tetrahydrocannabinols 172
   A. Studies in the Rat 172
   B. Distribution in the Rabbit, Dog, and Monkey 175
   C. Identification of Metabolites in the Rabbit 178
   D. Metabolism in Man 180
IV. Summary 181
   References 182

I. Introduction

The past decade has seen a tremendous upsurge in scientific research on cannabis. The early part of this period was devoted to identification and isolation of various components of the plant, and this was quickly followed by the development of several methods of synthesis. These advances in the chemistry of the cannabinoids provided a basis for subsequent biological research. For the first time, adequate supplies of pure materials were available for pharmacological studies of a more precise nature than had previously been possible.

The preparation of chemically and radiochemically pure labeled compounds was achieved by application of the newly reported chemistry. The

167

result has been that within the last 3 years substantial progress has been made in determining the course of metabolism of the tetrahydrocannabinols (THC's). The efforts of this brief period will be the subject of the following pages. (Data on cannabinoid labeling are summarized in Table I.)

TABLE I

LABELED CANNABINOIDS

Substance	Positions labeled	Specific activity (Ci/mole)	Reference
^{3}H-Δ^1-THC	4′, 6′	44	Nilsson et al. (1969)
	4′, 6′, 2, 6	0.24^a	Timmons et al. (1969)
	Unspecified		Idänpään-Heikkilä et al. (1969)
^{14}C-Δ^1-THC	Generally	2.1	Miras (1965)
	1′, 3′	5.5	Wall (1971)
^{3}H-Δ^6-THC	2	1.44, 5000^b	Burstein and Mechoulam (1968)
	4′, 6′, 2, 6	0.24	Timmons et al. (1969)
	Unspecified		Idänpään-Heikkilä et al. (1969)
^{14}C-Δ^6-THC	1′, 3′	0.097	Nilsson et al. (1969)
(±)-^{14}C-Δ^6-THC	7	0.47	Nilsson et al. (1969)
^{14}C-Cannabinol	1′, 3′	0.028	Widman et al. (1971)
D_4-Δ^1-THC	4′, 6′, 2, 6		Timmons et al. (1969)
D_4-Δ^6-THC	4′, 6′, 2, 6		Timmons et al. (1969)
D_1-Δ^6-THC	2		Burstein and Mechoulam (1968)

^{a} Calculated from the value given for Δ^6-THC.
^{b} This activity was reached by a modified procedure (see text).

II. Preparation of Labeled Tetrahydrocannabinols

A. BIOSYNTHETICALLY ^{14}C-LABELED THC

The earliest published report on the labeling of cannabinoids was made by Miras (1965) at a Ciba Foundation Study Group meeting. Few details were presented. However, in 1967 a full report was made (Joachimoglu et al., 1967) on the work of this group in Athens. They described a biosynthetic approach in which they raised cannabis plants in an atmosphere containing ^{14}CO$_2$. The flowering tips of the female plants were extracted with methanol, and the THC fraction was isolated by alkaline extraction and chromatography.

The THC was characterized by its ultraviolet absorption maxima and chromatographic mobility, and the authors reported a specific activity of 2.1 Ci/mole. They did not specify which isomer was obtained; however, it was probably the Δ^1-THC since this is the major component in cannabis. A serious problem with this approach is that of insuring radiochemical purity since all the plant components are generally labeled; considerable care should be taken to insure homogeneity. Joachimoglu *et al.* carried out distribution and excretion studies, which will be described in a later section of this review.

B. TRITIUM-LABELED THC

Several years later Burstein and Mechoulam (1968) described a method for the stereospecific introduction of tritium in Δ^6-THC. The facile isomerization of Δ^1-THC to Δ^6-THC in benzene with *p*-toluenesulfonic acid as a proton source was the basis for the incorporation of the isotope (Fig. 1, R = H).

By using acid in which the exchangeable hydrogen was equilibrated with tritiated water, it was possible to achieve a high incorporation of isotope into the molecule. The location of the label was demonstrated by carrying out an identical experiment using deuterated water. Examination of the nuclear magnetic resonance spectrum of the product showed that a deuterium atom had been introduced at the 2β position (Fig. 1, R = D). This resulted from the expected axial addition to the double bond of Δ^1-THC to give the carbonium ion intermediate shown in Fig. 1.

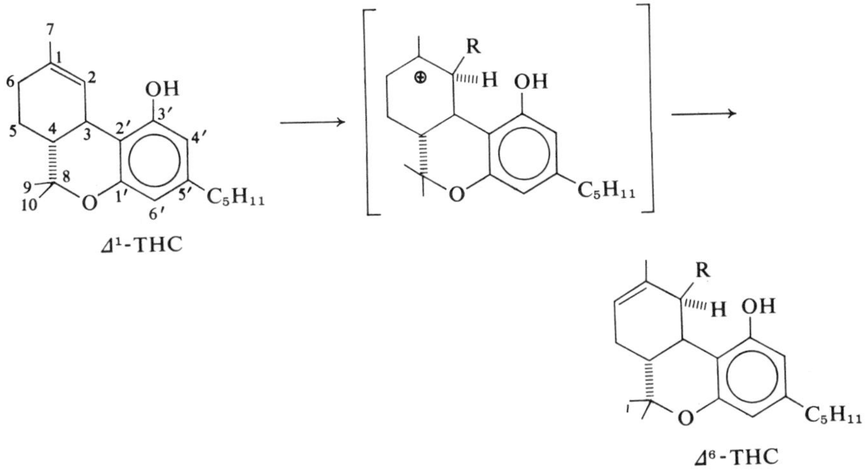

Fig. 1. Introduction of tritium by isomerization; R = H, D, or T.

Under the conditions of the experiment, the only major product obtained is the Δ^6 isomer so that thin-layer chromatography yields homogeneous material. Using commercially available tritiated water it was possible to prepare material with a specific activity of 1.44 Ci/mole. Since that time, we have been able to make a product with an activity of 5.0 Ci/mmole by using a modified procedure. This involves *in situ* oxidation of tritium gas over platinum oxide and exchange of the T_2O with *p*-toluenesulfonic acid under anhydrous conditions. This high specific activity Δ^6-THC is less stable than the lower activity material and after about 6 months at $-5°C$ showed extensive decomposition. Both preparations have been used in metabolic studies, which will be discussed below.

A second method for the tritiation of THC by acid catalysis has been reported by Nilsson *et al.* (1969). They reacted Δ^1-THC with tritiated water in the presence of phosphoric acid. It is known that aromatic hydrogens either ortho or para to a phenolic group are quite labile, and it was assumed that the isotope was incorporated at either the 4' or 6' positions or both (Fig. 2). The product was mainly THC as determined by thin-layer chromatography, and most of the radioactivity was in this zone. Nilsson *et al.* definitely

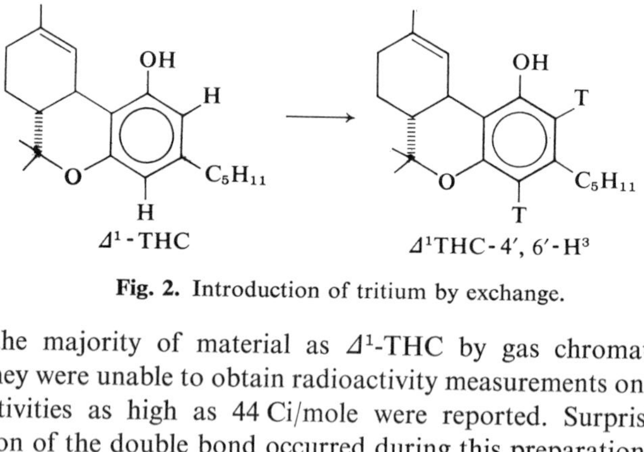

Δ^1-THC Δ^1THC-4', 6'-H³

Fig. 2. Introduction of tritium by exchange.

identified the majority of material as Δ^1-THC by gas chromatography; however, they were unable to obtain radioactivity measurements on the peak. Specific activities as high as 44 Ci/mole were reported. Surprisingly, no isomerization of the double bond occurred during this preparation.

More recently, Timmons *et al.* (1969) have published procedures for the tritiation of both THC isomers. Briefly, this involves the addition of tritiated trifluoroacetic acid to Δ^6-THC to give an adduct of unknown configuration (Fig. 3, R = H). Distillation of the trifluoroacetate causes a loss of acid to give back Δ^6-THC, which now contains tritium (Fig. 3, R = T). The reaction quite likely proceeds by trans addition, whereas the pyrolysis must proceed by a cis elimination, leaving the tritium at position 6.

Some indication of the location of the incorporated isotope was obtained by a comparable deuteration experiment (Fig. 3, R = D). By mass spectral and nuclear magnetic resonance analyses it was found that part of the deuterium was located on the aromatic ring. The remainder of the isotope was assumed to be at positions 2 and 6 because of the mechanism of the reaction. However, Timmons *et al.* presented no direct evidence on this point. Position

2 was implicated since Δ^1-THC may be formed as a transient intermediate and could incorporate isotope in the same manner as in our preparation [see Fig. 1 (Burstein and Mechoulam, 1968)]. If such an equilibration does occur, we should have seen a decrease of intensity in the vinyl (C-6) proton signal of our deuterated Δ^6-THC. We in fact observed no appreciable decrease, indicating the absence of such a reaction.

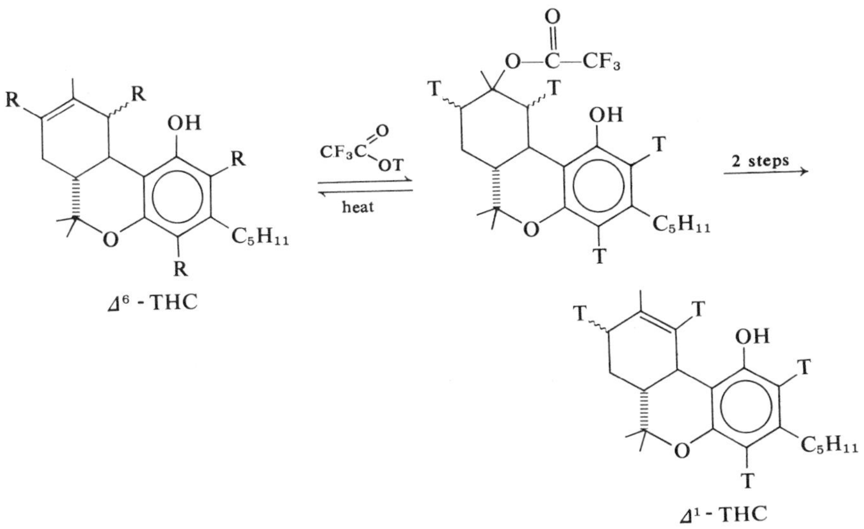

Fig. 3. Tritiation procedures involving a trifluoroacetate adduct; R = H, T, or D.

In the same publication, Timmons *et al.* (1969) also described a method for obtaining tritiated Δ^1-THC from the trifluoroacetate intermediate (Fig. 3, R = H). The ester was converted to the tertiary chloride by displacement with lithium chloride, and this was treated with base to give Δ^1-THC. No specific activity value was reported for this isomer. However, Δ^6-THC, which was obtained from the same intermediate, had a specific activity of 0.24 Ci/mole.

C. ^{14}C-LABELED THC

Nilsson *et al.* (1969) have developed two routes for preparing ^{14}C-labeled THC. One method utilizes the synthesis described by Farenholtz *et al.* (1967) for making racemic Δ^6-THC, which can then be isomerized to the Δ^1 isomer. Olivetol is converted in six steps to the ketone shown in Fig. 4. Addition of ^{14}C-methyl magnesium bromide followed by dehydration with *p*-toluene-sulfonic acid leads to ($\pm$)-Δ^6-THC in about 50% yield based on the ketone.

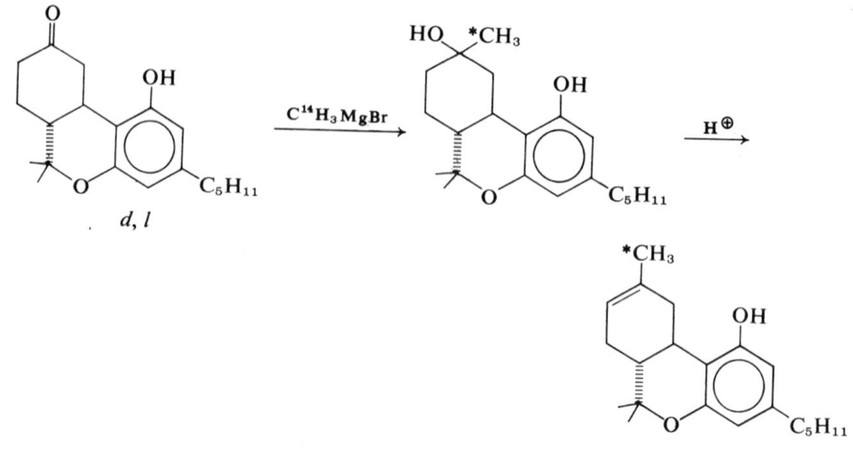

Fig. 4. Synthesis of racemic ^{14}C-labeled Δ^6-THC.

A more useful approach reported by Nilsson *et al.* is based on the preparation of ^{14}C-labeled olivetol by a known route (Anker and Cook, 1945). Condensation of the olivetol with $(+)$-*trans-p*-mentha-2,8-dien-1-ol gave $(-)$-Δ^6-THC of specific activity 97 mCi/mole in about 60% yield (Fig. 5).

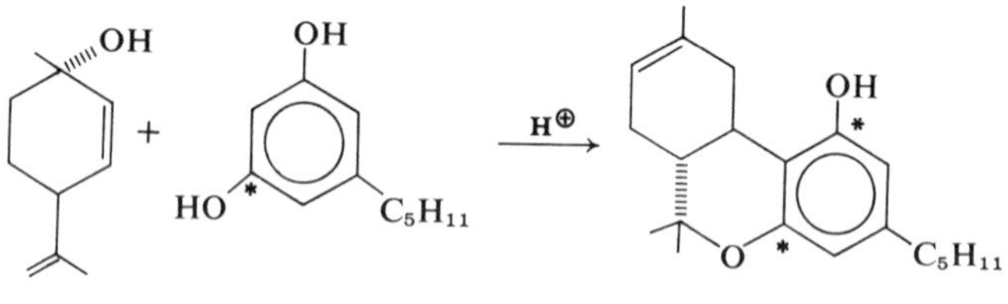

Fig. 5. Synthesis of optically active ^{14}C-labeled Δ^6-THC.

Of the published methods for making ^{14}C-labeled THC this would seem to be the one of choice. The Δ^1 isomer can be prepared by isomerization of the labeled Δ^6-THC (Wall, 1971).

III. Metabolism of Labeled Tetrahydrocannabinols

A. STUDIES IN THE RAT

Using biosynthetically prepared ^{14}C-labeled material (see previous section), Joachimoglu *et al.* (1967) studied distribution and excretion in the rat. Their material was not well characterized and was probably a mixture of Δ^1- and Δ^6-THC, with possibly other radioactive cannabinoids present. Nevertheless, they did present some data that are in good agreement with the results of recent, more sophisticated experiments (*vide infra*).

The distribution of radioactivity was studied at 10- and 60-minute intervals following intraperitoneal injection of the drug. After 10 minutes only traces were found elsewhere in the body, whereas at the end of an hour the liver was the only organ with a significant amount of ^{14}C (7.9% of the dose). Examination of the urine, bile, and feces over a 30-hour period showed that in this species the major route of excretion is via the bile and that most of the material is not reabsorbed. The authors found no free THC in either the bile or the urine. However, they did not isolate or characterize any of the metabolites.

Agurell *et al.* (1969) reported an *in vivo* study on the rat in which they used their tritium-labeled Δ^1-THC described earlier in this chapter. After intravenous injection of the drug, about 1 week was required for elimination of half of the dose. The majority of radioactivity appeared in the feces, which agrees with the findings of other workers (Joachimoglu *et al.*, 1967). Extraction of the urine with petroleum ether removed only a trace of the radioactivity, which was possibly unmetabolized THC. Ether extraction of the first 24-hour urine removed as much as 40% of the radioactivity, which seems to indicate metabolized but unconjugated THC. Neither this material nor the more polar fraction has thus far been identified or further characterized.

Klaisner and Dingell (1970, 1971) have obtained results that further confirm the previous reports of fecal excretion as the major route of elimination of Δ^1-THC in the rat. They injected $1',3'-^{14}C-\Delta^1$-THC (obtained from the National Institutes of Mental Health) intravenously in a mixture of propylene glycol and rat serum. This combination is particularly effective in preparing THC for injection, a problem that has caused difficulties in the past. They also performed perfusions on the isolated rat liver, which showed a rapid biliary elimination (80% within 2 hours) of the drug.

While the data of Klausner and Dingell are qualitatively similar to those of Agurell *et al.*, their rates of elimination of radioactivity are more rapid. More than one-half of the dose is eliminated by the third day, in contrast to about a week in the above report (Agurell *et al.*, 1969). They felt that this may have been due to differences in the animals or in the injecting vehicle. Another possibility is the nature of the labeling of the drug. If the tritium used by Agurell *et al.* was being lost in part either by exchange or by displacement, such a discrepancy could occur. A study with THC containing both ^{14}C and ^3H might resolve this point.

Only traces of radioactivity could be removed by petroleum ether extraction of the urine. On the other hand, with diethyl ether about 60% of the radioactivity was extracted. These results again are quite similar to those of Agurell *et al.* Unmetabolized, unconjugated THC would be soluble in petroleum ether, whereas oxidation products or conjugates would not. Since most common conjugates of lipid-soluble materials do not dissolve in diethyl ether it would seem that a major portion of the metabolites are unconjugated. The authors did not present any evidence for the chemical nature of the metabolic products.

Studies in the rabbit (*vide infra*) led to the establishment of 7-hydroxy-Δ^6-THC (Table II) as a major Δ^6-THC metabolite (Ben-Zvi *et al.*, 1970a; Burstein *et al.*, 1970). Almost simultaneously, similar structures (Table II) were obtained for the major metabolite of Δ^1-THC in the rat (Wall *et al.*, 1970) and in the rabbit (Nilsson *et al.*, 1970). Still another group (Foltz *et al.*, 1970) at about the same time showed that the major product of Δ^6-THC in the rat is 7-hydroxy-Δ^6-THC, the same as that isolated by Burstein *et al.* from the rabbit.

The Battelle group (Foltz *et al.*, 1970) used tritiated material obtained from the National Institutes of Mental Health which had been prepared by Timmons *et al.* (1969). They also used ^{14}C-labeled material, but no information on the source was given. Examination of the livers of their rats one-half hour after injection showed a radioactivity content of about 13% of the dose. Of this about 65% had the same tlc mobility in several systems as synthetic 7-hydroxy-Δ^6-THC. Incubation of the drug with a rat liver preparation allowed the isolation of sufficient metabolite for identification, which was deduced by mass spectral and nuclear magnetic resonance studies and confirmed by synthesis. The latter was accomplished by selenium dioxide oxidation of Δ^6-THC followed by sodium borohydride reduction. However, no details of the reaction conditions or the yields were given.

Using an *in vitro* system, Wall *et al.* (1970) found that 7-hydroxy-Δ^1-THC is the major metabolite of Δ^1-THC in the rat. In a large-scale experiment with the 10,000 g supernatant from 500 gm of rat liver, 1.0 gm of tritiated Δ^1-THC was converted to several products. Twenty-five percent of the Δ^1-THC was recovered unchanged. Free 7-hydroxy-Δ^1-THC accounted for 30% and an additional 15% was isolated as the 7-monoacetate. The authors noted that the latter was probably an artifact due to the method of isolation. A second, more polar product was obtained in 30% yield and the mass spectrum showed that it was a dihydroxy-THC. Analysis of the nuclear magnetic resonance spectrum showed that it was 6,7-dihydroxy-Δ^1-THC; the α orientation was assigned to the 6-hydroxyl (Table II). The structures of both metabolites were based entirely on physical measurements. However, the identification of 7-hydroxy-Δ^1-THC has also been confirmed by comparison with a synthetic sample by Ben-Zvi *et al.* (1970b).

The metabolism of Δ^6-THC was also studied by Wall (1971) using the conditions described above for the Δ^1 isomer. In addition to the 7-hydroxy metabolite (Table II) reported by previous laboratories, he found two dihydroxylated substances in his incubation extract. Nuclear magnetic resonance analysis showed these to be the epimeric 5α- and 5β,7-dihydroxy-Δ^6-THC's (Table II). The total conversion to metabolites was 40–60% in rats that were pretreated with phenobarbital. The proportions of mono- and dihydroxylated products were reported to vary with "experimental conditions." Since the monohydroxy-THC's are active (see Chapter 2), the second hydroxylation may be the initial detoxification step *in vivo*.

The characteristics of the hepatic oxygenase responsible for the production of 7-hydroxy-Δ^1-THC have been studied in some detail by Burstein and Kupfer (1971). We showed that the reaction indeed took place in the microsomal fraction and that no activity was present in the 100,000 g supernate. The presence of oxygen and NADPH were required and CO inhibited the reaction, suggesting the involvement of cytochrome P-450. Inhibition was observed with SKF-525A, but very little if any effect was found when hexobarbital was added to the incubation medium. Preparations from male rats showed significantly higher activity than those from females, again indicating a mixed-function oxidase enzyme system (Gillette *et al.*, 1969).

Little has been reported on the metabolism of cannabinoids other than the THC's. The Swedish group (Widman *et al.*, 1971) has investigated the fate of cannabinol in the rat. They prepared ^{14}C-cannabinol from the corresponding Δ^1-THC by heating with sulfur. Incubation with the 10,000 g supernatant of rat liver caused hydroxylation at the 7 position (Table II), as in the cases of both THC isomers. This product accounted for 45% of the metabolized material. This finding has been confirmed by Wall (1971) using unlabeled cannabinol and analyzing the incubation extract by gas chromatography–mass spectrometry.

B. DISTRIBUTION IN THE RABBIT, DOG, AND MONKEY

The metabolism of THC's in the rabbit was first studied simultaneously in our laboratories and by Agurell and co-workers in Stockholm. Our efforts centered on the conversions of Δ^6-THC, while the Swedish group examined both the distribution and the metabolic fates of Δ^1-THC.

Agurell *et al.* (1970) have published a rather thorough study of the elimination and distribution of ^{3}H-Δ^1-THC in the rabbit; their material was probably labeled on the aromatic ring (Fig. 2). They found that in contrast to the rat most of the radioactivity in the rabbit is excreted in the urine and at a considerably faster rate. After 24 hours, approximately 35% has been eliminated by this route, while only 10% has been eliminated in the feces. These results compare well with our data (Burstein *et al.*, 1970), which were obtained with

TABLE II
Cannabinoid Metabolites[a]

Precursor	Metabolite	Conditions	Reference
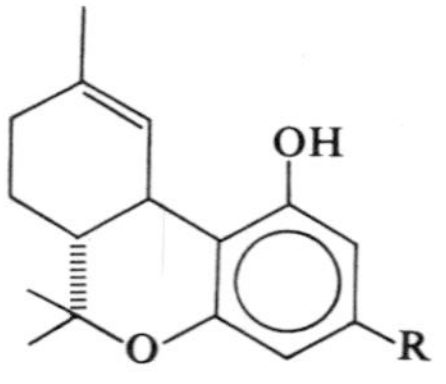 Δ^1-THC	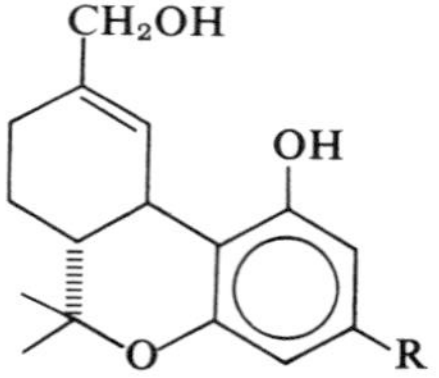	Rabbit liver Rat liver Rat liver microsomes Man	Nilsson et al. (1970) Wall et al. (1970) Burstein and Kupfer (1971) Lemberger et al. (1970)
	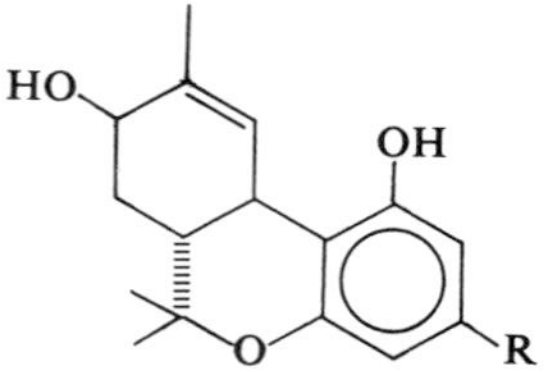	Rabbit liver	Wall (1971)
	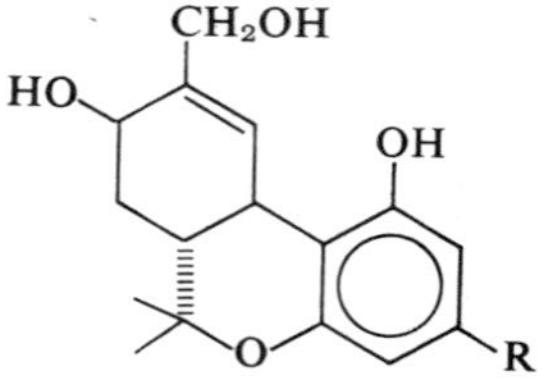	Rat liver	Wall et al. (1970), Wall (1971)
	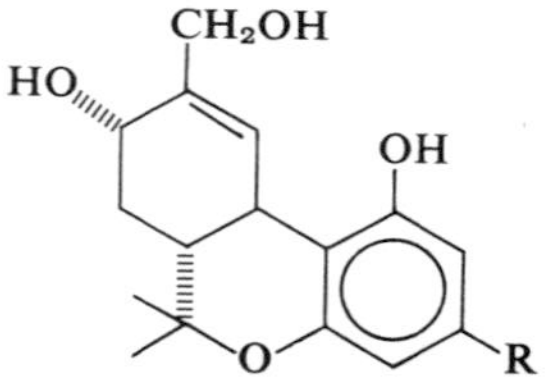	Rat liver	Wall et al. (1970), Wall (1971)

176

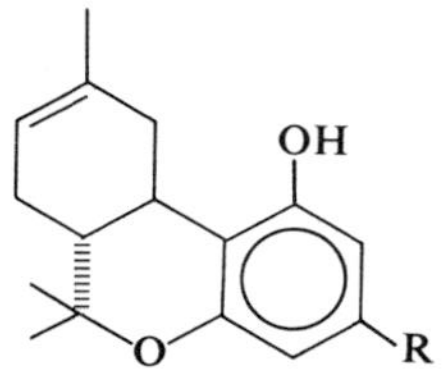

Δ⁶-THC

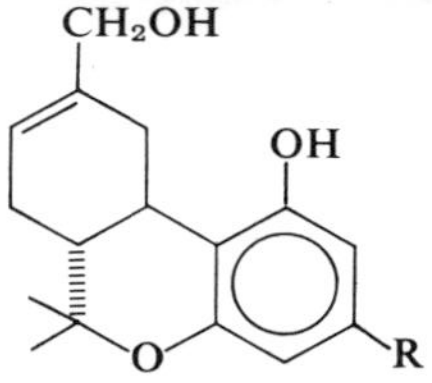

CH₂OH ⊕ Rabbit Burstein et al. (1970)
Rat Foltz et al. (1970)

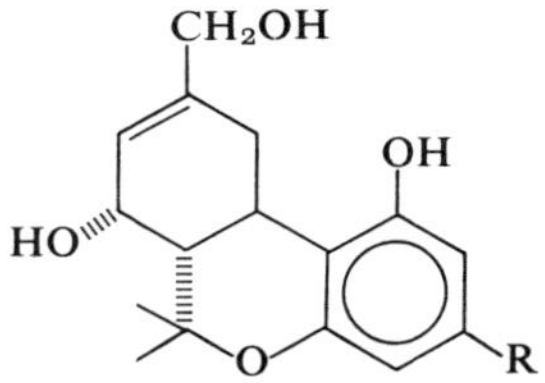

CH₂OH ⊖ Rat liver Wall (1971)

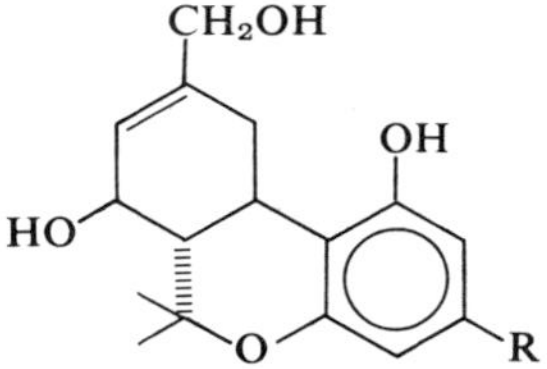

CH₂OH ⊖ Rat liver Wall (1971)

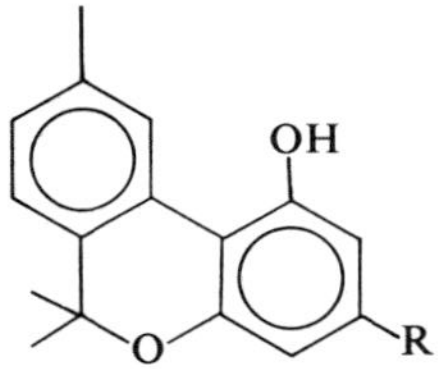

CH₂OH Rat liver Widman et al. (1971)

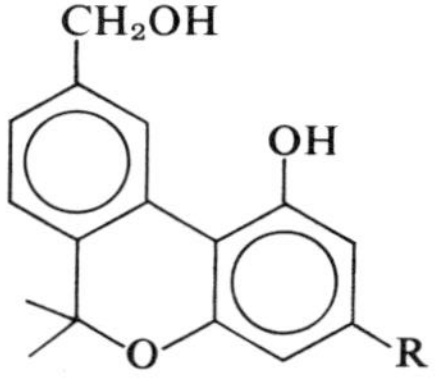

⊖ Cannabinol

^{a} Key: ⊕, biological activity; ⊖, no biological activity (see Chapter 2); $R =$ —CH$_2$CH$_2$CH$_2$CH$_3$.

^{3}H-Δ^6-THC; in both instances the drug was administered intravenously. We also examined the effect of dose on the rate of urinary excretion using tracer amounts (less than 1 μg). As might be expected, the low dose was eliminated more rapidly.

As part of a fluorometric assay method for THC, Bullock et al. (1970) measured the urinary excretion rate of tritiated Δ^1-THC in the dog. During 4 days, about 12% appeared in the urine, a large part of which was ether extractable (Bullock, 1970). The fate of the remaining radioactivity was not determined. However, they showed that the half-life of the drug in dog plasma is about 35 minutes. During this period the level of metabolites increases, reaching a plateau in approximately 1 hour.

A study of the distribution of tritium from injected Δ^1-THC showed some rather interesting patterns (Agurell et al., 1970). After 2 hours, rabbits had the highest levels in kidney and lung tissue; similar results were also observed by these authors and by Klausner and Dingell (1971) in the rat. There is still a considerable amount of radioactivity present after 72 hours; however, the spleen and body fat are now the principal areas. The earlier results (Joachimoglu et al., 1967) in the rat are not in agreement; however, those authors injected by the intraperitoneal route.

A report by McIsaac et al. (1971) on the distribution of ^{3}H-Δ^1-THC in the monkey brain has shown a possible correlation between dose level, time, and behavioral response. They found that measurable amounts of unchanged drug were localized in various areas of the brain within 15 minutes after intravenous injection. The initial pattern shifted during the following 24 hours, by which time only a small amount of evenly distributed radioactivity remained. The above authors, using other species, also found that only a small fraction of the administered radioactivity was localized in the brain; unfortunately, the nature of the material was not ascertained. Apparently, the amount of THC required at the active site for behavioral response is quite small. If the monkey also produces 7-hydroxy-THC, its role in the temporal brain distribution picture will also have to be examined in view of its reported pharmacological activity (Ben-Zvi et al., 1970a; Foltz et al., 1970; Nilsson et al., 1970; Wall et al., 1970).

C. IDENTIFICATION OF METABOLITES IN THE RABBIT

Parenterally administered ^{3}H-Δ^6-THC was excreted in rabbit urine as several water-soluble metabolites (Burstein et al., 1970). The substances resisted cleavage by enzymatic preparations, and strong acid conditions also proved unsatisfactory. Carefully defined acidic treatment (Burstein et al., 1960) did, however, liberate some benzene-soluble material. This substance showed the same chromatographic mobilities as the major conversion product that we obtained by rabbit liver incubation. Because of the relative ease in obtaining an unconjugated metabolite from the *in vitro* method, that approach was used in our structural studies.

The metabolite was protected by acetylation to minimize decomposition during isolation, and the derivative was analyzed by mass spectrometry (Burstein *et al.*, 1970). It was possible to determine from the mass spectrum that the metabolite was a hydroxylated THC in which the new group was probably allylic to the double bond. Next, it was shown that the carbon skeleton was intact by conversion of the metabolite to cannabinol. This was readily accomplished in good yield by treatment with acid (Fig. 6).

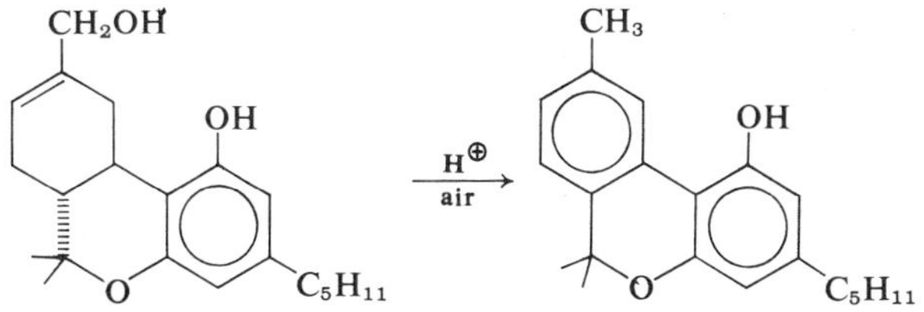

Fig. 6. Acid-catalyzed conversion of 7-hydroxy-Δ^6-THC to cannabinol.

The possibility of hydroxylation at the 2 position was readily excluded by oxidation of the phenolic methyl ether since the product was still labeled with tritium. The remaining possibilities (positions 5 and 7) were resolved by synthesis of authentic 7-hydroxy-Δ^6-THC (Ben-Zvi *et al.*, 1970a).* Several steps are involved and the overall yield is quite small. Nevertheless, sufficient material was obtained for characterization and comparisons.

An improved method involving direct oxidation with selenium dioxide (see also Section III,A) was later developed in which the overall yield is considerably higher (Ben-Zvi *et al.*, 1970b). The synthetically obtained 7-hydroxy-Δ^6-THC was identical in a number of different comparisons with the rabbit metabolite.

Similar findings were reported by Agurell *et al.* (1970) using ^{3}H-Δ^1-THC. They also found several water-soluble metabolites in rabbit urine that were not cleaved by β-glucuronidase treatment. Although acidification did not produce appreciable petroleum-ether-soluble material (presumably unchanged THC), it did greatly increase the amount of ether-extractable metabolite. The identity of this extract was not determined; however, evidence was given which indicated that there might be a carboxylic function on the molecule. This consisted of a study of the distribution of tritium between ether and an aqueous phase at various pH values. If the figures given represent a measure

---

* For a detailed discussion of THC metabolite syntheses, see Chapter 1, Section IV,F.

of an acidic metabolite, it could account for as much as 30–40% of the urinary metabolites.

As in our case, the above authors then turned to an *in vitro* approach for identification (Nilsson *et al.*, 1970). ^{14}C-Labeled material (Nilsson *et al.*, 1969) was incubated with the 10,000 g supernatant of rabbit liver after the addition of the appropriate cofactors. Under their conditions about 40% of the $\varDelta^1$-THC was converted to metabolite. Chromatography showed this to contain over 95% of a single substance, and analysis of the nuclear magnetic resonance and mass spectra showed that this material was 7-hydroxy-$\varDelta^1$-THC.

Using approximately the same conditions, Wall (1971) confirmed the above finding. In addition he reported the isolation of 6α,7-dihydroxy-$\varDelta^1$-THC, which he had previously also found in the rat. A third metabolite, 6β-hydroxy-$\varDelta^1$-THC, was isolated in 15% yield and its structure determined by nmr. The latter substance was synthesized by Mechoulam's group and was found to be active in monkeys (see Chapter 2).

D. METABOLISM IN MAN

The published information on THC metabolism in man is rather limited. Agurell (1970) reported that ^{3}H-$\varDelta^1$-THC gives rise to radioactivity in the urine; between 10 and 15% was excreted in the first 24 hours. Christiansen and Rafaelsen (1969) studied the urine from 10 volunteers who drank a suspension of 750 mg of cannabis resin in water. They did not specify the THC content. However, they indicated that the dose produced "effects."

The urine was treated with a β-glucuronidase–sulfatase mixture at pH 5.5 and then extracted with petroleum ether. Thin-layer chromatography of the extract revealed several substances that were not present in normal urine. One of the spots had the same mobility as cannabidiol, and there was no THC or cannabinol. Urine that was not treated with enzyme showed no substances that were mobile in the thin-layer system used. Although the experiment had obvious weaknesses it does suggest that man, like other species, completely metabolizes THC. The conjugates would, however, appear to be more easily hydrolyzed, although the lack of quantitative data leaves this point uncertain.

Lemberger *et al.* (1970, 1971) have published data on the excretion of ^{14}C-$\varDelta^1$-THC, which they administered intravenously to three subjects who claimed no previous use of cannabis. The THC (0.5 mg in 1 ml of ethanol) was given by infusion with a 5% dextrose in water solution into the subject's arm vein. Presumably, a fine suspension was formed, carried into the blood stream, and bound by the plasma constituents.

By withdrawing blood samples from the opposite arm, Lemberger *et al.*

were able to measure the plasma levels of radioactivity at intervals over 72 hours. The samples were fractionated into unchanged THC and metabolites by differential solvent extraction with heptane and ether. The heptane extract was shown to contain mainly unchanged Δ^1-THC by tlc comparison with a standard. A small fraction of the material had the same mobility as 7-hydroxy-Δ^1-THC, suggesting a route of metabolism similar to that in other species. No characteristics of the ether extracts were given. The THC levels dropped rapidly at first ($t_{1/2}$ = 30 minutes) and then decreased more slowly ($t_{1/2}$ = 50–60 hours). The metabolite(s) appeared within a few minutes after injection of the drug and showed a parallel disappearance from the plasma. However, the observed levels were about double those of the Δ^1-THC.

Studies were also done with chronic users under the same conditions (Lemberger *et al.*, 1971). In this case a mean half-life of 28 hours was observed; no other differences were found between the users and nonusers. The authors suggested that this increase in excretion rate is due to stimulation of the metabolic conversion of THC. This hypothesis is in accord with our finding, discussed earlier, that the 7-hydroxylase is a mixed-function oxidase (Burstein and Kupfer, 1971) since such systems are known to undergo substrate induction (Conney, 1967).

IV. Summary

The preparation of pure labeled Δ^1- and Δ^6-THC has been achieved, making these materials accessible to investigators studying their biological properties. Although several methods exist for the synthesis of tritiated materials, the most practical route for ^{14}C labeling is via ring-labeled olivetol. This preparation has thus far proven to be quite satisfactory for metabolic studies since there are no indications of important metabolites being formed that involve changes in the aromatic ring. A procedure for the synthesis of high specific activity ^{3}H-Δ^1-THC still has not been developed. This will become important if a workable radioimmunoassay for Δ^1-THC is achieved (see Chapter 3).

The pattern of metabolism, especially in the liver *in vitro*, is becoming fairly clear. The 7-methyl group appears to be the principal point of attack for the hydroxylase systems, which utilize THC. This seems to be due to the primary allylic nature of the position, which also makes it vulnerable to chemical oxidation (see Chapter 1). This reaction, which is mediated by a mixed-function oxidase, is of considerable significance since the 7-hydroxy compounds show high activity in all the animal assays used for THC. The available evidence in man indicates that these compounds are probably involved in the mechanism of action of Δ^1- and Δ^6-THC.

Deactivation of the drug can be brought about by further hydroxylation at one of the secondary allylic positions. Several of these compounds have been isolated thus far and none shows any appreciable activity. Interestingly, monohydroxylation at a secondary position gives an active molecule. The pathways leading to deactivated drug will have to be studied, particularly *in vivo* in man.

An area that has been elucidated only to a limited extent is the nature of the ultimate metabolites. Although small amounts of the 7-hydroxy compounds have been found in the urine of rabbits and man, the major fraction of material consists of acidic substances. The evidence to date indicates that it is made up of several quite polar substances. It is not clear whether these are conjugates or conversion products of THC. Determination of the chemical structures of these substances may throw light on how a unique psychotomimetic like THC operates.

References

Agurell, S. (1970). *In* "The Botany and Chemistry of Cannabis" (S. H. Curry and C. R. B. Joyce, eds.), p. 175. Churchill, London.

Agurell, S., Nilsson, I. M., Ohlsson, A., and Sandberg, F. (1969). *Biochem. Pharmacol.* **18**, 1195.

Agurell, S., Nilsson, I. M., Ohlsson, A., and Sandberg, F. (1970). *Biochem. Pharmacol.* **19**, 1333.

Anker, R. M., and Cook, A. H. (1945). *J. Chem. Soc.* 311.

Ben-Zvi, Z., Mechoulam, R., and Burstein, S. H. (1970a). *J. Amer. Chem. Soc.* **92**, 3468.

Ben-Zvi, Z., Mechoulam, R., and Burstein, S. H. (1970b). *Tetrahedron Lett.* 4495.

Bullock, F. J. (1970). Private communication.

Bullock, F. J., Bruni, R. J., and Werner, E. (1970). Paper presented at the 160th Nat. Amer. Chem. Soc. Meeting, Chicago, Illinois.

Burstein, S. H., and Kupfer, D. (1971). *Chem.-Biol. Interact.* **3**, 316.

Burstein, S. H., and Mechoulam, R. (1968). *J. Amer. Chem. Soc.* **90**, 2420.

Burstein, S., Jacobson, G. M., and Lieberman, S. (1960). *J. Amer. Chem. Soc.* **82**, 1226.

Burstein, S. H., Menezes, F., Williamson, E., and Mechoulam, R. (1970). *Nature (London)* **225**, 88.

Burstein, S. H., Menezes, F., and Williamson, E. (1970). Unpublished results.

Christiansen, J., and Rafaelson, O. J. (1969). *Psychopharmacologia* **15**, 60.

Conney, A. H. (1967). *Pharmacol. Rev.* **19**, 317.

Fahrenholtz, K. E., Lurie, M., and Kierstead, R. W. (1967). *J. Amer. Chem. Soc.* **89**, 5934.

Foltz, R. L., Fentiman, A. F., Jr., Leighty, E. G., Walter, J. L., Drewes, H. R., Schwartz, W. E., Page, T. F., Jr., Truitt, E. B., Jr. (1970). *Science* **168**, 844.

Gillette, J. R., Conney, A. H., Cosmides, G. J., Estabrook, R. W., Fouts, J. R., and Mannering, G. J., eds. (1969). "Microsomes and Drug Oxidations." Academic Press, New York.

Idänpään-Heikkilä, J., Fritchie, G. E., Englert, L. F., Ho, B. T., and McIsaac, W. M. (1969). *N. Engl.-J. Med.* **291**, 330.

Joachimoglu, G., Kiburis, J., and Miras, C. (1967). *U.N. Secretariat Document ST/SOA/ SER. S/15.*

Klausner, H. A., and Dingell, J. V. (1970). *Pharmacologist* 12, 259.

Klausner, H. A., and Dingell, J. V. (1971). *Life Sci.* 10, 49.

Lemberger, L., Silberstein, S. D., Axelrod, J., and Kopin, I. J. (1970). *Science* 170, 1320.

Lemberger, L., Tamarkin, N. R., Axelrod, J., and Kopin, I. J. (1971). *Science* 173, 72.

McIsaac, W. M., Fritchie, G. E., Idänpään-Heikkilä, J. E., Ho, B. T., and Englert, L. F. (1971). *Nature (London)* 230, 593.

Miras, C. J. (1965). *In* "Hashish. Its Chemistry and Pharmacology" (G. E. W. Wolsten-holme and J. Knight, eds.), p. 37. Churchill, London.

Nilsson, I. M., Agurell, S., Nilsson, J. L. G., Ohlsson, A., Sandberg, F., and Wahlqvist, M. (1970). *Science* 168, 1228.

Nilsson, J. L. G., Nilsson, I. M., and Agurell, S. (1969). *Acta Chem. Scand.* 23, 2209.

Timmons, M. L., Pitt, C. G., and Wall, M. E. (1969). *Tetrahedron Lett.* 3129.

Wall, M. E. (1971). *Ann. N.Y. Acad. Sci.* 23.

Wall, M. E., Brine, D. R., Brine, G. A., Pitt, C. G., Freudenthal, R. I., and Christensen, H. D. (1970). *J. Amer. Chem. Soc.* 92, 3466.

Widman, M., Nilsson, I. M., Nilsson, J. L. G., Agurell, S., and Leander, K. (1971). *Life Sci.* 10, 157.

Addendum

Since the manuscript for this chapter was completed, the literature on the metabolism of the cannabinoids has nearly doubled. The following will therefore be a brief summary of the most important reports to date. Despite the vast increase in our knowledge of this subject, a good deal remains to be ascertained. This is in part due to the unfolding of what seems to be a fairly complex metabolic pattern for THC. Moreover, the possible roles for the other cannabinoids in the pharmacology of cannabis will likely stimulate an interest in their biotransformations as well. The structures of the new metabolites are shown in Table A-II.

TABLE A-I

NEW LABELED CANNABINOIDS

Substance	Positions labeled	Specific activity (Ci/mole)	Reference
^{3}H-Δ^1-THC	1″,2″	607.0	Gill and Jones (1972)
^{14}C-Δ^1-THC	1′,3′	11.7	Liebman *et al.* (1971)
^{3}H-Δ^6-THC	1″,2″	607.0	Gill and Jones (1972)
^{14}C-Δ^6-THC	2″	0.82	Gau *et al.* (1972)
D_1-Δ^1-THC	3	—	Mechoulam *et al.* (1972)
D_1-Δ^6-THC	3	—	Mechoulam *et al.* (1972)

PREPARATION OF LABELED TETRAHYDROCANNABINOLS

Several additional methods for synthesizing labeled THC have recently appeared in print (Table A-I). Liebman et al. (1971) have described a method for the preparation of ^{14}C-olivetol, which they subsequently converted to ^{14}C-Δ^1-THC in 56% radiochemical yield. Gau et al. (1972) reported a synthesis of ^{14}C-Δ^6-THC in which the ring system is generated first. The side chain is then introduced by alkylation with labeled butyl lithium. The advantage of this method would seem to lie in its flexibility since a variety of side chains could be incorporated.

Gill and Jones (1972) have synthesized side-chain-tritiated THC by reduction of an unsaturated precursor of olivetol with a tritium–hydrogen mixture. This method allows the preparation of high specific activity THC if carrier-free tritium is used, which would make it useful in a radioimmunoassay. For metabolic studies, caution is advised since both Δ^1- and Δ^6-THC are known to undergo side chain hydroxylation (Burstein et al., 1972; Maynard et al., 1971).

Mechoulam et al. (1972) modified their synthesis of THC by utilizing deuterated verbenol. This led to the preparation of 3α-D-Δ^6-THC which could be readily adapted to produce the tritiated analog. To date the 3 position has not been implicated in biotransformation, making this derivative attractive for such purposes.

METABOLISM IN THE RAT

The capabilities of rat lung for metabolizing Δ^1-THC were reported by Nakazawa and Costa (1971). Using the postmitochondrial fraction of lung homogenate, they showed by thin-layer chromatography that two metabolites not produced by liver were present in the lung extract. They further showed that 3-methylcholanthrene increased metabolism in the lung but not in the liver. These results may be of great importance since cannabis is very often taken by smoking.

The in vitro metabolism of cannabidiol (CBD) in rat liver has been examined by Nilsson et al. (1971). Once again hydroxylation at the 7 position is the major reaction; however, they also observed monohydroxylation on the side chain, probably at the benzylic carbon. Tentative data on a third product indicated hydroxylation of the allylic methyl at 10. The metabolism of CBD may be very relevant to that of THC since Jones and Pertwee (1972) have shown that the former does influence the action of the latter.

An interesting THC metabolite, 7-hydroxy-Δ^1-THC-diacetate, was isolated from rat bile by Mikes et al. (1971). The 7-monoacetate had been reported from liver homogenate by Wall (1971); however, he believed it to be an artifact of the isolation procedure. Apparently, the ester(s) is further acted upon *in vivo* since it has not been found in either urine or feces. The authors also reported finding unchanged Δ^1-THC and 6,7-dihydroxy-Δ^1-THC in both urine and feces. Treatment with glucuronidase liberated more Δ^1-THC and, surprisingly, cannabinol.

METABOLISM IN THE RABBIT

A preliminary report on the *in vivo* metabolism of ³H-7-OH-Δ^1-THC in the rabbit has been given by Agurell and co-workers (1971). They found that the major urinary metabolite(s), as for Δ^1-THC, appeared to be a carboxylic acid. We recently published data on the isolation and identification of two of the urinary metabolites of Δ^1-THC in the rabbit (Burstein *et al.*, 1972). Both substances contained a carboxyl function at 7 and a hydroxyl group on the side chain. In one instance the hydroxyl is at the benzylic position, while the second metabolite probably has its OH at the β position. This is the first report in which a major urinary metabolite of THC has been isolated and identified from any species.

METABOLISM IN THE DOG

Very little has been done in the dog to date; however, there is one report by Maynard *et al.* (1971). They incubated ¹⁴C-Δ^6-THC with the 9000 *g* supernatant from beagle liver and observed about 30% formation of metabolites. They succeeded in isolating and identifying two monohydroxylated derivatives. On the basis of nmr data they proposed side chain hydroxylation for both metabolites. One substance had a benzylic hydroxyl as in the cannabinoids mentioned above; the other was oxygenated at the γ position. Interestingly, no 7-hydroxy derivatives were reported.

METABOLISM IN THE MONKEY

A temporal study on the cannabinoid content of squirrel monkey brains was done by Ho *et al.* (1972). ³H-Δ^1-Tetrahydrocannabinol was injected intravenously and brain extracts were analyzed by thin-layer chromatography. Unchanged drug and 7-hydroxy-Δ^1-THC were both found to be present; the proportion of metabolite increased with time, although the total amounts of each had decreased. A smaller fraction of more polar material was also observed which behaved like an acidic substance.

A comparison of the excretion patterns of ³H-Δ^1-THC from squirrel and rhesus monkeys has been reported by Würsch *et al.* (1972). Using the data on man published by Lemberger *et al.* (1971a) for comparison, they found that the rhesus monkey more closely resembles man in this respect. They also observed an increasing polarity of the urinary metabolites on successive days.

TABLE A-II

New Metabolites of Cannabis Constituents

Precursor	Metabolite	Conditions	References
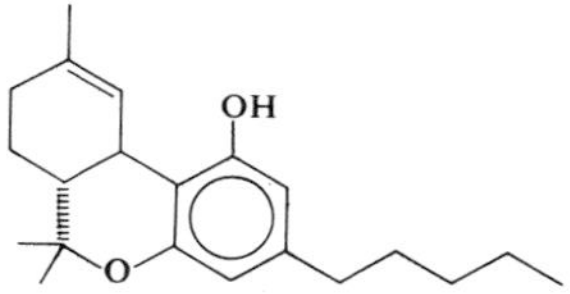 Δ¹-THC	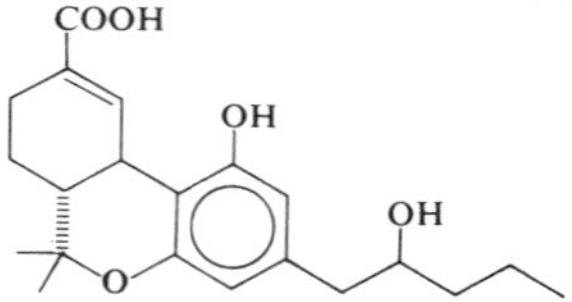	Rabbit urine	Burstein et al. (1972)
	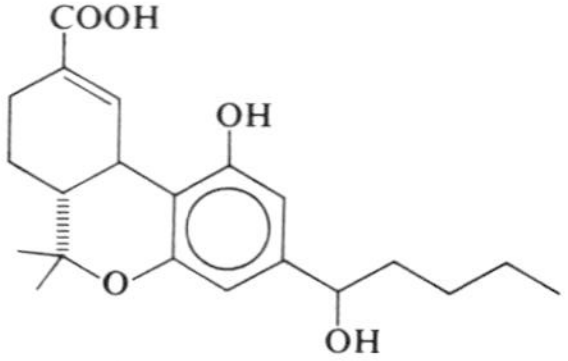		
	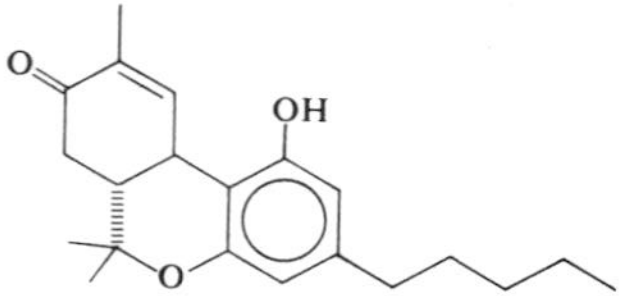	Squirrel monkey liver	Gurny et al. (1972)
	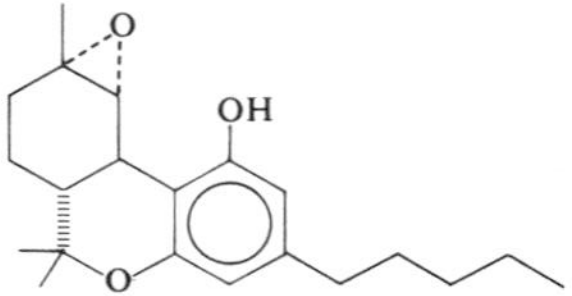		
	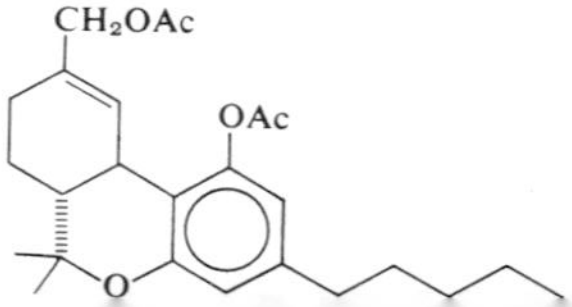	Rat bile	Mikes et al. (1971)

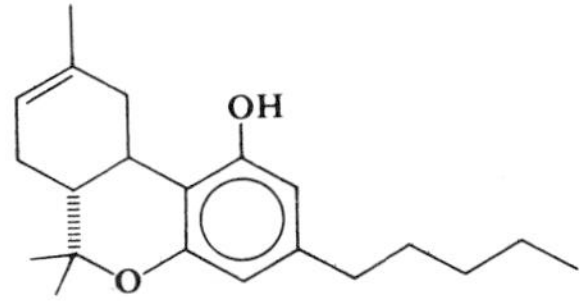

Maynard et al. (1971)

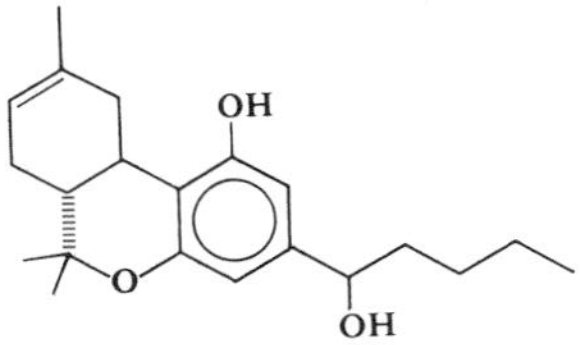

Dog liver

Gurny et al. (1972)

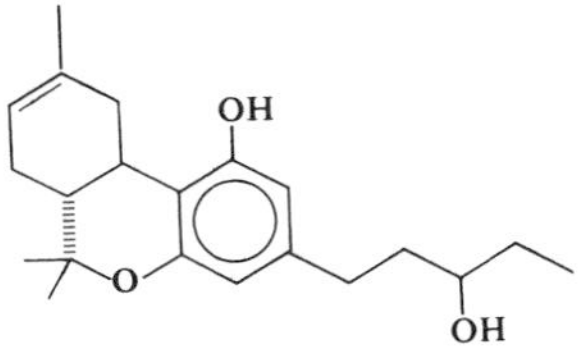

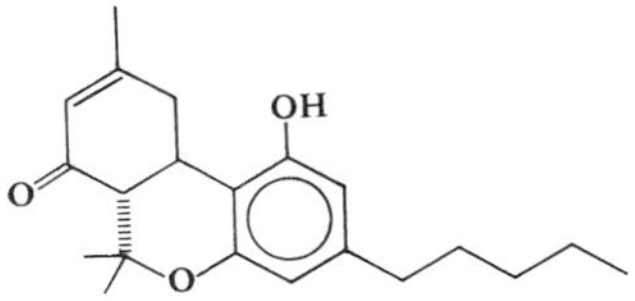

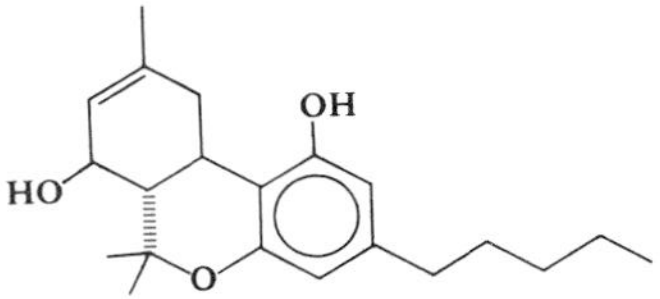

Squirrel monkey liver

Δ⁶-THC

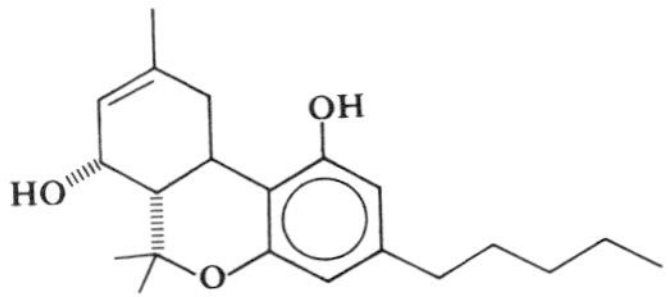

TABLE A-II (*continued*)

Precursor	Metabolite	Conditions	References
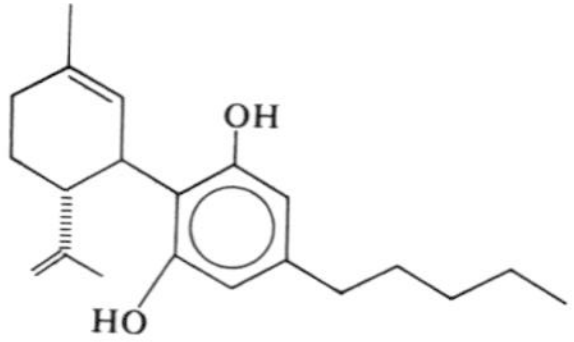 Cannabidiol	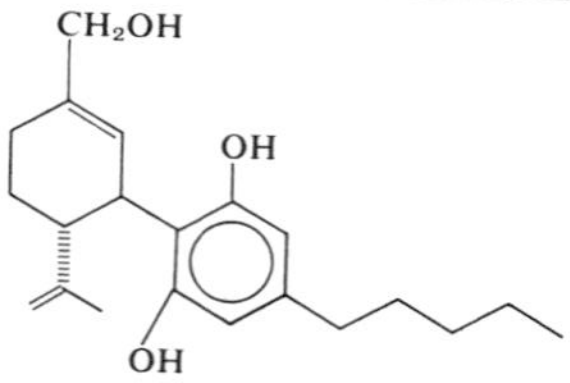 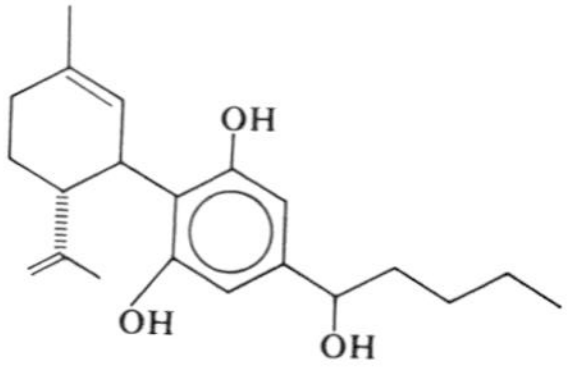 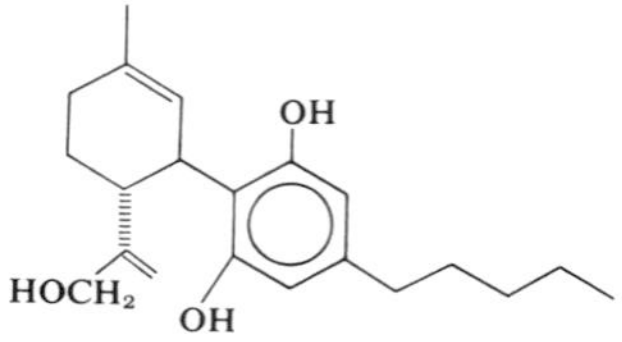	Rat liver	Nilsson *et al.* (1971)

Gurny *et al.* (1972) reported on liver transformations in the squirrel monkey. They found that Δ^6-THC gives rise to 5α- and 5β-hydroxy-Δ^6-THC as well as the 5-keto derivative. Δ^1-Tetrahydrocannabinol also formed the analogous 6-keto-Δ^1-THC and a new type of metabolite the 1,2-epoxide. This is the first report of either a ketone or epoxide type of metabolite for THC.

METABOLISM IN MAN

Lemberger *et al.* (1971a,b, 1972b) have summarized the results of their study on the effects of intravenous administration of ^{14}C-Δ^1-THC. Tentative evidence was given for the appearance of 7-OH-Δ^1-THC in plasma, urine, and feces; in the latter it was a major metabolite. A polar fraction was also observed in the urine which was probably an acid(s). This correlates nicely with our recent finding (see above) on the nature of the urinary metabolites in the rabbit.

The effects of 7-OH-Δ^1-THC in man have also been studied by Lemberger *et al.* (1972a). In general their observations showed that this substance "mimics" the parent drug, Δ^1-THC. Very little unchanged 7-OH-Δ^1-THC appeared in the urine; the majority of the radioactivity was associated with polar, acidic material.

Perez-Reyes *et al.* (1972) have given a preliminary report on metabolism of Δ^1-THC by oral administration. The nature of the products was the same as that found for other routes. Findings relevant to this point were reported by Greene *et al.* (1972), who showed that intestinal mucosa was capable of transforming Δ^1-THC to several metabolites. By thin-layer chromatography they concluded that the major product was 7-OH-THC.

References

Agurell, S., Nilsson, I. M., Nilsson, J. L. G., Ohlsson, A., Widman, M., and Leander, K. (1971). *Acta Pharm. Suecica* 8, 698.
Burstein, S., Rosenfeld, J., Wittstruck, T. (1972). *Science* 176, 422.
Gau, W., Bienick, D., and Korte, F. (1972). *Tetrahedron Lett.* 25, 2507.
Gill, E. W., and Jones, G. (1972). *J. Label. Compounds* 8, 237.
Greene, M. L., Sauders, D. R., Smith, K. (1972). *Gastroenterology* 62, 757.
Gurny, O., Maynard, D. E., Pitcher, R. G., and Kierstead, R. W. (1972). Abstract 551, Fifth Int. Congress on Pharmacology, San Francisco, July.
Ho, B. T., Estevez, V., Englert, L. F., and McIssac, W. M. (1972). *J. Pharm. Pharmacol.* 24, 414.
Jones, G., and Pertwee, R. G. (1972). *Brit. J. Pharmacol.* 45, 375.
Lemberger, L., Axelrod, J., Kopin, I. J. (1971a). *Ann. N.Y. Acad. Sci.* 191, 142.
Lemberger, L., Axelrod, J., and Kopin, I. (1971b). *Pharmacol. Rev.* 23, 371.

190 SUMNER H. BURSTEIN

Lemberger, L., Crabtree, R. E., and Rowe, H. M. (1972a). *Science* **177**, 62.
Lemberger, L., Weiss, J. L., Watanabe, A. M., Galanter, I. M., Wyatt, R. J., and Cardon, P. V. (1972b). *N. Engl. J. Med.* **286**, 685.
Liebman, A. A., Malarek, D. H., Dorsky, A. M., and Kaegi, H. H. (1971). *J. Label. Compounds* **7**, 241.
Maynard, D. E., Gurny, O., Pitcher, R. G., and Kierstead, R. W. (1971). *Experientia* **27**, 1154.
Mechoulam, R., Braun, P., and Gaoni, Y. (1972). *J. Amer. Chem. Soc.* **94**, 6159.
Mikes, F., Hofmann, A., and Waser, P. G. (1971). *Biochem. Pharmacol.* **20**, 2469.
Nakazawa, K., and Costa, E. (1971). *Nature (London)* **234**, 48.
Nilsson, I. M., Agurell, S., Leander, K., Nilsson, J. L. G., and Widman, M. (1971). *Acta Pharm. Suecica* **8**, 701.
Perez-Reyes, M., Lipton, M., Wall, M. E., Brine, D. E., and Timmons, M. C. (1972). Abstract 1075, Fifth Int. Congress on Pharmacology, San Francisco, July.
Wall, M. E. (1971). *Ann. N.Y. Acad. Sci.* **191**, 23.
Würsch, M. S., Otis, L. S., Greene, D. E., and Forrest, I. S. (1972). *Proc. West. Pharmacol. Soc.* **15**, 68.

CHAPTER 5

The Pharmacology of Cannabis in Animals

W. D. M. Paton and R. G. Pertwee

I. Introduction 192
  A. Physical and Chemical Properties of Cannabis Preparations . . 192
  B. The Preparations of Cannabis Most Commonly Used 195
  C. The Problem of Bioassay of Cannabis Activity 197
II. Actions of Cannabis. 205
  A. Behavioral and Experimental Psychology 205
  B. Neurological Effects 216
  C. Interactions with Convulsants and Amphetamines 221
  D. Hypothalamic and Endocrine Actions 222
  E. Vomiting and Scratching 225
  F. Interactions of Cannabis with Brain Amines 226
  G. Cannabis and Barbiturate Sleeping Time 228
  H. General Pharmacology 230
III. Toxicity and Teratogenicity. 235
  A. Acute Toxicity 235
  B. Chronic Toxicity. 238
  C. Teratogenicity and Action on the Fetus 238
IV. Metabolism and Fate of Tetrahydrocannabinol in the Body . . . 241
  A. The Metabolites 242
  B. The Disposition of the Metabolites 243
  C. Kinetics of Tetrahydrocannabinol Distribution and Disposal . . 244
  D. The Role of Metabolites in the Action of Tetrahydrocannabinol . 248
V. The Active Principles of Cannabis Other Than Δ^1-THC 250
VI. Cumulation and Tolerance 253
VII. General Discussion 257
  References 260
  Addendum 265

I. Introduction*

This chapter, and the following, attempt to survey the work with both animals and man that throws light on the pharmacology of cannabis. It is a field in which experimentation has been regrettably scanty, particularly investigations of an analytic kind. Indeed until recently the major contributions in experimental pharmacology had come from one man, S. Loewe, who was responsible for the pharmacological studies for the Mayor La Guardia report. The literature on cannabis is very extensive indeed. A good deal of it, however, merely draws on previous reviews or contributions. In addition, some of it reflects work done at a period when modern scientific techniques were not available. Broadly speaking, therefore, this review covers the work of the last 30 years, although a number of older experimental reports are mentioned.

There is a particular difficulty in interpreting the evidence in this field. This arises from the fact that much of the literature about cannabis concerns human use, with the drug being given in uncontrolled conditions, in a form of unknown potency, and with an unknown dose being given, commonly delivered in a smoke of unknown composition. It is indeed because of the limitations of these human experiments and the difficulty of interpreting the evidence that the animal work, fragmented though it is, assumes particular importance. It needs to be stressed that our approach has been pharmacological, regarding cannabis as a drug to be discussed in the same way as other modern drugs, and that this approach should not be abandoned because cannabis happens to be a drug that has been widely used by some indigenous populations, and now in other places, as an intoxicant. The interest of cannabis extends beyond the currently controversial aspects. As one example, to which we shall return later, we may note that it is one of the not very large number of materials which, while being intensely fat soluble (and in this way related to the volatile anesthetics), show a potency and a specificity of action and of chemical structure that the anesthetics lack.

A. PHYSICAL AND CHEMICAL PROPERTIES OF CANNABIS PREPARATIONS

The fat solubility of the main psychically active principles of cannabis has long been known. O'Shaughnessy (1842) gives a full description of the method of preparing the sweetmeat majoun. The following extract shows that the essential initial procedure is a partition of the active principles into clarified

---

* The chemical formulas of most cannabinoids discussed in this chapter are presented in an *appendix* at the end of the book.

butter (ghee) from a decoction of bhang, followed by washing the buttery extract:

> The *Majoon*, or hemp confection, is a compound of sugar, butter, flour, milk and *Sidhee* or *Bang*. The process has been repeatedly performed before us by Ameer, the proprietor of a celebrated place of resort for hemp devotees in Calcutta, and who is considered the best artist in his profession. Four ounces of *Sidhee* and an equal quantity of *ghee* are placed in an earthen or well-tinned vessel, a pint of water added, and the whole warmed over a charcoal fire. The mixture is constantly stirred until the water all boils away, which is known by the crackling noise of the melted butter on the sides of the vessel; the mixture is then removed from the fire, squeezed through cloth while hot—by which an oleaginous solution of the active principles and coloring matter of the hemp is obtained—and the leaves, fibres, etc., remaining on the cloth are thrown away.
>
> The green oily solution soon concretes into a buttery mass, and is then well washed by the hand with soft water so long as the water becomes colored. The coloring matter and an extractive substance are thus removed, and a very pale green mass, of the consistence of simple ointment, remains. The washings are thrown away;—Ameer says that these are intoxicating, and produce constriction of the throat, great pain, and very disagreeable and dangerous symptoms.

Subsequent work has largely exploited the fact that the active principles are extractable from the resin by petrol ether and has established that the substance responsible for most of the psychic effect is Δ^1-tetrahydrocanna-binol (Δ^1-THC). In a quantitative test, the octanol/water partition coefficient of $(-)$-Δ^1-THC was found to be over 500 (Gill et al., 1970) and later was re-ported to be of the order of 6000 (Gill and Jones, 1972).

This physical property of fat solubility is important for biological testing, since it brings with it a very low water solubility. For administration to animals, therefore, it is always necessary to add some suitable solvent or dispersing agent. The vehicles used in the past have included olive oil, sesame oil, alcohol, dimethylformamide, polyethylene glycol, gum arabic, glycerol, Tween 80, blood, serum albumin and PVP* (Fenimore and Loy, 1971). In each experiment it is necessary to ensure that the solvent concerned is not contributing additional actions and is not interfering with the action of some other drug when drug interactions are studied. For example, if one gave cannabis resin in olive oil intraperitoneally in relatively large volume and were studying a barbiturate interaction, the barbiturate could be extracted into the olive oil or (if also given intraperitoneally) be retained by it. The most commonly used vehicles have been olive oil given intraperitoneally, poly-ethylene glycol, or Tween 80–saline given by any chosen route within limits. Tween 80 is a highly surface-active material and causes frothing in isolated organ baths. It has been found (Paton and Pertwee, 1971) that the addition of cannabis resin greatly diminishes the frothing produced by, for instance,

---

* PVP = polyvinylpyrrolidone.

bubbling or shaking a solution of Tween 80, but the cannabis does not reduce the lowering of surface tension at an air–water interface. The state in which cannabis resin or one of its fat-soluble components exists, when carried in a nonlipid vehicle such as Tween 80, is almost certainly of micellar structure. The maximum solubility of THC in water was found to be of the order of 5 μg/ml. In experiments, therefore, in which these micellar suspensions are applied, for concentrations above 5 μg/ml, the micelles need to be regarded as a reservoir from which drug may enter into true solution. This may present problems regarding estimates of potency or of time course of action.

It has been shown that the psychically active principle of cannabis has a limited chemical stability, the two main practical questions being the effects of storage and of smoking. Lerner and Zeffert (1968) noted that the THC content of the outside of a sample of resin was much lower (1.9%) than that of the inside (8.0%), and that a fresh sample of red oil contained 30% Δ^1-THC, whereas an old red oil sample contained only 0.8% THC, mostly as Δ^6. Lerner (1969) suggested, from chemical analysis of samples of marijuana of varying age, that Δ^1-THC content decayed at about 5% per month. A solution of THC in petrol ether cannot be relied on for constant potency for more than about 24 hours, and a dispersion in Tween 80 may lose activity in a few hours (Paton and Pertwee, 1971). If THC is dissolved in a solvent such as carbon tetrachloride with a low tendency to radical formation, and if it is shielded from light and kept under an atmosphere of nitrogen, the stability seems to be adequate for at least some weeks. Valle *et al.* (1966) found that ethanolic solutions of resin, tetrahydrocannabinol, and pyrahexyl retained their activity for months, as tested by abolition of the rabbit blink reflex (see also Chapter 1, Section V,C).

When marijuana or hashish is smoked a number of possible changes may occur. These are discussed in Chapter 1, Section V,B. The better-known processes are (a) decarboxylation of the cannabinoid acids to the respective neutral cannabinoids, a process that in effect increases the amount of Δ^1-THC (Mechoulam, 1970; Yamauchi *et al.*, 1967), and (b) partial oxidation of Δ^1-THC to the inactive cannabinol (Shoyama *et al.*, 1969; Mikes and Waser, 1971). The cyclization of small amounts of cannabidiol to Δ^1-THC has been suggested (Mikes and Waser, 1971) but is yet to be confirmed. The amount of Δ^1-THC delivered from a cigarette to the body has been estimated to be from 2 to 50%, and almost all of the Δ^1-THC inhaled is retained (see Chapter 1 for details and references). The overall effect of these processes clearly depends greatly on the composition of the material and the smoking conditions. It is still not known how the retention and absorption of Δ^1-THC on smoking is distributed over the oropharyngeal and respiratory tracts. Nothing is known at present as to the fate of the other pharmacologically active substances in the resin, although from what is known of cigarette smoke it is to be expected that they too are carried into the body either as vapor or in smoke particles. The position becomes even more complicated with the evidence (Paton and Pertwee, 1972) that cannabidiol can interfere with liver metabolism and hence possibly with the fate of THC in the body.

The observation that cannabis or Δ^1-THC is more active when smoked than when taken orally is only to be expected and would be true for most drugs. By mouth, a drug is diluted by gastrointestinal contents, is exposed to alimentary and hepatic binding sites and enzymes and the pulmonary circulation before reaching the systemic arteries, and has a much spread out absorptive period; in contrast inhaled smoke has direct access to pulmonary capillary blood and reaches the systemic circulation with even less delay than does an intravenous injection.

B. THE PREPARATIONS OF CANNABIS MOST COMMONLY USED

Early work with cannabis was usually done either with crude material, with liquid extract, or with the tincture. The latter was in the "British Pharmacopoeia" for a period, being transferred to the "B.P. Codex" after 1914 and being removed from that after 1949. The preparation of the tincture was standardized as follows. An extract of the plant material was made by percolating with alcohol, then removing the alcohol, to give *extract of cannabis*; this extract, made up 5% by weight in 90% alcohol, constituted the *tincture of cannabis*. Smokers have used the tincture by adding a suitable amount of tobacco, allowing the alcohol to evaporate, and making a cigarette from the resin-impregnated tobacco. Gill *et al.* (1970) and Gill (1971b) have used this material to obtain a tincture base. It has been found (Gill, 1971a) to contain by weight 6.4% of Δ^1-THC, 3.4% of the *n*-propyl analog of Δ^1-THC, and 3.6% cannabidiol. The earlier figures given by Gill *et al.* (1970) for the Δ^1-THC and *n*-propyl analog content refer to the yield of material obtained when isolated from the tincture base, with accompanying preparative losses. The tincture, being an alcoholic extract, occupies an intermediate position between the raw material and the more purified materials obtained by petrol ether or ligroin extraction. The latter excludes more polar substances that appear in an alcoholic extract. Until all the actions of cannabis can be assigned to known substances, such a tincture appears to offer a convenient form of the crude material, freed principally from solid matter. Since the plant material is brought directly into contact with alcohol, and the extract is then kept in alcoholic solution, the fate of unstable constituents may differ from their fate in a block of untreated resin, and the conditions of exposure to oxygen or enzymes are different.

Loewe and his colleagues at first used as a standard the "red oil" obtained from the petrol ether extracts (potency $1.25 \times \Delta^3$-THC), then a more potent redistillate (potency 4.33 × Δ^3-THC), and finally, when it became available, the synthetic tetrahydrocannabinol now designated Δ^3-THC. In the last stages of the chemical work, a very active material was obtained, as the acetate, 16 times as active as Δ^3-THC (Wollner et al., 1942); this must have come close to pure Δ^1-THC. A brief series of articles by Alles and his colleagues (1942a,b) and Haagen-Smit et al. (1940) also included the preparation, by crystallization from methanol–acetic acid, of a material, again as acetate, producing ataxia in the dog at 100 μg/kg; this, too, must have approximated Δ^1-THC. Petrol ether extracts have been used by Valle and his colleagues (1966, 1967, 1968; Valle, 1969; Sampaio and Lapa, 1966), by Carlini and colleagues (Carlini and Kramer, 1965; Carlini, 1968; Salustiano et al., 1966; Silva et al., 1968; Carlini and Goldman, 1968; Carlini and Masur, 1969), and by Siegel and colleagues (Siegel, 1969; Siegel and Poole, 1969). Valle et al. make an extract with petrol ether of the dried powdered flowering heads, pass the extract through charcoal, remove the ether, take up in acetone, leave in the refrigerator for 24 hours to remove waxes, remove the acetone, and take up for use in ethanol. Carlini and associates extract the dried powdered flowering heads with petrol ether, take up with ethanol, and store at 4°C for 24 hours to remove waxes, giving a purification of about 10–11 times. The material used by Bose and his colleagues (1963a,b, 1964a,b), an extract of resin in 90% alcohol, and by Miras and his colleagues (Miras, 1965; Garattini, 1965; Miras et al., 1964), a methanol extract (containing about 30–35% of the original resin), are probably similar in character to the tincture base of cannabis.

It is unfortunately not possible to predict even roughly the amount of THC in an extract, even when its mode of preparation is known. A specimen of hashish may contain from mere traces up to 8% THC, and similar variations are recognized in the activity of cannabis plants from different regions. Under these conditions, very large variations in potency are possible. An interesting study of regional variations has been made by Curry and Patterson (1970) which allows some degree of "fingerprinting" of samples of cannabis. Figure 1 illustrates the main patterns they observed and incidentally shows the very large variations in THC content.

Because of the variations in composition and potency of extracts it is difficult to compare quantitatively the data of different studies. Fortunately, in a number of these the pure substances, Δ^3-THC or its hexyl derivative pyrahexyl, have been used and, in some of the later experiments, estimates of Δ^1-THC content are available. In the absence of these standards, one can only guess, from the doses of extract required to produce the effects studied, how purified the extract was, and thus the data are useful chiefly for their qualitative results.

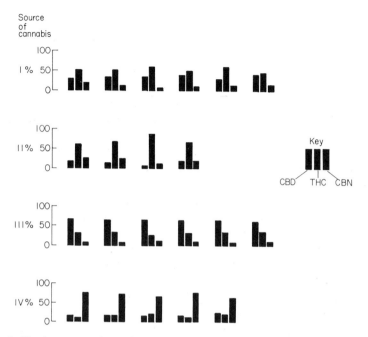

Fig. 1. Varying proportions of cannabidiol (CBD), Δ^1-THC, and cannabinol (CBN) in samples of cannabis from four different regions of the world. (Data from Curry and Patterson, 1970.)

C. The Problem of Bioassay of Cannabis Activity

As with all other impure substances of natural origin, a major problem for investigators has been the assay, necessarily by biological means, of their preparations. For some time a chemical test, the Beam test, assisted in purification, but it was in due course dissociated from the biological activity and in fact reflects mainly the presence of cannabidiol. Any biological effect could be used for such assay, and ataxia, corneal areflexia, analgesia, behavioral changes, synergism with barbiturates, and lethality to small animals or fish have been used for potency comparisons. Of these, the most important, being capable of quantitation with estimates of error, have been dog ataxia, rabbit corneal areflexia, and fish lethality, and these will be discussed in some detail. A recent mouse catalepsy test will also be described. Such assays remain important for assessing the possible contribution of substances other than Δ^1-THC, for comparing the potencies of different chemical structures, and perhaps in the future for giving estimates of potency of material for human use.

1. Dog Ataxia

This test was among those used by Marshall in assaying a number of charas fractions in 1897. It was also described by Dixon in 1899, and in detail, together with photographs of characteristic postures, by Fraenkel in 1903. Walton and his colleagues (1938) improved the test by defining six degrees of ataxia as follows. "First a slight depression; second, a barely recognisable ataxia; third, an obvious ataxia; fourth, a marked ataxia in which the animal frequently pitches forward and barely catches itself; fifth, inability to stand alone; sixth, inability to rise and plunge about." The subdivision into stages allows the time course of action to be followed; Fig. 2 (Walton, 1938) illustrates the gradation with dose of both intensity and duration of action. An excellent account of both the history and the conduct of the test up to 1931 is given by Munch in his textbook on bioassay; this includes the recognition of potency varying with region, of dogs becoming tolerant to cannabis if tested at too frequent intervals, of variability by a factor of at least 7 between different animals, and of the resulting importance of assaying preparations against a standard.

The test was initially conducted by determining the dose that just produced the same degree of response in several dogs as did the standard fluid extract. This did not, however, take any account of the dose–response curve, and therefore did not allow any adequate estimate of the error of the assay. Loewe took up this point and developed a method of successive approximation in which he obtained estimates of potency in relation to a standard (either a red oil, a further purified oil, Δ^3-THC or pyrahexyl) by approaching the true potency ratio from both above and below. From the results obtained, he reported the range of deviation of his assays—usually of the order of ± 5–15%. The actual procedure he used is somewhat cryptically described (Loewe, 1939, 1947), but it appears that he used animals carefully calibrated with a standard preparation and that he gave doses of unknown potency to produce effects bigger than, equal to, or smaller than a standard response. From this he obtained sets of potency ratios, which were estimated to be too high (H), too low (L), or correct (E). The mean of the latter (i.e., potency ratios apparently correct) gave his estimate of potency; the range of potency ratios over which there was overlap in different experiments between correctness (equality: E) and either too high (H) or too low (L) a potency ratio gave his estimate of variability. In a detailed example cited (Loewe, 1947) in which he adapted his data to an ordinary probit analysis, Loewe obtained a standard error of ± 2.54 for a potency ratio of 35, from 57 experiments. It is unfortunate that conventional estimates of error are not available for his data, which are the fullest available; but his method, very similar to that of the "straddling" technique used in bioassay of acetylcholine or histamine, is

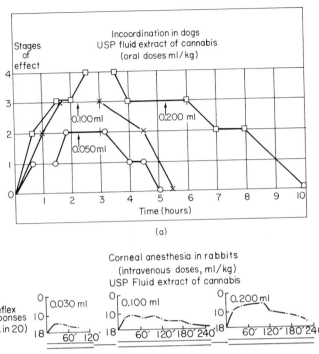

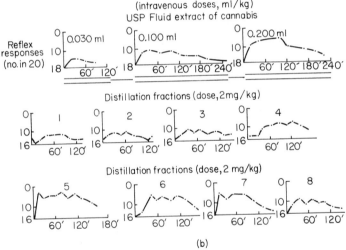

Fig. 2. Intensity and time course of action of fluid extract of cannabis. (a) Incoordination in dogs after oral dosage; (b) corneal areflexia in rabbits after intravenous dosage. (From Walton, 1938.)

relatively safe, because it takes account of the shape of the dose–response curve and probably does not err by more than 20%. A plot of his data (Fig. 3) is useful in showing, incidentally, that the responses in the dog appear to be normally distributed with arithmetic increases in dose and that the dose–response curve is rather flat—one of the chief reasons for the difficulty of precise assay.

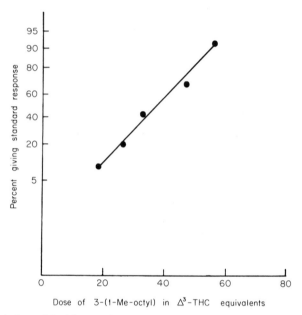

Fig. 3. Variation of incidence of response in dogs with dose of MOP in Δ^3-THC equivalents. Probit-log dose plot used. (Data from Loewe, 1947.)

One aspect hardly studied is that of how far the ataxia response is specific to cannabis, and further work is needed.

2. Rabbit Corneal Reflex

This test was introduced by Gayer (1928) after finding that a rabbit receiving an intravenous injection of cannabis became insensitive to painful stimulation, including a failure of eyelid closure in response to touching the cornea with von Frey hairs (the test was used by Walton; see Fig. 2). Loewe (1944) noted that the response differs from that of local anesthetics in that it is produced only by a systemic action of cannabis and that, although the lid reflex may be abolished, reflex neck muscle movements in response to corneal stimulation may persist. The test has been the subject of some controversy. Loewe was very critical of it, finding that there were large variations both among individual animals and among tests on particular animals and that in most animals susceptibility dwindled with time. Grlić (1962) and Miras (1965) have also found it unsatisfactory. It was used extensively, however, by Todd and his colleagues (Avison *et al.*, 1949), and Valle and his collaborators have improved the technique and have been able to estimate limits of error for their assay.

TABLE I

DATA FROM BIOLOGICAL TESTS USED IN ASSAYING CANNABIS PREPARATIONS

Preparation[a]	Dose to abolish corneal reflex in rabbits (mg/kg iv or relative potency)	Dose to produce ataxia in dogs (relative potency)	Dose to affect aggressiveness in mice (mg/kg)
Partially purified extracts (1, 2, 3, 4, 5)	3–30		
Purified extracts (6)	0.27		2.6
(5)	0.5		
Extract W	0.27		59.5
Extract N (7)	0.28		3.76
Extract C19 Fr 10 (3)	0.03		
Extract	1.10 × pyrahexyl	0.45 × pyrahexyl	
Extract aerated	0.33 × pyrahexyl	0.50 × pyrahexyl	
Wollner extract	1.23 × pyrahexyl	5.54 × pyrahexyl	
Wollner extract aerated (8)	1.22 × pyrahexyl	5.43 × pyrahexyl	
Pyrahexyl (1)	0.68		
(6)	0.83		5.4
(9)	0.03 (50% effect)		
(3)	0.125		
(10)	0.1		
Δ^3-THC (11)	1.0		
(10)	0.3 (acetate, 50% effect)		
(12)	4.6		3.84
(13)	> 32		
Δ^1-THC (1)	0.1		
(8)	0.1		
(12)	0.114		4.25
(14)	~0.5		
Δ^6-THC (14)	~0.5		

[a] References (numbers in parentheses) are as follows:

1. Valle *et al.* (1966)
2. Bose *et al.* (1964a)
3. Valle (1969)
4. Alles *et al.* (1942b)
5. Marx and Eckhardt (1933)
6. Salustiano *et al.* (1966)
7. Santos *et al.* (1966)
8. Loewe (1945a,b)
9. Avison *et al.* (1949)
10. Russell *et al.* (1941b)
11. Russell *et al.* (1941a)
12. Carlini *et al.* (1970)
13. Alles *et al.* (1942a)
14. Valle *et al.* (1968)

Table I shows some of the data available, from which a number of conclusions can be drawn. First, it is clear that a very substantial concentration of the areflexia activity is possible; in the early experiments doses of extract up to 30 mg/kg were required but, with further purification, extracts active at 0.1–0.3 mg/kg have been readily obtained. Second, the substance(s) involved must be quite potent; one of Valle's samples was active at 30 μg/kg. Third, activity appears to be distributed rather generally over purified extracts and the amyl or hexyl tetrahydrocannabinols; potencies of the order of 0.1–0.5 mg/kg are seen with $\varDelta^1$-, $\varDelta^3$-, $\varDelta^6$-THC, and pyrahexyl. There are, however, considerable variations in potency from one investigation to another. Part of this is probably due to the end point chosen; workers who obtained some of the lowest figures (Avison et al., 1949) took an interpolated 50% reduction of the reflex response; other workers (Valle et al., 1966, 1968; Valle, 1969; Santos et al., 1966; Salustiano et al., 1966) took abolition of the response or a reduction of at least 80%. In a particular investigation, however, standard errors of the order of ± 10–20% have been obtained (Valle, 1969).

There are three reasons for believing that there is more than one substance producing ataxia or behavioral change and areflexia. First is the experiment by Loewe (1945a) in which a cannabis extract and the Wollner extract were compared; they were found to be equiactive on the corneal reflex, but the Wollner extract was over 11 times more active by the ataxia test. Santos et al. (1966) obtained a similar result; a purified extract had nearly 16-fold greater potency on mouse aggressiveness, yet this was accompanied by no change in areflexia potency. It is difficult to see how such changes in relative potency can come about if a single substance produces both effects.

Second, Alles et al. (1942b) and Loewe (1945a) showed that the areflexia principle is proportionately more labile. Alles et al. found that it disappeared more readily on storage and was vulnerable to bubbling with air at 50°C. Loewe found that aeration had no effect on ataxia potency, whether a crude or highly purified (Wollner) extract was used; nor did it affect the areflexia potency of the Wollner extract, but it greatly reduced that of the crude extract. This last experiment also gives an estimate of the areflexia potency of $\varDelta^1$-THC, since the Wollner extract must have been not far from pure $\varDelta^1$-THC. Again, it seems that there must have been some substance other than THC present in the crude extract which was chiefly responsible for the areflexia. A problem is raised by the ataxia results, since $\varDelta^1$-THC would be expected to have been at least partly converted to the inactive cannabinol under the conditions of aeration described. Because of their variability, both the areflexia and ataxia assays need to be evaluated with caution. Even so, it must be noted that the differential lability was found by two groups of workers. It may be that some factor stabilizing $\varDelta^1$-THC was present or that a limited conversion occurred, say up to 20%, which was within the error of assay. The main point, however, is that the biological experiments provide some evidence for a greater lability to oxidation of the areflexia principle.

Third, there is the general point made by Loewe that over a range of substances there is a very large dissociation between the two potencies. Thus the *n*-heptyl derivative of Δ^3-THC was 10 times as active on areflexia as Δ^3-THC but only 1.05 times as active on ataxia. Extract 33 was equiactive with Δ^3-THC on areflexia but 8.66 times as active on ataxia. Similarly, the *n*-propyl Δ^3-THC had less than 5% of the areflexia potency of Δ^3-THC but 40% of the ataxia potency. The last results do not exclude the possibility of one molecule having both actions to a significant degree, but if it had not been shown that different structures could vary in their relative activities by these tests, some doubt would hang over the other evidence for the existence of different active substances in the extract.

Carlini *et al.* (1970) have taken the discussion further. They showed, first, with the compounds Δ^1-, Δ^3-THC, Todd's THC, and a tetrahydrodibenzopyran "Sy-Bi" that, as the chemical structure deviated from that of Δ^1-THC, areflexia was lost first, then catatonia and effect on motor activity, and, last, the effect on aggressiveness. Such an analysis depends largely on the compounds selected. Second, they showed, for five different extracts, that Δ^1-THC content correlated best with areflexia activity and quite well with catatonia; depression of motor activity and aggression correlated poorly. They did not examine dog ataxia. Analyzing their work, and comparing it with previous studies, they concluded that of the tests they used only the Gayer test was a useful procedure for measuring Δ^1-THC and that the failure of one of the extracts to have the depressant effect on motor activity expected from its Δ^1-THC content resulted from the presence of a stimulant antagonist, possibly cannabidiol. Their results are a little difficult to interpret because of the difference in ED_{50} dose levels of Δ^1-THC in their various tests: 0.114 mg/kg for areflexia, 18.8 mg/kg for motor activity, 37.2 mg/kg for catatonia, and 4.25 mg/kg for aggressiveness. The way the drugs are dealt with in the body, and the contribution by interfering substances, could vary considerably over the 300-fold range of doses involved. But their work underlines the possibility that the differences in properties of extracts may reflect variations in the content of substances that are antagonist as well as of those that are agonist in the various tests.

The identity of the crude extract areflexia substance is obscure. Neither cannabidiol (Valle *et al.*, 1968; Loewe, 1946a) nor cannabinol (Loewe, 1946a) could account for it. Its lability may hinder its identification. For the time being, the corneal reflex remains the only test for the active principle concerned; the articles by Valle give the fullest account of the details of a suitable technique. It is interesting that, in the most active preparations, the areflexia substance is over 100 times as active as morphine in the same test and much more active than reserpine, thiopentone, chlorpromazine, promethazine, LSD, or bulbocapnine (Valle *et al.*, 1967).

3. Ichthyotoxicity

The potency of extracts of cannabis has been assayed by the toxicity to 3–5 gm goldfish in 1 liter tank of water, the time to death shortening with increased potency. Loewe (1944) found, for example, that a concentration of 200 μg/ml of an extract with 52% of the potency of Δ^3-THC produced death in 68 minutes, but he did not use the test extensively. Duquénois (1939, 1950) tried goldfish, minnows, and sticklebacks, as well as tadpoles, earthworms, and other helminths, and obtained changes in swimming movements and ultimately death with 1 mg of resin in 80 ml water. Valle et al. (1967) have developed the test using guppies (*Lebistes reticulatis*). For assay, the percent mortality after 24 hours in groups of 20 guppies in 300 ml tap water is recorded to obtain the LD_{50}. Changes in reflectivity, pigmentation, motility, and swimming movements are also noted. Successive purifications of resin leads to increasing toxicity to guppies (from 15 μg/ml LD_{50} to 3 μg/ml), and the test shows Δ^1-THC to be more active than pyrahexyl. Positive tests are also given by concentrations of 2–5 μg/ml of reserpine, bulbocapnine, LSD-25, chlorpromazine (among other drugs), and the specificity of the response is still obscure. Valle (1969) noted that the resin maintains its ichthyotoxicity even after "being submitted to a prolonged flux of water steam," so that yet another substance may be responsible for this action.

4. Mouse Ring Immobility Assay

This method exploits an effect, shared by cannabis extracts and first noted by Loewe (1946a) for pyrahexyl or Δ^3-THC, that after adequate dosage a mouse placed in a prone position supported only by its thighs and jaws maintains this extended position until aroused. Pertwee (1972) has developed an assay based on the percentage of time spent immobile on a horizontal ring of 5.5 cm diameter during a 5-minute exposure. Cannabis tincture base is active in doses upwards of 100 mg/kg ip and 25 mg/kg iv; Δ^1-THC is active at 10 mg/kg ip and lower doses iv. The response (loosely referred to as "cataleptic") lasts for an hour or more depending on dose and route; with subcutaneous injections, the response develops slowly and may last over 12 hours. The response is dose related. Comparison of the tincture base, Δ^1-THC, and propyl-THC gave parallel dose–response curves; the THC content of the resin was adequate to account for its cataleptic effect. With suitably designed experiments, using randomized Latin square replications, limits of error of potency ratios can be obtained.

This characteristic behavior on the ring is not reproduced by barbiturates, but it is by chlorpromazine. If necessary, cannabis type of action can be distinguished from chlorpromazine by other features of its pharmacological profile, in particular its low activity in diminishing amphetamine toxicity (Salustiano et al., 1966).

5. Conclusions

Of the assays used, the dog ataxia and the mouse ring catalepsy test have been found both to provide estimates of error and to assess THC-like activity, and under particular circumstances (Carlini *et al.*, 1970) the Gayer test can do the same. Qualitative verification that particular compounds have a cannabislike action is possible by many other methods, including the use of monkeys (Scheckel *et al.*, 1968; Mechoulam *et al.*, 1970a,b; Grunfeld and Edery, 1969), gerbils (Grunfeld and Edery, 1969), and pigeon behavior (Frankenheim *et al.*, 1970). Although attention at present focuses on Δ^1-THC, the other assays are likely to be needed to investigate further aspects of cannabis pharmacology. It seems probable that, at present, no one assay is sufficient by itself if one wishes not only to assess relative potency, but also unequivocally to characterize an action as "cannabislike." The suggestion made earlier, of using a compound's "profile," however, should meet the need.

II. Actions of Cannabis

There is some difficulty in attempting a classification of these actions. The procedure here adopted will be to take certain broad fields of study (behavioral, electrophysiological, hypothalamic and endocrine, and general pharmacology) and to review the information about different species under these headings.

A. Behavioral and Experimental Psychology

In interpreting the phenomena now to be mentioned, some caution is necessary. Cannabis may affect hunger and thirst; it produces a cataleptoid state; there is some evidence that it changes sensory thresholds; it produces hypothermia; and fearfulness is not uncommonly reported. The change of response in some behavioral or psychological test is therefore the resultant of possible interactions between changes in drive, learning, aversion, perception, general neuromuscular coordination, and the general physiological state induced by the drug.

1. Monkeys

Scheckel *et al.* (1968) were the first to give an adequate account of the effects of THC (Δ^1- and Δ^6-THC as racemates) intraperitoneally using squirrel and rhesus monkeys. Squirrel monkeys given 4 or 8 mg/kg Δ^1-THC sat quietly with head down, seeming to peer at the apparatus. Doses of 16 mg/kg caused the monkeys to walk about, apparently hallucinating, or to crouch with heads moving from side to side or up and down as if watching some moving object. Some animals had blank expressions and gazed into space. With doses of 32 or 64 mg/kg, this apparent hallucinatory reaction was more obvious; the animals seemed to be in a state of panic, fighting imaginary objects, attempting to grasp what was not there. Movements were rapid, well coordinated, and associated with fine hand tremors. The animals tended to maintain one or two limbs in an unusual position and to look intently at wide-opened hands. Low doses took 1 hour to show their effect; higher doses were active in 20 minutes. The stimulant phase persisted about 3 hours and was followed by a period of depression, when the animals were crouched and almost motionless, lasting 1–2 days, occasionally for a week. Similar results, but shorter lasting since intravenous injection was used, were obtained by McIsaac et al. (1971).

In the rhesus monkey, Scheckel et al. noted only a loss of alertness and activity, without loss of appetite. Grunfeld and Edery (1969) give a fuller account of effects in rhesus monkeys given THC (Δ^1-THC, 100 μg/kg; Δ^6-THC, 500 μg/kg; and hexyl-Δ^6-THC, 500 μg/kg) intravenously. The animals became drowsy within 10 minutes; drowsiness was followed by ptosis, intermittent head drop abolished by noise, and reduction of motor activity. The animals assumed a typical posture termed the "thinker position," with a typical blank gaze, remaining thus for 1–1½ hours if undisturbed. Aggressive animals were tamed, grasping reflex was reduced but present, and offered food was not taken. The animals came round in about 3 hours. Injected conjunctivae were also observed (Mechoulam et al., 1970a) Lower doses produced smaller and briefer effects. The doses required to produce these effects in monkeys are smaller than those usually reported as necessary in other animals and comparable with those required in man (Isbell et al., 1967).

Scheckel et al. (1968) also found, in the squirrel monkey, that Δ^1-THC racemate in doses of 4 or 8 mg decreased the response rate by about 50% in a continuous avoidance procedure (involving lever pressing to postpone electric shocks to the feet, such that a response every 40 seconds avoided any shocks). However, with higher doses, lever pressing was often increased, possibly as a result of the general stimulant effect. It is interesting that Δ^6-THC racemate lacked the depressant effect of Δ^1-THC but shared the stimulant effect. In a further test in which an automatic gradual increase of shock stimulus strength was set back by the animal's response, both drugs in doses of 4–8 mg/kg tended to increase shock tolerance; it was doubtful if this was a purely analgesic effect or rather the result of a more variable performance. During this procedure, all the animals receiving Δ^1-THC vomited within 1 hour of receiving the drug; those that received Δ^6-THC did not. Finally, in the rhesus monkey, low doses of Δ^1-THC produced marked effects on a delayed matching response in which in fasted animals a food reward was given when a lever corresponding to a color (red or green) seen previously at a variable interval (up to around 60–100 seconds) was pressed. Figure 4 shows the effect of 4 mg/kg on the response. There was almost complete abolition on the first day; the response was still depressed on the seventh day after injection but normal on the ninth day. Effects were detectable with doses down to 250 μg/kg. The recovery from 4 mg/kg is shown in

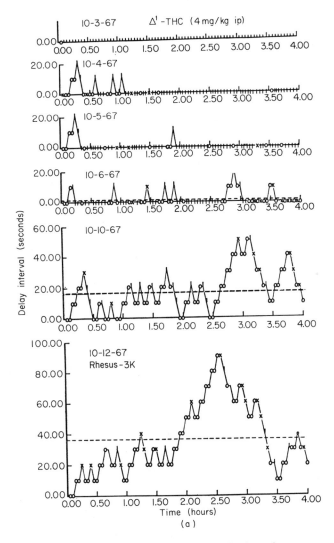

Fig. 4. See following page for legend.

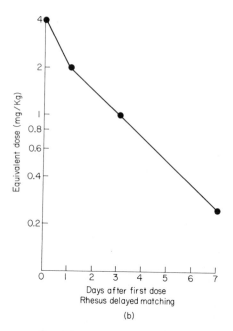

Days after first dose
Rhesus delayed matching

(b)

Fig. 4. (a) The long-term effect of one intraperitoneal dose of Δ^1-THC, 4 mg/kg ip, on a rhesus monkey in the delayed matching procedure. Open circles, correct response; x, an incorrect match; short vertical lines, failures to respond; dashed horizontal lines, average level of performance in that session. The responses in the second, fourth, and fifth panels were equivalent to those produced by 2, 1, and 0.25 mg/kg, respectively; that in the last panel was normal. (b) Plot of the recovery curve, expressed as the equivalent dose still remaining in the body, from the data of (a). (From Scheckel *et al.*, 1968.)

Fig. 4a, and on the appropriate panels have been inserted the doses corresponding to the effects at that stage. Figure 4b shows the exponential nature of the recovery. The Δ^6-THC had similar actions, but the effects lasted less than 3 days.

2. Dogs

There have been many descriptions of the effects of cannabis in dogs and of the ataxia assay derived from the earliest studies (Dixon, 1899; Chopra and Chopra, 1957; Marx and Eckhardt, 1933; Loewe, 1944, 1946a; Walton, 1938; Munch, 1931; Grunfeld and Edery, 1969; Dewey *et al.*, 1970d; Bose *et al.*, 1964a; Fraenkel, 1903). The general picture is as follows. Initially there may be some excitement and barking, and retching, vomiting, salivation, urination, or defecation may occur. Mydriasis may occur but is not constant. Then follows the state characterized by the ataxia described earlier, swaying of the head and body, twitching of muscles, awkward gait and slipping of the feet, reduced activity with a tendency to stand in one spot, head sinking lower and lower and then suddenly being jerked back again, and a tolerance of abnormal postures. Very characteristic is useless scratching (sometimes evoked simply by calling), which is seemingly continued for lack of will to stop. The animal is relatively unresponsive to discomfort or mild painful stimuli, yet can be completely but transiently aroused to a state near normality. The corneal reflex is said not to be abolished (Bose *et al.*, 1964a). A bad-tempered dog becomes docile, yet some animals appear to become fearful. Finally, the animal tends to go to sleep for some hours and to sleep more than usual for 24 hours.

The stimulant effects are commoner with intravenous administration. The duration of the main ataxia phase depends on dose (see Fig. 2) but ranges from 1 to 2 hours and above. Onset of action is prompt intravenously (within 10 minutes) but may take ¾–1 hour for oral administration. With intraperitoneal injection, an excitement phase occurs lasting about 10 minutes before depression and ataxia develop. Responses are very variable. The best illustration of this is the data given by Loewe (Fig. 3) in his study of the 1-methyloctyl homolog of Δ^3-THC (MOP) in which the dose had to be increased about threefold to pass from a 10 to a 90% incidence of standard ataxia response. Similarly, Fig. 2 shows how increasing the dose of a cannabis extract fourfold affects duration of action principally, and carries the animal only from stage 1 to stage 4 ataxia at peak effect. Threshold doses of Δ^1-THC for the dog are in the range 0.2–0.5 mg/kg intravenously (Dewey *et al.*, 1970d; Grunfeld and Edery, 1969).

The question of repeated dosage is discussed later. Munch (1931) noted that dogs retain a constant sensitivity unless tested too frequently; any temporary tolerance disappears after a week. Loewe (1944) allowed 3-day intervals between tests.

3. Cats

Effects of cannabis in cats were reported very early, but they were not followed up because of the lack of specific characteristics (Loewe, 1946a; Chopra and Chopra, 1957; Gayer, 1928; Dixon, 1899; Walton, 1938; Lipparini *et al.*, 1969; Munch, 1931; Hockman *et al.*, 1971). Some stimulation may occur in the early stages, with photophobia and high-pitched cries; salivation, retching, and vomiting occur (Walton, 1938; Hockman *et al.*, 1971) but seem less common than with dogs. Hockman *et al.* comment that the animals seemed oblivious of having vomited and defecated and sat in their excrement. The animal becomes less active and may go to sleep; ataxia, swaying, catatonia, snakelike movements, head nodding, and clumsiness are present but are less prominent than in the dog. Gayer (1928) found that corneal anesthesia was produced at about the same dose per unit body weight as in the rabbit, but Loewe (1946a) states that corneal areflexia is specific to the rabbit. Mydriasis throughout the whole period of intoxication has been reported (Lipparini et al., 1969; Hockman et al., 1971). The variability of response is as great in cats as in other species. Its sensitivity in comparison with other animals has not been defined; it is said to be about the same as or somewhat less sensitive than in dogs, less sensitive than in rabbits. Doses of 2 mg/kg of Δ^1-THC intraperitoneally produce a pronounced effect lasting 5–6 hours (Lipparini et al., 1969). Hunger during recovery was also noted (Lipparini et al., 1969). In an instrumental reward discrimination task, performance was disrupted by 2 mg/kg ip.

4. Rabbits

Among the effects in rabbits (Lipparini et al., 1969; Walton, 1938; Munch, 1931; Gayer, 1928; Marx and Eckhardt, 1933; Carlini et al., 1970; Geber and Schramm, 1969b), the corneal areflexia discovered by Gayer and already discussed has been the effect most often considered. But other typical actions have also been described: legs slipping (so that the animal crouches on its belly), clumsiness of movement, ataxia, head nodding, apparent fearfulness, hypersensitivity to acoustic stimuli and arousability, and tolerance of abnormal postures. Alternation of periods of immobility with periods of agitation occurs (Lipparini et al., 1969), and restlessness, hyperpnea, mydriasis, and exophthalmos have been observed. The corneal insensitivity was noted by Gayer as part of a general insensitivity to painful stimuli. Doses of 0.5–1 mg/kg Δ^1-THC iv are effective; after a dose of 2 mg/kg, effects lasted 5–6 hours (Lipparini et al., 1969).

5. Rats

Cannabis produces a reduction of spontaneous activity in rats (Lipparini et al., 1969; Garattini, 1965; Forney, 1971). However, Garattini (1965) found no other clear-cut effects from doses of extract adequate to produce other actions on tests of the Irwin type (Irwin, 1968): curiosity, reactivity, irritability, response to pain, muscle tone, and corneal, pinnal, or righting reflexes. Lomax (1971) also failed to find behavioral effects. Joachimoglu (1965), Carlini and Kramer (1965), and Moreton and Davis (1970) noted a first stage of excitement. Grunfeld and Edery (1969) found that 20 mg/kg Δ^1-THC made rats flaccid and ataxic and showed that the gait (as measured by the technique of Rushton et al., 1963) showed a more variable splay. The animals became cataleptic (Grunfeld and Edery, 1969; Lipparini et al., 1969; Carlini and Kramer, 1965); this effect is detectable with 3 mg/kg Δ^1-THC ip and is substantial and prolonged at 20 mg/kg (Grunfeld and Edery, 1969). In the early stages appetite may be increased, but looking for food is reduced in the depression phase of the response (Carlini and Kramer, 1965). With a dose of 80 mg/kg, jumping movements, circling, walking backward, and well-developed catalepsy occur (Schildkraut and Efron, 1971). The related compound, pyrahexyl (Abel and Schiff, 1969), caused reduction of food but not of water intake. With the latter compound (Abel, 1970), by the "open field" technique, activity was increased at lower doses and decreased at higher, rearing was reduced, and grooming and defecation were unchanged. In a test for curiosity (Abel and Schiff, 1969), although the frequency of nose poking into an aperture was unchanged, the time spent at the aperture was increased. Possibly related to the stimulant effect at the lower doses is the vocalization when the animal is touched, detectable at 1.5 mg/kg (Henriksson and Järbe, 1971).

In test procedures, treatment with Δ^1-THC or with an extract of cannabis smoke impairs the conditioned avoidance response (Grunfeld and Edery, 1969; Vieira *et al.*, 1967; Bailey *et al.*, 1971; Boyd *et al.*, 1963), without reducing the unconditioned response (Grunfeld and Edery, 1969). Rope climbing was not reduced by single doses of extract (20 mg/kg ip; Carlini, 1968), but was impaired after further daily dosage. In the same study, bar pressing for a water reward in an operant behavior test was, however, reduced by a first dose of 25 mg/kg. Bar pressing for food reward and responding with hypothalamic self-stimulation are also usually depressed (Bailey *et al.*, 1971). In a maze test, Carlini and Kramer (1965) found that a series of daily injections of extract (10 mg/kg ip), given 3 minutes before trial in a Lashley maze after a set of runs in a training box, improved performance, whereas animals that received the same injection 30 seconds after the trial showed a prolonged running time. In addition, in 5 out of 32 rats, a gross disruption of performance occurred. The timing of the trials in relation to the injection in these experiments was such that the first group (Group II in the paper) would be in the stimulant phase of cannabis action. Higher doses were not given because of a possible depressant action, but it seems likely that in the second group (Group III in the paper) of animals, depression was present due to cumulation of successive doses. Garattini (1965) showed a slight reduction of learning in suckling rats.

An interesting experiment by Jaffe and Baum (1971) showed that, in rats trained to conditioned avoidance of electric shock to the feet, cannabis extract, 62.6 or 125 mg/kg, could considerably delay extinction of the response. This could have represented a magnified fear, an alteration in perception, or a delay in learning a new response during the period of extinction.

An interesting series of experiments by Carlini and his colleagues (Carlini and Goldman, 1968; Carlini and Masur, 1969) has shown that chronic treatment with cannabis extract can produce aggressiveness in rats. They had noted increased aggressiveness in earlier chronic experiments in which hunger drive had been used in maze and rope-climbing tasks, yet in a deliberate test for effect on aggression they found that it was reduced by cannabis administered for short periods of time to fed rats. They therefore devised a procedure combining food restriction and cannabis treatment. In this the animals received cannabis intraperitoneally and were then tested at some time during the following 2 hours for aggressiveness; thereafter, but for 2 hours only, they had access to food. Thus, treated animals had access to food while they were still under the effects of a recent cannabis injection and after the test for aggression. Using this regime Carlini and his colleagues found that after 15–18 daily injections spontaneous fighting occurred between animals, starting 30–40 minutes after the injection and lasting 2–4 hours. If the animals were fed before the test or did not receive cannabis, there was no fighting. If the animals were starved but did not receive cannabis until a single injection on the 23rd day, no fighting occurred. If the animals were both starved and cannabis treated for 22 days, and on the 23rd day the animals were fed, cannabis on that day did not elicit aggressiveness. It is clear, therefore, that both relative starvation and chronic cannabis treatment are required for the effect. As measures of aggressiveness, numbers of fights, duration of fighting, and fighting induced by electric shock were used; with the latter method, increase in aggressiveness could be shown after only 7 days of treatment. The effect was most striking in females, but it was shown that this was probably due to body weight difference compared to males; males and females of equal weight showed equal aggressiveness. It was also found that environmental temperature had a profound effect; with temperatures around 15°–18°C aggressiveness appeared after only 1–2 days of treatment, whereas above 22°C aggressiveness appeared after 8–16 days of treatment. The threshold dose for the effect was of the order of 5 mg/kg ip; 10–20 mg/kg produced a big effect in eight daily injections.

Finally, Carlini and his associates showed that caffeine, amphetamine, or amytal did not produce this aggressiveness and that even in a cannabis-treated rat, in which the effect had been developed, it could not be elicited by mescaline, LSD, or amphetamine. The whole phenomenon is of considerable interest, particularly since it differs from other responses such as ataxia, catalepsy, and hypothermia in that repeated doses of cannabis, so far from producing tolerance, are required to evoke the effect.

One general comment also arises from these experiments. They show that food intake is deeply connected with cannabis action. In many of the experiments described earlier in this section, hunger drive was used, and it must be borne in mind that the cannabis may have been acting by changing the effective stimulus to, as much as the response by, the animal. In an analogous way, the ataxia and cataleptoid phenomena and the fearfulness and hyperreactivity may also change the effective stimulus in other tests.

6. *Mice*

Lethality of hashish extracts in mice was early used for assay, but the first account of other action in the species was written by Gayer (1928). He found 0.3 mg crude resin to be active, causing a fall in motor activity, catalepsy, corneal anesthesia, and he succeeded in taming a wild gray house mouse. He also noted arousability. Many other investigators have also noted a fall in spontaneous motor activity (Garattini, 1965; Garriott *et al.*, 1967, 1968; Holtzman *et al.*, 1969; Grunfeld and Edery, 1969; Dewey *et al.*, 1970d; Vieira *et al.*, 1967; Christensen *et al.*, 1971; Santos *et al.*, 1966), produced both by cannabis extracts and by Δ^1-THC, although some workers (Garriott *et al.*, 1967, 1968) have also noted a subsequent relative increase in spontaneous exploratory behavior when compared with controls (Fig. 5). By Irwin-type tests, little effect may be seen (Garattini, 1965), but ataxia (Holtzman *et al.*, 1969), catalepsy (Valle, 1969; Loewe, 1946a), hyperreactivity, especially to high tones (Holtzman *et al.*, 1969; Christensen *et al.*, 1971; Vieira *et al.*, 1967), aggression (Vieira *et al.*, 1967), or an initial phase of excitement (Joachimoglu and Miras, 1963) have been described. Ptosis (Grunfeld and Edery, 1969), narrowing of palpebral fissure (Vieira *et al.*, 1967), piloerection (Grunfeld and Edery, 1969), and diarrhea with high doses

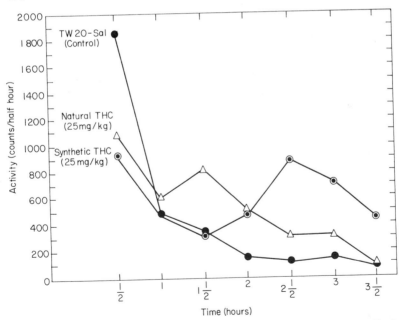

Fig. 5. The effect of "natural THC" (Δ^1-THC) and "synthetic THC" (Δ^3-THC) given ip on activity in mice compared with control injection. Note that with control injection, initial exploratory activity is high and falls away; the drugs greatly reduce initial activity, but it is greater than normal later. (From Garriott *et al.*, 1967.)

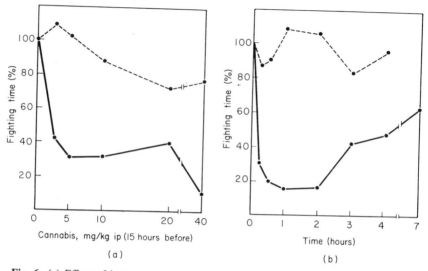

Fig. 6. (a) Effect of increasing amounts of marijuana extract on spontaneous motor activity (O----O) and on isolation-induced aggressiveness (O——O) of fighter mice. (b) Time course of action of 10 mg/kg extract ip on aggressiveness. (From Santos et al. 1966.)

(Loewe, 1946a) occur. Loewe (1946a) noted that motor excitation, with running, jumping, dancing, and pugnacity, could appear in particular mice even with very small doses of extract. As the dose increases, depression and sleep increase, with ultimate paralysis and death (Vieira et al., 1967). The cataleptic response has been developed into an assay procedure (Gill et al., 1970; Pertwee, 1972). Certain behavior, i.e., the Straub tail response, a crouched posture and gait, and provoked "freezing," have been likened to the responses to opiates (Christensen et al., 1971; Buxbaum et al., 1969).

In test situations, cannabis and Δ^1-THC impair performance on a rotating rod (Grunfeld and Edery, 1969; Joachimoglu, 1965; Joachimoglu and Miras, 1963) or swimming (Joachimoglu, 1965). A number of studies on experimentally induced aggression have been made. The fighting of mice previously isolated for about 4 weeks was reduced by doses of extracts (Miras type) of 100 mg/kg ip upwards, and 200 mg/kg matched 10 mg/kg chlordiazepoxide. Santos et al. (1966), using the aggression of a 20-hour isolated animal against an intruder, found that cannabis was much more potent in reducing aggression than in depressing motor activity (Fig. 6). The effect on aggression was maximal (over 80% inhibition) at about 1 hour after intraperitioneal injection and lasted over 7 hours, with a dose affecting spontaneous activity less than 20%. In a subsequent article by the same group (Salustiano et al., 1966) the cannabis extract with an ED_{50} against aggression of 2.6 mg/kg was about as active as chlorpromazine, twice as active as pyrahexyl, and more active than reserpine, chlordiazepoxide, benactyzine, and meprobamate. It was also noted that, at effective doses in this test, chlorpromazine greatly reduced spontaneous activity, unlike cannabis.

Finally, an interesting study in "social pharmacology" was reported by Siegel and Poole (1969). If mice treated with Δ^1-THC (2–10 mg/kg ip) or an extract (50–100 mg/kg ip) were introduced into a normal colony of 40–50 mice, they retreated from investigation, did not fight back against a dominant inhabitant, and stayed huddled together in a separate place. The effect lasted 6–8 hours, and the animals seemed hypersensitive. If the whole group were treated, they tended to disperse, avoiding contact with each other; if a fight started, it incited the whole colony to disoriented activity, but only for a short time. Dominance relationships were unaltered. If an untreated stranger was introduced, it was ignored, and its investigation could produce squealing and flight. These effects were similar to those produced by LSD and bufotenine, but cannabis had a considerable sedative effect which reduced the animals' activity.

It should be remembered that cannabis lowers the body temperature, particularly in mice (see later) and that hypothermia itself affects behavior.

7. Pigeons

There is less information on the general effect of cannabis or Δ^1-THC on birds, but McMillan *et al.* (1970a) noted that 2 hours after a large dose of 36 mg/kg im a pigeon could not stand, walk, or fly normally and refused food; after 8 hours, it lay on the cage floor with labored respiration, stood again at 48 hours, but did not eat until 72 hours after the injection. In a visual discrimination task (Siegel, 1969) requiring conditional responding to form and color for a food reward (the pigeons being maintained at 70% of their free-feeding weight), doses of extract at 20 mg/kg upwards slowed the time to complete a trial, and led to errors in which response appropriate to color predominated; color stimulation itself involved few errors. The effect of LSD was similar, and the authors suggest that the animals may have been reporting colored perceptual events when no color stimulus was present. With a test using operant conditioning with a multiple fixed-ratio, fixed-interval schedule of food presentation (Ford and McMillan, 1971; McMillan *et al.*, 1970a), Δ^1-THC in a dose of 1.8 mg/kg im eliminated the response for up to 7 hours and the effect of 5.6 mg/kg lasted 48 hours. Repeated injections led to a rapidly developing tolerance. The dimethylheptyl homolog of Δ^3-THC (DMHP) (0.3 mg/kg) and pyrahexyl (10 mg/kg) are also effective (Black *et al.*, 1970). The Δ^1-THC was found to be twice as potent as Δ^6-THC; Δ^1-THC did not produce the increase in key-pecking rates seen with barbiturates, amphetamines, and narcotics (Frankenheim *et al.*, 1970).

8. Other Animals

Guinea pigs were reported as unsuitable for assay of cannabis (Walton, 1938), and Loewe (1946a) noted that doses required to produce motor effects are higher than in rabbits and much higher than in dogs, and that excitement phenomena are rare. Hamsters receiving a ligroin extract of New Jersey marijuana (Geber and Schramm, 1969a) were calmed. Offered fresh carrot, normally active and curious hamsters receiving low doses (25–50 mg/kg sc) ate normally but did not maintain interest as long as controls; with high doses, they responded more slowly, less aggressively, and became disinterested. The effects of high doses were gone within 24 hours. With another extract (from Mexican marijuana) they were not calmed but excited for several hours. Overall, feeding and drinking habits were not impaired after these initial effects. Digging activity of gerbils was found (Grunfeld and Edery, 1969) to be inhibited by 10 mg/kg Δ^1-THC intraperitoneally; decrease of spontaneous activity and a cataleptic state from which they could be aroused by finger clicking or touching to a transient state of hyperexcitability were also seen. The animals recovered within 2 hours. The Δ^6-THC was roughly half as active. Pyrahexyl (Walters and Abel, 1970) in a dose of 2.3 mg/kg ip slightly speeded the acquisition of conditioned avoidance response and diminished response latency. The authors suggest that pyrahexyl increases the probability of "emitting a prepotent response." Frogs receiving 15 mg/20 gm body weight (Goodall, 1910) were profoundly narcotized, up to 48 hours, but cannabis did not appear to be toxic. The pupils were usually contracted. Duquénois (1950) outlined the effects of extracts on tadpoles, minnows, sticklebacks, earthworms and ascaris. Valle has reviewed effects on fish, for the purpose of assay (Valle et al., 1967; Valle, 1969).

B. NEUROLOGICAL EFFECTS

1. Electroencephalographic Studies

The earliest studies in animals are those of Williams et al. (1946), who found that, in acute spinal cats recovered from anesthesia, the inhalation of marijuana smoke caused the slower cortical rhythm (6–9 per second) to disappear and spontaneous muscle activity to appear in the temporalis muscle. This effect could also be interpreted as an arousal due to the irritant effect of the smoke. More concentrated smoke produced a marked slowing of cortical rhythms, but anoxia may have contributed to the effect. Bose et al. (1964a), using an alcoholic extract (Bose et al., 1963b) active in the dog ataxia test at 2.5 mg/kg, studied the electroencephalographic (EEG) changes in rabbits. The normal frontal EEG frequency (7–12.2 cps) was increased during the first half hour after 15–30 mg/kg of drug iv and subsequently decreased with recovery over 5 hours, during which time bursts of sharp waves of

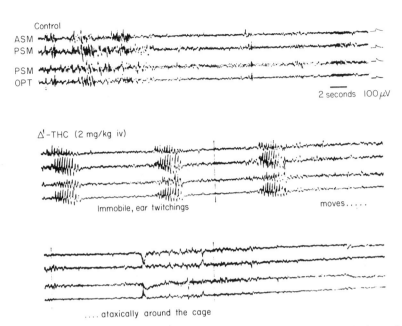

Control

ASM
PSM
PSM
OPT

2 seconds 100 μV

Δ^1-THC (2 mg/kg iv)

Immobile, ear twitchings   moves......

.... ataxically around the cage

Fig. 7. Effects of Δ^1-THC on EEG of rabbit with chronically implanted electrodes in anterior and posterior sensorimotor cortex (ASM, PSM) and optic cortex (OPT). Thirty minutes after 2 mg/kg iv, flattening of the tracing and spike-and-wave pattern are observed. (From Lipparini *et al.*, 1969.)

frequency 10–14 cps and increasing voltage appeared. In the parietal area (normal frequency 6.4–7.1 cps) slower activity (1.5–4.6 cps) of δ type occurred in the first hour, followed by a reduction of frequency, and then recovery with bursts of sharp waves. Bicher and Mechoulam (1968) showed that Δ^1- and Δ^6-THC, in a dose (8 mg/kg iv) in rabbits producing restlessness and increased motor activity, caused an acceleration of cortical activity, a lowering of threshold to electrical arousal by midbrain reticular stimulation, and prolongation of the duration of the arousal.

The fullest studies of this kind have been those of Lipparini *et al.* (1969), who combined EEG with behavioral tests. In the rabbit with chronically implanted electrodes, 0.5–1 mg/kg Δ^1- and Δ^6-THC iv produced a general reduction of voltage of EEG waves and disappearance of the theta (3½–8 cps) waves of the hippocampus. Spike-and-wave complexes appeared 15–20 minutes later (Fig. 7), at first isolated, but later (with high doses) almost continuous. Periods of agitation and ataxic movement around the cage, which were accompanied by a flattened EEG, alternated with periods of depression and immobility during which spikes and waves were more frequent, with some ear twitchings. Behavioral changes lasted for 5–6 hours after a dose of 2 mg/kg, but the spike and waves and flattening of the tracing disappeared much earlier, leaving only a marked synchronization in the later stages of the effect. In acute preparations, Δ^1-THC impaired, or in high doses abolished, the EEG activation due to reticular stimulation, although it did not alter the afterdischarge following stimulation of the dorsal hippocampus. With rats, a similar flattening of the EEG with bursts of 3- to 4-cps waves appeared after 10 mg/kg ip.

In cats, the effects were milder, consisting (with doses up to 6 mg/kg ip) of only a moderate synchronization of the EEG easily interrupted by stimuli and accompanied by reduced spontaneous mobility and sleepiness. Although conditional cues were ignored, other stimuli produced an arousal reaction with a different hypersynchronous component resembling the deactivation pattern seen with small doses of barbiturates. Hockman et al. (1971) have also observed this pattern of hypersynchronous activity, alternating with a sleep pattern or sometimes giving way to 5- to 100-second bursts of 2–3/second high-voltage waves. The hypersynchronous episodes were associated with staring into space or the apparent following of "nonexistent" stimuli.

Further studies in the rat (Masur and Khazan, 1970), in which sleep, REM sleep, and wakefulness had been correlated with EEG and electromyographic (EMG) activity, showed that crude cannabis and Δ^6-THC caused the appearance of bursts of large spike discharges (8–12 cps, up to 600 μV) immediately; these declined during the awake state but reappeared at the end of sleeping periods, overriding the electrical records of the REM sleep states that followed. It was suggested that cannabis facilitates rhythmic EEG bursts which correspond to the pontine–geniculate–occipital (PGO) activity preceding REM sleep in the cat. Further studies (Moreton and Davis, 1970) in rats with electrodes chronically implanted over frontal cortex, dorsal hippocampus, and neck muscles and given synthetic Δ^1-THC, 10 mg/kg ip, showed that the drug produced a pronounced reduction of paradoxical sleep, requiring 2 days for recovery, and that, in animals selectively deprived of paradoxical sleep for 72 hours, blockade of rebound paradoxical sleep occurred. There is not enough information to reconcile these two sets of observations, although one implication may be that cannabis does not interfere with or even potentiate the PGO spikes believed to usher in REM sleep, but does interfere with the sleep itself.

Finally, some observations in the cat with the dimethylheptyl homolog of Δ^3-THC (DMHP) may be mentioned (Boyd and Meritt, 1965a, 1966). With electrodes implanted in the reticular formation, DMHP (0.2 mg/kg) was found to raise the threshold to arousal, assessed both by EEG and by eye opening and head lifting, sometimes with an initial decrease; there was no detectable effect on the recruiting response, and the EEG generally showed increased synchronization. In further analysis of the recovery cycle after a shock to the radial nerve tested by a second shock delivered 10–200 msec later, variable results were obtained. In the mesencephalic medial lemniscus regular recovery cycles were obtained, sometimes accelerated, sometimes decelerated, but no changes in latencies or size of response occurred. In the reticular formation, recovery cycles were much more variable, and depression was commonest, sometimes with increased latency of response. In the ventrobasal complex of the thalamus, the response was usually reduced and recovery slowed. If one accepts the view that synchrony of cortical discharges facilitates sensory representation at the cortex, and that arousal impairs this, depressant effects at the reticular level would be expected to facilitate information transfer by the cuneate nucleus and in the thalamus; the authors suggest, therefore, that DMHP as well as thiopental (reported in same article) have a direct depressant action at these latter loci. A possible functional result would be that the *character* of the information reaching the cortex changes, the information being transferred more slowly (as shown by depressed recovery curves) but less selectively (as a result of the impairment of arousal).

2. Spinal Reflexes

Of the limited number of studies on reflexes, the first was by Dagirmanjian and Boyd (1960, 1962) using the dimethylheptyl and methyloctyl homologs of Δ^3-THC (DMHP and MOP). They found in cats under barbiturate–urethane anesthesia that the knee jerk was not affected, but the linguomandibular and ipsilateral flexor reflexes were depressed by 0.05–1 mg/kg DMHP or 0.2–0.4 mg/kg MOP. The linguomandibular reflex was the most sensitive. On the basis of brain section experiments they suggested that the drugs depressed facilitation originating in the reticular formation. In a further analysis (Boyd and Meritt, 1965b) in cats under pentobarbitone and chloralose, similar results were obtained, and it was further found that the drugs frequently reduced the facilitation but not the inhibition of reflexes produced by stimulation of the reticular formation (facilitation and inhibition), the fastigial nuclei (inhibition), and the caudate–internal capsule region (facilitation). The linguomandibular reflex has also been shown to be abolished in the dog under thiopentone by crude cannabis (5 mg/kg) and by pyrahexyl (2 mg/kg) (Sampaio and Lapa, 1966) and by THC 0.5 mg/kg; chlorpromazine (0.5 mg/kg) had a similar effect and the impairment was not prevented by atropine, antihistamines, or reserpinization. A marijuana preparation ("dihydrocannabinol") (Apter and Pfeiffer, 1956) did not affect the electroretinogram.

A detailed study of the response to trigeminal stimulation using hook electrodes inserted into the conjunctiva (Lapa *et al.*, 1968) showed that THC (0.4–1.6 mg/kg iv) reduced the pre- and postsynaptic focal responses at the V sensory nucleus without changing the latency of the responses and reduced the potential recorded at the entry of the nerve at the pons in parallel with the reduction of the focal response. A synaptic action was therefore unlikely. The dorsal root potential in response to stimulation of the posterior tibial nerve was almost unaffected. A selective action on trigeminal fibers was suggested, but since supramaximal stimulation was not used, the possibility was not excluded that in the presence of the drug the effectiveness of stimulation at the nerve endings in the conjunctiva was altered, for instance by a change of short-circuiting resistance due to vasodilatation or edema.

From these few studies, it seems probable that the action of cannabis is fundamentally not on basic reflexes but on the delicate influences that constantly modulate them.

3. Analgesia

The older literature (Walton, 1938) refers to analgesic effects of cannabis in man but, as Walton remarks, it does not usually produce analgesia without producing cortical effects, and these usually predominate. In addition, the degree of analgesia produced is less, and is much less predictable, than with opiates. For these reasons the popularity of hemp preparations at the end of the 19th century gradually declined. There is, too, general agreement in the older animal work that, after treatment with cannabis, animals respond less to painful stimuli, although such stimuli could arouse them from their cataleptic state.

In the first modern test (Davies et al., 1946), using the rat tail flick in response to a heated wire, a cannabis preparation in acetone (mixed with blood before injection intravenously) was about three times more active than morphine. But the experiment entailed injection of considerable amounts of acetone; the lethal dose of the preparation was surprisingly low (~ 5 mg/kg iv); and unlike morphine, it was inactive intraperitoneally. Using the same method, Avison et al. (1949) found that pyrahexyl was active at 100 mg/kg given sc in propylene glycol. Analgesia in rats produced by oral, subcutaneous, or intraperitoneal doses of an extract in gum arabic or ethylene glycol have also been described by Kabelik et al. (1960). Local anesthesia as tested by rabbit corneal reflex or infiltration of guinea pig skin was produced by concentrations of extract of 5% or more in ethylene glycol (Kabelik et al., 1960).

More recent work has shown that Δ^1-THC is particularly effective against chemically induced writhing, less so in the hot plate test, and least with the tail flick technique (Dewey et al., 1970d). By the writhing test, it is about as active as morphine (Buxbaum et al., 1969). It is claimed that reserpine potentiates the analgesia tested by the hot plate method (Cortez et al., 1966). With Δ^6-THC (Bicher and Mechoulam, 1968), similar results were obtained.

The amounts of tetrahydrocannabinol used ranged from about 1 to 10 mg/kg (Cortez *et al.*, 1966; Dewey *et al.*, 1970d; Bicher and Mechoulam, 1968; Buxbaum *et al.*, 1969). These results suggest some analogy with morphine, and it has been found that Δ^1-THC shares with morphine the ability to depress acetylcholine (ACh) output from guinea pig ileum (Gill and Paton, 1970), although with a very different time course. On the other hand, the potency of Δ^1-THC compared with morphine varies considerably with the test used, and the two drugs given together produce more than additive effects (Buxbaum *et al.*, 1969). Further, Bicher and Mechoulam (1968) found that whereas morphine abolishes the fall in blood pressure in response to stimulation of the sciatic nerve in the conscious rabbit, and facilitates cortical arousal, Δ^6-THC does not affect the hypotensive response and depresses arousal. In addition, although in the mouse THC potentiates the Straub tail response (Buxbaum *et al.*, 1969) and increases locomotor activity elicited by morphine, it antagonizes morphine-induced activity in the rat. It seems probable, therefore, that the mode of action is different and possibly more analogous to the analgesic action of anesthetics such as trichloroethylene, with which cannabis shares the property of high fat solubility. One possibility, that the analgesia (at least that produced by cannabis in small animals) is due to the hypothermia it produces, was excluded by Gill *et al.* (1970); they showed that the antagonism to writhing produced by a crude cannabis preparation giving a dose of about 3 mg/kg Δ^1-THC was still exerted in a thermally neutral environment. Under the same conditions chlorpromazine also reduced the writhing response.

C. Interactions with Convulsants and Amphetamines

The least complicated test for anticonvulsant activity employs electric shock. Loewe and Goodman (1947) found that charas THC, pyrahexyl, MOP, and DMHP were effective in the ratio 7:1:80: >200 in abolishing the tonic extensor component of maximal seizures in the rat, a set of potency ratios not far from those found for dog ataxia. They also found that these drugs were not only ineffective against metrazol, but gave a lethal synergism with it. On the basis of these results they compared the components with diphenylhydantoin and reported that the latter could also produce ataxia and catalepsy and that an anticonvulsant synergism existed between diphenyl-hydantoin and the cannabis compounds. This was followed by some suggestive clinical results against grand mal in man (Davis and Ramsay, 1949).

The only further reports consist of a confirmation (Garriott *et al.*, 1968) that Δ^1-THC (25 mg/kg) and pyrahexyl (50 mg/kg) reduce the tonic phase of electroconvulsion seizure, a statement that an incompletely purified extract (Kabelik *et al.*, 1960) could antagonize both leptazol in mice and strychnine

convulsions in frogs, and a passing remark (Valle, 1969) that cannabis potentiates strychnine in mice. Interesting additional comments are those by
Loewe and Adams (1947) that DMHP can itself produce convulsions, and
by Loewe (1944) that tetrahydrocannabidiol and 5-methyl-Δ^3-THC are
convulsants. This may be related to the description of seizure like discharges in
EEG records described by Lipparini et al. (1969) and to the phenomenon
familiar to workers with THC of a "jerkiness," or liability to an almost
convulsive hyperactivity in response to a stimulus, coexisting with reduced
mobility or a cataleptic state.

Loewe (1944) was also the first to report a synergism between amphetamine
and cannabis, using a red oil. Since then, three types of interaction have been
studied. First, amphetamine antagonizes the catalepsy induced by Δ^1- and
Δ^6-THC in monkeys (Grunfeld and Edery, 1969) and the depressed state
following DMHP administration (Hardman et al., 1970) in dogs and monkeys.
Second, amphetamine given after red oil, or Δ^1-THC, Δ^3-THC, DMHP, or
MOP (Bose et al., 1963a; Forney, 1971; Garriott et al., 1967; Dagirmanjian
and Boyd, 1962), has been found to have a considerably bigger effect on
spontaneous motor activity in mice. The augmentation was still detectable
3 days after the THC administration (Garriott et al., 1967). On the other
hand, methamphetamine action in the rat was not potentiated (Kubena and
Barry, 1970). With a dose of 0.5 mg/kg, the absolute level of activity produced
was the same whether 4–16 mg/kg THC was present or not; THC alone
depressed activity considerably. At a higher dose of methamphetamine
(2 mg/kg), Δ^1-THC at a dose of 4 mg/kg reduced the response. These results
are therefore more compatible with a mutual antagonism between the drugs.
Finally, cannabis has been tested against toxicity of amphetamine. With
amphetamine administered to aggregated animals, an increase of about 50%
in LD_{50} was obtained with high doses of THC (Salustiano et al., 1966), an
effect far smaller than that obtainable with chlorpromazine. Garattini (1965)
found the toxicity of amphetamine unaffected by up to 200 mg/kg hashish
extract. An increase in survival rate after treatment with 25 mg/kg methamphetamine following treatment with Δ^1-THC (Kubena and Barry, 1970)
has also been found, but with no estimate of the change in LD_{50}.

D. Hypothalamic and Endocrine Actions

1. Hypothermia

Ames (1958) noted that some subjects felt cold in their limbs and even
developed blanched fingers, suggesting a fall in body temperature. Waskow
et al. (1970) found a small but consistent fall in body temperature in man.
In animals, Miras (1965) and Garattini (1965) have both reported falls up to
2°–3°C after intraperitoneal injection of cannabis resin into rats. The falls

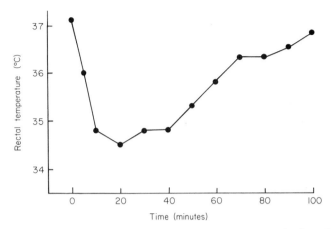

Fig. 8. Fall in rectal temperature of a mouse after intravenous injection of 25 mg/kg cannabis extract.

had a slow onset and lasted several hours. Gill *et al.* (1970) obtained similar results in mice, with falls up to 8°C, by injection of extract intravenously (Fig. 8) as well as intraperitoneally. Holtzman *et al.* (1969) obtained hypothermia in mice and Lomax (1971) in rats with doses of Δ^1-THC of 10 mg/kg or more. It has been reported that DMHP (Hardman *et al.*, 1970) lowers body temperature in dogs and monkeys. In principle, such a fall could be due to a reduction of energy production or an increase in heat loss. It has been found that cannabis injected in mice or rats into the cerebral ventricles is more effective than iv or ip injection (Garattini, 1965; Gill *et al.*, 1970), and this makes unlikely a peripheral metabolic effect. Further, it has been noticed that in mice during the fall in body temperature there is no overt shivering and that foot temperature rises transiently (Pertwee, 1971). This suggests that the mechanism involves an increase in heat loss, arising from a resetting of the thermoregulatory center. A peripheral direct vasodilatator action could also contribute to the hypothermia. However, THC does not block ganglia nor antagonize the effects of sympathetic stimulation or of noradrenaline, and only in relatively large doses is it hypotensive in the anesthetized cat (Gill *et al.*, 1970). Additional contributory factors in small animals would be reduction of motor activity and reduction of the huddling together of animals, known to be important for heat conservation (Prychodko, 1958) and said to be impaired when an entire group of animals receives the drug (Siegel and Poole, 1969).

It is evident that much remains to be done in analyzing the mechanism of the hypothermia. If the interpretation presented on the basis of the limited work reported is correct, that the primary effect is on thermoregulatory centers, then cannabis and THC in this respect resemble chlorpromazine, although at a much lower level of potency.

2. Appetite and Body Weight

A recurrent theme in reports on man is that of improved appetite after taking cannabis. There is scanty experimental information on this point. Carlini and Kramer (1965) found that 30–50 mg/kg of extract given ip to rats led to increased apparent appetite (along with increased activity and excitement) for a period, followed by a depressed stuporose state. In contrast, Abel and Schiff (1969), using pyrahexyl, found that repeated administration to rats led to depression of food intake and loss of weight compared to controls. A loss of weight as a result of food restriction and cannabis treatment was also found by Carlini and Masur (1969), but no control without cannabis was reported. Miras (1965) noted that rats fed 0.2% cannabis extract in food developed diarrhea, and growth was slowed. Dagirmanjian and Boyd (1962) found that animals treated with DMHP and MOP became bloated and lost weight. In unpublished experiments (Paton and Pertwee, 1971), 100 mg/kg cannabis extract injected sc daily led to a slower rate of increase in weight compared to controls over a period of 11 days; a 10-fold higher dose produced loss of body weight followed by death. In the cat Lipparini et al. (1969) found that after recovery from the effect of 2 mg/kg THC, the animal appeared hungry and eagerly performed the food-reward tests being used. Scheckel et al. (1968) noted in the monkey that, while Δ^1-THC impaired a food-rewarded task, the animal's appetite appeared normal. Grunfeld and Edery (1969) reported a rejection of food by rhesus monkey while under the effect of Δ^1-THC. In pigeons (McMillan et al., 1970a) refusal of food followed high dosage of Δ^1-THC. Rabbits and hamsters (Geber and Schramm, 1969b), although showing initial evidence of disinterest in food (carrots) after cannabis treatment for 2–4 days, showed no loss of weight compared to controls on doses ranging from 25 to 500 mg/kg cannabis extract sc. However, in rabbits with more prolonged treatment (Paton and Temple, 1971) a relatively slower weight gain was seen.

The only general conclusion one can provisionally draw is that, with chronic or high dosage, loss of body weight occurs, possibly due to impaired food intake, but that with single doses, or low dose levels, there is no specific effect and food intake simply parallels the general activity of the animal.

3. Corticosteroid and Thyroid Hormones

A dose of 1.25 mg/kg or more of Δ^1-THC causes a release of cortical hormones in the rat (Dewey et al., 1970b; Kubena et al., 1971), as shown by depletion of adrenal ascorbic acid and by a rise in peripheral plasma corticosterone. The effect is abolished by hypophysectomy and therefore is mediated by adrenocorticotropic hormone (ACTH) release. It differs from the action of morphine, in that the stimulation of ACTH release by morphine is prevented by pentobarbitone (Kubena *et al.*, 1971), whereas that by Δ^1-THC is not. Further, the effect of Δ^1-THC is abolished by pretreatment with pentobarbitone and morphine, a procedure known to block secretion of corticotropin-releasing factor (CRF) from the hypothalamus, so that it appears that Δ^1-THC can mobilize CRF. In a dose just insufficient itself to cause ACTH release, Δ^1-THC did not block the release induced by adrenaline (Dewey *et al.*, 1970b). There was no development of tolerance to this action of THC over periods of repeated injection for 5 or 8 days (Dewey *et al.*, 1970b; Kubena *et al.*, 1971), nor were cumulative effects noticed. It may be noted that, in man, doses of THC up to 1 mg/kg were not found to alter plasma cortisol, but this does not exclude pituitary activation at higher doses. A similar failure to observe in man the stimulant effect in animals of morphine on ACTH release has been reported (Munson, 1963).

It might be suggested that the ACTH release is a result of hypothermia. However, pentobarbitone (50 mg/kg) does not cause release (Dewey *et al.*, 1970b) although it produces a fall in body temperature, and it is known that lowering body temperature by cooling systemic blood (Egdahl *et al.*, 1955) gradually reduces ACTH output. It is likely, therefore, that Δ^1-THC in some way excites release of CRF; a puzzling feature remains as to why this action resists pentobarbitone in a dose sufficient to block morphine stimulation of ACTH release.

Evidence for depression of thyroid function was obtained by Miras (1965), who showed that cannabis extract depressed uptake of ^{131}I by the thyroid. It has subsequently been shown (Lomax, 1970) that Δ^1-THC, 2.5 mg/kg sc, inhibits release of iodine from the thyroid, that this inhibition can be overcome by thyroid-stimulating hormone, and that bilateral lesions in the region of the median mammillary nuclei of the hypothalamus, such as are known to abolish the inhibitory effect of morphine on thyroid function, also prevented the inhibitory action of THC. Lesions of the rostral nuclei including the ventromedial nuclei were ineffective (Lomax, 1970). It was concluded that THC, like morphine in its inhibitory action, may well act by depressing secretion of thyrotropin-releasing factor (TRF).

E. Vomiting and Scratching

Two responses, presumably of central origin, have been recorded with cannabis extract in dogs. Marx and Eckhardt (1933) and Chopra and Chopra (1957) mention vomiting, and Walton (1938) reports vomiting and retching as common and occurring as frequently with oral as with intravenous dosage. Loewe (1946a) found salivation, retching, nausea, and vomiting frequently in dogs, with all extracts that produced ataxia, after both oral and intravenous administration. Munch (1931) noted vomit of froth and mucus with above-threshold doses, and Bose et al. (1964a) observed salivation, retching, and vomiting with doses, intraperitoneally, 8 times above a threshold dose. In cats, salivation was noted (Walton, 1938); vomiting seems less common, but Hockman et al. (1971) found that Δ^1-THC in doses of 0.5 mg/kg upwards ip made cats vomit. In monkeys, Δ^1- but not Δ^6-THC induced vomiting (Scheckel et al., 1968). The mechanisms involved have not been analyzed, and there may be other emetics present in crude cannabis as well as Δ^1-THC.

Persistent, seemingly useless scratching produced by cannabis extracts was observed by Marx and Eckhardt (1933) and by Haagen-Smit et al. (1940). Walton (1938) noted that the animal continues to scratch apparently because it lacks the mental initiative to stop. Loewe (1944) found that it appeared only with doses large enough to produce ataxia, appeared before the ataxia, was less pronounced with higher degrees of ataxia, and seemed to be an intensification of the normal scratch reflex. As with vomiting, the reaction has not been analyzed, and it is only the association with ataxia that suggests that THC may be responsible. There is no evidence that cannabis can release histamine or produce an anaphylactoid response, so that the reaction is presumably central in origin. Interestingly enough, it has also been shown for morphine given into the cerebral ventricles.

F. Interactions of Cannabis with Brain Amines

1. 5-Hydroxytryptamine

Bose et al. (1964b) found that after injection of rats with cannabis extract, the 5-hydroxytryptamine (5-HT) content of whole brain increased consider-ably, from 0.36 to 1.4 μg/gm. Although Garattini (1965) did not find this increase, it has been confirmed with Δ^1-THC (although smaller rises were found) in mice (Holtzman et al., 1969; Welch et al., 1971) and rats (Magus and Harris, 1971; Schildkraut and Efron, 1971). The latter showed that the increase was localized to hypothalamus plus midbrain and to cerebellum, with no significant rise in medulla plus pons or in cerebral cortex. It was shown that Δ^1-THC (20 mg/kg) reduced the rate of brain HT synthesis, as measured by the rate of rise after administration of pargyline; THC also retarded the rate at which reserpine depleted brain HT. Monoamine oxidase activity was not affected by THC in vitro, nor was the monoamine oxidase activity in tissues taken from THC-treated animals altered. From what is now known of the presence of THC metabolites in the tissues, this evidence suggests that these, too, lack activity against monoamine oxidase. In the light of this evidence against increased synthesis or decreased destruction of HT, the rise in brain HT produced by THC must be due to decreased release.

Since THC retarded the action of reserpine, which is believed to act by interfering with the vesicular membrane, Sofia and Dixit (1971) and Sofia *et al.* (1971) suggest that THC may be acting at the same level; this would be compatible with its highly lipophilic property. If the theory of thermoregulation by monoamines is adopted, it is reasonable that a drug which produces hypothermia should produce a fall in HT release, provided that the hypothermia is brought about by an adjustment downward of the thermostatic mechanism.

Interaction with injected tryptamine has also been studied (Garattini, 1965). Injected iv into rats, a characteristic pattern of salivation, tremors, and backward movement occurs. Hashish extract neither protected against nor enhanced the response.

2. Catecholamines

Consistent evidence for a significant effect on brain catecholamines is lacking. Garattini (1965) briefly reported a lack of effect of hashish extract on rat brain or heart noradrenaline content with single doses, with 12 daily doses ip, or with intracerebral injection, under conditions in which reserpine, 1.25 mg/kg ip, had a marked effect. Holtzman *et al.* (1969) found, for mouse brain after 10–500 mg/kg Δ^1-THC, that the lower doses produced a fall in noradrenaline content by up to 20%, and very high doses, which produced profound hypothermia and stupor, caused a rise. Unspecific effects due to stimulation at lower doses or to the results of stupor and hypothermia at higher doses could not be excluded. Maître *et al.* (1970) showed that a cannabis extract, Δ^1-THC, Δ^3-THC, and a xanthane derivative, had no effect on noradrenaline content or uptake of ^{3}H-NAD by rat heart nor on NAD and dopamine (DA) content of brain. They observed an increase in rate of formation of ^{3}H-DA and ^{3}H-NAD from injected ^{3}H-tyrosine. The significance of this is doubtful, however, since they also found that Δ^1-THC reduced the endogenous tyrosine level in the plasma so that the specific activity of the tyrosine being delivered to the brain would be raised, and since it is also possible that the cannabinoids altered the rate of delivery of label to the brain, for instance by changes in brain blood flow. Schildkraut and Efron (1971), with doses of 80 mg/kg to rats, found a small (13%) increase in disappearance of ^{3}H-NAD from brain 190 minutes after its intracisternal injection, a rise of 10–16% in metabolites, and no significant change in endogenous NAD. In another experiment, examining effects 6 minutes after intracisternal injection, ^{3}H-NAD removal was if anything slowed, but a small rise in metabolite formation was again seen. Finally, Welch *et al.* (1971) found in mice that neither Δ^1-THC nor cannabinol changed brain content of NAD or DA, although brain HT rose. They also observed after THC administration, but not with cannabinol, a 25–36% reduction in adrenaline content of suprarenal; cannabinol (CBN) did not antagonize this action of THC.

It appears, therefore, (a) that Δ^1-THC has no consistent effect on NAD or DA content of brain; (b) by comparing the results with those obtained, for instance, with desipramine or a monoamine oxidase inhibitor, that Δ^1-THC does not interfere with amine uptake or metabolism; (c) that the small effects noted on rate of ^{3}H-tyrosine incorporation and on ^{3}H-NAD disappearance may be attributable to secondary mechanisms.

G. CANNABIS AND BARBITURATE SLEEPING TIME

The first observation on the interaction of cannabis and barbiturates was made by Loewe in 1944. He showed that the hypnotic effect of Pernocton (butallylonal, a brominated barbiturate) in mice was prolonged by cannabis extracts, that red oil and cannabidiol (CBD) were particularly active (the former probably by reason of its CBD content), and that a semisynthetic THC and cannabinol were relatively inactive. Bose et al. (1963a) confirmed this for cannabis extract with hexobarbital in rats, also showing that the extract augmented the prolongation of sleeping time by reserpine and (a still unexplained result) that it antagonized the prolongation by a large dose (20 mg/kg) of 5-HT-creatinine sulfate. Miras (1965) claimed that the prolongation was still detectable in the rat 30 days after the last of 2–3 injections of resin, although Layman and Milton (1971b) found no effect 14 days after administration of 100 mg/kg extract in mice. Garattini (1965) found that cannabis extract prolonged pentobarbitone sleeping time in rats and that cannabis had the same effect in a dose of 2 and 4 mg intracerebrally.

Prolongation of sleeping time has also been shown for Δ^1-THC (Kubena and Barry, 1970; Forney, 1971), Δ^3-THC, pyrahexyl (Garriott et al., 1967), the Δ^6 metabolite 7-hydroxy-Δ^6-THC (Truitt, 1970), DMHP and MOP (Dagirmanjian and Boyd, 1962), and certain cannabinoid derivatives (Garriott et al., 1968). Usually doses of the order of 25–50 mg/kg were required, but DMHP and MOP were detectably active at 0.2 and 0.4 mg/kg, respectively. A failure to find an effect after administration of 25 mg/kg of a red oil containing 25% Δ^1-THC, the residue being mainly cannabinol (Garriott et al., 1967), confirms Loewe's finding of the relative inactivity of cannabinol.

Some studies of mechanism with Δ^1-THC have been made. Kubena and Barry (1970) showed that Δ^1-THC prolonged barbitone as well as pentobarbitone sleep in rats and concluded that, since barbitone is not metabolized, the effect could not be on metabolic processes, but involved a central potentiating effect. Sofia and Barry (1970) also found that Δ^1-THC potentiated barbitone sleep, that SKF 525-A alone had a small but significant effect, and that the two drugs together produced a very considerable mutual potentiation. They concluded that the effect was due to THC, not its metabolite, and that

Δ^1-THC has a central depressant action showing itself by a synergism with the biochemically stable barbitone. Prolongation of ethanol as well as of barbitone sleep has been reported (Forney, 1971). Prior treatment with phenobarbitone, in order to induce enhanced microsomal activity, did not increase Δ^1-THC metabolism. In contrast, both Δ^1- and Δ^6-THC (Dewey *et al.*, 1970a) have been shown to inhibit demethylation of aminopyrine and ethylmorphine. Five daily injections of Δ^1-THC in rats did not stimulate microsomal activity.

A major difficulty in interpreting the experiments reviewed above is that the body temperature of the rats and mice used was not controlled. However, it is known (see p. 222) that cannabis and Δ^1-THC produce hypothermia. It is also known that hypothermia can (a) depress liver metabolism, (b) interfere with elimination of drugs from the body in other ways, e.g., by reducing renal blood flow or the rate of redistribution of a drug, and (c) exert a central depressant effect of its own. The effect of cannabis extract and of Δ^1-THC and the other cannabinols on pentobarbitone, Pernocton, and hexobarbitone sleep could therefore be due simply to depression by hypothermia of microsomal activity, and the effect on barbitone or ethanol sleep could be by interference with renal elimination or by summation with a hypothermic depression.

For this reason, experiments on barbiturate sleeping time have been repeated (Gill *et al.*, 1970; Paton and Pertwee, 1972) on mice at the thermally neutral temperature of 30°–32°C. These experiments showed, first, that under these conditions cannabis extract (50 mg/kg or more) prolonged pentobarbitone sleeping time. Further, Δ^1-THC was also effective, although only to a limited degree, giving an increase of not more than 90% in doses of 12.5 mg/kg or more. Since it constituted only 6.4% of the extract, it could not account for the latter's activity. The carotenes and the water-soluble fraction of the extract were inactive, but cannabidiol was very active; a dose of 12.5 mg/kg produced a three-fold increase in sleeping time, and 50 mg/kg produced a 4.6-fold increase. It is likely, therefore, as Loewe implies, that cannabidiol is mainly responsible for this effect of cannabis extracts. Second, it was found that cannabis extract did not potentiate sleeping time induced by injections of ether in oil. This excluded a summation of central depressant effect for crude cannabis. Finally, the cannabis extract was shown to inhibit the metabolism of antipyrine by the 9000 g supernatant fraction from homogenate of mouse liver; again THC had only a small (although significant) effect of this kind, whereas cannabidiol was much more active, producing 50% inhibition at about 90 μM, a potency comparable with that of SKF 525-A. It seems probable, therefore, that prolongation of barbiturate sleeping time by cannabis extracts is due to their cannabidiol content and is mediated by a direct effect on the microsomal enzyme systems.

With Δ^1-THC, however, it was not so clear that the *in vitro* effects could account for the sleeping time results, and the possibility of a synergism of a central depressant effect of $\varDelta^1$-THC (as opposed to crude cannabis) with ether had not been adequately excluded. It remains possible, therefore, that with controlled temperature, such a synergic central depressant interaction with barbitone and ethanol may be shown to exist.

The interest of these studies lies partly in the fact that an action of cannabis on microsomal processes would be important in practice, since it would imply that the cannabis user might respond abnormally to other drugs, and partly in the fact that a specific and clearly defined central effect, which was less variable and more easily studied than the cataleptic or other behavioral responses, could facilitate investigation.

H. General Pharmacology

1. Respiration

Cannabis extracts have been shown to depress the respiratory rate in unanesthetized dogs (Bose et al., 1964a; Loewe, 1944, 1946a; Dixon, 1899), the breathing becoming slower and deeper (Bose et al., 1964a; Dixon, 1899). With low doses slight stimulation was seen (Bose et al., 1964a). Miras (1965) noted that cessation of respiration is the first sign of death in toxicological experiments, and de Farias (1955) also noted that respiration fails before the circulation. The same has been found for DMHP and MOP in mice (Dagirmanjian and Boyd, 1962), in which THC is also stated to cause death by respiratory arrest (Christensen et al., 1971). The doses required for some respiratory effect are modest, of the order of 10 mg/kg of an active extract given iv (Bose et al., 1964a) or 0.25 mg of a highly purified material that produced definite ataxia (Loewe, 1944). The solvents used for the cannabis preparation may, however, contribute to the effect even if they are by themselves apparently ineffective. The pulmonary edema produced by pyrahexyl in the dog (Loewe, 1946a) may also be partly due to the solvent used. Similar findings have been made in anesthetized dogs and cats (Miras, 1965; de Farias, 1955). Further, $\varDelta^1$-THC has been found to be a respiratory depressant in cats under chloralose (Gill et al., 1970), producing a substantial depression at 2 mg/kg, and also in anesthetized rats (Forney, 1971). The homologs DMHP (0.1 mg/kg) and MOP depress respiration in the cat under dial and urethane (Dagirmanjian and Boyd, 1960, 1962). Carotid sinus denervation did not affect the respiratory effect (Dagirmanjian and Boyd, 1960). It must be noted that respiratory minute volume is in general more readily depressed in anesthetized animals; thus Lerman and Paton (1960) found that the steroid anesthetic hydroxydione in a dose of 10 mg/kg could abolish respiration in a cat under chloralose, although in a decerebrate animal doses 4–14 times higher produced either no depression or only a transient depression. One may conclude, although adequate respiratory studies are lacking, that cannabis and Δ^1-THC in quite low doses can affect respiratory *rate*; that the lethal effect is probably due to respiratory failure; and if the last conclusion is accepted, then by comparing the doses affecting rate with the lethal doses, it follows that much larger doses are required to depress minute volume than rate.

2. Cardiovascular Effects and the Autonomic Nervous System

Among the earliest tests of cannabis extracts on the cardiovascular system were those of Dixon (1899). He found that injection of an emulsion of cannabis in gum acacia produced a slowing of the heart and fall of blood pressure abolished by cutting the vagi. It seems probable that, because of the particulate nature of his material, he was producing a Bezold-Jarisch response, elicitable, for instance, by starch grain emboli, and that the response was not due to cannabis per se; this conclusion is supported by the failure of other workers to reproduce such effects. For the same reason, doubts hang over his observation that after vagotomy the cannabis extract produced dropped beats and cardiac asystole; these, too, could be due to embolism.

In general, a gradual and sustained fall of blood pressure has been shown to be produced by extracts in the dog (Marx and Eckhardt, 1933; Loewe, 1944), by Δ^1-THC in the dog, cat, and rat (Dewey *et al.*, 1970c,d; Gill *et al.*, 1970; Forney, 1971), by Δ^6-THC in the dog (Dewey *et al.*, 1970d), and by DMHP and MOP in the cat (Dagirmanjian and Boyd, 1960, 1962; Hardman *et al.*, 1970), although in some experiments (Bose *et al.*, 1963b; Miras, 1965) insufficient material appears to have been given to produce an effect. Associated with the hypotension, the pulse rate decreases in anesthetized dogs (Loewe, 1944; Marx and Eckhardt, 1933; Dewey *et al.*, 1970c), in the anesthetized cat (Dagirmanjian and Boyd, 1962; Miras, 1965), and in the anesthetized rat (Forney, 1971); the bradycardia but not the hypotension is abolished by vagotomy or atropine (Loewe, 1946a; Forney, 1971). Loewe (1944), however, showed an interesting figure of responses in an unanesthetized dog, in which a low dose of tetrahydrocannabinol produced a marked slowing of respiration, a fall in blood pressure, and a rise in pulse rate paralleling the ataxia that developed; there are other instances in which bradycardia and hypotension were dissociated (Dagirmanjian and Boyd, 1962; Miras, 1965; Forney, 1971).

The mechanism of the hypotension does not involve any peripheral interference with the sympathetic nervous system. In its presence, adrenaline and noradrenaline are potentiated by DMHP and MOP (Dagirmanjian and Boyd, 1962) and by Δ^1- and Δ^6-THC (Dewey *et al.*, 1970d). The potentiation is probably mostly attributable to a lower level of blood pressure. Miras (1965) and Bose *et al.* (1963b), in experiments in which extract did not cause a fall in blood pressure, found that the response to adrenaline was prolonged.

Isoprenaline becomes somewhat less active, as might again be expected with a lower pressure. Dichloroisoprenaline did not antagonize the fall in pressure (Dagirmanjian and Boyd, 1962), so that activation of β receptors is not involved in the hypotension. The Δ^1-THC does not block transmission in autonomic ganglia, either the superior cervical ganglion in the rat (Dewey *et al.*, 1970c; Dagirmanjian and Boyd, 1962) or the vagal ganglia (de Farias, 1955; Gill *et al.*, 1970) or the ganglia in the chorda tympani pathway to the salivary gland (Gill *et al.*, 1970). Acetylcholine is still pressor in the atropinized cat in the presence of DMHP (Dagirmanjian and Boyd, 1962). The hypotension is not affected by vagotomy but is reduced by prior treatment with hexamethonium (Dagirmanjian and Boyd, 1962) and is abolished in cat, dog, and monkey by section of the spinal cord at C1 (Dagirmanjian and Boyd, 1962; Hardman *et al.*, 1970). In addition, it has been found in the dog that Δ^1-THC increases femoral blood flow and decreases peripheral resistance (Dewey *et al.*, 1970a), and Dixon (1899) reported that cannabis in the dog produces a slight vascular dilatation of the testes. All these results point to the conclusion that the hypotensive effect of Δ^1-THC and its analogs is mediated by a central withdrawal of sympathetic tone; this alone, by leaving vagal action unopposed, could be responsible for the commonly observed bradycardia.

Compatible with this action also is the constriction of the pupil noted by Loewe (1944) which, since petrol ether extracts of cannabis and Δ^1-THC lack other parasympathomimetic actions, would otherwise be puzzling. It is also concordant with the depression of the carotid occlusion response (Bose *et al.*, 1964b; Dewey *et al.*, 1970c; Dagirmanjian and Boyd, 1960) and, since the peripheral vasodilatation will predispose to heat loss, with hypothermia. The hypothermia, indeed, by its own central depressant effect, will then be expected to reinforce the hypotension.

Two further observations should be mentioned. First, Bicher and Mechoulam (1968) showed that the fall in blood pressure obtained after stimulating the sciatic nerve in the rabbit was not altered by Δ^6-THC (2–5 mg/kg), although it was abolished by morphine (4 mg/kg). This indicates that Δ^6-THC does not have a general unspecific effect on the central nervous system and also represents a difference from morphine, which in other respects it often resembles. Second, the lethal effect of Δ^1-THC in the dog was reduced by repeated catecholamine injection (Dewey *et al.*, 1970c); here again, a difference from a number of general anesthetics may be represented.

3. Gastrointestinal Effects and Actions at Cholinergic Synapses

The effects of cannabis on the alimentary tract of whole animals have been little studied. Miras (1965) reported that rats receiving 0.2% resin in food developed diarrhea, while Loewe (1944, 1946a) found that mice developed diarrhea on high oral doses of "THC," and dogs given a toxic oral dose of pyrahexyl had a profuse bloody diarrhea. On the other hand, Dagirmanjian and Boyd (1960) found that DMHP produced in a proportion of anesthetized cats a relaxation of ileum *in situ* (absent after atropinization), and Dewey *et al.* (1970a) showed that Δ^1-THC, 10–30 mg/kg, produced a 34% inhibition of the passage of charcoal in mouse intestine, an effect comparable to that of 0.5–1 mg/kg morphine. Δ^6-THC was less active. Bose *et al.* (1963b, 1964a), in experiments on strips of tissue *in vitro*, found that the resin depressed duodenum, ileum, uterus, colon, and auricle and the responses to carbachol, ACh, 5-HT, barium, adrenaline, and Pitocin; but since his preparation contained 15 times as much ethanol as resin, and few doses are specified, it is impossible to be sure that these effects were not due to ethanol. Gill and Paton (1970) found that Δ^1-THC depressed the nerve-evoked twitch of guinea pig ileum in concentrations of 10^{-6} gm/ml upwards, with a characteristically slow onset and persistence of action; the effect of ACh was not reduced, so that the Δ^1-THC must impair the output of ACh from the cholinergic nerve endings of Auerbach's plexus. Layman and Milton (1971a) confirmed this depression of the twitch, which they found was not shared by cannabidiol. They, like Dewey *et al.* (1970a), found that THC could impair the response of the intestine to ACh, but only in preparations or at concentrations that also depressed the response to histamine. Layman and Milton (1971a) also found that *resting* release of ACh was reduced by both THC and CBD; 35% reduction was produced by concentrations of 1.59×10^{-5} and 1.29×10^{-6} M, respectively. It is not yet clear why CBD (unlike THC) should be effective on resting ACh release, yet ineffective on the ileum twitch.

It seems clear, therefore, that Δ^1-THC affects the cholinergic neuro-effector system of the gut, but at other cholinergic synapses no action has been found. Its failure to block autonomic ganglia is mentioned above. Its failure to block choline-induced salivary secretion (Gill *et al.*, 1970) implies that it lacks atropinic as well as ganglion-blocking action. It does not affect the indirectly excited twitch of rat diaphragm or the response of frog rectus to ACh (Layman and Milton, 1971a); DMHP is also ineffective on the indirectly or directly excited twitch of cat muscle (Dagirmanjian and Boyd, 1960), and indeed a curarelike action would be quite incompatible with the general pharmacology of cannabis and the cannabinols. There is no direct evidence as to whether Δ^1-THC can affect the splanchnic–suprarenal synapse.

If it is accepted that in the whole animal cannabis and Δ^1-THC impair the nerve mechanisms of the gut, yet also produce a withdrawal of sympathetic tone, one would expect a very variable resultant effect, since withdrawal of sympathetic control leads to increase in intestinal activity. This may account for the variable effects in the whole animal mentioned above. The complexity of the response is increased by the fact that preparations of cannabis may contain, as well as Δ^1-THC, an atropinelike substance (which tends to constipate) and ACh-like trigonelline esters (which could stimulate the alimentary tract) (Gill et al., 1970).

4. Blood Sugar

Increase of appetite has been reported after cannabis consumption, and the question arises of its effect on the blood sugar. Marx and Eckhardt (1933) found that resin given iv or orally to dogs produced a modest hypoglycemia, down to about 85 mg/100 ml, the effect being greater as the initial blood sugar was higher. On the other hand, Dahi (1951), giving very large doses of pyrahexyl, obtained rises in blood sugar in rats and guinea pigs lasting 5–10 hours, with evidence of inhibition of liver glycogen synthesis; unfortunately he did not control the effect of his solvent, propylene glycol, and he might have produced a shocklike state with adrenaline release. Miras (1965) noted in rats much wider fluctuations than normal in blood sugar but no consistent change. Paton and Temple (1971) found that cannabis extract injected daily into rabbits produced (a) a statistically insignificant rise in resting blood sugar (115–124 mg/100 ml); (b) no significant change in very variable glucose tolerance curves; (c) a modest increase in the hyperglycemia produced by sc injection of adrenaline after 5 days, which was absent after 36 days; and (d) an increased hypoglycemia in response to 1 IU/kg of insulin at 18 days of treatment, which also became insignificant with continued administration. It seems clear that there is no very striking effect by cannabis on blood sugar itself, yet the results suggest some interference with control of glucose utilization, for instance a depression in the rate of output of insulin in response to a given blood glucose level, to which tolerance can develop.

5. Other Actions

Although diuresis has been reported in man, the only experimental work in animals appears to be the report by Barry et al. (1970), who found that Δ^1-THC in rats increased the urine flow over an 8-hour period twofold compared to controls. They drew an analogy with alcohol, which like Δ^1-THC produces both a diuresis [shown for alcohol to be mediated by reduction of antidiuretic hormone (ADH) output] and a stimulation of ACTH release.

As to reproductive organs, Miras (1965) reported that the reproductive activity of rats being fed 0.2% resin in their food was significantly lower than that of controls, that there was a rather greater incidence of death in mothers 2–3 days after delivery (although most were then not receiving the resin), and that the newborn rats developed normally. The report by Dixon (1899) of evidence for a vasodilatation of the testes in the dog has been mentioned above. Effects on the fetus are discussed in a later section.

Antibiotic activity has been demonstrated for cannabis (Kabelik *et al.*, 1960; Krejči, 1970; Ford and McMillan, 1971). One active component appears to be cannabidiolic acid, but there is also a phenolic component which (in contrast) becomes more potent as pH rises. Gram-positive organisms are susceptible, including penicillin-resistant staphylococci, but gram-negative organisms are not. Activity at dilutions of $1:10^6$ in broth was found, but on agar plates (Oxford method) or in the presence of blood or serum it is severely reduced. Some clinical success with tinctures or boracic acid dusting powders containing resin has been reported. Compared with modern antibiotics, however, the potency is relatively low, and inactivation by tissue fluid is a drawback.

Effects on brain metabolism reported include (a) a reduction of oxygen consumption of rat brain homogenate by an alcoholic extract of cannabis in concentrations of about 0.1–0.3 mg resin/ml homogenate upwards (Bose *et al.*, 1963a), (b) a 50% inhibition of the anaerobic glycolysis of rat brain homogenate by 3.6×10^{-4} M pyrahexyl (Dahi, 1951), and (c) an increase in brain DNA (but not RNA) content in rats receiving six daily injections of 100 mg/kg cannabis extract ip (Carlini and Carlini, 1965).

In tests of ^{86}Rb transport by human and rat erythrocytes (Porter and Scott, 1970) with $\varDelta^1$-THC in alcohol, detectable inhibition of both active uptake and passive movement was found at 25 μg/ml upwards for human cells and 10 μg/ml for rat cells. Ethanol was active at about 4 mg/ml and ouabain at 0.018 μg/ml.

In a test for carcinogenicity the tar obtained from marijuana (5% $\varDelta^1$-THC) made up into cigarette form and combusted has a similar effect on mouse skin as do cigarette tar and carcinogens such as the polycyclic hydrocarbons (Magus and Harris, 1971). The tar yield was 1.8 gm/100 gm of combusted material, against 4 gm/100 gm for a commercial cigarette.

III. Toxicity and Teratogenicity

A. ACUTE TOXICITY

Table II summarizes the more recent data concerning the doses liable to kill in a single dose. Most of the data are estimated lethal doses, but limits of error are cited by Phillips *et al.* (1971). The original articles should be consulted for details. The table makes clear how limited is the available information. Loewe (1944) collated some of the older information on liquid extract given by various routes to various species. The cause of death is rarely analyzed, but (as discussed earlier) it seems likely that it is usually due to respiratory failure. A difficulty arises from the varied excipients used. Thus, the very low lethal dose cited by Davies *et al.* (1946) was obtained with a

TABLE II

Preparation	Mouse				Rat			Gu p i
	iv	ip	Oral	sc	iv	ip	Oral	
Hashish	—	940	—	—	—	800	—	
Sublimate	—	3,200	—	—	—	3,000	—	
Extract	—	5,000	—	—	—	—	—	
	—	—	1,830	—	—	—	—	
Distillate	—	—	—	—	5	—	—	
	—	—	—	—	—	—	—	
$[\alpha]-160°$ (a mixture)	—	—	—	—	—	—	—	
$[\alpha]-265°$ (Δ^6-THC)	—	—	—	—	—	—	—	
Δ^1-THC (Wollner acetate)	175	—	>21,600	>11,000	—	—	—	
Δ^1-THC racemate	—	—	—	—	—	—	—	
Δ^1THC	42.5	454.5	481.9 (ig)	—	28.6	372.9	666.1 (ig)	
	—	—	—	—	—	—	—	
	—	—	—	—	—	—	—	
Δ^6-THC	—	~1,200	~1,500	—	—	—	—	
Pyrahexyl	200, 170 140	—	13,500	>34,000	—	—	—	850
Δ^3-THC	>200	—	—	—	—	—	—	
Cannabinol	—	—	13,500	—	—	—	—	
Cannabidiol	—	—	>12,700	—	—	—	—	
	—	—	—	—	—	—	—	
Varied dibenzopyrans	—	178−>500	—	—	—	—	—	

[a] Expressed as milligrams per kilogram body weight.

hashish distillate dissolved in acetone and mixed with blood before intravenous administration. Loewe (1946a) quotes the oral LD$_{50}$ in mice for the solvents he used as follows: propylene glycol, 26 ml/kg; dipropylene glycol, 20 ml/kg; and ethanol, "much lower." The glycols have been commonly used as a result. Yet it is probable that some of the figures given are underestimates of the true lethal dose for the extract or substance concerned, since even if doses of solvent well below the lethal are used, the solvent could still make a contribution to the lethal effect.

Subject to this caveat, it is evident that toxicity by the intravenous route is higher than by the less direct routes, by a factor ranging from 10 to 100 or

ACUTE TOXICITY OF CANNABIS EXTRACTS AND DERIVATIVES[a]

bbit	Dog		Squirrel monkey	Pigeon	Reference
v	iv	Oral	ip	im	
—	—	—	—	—	Joachimoglu (1965)
—	—	—	—	—	Joachimoglu (1965)
—	—	—	—	—	Gill et al. (1970)
—	—	—	—	—	Kabelik et al. (1960)
—	—	—	—	—	Davies et al. (1946)
–8.4	—	—	—	—	Loewe (1944)
—	32.5–43.2	—	—	—	Loewe (1944)
—	>17	—	—	—	Loewe (1944)
155	100	—	—	—	Phillips et al. (1971)
—	—	—	16	—	Scheckel et al. (1968)
—	—	—	—	—	—
—	3 (anesthetized animal)	—	—	—	Dewey et al. (1970c)
—	—	—	—	180 (lethal to some nontolerant birds)	McMillan et al. (1970b)
—	—	—	—	—	Bicher and Mechoulam (1968)
143	223	<930	—	—	Loewe (1946a)
—	—	—	—	—	Avison et al. (1949)
—	—	—	—	—	Avison et al. (1949)
<126	>254	—	—	—	Loewe (1946a)
—	—	—	—	—	Loewe (1946a)
—	60	—	—	—	Loewe (1944)
—	—	—	—	—	Garriott et al. (1968)

more. It has also been noted by both Loewe (1946a) and Phillips et al. (1971) that death is usually quick (5–15 minutes) when it follows intravenous administration, but it is delayed by 10–36 hours, or even longer, for other routes.

In general, there is no very convincing evidence that species vary greatly in their susceptibility to the lethal action of these substances. The main exception in Table II is the squirrel monkey, in which 16 mg/kg Δ^1-THC racemate injected intraperitoneally killed two out of five animals; this is a low dose compared to the lethal doses of 178 mg/kg upwards to 1200 mg/kg found for various cannabinols in mouse, rat, and guinea pig. The low lethal dose of Δ^1-THC intravenously in the dog cited by Dewey et al. (1970c) can probably be attributed to the potentiating effect of anesthesia. Nor is there any consistent evidence, within the cannabinols as a whole, of toxicity being particularly associated with any special chemical structure. Roughly speaking, the cannabinols have an intravenous toxicity of 30–200 mg/kg, and this range of variation may well reflect chiefly variations in technique. Extracts do, however, tend to have a lower general toxicity than the pure substances, if one judges by the intraperitoneal data, and the evidence is roughly compatible with the view that the toxicity is largely due to the content of tetrahydro-cannabinol. Intravenously, extracts have a high acute toxicity, but this could be due to the greater liability to embolic or other phenomena with a cruder material.

B. Chronic Toxicity

The only chronic toxicity test with cannabis extract, until recently, has been that by Miras (1965), who fed rats with 0.2% resin in standard Purina food; the results were mentioned above (p. 224). Table III summarizes the data obtained by Dagirmanjian and Boyd (1962) on DMHP and MOP, together with the finding by Carlini and Masur (1969), from their study of aggressive-ness induced by cannabis in food-restricted rats, that 1-month-old rats lost weight and died under daily dosage of cannabis. The table also includes unpublished data (Paton and Pertwee, 1971) showing that both by the intra-peritoneal and by the subcutaneous route, the LD_{50} falls to about 10–20% of the acute LD_{50} on repeated daily administration. These data show that the lethal action is cumulative, as would be expected from the lipophilicity of the active principles. No information is yet available on the chronic toxicity of Δ^1-THC, but similar findings are likely.

C. Teratogenicity and Action on the Fetus

Persaud and Ellington (1968) reported in 1968 that a dose of 4.2 mg/kg cannabis resin, given intraperitoneally in Tween 80–saline to pregnant rats on days 1–6 of gestation, produced an incidence of 57% abnormal fetuses (none in a control group receiving saline injections), and 29% fetal resorptions (control group 17%). The abnormalities were syndactyly 72%, encephalocoele 57%, eventration of viscera 30%, phocomelia 15%, and amelia 2%. All abnormal fetuses were stunted. Geber and Schramm (1969a,b) extended these observations to rabbits and hamsters. In the hamster they found a dose-related increase in skeletal abnormalities (phocomelia, omphalocoele, spina bifida, exencephaly, myelocoele) with doses of 100 mg/kg upwards of canna-bis extract given subcutaneously on days 6, 7, and 8 of gestation (Fig. 9). The effect was greater for experiments done during winter than for those

TABLE III

DATA ON LETHAL DOSES OF CANNABIS OR DERIVATIVES WITH REPEATED DAILY DOSAGE

Species	Route	Preparation	Dose (mg/kg)	Treatment	Reference
Mouse	iv	DMHP	27	7 doses	Dagirmanjian and Boyd (1962)
Mouse	iv	MOP	5	7 doses	
Rat	ip	Petrol ether extract	10	Repeated daily dosage to 1-month-old rats with food restriction	Carlini and Masur (1969)
Mouse	ip	Ethanolic extract	5000 (5/5 dead)	1 dose	Paton and Pertwee (1971)
			1000 (3/4 dead)	3 doses	
			500 (2/5 dead)	47 doses	
Mouse	sc	Ethanolic extract	5000 (10/10 dead)	1 dose	
			2500 (6/10 dead)	2 doses	
			1000 (9/10 dead)	3 doses	
			500 (0/10 dead)	7 doses	

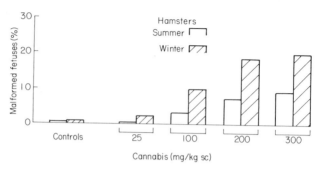

Fig. 9. Teratogenicity of cannabis extract injected subcutaneously in hamsters (excluding runts and edema) on days 6–8 of gestation, showing dose dependence of effect and effect of season on the response.

during summer. They also showed that the extracts produced some fetal deaths, stunting, and fetal edema; in a comparison between New Jersey and Mexican marijuana, the former produced more edema, the latter more stunting.

In rabbits given the New Jersey and Mexican extracts subcutaneously on days 7–10 of gestation, with sacrifice on day 16 or 17, the most striking effect was the decrease in litter size due to fetal resorptions. At 130 mg/kg, fetal resorption was 10%, compared to 2% for controls, and rose to 21–40% at 250 mg/kg. At this dosage, of the fetuses found 7–11% were dead, and there was 21–30% stunting, 5–19% skeletal abnormalities, and 8–21% fetal edema. New Jersey marijuana produced more edema and Mexican marijuana more abnormalities.

For mice given 16 mg/kg intraperitoneally on day 6, no fetal abnormalities were found by Persaud and Ellington (1967), but there was a high incidence of stunting, and with treatment on days 1–6 there was complete fetal resorption.

With cannabis extracts, therefore, a dose-dependent increase in fetal abnormalities can be produced; these abnormalities have been found in three species; the doses required are relatively low compared to those likely to be lethal to the mother; and fetal resorption and stunting also occur to a marked degree.

On the preliminary evidence so far available with Δ^1-THC, the picture appears to be different (Borgen and Davis, 1970). With doses given subcutaneously in oil to rats on days 1–20 of gestation, a retardation of maternal growth and prolongation of gestation was found at 10 mg/kg, a marked neonatal mortality apparently due to insufficient lactation by the mothers was found at 25 mg/kg upwards, and a reduction of litter size at 100 mg/kg upwards. No teratogenesis was seen, although in a later report (Pace *et al.*,

1971) of a study using other routes and other species, a few abnormalities are mentioned in rats and rabbits after the use of a marijuana extract distillate.

Experiments have been made on the question of placental transfer of Δ^1-THC. Idänpään-Heikkilä *et al.* (1969) gave single doses of tritiated Δ^1-THC of 2 mg/day to hamsters intraperitoneally or subcutaneously at the 6th or 15th days. By both routes, the fetus at 15, 30, 120 minutes, and 24 hours later contained more label than maternal plasma or brain, and the placental content was higher still. The transfer was higher in early than in late pregnancy. It was estimated that unchanged THC was responsible for 25 and 55% of the activity in fetus and in placenta, respectively. Pace *et al.* (1971) found, in tests on 13th–20th day of gestation, that the maximum concentration of ^{14}C-labeled THC in the fetus was 36% of that in maternal tissues. It seems clear that, as would be expected, THC can reach the fetus and that transfer is greater early in pregnancy.

Finally, certain chromosomal experiments must be mentioned. Martin (1969) found that, with cultured rat leukocytes, cultured rat embryonic tissue, or rat embryos, exposed to cannabis resin, no significant increase in chromosomal abnormality occurred, but at the higher concentrations there was mitotic inhibition. Neu *et al.* (1969) made exactly analogous observations on leukocyte cultures with Δ^6-THC in concentrations up to 40 μg/ml.

These last observations may provide an important clue to the whole problem of the fetal effects of cannabis and THC. They are highly lipophilic substances, resembling in this respect the volatile anesthetics. A number of anesthetics are also known to be teratogenic and to impair mitotic index (see Fink, 1968, for a review). The general picture of cannabis action is that of fetal resorption, stunting, and fetal abnormality in which limb defect is common. It appears possible that the primary action is not intensely specific but that the effects are produced because the drugs, by virtue of their affinity for lipid, are able to interfere with cell division at moments in ontogeny when temporary failure of mitosis may produce an irreversible impairment of development. The difference between the action of extracts and of THC, if substantiated, may indicate, however, that particular chemical structures favor this action. The question of the relevance of these findings to human use is discussed in the next chapter.

IV. Metabolism and Fate of Tetrahydrocannabinol in the Body*

The first attempt to study the fate of any cannabinoid in the body appears to be that of Loewe (1946b). Injecting large and sometimes lethal doses of

---

* *Editor's note:* Some of the material presented in this section (in particular Subsections A and B) is also discussed in Chapter 4. However, the emphasis and viewpoints of the authors are different to such an extent that the editor considers the overlap worthwhile.

pyrahexyl (41–326 mg/kg) intravenously into dogs, he was able to show, by bioassay on extracts of blood, that between 1 and 10% of the injected material could be detected in the blood 2–11 hours later and that 1% of an intravenous dose was recoverable from the lungs after 20 hours. Although this remains a unique application of bioassay to the problem, the assay was subject to great error, and Loewe could not, for instance, show a dose-related decline of activity in the blood. Further advance depended mainly on the use of radio-actively labeled tetrahydrocannabinols. The topics that will be discussed in this section include the formation of metabolites, the disposition and elimina-tion of these metabolites, the general pattern of distribution of radioactivity, and finally the question of the role of the metabolites in the effects produced by Δ^1-THC.

A. THE METABOLITES

The first clue to the fate of Δ^1-THC was obtained by Agurell et al. (1969). They found that ^{3}H-Δ^1-THC injected intravenously into rats was very slowly eliminated, half the dose remaining in the body after a week; that most of the dose appeared in metabolized form in the feces; that around 10% appeared in the urine; and that virtually none appeared as THC itself but in a more polar form extractable with ether. The activity remaining in the aqueous phase was extractable with n-butanol, but treatment with glucuronidase did not yield free Δ^1-THC. Later work (Agurell, 1970; Agurell et al., 1970) was extended to the rabbit, in which elimination is much faster, with about 35% of the activity appearing in the urine within 24 hours. Evidence was obtained of ether-soluble metabolites in the blood and in the urine and of a small quantity of a metabolite extractable by petrol ether from urine whose amount could be increased by glucuronidase treatment. The amount of ether-soluble metabolite in urine was increased by acidifying the latter. It was also shown that a metabolite was formed from Δ^1-THC by a microsome-rich liver homogenate.

The first evidence as to the structure of THC metabolites came from the experiments by Burstein et al. (1970), who showed, using 0.1 M perchloric acid in ethyl acetate to release the aglycone, that after injection of ^{3}H-Δ^6-THC into the rabbit, a derivative, probably hydroxylated in the 7 position, appeared in urine. This was later confirmed chemically (Ben-Zvi et al., 1970) and was followed by the demonstration of the formation of 7-OH-Δ^1-THC by liver homogenate (Nilsson et al., 1970; Wall et al., 1970), of 7-OH-Δ^6-THC in liver and by liver homogenate in vitro (Truitt, 1970; Foltz et al., 1970), and of 7-OH-cannabinol from cannabinol (Widman et al., 1971).

The conversion of Δ^1-THC to the 7-OH derivative by liver is known to be microsomal, to require NADPH and molecular oxygen, and to be inhibited by CO. It is therefore likely to involve the system containing cytochrome P-450. It is also inhibited by SKF 525-A. Activity is greater in male than in female animals (Burstein, 1971).

Hydroxylation can also occur at the 5 and 6 positions. Wall *et al.* (1970) found that a microsome-rich liver preparation converted 75% of Δ^1-THC, 30% to the 7-OH derivative, 30% to the 6,7-dihydroxy derivative, and 15% to an acetylated 7-OH-Δ^1-THC, probably an artifact of extraction. Later (Wall, 1971), 7-hydroxy derivatives of Δ^1, Δ^6-THC, and CBN, 5α- or 5β,7-dihydroxy-Δ^6-THC and 6β,7-dihydroxy-Δ^1-THC were identified as microsomal products *in vitro* with evidence of similar changes *in vivo*. Other metabolites were believed to be present, possibly as conjugates. An interesting additional observation is that by Christiansen and Rafaelsen (1969), who found in human subjects given cannabis by mouth that, after treatment of the urine with glucuronidase/aryl sulfatase at pH 5.5, cannabinol or THC present in the resin was not detectable, but cannabidiol and a probable metabolite appeared. This suggests that cannabidiol may be conjugated but not hydroxylated. In man, there are, in addition to the 7-OH derivative and its conjugate, more polar metabolites (Lemberger *et al.*, 1970).

It is clear from the above that a major role in the metabolism of the cannabinols is hydroxylation by liver microsomes. This is compatible with evidence discussed earlier about the inhibition of barbiturate metabolism by cannabinols (p. 228). Christensen *et al.* (1971) have made the further important finding that homogenates of spleen and blood are also capable, in the presence of NADPH, of metabolizing Δ^1-THC, but there is negligible conversion by brain and small intestine. It is also clear, however, that a number of unidentified metabolites exist.

The technique used by Burstein *et al.* (1970) to dehydrate 7-OH-Δ^1-THC to cannabinol has been put forward as the basis of a urine test (Anderssen *et al.*, 1971). Urine is first washed with petrol ether to eliminate any cannabis that has not passed through the body, to avoid false positives. It is then extracted with ether at pH 3.8, and the extracts are dried and refluxed with toluenesulfonic acid in benzene to form dehydration products. Positive findings were represented by characteristic chromatographic spots.

B. THE DISPOSITION OF THE METABOLITES

The end products of THC metabolism appear not only in urine, but to a considerable extent in bile and feces. There is considerable variation with species. In the rat, the greater part (80%) of the amount recoverable (Agurell *et al.*, 1969) appears in the feces and only about 10% in urine (Fig. 10), but in the rabbit, elimination is predominantly renal, about ¾ of the activity appearing in urine, The renal pathway is associated with a more rapid elimination;

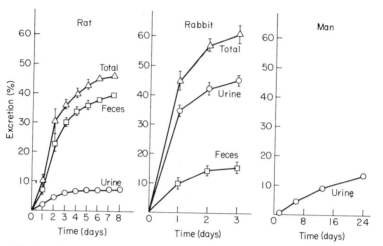

Fig. 10. Cumulative excretion of label after administration of ³H-Δ¹-THC in rat, rabbit, and man, in urine and feces. (From Agurell *et al.*, 1970.)

thus, in 24 hours, the rabbit excretes about 45% of the activity (35% urine, 10% feces), and the rat only 10% (roughly 8% in feces, 2% in urine). Man appears to be intermediate between the two; there is an output in 24 hours in urine of about 13% (Agurell, 1970). Over a week, about 30% appears in urine and 50% in feces (Lemberger *et al.*, 1970). Contributing to the delay in elimination in the rat is an enterohepatic circulation of metabolite. King and Forney (1967) showed that after intraperitoneal injection of CBN or Δ¹-THC into normal rats, 22 and 12%, respectively, appeared as conjugates in feces in 7 days; in rats with biliary fistulae, 23 and 44% of the doses given for CBN and THC, respectively, were found to appear as conjugates in the bile over the same period. It is clear that the THC (but not the CBN) metabolite is substantially reabsorbed after delivery in the bile to the intestinal contents. This work also showed that with THC given by mouth to animals with biliary fistulae, 20% of the drug appeared unchanged in the feces; this suggests that, as would be expected, bile is required for full absorption of THC from the intestine.

C. KINETICS OF TETRAHYDROCANNABINOL DISTRIBUTION AND DISPOSAL

After intravenous injection of Δ¹-THC, there is a rapid fall of THC content in the plasma, with an initial half-life of about 12 minutes in the rabbit (Agurell *et al.*, 1970) and 30 minutes in man (Lemberger *et al.*, 1970) (Fig. 11). There follows a much slower decline, with a half-life of 50–60 hours in man. Ether-soluble metabolite appears very quickly, reaching a peak

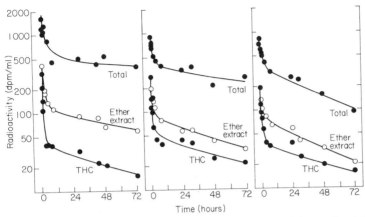

Fig. 11. Plasma levels of Δ^1-THC, ether-extractable radioactivity, and total radioactivity after iv injection of ^{14}C-Δ^1-THC (5.6–7.9 μg/kg) in three human subjects. (From Lemberger *et al.*, 1970.)

concentration several times greater than that of the THC between ½ and 2 hours in the rabbit. In man, metabolite is also formed very rapidly, reaching a concentration two to three times that of THC; there is then a rapid initial decline followed by a slower phase of disappearance paralleling to a remarkable extent that of THC. The total activity in the blood falls to 10–20% of its initial level in about 3 days.

The activity in the blood is almost certainly mostly protein bound; Δ^1-THC passes in only trace amounts into an ultrafiltrate of plasma (Agurell *et al.*, 1970). Its very low water solubility makes experiments difficult. If plasma is incubated with Δ^1-THC, and then subjected to disc electrophoresis on polyacrylamide gel, the drug is associated with the albumin (chiefly) and transferrin peaks. With agarose electrophoresis, the major peak in radioactivity did not coincide with the albumin band, and association with lipoprotein was suggested (Wahlqvist *et al.*, 1970). This was supported by immunoelectrophoretic study and by electrophoresis on agar combined with staining of lipoprotein. It turned out, indeed, that albumin did not carry Δ^1-THC at all. It was also found that the activity in rabbit blood 3 hours after injection was protein bound (at a time when THC activity is low), and it must be supposed that metabolites are similarly bound to lipoprotein. This binding, by reducing the concentration of free THC or metabolite in the plasma, must slow down the kinetics of their disposal. It is interesting that this disposal is nevertheless initially so fast, and it suggests that the cannabinoid–lipoprotein complex itself may be taken up by the tissues.

The distribution of radioactivity in the tissues after administration of labeled Δ^1-THC has been the subject of a number of studies; these are

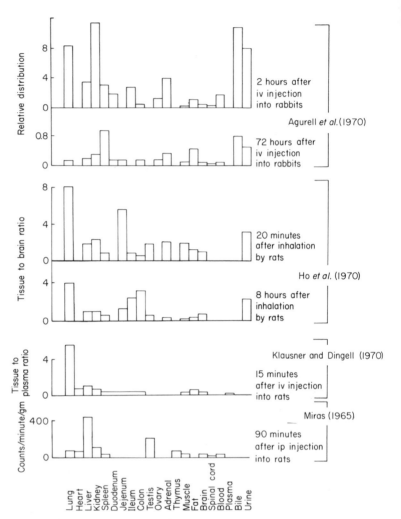

Fig. 12. Collation of data available on distribution of labeled Δ^1-THC in various tissues of the body in rats and rabbits.

summarized in Fig. 12. Certain trends are clear. A relatively high concentration in liver, bile, and kidney corresponds to these tissues being involved in excretion of metabolites. The route of administration must contribute to the high content in liver after intraperitoneal injection (with subsequent uptake by the portal system) and to that in lung after inhalation. Content in lung is also high with intravenous injection. The study by Ho *et al.* (1970) shows a distribution in the bowel reflecting the role of biliary excretion, with a higher content in jejunum than colon initially, the gradient being reversed after 8 hours with transport of the intestinal contents. Contents of testis, adrenal, and to a lesser extent ovary are relatively high. Ho *et al.* also described a concentration in salivary gland at 20 minutes not far short of that in lung. An interesting feature is that amounts in fat, brain, and spinal cord are relatively low. Some hours after the injection, a relative concentration in fat is detectable, but only in Klausner and Dingell's study (1970) was there any sign of selective concentration in brain. Interesting also is the persistence of activity in the spleen.

An autoradiographic study on mice (Kennedy and Waddell, 1971) injected with 30 mg/kg Δ^1-THC in an albumin suspension given intravenously has confirmed the rapid fall of activity in blood, the accumulation in liver and lung, the appearance of activity in bile and to a slightly lesser extent in urine, in intestine and stomach, and in maternal ovary and fetal yolk sac. Brain activity was low with no localization. Twenty-four hours later, there was an appreciable migration of activity to fatty tissues, particularly brown fat. A novel finding was a notable accumulation in dental pulp.

To interpret these results, it may be noted first that some correspondence between content and blood flow would be anticipated, since with substances so insoluble in water the content of a tissue is likely to be limited by the rate of delivery of drug or metabolites through the blood. This probably accounts for the low muscle, fat, and spinal cord values and contributes to the high lung, heart, liver, and kidney values. In a study of distribution of the very fat-soluble anesthetics, chloroform, halothane, and methoxyflurane, Chenoweth *et al.* (1962) noted that the content in brain corresponded to that of arterial blood and that high concentrations were found in the adrenal gland; the findings with Δ^1-THC may provide an analogy. The distribution in liver, kidney, intestine, and bile, as mentioned above, must reflect elimination, and the high content in salivary gland could represent a similar process, particularly if there is an anionic metabolite. Finally, the persistence of activity in the spleen after intravenous injection, otherwise puzzling, suggests that THC, even in the best "solvent", forms micelles in the blood of sufficient size to be taken up by the reticuloendothelial system.

Two studies have been made of distribution of activity in brain, one by McIsaac *et al.* (1971) using both autoradiography and tissue counts in monkey brain, and the other by Layman and Milton (1971b) in rat brain. In monkey brain, total activity 15 minutes after intravenous injection was relatively high in cortical white matter, cerebellum, geniculate nuclei, hippocampus amygdala, colliculi, caudate nucleus, putamen, and pons. White matter and tracts had low activity. The relative concentration in gray matter declined considerably within 1 hour, and by 24 hours activity was evenly distributed. It was shown that, at 15 minutes, 77% of activity present in brain represented Δ^1-THC itself, and this declined to 51% at 4 hours. In rat brain, after intraperitoneal injection, activity rose to a peak at 1 hour and declined slowly thereafter, demonstrable activity still being present at 30 days. No significant regional distribution was detected. Layman and Milton did not distinguish between Δ^1-THC and metabolite, but Christensen et al. (1971) showed that in mouse brain after intravenous injection the ratio of Δ^1-THC to metabolites 10 minutes later was 2.3; 7-OH-Δ^1- and 6,7-di-OH-Δ^1-THC accounted for over 70% of the metabolites, there being four times as much of the former.

The regional differences shown by McIsaac et al. (1971) particularly low activity in white matter and tracts, probably correspond chiefly to blood flow variations and, without more detailed knowledge than at present exists, no case can be made for any selective concentration. Such localization as there was became rapidly blurred, and it is probable that Layman and Milton saw no localization because absorption by the intraperitoneal route would be relatively slow. Ho et al. (1971) have indeed suggested that after intraperitoneal injection little is absorbed; this statement, however, is based on an autoradiographic comparison of the distribution 5 minutes after an intravenous injection of an unstated dose with the distribution 15 minutes and 2 hours after intraperitoneal injection of the same dose. The autoradiographic technique used is best adapted for showing concentration gradients rather than absolute amounts, and it is only to be expected that such gradients would be blurred at longer times with slower absorption. The statement, in addition, hardly takes account of the effectiveness of intraperitoneal dosage, or of Miras' (1965) finding that he could recover only 20% of intraperitoneally injected material from the peritoneal cavity.

D. The Role of Metabolites in the Action of Tetrahydrocannabinol

Mechoulam and his colleagues have conjectured that the effects of Δ^1-THC in the body are produced not by Δ^1-THC itself but by a metabolite (Grunfeld and Edery, 1969; Mechoulam, 1970). The original points made were (a) that this would explain the statements by habitués that marijuana has no effect the first time (since induction of an enzyme forming the active substance could occur), (b) that Δ^1- and Δ^6-THC are more active intraperitoneally than subcutaneously (perhaps this point was overstated; cf. Dewey et al., 1970d), possibly indicating a formation of active metabolites by the liver, and (c) that there was evidence of a sufficiently rapid formation of metabolite in rabbit to account for the known speed of action. The relative inactivity of marijuana on first exposure compared to later doses, which is by no means invariable, could of course be due to a process of cumulation, and skin blood flow is so slow compared to that of the intestine that much slower absorption from a subcutaneous site, for a water-insoluble compound, is inevitable. Nonetheless, it is interesting that the prediction of activity by a metabolite proved true, and the strong activity of 7-OH-Δ^1- and 7-OH-Δ^6-THC has been confirmed for rats, mice, and rhesus monkeys by Nilsson et al.

(1970), Truitt and colleagues (Truitt, 1970; Foltz *et al.*, 1970), Wall and his colleagues (Christensen *et al.*, 1971; Wall, 1971), and Ben-Zvi *et al.* (1970).

Christensen *et al.* (1971) have subsequently provided quantitative data on the mouse concerning the possible role of the metabolite, although details of the assay procedures have not yet been presented. In addition, it is not clear that control injections were made; it is possible that acute intracerebral injections could affect behavior, for instance by inducing cortical spreading depression. First, the 7-hydroxy metabolites of Δ^1- and Δ^6-THC were equipotent and about twice as active by the intravenous route as the parent compounds, themselves equipotent. The 6,7- and 5,7-dihydroxy compounds together with Δ^7-THC, cannabidiol, and cannabinol had 5% or less of the activity of Δ^1-THC. Second, the 7-hydroxy compounds were seven times more active by intracerebral than by intravenous administration, whereas the parent compounds were approximately equipotent by either route. Third, it was noticed that the parent compounds had a faster onset of activity after the intravenous than after the intracerebral route; with the 7-OH metabolites, onset of action was slightly faster than with parent compounds. Finally, it was shown that, 30 seconds after Δ^1-THC was given intravenously, 7-OH-Δ^1-THC was detectable in the blood and that, with Δ^1-THC given by either route, the metabolite concentration reached a maximum at a time (10 minutes) close to the time of maximum behavioral effect.

These results, together with the evidence presented earlier about the formation of metabolite, indicate that the metabolite is involved, but the possibility of action by Δ^1-THC itself is not excluded. Two possible difficulties for the theory have been avoided. First, metabolite formation was initially shown for liver preparations, yet it could well be the case that any metabolite formed in the liver is not released as such into the blood, but only in conjugated form into the bile. However, metabolite formation has been shown to occur also in blood and in the spleen (Christensen *et al.*, 1971) so that, for instance, the metabolite appearing in blood could be formed in blood itself. Second, it might be argued that it was not the 7-hydroxylated metabolite that was active, but a further metabolite formed from it in turn. But it appears that the next steps, either further hydroxylation or conjugation lead to inactivity. The question becomes, then, how to establish the truth or otherwise of the conjectures that the metabolite is either solely responsible or (alternatively) acts jointly with the parent compound. An attempt at a decisive correlation between behavioral effect and the amount of Δ^1-THC and 7-OH-Δ^1-THC in the part of the brain concerned is not promising, since the concentrations of the two components may well vary roughly in parallel (see McIsaac *et al.*, 1971; Lemberger *et al.*, 1970), behavioral activity is hard to quantitate, and the relevant part of the brain involved is not identified. Decisive proof probably requires the use of inhibitors of metabolite formation with which, if sufficiently specific inhibition could be obtained, it might be possible to show that in their presence Δ^1-THC became inactive, and the 7-OH derivative became more effective, because of abolition of further metabolism. For the time being, a cautious view would be that both Δ^1-THC and 7-OH-Δ^1-THC contribute to the effect roughly equally, the lower concentration of metabolite in brain being compensated by its higher activity.

The rate of appearance of metabolites seems to be so fast in animals presumably not previously exposed to cannabinols that there is no need to postulate induction of the enzyme responsible for their formation. Whether induction can occur is not yet clear. Dewey *et al.* (1970a) found in rats that five daily injections of Δ^1-THC intraperitoneally in a dose of 40 mg/kg did not stimulate microsomal activity; on the other hand, Lemberger *et al.* (1971) obtained evidence in man that the half-life of THC in plasma declined from 57 hours in nonusers of cannabis to 28 hours in users and that 22% of administered radioactivity was recovered in 1 week in the urine of nonusers against 33% for users, suggesting a somewhat enhanced metabolism of THC in the chronic user.

V. The Active Principles of Cannabis Other Than Δ^1-THC

The evolution of the chemical and biological work on cannabis made it clear that a tetrahydrocannabinol was chiefly, if not wholly, responsible for the actions of cannabis in animals (particularly dog ataxia and behavioral changes) that appeared to parallel the psychic effects in man. Once it was shown that Δ^1-THC was by far the major constituent, with small and variable amounts of Δ^6-THC, it followed that Δ^1-THC must be the main active principle. Interest in the other constituents arises in three ways, still to be fully explored. (1) There may still be contributory actions of the same type exerted by other substances; (2) other substances in crude cannabis might modify the effects of Δ^1-THC; and (3) other substances may produce other effects and be responsible for the difference between the actions of Δ^1-THC and extracts.

1. The experiments described by Mechoulam *et al.* (1970a), based on a sample of Lebanese hashish, provided convincing evidence that, at least for single doses of 0.25 mg/kg in the monkey, constituents of hashish other than Δ^1-THC in the amounts normally present neither contribute to the effect nor impair the action of Δ^1-THC. The experiment consisted of a comparison between the effects of (I) Δ^1-THC (250 μg/kg) alone; (II) combined administration of cannabicyclol (5.5 μg/kg), cannabidiol (288 μg/kg), cannabinol (43.5 μg/kg), cannabichromene (5.5 μg/kg), cannabigerol (16.5 μg/kg); and (III) the mixture in II with Δ^1-THC (250 μg/kg). The effects of I and III were indistinguishable, and II was inactive. It remains possible, however, although

it would be laborious to test the point, that a different result would be obtained with repeated dosage, higher dosage, other samples of hashish, or other species. Of the additional substances used, cannabidiol has been repeatedly found to lack THC-like activity by systemic administration (Lipparini *et al.*, 1969; Loewe, 1946a; Christensen *et al.*, 1971), although it has other actions discussed later, and was stated to be active if injected intracerebrally (Christensen *et al.*, 1971). Cannabinol was shown by Loewe (1945b) to produce ataxia in dogs, but a dose of 18 mg/kg was needed to produce grade III ataxia, and its activity is probably less than 1/200 that of Δ^1-THC; it, too, is stated to be active intracerebrally (Christensen *et al.*, 1971). It is now known that tetrahydrocannabinolic and cannabidiolic acids occur in cannabis, and these, too, have been found to be inactive (Mechoulam, 1970; Mechoulam *et al.*, 1971).

A new possibility arose with the identification in a tincture of Pakistani cannabis of the propyl homolog of THC (Gill *et al.*, 1970; Gill, 1971b), to which Gill has given the trivial name of tetrahydrocannabidivarol (Δ^1-THD). This represented (see p. 195) 3.4% of the tincture base, against 6.4% of Δ^1-THC; it was found to be about five times less active than Δ^1-THC on the mouse catalepsy test, and the time course of its action appears different. Preliminary experiments indicated that, while Δ^1-THC accounted for the bulk of the cataleptic effect of the extract, Δ^1-THD might contribute to the early part of the response. The Δ^1-THD has been reported in trace amounts in only one other sample, so that its role, and that of its (presumed) metabolite, remain to be assessed.

2. Apart from the experiment by Mechoulam *et al.* (1970a) and the suggestion of an antagonistic action by cannabidiol (Carlini *et al.*, 1970) already mentioned, the question of interaction of other constituents of cannabis with Δ^1-THC has not been studied. One aspect must, however, be mentioned. The evidence has been reviewed above that Δ^1-THC is metabolized by microsomal enzymes. Paton and Pertwee (1972) have confirmed Loewe's finding (1944) that cannabidiol is chiefly responsible for the prolongation of barbiturate sleeping time by cannabis extract, and they have further shown that cannabidiol is about as active as SKF 525-A in inhibiting phenazone metabolism by a microsome-rich preparation of mouse liver. The possibility of a metabolic interaction between cannabidiol and Δ^1-THC cannot, therefore, be excluded, particularly when the variations in relative amounts present are considered (Fig. 1). It is by no means clear what the result of that interaction would be.

3. The question of other actions exerted by substances in cannabis other than Δ^1-THC calls first for consideration of the actions that an extract and Δ^1-THC exert alike. These appear to be dog ataxia, mouse catalepsy and other behavioral changes, characteristic EEG effects, analgesia, synergism with amphetamine, hypothermia, depression of thyroid activity, and respiratory and circulatory depression. It was also concluded earlier that Δ^1-THC

could account for most of the acute toxicity of extracts given intraperitoneally, although with intravenous dosage the crudity of extracts could produce additional embolic or other phenomena. The remaining differences can be approached in two ways; one can determine (as did Gill et al., 1970) what actions an extract can exert other than those attributable to Δ^1-THC and then consider what chemical structures are responsible, or one can examine the very large number of known substances found in the extract and test their pharmacological actions.

The former approach has, as discussed above, made it likely that there is a substance (or substances) in cannabis, not yet identified, responsible for corneal areflexia (Gill and Paton, 1970). Gill et al. (1970) also found (a) in the petrol-ether-soluble fraction evidence of, in addition to propyl-THC, another active principle producing a nonspecific depression of smooth muscle; and (b) in the water-soluble fraction evidence of quaternary compounds, other than choline or trigonelline, with atropinelike and acetylcholinelike activities. Basic compounds have also been reported by Bercht and Salemink (1969) (see also Chapter 1, Section II). The atropinelike substance is present only in small amounts, and the comparison with atropine may be misleading, but it offers a possible explanation for two reported effects of cannabis in man, dry mouth and tachycardia, for which the peripheral actions of Δ^1-THC cannot account. They might equally, however, be explained by the effect of the inhaled smoke and by excitement. Consideration of the teratogenic experiments discussed above also suggests that there is a teratogen other than Δ^1-THC in cannabis.

Of the known chemical substances other than Δ^1-THC, cannabinol and cannabidiol require further discussion. In general, cannabinol has been found to be a relatively inactive compound (Loewe, 1946a; Mechoulam et al., 1970a; Christensen et al., 1971). Welch et al. (1971) did, however, report that at 10 mg/kg in mice it can reduce spontaneous activity and increase brain 5-HT content; unlike Δ^1-THC it does not cause a fall in adrenal gland epinephrine content. In the same article, allusion is made to unpublished evidence that cannabinol can prevent potentiation of barbiturate sleeping time by Δ^1-THC. Cannabidiol may be more significant, quite apart from its microsomal action. Lipparini et al. (1969) found that, while a dose of 2 mg/kg was inactive in the rabbit, 5 mg/kg produced head nodding and ataxia, and 10 mg/kg produced an anesthesialike state, lasting 3–4 hours, in which the EEG showed only increased synchronization and none of the spikes and waves or reduction of voltage produced by Δ^1-THC. Further, Layman and Milton (1971a) noticed an effect of cannabidiol on resting ACh output by guinea pig ileum. It is possible, therefore, that it could contribute what appears to be a rather nonspecific depressant effect to the action of a cannabis extract.

TABLE IV
PROVISIONAL SUMMARY OF ACTIVE PRINCIPLES OF CANNABIS

Actions of cannabis extracts in animals	Probably mainly attributable to
Dog ataxia Mouse catalepsy Animal behavioral changes EEG effects Analgesic Synergism with amphetamine Hypothermia Depression of thyroid activity Respiratory depression Vasomotor depression Vomiting	Δ^1-THC (? contribution by propyl-Δ^1-THC)
Barbiturate sleep prolongation	Cannabidiol
Corneal areflexia	Unknown (some contribution by Δ^1-THC)
"Atropinelike" action	Unknown
Muscarinic action	Unknown
Teratogenicity	Unknown
Nonspecific depressant	Unknown

Table IV summarizes the conclusions reached in this section. These conclusions are necessarily tentative, since the necessary quantitative data are lacking; a number of actions have been omitted, and the summary is presented only as a working approximation.

VI. Cumulation and Tolerance

Although the older literature contains evidence of tolerance, of a withdrawal response, and even perhaps of cumulation produced by cannabis, the appreciation of these effects has been distorted, as were those of the barbiturates, by a preoccupation with the more striking phenomena induced by the opiates. As a result, the statement that cannabis did not produce tolerance meant no more than it did not produce opiatelike effects, and other effects were discounted. Munch (1931) refers to decreasing sensitivity of dogs to cannabis, if tested too frequently. Loewe (1944) refers to periods of increasing sensitivity in the initial period of tests with cannabis and explains the subsequent tolerance he sometimes encountered as due to an adaptation to his test procedure. Chopra and Chopra (1957) mention the production of slight tolerance in monkeys, cats, and rats, of signs of the animals' liking for the drug, and of mild abstinence effects in cats and rats, all well short of the opiate-type responses.

The first quantitative appreciation of development of tolerance came from Carlini (1968) working on the behavioral responses of rats to cannabis extract. He divided his rats into two groups according to whether they became completely tolerant or not, and Fig. 13a,b shows the results, so divided, of repeated daily injections of 20 mg/kg on rope-climbing time. After one injection, performance was impaired; with continued injections this impairment increased for a few days, and then over about 10–15 days climbing time fell back to normal in the "tolerant" group and to time greater than normal in the "nontolerant" animals. This picture of the initial enhancement of the effect for a few days followed by development of partial or complete tolerance has been repeatedly confirmed in rats (Silva et al., 1968; Ford and McMillan, 1971; Bailey et al., 1971; Moreton and Davis, 1970; McMillan et al., 1971), with cannabis, Δ^1-THC, Δ^6-THC, and (for the enhancement phase) pyrahexyl (Abel and Schiff, 1969), and for a variety of behavioral tests including depression of the self-stimulation response (Bailey et al., 1971). The tolerance developed is not accompanied by cross tolerance with mescaline or LSD (Silva et al., 1968) or morphine (Myers, 1916; McMillan et al., 1971), and morphine antagonists do not precipitate an abstinence syndrome. Tolerance to LSD and mescaline develops more rapidly (Silva et al., 1968), in about 3 and 9 days, respectively. The tolerance developed can be as much as 10-fold in terms of dose (Ford and McMillan, 1971) and persists a considerable time after withdrawal of drug (Silva et al., 1968; Moreton and Davis, 1970; McMillan et al., 1971). Moreton and Davis (1970) noted that, in animals in activity cages, Δ^1-THC, 25 mg/kg subcutaneously, produced excitement and then depression, that with daily dosage the stimulant effect first disappeared, and that tolerance then developed to the depressant effect. It is doubtful how far induction of liver microsomal activity can contribute to the effect, since five daily doses of Δ^1-THC did not stimulate this (Dewey et al., 1970a). Tolerance to the hypothermic effect in rat has been shown by Lomax (1971), the hypothermia giving place on the sixth day to a small rise in body temperature; he noted that repeated morphine dosage also produces initial hypothermia which diminishes and is replaced by hyperthermia. Gill et al. (1970), using cannabis extract, made similar observations on mice, with the ring immobility (catalepsy) test and (Paton and Pertwee, 1971) with hypothermia. McMillan et al. (1971) found marked tolerance in the dog to Δ^1-THC. Lipparini et al. (1969), however, noticed no change in response in rabbits receiving 3 mg/kg Δ^1-THC for 6 days.

Particularly striking are reports on the pigeon (McMillan et al., 1970a,b; Black et al., 1970; Ford and McMillan, 1971). Tolerance to the effect on behavioral tests may develop after a single injection (Fig. 14), it may be as much as 60-fold in terms of dose, and it can develop with doses no more frequent than once a week. Cross tolerance develops between Δ^1-, Δ^6-THC, pyrahexyl, and DMHP. Development of tolerance is independent of whether

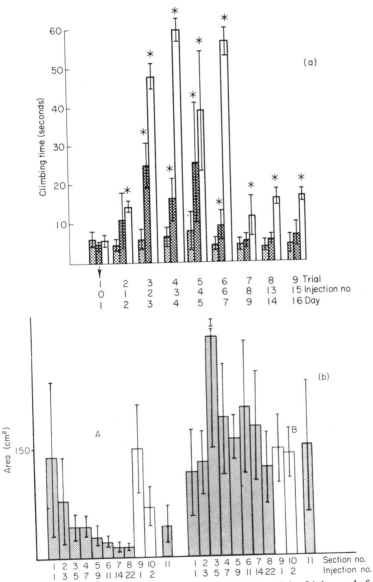

. **Fig. 13.** (a) Effect of 20 mg/kg marijuana extract injected ip 24 hours before on rope-climbing performance of rats. The animals were divided into "tolerant" (heavily stippled columns) and "nontolerant" (open columns) groups according to their response. Asterisk indicates results significantly different from controls (lightly stippled columns). (From Carlini, 1968.) (b) Effect of 10 mg/kg Δ^1-THC (stippled columns) on rope-climbing performance (effect–time integral) in "tolerant" (A) and "nontolerant" (B) rats. Open columns represent mescaline injection, 40 mg/kg, showing lack of cross tolerance. After mescaline injections a further test with Δ^1-THC was made, 8 days after the last dose of THC, showing tolerance still present. (From Silva *et al.*, 1968.)

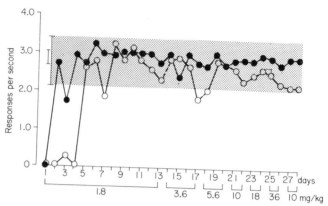

Fig. 14. Effect of repeated daily dosage of Δ^1-THC on performance of two pigeons (nos. 1989 and 6512) in fixed-ratio component of a multiple food presentation schedule. Normal values shown shaded. (From McMillan *et al.*, 1970a.)

the birds performed while under the influence of the drug (Black *et al.*, 1970). On withdrawal of the drug, signs of abstinence have not been seen; the degree of tolerance is much reduced after an interval of 4 weeks.

As pointed out by Gill *et al.* (1970), the pattern of enhancement of effect followed by tolerance is to be expected with repeated doses of a fat-soluble drug and is exemplified by the barbiturates. At least three factors must be involved: (a) the time course of elimination of drug from the body, which determines whether there is a residue, each time a further dose is given, from the previous dosage; (b) the induction of metabolizing enzymes, which by accelerating disposal of drug may diminish cumulation from previous doses, but may also increase or decrease the effect of a test dose according to whether metabolism activates or deactivates it; (c) the development of cellular tolerance, by which the cells involved come to be less responsive to a given concentration of drug. It must be noted that insofar as the drug cumulates, this masks the development of tolerance. Results such as those in Fig. 13 suggest that this may be happening in the rat. This species eliminates Δ^1-THC very slowly, and it could be suggested that it takes some days before a cumulative steady state is set up. The final level of drug achieved in the tissues would naturally vary with different animals. Thereafter, tolerance could show itself overtly. Function would return to normal only if the degree of tolerance were sufficient to overcome the result of cumulation. We suggest that this may explain the pattern observed by Carlini (1968) and that the animals he classed as nontolerant developed little less tolerance in dose-ratio terms than the others, but that they were more liable to cumulation. Induced microsomal activity would, of course, modify this picture, and further work to test whether treatment longer than 5 days (Dewey *et al.*, 1970a) would induce is required.

There are inadequate data to test this approach: the single negative report of tolerance in the rabbit (Lipparini *et al.*, 1969), an animal that eliminates Δ^1-THC considerably faster than the rat, is compatible with an approximate matching of cumulation and development of tolerance. On the same basis, it could be suggested that tolerance develops in the pigeon rapidly, because it disposes of the drug relatively rapidly from the start, but there are many other possibilities.

VII. General Discussion

One of the keys to understanding the pharmacology of cannabis is the lipophilicity of its main active principles, and in particular that of Δ^1-THC. The ability of Δ^1-THC to traverse cell membranes, and hence its activity by mouth, stems from this property, as does its ability to act on brain and to reach the fetus and its susceptibility to metabolism. Its metabolism by microsomal enzymes falls into the general patterns by which more polar metabolites are produced from nonpolar drugs, and large molecular weight substances are eliminated in the bile. A number of aspects of its distribution in the body, its binding to lipoprotein in the blood and its prolonged duration of action and cumulative toxicity, can be traced to the same physical property. That property, of course, also links it to the general anesthetics as a class, whose potency correlates over a remarkable range of substances with solubility in a biological phase of solubility parameter $\delta \simeq 9$ (Miller *et al.*, 1967), and perhaps to the especially lipophilic anesthetics such as trichloroethylene, halothane, and methoxyfluorane in particular. The analogy extends to a number of effects: the inhibition of arousal; the delaying of extinction of a conditioned avoidance response; the depressant effect on respiratory, vasomotor, and thermoregulatory centers and on ion transport in red cells; and the stimulant effect on ACTH release and (presumptive) inhibition of ADH release, properties shared with alcohol. There are, too, analogies between the cannabinoids and the barbiturates in the neurophysiological actions, in the way convulsant phenomena appear in tetrahydrocannabinol derivatives (just as they do in certain barbiturates), and in the manner in which successive doses lead first to cumulation and increased effect, and later to tolerance.

However, it is not possible to equate the action of cannabis and Δ^1-THC simply with the nonspecific narcosis produced by volatile anesthetics. First, Δ^1-THC is too active, and at an effective dose of the order of 0.1–0.5 mg/kg or less is far more potent than the anesthetics, of which at least 10–50 times as much is needed to produce detectable effects. Structures closely related to it, such as cannabinol or cannabidiol, also highly fat soluble, are lacking in the characteristic action. Second, while there are analogies, there are also many detailed aspects in which the properties of cannabis and anesthetics differ: the resistance of the ACTH release to barbiturates, the lack of an initial increase in pigeon key pecking, the extraordinary development of tolerance in the pigeon, and the difficulty of producing a state comparable with surgical anesthesia. Finally, there are a few instances in which it appears that, of two optically active pairs, cannabislike activity is greater in one isomer than the other. Thus, of the two Δ^3 isomers (the asymmetry arising at the C-1), the $(-)$ isomer is said to be 4 or 11–15 times as active as the $(+)$ isomer (Leaf et al., 1942; Loewe, 1950); $(-)$-Δ^1- and $(-)$-Δ^6-THC have been stated to be more active than their respective racemates (Scheckel et al., 1968), and $(+)$-Δ^6-THC has been said to be inactive at the ED_{50} of the $(-)$ derivative (Mechoulam and Gaoni, 1967) (see also Chapter 2). The evidence is still somewhat limited, and it is possible, for instance, that the isomers are metabolized differently, although it is not clear whether one would then predict a higher or lower activity for the more slowly metabolized isomer. The general question of the structure–action relationships for the cannabinols is discussed in Chapter 2 and will be mentioned in the next chapter, since data on man are also involved, but if one adds these to the stereoisomeric evidence, the indications that the cannabis effect is specific in terms of chemical structure are too great to allow a simple equation with anesthetics at this stage. Yet so high is the partition coefficient of Δ^1-THC, that it must in any cell be associated strongly with lipid constituents, and a reasonable view would be that its characteristic action arises from a specific structural fit into a hydrophobic environment in some cell membrane. One might also anticipate that effects related to anesthesia will be produced in some exponents in which relatively high doses are used.

If, then, one views the action of Δ^1-THC as at least in part specific, the question arises whether illuminating analogies with other compounds can be found. The most striking comparison is with morphine. Both drugs produce analgesia; the Straub tail and other behavioral responses in the mouse; vomiting, scratching, and bradycardia in dogs; an arousable "stupor" in all animals; hypothermia and, when tolerance has developed, hyperthermia; a depression of TSH release and rise in ACTH; a mixture of pupillary constriction and (particularly with excitement) dilatation; depression of respiratory rate and of the vasomotor center; and depression of the nerve-evoked twitch of guinea pig ileum without antagonizing acetylcholine. Yet important differences exist: the ratio of analgesic activity to that of morphine varies considerably with the test used; the hypotension to sciatic nerve stimulation in the rabbit is not blocked; morphine hyperactivity in the rat is not potentiated but antagonized; and the ACTH secretion evoked resists barbiturates. There is, in addition, no antagonism to Δ^1-THC by opiate antagonists. This may not be very significant, for although some structural resemblances between Δ^1-THC and the opiates can be traced, and may be important, the lack of an amino group must make it unlikely that morphine antagonists, for which amino substitution is the critical molecular change, should be effective. The lack of opiate-type withdrawal symptoms is also of uncertain significance, since the rate of disappearance of Δ^1-THC from the tissues after a period of treatment must be very much slower than that of an opiate after corresponding treatment. However, the evident absence of any cross tolerance with morphine may be a serious complication in the analogy between the drugs.

Chlorpromazine is another drug with which analogies may be drawn. With it is shared the ability to produce a "cataleptic" state; depression of aggressiveness, of arousal, and of the conditioned avoidance response; mild analgesia; hypothermia; prolongation of barbiturate sleep; and, in the mouse, ptosis and narrowing of the palpebral fissure. Yet cannabis is emetic rather than antiemetic, has little protective effect against amphetamine toxicity, and may synergize with the latter, and cannabis has less effect on spontaneous activity. Nor can chlorpromazine imitate the hypersensitivity that cannabis induces. In the same way, parallelisms with other drugs such as amphetamine, cocaine, phenytoin, or atropine, suggested by particular pharmacological actions, or with other nitrogen-free drugs such as chloralose and picrotoxin, fail to reveal any other substance whose profile matches that of cannabis, particularly the combination of analgesia, ataxia, "catalepsy," and hypersensitivity to sensory stimuli. Nor does one readily find another substance so "contradictory," capable of taming yet producing aggressiveness, of both enhancing and depressing spontaneous activity, of being an anticonvulsant yet generating epileptiform cortical discharges.

This discussion of possible analogies reflects, of course, the difficulty of classifying cannabis and of defining the best method of analyzing its action. Its low solubility in water, the metabolism of Δ^1-THC, the flat dose–response curve, and the long duration of its action such that only a single dose may be possible during an experiment present considerable problems for the experimenter. For the time being the animal work does not allow one to do more than characterize it as a potent, highly lipophilic substance; probably related in its properties to the anesthetics and perhaps also to morphine; acting perhaps chiefly at the levels of the reticular formation, the thalamus, and the cerebellum; able, on the cholinergic terminals of Auerbach's plexus at least, to reduce transmitter output; and having a protean and contradictory pattern of action.

References

Abel, E. L. (1970). *J. Pharm. Pharmacol.* **22**, 785.

Abel, E. L., and Schiff, B. B. (1969). *Psychonom. Sci.* **16**, 38.

Agurell, S. (1970). In "The Botany and Chemistry of Cannabis" (C. R. B. Joyce and S. H. Curry, eds.), pp. 175–191. Churchill, London.

Agurell, S., Nilsson, I. M., Ohlsson, A., and Sandberg, F. (1969). *Biochem. Pharmacol.* **18**, 1195.

Agurell, S., Nilsson, I. M., Ohlsson, A., and Sandberg, F. (1970). *Biochem. Pharmacol.* **19**, 1333.

Alles, G. A., Icke, R. N., and Feigen, G. A. (1942a). *J. Amer. Chem. Soc.* **64**, 2031.

Alles, G. A., Haagen-Smit, A. J., Feigen, G. A., and Dandliker, W. B. (1942b). *J. Pharmacol. Exp. Ther.* **76**, 21.

Ames, F. (1958). *J. Ment. Sci.* **104**, 972.

Anderssen, J. M., Nielsen, E., Schou, J., Steentoft, A., and Worm, K. (1971). *Acta Pharmacol. Toxicol.* **29**, 111.

Apter, J. T., and Pfeiffer, C. C. (1956). *Amer. J. Ophthalmol.* **42**, 206.

Avison, A. W. D., Morrison, A. L., and Parkes, M. W. (1949). *J. Chem. Soc.* 952.

Bailey, P. T., Pradhan, S. N., and Ghosh, B. (1971). *Fed. Proc. Fed. Amer. Soc. Exp. Biol.* **30**, 279.

Barry, H., III, Perhach, J. L., Jr., and Kubena, R. K. (1970). *Pharmacologist* **12**, 258.

Ben-Zvi, Z., Mechoulam, R., and Burstein, S. (1970). *J. Amer. Chem. Soc.* **92**, 3468.

Bercht, C. A. L., and Salemink, C. A. (1969). U.N. Secretariat Document ST/SOA/SER. S/21.

Bicher, H. I., and Mechoulam, R. (1968). *Arch. Int. Pharmacodyn. Ther.* **172**, 24.

Black, M. B., Woods, J. H., and Domino, E. F. (1970). *Pharmacologist* **12**, 258.

Borgen, L. A., and Davis, W. M. (1970). *Pharmacologist* **12**, 259.

Bose, B. C., Saifi, A. Q., and Bhagwat, A. W. (1963a). *Arch. Int. Pharmacodyn. Ther.* **141**, 520.

Bose, B. C., Vijayvorgiya, R., Saifi, A. Q., and Bhagwat, A. W. (1963b). *Arch. Int. Pharmacodyn. Ther.* **146**, 99.

Bose, B. C., Saifi, A. Q., and Bhagwat, A. W. (1964a). *Arch. Int. Pharmacodyn. Ther.* **147**, 285.

Bose, B. C., Saifi, A. Q., and Bhagwat, A. W. (1964b). *Arch. Int. Pharmacodyn. Ther.* **147**, 291.

Boyd, E. S., and Meritt, D. A. (1965a). *J. Pharmacol. Exp. Ther.* **149**, 138.

Boyd, E. S., and Meritt, D. A. (1965b). *Arch. Int. Pharmacodyn. Ther.* **153**, 1.

Boyd, E. S., and Meritt, D. A. (1966). *J. Pharmacol. Exp. Ther.* **151**, 376.

Boyd, E. S., Hutchinson, E. D., Gardner, L. C., and Meritt, D. A. (1963). *Arch. Int. Pharmacodynam. Ther.* **144**, 533.

Burstein, S. (1971). N.Y. Acad. Sci. Conference on Marijuana, Abstract 15a.

Burstein, S. H., Menezes, F., Williamson, E., and Mechoulam, R. (1970). *Nature (London)* **225**, 87.

Buxbaum, D., Sanders-Bush, E., and Efron, D. H. (1969). *Fed. Proc. Fed. Amer. Soc. Exp. Biol.* **28**, No. 2, 735.

Carlini, E. A. (1968). *Pharmacology* **1**, 135.

Carlini, G. R. S., and Carlini, E. A. (1965). *Med. Pharmacol. Exp.* **12**, 21.

Carlini, E. A., and Goldman, J. (1968). *Acta Physiol. Lat. Amer.* **18**, 274.

Carlini, E. A., and Kramer, C. (1965). *Psychopharmacologia* **7**, 175.

Carlini, E. A., and Masur, J. (1969). *Life Sci.* **8**, 607.

Carlini, E. A., Santos, M., Claussen, U., Bieniek, D., and Korte, F. (1970). *Psychopharmacologia* **18**, 82.

Chenoweth, M. B., Robertson, D. N., Erley, D. S., and Golhke, R. (1962). *Anesthesiology* **23**, 101.

Chopra, I. C., and Chopra, R. N. (1957). *Bull. Narcotics* **9**, No. 1, 4.

Christensen, H. D., Freudenthal, R. I., Gidley, J. T., Rosenfeld, R., Boegli, G., Testino, L., Brine, D. R., Pitt, C. G., and Wall, M. E. (1971). *Science* **172**, 165.

Christiansen, J., and Rafaelsen, O. J. (1969). *Psychopharmacologia* **15**, 60.

Cortez, L., Jr., Chaud Sob, J., and Louzada, N. L. (1966). III International Pharmacological Congress, San Paulo, Brazil, Abstract 667.

Curry, A. S., and Patterson, D. A. (1970). Private communication.

Dagirmanjian, R., and Boyd, E. S. (1960). *Fed. Proc. Fed. Amer. Soc. Exp. Biol.* **19**, 267.

Dagirmanjian, R., and Boyd, E. S. (1962). *J. Pharmacol. Exp. Ther.* **135**, 25.

Dahi, M. A. Y. (1951). *Fed. Proc. Fed. Amer. Soc. Exp. Biol.* **10**, 290.

Davies, O. L., Raventos, J., and Walpole, A. L. (1946). *Brit. J. Pharmacol.* **1**, 255.

Davis, J. P., and Ramsay, H. H. (1949). *Fed. Proc. Fed. Amer. Soc. Exp. Biol.* **8**, 284.

de Farias, R. C. (1955). *Bull. Narcotics* **7**, No. 2, 5.

Dewey, W. L., Kennedy, J. S., and Howes, J. F. (1970a). *Fed. Proc. Fed. Amer. Soc. Exp. Biol.* **29**, 650.

Dewey, W. L., Peng, T.-C., and Harris, L. S. (1970b). *Eur. J. Pharmacol.* **12**, 382.

Dewey, W. L., Yonce, L. R., Harris, L. S., Reavis, W. M., Griffin, E. D., Jr., and Newby, V. E. (1970c). *Pharmacologist* **12**, 259.

Dewey, W. L., Harris, L. S., Howes, J. F., Kennedy, J. S., Granchelli, F. E., Pars, H. G., and Razdan, R. K. (1970d). *Nature (London)* **226**, 1265.

Dixon, W. E. (1899). *Brit. Med. J.* **2**, 1354.

Duquénois, P. (1939). *Bull. Sci. Pharmacol.* **46**, 222.

Duquénois, P. (1950). *Bull. Narcotics* **2**, No. 3, 30.

Egdahl, R. H., Nelson, D. H., and Hume, D. M. (1955). *Science* **121**, 506.

Fenimore, D. C., and Loy, P. R. (1971). *J. Pharm. Pharmacol.* **23**, 310.

Fink, B. R., ed. (1968). "Toxicity of Anesthetics," Chaps. 22–26, pp. 259–323. Williams & Wilkins, Baltimore, Maryland.

Foltz, R. L., Fentiman, A. F., Jr., Leighty, E. G., Walter, J. L., Drewes, H. R., Schwartz, W. E., Page, T. F., Jr., and Truitt, E. B., Jr. (1970). *Science* **168**, 844.

Ford, R. D., and McMillan, D. E. (1971). *Fed. Proc. Fed. Amer. Soc. Exp. Biol.* **30**, 279.

Forney, R. B. (1971). N.Y. Acad. Sci. Conference on Marijuana, Abstract 7.

Fraenkel, S. (1903). *Arch. Exp. Pathol. Pharmakol.* **49**, 266.

Frankenheim, J. M., McMillan, D. E., and Harris, L. S. (1970). *Fed. Proc. Fed. Amer. Soc. Exp. Biol.* **29**, 619.

Garattini, S. (1965). *In* "Hashish. Its Chemistry and Pharmacology" (G. E. W. Wolstenholme and J. Knight, eds.), pp. 70–82. Churchill, London.

Garriott, J. C., King, L. J., Forney, R. B., and Hughes, F. W. (1967). *Life Sci.* **6**, 2119.

Garriott, J. C., Forney, R. B., Hughes, F. W., and Richard, A. B. (1968). *Arch. Int. Pharmacodyn. Ther.* **171**, 425.

Gayer, H. (1928). *Arch. Exp. Pathol. Pharmakol.* **129**, 312.

Geber, W. F., and Schramm, L. C. (1969a). *Arch. Int. Pharmacodyn. Ther.* **177**, 224.

Geber, W. F., and Schramm, L. C. (1969b). *Toxicol. Appl. Pharmacol.* **14**, 276.

Gill, E. W. (1971a). Personal communication.

Gill, E. W. (1971b). *J. Chem. Soc. C* 579.

Gill, E. W., and Jones, G. (1972). *Biochem. Pharmacol.* **21**, 2237.

Gill, E. W., and Paton, W. D. M. (1970). In "The Botany and Chemistry of Cannabis" (C. R. B. Joyce and S. H. Curry, eds.), pp. 165–173. Churchill, London.

Gill, E. W., Paton, W. D. M., and Pertwee, R. G. (1970). Nature (London) 228, 134.

Goodall, A. (1910). Pharm. J. Pharm. 84, 112.

Grlić, L. (1962). Bull. Narcotics 14, No. 3, 337.

Grunfeld, Y., and Edery, H. (1969). Psychopharmacologia 14, 200.

Haagen-Smit, A. J., Wawra, C. Z., Koepfli, J. B., Alles, G. A., Feigen, G. A., and Prater, A. N. (1940). Science 91, 602.

Hardman, H. F., Domino, E. F., Woods, L. A., and Seevers, M. H. (1970). Pharmacologist 12, 258.

Henriksson, B. G., and Järbe, T. (1971). J. Pharm. Pharmacol. 23, 457.

Ho, B. T., Fritchie, G. E., Kralik, P. M., Englert, L. F., McIsaac, W. M., and Idänpään-Heikkilä, J. (1970). J. Pharm. Pharmacol. 22, 538.

Ho, B. T., Fritchie, G. E., Englert, L. F., McIsaac, W. M., and Idänpään-Heikkilä, J. (1971). J. Pharm. Pharmacol. 23, 309.

Hockman, C. H., Perrie, R. G., and Kalant, H. (1971). Science 172, 968.

Holtzman, D., Lovell, R. A., Jaffe, J. H., and Freedman, D. X. (1969). Science 163, 1464.

Idänpään-Heikkilä, J., Fritchie, G. E., Englert, L. F., Ho, B. T., and McIsaac, W. M. (1969). N. Engl. J. Med. 281, 330.

Irwin, S. (1968). Psychopharmacologia 13, 222.

Isbell, H., Gorodetzsky, C. W., Jasinski, D. R., Claussen, U., von Spulak, F., and Korte, F. (1967). Psychopharmacologia 11, 184.

Jaffe, P. G., and Baum, M. (1971). Psychopharmacologia 20, 97.

Joachimoglu, G. (1965). In "Hashish. Its Chemistry and Pharmacology" (G. E. W. Wolstenholme and J. Knight, eds.), pp. 2–11. Churchill, London.

Joachimoglu, G., and Miras, C. (1963). Bull. Narcotics 15, No. 3–4, 7.

Kabelik, J., Krejčí, Z., and Šantavý, F. (1960). Bull. Narcotics 12, No. 3, 5.

Kennedy, J. S., and Waddell, W. J. (1971). Fed. Proc. Fed. Amer. Soc. Exp. Biol. 30, 279.

King, L. J., and Forney, R. B. (1967). Fed. Proc. Fed. Amer. Soc. Exp. Biol. 26, 540.

Klausner, H. A., and Dingell, J. V. (1970). Pharmacologist 12, 259.

Krejčí, Z. (1970). In "The Botany and Chemistry of Cannabis" (C. R. B. Joyce and S. H. Curry, eds.), pp. 49–55. Churchill, London.

Kubena, R. K., and Barry, H., III (1970). J. Pharmacol. Exp. Ther. 173, 94.

Kubena, R. K., Perhach, J. L., Jr., and Barry, H., III (1971). Eur. J. Pharmacol. 14, 89.

Lapa, A. J., Sampaio, C. A. M., Timo-Laria, C., and Valle, J. R. (1968). J. Pharm. Pharmacol. 20, 373.

Layman, J. M., and Milton, A. S. (1971a). Brit. J. Pharmacol. 41, 379P.

Layman, J. M., and Milton, A. S. (1971b). Brit. J. Pharmacol. 42, 308.

Leaf, G., Todd, A. R., and Wilkinson, S. (1942). J. Chem. Soc. 185.

Lemberger, L., Silberstein, S. D., Axelrod, J., and Kopin, I. J. (1970). Science 170, 1320.

Lemberger, L., Axelrod, J., and Kopin, I. J. (1971). N.Y. Acad. Sci. Conference on Marijuana. Abstract 12.

Lerman, H., and Paton, W. D. M. (1960). Brit. J. Pharmacol. Chemother. 15, 458.

Lerner, M., and Zeffert, J. T. (1968). Bull. Narcotics 20, No. 2, 53.

Lerner, P. (1969). Bull. Narcotics 21, No. 3, 39.

Lipparini, F., Scotti de Carolis, A., and Longo, V. G. (1969). Physiol. Behav. 4, 527.

Loewe, S. (1939). J. Pharmacol. Exp. Ther. 66, 23.

Loewe, S. (1944). In "The Marihuana Problems in the City of New York" (Mayor's Committee on Marihuana), pp. 149–212. Jaques Cattell Press, Lancaster, Pennsylvania.

Loewe, S. (1945a). *J. Pharmacol. Exp. Ther.* **84**, 78.
Loewe, S. (1945b). *Science* **102**, 615.
Loewe, S. (1946a). *J. Pharmacol. Exp. Ther.* **88**, 154.
Loewe, S. (1946b). *J. Pharmacol. Exp. Ther.* **86**, 294.
Loewe, S. (1947). *Science* **106**, 89.
Loewe, S. (1950). *Arch. Exp. Pathol. Pharmakol.* **211**, 175.
Loewe, S., and Adams, R. (1947). *Fed. Proc. Fed. Amer. Soc. Exp. Biol.* **6**, 352.
Loewe, S., and Goodman, L. S. (1947). *Fed. Proc. Fed. Amer. Soc. Exp. Biol.* **6**, 352.
Lomax, P. (1970). *Agents and Actions* **1**, 252.
Lomax, P. (1971). *Res. Commun. Chem. Pathol. Pharmacol.* **2**, 159.
McIsaac, W. M., Fritchie, G. E., Idänpään-Heikkilä, J., Ho, B. T., and Englert, L. F.
   (1971). *Nature (London)* **230**, 593.
McMillan, D. E., Harris, L. S., Frankenheim, J. M., and Kennedy, J. S. (1970a). *Science*
   169, 501.
McMillan, D. E., Harris, L. S., Turk, R. F., and Kennedy, J. S. (1970b). *Pharmacologist*
   12, 258.
McMillan, D. E., Dewey, W. L., and Harris, L. S. (1971). N.Y. Acad. Sci. Conference
   on Marijuana, Abstract 8.
Magus, R. D., and Harris, L. S. (1971). *Fed. Proc. Fed. Amer. Soc. Exp. Biol.* **30**, 279.
Maître, L., Staehelin, M., and Bein, H. J. (1970). *Agents and Actions* **1**, 136.
Marshall, C. R. (1897). *Lancet* **1**, 235.
Martin, P. A. (1969). *Lancet* **1**, 370.
Marx, H., and Eckhardt, G. (1933). *Arch. Exp. Pathol. Pharmakol.* **170**, 395.
Masur, J., and Khazan, N. (1970). *Life Sci.* **9**, 1275.
Mechoulam, R. (1970). *Science* **168**, 1159.
Mechoulam, R., and Gaoni, Y. (1967). *Fortschr. Chem. Org. Naturst.* **25**, 175.
Mechoulam, R., Shani, A., Edery, H., and Grunfeld, Y. (1970a). *Science* **169**, 611.
Mechoulam, R., Shani, A., Yagnitinsky, B., Ben-Zvi, Z., Braun, P., and Gaoni, Y.
   (1970b). *In* "The Botany and Chemistry of Cannabis" (C. R. B. Joyce and S. H.
   Curry, eds.), pp. 93–117. Churchill, London.
Mechoulam, R., Ben-Zvi, Z., Edery, H., and Grunfeld, Y. (1971). N.Y. Acad. Sci.
   Conference on Marijuana, Abstract 4.
Mikeš, F., and Waser, P. G. (1971). *Science* **172**, 1158.
Miller, K. W., Paton, W. D. M., and Smith, E. B. (1967). *Brit. J. Anaesth.* **39**, 910.
Miras, C. J. (1965). *In* "Hashish. Its Chemistry and Pharmacology" (G. E. W. Wolsten-
   holme and J. Knight, eds.), pp. 37–47. Churchill, London.
Miras, C. J., Simos, S., and Kiburis, J. (1964). *Bull. Narcotics* **16**, No. 1, 13.
Moreton, J. E., and Davis, W. (1970). *Pharmacologist* **12**, 258.
Munch, J. C. (1931). "Bioassays," pp. 67–88. Baillière, London.
Munson, P. L. (1963). *In* "Advances in Neuroendocrinology" (A. V. Nalbandov, ed.),
   pp. 427–444. Univ. of Illinois Press, Urbana.
Myers, H. B. (1916). *J. Pharmacol. Exp. Ther.* **8**, 417.
Neu, R. L., Powers, H. O., King, S., and Gardner, L. I. (1969). *Lancet* **1**, 675.
Nilsson, I. M., Agurell, S., Nilsson, J. L. G., Ohlsson, A., Sandberg, F., and Wahlqvist,
   M. (1970). *Science* **168**, 1228.
O'Shaughnessy, W. B. (1842). "The Bengal Dispensatory," pp. 579–604. Thacker, Cal-
   cutta, St. Andrews Library.
Pace, H. B., Davis, W. M., and Borgen, L. A. (1971). N.Y. Acad. Sci. Conference on
   Marijuana. Abstract 10.
Paton, W. D. M., and Pertwee, R. G. (1972). *Brit. J. Pharmacol.* **44**, 250.

Paton, W. D. M., and Pertwee, R. G. (1971). Unpublished results.

Paton, W. D. M., and Temple, D. (1971). Unpublished results.

Persaud, T. V. N., and Ellington, A. C. (1967). *Lancet* 2, 1306.

Persaud, T. V. N., and Ellington, A. C. (1968). *Lancet* 2, 406.

Pertwee, R. G. (1971). Unpublished results.

Pertwee, R. G. (1972). *Brit. J. Pharmacol.* 46, 753.

Phillips, R. N., Turk, R. F., and Forney, R. B. (1971). *Proc. Soc. Exp. Biol. Med.* 136, 260.

Porter, C. D., and Scott, K. G. (1970). *Res. Commun. Chem. Pathol. Pharmacology* 1, 733.

Prychodko, W. (1958). *Ecology* 39, 500.

Rushton, R., Steinberg, H., and Tinson, C. (1963). *Brit. J. Pharmacol. Chemother.* 20, 99.

Russell, P. B., Todd, A. R., Wilkinson, S., Macdonald, A. D., and Woolfe, G. (1941a). *J. Chem. Soc.* 169.

Russell, P. B., Todd, A. R., Wilkinson, S., Macdonald, A. D., and Woolfe, G. (1941b). *J. Chem. Soc.* 826.

Salustiano, J., Hoshino, K., and Carlini, E. A. (1966). *Med. Pharmacol. Exp.* 15, 153.

Sampaio, C. A. M., and Lapa, A. J. (1966). III International Pharmacological Congress, San Paulo, Brazil, Abstract 668.

Santos, M., Sampaio, M. R. P., Fernandes, N. S., and Carlini, E. A. (1966). *Psychopharmacologia* 8, 437.

Scheckel, C. L., Boff, E., Dahlen, P., and Smart, T. (1968). *Science* 160, 1467.

Schildkraut, J. J., and Efron, D. H. (1971). *Psychopharmacologia* 20, 191.

Shoyama, Y., Yamaguchi, A., Sato, T., Yamauchi, T., and Nishioka, I. (1969). *J. Pharm. Soc. Jap.* 89, 842.

Siegel, R. K. (1969). *Psychopharmacologia* 15, 1.

Siegel, R. K., and Poole, J. (1969). *Psychol. Rep.* 25, 704.

Silva, M. T. A., Carlini, E. A., Claussen, U., and Korte, F. (1968). *Psychopharmacologia* 13, 332.

Sofia, R. D., and Barry, H., III (1970). *Eur. J. Pharmacol.* 13, 134.

Sofia, R. D., and Dixit, B. N. (1971). *Fed. Proc. Fed. Amer. Soc. Exp. Biol.* 30, 279.

Sofia, R. D., Dixit, B. N., and Barry, H., III (1971). *Life Sci.* 10, 425.

Truitt, E. B., Jr. (1970). *Fed. Proc. Fed. Amer. Soc. Exp. Biol.* 29, 619.

Valle, J. R. (1969). *Int. J. Addict.* 4, 623.

Valle, J. R., Souza, J. A., and Neide Hyppolito (1966). *J. Pharm. Pharmacol.* 18, 476.

Valle, J. R., Baratella, J. R. S., Tangary, M. R., and Neide da Silva, E. (1967). *An. Acad. Brasil. Cienc.* 39, 445.

Valle, J. R., Lapa, A. J., Barros, G. G. (1968). *J. Pharm. Pharmacol.* 20, 798.

Vieira, F. J. A., Aguiar, M. B., Alencar, J. W., Prado Seabra, A., Tursch, B. M., and Leclercq, J. (1967). *Psychopharmacologia* 10, 361.

Wahlqvist, M., Nilsson, I. M., Sandberg, F., Agurell, S., and Grandstrand, B. (1970). *Biochem. Pharmacol.* 19, 2579.

Wall, M. E. (1971). N.Y. Acad. Sci. Conference on Marijuana, Abstract 3.

Wall, M. E., Brine, D. R., Brine, G. A., Pitt, C. G., Freudenthal, R. I., and Christensen, H. D. (1970). *J. Amer. Chem. Soc.* 92, 3466.

Walters, G. C., and Abel, E. L. (1970). *J. Pharm. Pharmacol.* 22, 310.

Walton, R. P. (1938). "Marihuana." Lippincott, Philadelphia, Pennsylvania.

Walton, R. P., Martin, L. F., and Keller, J. H. (1938). *J. Pharmacol. Exp. Ther.* 62, 239.

Waskow, I. E., Olsson, J. E., Salzman, C., and Katz, M. M. (1970). *Arch. Gen. Psychiat.* 22, 97.

Welch, B. L., Welch, A. S., Messiha, F. S., and Berger, H. J. (1971). *Res. Commun. Chem. Pathol. Pharmacol.* **2**, 382.

Widman, M., Nilsson, I. M., Nilsson, J. L. G., Agurell, S., and Leander, K. (1971). *Life Sci.* **10**, 157.

Williams, E. G., Himmelsbach, C. K., Wikler, A., and Ruble, D. C. (1946). *Pub. Health Rep.* **61**, 1059.

Wollner, H. J., Matchett, J. R., Levine, J., and Loewe, S. (1942). *J. Amer. Chem. Soc.* **64**, 26.

Yamauchi, T., Shoyama, Y., Aramaki, H., Azuma, T., and Nishioka, I. (1967). *Chem. Pharm. Bull.* **15**, 1075.

Addendum

BEHAVIORAL AND EXPERIMENTAL PSYCHOLOGY

There has been a great expansion in this type of work, which may be grouped under the following heads:

A. *With food or water reinforcement*

1. Operant studies with varying FR and FI parameters: Frankenheim *et al.* (1971), rat, pigeon; Conrad *et al.* (1972), chimpanzee; Pradhan *et al.* (1972), rat; Ferraro and Billings (1972), chimpanzee; Ferraro *et al.* (1971), chimpanzee; McMillan *et al.* (1972), pigeon, rat; Manning and Elsmore (1972), rat; Elsmore (1972), rhesus and macaque; Peterson *et al.* (1971), rat; Harris *et al.* (1972), rhesus

2. DRL (differential reinforcement of low rate of responding): Webster *et al.* (1971), rat; Zimmerberg *et al.* (1971), rhesus; Ferraro and Billings (1972), chimpanzee; Ferraro *et al.* (1971), chimpanzee; Harris *et al.* (1972), rhesus

3. Maze running: Carlini *et al.* (1970), rat; Orsingher and Fulginiti (1970), rat; Gonzalez and Carlini (1971), rat

4. Rope climbing: Bueno and Carlini (1972), rat

5. Worker/nonworker pairs: Masur *et al.* (1972a), rat

6. NSSA (nonspatial single alternation task): Drew and Miller (1972), rat

B. *With aversive stimulation*

1. CAR (conditioned avoidance response): Henriksson and Järbe (1971), rat; Orsingher and Fulginiti (1970), rat; Newman *et al.* (1972), rat; Pradhan *et al.* (1972), rat; Robichaud *et al.* (1972), mouse, rat; Harris *et al.* (1972), rhesus

2. CER (conditioned emotional response): Gonzalez *et al.* (1972), rat

3. Sidman avoidance schedule: Webster *et al.* (1971), rat; Herring (1972), rat

C. *Studies on aggression*

1. Chronic dosage with or without food deprivation: Carlini and Masur (1970), rat; Carlini *et al.* (1972), rat; Neto and Carlini (1972), rat; Thompson and Rosenkrantz (1971), rat; Carlini and Gonzalez (1972), rat
2. Isolated mouse aggression: Kilbey *et al.* (1972); Neto and Carlini (1972)
3. Food competition: Masur *et al.* (1971a, 1972b), rat
4. Aggression provoked by electric shock: Manning and Elsmore (1972); Carder and Olson (1972)
5. Fighting fish: Gonzalez *et al.* (1971)

D. *Miscellaneous*

1. Spontaneous motor activity: Carlini *et al.* (1970), mouse; Davis *et al.* (1972), rat; Potvin and Fried (1972), rat
2. Open field behavior: Drew *et al.* (1972), rat; Gonzalez and Carlini (1971), rat; Masur *et al.* (1971b), rat; Potvin and Fried (1972), rat
3. Saccharine choice: Elsmore and Fletcher (1972), rat
4. Habituation tests: Brown (1971), mouse
5. Self-stimulation: Pradhan *et al.* (1972), rat
6. Control of light intensity in pigeons: Ford and McMillan (1972)
7. State dependence: Kubena *et al.* (1972), rat; Kubena and Barry (1972), rat; Bueno and Carlini (1972), rat

These tests show that Δ^1-THC exerts a depressant effect on most forms of conditioned and unconditioned behavior, although at low doses some excitatory effects do exist. Only a few findings can be mentioned. Of special interest, since it provides a link with human experience, is a dose-related effect on time sense. Animals tended to respond prematurely, as though "felt" time were longer than "clock" time. The studies with DRL schedules, in which the animal learns to defer a response for a specific period such as 60 seconds, proved particularly sensitive to the drug. Memory may also become disrupted by the drug. Acquisition and retention of learning was impaired, as was transfer to the undrugged state of material learned during the drugged state ("symmetrical state-dependent learning"), and there was disruption of previously learned behavior. Experiments with worker/nonworker pairs led Masur *et al.* (1972a) to attribute impairment of learned behavior by cannabis to "deconditioning" rather than to a reduction in motivation or motor function. A new type of observation is the impairment by cannabis in the mouse of habituation to a new environment.

Considerable attention has been paid to the problem of aggression. On the one hand, the aggression induced by chronic dosage combined with starvation has been confirmed and shown to be augmented by treatment with *p*-chlorophenylalanine (which depletes brain 5-HT) or with DOPA (which can increase brain catecholamine). In addition, a more extensive analysis of factors influencing aggressiveness elicited by cannabis has been made. It has been found that effects of starvation per se (hypoglycemia, acidosis, lack of specific nutrients) are not responsible and that starvation is but one of several stressful conditions (cold, abstinence from morphine, electric shock, or simply chronic dosage) that can lead to cannabis-induced aggression. On the other hand, with fighting fish or with mice previously made aggressive by isolation, aggression is impaired. Under conditions of food competition, increased or diminished aggression occurred according to the nature of the test used. With shock-induced fighting and with stimuli sufficient to produce 50% fighting, THC was inactive. It seems likely, therefore, that the effect of cannabis depends on the initial level of "aggression" and that the drug may both facilitate its appearance when not initially present and attenuate it when preexisting.

Tolerance has also been frequently studied and has invariably been found in animal studies when tested for. A very interesting and theoretically important point is that the rate of development of tolerance varies with the animal and the function studied. In the pigeon tolerance develops with particular rapidity in 1–2 days, as it does to the initial excitant effect in rats. But tolerance takes 10–20 days to develop against other effects in the rat, such as on maze running, bar pressing, motor activity, rope climbing, or acquirement of a conditioned emotional response. In the dog, overreaction induced by cannabis disappears early, followed by ataxia, and the tolerance extends to the lethal effect; however, sedation and anorexia persist, as does the sensitivity in the rat of a preexisting conditioned emotional response to cannabis. The tolerance achieved can be considerable; in the pigeon it may be 100-fold and last for over 1 but less than 5 months.

A recurrent theme in these studies is comparison with other drugs. As with earlier studies, differences from the opiates (Frankenheim *et al.*, 1971; McMillan *et al.*, 1972), chlorpromazine (Masur *et al.*, 1972a; Frankenheim *et al.*, 1971; Zimmerberg *et al.*, 1971), chlordiazepoxide (Pirch *et al.*, 1972), barbiturates (Frankenheim *et al.*, 1971; Zimmerberg *et al.*, 1971; Carlini and Masur, 1970), amphetamine (Frankenheim *et al.*, 1971; Zimmerberg *et al.*, 1971; Carlini and Masur, 1970), mescaline (Webster *et al.*, 1971; Zimmerberg *et al.*, 1971; Masur *et al.*, 1971a; Carlini and Masur, 1970), LSD (Zimmerberg *et al.*, 1971; Carlini and Masur, 1970), and caffeine (Carlini and Masur, 1970) are noted. Somewhat confusing are comparisons drawn with the behavioral effects of physostigmine (Frankenheim *et al.*, 1971), atropinelike substances (Brown, 1971), and sympathomimetic amines (Frankenheim *et al.*, 1971). The demonstration of cross-tolerance with ethanol (Newman *et al.*, 1972) makes important a test on cross-tolerance with barbiturates. Female rats have been found more sensitive than male rats by a variety of behavioral tests by Cohn *et al.* (1971).

From studies thus far, it appears that there is no one behavioral response on which Δ^1-THC is uniquely and specifically active but rather that it has a fairly wide pattern of action, from which (if desired) a diagnostic profile of two or three tests could readily be drawn. Equally, it overlaps in its effects with many drugs, yet it cannot be matched as a whole with any of them.

METABOLISM AND FATE IN THE BODY

The metabolic transformations that Δ^1-THC and its congeners may undergo have shown themselves to be unexpectedly complex, and to the hydroxylations previously recognized must be added the following: (in Δ^6-THC) hydroxylations on C-5 and on the side chain and keto formation in C-5; (in Δ^1-THC)1,2-epoxidation, keto formation on C-6, 7-carboxylation, and the formation of less polar metabolites, possibly dimers (Maynard *et al.*, 1971; Gurny *et al.*, 1972; Nakazawa and Costa, 1971a,b; Burstein *et al.*, 1972; Agurell *et al.*, 1972). The distribution of a given dose of THC over many different metabolic products offers considerable difficulties for detection or dosimetry. So far as pharmacological activity goes, however, this appears still to be mostly restricted to Δ^1-THC and the 7-OH derivative. The 6β-OH and 1,2-epoxy metabolites are active but, in rhesus monkeys at least, appear to be only about one-quarter of the potency of Δ^1-THC (Ben-Zvi *et al.*, 1971; Mechoulam *et al.*, 1972).

It has been shown, in perfusion experiments, that the rat liver can extract almost all the Δ^1-THC delivered to it, and 80% of metabolized label appears in the bile in only 2 hours (Klausner and Dingell, 1971). High fecal excretion has been confirmed in the rat and extended to the mouse, and evidence has been obtained in the rat for an enterohepatic circulation (Klausner and Dingell, 1971; Harbison and Mantilla-Plata, 1972; Dewey and Turk, 1972). It is possible that such a circulation could lead to a prolongation of THC action, but since the biliary products appear to be almost entirely the more polar and inactive metabolites, it would be necessary for these to include significant amounts of a conjugate, presumably of 7-OH-Δ^1-THC, which can be hydrolyzed and reabsorbed. An interesting species difference has appeared, namely that the squirrel monkey absorbs only a small amount of THC given orally, unlike the rhesus monkey (Forrest *et al.*, 1972). As would be expected, bile is necessary for intestinal absorption of THC; in an animal with a biliary fistula, a considerable amount of THC orally administered appears as such in the feces, whereas normally it is all metabolized to a methanol- or water-soluble form (Dewey and Turk, 1972). Metabolism has also been found to take place in rat lung homogenates; a number of metabolites appear, probably including 7-OH-Δ^1-THC, and there are two metabolites not formed by liver homogenates. This activity is strongly induced by 3-methylcholanthrene, which leaves liver activity unchanged, and such pretreatment is stated to increase the effect in rats of Δ^1-THC on motor activity (Nakazawa and Costa, 1971a,b). It is worth noting that brain homogenates do *not* appear to form the 7-OH metabolite from THC (Christensen *et al.*, 1971), so that both THC and metabolite found in brain presumably derive from the blood.

With liver microsomal preparations, metabolism of THC is inhibited by SKF 525A, nortriptyline, and desmethylimipramine, and in turn THC itself inhibits aminopyrine and hexobarbitone breakdown and estradiol and *p*-nitrophenol conjugation (Dingell *et al.*, 1971). Cannabidiol is, however, a much more active inhibitor, comparable to SKF 525A (Paton and Pertwee, 1972). Burstein and Kupfer (1971) noted that hexobarbital does not inhibit rat liver microsomal hydroxylation of Δ^1-THC, suggesting that more than a simple competitive inhibition is involved. A water-soluble form of THC, the γ-morpholinobutyric acid ester, has been shown to be hydrolyzed by the microsomes (Zitko *et al.*, 1972) sufficiently rapidly for its potency and kinetics to be comparable to those of THC. It should be a useful tool under conditions in which microsomal activity is not impaired.

DISTRIBUTION OF THC AND ITS METABOLITES

The binding of THC in blood has been confirmed. Dingell *et al.* (1971) found in the rat that 90% is associated with total protein, and 2/3 of this in the "chylomicron" fraction. Klausner and Dingell (1971) followed the decline in whole body radioactivity in the rat after an intravenous dose of labeled Δ^1-THC in a propylene glycol–serum excipient: Total radioactivity fell with a half-time of 14 hours, but THC activity (taken as the petrol-ether-soluble component) fell biphasically, with a half-time of 30 minutes, for about 2 hours, followed by a much slower decline with a half-time of 21 hours. This corresponds to data on human blood levels and suggests that, after a rapid phase of THC distribution and metabolism, a prolonged phase of release of THC from a site immune to metabolism takes place. It may be noted that THC binds not only to plasma constituents but also to microsomes and nuclear fractions in homogenates (Dingell *et al.*, 1971).

Distribution of label including metabolites has been analyzed, either by measuring total radioactivity or diethyl-ether-extractable activity or by autoradiography [Harbison and Mantilla-Plata (1972), Klausner and Dingell (1971), tissue samples; Freudenthal *et al.* (1972), Kennedy and Waddell (1972), autoradiography], and it is becoming possible to build up a consistent pattern. The high localization in lung and spleen has been confirmed, but attributed at least in part to circulation of droplets or microemboli of injected material when given intravenously. Liver and kidney show high activity corresponding to their excretory roles. Plasma, muscle, brain, and heart run roughly parallel, as does placenta and (at a level about 30% of placental) the fetus and amniotic fluid. Fat levels depend on conditions of administration; quite low levels follow intravenous dosage, but with more sustained exposure such as after intraperitoneal or subcutaneous injection, high fat concentrations occur, with fat:plasma ratios of the order of 20:50 and persistence of label in fat. High activity in the adrenal gland has been confirmed, and it is found also in the corpora lutea of the ovary, the Harderian glands of the orbit, hair follicles, the mammary glands, and brown fat. In the fetus, the central nervous system has the highest activity.

An important point arises from the manner in which THC is given, in addition to the possible formation of microemboli noted above. The partition coefficients for Δ^1-THC and the 7-OH metabolite are so high that the amount of drug in free aqueous solution must be very low. In transport around the body, therefore, one must be dealing either with transfer of a more hydrophilic complex of cannabinoid with some other molecule, or with a continuous partition between lipophilic carrier in blood and lipophilic acceptor in tissue (Paton et al., 1972). Klausner and Dingell (1971) found faster metabolic kinetics than had Agurell et al. (1969), and suggested that this may be due to their use of propylene glycol. Agurell et al. (1972) noted that the distribution rate depends on the solvent used.

Interest attaches to brain levels of cannabinoids, especially in relation to the question of the role of the 7-OH metabolite. Ho et al. (1972) found that up to 4% of radioactivity entered the brain after iv administration of 10 mg/kg labeled Δ^1-THC, 84% as Δ^1-THC, 8% as the 7-OH metabolite. Gill and Jones (1972) have correlated levels of Δ^1-THC and 7-OH-Δ^1-THC in mouse whole brain with "cataleptic" effect using the "ring" test (Pertwee, 1972) after intravenous injection of Δ^1-THC. The Δ^1-THC levels in brain were about six times that of metabolite, and temporal changes in both correlated well with pharmacological effect. Treatment with SKF 525A had the interesting effect of increasing brain THC content slightly and metabolite content about three-fold, implying a relatively greater inhibition of metabolic processes *after* the 7-hydroxylation. This was associated with a moderate but not significant increase in immobility. Subsequently, Gill et al. (1972) studied brain levels and catalepsy after injection of the metabolite. From these data they derived brain concentration–response curves, which estimated the metabolite as 6.9 times as active as Δ^1-THC, and concluded that both substances contributed to the pharmacological effect of Δ^1-THC. The data imply that both Δ^1-THC and the metabolite produce significant effects, when they are present in a concentration of about 1.0 and 0.2 nmole/gm whole brain, respectively. Jones and Pertwee (1972) went on to show that cannabidiol, like SKF 525A, increased

THC and 7-OH metabolite levels in brain; in addition, they noted a significant fall in "polar metabolites," supporting the idea of a proportionately greater inhibition of the later metabolic pathways.

TOXICITY AND TERATOGENICITY

Acute Toxicity

Dewey *et al.* (1972a) reported LD_{50} values for Δ^1-THC in mouse and rat, respectively, as follows: intravenous, 60 and 100 mg/kg; intraperitoneal, 168 and 430 mg/kg; oral, 1900 and 2000 mg/kg. Values for Δ^6-THC were similar. They also found (Dewey *et al.*, 1972a) a dose of 24 mg/kg iv invariably lethal to dogs, although Braude (1972) cites a higher figure. Mantilla-Plata and Harbison (1971) were able to show in mice that phenobarbitone pretreatment lowered the death rate following administration of Δ^1-THC 400 mg/kg ip from 90 to 45% and that SKF 525A raised it again to 90%. Zitko *et al.* (1972) found the toxicity of their soluble ester of Δ^1-THC comparable with that of Δ^1-THC.

Chronic Toxicity

Paton *et al.* (1972) have reported on the chronic toxicity of cannabis extract compared with that of ethanol. The toxicity of cannabis is strongly cumulative and is attributable to the petrol ether fraction. While Δ^1-THC readily produces weight loss, it cannot itself account for all the toxicity, which is probably also attributable to synergism with the propyl derivative and cannabidiol. The petrol-ether-insoluble fractions (which include water-soluble substances) were relatively inactive. Braude (1972) also reported on cumulative toxicity; an interesting feature, in rats, receiving 500 mg/kg Δ^1-THC daily by mouth, was a great reduction in body fat, especially in female animals. Dewey *et al.* (1972b) were able to obtain some evidence of tolerance in dogs to the intravenous toxicity of Δ^1-THC (one animal survived 161 mg/kg iv); at the same time they had deaths at 12 and 16 mg/kg. The data suggest an interaction of cumulation and tolerance development.

Manning *et al.* (1971) have shown that the weight loss produced in rats by daily intraperitoneal injections of Δ^1-THC (4 mg/kg) is also produced by oral dosage, so that the sterile peritonitis induced by intraperitoneal Δ^1-THC was not the cause. Even at 0.5 mg/kg, Δ^1-THC given orally detectably impaired weight gain. They also noted that while no deaths attributable to Δ^1-THC occurred in these experiments, six out of eight animals died in a similar study when ip injection of THC was combined with shock avoidance tests. It seems probable that, as with other drugs, lethality is increased by stress.

Fetal and Maternal Effects

Δ^1-Tetrahydrocannabinol has been tested in rats, mice, and rabbits. In the rat (Borgen *et al.*, 1971) the most striking effect was on the mother, doses of 10 mg/kg causing impairment of maternal growth and of lactation; at higher doses, enlargement of adrenal and thyroid appeared. The failure of lactation was associated with a greatly increased postnatal mortality in the litters. In the fetuses, no deformity or stunting was found in doses up to 200 mg/kg sc in olive oil; litter size fell at a dose of 100 mg/kg upwards. Their earlier report (Pace *et al.*, 1971) noted a high incidence of small subdermal hemorrhages in the fetuses, which disappeared within a few days after birth. Harbison and Mantilla-Plata (1972) found that in the mouse 200 mg/kg Δ^1-THC given intraperitoneally produced 65% fetal resorption at the most vulnerable period (8–9 days); the weight of surviving fetuses was also reduced, this effect being greatest with treatment on days 10–11. Braude (1972) reported that in rabbits receiving Δ^1-THC in doses up to 5 mg/kg there was no deformity or stunting but possibly an increase in resorptions. There have been no reports of teratogenesis studied with an extract comparable in composition to the crude material as used. The evidence continues to suggest that, while Δ^1-THC can reach the fetus, its action there is restricted to increasing resorption and stunting at higher doses and that teratogenesis is due to some other factor.

ELECTROPHYSIOLOGY, SLEEP, AND ANTICONVULSANT ACTION

Although the effects of Δ^1-THC vary with species, a consistent picture is emerging of its effects on electroencephalographic and related potentials, consisting of a reduction in normal waking electrical activity, hypersynchrony, and bursts of spike activity. Colasanti and Khazan (1971) found that 2.5–10 mg/kg Δ^1-THC ip in the rat reduced the waking EEG voltage and caused the appearance of superimposed multiple spike discharges, they comment on the resulting state of CNS arousal with behavioral sedation. Pirch *et al.* (1971, 1972) observed a similar picture elicited by 10–40 mg/kg orally, 20 mg/kg ip, or 1.25–2.5 mg/kg iv. On administration of repeated daily doses, the depressant effect on integrated voltage first increased and then tolerance developed, so that after 5–12 doses it had returned to control levels. On withdrawal of drug, a rebound increase in integrated voltage occurred, maximal 2–3 days after withdrawal. In contrast, the episodes of high-voltage "spindlelike" activity increased for 3–5 days of administration and persisted throughout 35 days of treatment. The results are strongly reminiscent of the findings of Carlini and his colleagues in rats, with evidence of cumulation followed by tolerance and of an aggressive behavior developing and then persisting throughout treatment. Martinez *et al.* (1971, 1972) describe effects in rhesus monkeys; doses of 0.05–12 mg/kg produce high-voltage slow-wave activity (about three times the voltage of control desynchronized activity) together with 12–20-cps bursts. These bursts were found in amygdala, pons, putamen, cerebellar peduncle, and fastigial nuclei, but not in the hippocampus. They appeared most readily in amygdala and the peduncles, and a dose of only 0.05 mg/kg could produce this subcortical "convulsive" activity without cortical changes. The authors link the slow movement and rigidity of the animal with the cerebellar effects in particular. Segal and Kenney (1972) found that Δ^1-THC in the cat raised the threshold to reticular arousal (although not the threshold to peripheral arousal); a dose of 20 mg/kg initially itself caused arousal, followed by increased synchronization and slow-wave activity, with spikes superimposed. Δ^6-Tetrahydrocannabinol was found to raise reticular threshold but otherwise to be depressant.

Moreton and Davis (1971) studied sleep rhythms in rats, finding that 5–10 mg/kg Δ^1THC reduced both paradoxical sleep (PS) and slow-wave sleep and blocked rebound in PS-deprived animals. Tolerance developed to the suppression of PS, but no rebound was found on withdrawal.

Sofia et al. (1971b,c) have confirmed, with Δ^1-THC, Loewe's conclusions on purified extracts that cannabis resembles phenytoin in antagonizing electroshock convulsions while enhancing metrazol and strychnine effects. They also used the effect on electroshock convulsion latency to test various excipients for Δ^1-THC given intraperitoneally. The effect of the drug was greatest in 10% propylene glycol plus 1% Tween-80–saline vehicle, next best in 3% PVP, and irregular in 1% Tween-80–saline or in bovine serum albumin–saline.

Brain Amines and Other Constituents

The assessment of the role of brain amines in THC action remains difficult. Ho et al. (1971a), administering Δ^1-THC to rats by repeated exposure to a smoke, found no change in whole brain noradrenaline or 5-HT but some fall in normetanephrine and 5-HIAA. They also reported a reduction in uptake of radioactivity and lower labeling of catecholamines after injection of ^{3}H-tyrosine. Sofia et al. (1971a) found that Δ^1-THC in a concentration of 10^{-7} M or higher reduced ^{14}C-5-HT uptake by rat brain homogenates (synaptosomes), having an activity of about $\frac{1}{6}$ that of desipramine. Kilbey et al. (1972) found no change in mouse whole brain noradrenaline, 5-HT, or dopamine after iv administration of 2.5 mg/kg, a dose sufficient to produce substantial behavioral effects. Constantinidis and Miras (1971) found that a dose of 300 mg/kg of hashish sublimate given ip to rats increased the green fluorescent varicosities of the hypothalamus, in both intensity and number, and reduced the depleting effect of reserpine. It also increased the potentiation of the fluorescence by intraventricular noradrenaline, but it did not modify the effect of DOPA or DOPA with nialamid. They suggest a facilitation of noradrenaline uptake. Pal and Ghosh (1972) reported a small rise in urinary secretion of 5-HIAA in the rat after substantial doses of Δ^1-THC.

Gallager et al. (1971, 1972) found no change in rat brain 5-HT or 5-HIAA, nor in 5-HT turnover, after iv or ip administration of Δ^1-THC, and a transient rise in 5-HT and 5-HIAA after intraventricular administration of THC. Since behavioral effects were produced at all doses, dissociation between amine changes and behavior was evident. Leonard (1971) found that Δ^6-THC had no effect on concentration or turnover of noradrenaline, dopamine, or 5-HT in whole brain from rats given 100 mg/kg ip. There was a slight decrease in brain and blood tyrosine and in brain GABA* levels. Maitre (1972) showed in rats that Δ^1-THC did not alter total noradrenaline or dopamine brain content but that Δ^6-THC and DMHP increased the rate of incorporation of noradrenaline, especially into hypothalamus, and of dopamine, especially into corpus striatum. Evidence of increased rate of turnover was also obtained, and tolerance was found to develop. Finally, Neto and Carlini (1972) observed that DOPA and/or p-chlorophenylalanine treatment potentiate the aggression induced by food deprivation and chronic treatment. It remains difficult to know what the real changes are, and how far they are primary or secondary. It may be that the main effects are in subcortical structures rather than in whole brain.

Evidence has been obtained that Δ^1-THC interferes in vitro with uptake of radioactivity from L-leucine-U-^{14}C and from uridine-2-^{14}C into protein and nucleic acid of rat brain cortex slices (Jakubovič and McGeer, 1972). Jakubovič and McGeer, also showed considerable uptake of labeled Δ^1-THC by the brain slices; in the presence of a 0.1 nM suspension of Δ^1-THC in the incubation medium giving a concentration of free THC of 7 nmoles/ml, there was an uptake of 500 nmoles/gm initial wet weight. A preliminary report by Rosenkrantz et al. (1972) notes that, when given repeatedly to rhesus monkeys, Δ^1-THC reduces lipid, RNA, and protein content of brain, but not phospholipid content.

Analgesia

Considerable variations in estimates of analgesic potency occur, probably due in part to strain differences (see Buxbaum, 1972). In general, analgesic action can be shown by all tests, including tail flick, hot plate, or intraperitoneal phenylbenzoquinone or acetic acid techniques, in mice, rats, cats, and monkeys (Kaymakçalan and Deneau, 1971, 1972; Gallager et al., 1971, 1972; Dewey et al., 1971, 1972a; Sofia and Barry, 1972; Buxbaum, 1972). In general, Δ^1-THC is most effective on the intraperitoneal irritant test, then on the hot plate, and least on tail flick. Estimates of potency relative to morphine range from equipotent to one-eighth, according to conditions. The time

* GABA = γ-aminobutyric acid.

course of THC action is evidently slower and more prolonged than that of morphine, and intensity of action appears to be more limited (Dewey *et al.*, 1972a). Evidence that SKF 525A increased the analgesia produced by Δ^1-THC (Sofia and Barry, 1972), as did hepatectomy (Kaymakçalan and Deneau, 1972), has been taken to imply that it is the parent compound, not the 7-OH metabolite, that is active. But since it is now known that SKF 525A *increases* levels of metabolite in mouse brain (Gill and Jones, 1972), and since hepatectomy may do less to impair production of the metabolite (which is found in other tissues as well as liver) than its inactivation, the evidence is not conclusive and may even point to the opposite conclusion.

It is interesting that further evidence has accrued that animals tolerant to morphine continue to respond to Δ^1:THC, but if treated chronically with Δ^1-THC they become resistant to morphine (Dewey, *et al.*, 1971; Kaymakçalan and Deneau, 1972). The latter authors also found that tolerance to the analgesic effect of THC was readily produced and lasted 1 month, that the analgesic effect of Δ^1-THC was additive with morphine, and that Δ^1-THC increased the excitant action of morphine. Buxbaum (1972) makes the important comment that animals treated with Δ^1-THC may show behavioral signs of pain in the hot plate test, without moving off the plate. Morphine does not do this, and the full nature of Δ^1-THC's analgesic action remains to be established.

CARDIOVASCULAR, RESPIRATORY, AUTONOMIC, GASTROINTESTINAL, AND HYPOTHERMIC EFFECTS

Bradycardia is shown as consistently in animals as tachycardia in man. It has been observed in rats, cats, dogs, and monkeys (Kaymakçalan and Deneau, 1971, 1972; Milzoff *et al.*, 1971, 1972; Kubena *et al.*, 1971; Lahiri *et al.*, 1972; Cavero and Jandhyala, 1972; Dewey *et al.*, 1972b). The effect is dose related and is reduced or abolished by cutting the vagus or giving atropine. On repeated administration in dogs, it is possible that some tolerance occurs (Kaymakçalan and Deneau, 1972). Oskoui (1972) reported an increase in vagal nerve activity. The evidence is therefore good that most, and sometimes all, of the bradycardia is mediated by the vagus. Dewey *et al.* (1972b) found a marked rise in pretreatment pulse rate with daily injections, which calls for further study. Oskoui (1972) also noted a reduction in sympathetic nerve activity which could produce slowing of the heart. It must be stressed that, given little or no direct effect of Δ^1-THC on heart rate, the changes seen depend on the pattern of discharge in sympathetic and vagal fibres, a pattern likely to change profoundly under different conditions. In isolated heart preparations, Δ^1-THC had no effect on rate (Lahiri *et al.*, 1972).

A fall in *blood pressure* has been observed in rats, cats, dogs, and monkeys (Milzoff *et al.*, 1971, 1972; Kubena *et al.*, 1971; Hosko and Hardman, 1971;

Oskoui, 1972; Cavero and Jandhalya, 1972; Ho et al., 1971b; Zitko et al., 1972; Paton et al., 1972; Martinez et al., 1972), but Dewey et al. (1972b) found no change in blood pressure in response to repeated doses in unanesthetized dogs. The fall is inevitably complex, and contributions occur from increased vagal activity, reduced vasomotor and sympathetic activity, direct effects on the myocardium, and secondary results of respiratory effects. Cavero and Jandhyala (1972) found a fall both in cardiac output and in total peripheral resistance, and Manno et al. (1970) observed in perfused heart a small decline in strength of beat with low doses and a biphasic response (augmentation followed by a nonreversible impairment) with higher doses. No significant ganglion-blocking action has been found, as judged by the response to preganglionic vagal, chorda tympani, or cervical sympathetic stimulation, or to DMPP* injection. Noradrenaline is potentiated by an amount very close to the antecedent blood pressure fall (Paton et al., 1972; Zitko et al., 1972). The carotid occlusion response is blocked (Milzoff et al., 1972). Hosko and Hardman (1971) made the important observation that Δ^1-THC reduces the pressor effect of selective stimulation at hypothalamic, reticular, and medullary vasomotor sites, the hypothalamic site being least sensitive.

 Respiration has been found to be depressed in rats, cats, and dogs (Milzoff et al., 1971; Kubena et al., 1971; Hosko and Hardman, 1971; Paton et al., 1972), and Oskoui (1972) reported a reduction in phrenic nerve discharge. Vagotomy may reduce the effect. Cavero et al. (1972a,b) observed a rise of respiratory rate in dogs and hypoxemia abolished by artificial ventilation. In isolated perfused rat lung, injection of 0.4–1.6 mg into the pulmonary artery produced an increase (17%) in tidal volume and reduction in perfusion rate ($\sim 50\%$)—an unusual pattern produced by a rather large dose of drug (Sperling and Coker, 1972).

 Cavero et al. (1972a,b), in a careful study on dogs under pentobarbital, showed that Δ^1-THC given in ethanolic solution shifted the frequency response curves to *vagal stimulation* to the right and attenuated *salivation* response to chorda tympani stimulation; the drug did not antagonize the action of carbachol. The difference from the results reported by Gill et al. (1970) in the cat under chloralose may be due to differences in species, anesthetic, or excipient.

 Dewey et al. (1972a) found that Δ^1-THC administered subcutaneously produced in the intestine a delay in propulsion of a charcoal test meal, being about one-tenth the potency of morphine. They also found Δ^1-THC to be a weak noncompetitive depressant of intestinal strips. In the rat vas deferens, little effect was seen, but there was some potentiation at low doses, with depression at high doses, of responses to noradrenaline, Paton et al. (1972)

 * DMPP = 1,1-dimethyl-4-phenyl piperazinium.

describe the persistent reduction of acetylcholine output by Δ^1-THC from guinea pig ileum strips and, in the guinea pig vas deferens, a depression of tetrodotoxin-sensitive contractions evoked by brief trains of stimuli, with a facilitation of response to massive single shocks. The evidence indicated that Δ^1-THC could have both a presynaptic and a postsynaptic effect.

There are further reports on *hypothermia* in mice, rats, hamsters, gerbils, cats, dogs, and monkeys (Kaymakçalan and Deneau, 1971; Leonard, 1971; Abel, 1972), and Δ^1-THC and cannabis extract have also been found to be antipyretic (Paton *et al.*, 1972). Abel, in an extensive analysis, has shown the hypothermia to vary with species, the order of intensity being mice > hamsters > gerbils = rats; it is also much greater in young chicks and depends on environmental temperature (at 31°C, a small temperature rise was seen). As a result of tests with adrenoceptive and monoamine oxidase blocking agents, and on brain amine levels, it was provisionally concluded that the effect of Δ^1-THC on thermoregulation was not due to an action on biogenic nerve amines such as noradrenaline or 5-HT.

MISCELLANEOUS

Alkaloids

Further evidence of basic substances in cannabis has been provided by Klein *et al.* (1971). With doses of crude alkaloid mixture up to about 2.5 mg/kg, spontaneous activity of mice was depressed, but no other effect was seen nor was there change in barbiturate sleeping time.

Cell Pathology

Leuchtenberger and Leuchtenberger (1971) investigated with cultured explants from mouse lung and by comparing cannabis and cigarette smokes, changes in the epithelioid cells. Cannabis smoke produced relatively larger nucleoli and the cells tended to fuse; there was impairment of contact inhibition, a rise in mitotic index and in DNA synthesis, an increase in tritiated thymidine uptake, and signs of mitotic lag in metaphase and anaphase. They also found cannabis smoke less cytotoxic than cigarette smoke, but they thought this might have been due to the stickiness of the resin reducing the amount of smoke delivered by the cannabis cigarette.

Okamoto *et al.* (1972) found that marijuana and tobacco smoke condensate are equally active in inducing aryl hydrocarbon hydoxylase in hamster lung; benzopyrene is about 1000 times more active.

Price *et al.* (1972) showed that Δ^1-THC (but not Δ^6-THC, CBN, or CBD) had a detectable activity in producing carcinogenic transformation of rat embryo cells inoculated with a murine leukemia virus; the activity was weak compared to that of methylcholanthrene, but it was exerted at a very low dose and produced highly malignant tumors.

Drug Interactions

The report that *phenitrone* can antagonize THC has not been confirmed. Spaulding *et al.* (1971) noted that phenitrone produced a behavioral effect slightly like that of Δ^1-THC in the dog, a transient fall in blood pressure, and some hypothermia and reduction in activity in mice. But in doses up to 40 mg/kg it did not antagonize Δ^1-THC-induced ataxia, hypotension, or bradycardia in dog, nor hypothermia in mice. There was some impairment of THC action on the tail flick test. Berger and Krantz (1972) found that phenitrone in doses up to 50 mg/kg did not antagonize Δ^1-THC on mouse sleeping time or ataxia, nor on dog ataxia. Lomax and Campbell (1971) found that it augmented rather than reduced hypothermia.

Cannabinol, which in a dose of 50 mg/kg prolongs barbiturate sleeping time and reduces motor and exploratory activity in mice, was found by Krantz *et al.* (1971) to reduce the sleeping-time effect of Δ^1-THC. Interaction among these drugs, and their metabolites, may be important. Effects mediated by interaction at binding sites in blood constituents have not been controlled.

Following up the observation by Paton and Pertwee (1972) that *cannabidiol* has an activity not far short of SKF 525A in inhibiting liver microsomal activity, Jones and Pertwee (1972) have shown that cannabidiol causes an increase in the levels both of Δ^1-THC and of metabolite in the brains of mice treated with labeled Δ^1-THC. The effect could well be due to an effect on the liver, but it is not yet known whether THC metabolism at other sites is also inhibited. The effect was seen with a high cannabidiol/Δ^1-THC ratio; its magnitude evidently varies both with this ratio and with the extent to which microsomal activity has been induced before the test.

Thiopentone anesthesia in rabbits is potentiated by cannabis extract; about 25% less thiopentone given intravenously is needed to induce a given depth of anesthesia (Paton and Temple, 1972).

The toxicity of *physostigmine* in rats is augmented by Δ^1-THC (Rosenblatt *et al.*, 1972), but this does not occur after atropine or methylscopolamine treatment. It seems likely that Δ^1-THC impairs a protective reaction to the peripheral anticholinesterase effects of physostigmine.

Paton and Pertwee (1972) found that cannabis extract, in amounts sufficient to prolong barbiturate sleeping time in mice under normothermic conditions, did not prolong *ether sleeping time*. It should be noted that this does not exclude such an effect by pure Δ^1-THC, since the effect of the extract studied was chiefly due to cannabidiol.

Phillips *et al.* (1971) found in mice that Δ^1-THC enhanced and prolonged the stimulant effect of *caffeine*; with *amphetamine*, lower doses of THC prolonged the stimulant effect, and a high dose reduced it.

Mitochondria, Microsomes, and Red Blood Cells

Chari-Bitron and Bino (1971) found that $\varDelta^1$-THC caused an increase in ATPase activity of rat liver mitochondria, augmented by Mg^{2+}, which they interpreted as due to membrane destabilization. Mahoney and Harris (1972) have extended this type of work. They found that $\varDelta^1$-THC, in a concentration of 15–60 nmoles/mg mitochondrial protein, increased state 4 respiration and at 60 nmoles/mg or higher caused a rapid and large mitochondrial swelling; Mg^{2+} greatly augmented the effect. The drug is therefore fairly reactive in uncoupling mitochondrial respiration. At 120 nmoles/ml, in the presence of Mg^{2+}, $\varDelta^1$-THC caused flocculation of phospholipid micelles. They suggest that $\varDelta^1$-THC acts on the membrane to produce a state in which its stability depends more than normally on its negative charges, which Mg^{2+} then neutralizes.

$\varDelta^1$-Tetrahydrocannabinol has been shown by Cohen *et al.* (1971) to combine with the microsomal system of rat liver, as shown by the difference spectrum due to binding by hemoprotein; a spectral dissociation constant (K_s) of 18.5 and 9.1 μM was found for untreated and phenobarbitone-pretreated animals, respectively. The drug also inhibited metabolism of ethylmorphine N-demethylase competitively (K_i, 15.4 μM), although in phenobarbitone-pretreated animals the inhibition was mixed at higher concentration. The data indicated a type 1 action. The agreement obtained between the values for K_s and K_i suggest that the K_m for $\varDelta^1$-THC metabolism might also be of the order of 15 μM. Kupfer *et al.* (1972) obtained similar results, and give data for $\varDelta^6$-THC and cannabinol. In addition, 7-OH-$\varDelta^6$-THC was found not to induce a spectral change, nor to interfere with that induced by $\varDelta^6$-THC. They also give a preliminary value of the K_m for $\varDelta^1$-THC, on rat liver microsomes, of 28 μM. The data explain the failure reported by Burstein and Kupfer (1971) of hexobarbital (K_m, $3 \times 10^{-4} M$) to inhibit $\varDelta^1$-THC hydroxylation. The effects of *cannabidiol* have been mentioned earlier.

Tested on hypotonic *hemolysis* of rat blood cells, $\varDelta^1$-THC was detectably active at 10^{-6} M (Chari-Bitron, 1971). The effect was less as temperature increased, and it was reversed by prior incubation of the cells in the cold. Lysis was never seen, even at 8×10^{-5} M concentration. Addition of bovine serum albumin also inhibited the effect. Raz *et al.* (1972) have found that both $\varDelta^1$-THC and cannabidiol reversibly stabilize human erythrocytes against hypotonic hemolysis.

Withdrawal Phenomena

Deneau and Kaymakçalan (1971) and Kayamakçalan and Deneau (1972) describe withdrawal phenomena in monkeys. Moreton and Davis (1971) failed to find withdrawal effects on sleep rhythms in rats, Dewey *et al.* (1972b) saw no withdrawal in dogs, and McMillan *et al.* (1972) found none in pigeon behavioral tests. Pirch *et al.* (1972), however, found a rebound increase in the integrated cortical EEG of rat, maximal on second and third days, and Davis *et al.* (1972) noted in rats a small but significant rise in motor activity on the second day after withdrawal. These reports support the suggestion that, as a result of the kinetics of the drug, withdrawal effects, if present, would be delayed and spread out.

GENERAL DISCUSSION

The developments briefly reviewed in this addendum are generally in line with previous work and continue to present the picture of Δ^1-THC as a drug which, in a tantalizing way, resembles others and yet has subtle and unusual characteristics of its own that are still hard to understand.

In unraveling these complexities, three suggestions emerge from recent work that may be helpful. First, in neurochemical studies, evidence is appearing that the significant changes may be in the deeper structures of the brain; work with whole brain may well mask important effects recognizable by a more selective approach. Second, dose level may be very important. It is suggestive, if one considers the data on brain amines, that evidence for depletion of amines comes from those experiments in which the brain dose was probably small and that evidence for elevation of amine content was obtained when brain dose was probably very high, whereas null effects were observed with intermediate dose. There is no more than a suggestion of a rather critical biphasic dose dependence, but it is not unreasonable that it should occur, with lower doses being stimulant and a depressant action becoming increasingly important as dose increases. If such is the case, the rather confusing data available might form a much more coherent pattern. Third, if one links the findings on aggression by Carlini's group with the generation by cannabis of spike discharges in the EEG which persist during continued treatment, the possibility emerges that cannabis has mixed depressant and stimulant actions, with tolerance developing to the former but not to the latter. Such a view would imply that tolerance is not due to changed metabolism of Δ^1-THC. One thus comes again to the conception of a biphasic action. It is premature to attempt to allocate particular actions to a "depressant" or "stimulant" class. Nevertheless, the evidence for reduction in sympathetic tone, as shown by vasomotor impairment and hypothermia, suggests that this may be one of the clearest depressant effects. Possibly related to this is an apparently widespread inhibition of neurohypophyseal hormonal mobilization, with circumstantial evidence for impairment of release of thyrotropin, vasopressin, and prolactin. One should also note that a considerable number of observations on anesthetized animals are now available. It needs to be remembered that anesthesia can potentiate or alter many physiological responses, and that anesthetics vary significantly; such factors may be particularly important with a lipophilic substance such as Δ^1-THC.

Two theoretical proposals may also be helpful. The first is the suggestion by Gill *et al.* (1972) that there is a significant resemblance in chemical structure between Δ^1-THC and its 7-OH metabolite, and cholesterol. Such an analogy has wide-ranging implications—for the nature of the interaction between the cannabinoids and cell membranes, for the interpretation of central effects (steroids exist both with anesthetic and with convulsant activity), in the interpretation of cannabinoid metabolism, for whose complexity steroid metabolism forms a fitting companion, and for possible interactions between the cannabinoids and steroids in the body at various receptor and binding sites.

Second is the suggestion (Paton *et al.*, 1972) that not only is the lipophilicity of Δ^1-THC at the center of its pharmacological action, but that there is a limit or "cutoff" to this action set by its physicochemical properties in relation to those of the cell membrane. Evidence is accumulating for the action of THC at the membrane level, as shown by its effects on mitochondria, microsomes, red blood cells, and synaptosomes. The measurement by Jakubovič and McGeer (1972) of Δ^1-THC uptake by cortex slices, yielding a partition between whole tissue and medium of about 100, agrees well with the expected partition coefficient (1200) based on a corrected octanol/water partition, if one supposes the whole brain tissue to contain about 10% lipid. This degree of uptake must be expected to apply generally, whenever equilibrium is approached. But there are signs that the capacity of tissues to take up Δ^1-THC may be limited, e.g., the absence of any report of the production of typical surgical anesthesia (usually possible with any lipophilic substance capable of reaching a concentration of around 0.05 M in lipid), the cutoff in THC effect on liver microsomes as compared to cannabidiol, and its inability to hemolyze red cells, as other lipophiles do in higher concentrations. This suggests that Δ^1-THC, unlike a lipophile such as chloroform, is not infinitely miscible with membrane lipid, but can achieve only a limited concentration. One may make a provisional estimate of this limit, if one takes 7 nmoles/ml as a saturated solution of Δ^1-THC in water and if the partition coefficient of 1200 applies to saturated conditions; then, the concentration limit in membrane lipid would be of the order of 0.01 M—sufficient (for instance) to contribute to, but not produce, anesthesia. Such an approach must be far too simple and cannot account for the variation of cannabinoid potency among optical isomers, but a "cutoff" of this kind could well contribute a certain selectivity of action as well as explain a number of anomalies.

References

Abel, E. L. (1972). *In* "Cannabis and its Derivatives: Pharmacology and Experimental Psychology" (W. D. M. Paton and J. Crown, eds.). Oxford Univ. Press, London and New York.

Agurell, S., Nilsson, I. M., Ohlsson, A., and Sandberg, F. (1969). *Biochem. Pharmacol.* **18**, 1195.

Agurell, S., Dahmen, J., Gustaffson, B., Johansson, U.-B. Leander K., Nilsson, I., Nilsson, J. L. G., Nordqvist, M., Ramsay, C. H., Ryrfeldt, Å., Sandberg, F., and Widman, M. (1972). *In* "Cannabis and its Derivatives: Pharmacology and Experimental Psychology" (W. D. M. Paton and J. Crown, eds.). Oxford Univ. Press, London and New York.

Ben-Zvi, Z., Mechoulam, R., Edery, H., and Porath, G. (1971). *Science* **174**, 951.

Berger, H. J., and Krantz, J. C. (1972). *J. Pharm. Pharmacol.* **24**, 492.

Borgen, L. A., Davis, W. M., and Pace, H. B. (1971). *Toxicol. Appl. Pharmacol.* **20**, 480.

Braude, M. (1972). *In* "Cannabis and its Derivatives: Pharmacology and Experimental Psychology" (W. D. M. Paton and J. Crown, eds.). Oxford Univ. Press, London and New York.

Brown, H. (1971). *Psychopharmacologia* **21**, 294.

Bueno, O. F. A., and Carlini, E. A. (1972). *Psychopharmacologia* **25**, 49.

Burstein, S. H., and Kupfer, D. (1971). *Chem.-Biol. Interact.* **3**, 316.

Burstein, S., Rosenfeld, J., and Wittstruck, T. (1972). *Science* **176**, 422.

Buxbaum, D. M. (1972). *Psychopharmacologia* **25**, 275.

Carder, B., and Olson, J. (1972). *Physiol. Behav.* **8**, 599.

Carlini, E. A., and Gonzalez, C. (1972). *Experientia* **28**, 542.

Carlini, E. A., and Masur, J. (1970). *Commun. Behav. Biol.* **5**, 57.

Carlini, E. A., Hamaoui, A., Bieniek, D., and Korte, F. (1970). *Pharmacology* **4**, 359.

Carlini, E. A., Hamaoui, A., and Märtz, R. M. W. (1972). *Brit. J. Pharmacol.* **44**, 794.

Cavero, I., and Jandhyala, B. S. (1972). *Fed. Proc. Fed. Amer. Soc. Exp. Biol.* **31**, 505.

Cavero, I., Kubena, R. K., Dziak, J., Buckley, J. P., and Jandhyala, B. S. (1972a). *Res. Commun. Chem. Pathol. Pharmacol.* **3**, 483.

Cavero, I., Buckley, J. P., and Jandhyala, B. S. (1972b). *Eur. J. Pharmacol.* **19**, 301.

Chari-Bitron, A. (1971). *Life Sci.* **10**, 1273.

Chari-Bitron, A., and Bino, T. (1971). *Biochem. Pharmacol.* **20**, 473.

Christensen, H. D., Freudenthal, R. I., Gidley, J. T., Rosenfeld, R., Boegli, G., Testino, L., Brine, D. R., Pitt, C. G., and Wall, M. E. (1971). *Science* **172**, 165.

Cohen, G. M., Peterson, D. W., and Mannering, G. J. (1971). *Life Sci.* **10**, 1207.

Cohn, R., Barnes, P., Barratt, E., and Pirch, J. (1971). *Pharmacologist* **13**, 297.

Colasanti, B., and Khazan, N. (1971). *Pharmacologist* **13**, 246.

Conrad, D. G., Elsmore, T. F., and Sodetz, F. J. (1972). *Science* **175**, 547.

Constantinidis, J., and Miras, C. J. (1971). *Psychopharmacologia* **22**, 80.

Davis, W. M., Moreton, J. E., King, W. T., and Pace, H. B. (1972). *Res. Commun. Chem. Pathol. Pharmacol.* **3**, 29.

Deneau, G. A., and Kaymakçalan, S. (1971). *Pharmacologist* **13**, 246.

Dewey, W. L., and Turk, R. F. (1972). *Fed. Proc. Fed. Amer. Soc. Exp. Biol.* **31**, 506.

Dewey, W. L., Harris, L. S., Dennis, B., Fisher, S., Kessaris, J., Kersons, L., and Watson, J. (1971). *Pharmacologist* **13**, 296.

Dewey, W. L., Harris, L. S., and Kennedy, J. S. (1972a). *Arch. Int. Pharmacodyn.* **196**, 133.

Dewey, W. L., Jenkins, J., O'Rourke, T., and Harris, L. S. (1972b). *Arch. Int. Pharmacodyn.* **198**, 118.

Dingell, J. V., Wilcox, H. G., and Klausner, H. A. (1971). *Pharmacologist* **13**, 296.

Drew, W. G., and Miller, L. L. (1972). *Fed. Proc. Fed. Amer. Soc. Exp. Biol.* **31**, 551.

Drew, W. G., Miller, L. L., and Wikler, A. (1972). *Psychopharmacologia* **23**, 289.

Elsmore, T. F. (1972). *Psychopharmacologia* **26**, 62.

Elsmore, T. F., and Fletcher, G. V. (1972). *Science* **175**, 911.

Ferraro, D. P., and Billings, D. K. (1972). *Psychopharmacologia* **25**, 169.

Ferraro, D. P., Grilly, D. M., and Lynch, W. C. (1971). *Psychopharmacologia* **22**, 333.

Ford, R. D., and McMillan, D. E. (1972). *Fed. Proc. Fed. Amer. Soc. Exp. Biol.* **31**, 505.

Forrest, I. S., Green, D. E., Otis, L. S., and Würsch, M. S. (1972). *Fed. Proc. Fed. Amer. Soc. Exp. Biol.* **31**, 506.

Frankenheim, J. M., McMillan, D. E., and Harris, L. S. (1971). *J. Pharmacol. Exp. Ther.* **178**, 241.

Freudenthal, R. I., Martin, J., and Wall, M. E. (1972), *Brit. J. Pharmacol.* **44**, 244.

Gallager, D. W., Sanders-Bush, E., and Sulser, F. (1971). *Pharmacologist* **13**, 296.

Gallager, D. W., Sanders-Bush, E., and Sulser, F. (1972). *Psychopharmacolgia* **26**, 337.

Gill, E. W., and Jones, G. (1972). *Biochem. Pharmacol.* **21**, 2237.

Gill, E. W., Jones, G., and Lawrence, D. K. (1973). *Biochem. Pharmacol.* **122**, 175.

Gill, E. W., Paton, W. D. M., and Pertwee, R. G. (1970). *Nature (London)* **228**, 134.

Gonzalez, S. C., and Carlini, E. A. (1971). *Psychonom. Sci.* **24**, 203.

Gonzalez, S. C., Matsudo, V. K. R., and Carlini, E. A. (1971). *Pharmacology* **6**, 186.

Gonzalez, S. C., Karniol, I. G., and Carlini, E. A. (1972). *Behav. Biol. A,* **7**, 83.

Gurny, O., Maynard, D. E., Pitcher, R. G., and Kierstead, R. W. (1972). *J. Amer. Chem. Soc.* **94**, 7928.

Harbison, R. D., and Mantilla-Plata, B. (1972). *J. Pharmacol. Exp. Ther.* **180**, 446.

Harris, R. T., Waters, W., and McLendon (1972). *Psychopharmacologia* **26**, 297.

Henriksson, B. G., and Järbe, T. (1971). *Psychopharmacologia* **22**, 23.

Herring, B. (1972). *Psychopharmacologia* **26**, 401.

Ho, B. T., Taylor, D., Englert, L. F., and McIsaac, W. M. (1971a). *Brain Res.* **31**, 233.

Ho, B. T., An, R., Fitchie, G. E., Englert, L. F., McIsaac, W. M., Mackay, B., and Ho, D. H. W. (1971b). *J. Pharm. Sci.* **60**, 1761.

Ho, B. T., Estevez, V., Englert, L. F., and McIsaac, W. M. (1972). *J. Pharm. Pharmacol.* **24**, 414.

Hosko, M. J., and Hardman, H. F. (1971). *Pharmacologist* **13**, 296.

Jakubovič, A., and McGreer, P. L. (1972). *Can. J. Biochem.* **50**, 654.

Jones, G., and Pertwee, R. G. (1972). *Brit. J. Pharmacol.* **45**, 375.

Kaymakçalan, S., and Deneau, G. A. (1971). *Pharmacologist* **13**, 247.

Kaymakçalan, S., and Deneau, G. A. (1972). *Acta Med. Turc.* Suppl. 1.

Kennedy, J. S., and Waddell, W. J. (1972). *Toxicol. Appl. Pharmacol.* **22**, 252.

Kilbey, M. M., Fitchie, G. E., McLendon, D. M., and Johnson, K. M. (1972). *Nature (London)* **238**, 463.

Klausner, H. A., and Dingell, J. V. (1971). *Life Sci.* **10**, 49.

Klein, F. K., Rapoport, H., and Elliott, H. W. (1971). *Nature (London)* **232**, 258.

Krantz, J. C., Berger, H. J., and Welch, B. L. (1971). *Amer. J. Pharm.* **143**, 149.

Kubena, R. K., and Barry, H., III (1972). *Nature (London)*, **235**, 397.

Kubena, R. K., Cavero, I., Jandhyala, B. S., and Buckley, J. P. (1971). *Pharmacologist* **13**, 247.

Kubena, R. K., Barry, H., III, Segelman, A. B., Theiner, M., and Farnsworth, N. R. (1972). *J. Pharm. Sci.* **61**, 144.

Kupfer, D., Jansson, I., and Orrenius, S. (1972). *Chem.-Biol. Interact.* **5**, 201.
Lahiri, P. K., Laddu, A. R., and Hardman, H. F. (1972). *Fed. Proc. Fed. Amer. Soc. Exp. Biol.* **31**, 505.
Leonard, B. E. (1971). *Pharm. Res. Commun.* **3**, 139.
Leuchtenberger, C., and Leuchtenberger, R. (1971). *Nature (London)* **234**, 227.
Lomax, P., and Campbell, C. (1971). *Experientia* **27**, 1191.
McMillian, D. E., Ford, R. D., Frankenheim, J. M., Harris, R. A., and Harris, L. S. (1972). *Arch. Int. Pharmacodyn.* **198**, 132.
Mahoney, J. M., and Harris, R. A. (1972). *Biochem. Pharmacol.* **21**, 1217.
Maitre, L. (1972). *In* "Cannabis and its Derivatives: Pharmacology and Experimental Psychology" (W. D. M. Paton and J. Crown, eds.). Oxford Univ. Press, London and New York.
Manning, F. J., and Elsmore, T. F. (1972). *Psychopharmacologia* **25**, 218.
Manning, F. J., McDonough, J. H., Elsmore, T. F., Saller, C., and Sodetz, J. (1971). *Science* **174**, 424.
Manno, B. R., Manno, J. E., Kilsheimer, G. S., and Forney, R. B. (1970). *Toxicol. Appl. Pharmacol.* **17**, 311.
Mantilla-Plata, B., and Harbison, R. D. (1971). *Pharmacologist* **13**, 297.
Martinez, J. L., Stadnicki, S. W., and Schaeppi, U. H. (1971). *Pharmacologist* **13**, 246.
Martinez, J. L., Stadnicki, S. W., and Schaeppi, U. H. (1972). *Life Sci.* **11**, 643.
Masur, J., Martz, R. M. W., Bieniek, D., and Korte, F. (1971a). *Psychopharmacologia* **22**, 187.
Masur, J., Martz, R. M. W., and Carlini, E. A. (1971b). *Psychopharmacologia* **19**, 388.
Masur, J., Martz, R. M. W., and Carlini, E. A. (1972a). *Psychopharmacologia* **25**, 57.
Masur, J., Karniol, I. G., and Neto, J. P. (1972b). *J. Pharm. Pharmacol.* **24**, 262.
Maynard, D. E., Gurney, O., Pitcher, R. G., and Kierstead, R. W. (1971). *Experientia* **27**, 1154.
Mechoulam, R., Varconi, H., Ben-Zvi, Z., Edery, H., and Grunfeld, Y. (1972). *J. Amer. Chem. Soc.* **94**, 7930.
Milzoff, J. R., Forney, R. B., Stone, C. J., and Allen, D. O. (1971). *Pharmacologist* **13**, 247.
Milzoff, J. R., Martz, R., and Harger, R. N. (1972). *Fed. Proc. Fed. Amer. Soc. Exp. Biol.* **31**, 505.
Moreton, J. E., and Davis, W. M. (1971). *Pharmacologist* **13**, 246.
Nakazawa, K., and Costa, E. (1971a). *Pharmacologist* **13**, 297.
Nakazawa, K., and Costa, E. (1971b). *Nature (London)* **234**, 49.
Neto, J. P., and Carlini, E. A. (1972). *Eur. J. Pharmacol.* **17**, 215.
Newman, L. M., Lutz, M. P., Gould, M. H., and Domino, E. F. (1972). *Science* **175**, 1022.
Okamoto, T., Chan, P., and So, B. (1972). *Life Sci.* **11**, 733.
Orsingher, O. A., and Fulginiti, S. (1970). *Pharmacology* **3**, 337.
Oskoui, M. (1972). *Fed. Proc. Fed. Amer. Soc. Exp. Biol.* **31**, 505.
Pace, H. B., Davis, W. M., and Borgen, L. A. (1971). *Ann. N.Y. Acad. Sci.* **191**, 123.
Pal, B., and Ghosh, J. J. (1972). *Biochem. Pharmacol.* **21**, 263.
Paton, W. D. M., and Pertwee, R. G. (1972). *Brit. J. Pharmacol.* **44**, 250.
Paton, W. D. M., and Temple, D. M. (1972). *Brit. J. Pharmacol.* **44**, 346P.
Paton, W. D. M., Pertwee, R. G., and Temple, D. M. (1972). *In* "Cannabis and its Derivatives: Pharmacology and Experimental Psychology" (W. D. M. Paton and J. Crown, eds.). Oxford Univ. Press, London and New York.
Pertwee, R. G. (1972). *Brit. J. Pharmacol.* **46**, 753.

Peterson, D. W., Cohen, G. M., and Sparber, S. B. (1971). *Life Sci.* **10**, 1381.

Phillips, R. N., Neel, M. A., Brown, D. J., and Forney, R. B. (1971). *Pharmacologist* **13**, 297.

Pirch, J. H., Barnes, P. R., and Barratt, E. (1971). *Pharmacologist* **13**, 246.

Pirch, J. H., Cohn, R. A., Barnes, P. R., and Barratt, E. S. (1972). *Neuropharmacol.* **11**, 231.

Potvin, R. J., and Fried, P. A. (1972). *Psychopharmacologia* **26**, 369.

Pradhan, S. N., Bailey, P. T., and Ghosh, B. (1972). *Res. Commun. Chem. Pathol. Pharmacol.* **3**, 197.

Price, P. J., Suk, W. A., Spahn, G. J., and Freeman, A. E. (1972). *Proc. Soc. Exp. Biol. Med.* **140**, 454.

Raz, A., Schurr, A., and Livne, A. (1972). *Biochim. Biophys. Acta* **274**, 269.

Robichaud, R. C., Hefner, M. A., Anderson, J. E., and Goldberg, M. E. (1972). *Fed. Proc. Fed. Amer. Soc. Exp. Biol.* **31**, 551.

Rosenblatt, J. E., Janowsky, D. S., Davis, J. M., and El-Yousef, M. K. (1972). *Res. Commun. Chem. Pathol. Pharmacol.* **3**, 479.

Rosenkrantz, H., Luthra, Y. K., Sprague, R. A., Thomspon, G. R., and Braude, M. C. (1972). *Fed. Proc. Fed. Amer. Soc. Exp. Biol.* **31**, 506.

Segal, M., and Kenney, A. F. (1972). *Experientia* **29**, 816.

Sofia, R. D., and Barry, H., III (1972). *Fed. Proc. Fed. Amer. Soc. Exp. Biol.* **31**, 506.

Sofia, R. D., Extel, R. J. Dixit, B. N., and Barry, H., III (1971a). *Eur. J. Pharmacol.* **16**, 257.

Sofia, R. D., Kubena, R. K., Barry, H., III (1971b). *J. Pharm. Pharmacol.* **23**, 889.

Sofia, R. D., Solomon, T. A., Barry, H., III (1971c). *Pharmacologist* **13**, 246.

Spaulding, T. C., Dewey, W. L., and Harris, L. S. (1971). *Pharmacologist* **13**, 296.

Sperling, F., and Coker, A.-A. O. (1972). *Fed. Proc. Fed. Amer. Soc. Exp. Biol.* **31**, 505.

Thompson, G. R., and Rosenkrantz, H. (1971). *Pharmacologist* **13**, 296.

Webster, C. D., Willinsky, M. D., Herring, B. S., and Walters, G. C. (1971). *Nature (London)* **232**, 498.

Zimmerberg, B., Glick, S. D., and Jarvik, M. E. (1971). *Nature (London)* **233**, 343.

Zitko, B. A., Howes, J. F., Razdan, R. K., Dalzell, B. C., Dalzell, H. C., Sheehan, J. C., and Pars, H. G. (1972). *Science* **177**, 442.

CHAPTER 6

The Actions of Cannabis in Man

W. D. M. Paton and R. G. Pertwee

.

I. Introduction 288
  A. Factors Influencing the Reported Action of Cannabis . . . 288
  B. The Placebo Reaction 289
II. Effects of Cannabis Involving Perception 291
  A. Visual Perception 291
  B. Auditory Perception 293
  C. Taste and Smell 294
  D. Temperature and Other Sensations 294
  E. Pain. 294
  F. Somesthetic Sensation 295
  G. Imagery, Dreaming, Fantasies, and Hallucinations 296
III. Perception of Time 297
IV. Memory 301
V. Thought Processes 305
VI. Sense of Unreality and Depersonalization 308
VII. Feelings of Insight and Significance. 309
VIII. Mood and Emotions 310
  A. Euphoria 310
  B. Dysphoria, Aggressiveness, Paranoia, and Fear of Death . . 311
IX. Sleep and Sleepiness, Disinterest, Detachment: The Amotivational
  Syndrome 312
X. "Drunkenness" and Light-headedness 314
XI. Sexual Feeling 314
XII. Laughter 315
XIII. General Motor Activity 316

XIV. Ataxia, Tremor, Reflexes, and Catalepsy 317
XV. Electroencephalography 320
XVI. Autonomic and Other Related Effects 320
XVII. Visceral and Metabolic Effects 324
XVIII. The Temporal Pattern of Cannabis Action 326
XIX. Conclusion: Cannabis Action in the Light of Other Psychic Phenomena 326
  A. Anesthetics 327
  B. Alcohol 328
  C. Epilepsy 328
  D. Sensory Deprivation 329
  References 330

I. Introduction

In this chapter it is necessary to come to grips, not only with the effects of cannabis in man that correspond to those observable in animals, but also with the psychic effects. The literature concerning the latter is very large, much of it is descriptive, and many of the experiments reported were uncontrolled. At the same time, it is remarkable how far some of these accounts (which even if anecdotal are thorough, thoughtful, and sometimes written in far better English than is usual today) are endorsed by modern work. We have, therefore, included some qualitative material from the older work, where it is quite clear that a genuine effect was obtained, even if quantitative data such as dosage are unavailable.

Valuable official reviews include a report by the World Health Organization (1971), the first and second reports from the National Institute of Mental Health (1971, 1972), and the final report of the Le Dain Commission (1972). Bibliographies have been prepared by the UNESCO Commission on Narcotic Drugs (1965), by Gamage and Zerkin (1969, the annotated Stash bibliography), and by Waller and Denny (1971), also annotated. Other reviews include those of Murphy (1963), Pillard (1970), Hollister (1971b), and Nahas (1972); reviews containing a good deal of user testimony include those of Tart (1970), Halikos et al. (1971), and McGlothlin et al. (1970).

There have also been a number of relevant symposia at the New York Academy of Sciences (Singer, 1972), a Federation Meeting (1971), the Swedish Academy of Pharmaceutical Sciences (Agurell and Nilsson, 1971), and the Institute for the Study of Drug Dependence (Paton and Crown, 1972).

A. FACTORS INFLUENCING THE REPORTED ACTION OF CANNABIS

In comparing various reports, apparent conflicts sometimes arise, and certain contributing factors need to be mentioned. (a) The cannabis preparations used vary considerably, the most important difference being between marijuana (dried cannabis flowering tops) and forms such as hashish which are much richer in resin. A wide range of dose is possible among the different preparations, and (for instance) a failure to detect some effect after giving marijuana that is seen after hashish administration very often simply reflects the difference in dose. Related to this is whether single or repeated dosage is involved; with the latter, since cumulative effects can occur, effects not seen with single doses may appear. It should be noted, too, that the stated THC content of marijuana or extracts has not always been reliable (see Manno *et al.*, 1970, 1971). Caldwell *et al.* (1969b) found that marijuana nominally containing 1.3% THC in fact contained 0.2–0.5% THC. Similarly, the THC content of material used by Clark and Nakashima (1968), Weil *et al.* (1968), Weil and Zinberg (1969), and Crancer *et al.* (1969) must be expected to be one-third to one-sixth less than stated. This means that rather low doses were used and negative findings are not surprising, but the positive effects observed illustrate in an unexpected way the potency of THC. (b) Similarly, the effect of a given dose depends on the route of administration, as does the duration of action; when a preparation is smoked rather than ingested, less is needed for an effect, the onset is much quicker, and the duration may only be of 1–3 hours, although much more prolonged actions occur with oral administration. (c) It is a truism that the phenomena seen depend on what is looked for, and recent work illustrates well how a simple routine task may be unaffected whereas a mentally more demanding task is impaired. This has a further effect on the apparent duration of action of the drug. Thus, Tinklenberg *et al.* (1970) found that after doses of 20–50 mg THC given orally the impairment of forward digital memory had almost recovered in $3\frac{1}{2}$ hours, but backward digital memory was still significantly affected. (d) A characteristic feature of cannabis action, at least with lower doses, is its "wavelike" incidence of effect and the ability of the subject to bring himself back to normal for a period if required. This means that the timing and duration of a test may be such as to coincide with or induce a period of normality and allow an effect to be missed. (e) The past history of a subject and the extent to which he may be sensitized to cannabis by cumulation or desensitized by tolerance—a question discussed later—must be borne in mind. (f) Finally, in work on cannabis the so-called placebo reaction is particularly important.

B. THE PLACEBO REACTION

Becker (1953) has described one pattern of use in which the user is taught how to smoke cannabis, what the characteristics of the "high" are, and how to appreciate it. This represents a state of expectation and readiness for cues to a given behavioral pattern in which placebo response could operate as readily as it does (for instance) in a doctor–patient interaction. The need for a placebo control has long been recognized. The authors of the Mayor La Guardia report (Mayor's Committee on Marihuana, 1944, p. 69) attempted to prepare a satisfactory control pill but were not able to make the control and marijuana-containing pills taste the same. The first use of a placebo control appears to have been in the experiments reported by de Farias in 1955. Cigarettes of corn silk as well as of *maconha* were prepared, the seven subjects not knowing which they would receive. For the three receiving corn silk, symptoms of burning or roughness of the tongue, throat, and cheeks were reported, but there was no change in pulse rate, pupil, or psychic state. In a further experiment on nine subjects, an interesting procedure was used in which the group of subjects was led to believe that the cigarettes were of two types, but in fact all the subjects were given *maconha*. The next use of placebos appears to be that of Weil *et al.* (1968), who took the chopped outer covering of mature stalks of male hemp plants for making placebo cigarettes; the nine subjects smoked cigarettes but had not taken marijuana. The placebo cigarettes produced a mean rise of pulse rate of 8/minute at 15 minutes (which disappeared at 90 minutes) and conjunctival reddening in one of the subjects. The placebo material was found to be free of THC and probably represented an adequate control, but it was not stated whether other cannabinoids were also absent.

Subsequent procedures have involved marijuana from which cannabinoids have been extracted chemically, and these probably represent the most reliable control thus far for smoked material. With this, a picture of the placebo response can be built up. Thus, in one experiment (Hollister, 1970) the inhalation of the smoke of cigarettes made with cannabinoid-free marijuana produced symptoms in all of six subjects, experienced cigarette smokers, but only in the first 30 minutes. The symptoms consisted of dizziness, light-headedness, and (in one) tingling of hands and nausea; an average increase of pulse rate of 8/minute, and in some subjects reddened conjunctivae, were seen. Manno *et al.* (1970), using eight cigarette or marijuana smokers and a similar control material, found no significant rise in pulse rate but did observe a number of symptoms; the total symptom score on placebo, involving seven subjects, was 78 against 227 involving all eight subjects on marijuana. Four out of eight subjects receiving placebo guessed that they had had marijuana, but all those receiving marijuana identified it correctly. Jones and Stone (1970), using 10 regular consumers of marijuana, and control cigarettes made from alcohol-extracted marijuana, tested their subjects' ability to rate the potency of marijuana. The subjects gave a mean rating of 66 to the active material when smoked (on a scale of 0–100 ranging from the worst to the best material they had ever had), but a mean rating of

57 (not significantly different) to placebo. In these experiments the placebo had no effect on pulse rate, time estimation, EEG, or salivary flow, nor were the scores (based on answers to questionnaires) raised for euphoria, dysphoria, thinking, or perception. It is interesting that subjects had no difficulty in distinguishing marijuana given *orally* from placebo or alcohol. Finally, Kiplinger *et al.* (1971) found, with 15 subjects (8 experienced and 7 naive) that only 3 out of 15 identified placebo cigarettes as marijuana, although the majority (12/15) did this for cigarettes with a THC content of 6.25 μg/kg, and all did for a content of 25 μg/kg. The placebo produced no change in pulse rate, but it did cause a small increase in the index of conjunctival injection.

One may conclude from these studies that the "placebo" response includes local effects of the smoke on tongue and throat, a small tachycardia, occasional conjunctival reddening, and a number of relatively short-lived symptoms, and that the subject's testimony about the "high" or the rating of the marijuana is unreliable. It also appears, however, that specific tests, either by experiment or questionnaire, provide rather reliable indices of cannabis or THC action.

In reviewing the material on subjective and objective effects of cannabis in man, we found it unhelpful to segregate rigidly these two types of report. We also found a provisional theory helpful: that a primary action of cannabis is on perception and that a number of effects flow from this, namely (a) changes in time sense; (b) changes in memory and hence in thought processes as a whole; (c) changes in sense of identity and feelings of reality, insight, and truth; (d) changes in mood; and (e) changes in behavior. In what follows, the information is classified by these broad heads, combining objective psychometric tests with subjective reports as seems most likely to be useful to the reader. Somatic effects, wherever relevant, are also referred to. Later sections take up subjective or experimental results that have to do with somatic effects, not already discussed, and with a number of special topics.

II. Effects of Cannabis Involving Perception

A. VISUAL PERCEPTION

1. Colors

The subject may see colors, blue, green, yellow, red, scarlet, and white, flowing or in patches (Bromberg, 1939), or flashes of light (Allentuck and Bowman, 1942); simple colored patterns when the eyes are closed (Tayleur-Stockings, 1947; Hollister *et al.*, 1968); things looking darker (Pond, 1948); increased vividness and freshness of colors and, when the eyes are closed, gold with blue and red stripes, prismatic colors, a reddish glow, a fiery meteor, or light like a forked flame (Ames, 1958); dimming or brightening of colors (Soueif, 1967); sparkling points of light and color spots and designs (Keeler et al., 1968); and clouds with bright lights (Talbott and Teague, 1969). Ames (1958) reported that many subjects seemed to experience a greater intensity and duration of afterimages. Clark and Nakashima (1968) found that the afterimage time of an Archimedes spiral test (much enjoyed by the subjects) was not significantly affected.

2. Perception of Depth

The sense of spatial dimension is disturbed and confused (Baker-Bates, 1935; Chopra and Chopra, 1957; Hollister et al., 1968); distances may seem elastic, with objects seeming either small (micropsia) or large (macropsia) (Allentuck and Bowman, 1942); there may be an increased sense of distance, with the walls advancing and receding (Parker and Wrigley, 1947; Ames, 1958); or a curb may seem too high to step off (Bromberg, 1939). In Soueif's (1967) series of experiments, most subjects found that distances became larger, and about half found objects bigger. The sense of a third dimension may be lost, so that people look as though cut out of cardboard, and objects are flat with bright colors and a sharp outline (Ames, 1958). But in a case with an inadvertent large dose of "dagga," objects were seen to stand out with "a lively 3-D effect," and a face had a "lovely depth" inviting sculpture (Ames, 1958). A test by Clark and Nakashima (1968) on depth perception (positioning vertical white rods at 16 ft), in which the dose of extract was sufficient to produce a mild high in all subjects, showed no consistent effect.

3. Shape, Pattern, and Contrast

Although distortion of objects has been reported, this appears to be of size rather than (for instance) the perception of something straight as wavy; in one case there is mention of the limbs of trees appearing to undulate (Keeler et al., 1968). Much more common is the seeing of geometrical patterns. Objects may seem to vibrate (Hollister et al., 1968). There is also the report of increased contrast and sharper edges to objects (Tayleur-Stockings, 1947; Ames, 1958; Hollister et al., 1968). It is interesting that, although many distortions are possible, linearity seems to be conserved under cannabis.

4. Acuity

There are passing references by subjects to increased acuity of vision (Chopra and Chopra, 1957; Isbell et al., 1967), but Caldwell et al. (1969a) found no change in the ability of subjects to match light intensities. Users find lights more brilliant, and prefer surroundings with low illumination

(Marcovitz and Myers, 1944; Chopra and Chopra, 1957), which could imply either a lowered visual threshold to light intensity or pupils that would be relatively dilated at a high illumination. No test appears to have been made on visual threshold, but the occurrence of pupillary dilation (which could be due to the drug directly or to associated excitement) is not unequivocal (see below). Waskow *et al.* (1970) noted, in addition to strained eyes and blurring of vision, that the visual field seems clearer in the center than in the periphery.

B. AUDITORY PERCEPTION

The subject's impression that hearing becomes more acute is commonly reported to the extent that an addict may have a horror of noise and may be affected by the ticking of a watch or the buzzing of a mosquito (Tayleur-Stockings, 1947; Bouquet, 1951; Chopra and Chopra, 1957; Isbell *et al.*, 1967). No change was found in some studies (Pond, 1948; Weil *et al.*, 1968). In tests of auditory perception, no difference in auditory threshold or in pitch discrimination, and only a small impairment of intensity discrimination, have been found by some workers (Caldwell *et al.*, 1969a; Mayor's Committee on Marihuana, 1944). But Williams *et al.* (1946) found in three out of twelve subjects an improvement in auditory acuity at 1000 and 2000 Hz, no change in eight subjects, while one became very drowsy and got worse. Clark *et al.* (1970) make the interesting comment that a subject may become aware of stimuli to which he is normally habituated. Keeler (1968a) reported a sensation of "hearing" sounds for a few seconds after they have stopped. It could well be that any change is in habituation rather than in perceptual acuity itself. Ringing and buzzing in the ears are sometimes reported (Allentuck and Bowman, 1942; de Farias, 1955).

The appreciation of, and emotional response to, musical sounds may be increased (Bouquet, 1951), but neither cannabis nor pyrahexyl improves musical ability as assessed by a battery of tests for discrimination of pitch, intensity, rhythm, time, and timbre or for tonal memory (Mayor's Committee on Marihuana, 1944; Aldrich, 1944; Williams *et al.*, 1946). It was noted, in the last-mentioned tests by Aldrich with pyrahexyl, that eight out of twelve subjects felt mistakenly that they improved in performance under the drug (three claimed no change, one did not know), and Williams *et al.* confirmed this for cannabis. Indeed, so far from improvement, evidence points to the possibility of impairment. Williams *et al.* noted a rise in errors. With pyrahexyl a depression of performance was seen following drug treatment compared with the second of two control runs, but performance was not reduced below that in the first run, suggesting that the drug had impaired the improvement with practice. Caldwell *et al.* (1969a) make the same suggestion for the small impairment in intensity discrimination (from 1.51 to 0.94 db) after marijuana administration.

C. Taste and Smell

Taste was reported to be more acute by Tayleur-Stockings (1947) and as being disturbed, as was the sense of smell, in the later stages of intoxication (Chopra and Chopra, 1957). Ames (1958) noted that her subjects were not hungry but ate with relish, commenting that "even hospital food was delicious." In her case of overdosage, the subject experienced a bitter taste in the mouth about 3 hours after ingestion of dagga, along with vomiting and abdominal cramps, but the amount of liquorice excipient taken could have contributed to this.

D. Temperature and Other Sensations

A pleasant feeling of warmth (Tayleur-Stockings, 1947; Ames, 1958), alternations of hot and cold sensations and "flashes" (Hollister et al., 1968), and sweating followed by feeling chilly, or extremities feeling "blue" or cold have been described (Bromberg, 1939; Gaskill, 1945; Pond, 1948; Ames, 1958). No experimental tests of temperature sensation have been made, and the feelings reported could be central or secondary to vasomotor changes. Any change in body temperature is evidently small (see below).

E. Pain

The experimental evidence in animals that cannabis is analgesic was reviewed in the previous chapter. In man, no experimental study has been described, but there are a good many limited reports of such an analgesic action. One of the clearest early reports is by Christison (1848), who took 4 grains of extract orally for toothache, obtaining within an hour cessation of pain, along with pleasant numbness of limbs, giddiness, flight of ideas, sleepiness, and increase in force of the pulse. The following morning, ordinary appetite, torpidity, defect of memory, and extreme apparent protraction of time occurred. At about 2 p.m. they were terminated when Christison drank lemonade. Evidently a fairly large dose (as judged by other effects) was analgesic. Chopra and Chopra (1957) state that sense of pain is definitely dulled, and Parker and Wrigley (1947) found that 60 mg pyrahexyl produced marked analgesia. Ames (1958) reported that one subject under cannabis found venepuncture agonizing, whereas analgesia was produced in another subject. Since Christison (1851) also reported that cannabis could increase the intensity of labor pains, it seems that the analgesic activity in man is limited, perhaps of the order of antipyretic analgesics, and may be overridden by other actions.

F. SOMESTHETIC SENSATION

A wide range of feelings hard to classify has been described. These may refer to the whole body and be described as feelings of floating, drifting in space or weightlessness, and the feeling of falling or light-headedness, dizziness and vertigo (Baker-Bates, 1935; Bromberg, 1939; Allentuck and Bowman, 1942; Gaskill, 1945; Tayleur-Stockings, 1947; Parker and Wrigley, 1947; Pond, 1948; de Farias, 1955; Chopra and Chopra, 1957; Ames, 1958; Hollister *et al.*, 1968; Weil *et al.*, 1968; Waskow *et al.*, 1970; Grossman, 1969; Klee, 1969; Manno *et al.*, 1970; Hollister, 1970). More localized feelings include heaviness of head or eyes; teeth feeling sore and full of holes; head swelling; legs or arms feeling light, heavy, large, or lengthening; awareness of the ribs, scars on the body, the penis, eyes, face, fingernails; the heart vibrating the whole body; or the air seeming heavy (Bromberg, 1939; Allentuck and Bowman, 1942; de Farias, 1955; Ames, 1958; Hollister *et al.*, 1968; Keeler *et al.*, 1968; Waskow *et al.*, 1970; Manno *et al.*, 1970). Paresthesiae include tinglings, numbness, thrilling, vibrations, lips burning and later numb, aching in legs, and a feeling of being wrapped in cotton wool or of a pleasantly warm feeling like a watered-down orgasm (which was accompanied by inability to pass urine) (de Farias, 1955; Chopra and Chopra, 1957; Ames 1958; Hollister *et al.*, 1968; Talbott and Teague, 1969; Manno *et al.*, 1970; Waskow *et al.*, 1970). Throughout these accounts, which one should consult in the original to appreciate the variety of the reports, runs the theme of the wavelike character of the experience, with heaviness and lightness, feelings of heat or cold, or normality and abnormality alternating.

If one collates these perceptual changes, there seems on the one hand no real evidence that perceptual acuity is enhanced. On the other hand, many of the phenomena could be described as the result of a much greater significance or awareness being attached to normal sensory events, giving them a vividness and force normally missing. Some phenomena appear to be new, such as perception of patterns, vibrations, or thrills, but many, if not most, could represent a central impact of otherwise normal peripheral sensory activity, resulting sometimes simply in vividness, at other times in misinterpretation (e.g., of depth of objects or body size). This could arise (as mentioned above) by a loss of a normal habituation to customary stimuli or by the removal of other "gating" mechanisms. One must also note the comments that contrast seems enhanced (and this, by altering visual cues for distance might influence depth perception), that linearity seems to be conserved, that no special color is picked out, and that afterimages seem to last longer and a sound to continue after it has ceased. The sharpening of contrast indicates that "surround inhibition" is not impaired, and the data generally suggest that cannabis action takes place at the higher levels of sensory analysis.

G. Imagery, Dreaming, Fantasies, and Hallucinations

When one considers the phenomena under this head produced by cannabis, it is most profitable to arrange them in a kind of continuous spectrum. At one end, one notes the enhanced vividness of sensory experience. If this is strongly developed, unusual comparisons are made, such as that "the world looks as though it is cut out of cardboard," and an increased readiness to indulge in such fantasy, as well as a suggestibility to outside ideas, facilitates the process. All this seems, however, still at a stage where insight is preserved, and there is an adequate external sensory basis for the phenomena. A further development could be regarded as that when erroneous interpretations are made of these vividly evoked comparisons and images, so that (for instance) a wall appears to be covered with brilliant fantastic foliage. Finally, one comes closest to the stricter meaning of hallucination, where objects are seen or sounds are heard with no recorded external sensory basis. It is obvious from considering such a spectrum that there is no rigid line to be drawn, and, indeed, it is not clear how one establishes, even with what appears to be the most thoroughgoing hallucination, that it was not in fact based on *some* external sensory input or was not essentially a very vivid and unwilled fantasy or image.

If one considers the published reports, it is clear, as discussed in an earlier section, that sensory experience, particularly visual, can become subjectively much more vivid than normal under cannabis. Cannabis also gives rise readily to visual imagery, particularly when the eyes are closed or when one looks at a (presumably) bare surface such as a wall or ceiling (Bouquet 1951; Ames, 1958; Hollister *et al.*, 1968; Waskow *et al.*, 1970; Weil, 1970). Analogies are obvious and have been noted (Pond, 1948) with hypnagogic imagery, in which (again) eyes are closed. When well developed, these may be termed by the authors hallucinations. Thus, Ames (1958) describes a number of such experiences with eyes closed: Seeing "my brain like a ballerina's dress going round and round in the middle of a glass cube." Or, "Now I see a fat man in military costume running down stairs. He is in military uniform, has a snow-white beard and he is in a Roman tunic." Or, "I see a block of flats with a garage and stable gates and a man is leaning on the gate—it keeps changing and there are flickering bands of light going across like a forked flame." Finally, there are reports, although they are not common and are rarely described in detail, of both visual and auditory hallucinations (Baker-Bates, 1935; Bromberg, 1939; Allentuck and Bowman, 1942; Bouquet, 1951; Chopra and Chopra, 1957; Isbell *et al.*, 1967; Keeler,

1967, 1968b; Klee, 1969; Baker and Lucas, 1969; Grossman, 1969; Talbott and Teague, 1969; Weil, 1970; Keeler *et al.*, 1971). Thus, the subject may see objects flying, skulls, or arms and legs from a dissecting room; a fellow soldier may be identified as Ho Chi Minh and attacked; there may be auditory hallucinations compared with those of alcoholic psychosis; there may be a feeling of the internal organs rotting. Hallucinations may have a sexual or religious basis, may be distressing, and associated with delusions. An interesting case is that reported by Graff (1969) in which marijuana was taken by a girl after it had been soaked in scopolamine; this was followed by uncontrollable visual hallucinations (that a girl friend was a Negro man and that men were coming in the window) and auditory hallucinations (hearing monkeys and owls). Evidently the two drugs are not mutually antagonistic and are probably synergic.

Reviewing the reports, it appears that it is only with high doses, for instance (Grossman, 1969) when consumption rises from 1–2 cigarettes a week to 4–5 doses a week for a period of months or when (Baker and Lucas, 1969), after only one or two previous cigarettes, the subject smokes continuously for 1–2 hours, that the frankly hallucinatory phenomena appear. The content of the imagery and hallucinations does not seem to offer any particular clue to the action of cannabis beyond the general emphasis on visual phenomena already noted in the discussions on perceptual effects.

III. Perception of Time

One of the most regular effects of cannabis is to change time perception, and almost all investigators use phrases such as "alteration in sense of time," "tremendous increase in sense of time," "distortion of time perception," or "disoriented in time" (Gaskill, 1945; Parker and Wrigley, 1947; Isbell *et al.*, 1967; Keeler, 1967; Talbott and Teague, 1969; Waskow *et al.*, 1970; Hollister, 1970). Sometimes the phrases express a confusing state: "a combination of fastness and slowness" or "time intervals appear elastic" (Bromberg, 1939; Allentuck and Bowman, 1942). In Soueif's (1967) study, some subjects (particularly urban) reported time as being slowed, whereas others (particularly rural) reported it as going faster. More specific are statements such as time seems slower or stands still; events occurring immediately after each other are separated by an eternity; a venepuncture taking less than a minute seemed to last 15 minutes; a long time seemed to have passed even during the utterance of a sentence; a few minutes seemed like hours (Bromberg, 1939; Ames, 1958; Weil *et al.*, 1968; Hollister *et al.*, 1968; Tinklenberg *et al.*, 1970).

Statements of the last type suggest, correctly, that this type of effect could be measured. Difficulty arises in trying to move from spontaneous comment to deliberate experiment, since self-awareness by the subject of the distortion of time sense might evoke an attempt at compensation or might (by changing his state of attention) change the response in some other way. Some difficulty also arises in nomenclature, particularly with terms such as "time contraction" or "chronosystole," and care is needed to distinguish between, on the one hand, the lapse of time as felt or reported by the subject and, on the other, "clock time." Three types of measurement have been made: (a) The observer asks the subject how long some interval, measured on a clock, seemed to him. This can be called "felt" or "reported" time. The intervals used vary in length and in how far they are filled with speech or other activity. In this case felt or reported time is the dependent variable. (b) The observer asks the subject to say when a named time interval has elapsed and to note the corresponding clock time. Here "clock" time is the dependent variable. This is sometimes called "time production." These two tests are similar in principle in directly comparing reported and clock time, but the mental activity of comparison takes place at different times in relation to the elapsed interval. (c) Finally, the observer may demonstrate to the subject a given time interval, e.g., by sounding a tone of a given duration or by tapping, and ask the subject to reproduce the interval or a fraction of it. This has been termed "time reproduction." Since it requires the subject only to reproduce an interval without commenting on how long it seems to him, it is not clear how far it reflects changes in time perception.

In experiments on "reported" time, a low dose of smoked marijuana led to the reporting by three out of nine subjects that a period of speech lasting 5 minutes appeared to last about 10 minutes (Weil et al., 1968), to an overestimation by about one-third of tasks lasting on the average 15, 90, or 180 seconds (Clark et al., 1970), and to a significant rise in the estimation of an interval of 15 seconds from a control level of 14.9 to 15.6 seconds (Jones and Stone, 1970). In the last-named study, a contrasting effect of alcohol was found, the report of an interval of 15 seconds falling from 14.7 to 11.7 seconds. In all these experiments with cannabis, despite large quantitative differences, the ratio of reported or felt time to clock time increased. Similar results have been obtained with time "production." These experiments are complicated by the fact that the time produced even in normal subjects is usually briefer than the nominal clock interval. Williams et al. (1946) found that after subjects smoked two marijuana cigarettes, the interval of 20 seconds produced by the subjects fell from a control value of 12.7 seconds on the clock to 9.8 seconds. Jones and Stone (1970) found a small fall in production of a 15-second interval from 14.9 to 14.5 seconds. Although the effects are small, again the ratio of felt time to clock time is raised. Less helpful have been experiments on time "reproduction." Pond (1948) failed to find any change after pyrahexyl administration in the ability to tap out, after the examiner's demonstration, a series of 5-second intervals, even in subjects reporting a change in time perception. Hollister and Gillespie (1970) found, in subjects asked to produce an interval half that of a demonstrated interval, that this was normally underestimated and that marijuana and amphetamine (but not alcohol) reduced the underestimation; the full data, however, are not given.

It can be concluded, by comparing the general statements made together with these experimental data, that felt or reported time under cannabis is greater than clock time. In addition, it seems likely that some of the ambiguity in the reports, as to whether time goes faster or slower, simply reflects the choice of dependent variable, i.e., whether clock time or felt time is taken as *given*. It is also clear that relatively low doses of cannabis are required to produce an effect, namely of the order of 50–100 $\mu g/kg$ Δ^1-THC smoked (Isbell *et al.*, 1967; Jones and Stone, 1970; Clark *et al.*, 1970) or 100–200 $\mu g/kg$ taken orally (Isbell *et al.*, 1967; Jones and Stone, 1970). It is noticeable, however, that the experimentally measured effects are much less dramatic than spontaneous reports, and it raises the question as to how far a subject can bring himself "down" for the purpose of a relatively brief deliberate test in a way he would not otherwise do. It would be interesting to know how far this effect on time perception is deliberately reversible.

The phenomena described do not, however, give a complete picture of the effects produced. Also described are timelessness, time standing still, loss of sense of time, something like a fragmentation of the normally smooth succession of events, with long intervals between events, as though individual frames of a movie were being shown; a tendency to concentrate on the present; and a blurring of the distinction between past, present, and future—a temporal disintegration found to be significantly correlated with the degree of depersonalization (Ames, 1958; Hollister *et al.*, 1968; Waskow *et al.*, 1970; Jones and Stone, 1970; Melges *et al.*, 1970b, 1971). The effect is euphorigenic, so long as it is known to be time limited. However, panic can result from responses such as the following, from one of the subjects of Melges *et al.* (1970b): "helplessly drifting for ever, locked in infinity . . . a never-ending slosh, with my mind bouncing like a yo-yo." Timelessness, time fragmentation, or loss of time direction are not a necessary consequence of a relative augmentation of felt time, and they suggest a more fundamental change than, for instance, that of modulating some internal pacemaker.

Investigators who experiment with these phenomena face many difficulties, of which two have been mentioned: that the subject may, in the experimental situation, try to compensate for his abnormality, and that cannabis has a wavelike pattern of action that could allow the subject to come "down" for a period. In addition, it must be noted that many factors affect time estimation and awareness (Goldstone, 1967). Thus, a clock-second stimulus is judged to be equivalent in time to a shorter auditory than a visual stimulus and to a shorter still tactile stimulus, and these comparisons vary with conditions of the experiment. A loud auditory stimulus is felt to be longer than a soft. Age, body temperature, mood, and psychiatric state can all modify time estimation. For fuller experiments in this field, the influence of these factors will need control.

To approach an interpretation of the effects of cannabis on the sense of time, one cannot do better than quote William James (1890).

> We have every reason to think that creatures may possibly differ enormously in the amounts of duration which they intuitively feel, and in the fineness of the events that may fill it. Von Baer has indulged in some interesting computations of the effect of such differences in changing the aspect of Nature. Suppose we were able, within the length of a second, to note 10,000 events distinctly, instead of barely 10, as now; if our life were then destined to hold the same number of impressions, it might be 1000 times as short . . . The motions of organic beings would be so slow to our senses as to be inferred, not seen. The sun would stand still in the sky, the moon be almost free from change, and so on . . . .
>
> "A gnat's wings," says Mr. Spencer (Psychology §91), "make ten or fifteen thousand strokes a second. Each stroke implies a separate nervous action. Each such nervous action or change in a nervous centre is probably as appreciable by the gnat as is a quick movement of his arm by a man. And if this, or anything like this, is the fact, then the time occupied by a given external change, measured by many movements in the one case, must seem much longer than in the other case, when measured by one movement."
>
> In hashish intoxication there is a curious increase in the apparent time-perspective. We utter a sentence, and ere the end is reached the beginning seems already to date from indefinitely long ago. We enter a short street, and it is as if we should never get to the end of it. This alteration might conceivably result from an approach to the condition of Von Baer's and Spencer's short-lived beings. If our discrimination of successions became finer-grained, so that we noted ten stages in a process where previously we only noted one; and if at the same time the processes faded ten times as fast as before; we might have a specious present of the same subjective length as now, giving us the same time-feeling and containing as many distinguishable successive events, but out from the earlier end of it would have dropped nine tenths of the real events it now contains. They would have fallen into the general reservoir of merely dated memories, reproducible at will. The beginning of our sentences would have to be expressly recalled; each word would appear to pass through consciousness at a tenth of its usual speed. The condition would, in short, be exactly analogous to the enlargement of space by a microscope; fewer real things at once in the immediate field of view, but each of them taking up more than its normal room, and making the excluded ones seem unnaturally far away.
>
> Under other conditions, processes seem to fade rapidly without the compensating increase in the susceptibility of successions. Here the apparent length of the specious present contracts. Consciousness dwindles to a point, and loses all intuitive sense of the whence and whither of its path. Express acts of memory

replace rapid bird's-eye views. In my own case, something like this occurs in extreme fatigue.

This passage postulates several processes: that the mind receives impressions which fade, that these impressions must normally overlap so that at any moment traces of past events coexist with present traces, and that the sense of time depends on the receipt of these impressions and its nature on their frequency and overlap. These processes are plausible. The first could be related to the collection of processes termed "short-term memory"; the second is a natural consequence of its existence; the third is a pure assumption, not uncommonly made, implying that experience leads to an association of a given frequency of impressions with an appropriate passage of clock time. To them should be added the possibility of adaptation by the system, i.e., that its function would depend on its immediate past history, and the possibility, discussed above, that the inflow of sensation could be increased by a lifting of inhibition at earlier points on the sensory pathways. It might also be increased if the fading of an impression allows a new impression to appear more readily. With such an approach, it seems that an account can be given of all the phenomena described. If cannabis can shorten the trace and lead to an increased sensory input, then one could understand the drawing-out of time, the feeling of timelessness (if impressions no longer overlapped sufficiently to be related to each other), the sense of disorientation, and the confusion of past, present, and future.

IV. Memory

In the older literature, effects of cannabis on memory receive relatively little attention and usually refer to amnesia after gross overdosage. But in more recent work, especially in which an observer is present asking questions and conducting tests, it has become much clearer that an effect on memory is relatively common and is found with relatively low dosage. Possibly the earliest report is that of Bromberg (1939), who noted that subjects were confused in their recall of thoughts and suggested that this might be due to the sense of an increased speed of thought. Ames (1958) gives a much fuller account of the failure to recall and of forgetting what was said a few seconds earlier, a phenomenon frequently mentioned by later observers. Interestingly, her subjects, if reminded, could resume the thread of conversation, but, if they were left to themselves, the difficulty of recall became obvious. Despite this, the subjects' subsequent recollections of what happened during the experience corresponded well with the observers' notes. She also noted that the inability of recall was associated with the "dips" in the experience during which haziness and sense of unreality were present. All this suggests that, at this level of study, experience enters the memory stores normally and that the primary point of attack by cannabis comes at some later point. Hollister *et al.* (1968) mention impairment of memory by about 500 μg/kg THC orally or 370 μg/kg synhexyl orally. Soueif (1967) and Talbott and Teague (1969) describe a frequent loss of memory specifically for recent events, and the latter authors comment on the short attention span of their subjects.

Turning to more detailed studies, it is first possible to conclude that cannabis has little or no effect on long-term established memories. This was already probable from the fullness of the memory of cannabis experiences; the elaborate imagery described in an earlier section and the recrudescence of long-buried recollections also imply the same. More analytically, the ability of subjects for memory by rote, to say the alphabet, or to count backward, procedures dependent on past learning, were not affected (Williams *et al.*, 1946; Melges *et al.*, 1970a; Waskow *et al.*, 1970). Further, Abel (1971b) found that the number of words recalled or recognized during a marijuana "high," after learning them *before* the marijuana was given, was not reduced (although errors increased).

The effect on short-term memory, suggested by Ames, Soueif, and Talbott and Teague, has been shown in various ways. [This term is now being replaced by more specific terms (see Craik, 1971), but it is sufficiently precise for the discussion of the available evidence.] The effect becomes more pronounced the more demanding the test. Thus, in tests on forward or backward digit span (i.e., the longest series of digits that can be repeated forward or backward), some observers found no impairment by 20 mg THC orally (Waskow *et al.*, 1970), while others (Tinklenberg *et al.*, 1970) found a modest reduction in span with doses of 20 mg THC or above. Similarly, with serial addition or subtraction, the former group found impairment (with serial addition), but the latter (Melges *et al.*, 1970a) found no effect (with serial subtraction). With a test requiring alternate subtraction of 7 and addition of 1, 2, or 3 to reach a specific goal (some number lying between 46 and 54, starting from 106–114), Melges *et al.* (1970a) found pronounced effects on time taken and errors with 20 mg THC or above, and the impairment lasted over 5 hours. Similarly, Tinklenberg *et al.* (1970) found that the ability to rearrange and say back in correct numerical order a series of random digits was also sensitive to 20 mg THC orally and that the impairment could last up to 24 hours in some subjects. In both of the last two tests, the effect of THC became greater as dose was increased. Tinklenberg *et al.* (1970) also noted, as Ames had done, that the impairment was episodic and suggested that their urging the subjects to try to overcome their disability may have mitigated the effects. Another demanding task was used by Clark *et al.* (1970)

in which the subjects had to learn to associate each of a series of numbers, randomly presented, with particular push buttons and then reproduce this. Learning by the subjects was impaired while they were under the influence of cannabis (0.25–0.6 mg/kg THC orally), and the effects lasted up to 6 hours. It was appreciated that the impairment might have been due to failure of motivation, but the authors reported that the subjects were aware, "some painfully so," of the impairment of their performance, suggesting that failure of motivation was not the cause.

Another approach uses words rather than digits. Clark *et al.* (1970) showed that cannabis impaired comprehension in a reading test, and Abel (1970) showed that the smoking of marijuana cigarettes (sufficient to produce a "high," but THC dose was unmeasured), reduced the recall, after hearing a test story, of significant content words, of pairs or quadruplets of words from the story, and of idea units from the story. Later, Abel (1971a) in more extensive experiments showed that, while the capacity to solve anagrams was not impaired, subjects under the influence of marijuana improved less with practice, the recall of the anagram words and of content words and idea units after a test story was reduced, and errors increased. Finally, effects on immediate and delayed recall of words from carefully prepared lists were analyzed (Abel, 1971b,c). First, it was shown that the number of words remembered from lists read to the subjects before smoking marijuana was not reduced after smoking marijuana, either for free recall or recognition when interspersed with new words, but a considerable increase in false recognition took place, as though less stringent criteria for accepting recognition of a word were being used. A test of motivation during the exposure showed no difference from a control group, confirming the conclusion of Clark *et al.* (1970) that these effects are not simply due to subjects no longer being concerned with doing well in such tests. Finally, both immediate and delayed free recall were tested when both learning and test were done with subjects under the influence of marijuana. It was found that, when subjects were tested immediately after being read a list of words, the recall of the two or three most recently heard words, of a list of 12, was not impaired, but the recall of earlier words was reduced; the ability after an interval to reproduce words from the lists was also impaired. Abel infers that the initial processing information (entry into the "sensory register") is therefore not damaged by cannabis but that information is poorly retained in the short-term memory and therefore not passed on to a long-term memory. He suggests that this arises because cannabis impairs the rehearsal of information required for successful short-term remembering, this itself being a result of a failure of concentration. Miller *et al.* (1972) repeated part of these experiments, with both learning and test done after the smoking of marijuana, using material of known composition (25 μg/kg THC delivered) and placebo controls. They confirmed Abel's findings, and in addition failed to find any effect of cannabis on Stroop color–word performance.

Although this evidence demonstrates an effect of cannabis on recent memory, it is not yet clear as to how the effect is brought about. One may assume a simple model whereby information first enters the mind; it is then subject to a brief period of relatively rapid forgetting (the stage of short-term memory); if not lost, it next passes to longer-term stores with a lower rate of loss; finally, to bring a memory to consciousness a process of "retrieval" is necessary. There is no evidence of impairment of the first stage, and the main issue is whether under cannabis information is lost more rapidly from short- or long-term stores or whether this loss is at the normal rate but retrieval is more difficult. It seems clear from the general pattern of cannabis experience, as well as from Abel's results, that material placed in the long-term stores before cannabis is taken remains there and can be normally retrieved while one is under the influence of cannabis. It also seems that a good deal of information received *during* a cannabis experience enters the long-term stores and can be normally retrieved subsequently; this is implied by the general accounts but also more strictly by Ames' remark that her subjects' recollections of the experiment corresponded well with the observers' records. However, Abel has found that, for information both learned and tested for (by delayed free recall) while the subject is under cannabis, there is an impairment of long-term memory. Because he found no impairment during the cannabis experience in retrieval of long-term material learned *before* cannabis administration, his own view is that the retrieval mechanism is also unimpaired for short-term memory and that cannabis increases short-term (and therefore also long-term) forgetting. This is not at once reconcilable with Ames' report, and it is possible that information learned while subjects are under the influence of cannabis enters short- and long-term stores to the usual extent but cannot be normally retrieved until the effect of the drug has worn off. The decisive experiment, of quantitative testing *after* the drug exposure for recollection of neutral information presented during exposure to cannabis, does not appear to have been done. It carries an added interest in the light of comparisons between cannabis and anesthetics, for there is evidence, for instance, that nitrous oxide actually *reduces* forgetting as well as slows up the learning process (Summerfield and Steinberg, 1957, 1959).

There are a number of ways in which the effects of cannabis could interfere with memory or retrieval. An obvious one is that the subject's motivation could be weakened, giving rise to what would in effect be a spurious reduction of performance. But, as already mentioned, no reduction of motivation has been found under conditions in which memory deficit appeared. It is, of course, to be expected that cooperation in such experiments would fail with more intense intoxications. A second possibility, suggested in fact by some reports, is that there is increased "interference" due to the perceptual changes or to the enhanced stream of thought and imagery. It is known that forgetting increases in proportion as other irrelevant material is presented, and Summerfield and Steinberg (1957, 1959) obtained evidence that the reduction of forgetting produced by nitrous oxide is due to a reduction of the interference by such irrelevant information. Is also seems possible that this stream of thought and imagery could interfere with the full efficiency of retrieval. Third, it was suggested by Abel that the primary effect is a failure of the concentration required for the rehearsal of short-term material which allows it to be retained and to pass into long-term stores. This, too, is a plausible suggestion in the light of the general character of cannabis effects. Finally, one could suggest, in a different experimental idiom, that the drug directly interferes with the neurochemical processes involved in memory and retrieval, perhaps by reducing transmitter output in the pathways concerned so as to reduce the intensity or duration of a memory trace or to make sampling of stored information less effective.

The action is unlikely to be simple and may represent a balance of effects. One would expect, on the one hand, that cannabis would increase interference with remembering, by virtue of its increase in the stream of imagery and thought. On the other hand, its selective action and partial analogy with anesthetics suggest that it would reduce the effect of interference. Finally, any theory must take account of the episodic character of the memory defect and allow for a temporary improvement of memory either during spontaneous remissions or under an external stimulus.

V. Thought Processes

Characteristically, the subject under cannabis feels what is described as an "increased speed of thought," thoughts rapid or racing, flight of ideas, crowding of perceptions, flooded with thoughts, an increase in new associations (Bromberg, 1939; Tayleur-Stockings, 1947; Bouquet, 1951; de Farias, 1955; Ames, 1958; Soueif, 1967; Hollister et al., 1968; Talbott and Teague, 1969). With this may go the feeling that thoughts are out of control, of mental confusion or fragmentation of thoughts, of difficulty in sorting out mental processes towards "a single idea goal" or of maintaining sequential thought against the intrusions of irrelevant associations, of disjointedness and rapid change of topic of thought, of a daydreamy state with wandering thoughts, and of easy distractibility (Bromberg, 1939; Tayleur-Stockings, 1947; de Farias, 1955; Ames, 1958; Soueif, 1967; Hollister et al., 1968; Talbott and Teague, 1969; Clark et al., 1970; Melges et al., 1970b; Hollister,

1970; Tinklenberg *et al.*, 1970). The subject may feel that his thinking powers are still competent and clear, or unusually brilliant or clearheaded, or even that efficiency of thought is so enhanced that no mental feat is beyond him (Bromberg, 1939; de Farias, 1955; Ames, 1958; Soueif, 1967). On the other hand, an awareness may be present of difficulty in understanding, that something read repeatedly "will not stick," of sudden meaninglessness, or of some impairment in logical integration of facts (Tayleur-Stockings, 1947; Ames, 1958; Hollister *et al.*, 1968). This mental effect, like others, is episodic, and a period of languor may be followed by a period when the mind feels "precision clear" (Ames, 1958).

Corresponding with these effects are a difficulty in paying attention, a reduced attention span, and difficulty in concentrating (Allentuck and Bowman, 1942; Pond, 1948; Williams *et al.*, 1946; Hollister *et al.*, 1968; Talbott and Teague, 1969; Hollister, 1970). The loss of attention is episodic (Tinklenberg *et al.*, 1970). This affects the ability to act, and subjects report how difficult a simple sequence of actions such as putting on a kettle becomes because of difficulty in concentrating on a task (Parker and Wrigley, 1947) or the difficulty of completing a sentence (Baker-Bates, 1935; Parker and Wrigley, 1947; de Farias, 1955; Ames, 1958; Weil and Zinberg, 1969; Melges *et al.*, 1970a). Circumstantial talk, lackadaisical behavior, and difficulty in self-expression or in speaking (Allentuck and Bowman, 1942; Williams *et al.*, 1946; Hollister *et al.*, 1968; Hollister, 1970) are noted by observers. Action fails, too, because the subject is unable to keep up with the pressure of ideas, and, in attempting to write, it might be impossible for him to write a single intelligible sentence (de Farias, 1955). Related to these phenomena, perhaps, is the feeling of loss of control or of will power (Pond, 1948; Bouquet, 1951; Waskow *et al.*, 1970).

A number of formal tests of cognitive function have been made. Williams *et al.* (1946) found that chronic marijuana administration caused a small reduction in mental age by the Stanford–Binet test (against the rise expected from practice with the test); in other tests, those involving speed alone showed improvement, but when coordination and manual skill were involved, there was a loss in accuracy. Analogous observations were made with pyrahexyl, during which a slower reaction to questions was also noted, together with the belief by subjects that pyrahexyl made their thinking and the tasks presented to them easier. Melges *et al.* (1970b) found that THC (about 0.5 mg/kg orally) produced a significant degree of confusion, judged by a Temporal Integration Inventory. With a Number Facility Test, THC led to a slower (although still accurate) performance, whereas a Flexibility of Closure Test (involving the retracing of a design) showed a reduction of accuracy without any reduction in number of attempts in the test (Hollister *et al.*, 1968; Hollister and Gillespie, 1970). Clark *et al.* (1970) found an impairment of comprehension in a silent reading test, the impairment being proportional to the complexity of the test. Weil and Zinberg (1969) give an account of the effect of cannabis smoking on the character of a spontaneous 5-minute spoken narrative by the subject. Results were variable, but there was a trend toward a less coherent or unified product, with thoughts less completed, less awareness of the listener, a shift from past or future to the present, and more associations and imagery.

Some tests appear to be relatively insensitive, such as simple pursuit-meter procedures (Weil *et al.*, 1968), digital symbol substitution tests (Weil *et al.*, 1968; Jones and Stone, 1970), and simple repetition of numbers or alphabet. Hollister and Gillespie (1970) found a small increase in simple reaction time. Clark *et al.* (1970) found a similar increase in reaction time but were more impressed by the episodic variability in the response, with occasional complete failures. Possibly the most sensitive objective tests yet described are those using delayed auditory feedback (DAF), in which the subject is required to perform some task such as serial addition or reverse reading while his verbal response is played back to him with a delay of about 0.25 second (Manno *et al.*, 1970, 1971; Kiplinger *et al.*, 1971). The delayed feedback converts a simple procedure into a surprisingly difficult one. With some tasks, as little as 6.25 μg/kg THC delivered in the smoke produced a substantial effect. The same group (Manno *et al.*, 1970) found that THC also impaired performance on sophisticated pursuit-meter tasks requiring the following of various patterns. They have also studied (1971b) the interaction with alcohol, comparing the effects of alcohol (in a dose giving a blood level of 50 mg/100 ml) with that of a delivered dose of 2.5 and 5 mg THC by smoking. They found that the effect of alcohol was comparable to (or somewhat less than) that of THC on most of the DAF tests and in producing conjunctival injection, and much less on the pursuit-meter, on pulse rate, or on the Cornell Medical Index. When combined, however, the effects in general summed, including pursuit-meter, DAF, pulse rate, conjunctival injection, and Cornell Medical Index results. No sign of mutual antagonism was found by these tests, save that subjects seemed to the observers more depressed and quieter when marijuana and alcohol were combined than with either drug alone.

In addition to the phenomena described, certain other changes occur, which may be connected with each other. Suggestibility is enhanced (Pond, 1948; Bouquet, 1951; Ames, 1958; Caldwell *et al.*, 1969a), and it has been speculated that this occurs with cannabis in a way that it does not with (say) the opiates or alcohol, because not only is free association and imagery facilitated, but perceptual awareness and responsiveness to external stimuli are not blunted. With this may be linked the much-quoted influence of "set and setting" on the response to cannabis. There is little demonstrative evidence of this, although experience with placebo responses makes it plausible, and subjects may comment that they felt the "sterile" laboratory environment reduced the effect of marijuana (Caldwell *et al.*, 1969a). Waskow *et al.* (1970) found some evidence that the degree of euphoria was increased if music was played, and subjects have reported that they could "turn off a high" for a short space when the stimulus of some task was presented (Caldwell *et al.*, 1969a). In addition, lack of congeniality of surroundings as a stimulus to side effects was noted by Galanter *et al.* (1972). More conclusive is the finding of Jones (1971) that the response to cannabis, as with many other centrally acting drugs, depends on whether the subject is alone or in a group. Thus, in a group a given dose of cannabis smoked was found to produce more euphoria, perceptual change, and change in thinking, and less dysphoria and sedation than when the drug was smoked in solitude. Even so, the existence of additional objective evidence to show the influence of the subject's expectations or his environment on the effect of cannabis would be desirable.

It is clear that insight generally is preserved in these test situations in the sense that, however striking the effects are, the subject knows they are due to the drug. But it appears that this insight has its limitations, and defect of judgment has also been reported (Gaskill, 1945; Williams *et al.*, 1946; Chopra and Chopra, 1957; Talbott and Teague, 1969; Caldwell *et al.*, 1969a), with subjects believing they have performed better than was in fact the case. Finally, a tendency to introversion, described in one study as "hypertrophy of the ego," has been noted (Pond, 1948; Bouquet, 1951). Ames' (1958) case of overdosage describes how time and space were compressed to one bright minute of gay brilliant talk, himself "the care-free centre of it all." Melges *et al.* (1970b) found a correlation between egotism and aggression in answer to the questionnaire, which reflected the cocky devil-may-care attitude of the THC-induced mood.

VI. Sense of Unreality and Depersonalization

A frequent report is that of feelings of unreality (Bromberg, 1939; Ames, 1958; Isbell *et al.*, 1967; Hollister *et al.*, 1968; Talbott and Teague, 1969; Grossman, 1969; Kaplan, 1971). It has been expressed as "losing contact with reality," "loss of feeling real," "seeing reality in glimpses," "conscious of reality leaving him," "perceiving voice thoughts and appearance as unreal," "being in an unreal state." Related to it are feelings of change of personality or loss of personality (Baker-Bates, 1935; Pond, 1948; Bouquet, 1951; de Farias, 1955; Chopra and Chopra, 1957; Ames, 1958; Isbell *et al.*, 1967; Keeler, 1967; Hollister *et al.*, 1968; Talbott and Teague, 1969; Grossman, 1969; Melges *et al.*, 1970b). This may be a feeling of nonexistence, that one is dead, or that one is someone else (e.g., the Virgin Mary or part of the Holy Trinity). Most common is a sense of duality, like watching a film of one's own performance, watching (from the outside) oneself in a big transparent bubble, or feeling like two people, one laughing, the other anxious; imagining that one is outside one's own body or that the mind split in two parts, good and evil; or feeling detachment such that a headache seems to be someone else's headache. The more developed forms appear to require repeated recent use of cannabis for their appearance, but Melges *et al.* (1970b) found that single doses of 20 mg THC or more given orally produced a significant rise in depersonalization as judged by a depersonalization inventory. In one study with pyrahexyl, Pond (1948) found that, in patients with preexisting depersonalization, the drug made it worse. Melges *et al.* (1970b) showed that depersonalization and temporal disintegration are statistically associated, and suggested that the loss of a sense of past, present, and future, and hence of goal direction or of the ability to compare experience with expectation, may be an important cause of the depersonalization.

VII. Feelings of Insight and Significance

The increased vividness of sensory experience, described earlier, may naturally carry with it a feeling of increased significance and meaning of much the same sort that certain poetry can evoke, and unexpected things such as an ant heap (Chapple, 1966) can become meaningful. Further than this is a feeling of clarity of thought and a sense of deeper insight into the subject's own personality, of seeing how to solve personal problems or being able to achieve a better recognition of the important goals in life (Bromberg, 1939; Ames, 1958; Chapple, 1966; Soueif, 1967; Keeler, 1967). Marcovitz and Myers (1944) noted a feeling of superiority in the habitual user, of taking over the claims of the creative artist to freedom from the need to work, but without even a pretence of creating—arising from this image of himself. J. R. Anderson, in his fascinating account of cannabis use in Walter de la Mare's (1930) "Desert Islands and Robinson Crusoe," describes how under cannabis he felt he could "see" a mathematical proposition in the theory of infinite series. One of de Farias' (1955) subjects felt able to interpret the interplay of the forces between the ego and the superego. Related to these feelings may be the feeling of ecstasy sometimes reported (Tayleur-Stockings, 1947; de Farias, 1955; Chopra and Chopra, 1957): "imaginative ecstasy" or "a dreamy apathy and contentment with large doses reaches the stage of ecstasy." On the obverse side, some of the imaginings, although intensely significant, are painful: "indescribably evil things happen to her," or an unbelievable experience, fantastically real, of Hell and Purgatory, and of a pain "that I knew would lead to better things."

VIII. Mood and Emotions

A. EUPHORIA

There is, as Pond (1948) pointed out, an ambiguity in this term; it may be used to express a *normal* feeling of well-being or an *abnormal* elevation of mood inappropriate to the circumstances. Both states can be produced by cannabis, as illustrated by the following phrases: contented; pleasurable; happy; relaxation and well-being; a refreshing and stimulating feeling; a pleasant feeling if one hadn't anything to do; exhilaration; physical well-being, happiness, self-confidence; delicious, confused lassitude; fatuous giggling, "I would laugh at things not worth laughing about"; feisty, whoopy, frolicsome; gay, excited; (Baker-Bates, 1935; Bromberg, 1939; Allentuck and Bowman, 1942; Marcovitz and Myers, 1944; Gaskill, 1945; Williams *et al.*, 1946; Tayleur-Stockings, 1947; Parker and Wrigley, 1947; Pond, 1948; de Farias, 1955; Chopra and Chopra, 1957; Ames, 1958; Hollister *et al.*, 1968; Waskow *et al.*, 1970; Jones and Stone, 1970; Melges *et al.*, 1970b).

At the same time, the elevation of mood may be absent in naive subjects (Weil *et al.*, 1968), is sometimes a minor element (Waskow *et al.*, 1970), and is usually described in mild terms or as falling short of euphoria (Ames, 1958; Jones and Stone, 1970). It is not, of course, invariably present. It occurs during the earlier part of the experience, lasting longer than with LSD (Hollister *et al.*, 1968), but giving way to drowsiness. To some extent, the euphoria has to be learned (Weil *et al.*, 1968; Becker, 1967; Waskow *et al.*, 1970). Soueif (1967) suggests that dependence is liable to start only after the subject has in fact learned to find the experience pleasant. He also makes the interesting comments that his users started smoking cannabis in search of euphoria, out of curiosity, or for sexual reasons (in descending order of priority), but continued with it for reasons of habit, because it was soothing, or for euphoria (again in descending order). Users felt that on the drug they became more submissive, less contradictory, more sociable, less depressed, and tended to need it to avoid feeling low. Ames (1958) noted that the two subjects who spoke about it with most appreciation ("extraordinarily delightful," "a golden dream") were also the only two who were willing to take the drug again.

The euphoria is infectious. It may be associated with feelings of friendliness or of power (to show how strong he was, a subject jumped off a 20-ft balcony), excitement, an increased sensual quality to thoughts, a feeling of loss of inhibitions, or (possibly rather important in young subjects) a feeling of greater confidence. An alternation may occur between feeling happy and gay one moment and anxious the next (Baker-Bates, 1935; Bromberg, 1939;

Gaskill, 1945; Chopra and Chopra, 1957; Chapple, 1966; Soueif, 1967; Hollister *et al.*, 1968). Wilson and Linken (1968) recorded an amusing comment by a subject that "African hash made her giggly, Cypriot hash made her sexy, and Indian hash made her sleepy." Quantitation of mood change by use of suitable checklists or the Cornell Medical Index and Addiction Research Center Inventory have shown that they are dose related. Kiplinger *et al.* (1971) found detectable effects at more than 6 μg/kg THC smoked. Hollister and Gillespie (1970) found, with a checklist, that marijuana reduced the "active" factor, raised (but not significantly) the "stimulated" factor, and did not affect the "drowsy" factor. In contrast, amphetamine raised the "active" and "stimulated," and reduced the "drowsy" factors, and alcohol reduced the "active" factor and raised the "drowsy" factor insignificantly, with no effect on the "stimulated" factor. Hollister (1969) also reported that neither THC nor pyrahexyl caused any change in plasma cortisol in the absence of secondary fear or anxiety; this is compatible with its sedative action, and excludes the possibility that the euphoria might be due to cortisol.

B. Dysphoria, Aggressiveness, Paranoia, and Fear of Death

For a drug supposedly taken for pleasure, dysphoria and anxiety are surprisingly common results of taking cannabis. Malaise, nausea, vomiting, giddiness, visceral feelings of panic, muscle discomfort, headache, palpitations, uneasiness and "feeling tight inside" are reported symptoms, and it appears in general that onset of action, even in the experienced, commonly has unpleasant somatic effects (Bromberg, 1939; Allentuck and Bowman, 1942; Gaskill, 1945; Tayleur-Stockings, 1947; de Farias, 1955; Ames, 1958; Scher, 1970; Waskow *et al.*, 1970; Jones and Stone, 1970). Perhaps to be associated with these are feelings of anxiety or panic (which may be felt to be without cause), guilt, apprehension, and irritability (Baker-Bates, 1935; Bromberg, 1939; Allentuck and Bowman, 1942; Ames, 1958; Keeler, 1967; Talbott and Teague, 1969; Hollister, 1969; Weil, 1970; Persyko, 1970). A recurrent report is that of acute anguish and fear of death (Bromberg, 1939; Gaskill, 1945; de Farias, 1955; Chopra and Chopra, 1957; Ames, 1958; Talbott and Teague, 1969; Grossman, 1969; Persyko, 1970). Or the fear may be of injury, insanity, deformity or homosexuality; of loss of control or sense of identity; or that, because the subject can no longer control his own thinking, it will be controlled by others (Ames, 1958; Keeler, 1967; Melges *et al.*, 1970b). A paranoid state is common—as Weil (1970) remarks, a transient paranoia is familiar to most users—with feelings of persecution, of being watched and talked about, of betrayal, of distrusting the world with everyone an enemy (Allentuck and Bowman, 1942; Williams *et al.*, 1946; Chapple,

1966; Tylden, 1967; Keeler, 1967, 1968a; Talbott and Teague, 1969; Kaplan, 1971).

Aggressiveness (as judged by questionnaires) usually declines, perhaps from the sedative action of cannabis (Hollister *et al.*, 1968), but nevertheless suicidal actions, fighting, and firing of guns occur (Bromberg, 1939; Marcovitz and Myers, 1944; Gaskill, 1945; Klee, 1969; Talbott and Teague, 1969; Kaplan, 1971). Melges *et al.* (1970b) concluded, however, that the aggressiveness is egotistic rather than hostile, a note echoed by Marcovitz and Myers' (1944) account of the feeling of superiority displayed by cannabis users and Tylden's (1967) reference to their crushing arrogance.

The incidence of these types of effect depends, of course, on conditions of use. Chopra and Chopra (1957) found that in 12 out of 100 regular users, cannabis produces depression. Anxiety was present in 6 out of Talbott and Teague's (1969) 12 cases. Jones and Stone (1970) found that smoked THC produced euphoria in 30% of their subjects and dysphoria in 15%; when THC was given orally, the figures were 12% euphoria and 25% dysphoria. Keeler (1968a) noted paranoid thinking in 28 of 40 continuing users, and Talbott and Teague (1969) found it in 10 out of their 12 cases. One must note, too, the incidental report in a survey by Ungerleider *et al.* (1968), primarily concerned with adverse reactions to LSD, of over 1800 adverse reactions to cannabis reported by California psychiatrists. It is clear that these reactions may be transient, that they may be succeeded by euphoria, and that alternation of mood, or even coexistence of anxiety and hilarity, occur. But the extent of these reports illuminates the significance of the statements about learning to use cannabis. Soueif (1967) remarks that the initiate has to be cajoled, and dependence begins when he learns how to find the experience pleasant. Waskow *et al.* (1970) endorse Becker's (1953, 1967) remark that the user has to learn to redefine sensations as pleasurable, and there is a considerable popular literature in the same vein.

The question of these dysphoric experiences is of some interest, since it has been suggested that cannabis might be useful clinically for the elevation of mood, for instance in the treatment of depression. It seems likely that Pond's (1948) assessment of pyrahexyl as inferior for this purpose to amphetamine is true for cannabis itself. Parker and Wrigley (1950) conducted a trial in which pyrahexyl was no better than placebo in treating depression. Its failure was attributed mainly to wavelike intermittency of action.

IX. Sleep and Sleepiness, Disinterest, Detachment: The Amotivational Syndrome

While the pattern of the cannabis experience depends on the social environment in which the drug is taken, drowsiness or sleepiness is common in the later stages and may be overpowering (Allentuck and Bowman, 1942; Gaskill, 1945; de Farias, 1955; Chopra and Chopra, 1957; Chapple, 1966; Tart and Crawford, 1970; Hollister *et al.*, 1968; Waskow *et al.*, 1970; Hollister, 1970). Similar statements are true for pyrahexyl (Parker and Wrigley, 1947; Tayleur-Stockings, 1947; Pond, 1948). Cannabis may be used as a hypnotic. Williams *et al.* (1946) found that subjects taking pyrahexyl *ad lib* slept as long as normally, but on marijuana slept longer. Sometimes sleepiness may occur early and drowsiness may have a sudden onset and come in bursts. The subject is arousable during these episodes (Pond, 1948; Ames, 1958; Hollister *et al.*, 1968). Soueif (1967) noted that the habitual hashish taker has a fitful and disturbed sleep, finding it hard to get to sleep and waking early. The effect on sleep is dose related. Tart and Crawford (1970) reported some users' experience that, while low doses of marijuana are sedative, high doses over-stimulate and make sleep poor. Pivik *et al.* (1969, 1972) reported a tendency for cannabis, THC, and pyrahexyl to reduce REM activity in the second half of a period of sleep, to prolong sleeping time, and to reduce REM sleep after a period of REM deprivation.

Related to this is a general tendency toward disinterest, lethargy, listless-ness, and feeling weak and tired. Pond (1948) noted with pyrahexyl a decreased interest in work and a contentment in dozing and sitting about. Williams *et al.* (1946), with pyrahexyl given *ad lib*, recorded lethargy and loss of interest in surroundings; with marijuana, there was an initial rise in general activity, followed by indolence, loss of interest, and neglect of hygiene. An interesting feature was that two of their (prison) subjects expressed the intention of painting or practicing music during the experimental period but gave these up in the event. Marcovitz and Myers (1944) noted two habitual users' remarks: "Don't care what happens to me" and "I ain't for working." Bromberg (1939), de Farias (1955), Chopra and Chopra (1957), Chapple (1966), Scher (1970), and Waskow *et al.* (1970) similarly recorded listlessness, lethargy, sluggishness, and negativism.

Again related to this is detachment (Ames, 1958; Clark *et al.*, 1970). Parker and Wrigley (1947), with pyrahexyl, mention the feeling of detachment in the face of a child's danger, the child running around a room with a large jagged piece of glass in his mouth. Ames (1958) refers to being aware but feeling insulated from anxiety.

The group of symptoms of this kind has come to be referred to as the "amotivational syndrome," well reviewed in the National Institute of Mental Health (1971) report. What is referred to here ranges from social deterioration comparable to that of the fully developed alcoholic to a much less tangible loss of drive or efficiency (vaguely sensed by the subjects). A question, of course, arises as to how far cannabis use *causes* such a syndrome or is simply associated with it. The investigations cited above in which single doses produced, reversibly, feelings of listlessness and drowsiness, of detachment from events that would otherwise evoke action, and of insulation from anxiety (which could well remove, *inter alia*, anxiety about the consequences of inaction) make it clear that cannabis alone could produce the syndrome. In interpreting the reports, too, it must be remembered that the effects are dose related, and it is to be expected that patterns of very varying intensity would be seen, depending on both size of dose taken and (because of the drug's cumulative tendency) the frequency of use. The pattern of symptoms has prompted the suggestion that there may be an organic basis (West, 1970), and the question of neuropathy in taken up in Chapter 7.

X. "Drunkenness" and Light-headedness

A recurrent theme in subjective reports of the effects of cannabis is a comparison with the effects of alcohol. "Light-headedness" is a common term. It is described as being like the early stages of alcohol intoxication or like having a few glasses of wine, feeling almost drunk, or feeling or looking intoxicated (Baker-Bates, 1935; Tayleur-Stockings, 1947; Pond, 1948; de Farias, 1955; Ames, 1958; Weil *et al.*, 1968; Hollister *et al.*, 1968; Talbott and Teague, 1969; Grossman, 1969). Indeed, some authors have even described a hangover which was compared to that after alcohol (Allentuck and Bowman, 1942; de Farias, 1955; Hollister *et al.*, 1968) although such reports are rare. Talbott and Teague (1969) comment on the way that, in a group of habitual users, most adverse reactions were handled by a man's peers like belligerent drunkenness, by time, patience, and sobering-up. A man may act as though drunk but not smell of alcohol (Marcovitz and Myers, 1944; Grossman, 1969). For many subjects, of course, sensory changes may give rise to an experience quite unlike that produced by alcohol.

The psychometric tests discussed earlier (Hollister and Gillespie, 1970) point to a similar conclusion, that cannabis has resemblances to alcohol but also that it differs—notably, in their experiments, in the effect of time sense.

XI. Sexual Feeling

The much-debated question as to whether cannabis contributes to sexual offences, a matter of sociological and criminological statistics, is beyond the scope of this review. It must be remembered, too, that almost any substance can act as an aphrodisiac or an antiaphrodisiac if it is believed to be one or the other. Nevertheless, there appears to be more than a trivial connection between cannabis use and sexual feeling. Reports of sexual stimulation or of sexual fantasies and of sexual fears are common (Bromberg, 1939; Mayor's Committee on Marihuana, 1944; Marcovitz and Myers, 1944; Gaskill, 1945; Chopra and Chopra, 1957; Hollister *et al.*, 1968; Talbott and Teague, 1969). The study by Hollister *et al.* (1968) is particularly useful, in that although sexual thoughts were reported after cannabis or pyrahexyl was taken, they were not after LSD administration—a control on the possibility that any such inquiry would always reveal them. The well-established ability of cannabis to promote fantasy provides an obvious basis for much of this. Marcovitz and Myers (1944) go further and comment on the combination, in the habitual user, of indifference to the opposite sex and extreme promiscuity, and of the feeling of unrivaled sexual potency yet without affection; their subjects, however, would, if choice were necessary, have chosen marijuana rather than women. Chopra and Chopra (1957) describe how cocaine came to replace cannabis for aphrodisiac purposes, but as cocaine supplies dwindled cannabis returned. Yet they also note that cannabis may be used as an aphrodisiac by the dissolute and to quell sexual thoughts by the devout—a paradox resolvable if it is basically imagery and fantasy that cannabis fosters. They add that only 10% of their subjects used cannabis for sexual stimulation. To the fostering of fantasy may well be added what may be described as a release of inhibition or relaxation of taboos, and this may underlie the reports of perversion and fear of homosexual assault.

Certain more specific factors should not be discounted. First, cannabis causes a relaxation of sympathetic tone (see p. 231), and this is likely to cause a mild genital vasodilation. Second, time sense is altered, so that a sexual experience could seem to be prolonged; indeed, a partial reduction of sympathetic activity with delay of ejaculation might produce a genuine prolongation. Finally, even if there is only limited evidence that sensory thresholds are lowered, it is clear that many sensory stimuli are more intensely felt. It is likely, therefore, that the effect of cannabis on sexuality varies in a complex manner with the individual and that it is the resultant of fantasy, relaxed inhibitions, direct pharmacological effects, and sensory intensification and is modulated in its expression by the extent to which lassitude or activity prevails.

XII. Laughter

A characteristic effect of cannabis in many subjects is laughter, hilarity, and mirth, and it is infectious (Baker-Bates, 1935; Allentuck and Bowman, 1942; Marcovitz and Myers, 1944; Williams *et al.*, 1946; de Farias, 1955; Ames, 1958; Chapple, 1966). This is a natural consequence of an elevation of mood. However, the laughter is often inappropriate and is described as foolish or fatuous. It may alternate rapidly with depression or apprehension, and sometimes it proves uncontrollable (Baker-Bates, 1935; Bromberg, 1939; Parker and Wrigley, 1947; de Farias, 1955; Chapple, 1966; Hollister *et al.*, 1968). Here one is reminded of the epidemic laughter of the disease kuru and of the neurological syndrome of spontaneous, unprovoked laughter to which Daly and Mulder (1957) gave the name "gelastic epilepsy." There is evidence that this is associated with diencephalic or hypothalamic lesions (and perhaps with temporal lobe epilepsy), and Martin (1950) has suggested that there may be a laughter "center," which could under suitable con-ditions give rise to a sham mirth comparable to the well-known sham rage. It is interesting that Gumpert *et al.* (1970) were able to control, with intravenous diazepam, a case in which attacks of laughter were combined with limb and head movement. It seems quite probable, therefore, that the uncontrollable laughter produced by cannabis may represent the release of (among other structures) the nerve networks subserving laughter, allowing paroxysmal activity, alternating with that of other similarly disinhibited networks.

XIII. General Motor Activity

Although cannabis causes initial restlessness, excitement, and sometimes boisterous, impulsive behavior, pacing and dancing (Baker-Bates, 1935; Bromberg, 1939; Gaskill, 1945; Williams *et al.*, 1946; Tayleur-Stockings, 1947; de Farias, 1955; Chopra and Chopra, 1957; Grossman, 1969; Talbott and Teague, 1969), the main picture is of reduced physical activity apart from speech. The feelings of lethargy, laziness, and disinterest discussed earlier have the expected result. Activity can sometimes be "automatic," with, for example, an individual stopping at a traffic light or pushing a button in a test without being aware of it (Weil *et al.*, 1968). The loss of desire to work leads naturally to the type of result reported by Soueif (1967) where hours worked varied inversely with hashish consumption and to the usual case histories (e.g., Tylden, 1967). The only qualification to this is Tayleur-Stockings' (1947) suggestion that in depressed patients pyrahexyl led to an elevation of mood and feeling more energetic. But Pond (1948) found that pyrahexyl reduced the time by about 60% for which a patient, asked to hold one leg up as long as he could, would do so.

For speech the reverse is the case. Loquacity, continuous circumstantial talk, volubility, rapid speech, rapid disorderly conversation, and slurred speech are typical reports (Baker-Bates, 1935; Bromberg, 1939; Allentuck and Bowman, 1942; Williams *et al.*, 1946; Chopra and Chopra, 1957; Chapple, 1966; Grossman, 1969). Fluency in conversation was esteemed by

Soueif's (1967) subjects. The talk is felt to be witty, humorous, and brilliant, even though the conversation may in fact be hard to follow (Bromberg, 1939). This arises from the easy distractibility of the subjects, from failure to remember what was just said or was going to be said, from difficulty in completing sentences, and from the pressure of free associations (Baker-Bates, 1935; Parker and Wrigley, 1947; Hollister *et al.*, 1968; Melges *et al.*, 1970a). One could imagine that the enhanced imagery and lowered inhibition could well overcome an otherwise decreased tendency to speech, because of the close link between thought and speech. But there may be an additional element, following Bromberg's (1939) suggestion that the need of the marijuana user for a social setting may be a reaction to an inner anxiety that arises from the threat to the individual presented by somatic illusions. Considering the frequency of unpleasant or dysphoric phenomena, it would not be surprising if reassurance by conversation were sought. Such factors could explain the interesting way in which almost all spontaneous motor activity, save speech, tends to be reduced.

Involuntary hyperactivity may also occur. Restlessness and impulsive activity have been mentioned above. In a few subjects, probably with higher or repeated doses of cannabis, involuntary twitching (Allentuck and Bowman, 1942), jerking movements during sleep (Williams *et al.*, 1946, pyrahexyl), and painful muscle spasms (Ames, 1958) have been recorded. In one of Grossman's (1969) cases, there was some sort of convulsion, with crying and uncontrollable arm movements, and Ames noted jumping with arching of the back in patient A, muscle twitches of limbs and abdomen in patient F, and painful, prolonged arm and leg movements in patient G which could only be momentarily controlled when the patient was urged to do so. These phenomena strongly suggest, as with laughter, a disinhibiting process allowing myoclonic jerks or liability to choreiform activity.

XIV. Ataxia, Tremor, Reflexes, and Catalepsy

The most striking neurological effect of cannabis is ataxia, and it has been frequently reported (Baker-Bates, 1935; Allentuck and Bowman, 1942; Gaskill, 1945; Williams *et al.*, 1946; Pond, 1948; Tayleur-Stockings, 1947; de Farias, 1955; Ames, 1958; Chapple, 1966; Hollister *et al.*, 1968; Clark *et al.*, 1970; Kiplinger *et al.*, 1971). It may be noted as a loss of accuracy when coordination or manual skill is required, as difficulty in fine movements such as picking up a pin, as an unsteady gait, or as difficulty in articulation. Deliberate tests, such as the finger-to-finger test, heel-to-toe walking, or the Romberg test, also reveal it. The best study remains that of the Mayor's Committee on Marihuana (1944), in which the effect of cannabis extract on the sway of the erect subject's head in two dimensions was recorded and integrated. The data presented illustrate not only the effects but also the relation to dose of cannabis given, the time course of cannabis action when the preparation is given orally and when it is smoked, and the relative insensitivity of the habitual user compared to the naive subject (Fig. 1). Similar results were obtained at that time with the stylus-in-a-hole hand-steadiness test. Clark *et al.* (1970) have confirmed the latter studies, and

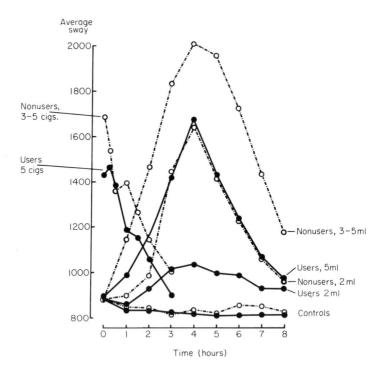

Fig. 1. Ataxia (eyes open) with cannabis taken orally or smoked (●, users; ○, nonusers).

Kiplinger *et al.* (1971) have used a similar head-sway method to show that ataxia is produced by smoked Δ^1-THC in doses of the order of 6–50 μg/kg. It should be noted that the ataxia is not gross, and Williams *et al.* (1946) reported that their subjects, taking cannabis *ad lib*, would throw and catch a ball normally.

Tremor or tremulousness also occurs in some subjects (Baker-Bates, 1935; Allentuck and Bowman, 1942; Pond, 1948; Hollister *et al.*, 1968; Talbott and Teague, 1969; Hollister, 1970). Thompson and Proctor (1953) describe a circumoral tremor and tremor of the protruded tongue and of the extremities. The tremor has not been well defined and appears to be irregular and to merge into twitchings and other muscle movements.

Reflex responses are also poorly characterized. There is a general impression that reflexes tend to increase (Allentuck and Bowman, 1942; Tayleur-Stockings, 1947; Hollister *et al.*, 1968; Talbott and Teague, 1969), but Domino (1971) required sophisticated instrumentation to show a slight increase in the knee jerk, and Isbell *et al.* (1967) found no change in knee-jerk threshold, with otherwise effective doses of Δ^1-THC. The most pronounced response is that mentioned by Gaskill (1945) whereby, during a subject's recovery from a vasovagal attack induced by cannabis, hyperactive reflexes with clonus were seen.

It is evident that there is no gross muscular paralysis, but there is evidence of impaired strength of voluntary movement. Pond (1948) found that leg lifting was less well sustained under pyrahexyl; the case reported by Baker-Bates (1935) progressed to a condition of loss of power in the legs and inability to stand; and Hollister *et al.* (1968) obtained quantitative ergographic data showing a decrement in finger strength over a period of 1 minute. These results, correlated with other data, seem to indicate that the defect is central rather than peripheral.

Although a "cataleptic" state is readily demonstrable in animals, no equivalent test has been devised for man. Perhaps this could be done, since a user remarked to one of the authors that, during one experience, he "had not known he was high until he realized he had been sitting in an uncomfortable position for a long time." There are, however, two reports of well-developed catalepsy after substantial dosage, with cataleptic postures, gross statuesque positions, and cerea flexibilitas (Bromberg, 1939; Allentuck and Bowman, 1942).

Cannabis increases reaction time (Clark and Nakashima, 1968; Hollister and Gillespie, 1970; Clark *et al.*, 1970); the effect is more noticeable with a more complex test involving choice. Irregularity in response also characteristically increases. Cannabis also impairs performance in pursuit-meter tests. Weil *et al.* (1968) found impairment for naive subjects in a simple pursuit-rotor test; Manno and his colleagues (Manno *et al.*, 1970, 1971; Kiplinger *et al.*, 1971) used a variety of pursuit patterns and were able to show a dose-related impairment of performance for all tests. Crancer *et al.* (1969) reported a study with a driving simulator, but there is a doubt as to the potency of the marijuana used (see Manno *et al.*, 1971); it may have been 1/6 of the believed potency, giving a dose of 3–4 mg THC. It is possible to conclude from the study only that subjects who claimed a "social high" and had detectable changes in heart rate after they smoked cannabis displayed speedometer but no other errors.

XV. Electroencephalography

The EEG changes seen depend on dose and time of observation. Wikler and Lloyd (1945) obtained variable results on frequency of the α rhythm, which was complicated in a number of patients by increase in fast waves due to muscle action potentials; an average fall in frequency of 19% was observed in 8 of 18 subjects. Williams *et al.* (1946), with subjects taking pyrahexyl and marijuana daily, found that the percentage of α rhythm tended to fall; in two subjects, much slower δ activity was noted; these changes disappeared within 4 days of withdrawal of the drug. Ames (1958) found a lower proportion of α activity; in a case of overdose, it was replaced entirely by fast activity; in addition, in two subjects under the influence of cannabis, slower 6–7 count/second synchronous rhythms were found in the temporal regions. Hollister *et al.* (1970b) also noted a shift from normal α to 7 cycles/second rhythm during peak action of THC, some synchronization of posterior leads, and on analysis obtained evidence of some peaking of frequencies (i.e., less scatter). Volavka *et al.* (1971) agree that, with daily smoking, EEG synchronization occurs, but they also note, with cannabis smoking, an early and transient rise in α and decline in θ and β frequencies. Campbell (1971) observed a marked rise in EEG abnormalities in cannabis users, particularly of θ activity, in bursts or sustained.

As with the animal data, there seems to be a tendency both toward "arousal," with a replacement of the normal α rhythm by fast activity, and toward hypersynchrony such as may occur with sedation. Since it has long been known that drugs can produce a marked dissociation of the normal relation between behavior and the EEG, an interpretation of these findings would be premature.

XVI. Autonomic and Other Related Effects

The smoking of cannabis characteristically produces a dry mouth. This may become intense and affect the tongue, throat, and nose, with a feeling of thirst and difficulty in swallowing. There may be some burning and irritation of the tongue, a resinous taste, and an anesthesia of the tip of the tongue (compared with the effect of menthol). Numbness and paresthesiae around the mouth have been noted. Corn silk control cigarettes produced only roughness of the tongue. Dryness of the mouth also follows oral administration of cannabis or pyrahexyl. Inhalation may produce an urge to cough or coughing fits and a sense of oppression in the chest but also a sense of warmth radiating to the chest. Some subjects cannot inhale the smoke (Baker-Bates,

1935; Bromberg, 1939; Allentuck and Bowman, 1942; Williams *et al.*, 1946; Tayleur-Stockings, 1947; de Farias, 1955; Chopra and Chopra, 1957; Ames, 1958; Tylden, 1967; Hollister *et al.*, 1968; Klee, 1969; Talbott and Teague, 1969; Waskow *et al.*, 1970; Hollister, 1970).

There is some evidence of irritant effects with chronic use: chronic pharyngitis and laryngitis, edema of the uvula, with hoarseness and catarrh, an increase in flow of bronchial mucus after an initial reduction, sinusitis, and changes in alveolar macrophages. Inspiratory or expiratory dyspnea may occur. Bronchitis or asthma was diagnosed in 10 of 31 subjects believed to be heavy users, and improvement in maximal ventilatory volume, vital capacity, and forced expiratory volume (1 minute) occurred on stopping hashish consumption (Baker-Bates, 1935; Chopra and Chopra, 1957; Ames, 1958; Mann *et al.*, 1971; Tennant *et al.*, 1971).

The conjunctiva characteristically becomes reddened due to vasodilatation. Sometimes there is swelling of the eyelids and pseudoptosis. The effect appears usually to cause no discomfort; unlike other effects of cannabis it does not wax and wane, and it persists for many hours. It occurs with oral administration as well as on smoking; it is produced by Δ^1-THC as well as by cannabis and by pyrahexyl. The effect is dose related (6 μg Δ^1-THC has been claimed to produce a detectable action) and develops rather more slowly than other actions, reaching a peak, when Δ^1-THC is smoked, in about an hour. Control experiments show that smoking itself produces little effect. In time, a yellow discoloration of the sclera develops (Allentuck and Bowman, 1942; Williams *et al.*, 1946; de Farias, 1955; Chopra and Chopra, 1957; Ames, 1958; Isbell *et al.*, 1967; Tylden, 1967; Weil *et al.*, 1968; Talbott and Teague, 1969; Isbell and Jasinski, 1969; Hollister, 1970; Kiplinger *et al.*, 1971).

There is an apparent conflict of evidence as to the effect of cannabis on the pupil. In the older literature dilatation, although sometimes only slight, is noted (e.g., Baker-Bates, 1935; Allentuck and Bowman, 1942; Marcovitz and Myers, 1944; Tayleur-Stockings, 1947; Chopra and Chopra, 1957; Ames, 1958). More recent findings, however, record no change (Isbell *et al.*, 1967; Hollister *et al.*, 1968; Weil *et al.*, 1968; Isbell and Jasinski, 1969; Domino, 1971). On the whole, dose rates are probably lower in the recent studies, so that it may simply be a matter of dose. It is also unfortunate that conditions of illumination are never specified. This may be particularly important since several workers noted a sluggish reaction to light (Allentuck and Bowman, 1942; Thompson and Proctor, 1953, de Farias, 1955). It is not at all unlikely that cannabis can diminish pupillary responses generally, so that with a structure doubly innervated from the autonomic nervous system, the net effect would depend on the tonic activity of dilator and constrictor pupillary muscle fibers under test conditions. Thus, it could well be that in bright light cannabis would indeed dilate the pupil. A further factor, of course, is that any excitement caused could also be accompanied by dilatation. It is clear, however, that pupillary dilatation is not diagnostic of cannabis use. A reduction by an average of 25% in intraocular pressure has been reported (Hepler and Frank, 1971) in 11 subjects smoking 2 gm of marijuana containing 0.9% THC. No data on blood pressure have been reported, so that it is not clear whether this, as is commonly the case, paralleled a fall in blood pressure or represents some more specific effect.

An increase in pulse rate is one of the most consistent effects of cannabis and THC, both smoked and given orally. Smoking a control cigarette may produce a rise of 6–8 beats/minute (Weil et al., 1968; Manno et al., 1970; Hollister, 1970) but, with THC or cannabis, heart rates up to 160/minute have been observed. The response is dose related and is certainly detectable at 50 μg/kg THC smoked. Pyrahexyl and Δ^3-THC appear to be less active than Δ^1-THC. The peak effect is found at around 20 minutes after smoking. The size of the response varies considerably from one subject to another. Normally the ECG is not altered, but with high doses irregularity of the pulse may appear, together with premature ventricular beats and flattened T waves. Sinus arrhythmia is abolished, and the slowing of the heart produced by the Valsava maneuver (expiratory effort against a closed glottis) is reduced. The increase in heart rate is greater with exertion. The tachycardia may bring precordial discomfort and palpitations; panic also occurs with severe tachycardia and it could, of course, be both a cause and a result of the change of heart rate. It has been noted that the subject who has become tolerant to the tachycardia produced by LSD still shows an acceleration of the heart with THC. An interesting feature is that the pulse may later become slow and that the chronic user may have a rather slow pulse rate (Baker-Bates, 1935; Allentuck and Bowman, 1942; Gaskill, 1945; Williams et al., 1946; Parker and Wrigley, 1947; Tayleur-Stockings, 1947; de Farias, 1955; Chopra and Chopra, 1957; Ames, 1958; Isbell et al., 1967; Weil et al., 1968; Hollister et al., 1968; Isbell and Jasinski, 1969; Waskow et al., 1970; Weil, 1970; Manno et al., 1970; Hollister, 1970; Domino, 1971; Kiplinger et al., 1971; Forney, 1971; Renault et al., 1971; Johnson and Domino, 1971).

Changes in blood pressure also appear to be complex. Various authors reported no change, a rise that may parallel the tachycardia, a modest (5–10 mm) fall developing rather slowly, or a fall after a preliminary rise. Peripheral vasodilatation and patchy flushing of the face as well as pallor have been noted. Vasovagal syncope and collapse have also been seen (Allentuck and Bowman, 1942; Gaskill, 1945; Williams et al., 1946; de Farias, 1955; Chopra and Chopra, 1957; Ames, 1958; Isbell et al., 1967; Hollister et al., 1968; Isbell and Jasinski, 1969; Waskow et al., 1970; Johnson and Domino, 1971). Three factors are likely to be operating:

excitement, change of heart rate, and the central vasomotor depression, leading to vasodilatation and fall of blood pressure, seen in animals. The latter effect is probably normally slight, unless the dose is relatively high, or the effect is enhanced by postural stress; the two former effects both tend to raise blood pressure. The variable picture seen, therefore, is only to be expected, and it will require standardization of conditions to disentangle these factors. Perhaps the most important point is that postural hypotension can occur and could be a cause of collapse after cannabis.

The question of sweating has not been adequately studied. Both dryness of the skin and perspiration have been recorded with cannabis, Δ^1-THC, or Δ^3-THC (Bromberg, 1939; Allentuck and Bowman, 1942; de Farias, 1955; Chopra and Chopra, 1957; Waskow *et al.*, 1970; Hollister, 1970). From the effect on heart rate and dryness of the mouth, one might predict an atropine-like inhibition of sweating. But excitement on the one hand, and changes in skin blood flow on the other, could radically distort the picture. In the chronic user, Chopra and Chopra (1957) reported the skin as pale, dry, and scaly, hair lusterless, with decay of teeth and nails; while these may be in part nutritional effects, it is also possible that continued cannabis use impairs sweat and sebaceous secretion and alters the salivary environment of the teeth.

Related to the cardiovascular effects is the question of changes in body temperature. Subjectively, feelings of warmth are common, but, particularly in the later stages of cannabis action, coldness and pallor of the extremities and shivering also occur. Chronic users are sensitive to the weather (de Farias, 1955; Chopra and Chopra, 1957; Ames, 1958). Objectively, small but significant falls of oral temperature have been found in response to test doses, on the average of 0.2°–0.4°C (Hollister *et al.*, 1968; Waskow *et al.*, 1970). Williams *et al.* (1946), however, in their study on chronic use, found a small fall with pyrahexyl and a slight rise with marijuana. Here again, conflicting forces may be at work. On the one hand, any peripheral vasodilatation of skin corresponding to that of the conjunctiva tends to cause loss of heat; on the other hand, excitement, motor activity, and impairment of sweating tend to increase body temperature. Perhaps the fact of feeling cold toward the end of the experience points to a mild impairment of thermoregulation, with vasodilatation, initially; as the effect of cannabis wears off, and normal regulation reestablishes itself, pallor, feeling cold, and shivering would be expected. Such a picture would correspond to the animal data and would, of course, find an analogy in the effect of alcohol.

Finally may be mentioned headache. This is not uncommon with higher dosage (Baker-Bates, 1935; Gaskill, 1945; Williams *et al.*, 1946; Parker and Wrigley, 1947; de Farias, 1955; Jones and Stone, 1970) and seems to occur later rather than early. While a central effect cannot be excluded, it is not improbable that it is of vascular origin, comparable with that produced by glyceryl trinitrate or histamine.

XVII. Visceral and Metabolic Effects

Nausea, usually slight, and occasional vomiting have been noted with cannabis, Δ^1-THC, and pyrahexyl, taken orally or smoked. The vomiting need not detract from the euphoria. Ames (1958) noted that it tended to follow movement from one room to another, and this suggests that it may in fact be due to, or facilitated by, postural hypotension. There are analogies with morphine in all these features (Allentuck and Bowman, 1942; Gaskill, 1945; Williams et al., 1946; Tayleur-Stockings, 1947; de Farias, 1955; Jones and Stone, 1970). On the lower alimentary tract, both reduction in gastric and intestinal motility and a flatulent dyspepsia with alternating diarrhea and constipation have been described. Anecdotally, cannabis smoking is reputed to favor bowel action, and giving it up supposedly produces constipation. The underlying alimentary response is likely in fact to be complex, just as with the pupil, since the intestine is dually innervated (Adams, 1942; Chopra and Chopra, 1957).

The effect on appetite has attracted far more attention. The usual report is of increased appetite usually around 3 hours later, but noticeable earlier. Sometimes it is described as "ravenous"; there may also be no specific mention of hunger, but rather an enhanced relish. A craving for sweets is recognized, and some experimental evidence has in fact been obtained (Abel, 1971a) for an increased consumption of marshmallows after cannabis smoking, compared to controls. Hollister (1971a) however, found little effect on intake of food or milk-shake consumption and regarded the drug as an unreliable stimulant of hunger or appetite, but he made the interesting observation that the subjects on marijuana appeared to be satiated less easily (see also Adams, 1942). With chronic administration, the stimulant effect on appetite disappears, and depression of appetite follows; the drug has been used to inhibit hunger pangs (Allentuck and Bowman, 1942; Williams et al., 1946; Tayleur-Stockings, 1947; Pond, 1948; de Farias, 1955; Chopra and Chopra, 1957; Ames, 1958; Tylden, 1967; Hollister et al., 1968; Clark et al., 1970). Corresponding to these findings are the limited data on body weight. Chopra and Chopra (1957) found that moderate use of bhang (a decoction of cannabis) did not produce weight loss, although well-to-do subjects became flabby; subjects given higher doses became thin and emaciated, and Tylden records the same (1967). The only quantitative data are those of Williams et al. (1946), who found that with pyrahexyl taken ad lib body weight rose by about 4 kg on the average in 2 weeks, followed by a slow decline, the food intake following the same course. With marijuana *ad lib* weight rose by 2 kg in 1 week and then stabilized or slowly declined.

With regard to metabolic studies, no striking changes have been found. In spite of a reference by Tayleur-Stockings (1947) to mild hypoglycemia, there is general agreement that there is no change in blood sugar with ordinary doses (Ames, 1958; Isbell *et al.*, 1967; Hollister *et al.*, 1968; Weil *et al.*, 1968; Manno *et al.*, 1970; Hollister, 1971a). Podolsky (1971) found a slightly higher blood sugar in glucose-tolerance tests after cannabis. A transient rise in urinary excretion of adrenaline after oral administration of Δ^1-THC and a lack of effect on plasma cortisol (unless distress occurred) or on platelet 5-hydroxytryptamine content were reported by Hollister *et al.* (1970a); the responses correspond to those of mild excitement. Similarly, no significant change in free fatty acids, leukocyte or eosinophil count, or plasma potassium have been found, nor was there any change in volume of plasma, blood, or extracellular space (Williams *et al.*, 1946; Hollister *et al.*, 1968; Manno *et al.*, 1970). There is some sign of a renal effect. A slight diuresis or frequency has been reported (Allentuck and Bowman, 1942; Tayleur-Stockings, 1947; Parker and Wrigley, 1947). Ames (1958), giving cannabis orally to seven subjects, found that, on the average, urine flow increased from 102 to 252 ml/hour, and this was accompanied by an increase in sodium and bicarbonate excretion and alkalinity of the urine, there being no change in the filtered load. Hollister *et al.* (1968), however, found a slight fall in creatinine and phosphate clearance.

There has been little study of effects on liver function, even though it is known that a substantial part of the metabolites is eliminated in the bile, that THC and cannabinol are metabolized by liver microsomal enzymes, and that (in animals) cannabidiol inhibits these enzymes. Kew *et al.* (1969), in following up a case of hematemesis due to cirrhosis of the liver (not attributable to alcohol) in a young cannabis smoker, found signs of hepatic degeneration in three out of twelve cannabis users and dysfunction in eight out of twelve. Hochman and Brill (1971) reported that, out of 50 users taking cigarettes containing 15–30 mg THC three or more times a week, 10 had liver disturbances. On the other hand, they also found that all 10 were in fact heavy alcohol users (more than 1 quart alcohol per week or four or more drinks an evening) and that the liver dysfunction disappeared if they abstained from alcohol. They raise the significant possibility that cannabis and alcohol may synergize.

Chopra and Chopra (1957) reported that there is some anemia in chronic users (but this must be difficult to disentangle from nutritional effects). Porter and Scott (1970) found that Δ^1-THC reduces rubidium-86 transport by red cells, a concentration of 5 μg/ml THC producing a threshold effect about comparable with that of 2 mg/ml ethanol; ouabain, 0.02 μg/ml, produced about 40% inhibition.

XVIII. The Temporal Pattern of Cannabis Action

The general pattern of cannabis effects, subject as it is to variation with dose, individual, and route of administration, is roughly as follows for smoked cannabis in commonly used doses. First come acute, sometimes unpleasant, somatic effects. Tachycardia, ataxia, dizziness, and muddled thinking follow, with tachycardia reaching its peak around 20 minutes after inhalation of the smoke. Euphoria, laughter, and loquacity develop. Conjunctival injection reaches its peak at around 1 hour. Fall in blood pressure, drowsiness, disinterest, and sometimes headache are late effects. With oral administration, there is an appreciable latency of ½–1 hour, the peak effect is around 3 hours, and recovery takes 5 hours or longer. In a recent study, Galanter et al. (1972) reported that the changes in level of Δ^1-THC in the plasma correlated well with the changes in heart rate, being at a peak at 15 minutes and declining to normal in 1½–2 hours, whereas the subjective "high" and the score on a symptom checklist peaked at 1–2 hours and lasted 3–4 hours. Blood levels of metabolites were not determined. Lemberger et al. (1972) determined these and found a better correlation of psychic effect with level of metabolites in plasma than of Δ^1-THC; the correlation after smoking, however, was not very satisfactory, and the combined role of other metabolites, as well as of the parent compound, and of their distribution from plasma to brain in man, remains to be clarified. A further important factor when cannabis itself rather than pure THC is used is its cannabidiol content, since Jones and Pertwee (1972) have shown that, as expected from its microsomal inhibitory action, cannabidiol interferes with THC metabolism, causing in mice a relative rise in brain content both of THC and of its 7-OH metabolite.

XIX. Conclusion: Cannabis Action in the Light of Other Psychic Phenomena

In Chapter 5 attention was drawn to the analogies that exist in various respects between cannabis on the one hand and the anesthetics, the opiates, chlorpromazine, and other drugs such as amphetamines on the other. From the work discussed in this and the preceding chapter, the relationship to anesthetics and alcohol arises again, and one also finds common ground with epileptic phenomena and the effects of sensory deprivation. Before considering the possible significance of these relationships, some discussion of each comparison is required.

A. ANESTHETICS

Humphrey Davy's account in 1839 of the inhalation by himself and his friends of nitrous oxide still presents the most vivid account of the effects of threshold anesthesia: pleasurable thrilling sensations, a gentle pressure on all the muscles, objects dazzling, hearing more acute, muscular power felt to be greater, mind full of visual imagery, pleasant mental indolence, synesthesia ("I felt like the sound of a harp"), as well as occasional dysphoria and precordial unease, the sense of insight and intense significance. All these find their counterpart in the cannabis experience. Nor is this merely pioneering enthusiasm. One finds the same pattern in a study (Bergström and Bernstein, 1968) of the use of nitrous oxide/oxygen anesthesia, without barbiturate induction, for caesarian section; the patients' report of "dreams" during the operation carries similar imagery and significance and in one case was compared with an account of LSD intoxication. A similar range of effects of nitrous oxide, including compulsive laughter, euphoria, dizziness, dreaminess, impaired concentration and memory, tingling, numbness, and perceptual disturbances, was reported in a carefully controlled study by Steinberg (1956). Among effects of subanesthetic doses of nitrogen and of CO_2 described during work on submarine escape by Case and Haldane (1941) were euphoria, confusion, impaired mental arithmetic, reduced ability to carry out tasks, alternating depression and elation, mystical consciousness, sense of sin and need for divine grace, fear of impending death, and feelings of eternity. In Chapter 7 the evidence for enhanced tolerance of barbiturates in chronic hashish users is mentioned.

There is, therefore, if one includes the animal data, a very extensive overlap in actions between cannabis and the anesthetics. There are, however, two significant differences. Under cannabis, time perception is altered so that "felt" time becomes longer than clock time (see p. 299) and forgetting is increased (see p. 301). With nitrous oxide, on the other hand, forgetting is reduced (Summerfield and Steinberg, 1957, 1959), and Robson *et al.* (1960) found that under nitrous oxide, the clock time corresponding to a given felt time (15 seconds produced by the subject) was considerably increased. Similarly, Case and Haldane (1941) found that under CO_2 30 seconds of felt time took 60 seconds to produce. Robson *et al.* also showed, with cats conditioned to transit in a cage every 30 seconds, that nitrous oxide prolonged the transit time. There are, too, some minor differences; thus, the intermittent wavelike incidence of the cannabis effect, and the suddenness of its onset, are not typical of anesthetic action.

B. Alcohol

In its properties, alcohol is essentially an anesthetic, differing from others chiefly in being a metabolizable source of calories and in being taken by mouth in dilute form, usually with food. Particular interest attaches to comparison between it and cannabis, partly in respect of their general roles as intoxicants, but particularly in relation to their effects on car driving or performance of other skilled acts. This is currently under intensive study. Recent reports are those by Jones and Stone (1970), Manno *et al.* (1971), Hollister and Gillespie (1970), Hollister (1971a,b), and Rafaelsen (1972). An earlier report by Crancer *et al.* (1969) is not very helpful, since (as noted above) the dose of THC given is uncertain, and the driving simulator was one in which the subject's reactions did not influence the driving situation presented. Very approximately, it appears that over a variety of tests, 2.5–5 mg THC smoked has a greater effect than 50 mg/100 ml alcohol in the blood and a lesser effect than 100 mg/100 ml and that 10–20 mg THC taken orally is equivalent to 100 mg/100 ml alcohol. These comparisons, however, depend strongly on the parameter measured: Cannabis produces relatively greater euphoria, perceptual changes, change of time sense, and effect on solution of arithmetical or other problems, and less dysphoria and sleepiness. Jones and Stone (1970) also observed a clear difference in the direction of the time effect, cannabis making "felt" time longer, alcohol making it shorter, as compared to clock time.

C. Epilepsy

It is well known that during the epileptic aura a variety of perceptual changes occur, which have sometimes been reproduced by stimulation of appropriate areas of cortex during surgery. Penfield and Jasper (1954) cite the following examples: objects appearing larger or seeming smaller and farther away; sensations of numbness, tingling, chilliness; lights twinkling or pulsating; red, blue, green, yellow, and purple colors or glittering, silvery, golden, or whirling lights; dreamlike episodes; feelings of familiarity or strangeness; sensations of loneliness or fear; and feelings of unreality, of floating away, or of increased awareness. It is interesting that anger, joy, pleasure, or sexual excitement were not reported. If one sets alongside these observations the reports of cannabis producing in animals hypersynchrony and epileptiform cortical bursts, and in man compulsive laughter and occasional compulsive motor activity, one has to take seriously the possibility that part at least of the cannabis picture consists of bursts of epileptiform activity affecting the higher levels of cortical integration. There is little published evidence at present to suggest that cannabis itself can induce an epileptic fit, and both the sedative effect of the latter stages of its action and its limited phenytoinlike antiepileptic action would make this unlikely. But a good deal would be explained if part of its action were by a release of inhibitory processes which allowed abnormal hypersynchrony and discharges to take place.

D. SENSORY DEPRIVATION

The studies pioneered by D. O. Hebb, in which sensory and perceptual input is reduced in human subjects as far as possible, have yielded a fascinating syndrome, although there is considerable divergence both in technique and in results (see review by Brawley and Pos, 1967). Findings include temporal and spatial disorientation, depersonalization, hallucinatory and delusory phenomena, increased suggestibility, changes in time perception, and changes in cognitive and motor function. To these may be related a variety of clinical observations on the blind, deaf, isolated, imprisoned, hospitalized, or solitary. Some overlap with cannabis-induced phenomena is obvious, but two differences appear, namely, stimulus hunger and a shortening of felt time against clock time, with sensory deprivation.

When one reviews all of these analogies (and the list is far from complete), together with what is said on p. 350 on the relationship of the cannabis experience to schizophrenia, it becomes increasingly implausible to attempt to equate them all, as though an identical mechanism lay beneath each of the patterns described. More attractive is the Sherringtonian idea of the "final common path," by which varied processes may, in their final convergence on the output mechanisms, share a common effector expression. One would then have to regard such mental entities as mood, feelings of insight, significance, or self-identity, memory, perceptual imagery and mental representation, orientation and judgment in space and time, suggestibility, and effective cognitive function as being in some sense an "output" from prior mental operations. If one had to choose a single mental function, interference with which could radically alter these entities, it might be that of selective attention and concentration. Impairment of the capacity to select and to attend, whether by lack of sensory input on which to focus, by a flooding of sensory flow, or by an attack on the selective processes by drugs or disease, could well underly these fascinating phenomena. The study of cannabis, which so conspicuously impairs the capacity to attend and to concentrate, could provide a major contribution toward the understanding of the processes involved in perception and selective attention.

W. D. M. PATON AND R. G. PERTWEE

References

Abel, E. L. (1970). *Nature (London)* **227**, 115.
Abel, E. L. (1971a). *Nature (London)* **231**, 260.
Abel, E. L. (1971b). *Nature (London)* **231**, 58.
Abel, E. L. (1971c). *Science* **173**, 1038.
Adams, R. (1942). *Harvey Lect.* p. 168.
Agurell, S., and Nilsson, J. L. G. (1971). *Acta Pharm. Suecica* **8**, 671.
Aldrich, C. K. (1944). *Pub. Health Rep.* **59**, 431.
Allentuck, S., and Bowman, K. M. (1942). *Amer. J. Psychiat.* **99**, 248.
Ames, F. (1958). *J. Ment, Sci.* **104**, 972.
Baker, A. A., and Lucas, E. G. (1969). *Lancet* **1**, 148.
Baker-Bates, E. T. (1935). *Lancet* **1**, 811.
Becker, H. S. (1953). *Amer. J. Sociol.* **59**, 235.
Becker, H. S. (1967). *J. Health Soc. Behav.* **8**, 163.
Bergström, H., and Bernstein, K. (1968). *Lancet* **2**, 541.
Bouquet, J. (1951). *Bull. Narcotics* **3**, 22.
Brawley, P., and Pos, R. (1967). *Can. Psychiat. Ass. J.* **12**, 105.
Bromberg, W. (1939). *J. Amer. Med. Ass.* **113**, 4.
Caldwell, D. F., Myers, S. A., Domino, E. F., and Merriam, P. E. (1969a). *Percept. Mot. Skills* **29**, 755.
Caldwell, D. F., Myers, S. A., Domino, E. F., and Merriam, P. E. (1969b). *Percept. Mot. Skills* **29**, 922.
Campbell, A. M. G., Evans, M., Thomson, J. L. G., and Williams M. J. (1971). *Lancet* **2**, 1219.
Campbell, D. R. (1971). *Can. Psychiat. Ass. J.* **16**, 161.
Case, E. M., and Haldane, J. B. S. (1941). *J. Hyg.* **41**, 225.
Chapple, P. A. (1966). *Brit. J. Addict.* **61**, 269.
Chopra, I. C., and Chopra, R. W. (1957). *Bull. Narcotics* **9**, 4.
Christison, R. (1848). "A Dispensatory or a Commentary on the Pharmacopoeias of Great Britain." A. & C. Black, Edinburgh.
Christison, R. (1851). *Mon. J. Med. Sci.* **13**, 117.
Clark, L. D., and Nakashima, E. N. (1968). *Amer. J. Psychiat.* **125**, 379.
Clark, L. D., Hughes, R., and Nakashima, E. N. (1970). *Arch. Gen. Psychiat.* **23**, 193.
Craik, F. I. M. (1971). *Brit. Med. Bull.* **27**, 232.
Crancer, A. J., Dille, J. M., Delay, J. C., Wallace, J. E., and Haykin, M. D. (1969). *Science* **164**, 851.
Daly, D. D., and Mulder, D. W. (1957). *Neurology* **7**, 189.
Davy, H. (1839). "Collected Works," Vol. 3, p. 272. Smith Elder & Co., London.
de Farias, R. C. (1955). *Bull. Narcotics* **7**, 5.
de la Mare, W. (1930). "Desert Islands and Robinson Crusoe." Faber & Faber, London.
Domino, E. F. (1971). *Ann. N.Y. Acad. Sci* **191**, 166.
Federation Meeting (1971). *Pharmacol. Rev.* **23**, 263.
Forney, R. B. (1971). *Ann. N.Y. Acad. Sci.* **191**, 74.
Galanter, I. M., Wyatt, R. J., Lemberger, L., Weingartner, H., Vaughan, T. B., and Roth, W. T. (1972). *Science* **176**, 934.
Gamage, J. R., and Zerkin, E. L. (1969). "A Comprehensive Guide to the English-Language Literature on Cannabis (Marihuana)." Stash Press, Beloit, Wisconsin.
Gaskill, H. S. (1945). *Amer. J. Psychiat.* **102**, 202.
Goldstone, S. (1967). *Ann. N.Y. Acad. Sci.* **138**, 767.

Graff, H. (1969). *Amer. J. Psychiat.* **125**, 1258.

Grossman, W. (1969). *Ann. Intern. Med.* **70**, 529.

Gumpert, J., Hansotia, P., and Upton, A. (1970). *J. Neurol., Neurosurg. Psychiat.* [N.S.] **33**, 479.

Halikos, J. A., Goodwin, D. W., and Guze, S. B. (1971). *J. Amer. Med. Ass.* **217**, 692.

Hepler, R. S., and Frank, M. (1971). *J. Amer. Med. Ass.* **217**, 1392.

Hochman, J. S., and Brill, N. Q. (1971). *Lancet* **2**, 818.

Hollister, L. E. (1969). *J. Clin. Pharmacol.* **9**, 24.

Hollister, L. E. (1970). *Nature (London)* **227**, 968.

Hollister, L. E. (1971a). *Clin. Pharmacol. Ther.* **12**, 44.

Hollister, L. E. (1971b). *Science* **172**, 21.

Hollister, L. E., and Gillespie, H. K. (1970). *Arch. Gen. Psychiat.* **23**, 199.

Hollister, L. E., Richards, R. K., and Gillespie, H. K. (1968). *Clin. Pharmacol. Ther.* **9**, 783.

Hollister, L. E., Moore, F., Kanter, S., and Noble, E. (1970a). *Psychopharmacologia* **17**, 354.

Hollister, L. E., Sherwood, S. L., and Cavasino, A. (1970b). *Pharmacol. Res. Commun.* **2**, 305.

Isbell, H., and Jasinski, D. R. (1969). *Psychopharmacologia* **14**, 115.

Isbell, H., Gorodetsky, C. W., Jasinski, D. R., Claussen, U., von Spulak, F., and Korte, F. (1967). *Psychopharmacologia* **11**, 184.

James, W. (1890). "Principles of Psychology," Vol. I. Macmillan, New York.

Johnson, S., and Domino, E. F. (1971). *Clin. Pharmacol. Ther.* **12**, 762.

Jones, G., and Pertwee, R. G. (1972). *Brit. J. Pharmacol.* **45**, 375.

Jones, R. T. (1971). *Pharmacol. Rev.* **23**, 359.

Jones, R. T., and Stone, G. C. (1970). *Psychopharmacologia* **18**, 108.

Kaplan, H. S. (1971). *N.Y. State J. Med.* **71**, 433.

Keeler, M. H. (1967). *Amer. J. Psychiat.* **124**, 674.

Keeler, M. H. (1968a). *Amer. J. Psychiat.* **125**, 386.

Keeler, M. H. (1968b). *Dis. Nerv. Syst.* **29**, 314.

Keeler, M. H., Reifler, C. B., and Liptzin, M. B. (1968). *Amer. J. Psychiat.* **125**, 384.

Keeler, M. H., Ewing, J. A., and Rouse, B. A. (1971). *Amer. J. Psychiat.* **128**, 213.

Kew, M. C., Bersohn, I., and Siew, S. (1969). *Lancet* **1**, 578.

Kiplinger, G. F., Manno, J. E., Rodda, B. E., and Forney, R. B. (1971). *Clin. Pharmacol. Ther.* **12**, 650.

Klee, G. D. (1969). *Psychiat. Quart.* **43**, 719.

Le Dain Commission (1972). "A Report of the Commission of Inquiry into the Non-Medical Use of Drugs." Information Canada, Ottawa.

Lemberger, L., Weiss, J. L., Watanabe, A. M., Galanter, I. M., Wyatt, R. J., and Cardon, P. V. (1972). *N. Engl. J. Med.* **286**, 685.

Mann, P. E. G., Cohen, A. B., Finley, T. W., and Ladman, A. J. (1971). *Lab Invest.* **25**, 111.

Manno, J. E., Kiplinger, G. F., Bennett, I. F., Forney, R. B., and Haine, S. E. (1970). *Clin. Pharmacol. Ther.* **11**, 808.

Manno, J. E., Kiplinger, G. F., Scholtz, W. S., and Forney, R. B. (1971). *Clin. Pharmacol. Ther.* **12**, 202.

Marcovitz, E., and Myers, H. J. (1944). *War Med.* **6**, 382.

Martin, J. P. (1950). *Brain* **73**, 453.

Mayor's Committee on Marihuana. (1944). "The Marihuana Problem in the City of New York." Jaques Cattell Press, Lancaster, Pennsylvania.

McGlothlin, W. H., Arnold, D. O., and Rowan, P. K. (1970). *Psychiatry* **33**, 433.
Melges, F. T., Tinklenberg, J. R., Hollister, L. E., and Gillespie, H. K. (1970a). *Science* **168**, 1118.
Melges, F. T., Tinklenberg, J. R., Hollister, L. E., and Gillespie, H. K. (1970b). *Arch. Gen. Psychiat.* **23**, 204.
Melges, F. T., Tinklenberg, J. R., Hollister, L. E., and Gillespie, H. K. (1971). *Arch. Gen. Psychiat.* **24**, 564.
Miller, L., Drew, W. G., and Kiplinger, G. F. (1972). *Nature (London)* **237**, 172.
Murphy, H. B. M. (1963). *Bull. Narcotics* **15**, 15.
Nahas, G. G. (1972). *N.Y. State J. Med.* **72**, 856.
National Institute of Mental Health. (1971). "Report on Marihuana and Health." US Govt. Printing Office, Washington, D.C.
National Institute of Mental Health. (1972). "Report on Marihuana and Health." US Govt. Printing Office, Washington, D.C.
Parker, C. S., and Wrigley, F. (1947). *Lancet* **2**, 223.
Parker, C. S., and Wrigley, F. (1950). *J. Ment. Sci.* **96**, 276.
Paton, W. D. M., and Crown, J., eds. (1972). "Cannabis and its Derivative: Pharmacology and Experimental Psychology." Oxford Univ. Press, London and New York.
Penfield, W., and Jasper, H. (1954). "Epilepsy and the Functional Anatomy of the Human Brain." Little Brown, Boston, Massachusetts.
Persyko, I. (1970). *J. Amer. Med. Ass.* **212**, 1527.
Pillard, R. C. (1970). *N. Engl. J. Med.* **283**, 294.
Pivik, R. T., Zarcone, V., Hollister, L. E., and Dement, W. (1969). *Psychophysiology* **6**, 261.
Pivik, R. T., Zarcone, V., Dement, W. C., and Hollister, L. E. (1972). *Clin. Pharmacol. Ther.* **13**, 426.
Podolsky, S. (1971). *Ann. N.Y. Acad. Sci.* **191**, 54.
Pond, D. A. (1948). *J. Neurol., Neurosurg. Psychiat.* [N.S.] **11**, 271.
Porter, C. D., and Scott, K. G. (1970). *Res. Commun. Chem. Pathol. Pharmacol.* **1**, 733.
Rafaelson, O. J. (1972). *In* "Cannabis and Its Derivatives: Pharmacology and Experimental Psychology" (W. D. M. Paton and J. Crown, eds.), p. 184. Oxford Univ. Press, London and New York.
Renault, P. F., Schuster, C. R., Heinrich, R., and Freeman, D. X. (1971). *Science* **174**, 589.
Robson, J. G., Delisle Burns, B., and Welt, P. J. L. (1960). *Can. Anaes. Soc. J.* **7**, 399.
Scher, J. (1970). *J. Amer. Med. Ass.* **214**, 1120.
Singer, A. J. (1972). *Ann. N.Y. Acad. Sci.* **191**, 1.
Soueif, M. I. (1967). *Bull Narcotics* **19**, 1.
Steinberg, H. (1956). *Brit. J. Psychol.* **47**, 183.
Summerfield, A., and Steinberg, H. (1957). *Quart. J. Exp. Psychol.* **9**, 146.
Summerfield, A., and Steinberg, H. (1959). *Proc. Int. Congr. Neuropharmacol., 1st, 1958* p. 481.
Talbott, J. A., and Teague, J. W. (1969). *J. Amer. Med. Ass.* **210**, 299.
Tart, C. T. (1970). *Nature (London)* **226**, 701.
Tart, C. T., and Crawford, H. J. (1970). *Psychophysiology* **7**, 348.
Tayleur-Stockings, G. (1947). *Brit. Med. J.* **1**, 919.
Tennant, F. S., Preble, M., Prendergast, T. J., and Ventry, P. (1971). *J. Amer. Med. Ass.* **216**, 1965.
Thompson, L. J., and Proctor, R. C. (1953). *N.C. Med. J.* **14**, 520.

Tinklenberg, J. R., Melges, F. T., Hollister, L. E., and Gillespie, H. K. (1970). *Nature* (*London*) 226, 1171.

Tylden, E. (1967). *Brit. Med. J.* 3, 556.

UNESCO Commission on Narcotic Drugs. (1965). "Cannabis Bibliography." United Nations (UNESCO), New York.

Ungerleider, J. T., Fischer, D. D., Goldsmith, R. S., Fuller, M., and Forgy, E. (1968). *Amer. J. Psychiat.* 125, 325.

Volavka, J., Donbush, R., Feldstein, S., Clare, G., Zaks, A., Fink, M., and Freedman, A. M. (1971). *Ann. N.Y. Acad. Sci.* 191, 206.

Waller, C. W., and Denny, J. J. (1971). "Annotated Bibliography of Marihuana 1964–1970." School of Pharmacy, University of Mississippi, University, Mississippi.

Waskow, I. E., Olsson, J. E., Salzman, C., and Katz, M. M. (1970). *Arch. Gen. Psychiat.* 22, 97.

Weil, A. T. (1970). *N. Engl. J. Med.* 282, 997.

Weil, A. T., and Zinberg, N. E. (1969). *Nature* (*London*) 222, 434.

Weil, A. T., Zinberg, N. E., and Nelsen, J. M. (1968). *Science* 162, 1234.

West, L. J. (1970). *Ann. Intern. Med.* 73, 459.

Wikler, A., and Lloyd, B. J. (1945). *Fed. Proc., Fed. Amer. Soc. Exp. Biol.* 4, 141 (abstr.).

Williams, E. G., Himmelsbach, C. K., Wikler, A., Ruble, D. C., and Lloyd, B. J. (1946). *Pub. Health Rep.* 61, 1059.

Wilson, C. W. M., and Linken, A. (1968). *In* "Adolescent Drug Dependence" (C. W. M. Wilson, ed.), p. 93. Pergamon, Oxford.

World Health Organization. (1971). *World Health Organ., Tech. Rep. Ser.* 478.

CHAPTER 7

Clinical Aspects of Cannabis Action

W. D. M. Paton, R. G. Pertwee, and Elizabeth Tylden

I. Cannabis and Psychiatric Problems. 335
  A. Introduction 335
  B. Psychopathological Phenomena 338
  C. Cannabis Action—A Model Psychosis? 350
  D. Duration of Mental Effect in Relation to Duration of Cannabis Use 351
  E. Cannabis and Dependence Liability 353
II. Toxicity in Man 357
III. Therapeutic Potential of Cannabinoids. 361
  References 362

I. Cannabis and Psychiatric Problems

A. INTRODUCTION

Any assessment of the extent to which psychiatric problems arise from cannabis use must take into account cultural and other sociological factors as well as the main pharmacological and psychological effects of cannabis. The latter are reasonably well defined, and there is a remarkable consistency in the clinical and experimental reports, whether based on observations of rich or poor, white or black, educated or uneducated people of Eastern or Western, industrialized or unindustrialized countries. Cannabis effects can, in addition, be deliberately reproduced under controlled laboratory or hospital conditions. This is not to say that certain effects of cannabis administration are not influenced, for instance, by the expectations of the subject. The placebo response, discussed in Chapter 6, occurs with cannabis users

335

as with those using other psychoactive drugs, and, as with the latter, the effect is greatest when the response by the subject consists entirely of personal testimony (e.g., an answer to the question, Are you high?). Placebos, however, do not produce reddened conjunctiva, tachycardia, fine ataxia, impaired memory and concentration, nonsequential thought, alteration of time sense, changes in behavior, paranoia, or depersonalization. In addition, the experiences of many cannabis takers run counter to their expectation.

The evaluation of cultural and sociological factors is less straightforward. Primarily they modify the interpretation of behavior, particularly in relation to accepted standards of normality. In psychiatry, as in medicine generally, there is blurring between diagnostic categories. In medicine, for instance, it is no longer possible to distinguish sharply patients with hypertension from those with normal blood pressure; there is a continuous distribution of pressures, and the decision whether to diagnose hypertension and initiate appropriate treatment ultimately rests on an actuarial assessment of benefit against treatment risk. With mental disorder one is dealing with constellations of overlapping symptoms rather than with the discrete clinical entities of Kretchmer and Kraepelin. Patterns of disturbed behavior are, we know, much more variable in character than the "classical" syndromes, and it is correspondingly difficult to pigeonhole diagnosis. Classical names such as depressive illness and schizophrenia are convenient labels covering overlapping areas. This leaves ample scope for arbitrary choice and debate. Hoffer and Osmond welcomed the psychedelic drugs as creating model psychoses. R. D. Laing and T. Leary, however, do not regard drug experience as abnormal, let alone a form of psychosis. They have been profoundly moved by their own drug experience, which happened to be enjoyable, and have become, like Aldous Huxley, proselytizers. They appear to have developed three main hypotheses: that the society in which a person grows up is largely responsible for his many discomforts, whether mental, spiritual, or physical; that any avenue of escape is permissible, even by suicide, drugs, or grossly abnormal behavior; and that destruction of the social matrix within which a person finds himself is also permissible, if in that way a solution is to be found. In their view LSD, and to a lesser extent cannabis, provide access to inaccessible stores in the memory which, once rationalized, enable the individual to become integrated, The repressed memories may be unpleasant, but for the removal of guilt they must be both discovered and faced. The experience may be permanently incapacitating, but for Laing and Leary this is merely a manifestation of the survival of the fittest. Those who commit suicide or become incapable of further useful activity are regarded as expendable; quite apart from their drug experience they would in any case have gone mad or committed suicide. On such a view, evidence of mental or physical harm or social damage is of little import. The opposite pole is a biological conception, centering on a view of normal health, for instance of the normal young, whether puppy or child, cheerful, active, exploring, learning.

The uncertainty is not restricted to questions of drug-induced psychosis. It has been questioned, too, whether puerperal psychosis exists, even though each year, in England, four out of every thousand women delivered become sufficiently mentally disturbed to warrant admission to a psychiatric unit and even though the law recognizes the prevention of puerperal psychosis as a justification for abortion. The uncertainty spreads from psychiatrist to layman, and the latter, too, can take the view that psychosis is simply a matter of social definition.

But social and cultural factors contribute more than radical controversy over the nature of psychiatric illness. The social patterns of drug use vary; cannabis is used chiefly by the middle-class intelligentsia-to-be in Western countries but by religious or low-privileged social groups in India (Chopra, 1971). There must be considerable differences in conditions of use and in the assessment of the social benefits or damage that follow, when groups with such different expectations of life and welfare are compared. Equally, the effects reported for a literate, educated individual coming to drug use only in adolescent or adult life will be quite different from those reported for the illiterate users of drugs from childhood. The literary accounts of the cannabis state, written by those who learned to smoke after formal education had been completed, cannot be matched by the accounts of the life-long peasant users of South America, South Africa, or Egypt. In an underprivileged environment, the balance of advantage and harm will inevitably be different—few would grudge the Jamaican sugarcane worker anything that relieves his lot. So, too, the reasons for starting and continuing cannabis use, factors of crucial importance for any effort in preventive medicine, will vary. These have been analyzed with some subtlety for Western countries, relatively new to the drug. Identified motives include pleasure (the hedonists' culture); relief from social embarrassment, anxiety, or depression; conformity to the peer group; participation in ritual with religious undertones; exploration of the mind; protest, with symbolic expression of claims to liberty of the individual; and simple experiment. The importance of learning has also been stressed, not only of the technique of smoking, but also of how to interpret and appreciate the experience. In less privileged and less sophisticated environments, however, custom, and the fact that the plant, like Mount Everest, "is there," could be equally important. Last, social and cultural factors of interpretations will influence reactions to drug use. Thus, those who see it simply as pleasurable, enlightening, significant, when confronted by the hiatus that is left when the effect of a dose is finished and by its aftereffect, would discount potential damage and urge unlimited access so that the pleasure and insight can be indefinitely prolonged.

The purpose of this preliminary discussion is partly to stress the difficulties that arise in considering abnormal psychiatric states, whether or not they are produced by cannabis. But it also serves to bring out how far the data on drugs inevitably consist of testimony. While such testimony must always be allowed to speak for itself, and although introspection has contributed greatly to psychology, a moment's reflection on one's own ability to give, say in response to a questionnaire, an accurate brief account of one's own motives, attitudes, and beliefs, let alone one's own actions, makes obvious the need for objective external observations.

B. PSYCHOPATHOLOGICAL PHENOMENA

There is some general agreement, if not in interpretation, at least on the phenomena seen in cannabis users who come to psychiatric attention. These will not be reviewed in full. Table I lists some of the major reports available, which need to be read in detail to be adequately assessed. The following illustrative case histories have been selected to show the various aspects of the problem that have been reported, as well as some of the general characteristics of cannabis action.

1. Acute Somatic Reaction (from Smith and Mehl, 1970, Case 1)

A 23-year-old white female secretary, an experienced marijuana user, shared several "joints" with a few friends in a quiet setting. She got very "high," and about an hour after smoking she felt nauseated and had diarrhea. With effort she stood up and walked to the bathroom but neither vomited nor had a bowel movement. When she left the bathroom she felt dizzy and looked very pale. After sitting down again and eating something she felt better but remained weak and slightly nauseated until she fell asleep later that night. There was no "hangover" or residual symptoms the next day.

TABLE I

REPORTS OF PSYCHOPATHOLOGICAL PHENOMENA ATTRIBUTED TO CANNABIS[a]

Group studied	Age range	Country	Comment	Reference
80 hashish users	7–50	Russia	Psychotic response to single doses; 21 transitory, 7 persistent psychoses	Skliar (1934)*
34 users	19–33	Panama	Soldiers: psychopathy	Siler et al. (1933)
1 case	22	England	Acute intoxication to first exposure	Baker-Bates (1935)*

TABLE I (*continued*)

Group studied	Age range	Country	Comment	Reference
3 cases	19–30	US	1 suicide	Curtis and Wolfe (1939)*
29 cases	16–38	US	14 acute intoxications, 8 to first exposure; 17 toxic psychoses	Bromberg (1939)*
77 subjects	—	US	9 cases of psychosis discussed	Allentuck and Bowman (1942)
150 users	—	India and Burma	Soldiers: 1 psychosis, accentuation of psychopathy	Gaskill (1945)
35 addicts	18–31	US	Soldiers: 5 attempted suicides	Marcovitz and Myers (1944)*
9 subjects	26–33	US	1 psychotic reaction on pyrahexyl withdrawal	Williams *et al.* (1946)*
60 addicts	22.4 (median)	US	Psychopathic behavior	Charen and Perelman (1946)
600 cases	—	India	Cases collected 1928–1939	Chopra and Chopra (1957)
824 psychiatric patients	15–>55	Morocco	27% cases of specific cannabis psychoses; also aggravated and associated psychoses	Benabud (1957)
39 cases	—	Nigeria	Toxic psychoses and schizophreniform reactions	Asuni (1964)
140 cases	Mostly 20–35	Morocco	Varied reactions	Christozov (1965)
General psychiatric admissions	—	South Africa	Schizophreniform reactions	Toker (1966)
General psychiatric admissions	25 (median)	Nigeria	110 toxic psychoses, often schizophreniform	Boroffka (1966)
40 cannabis users	—	England	2 schizophreniform psychoses, personality changes	Tylden (1967)*
6 LSD users	—	England	1 recrudescence of LSD effects after cannabis	Bewley (1967)*
4 cases	19–24	England	Brief case reports; LSD also used	Dally (1967)*

TABLE I (*continued*)

Group studied	Age range	Country	Comment	Reference
11 cases	—	US	Anxiety, depersonalization, paranoia	Keeler (1967)
54 users	18–30	US	Incidence of psychopathology correlated with dose	Keeler (1968)
4 users	21–23	US	Recurrence of marijuana effect, 2 cases of anxiety	Keeler et al. (1968)*
4 cases	—	England	Schizophreniform reactions	Tylden (1968b)
560 patients	All ages	Morocco	Confusional, schizophrenic, and dissociative states	Defer and Diehl (1968)
50 patients	—	Denmark	7 cases of psychotic reaction to cannabis	Jørgensen (1968)
—	—	US	1887 adverse reactions to cannabis, according to medical questionnaire; no details	Ungerleider et al. (1968)
112 drug users	—	US	8 schizophreniform reactions	Hekimian and Gershon (1968)
50 patients	—	England	8 toxic psychoses, 29 other reactions	Baker and Lucas (1969)
11 cases (10 adolescent)	14–22	US	Schizophreniform reactions	Milman (1969)*
114 drug psychoses	—	US	8% cases panic or schizoid response attributed to cannabis	Keup (1969)
6 cases	23–25	India	Ganja used by Westerners	Grossman (1969)*
12 cases	19–26	Vietnam	Soldiers: toxic psychoses, 10 paranoid, to first exposure	Talbott and Teague (1969)*
1 case	26	US	Intensive study of acute psychosis to first exposure	Klee (1969)*
1 case	23	US	Psychotic reaction, second exposure	Perna (1969)*

TABLE I (*continued*)

Group studied	Age range	Country	Comment	Reference
40–50 patients per month	—	Vietnam	5 cases per month with marijuana-associated psychosis; soldiers	Colbach and Crowe (1970)*
1 case	39	England	Two psychotic episodes	George (1970)*
—	24–49	US	6 illustrative case reports, ranging from depression to exacerbation of schizophrenia	Weil (1970)*
11 cases	19–22	US	Anxiety, psychosis, recurrence	Bialos (1970)*
—	15–34	US	8 illustrative case histories, Haight–Ashbury	Smith and Mehl (1970)*
—	—	Bahamas	Specific psychoses of semipermanent nature	Spencer (1970)
38 patients	13–24	US	8 cannabis psychoses: 4 attempted suicides; remainder borderline	Kolansky and Moore (1971)*
20 cases	19–24	Vietnam	Soldiers: acute psychoses	Bey and Zecchinelli (1971)
50 adolescents	13–18	US	Behavior disorders and depressive reactions	Kornhaber (1971)
5 adolescents	—	Canada	Amotivation	Thurlow (1971)
431 trainees	—	—	Flashback, 5 on marijuana only, ∝ use of drug	Blumienfeld (1971)
5 cases	16–27	US	Schizophreniform responses	Kaplan (1971)*
13 cases	16–22	Canada	Psychoses with EEG abnormalities	D. R. Campbell (1971)

a Some reports deal only with cases in which a psychopathological response was attributed to cannabis; the number of these is then entered under "Group studied." Other reports deal with a group of subjects in only some of whom was there such a response; the character and size of the group is indicated, and the number of cases (if stated) is entered under "Comments." The word "addict" is used by some authors, not in the sense of the WHO definition of addiction, but as a general term denoting nonmedical drug use. Reports containing case histories are denoted by an asterisk.

2. Panic Reaction with "Flashback" (from Keeler et al., 1968, Case 1)

A 21-year-old man smoked more than four marijuana cigarettes. He experienced confusion, disorientation, panic, and the sensation of loss of control of his hands; he could not talk and hallucinated colored spots and designs during the drug reaction. For 3 weeks thereafter he experienced confusion and disorientation and hallucinated designs similar to those that appeared during the marijuana experience. This took place most often when he was attempting to go to sleep. These events precipitated anxiety which required hospitalization. There was no evidence of schizophrenia or affective disorder. His symptoms gradually subsided during the next week.

3. Depressive Reaction with Anxiety (from Bromberg, 1939, Case 7)

A white man aged 31, admitted to a hospital on March 27, 1934, with a history of having smoked just one marijuana cigarette, was depressed, retarded, and apprehensive. He was oriented, and his memory showed no defects. Physical examination gave negative results. He said, "My hand began to feel blue all of a sudden. I felt like laughing and I felt funny in my head. It was the queerest feeling I ever had. I felt like I was kind of fainting away like. I sweat and then I'd get kind of chilly. I got the scare of my life. I thought I was going to die and everything else. I knew what was happening all the time. I thought my hands were beginning to get blue. My throat began to get kind of dry. It was a little better than getting drunk. I did not want to step down from the curb—it seemed to be so high. I was sitting down and afraid to get up." The patient improved and on the second day was less apprehensive and was pleasant and cheerful. He was discharged as recovered after 2 days.

4. Acute Psychotic Episodes

(a) (from Colbach and Crowe, 1970, Case 1)

A 22-year-old switchboard operator had been in Vietnam 8 months, and for approximately 4 months he had smoked as many as 10 cigarettes daily. He was a high-school dropout, with a police record for a variety of misdemeanors. He was always a nervous person, whose mother had spent 5 years in a state mental institution. He was brought to a hospital after he had tried to call Ho Chi Minh, stating that he had a plan to end the war. He was temporally disoriented, had unsystematized grandiose delusions, reported visual and auditory hallucinations, and had very disorganized thinking. After 10 days of hospital treatment, only his initial disorientation had improved. Three weeks after evacuation to Japan, his symptoms cleared completely. A careful work-up, including psychological testing, showed no evidence of a formal thought disorder. He was given a diagnosis of a mild personality disorder and returned to duty in Vietnam. When seen 2 months later, he was functioning quite well and denied any further marijuana usage.

(b) (from Kaplan, 1971, Case 2)

The patient is a 16-year-old female high-school student in a private school. Four months prior to referral she had been smoking marijuana intensively with her friends for about a week. On the night preceding the onset of her illness she had a frightening nightmare and the following day developed intense anxiety while at school. She felt tremulous and perceived her voice, thoughts, and appearance as being strange and unreal. After initial psychotherapy her symptoms continued unimproved, necessitating her discontinuing school. The patient was seen 4 months after the onset of the illness and was treated with high doses (800 mg daily) of chlorpromazine and with psychotherapy. She improved gradually, and medication was discontinued 3 months thereafter. Eight months after the episode the patient was left with some moderately severe phobias (she is afraid the symptoms will recur), a mild degree of mental blocking, and personality constriction, which continue to improve gradually. Perceptual symptoms have recurred briefly at times of stress and responded quickly to small doses of phenothiazine.

The patient has no prior history of psychosis. She was a happy, popular girl prior to this episode. She had used marijuana for a week previous to this episode when she was 15 and reported that she had had similar symptoms lasting only 2 days which cleared spontaneously. Examination of the family reveals the father has chronic borderline schizophrenia.

At the time of the occurrence of the present episode the patient's parents were in the process of divorce, and her older sister, to whom she is very close, had recently left for college. She has not used marijuana since the last episode.

(c) (from Talbott and Teague, 1969, Case 1)

A 26-year-old, single, white man, second lieutenant registered nurse with no history of psychiatric difficulties, was hospitalized after smoking his first cigarette containing cannabis derivatives. Immediately after smoking, he became aware of a burning, choking sensation in his throat and following this, he went to a civilian bar. Shortly thereafter he felt apprehensive, anxious, and suspicious. The symptoms rapidly increased in intensity and the subject became fearful that the "nationals" in the bar meant him harm. He fled in terror and returned to the bachelor officers' quarters. Shortly thereafter, one of us was called to see him.

When examined the patient was anxious and disoriented as to time, but not as to place and person. Anxiety, as well as the fear of being harmed by nationals, seemed to intensify and decrease in wavelike fashion. The fear of being harmed at its intensified peak we believed to be delusional. He was unable to identify the nature of the harm he feared. Affect was judged to be appropriate but labile. Thinking was rapid and disjointed, as if he were unable to follow a line of thought and as if he were experiencing a wide variety of thoughts (in rapid fashion) dissimilar in nature except for a common apprehensive quality. Proverbs were handled adequately, but with poor concentration and he quickly returned to his fears of being harmed. He did not acknowledge loosening of associations. Judgment and insight were impaired, and any evaluation of intelligence was precluded by his general condition. There were no hallucinations.

Abnormal physical findings included the following: there was a generalized impairment of coordination, as demonstrated by heel-to-toe walking and finger-to-nose testing; there was a positive Romberg sign; there was some injection of the conjunctivae; reflexes were generally and symmetrically hyperactive; and vital signs reflected a psychomotor agitation or excitement.

The patient was hospitalized and treated with phenothiazines and sedatives. He was also seen in brief psychotherapy. The patient was able to be discharged to his quarters in 36 hours and was returned to duty in 48 hours. No recurrence of symptoms was noted in the next 3 months. Further work-up revealed no other evidence of psychiatric difficulties sufficient to diagnose a preexisting psychiatric condition. The patient was not seen by another psychiatrist. A second cigarette containing cannabis derivatives was in his possession and was examined. The patient's condition was diagnosed as acute toxic psychosis.

5. *Precipitation of Psychosis* (from Grossman, 1969, Case 1)

Patient, L. M., a 25-year-old single man, was referred by some of his friends who asked us to see him because he was "acting crazy." They related that he had been using bhang and ganja regularly during the 2 years since he had arrived in India but that his usage was infrequent (once or twice weekly) until 3–4 months previously, when he was noted to increase his usage of these products to four or five times per week. At this point he was noted to sleep less and talk more and more about his personal conflicts indiscriminately to all with whom he came in contact.

When first seen by us, the patient presented a dishevelled, disorderly appearance and was physically hyperactive, striding up and down the room waving his hands. He talked continuously in a loud voice, and his thoughts seemed quite disorganized. His mood was quite labile but with strong overtones of hostility. His thought content was bizarre with gross delusional elements present. He said that he intermittently heard voices telling him to "proceed to Mohammed's temple and be drawn to the floor by the hairs about the anus." At one point he emptied a pail of water over his head and threw water at the others in the room. Further conversation with the patient and his neighbors revealed that in the last few days the patient had hardly slept at all and had on one occasion walked down the street of their village completely naked accosting females with the greeting "come to bed with me and have God."

The patient was sedated with amytal and thorazine and was returned to the United States for psychiatric hospitalization. He was hospitalized for 2 months, and the discharge diagnosis was schizoaffective reaction, manic phase. The psychiatrist in charge of his case felt that "ganja played a definite role in precipitating his illness." The patient is currently doing well, working, and seeing a psychiatrist regularly. There was no other history of drug abuse or usage of LSD, amphetamines, or opium derivatives.

6. Exacerbation of Preexisting Defect of Personality Structure

(a) (from Smith and Mehl, 1970, Case 2)

A 21-year-old, white, unemployed male experienced an acute psychosis after smoking marijuana with three other people in Golden Gate Park, San Francisco. When he came to the Haight–Ashbury Clinic—about 1 hour after smoking marijuana—he was talking in such a fashion that he would increase his speed until he was simply babbling. He would then return to a fairly rational state only to begin increased talking again. Flight of ideas, depersonalization, and transformation of personality were evident. One hundred milligrams of Thorazine given over a 2-hour period returned him to a reasonably normal state. During the next 4 days, he "tripped out" several times, although he used no drugs during this period. It was difficult to determine whether these were true "drug flashbacks" or recurrent psychotic episodes. Further questioning indicated that he had recurrent feelings of depersonalization and perceptual alteration during these 4 days. He was on welfare, had recently been arrested, had a history of epilepsy, had a brief psychotic break at age 12, and gave the impression of a marginally adjusted borderline psychotic. Two weeks after his initial adverse reaction he reported that he felt fine and no further follow-up could be obtained.

In cases such as this, the psychosis is characteristic of the personality structure of the user, not of the drug. The drug intoxication merely triggers the psychosis, as seen with a variety of other drugs including alcohol, amphetamine, and LSD.

(b) (from Weil, 1970, Case 6)

R.S., a 26-year-old writer who had been given the diagnosis of ambulatory schizophrenia but had never been hospitalized, smoked marijuana for the first time at a party in New York but did not consume enough to become high. After a few minutes of euphoria, she had the experience that things became "unreal and weird," and she grew anxious. Her anxiety increased, and she became very withdrawn. The "weird" sensations persisted for 48 hours and then subsided. Afterward, she said she "would never touch pot again."

7. *Prolonged Aftereffects in Young Subjects* (from Kolansky and Moore, 1971, Case 3)

Shortly after a 14-year-old boy began to smoke marijuana, he began to demonstrate indolence, apathy, and depression. Over a period of 8 months, his condition worsened until he began to hallucinate and to develop paranoid ideas. Simultaneously he became actively homosexual. There was no evidence of psychiatric illness prior to smoking marijuana and hashish. At the height of his paranoid delusions, he attempted suicide by jumping from a moving car he had stolen. He was arrested and, during his probation period, he stopped smoking and his paranoid ideation disappeared. In two 6-month follow-up examinations, he was still showing some memory impairment and difficulty in concentration. Of note was the fact that he still complained of an alteration in time sense and distortion of depth perception at the time of his most recent examination.

8. *The "Amotivational Syndrome"*

The following extracts from West (1970) express vividly a variable picture familiar to many teachers and described in many other reports (Charen and Perelman, 1946; Tylden, 1967; McGlothlin and West, 1968; Bromberg, 1939; Scher, 1970; Kornhaber, 1971; Mirin *et al.*, 1971; Thurlow, 1971; Kolansky and Moore, 1971). Its connection with cannabis-induced lethargy, sleepiness, and disinterest has already been discussed (p. 312).

> I knew a young man—let's call him Paul—one of my favourite hippies, whose career I followed for several years. Paul was on his way to becoming a Ph.D. in one of the social sciences. He had an outstanding academic record. He began to smoke marijuana in his junior year in college. It did indeed improve his interpersonal relations: he had more friends, overcame some sexual inhibitions, enjoyed himself more at parties, and so forth. He continued to use marijuana after graduation and in graduate school. He still uses it several times a week.
>
> After about three years of smoking marijuana, when Paul was in his first year of graduate school, his performance began to diminish. He seemed to have less motivation to complete the work he had set out to accomplish. His drive to achieve his goals was lessened. Paul told me that one day he realized that a whole year had gone by and he had not read a single book from cover to cover. It was not only that he felt much less desire to know what the contents of the book might be. It was not even only that he felt (which he did) that there was no *point* in knowing what was in the book. He was also aware of the fact that his capacity to concentrate was so impaired that reading was likely to be laborious and no longer a pleasure. . . .

There are a great many young people, including some of the brightest and some of the best, who have been using marijuana now more or less regularly for three to four years. Addiction or even habituation is denied. The smoking is said to be simply for pleasure. Untoward effects are usually although not always denied. But the experienced clinician observes in many of these individuals personality changes that seem to grow subtly over long periods of time: diminished drive, lessened ambition, decreased motivation, apathy, shortened attention span, distractibility, poor judgment, impaired communication skills, loss of effectiveness, introversion, magical thinking, derealization and depersonalization, diminished capacity to carry out complex plans or prepare realistically for the future, a peculiar fragmentation in the flow of thought, habit deterioration, and progressive loss of insight.

The interpretation of these phenomena is still controversial. As explained above, it is even questioned by some whether the term "psychosis" should be applied to any of them, although it would be so applied to patients as ill as this who had not taken cannabis. The question, like that of whether cannabis is truly addictive, is to a large degree semantic. With the question of addiction the real issue is whether cannabis induces drug-seeking behavior influenced by physical withdrawal symptoms; with psychic phenomena the issues are the extent to which the drug impairs individual development and social adaptation, the incidence of that impairment, and the prognosis.

There seems no doubt that cannabis can produce very serious psychic effects and can disrupt an individual's social framework, and (as discussed below) the prognosis of the psychic effect after the drug is given up depends on how long the drug was taken. But there is considerable uncertainty as to how frequently phenomena of the type described above occur. It is probable that only a fraction of these episodes comes to the notice of doctors, let alone health authorities. People who take drugs, including alcohol, tend to live with the disabilities they incur. This is possibly because they are often only transient (see Table III below). It is well known that far more alcoholics exist (perhaps by a factor of 10) than are known to physicians, and Blum et al. (1969), reporting on drug adverse reactions generally, estimated that there were 14 "bad outcomes" in the student population for each one noted in official health records. The evidence is well reviewed in the Le Dain Commission's final report (1972). Drug users themselves report that one-quarter to one-third have had an unpleasant experience at some time. Student health authorities see very approximately one adverse cannabis reaction or less per 1000 students. It is estimated that something of the order of 1 per 1000 admissions to a psychiatric hospital in the United States or the United Kingdom is associated with cannabis, although the actual number is not known since patients frequently suppress a history of drug use. Colbach and Crowe (1970) in Vietnam in 1969 saw schizophrenia-like psychoses associated with heavy marijuana use at a rate of about 60 per year, representing about

10% of all psychiatric patients seen drawn from 45,000 men. One may set alongside such figures (following the Le Dain report) a rough estimate for the incidence of schizophrenic breakdown in such groups. The report makes the reasonable estimates that 1% of the population suffers such breakdown at some time [Henderson and Gillespie (1962) give the figure for the U.K. of 0.85%], that half these cases begin between the ages of 15 and 25, and that initial breakdown is spread evenly over these years. On these assumptions one would expect an incidence of schizophrenia in this group of about 5 per 10,000 annually. It seems clear, however, that although the incidence of psychotic behavior attributed to cannabis which comes to medical attention appears to be of the same order of magnitude as that of schizophrenia, a true estimate of the incidence of all psychotic episodes experienced by users would be far larger. It follows that the number of adverse reactions to cannabis is probably much higher than can be attributed to incipient schizophrenic behavior. Even so, it could be that some cases apparently associated with cannabis use would have become mentally ill in any case. But it could also be that, as a result of cannabis use, breakdown of a schizophrenic type is being substantially increased. The accuracy of the data is too low to exclude either possibility. Whatever view is taken, admissions of young adults and adolescents to psychiatric hospitals have risen sharply in the last decade.

One of the problems that arises is the difference in recorded experience in the Eastern countries, where cannabis is the main drug of dependence, from that in the West. In many respects, however, the experiences are comparable. The characteristic state of chronic mental illness, referred to as Oneiric delirium by Moroccan writers, is very similar to the acute state of intoxication called a "high" in the West. It is far more common in men than in women, corresponding to the rare use of cannabis by women in India, Africa, or Morocco. In all countries, schizophrenic episodes, paranoid reactions, and intense anxiety have been reported, whereas mania or depression occur but are less common; the amotivational syndrome has also been reported throughout the world literature. Nonetheless, the incidence of recorded chronic mental illness is much higher in the East. There are two main explanations for this. The first is that cannabis consumption is still relatively low and of relatively recent duration in the West. The World Health Organization report (1971) makes a valuable attempt to assess this difference and estimates for regular users a median daily dose up to 150 mg THC per day in India, with a maximum of 720 mg, against a median of 15–40 mg in the United States and a maximum of around 100 mg. For casual users in the United Kingdom and the United States, of course, still lower doses are currently in use. The alternative view is that cases of psychosis have been misclassified or misdiagnosed in the East. The problem remains to be resolved. The position must, of course, be expected to change. Mirin et al. (1971) found that heavy users take on the average 16 months to move from occasional to daily use, so that one may expect a time lag of 1–2 years in the response to any change in availability.

The development of multiple drug use also produces complicated diagnostic problems (Tylden, 1968a, 1970; Mirin *et al.*, 1971; Brill *et al.*, 1971). Table II illustrates this for English experience, comparing the pattern of use in 1965 with that in 1970. The main possible confusion is with LSD, which, like cannabis, can produce psychotic effects in one small dose. In contrast, the amount of amphetamine that must be taken is large (40–50 tablets a day for several weeks) and such patients are hypermanic, loquacious, sleepless,

TABLE II

CHANGING PATTERN OF OTHER DRUG HABITS IN CANNABIS USERS[a]

Habit	1965	1970
Number of cannabis users investigated	143	233
Also taking heroin (%)	15	15
Also taking LSD (%)	1	34
Also taking barbiturates or other sedatives (%)	nil	10
On multiple drugs (%)	2	21
Taking cannabis alone (%)	80	11

[a] Age range, 14–25. From Tylden (1970).

and may be violent; there are hallucinations of terrifying animals and people; patterns of thought may be more connected than with cannabis; the amphetamine psychosis should subside spontaneously in 3–5 days unless there is activation of latent schizophrenia. Because of the effects of amphetamines, takers are resistant to sedation, and barbiturates may enhance the amphetamine effect. Phenothiazines and diazepines are more effective with cannabis. Similarly, delirium tremens develops only after long and heavy exposure to alcohol. Opiates do not produce a psychosis, although subjects may be depressed, anxious, and restless in withdrawal; temporary normality is restored by a further dose of opiates, whereas cannabis and LSD psychotic responses are made worse by further exposure.

It is interesting that cannabis and LSD share not only high potency as psychotogens, but also the phenomenon of flashback, i.e., recurrence many days later of the psychic phenomena experienced immediately after a drug is taken. The first became well known with LSD but has been repeatedly reported for cannabis; the recurrence may involve not only cannabis but also mescaline and LSD experiences (Bewley, 1967; Keeler *et al.*, 1968; Weil, 1970; Bialos, 1970; Blumienfeld, 1971). The recurrence is sometimes pleasurable, sometimes distressing. In the study by Moskowitz (1971), patients experiencing LSD flashbacks, occurring between 2 and 28 times per week, 1–14 months after LSD exposure, responded to haloperidol, with trihexylphenidyl to control parkinsonian symptoms. The period of weeks or months over which flashback may occur is so long that even with cannabis it is highly improbable that it is due to residual drug action; with LSD and mescaline, this possibility must be excluded. It is remotely possible that the drugs produce some permanent biochemical change in the brain, but since it may occur after a single dose, this also seems improbable. The most likely explanation is that the original perceptual experience, like an intense emotional experience, enters the memory stores at the time, almost *en bloc* and without competition. For some subjects, it seems to have been the most impressive experience in their lives up to that time.

C. Cannabis Action—A Model Psychosis?

Considerable interest attaches to drug-induced psychotic states, because of the light they might throw on natural disease. The hope that mescaline or LSD actions might lead to an understanding of schizophrenia has been disappointed, and differences in the mental states are recognized. It must be said, however, that it is about as overoptimistic to expect to equate some drug-induced process with "cancer" as it is to do the same with an equally complex and varied condition such as the schizophrenias. Nevertheless, reactions to cannabis have been so often diagnosed as schizophrenia or described as schizophreniform that relevant features of the cannabis effect deserve comment.

First, cannabis causes fragmentation of thought, distractibility, and inability to select what is relevant from the material presented by the nervous system to the mind, and it impairs recent memory. These effects are produced at ordinary doses; they may not be apparent to casual inspection but become so as soon as any task is undertaken demanding sustained logic or maintenance of some objective during mental effort. The type of impairment is similar to types of nonsequential thinking in the schizophrenic. Second, confusion, disassociation, and depersonalization can occur. Third, paranoid thought is extremely common, ranging from a mere tendency to be suspicious (usually attributed to consciousness of the illegality of cannabis use but in fact extending beyond this) to frankly paranoid thinking and actions. With this can go intense anxiety, although abrupt fluctuation of mood occurs. Fourth, there is incongruity of affect, laughing or weeping without apparent cause. Fifth, hallucinations can occur, but they are not common, being seen only with high dosage, and free visual imagery is the most common effect. Sixth, there can be a withdrawnness, a preoccupation with the *milieu intérieur*, reminiscent of, but different from, the withdrawal in catatonia. There is, indeed, some resemblance to schizophrenia treated with large doses of chlorpromazine or by lobotomy. A similar impression may be gained from the fact that, while subjects may say they love other people more and are in closer contact with them emotionally, this is not expressed in normal gesture, and a sense of flatness is gained, similar to that produced by chlorpromazine. Another difference from schizophrenia lies in the handling of nonsequential thinking. The cannabis user plays games with his thoughts and feelings but is prepared to offer some rationalization of his sequence of thought or change of effect; the schizophrenic does not feel the need to do this.

It is sometimes suggested that the psychotic episodes of cannabis users resemble schizophrenia because they are in fact due to the individuals either fortuitously initiating a schizophrenic breakdown at the time of use or being in a latent condition that is triggered off by cannabis. Hekimian and Gershon (1968), for instance, suggest that 50% of cannabis and amphetamine users were schizophrenic before using drugs. It is also suggested that schizophrenics are particularly attracted to the drugs, although this is hardly borne out by a case history such as that of Weil's (1970) cited above. It is not possible to accept that all such episodes can be accounted for in this way, for three reasons. First, in a number of cases, psychiatric examination was made before drug use and did not show a schizophrenic state. Second, many cases, particularly if previous drug use was not prolonged, recover completely. Third, the picture produced can be convincingly regarded as an extension of the effects readily and consistently seen in cognitive and other studies in many laboratory experiments. There is no reason to doubt, at present, that *any* subject could be made with cannabis to pass into a schizophrenia-like psychotic state, if the dose were sufficiently high, although the pattern of response would naturally be related to the subject's personality structure. In addition, it would be a mistake to equate the cannabis-induced mental state with schizophrenia. Certain differences have been noted, and no doubt others will emerge. The important and interesting thing is that with cannabis, as with LSD, it is possible to produce in graded and reversible form, with only minor somatic effects, a condition showing many of the features of a natural psychosis.

D. Duration of Mental Effect in Relation to Duration of Cannabis Use

If some constituent of cannabis, or a metabolite, accumulates in the body, one effect to be expected is that any toxic action produced would be more persistent after repeated dosage than after a single exposure. The basis for such cumulation lies in the fat solubility of THC and its 7-OH metabolite, the cumulative toxicity of cannabis in animals, and the persistence of THC and its metabolites in the body (Gill *et al.*, 1970; Agurell, 1970; Lemberger *et al.*, 1970, 1971; Paton *et al.*, 1972). The same result would follow if the effects of the substances accumulated, rather than (or as well as) the substances themselves. There is little information suitable for analysis in this way, but the report by Bromberg (1939) allows a preliminary approach. In this report, 31 cases of mental reaction to marijuana are recorded, 14 classified as acute intoxication, 17 as toxic psychosis. The evidence cited, available for all but two patients, about the duration of marijuana use on the one hand and of the mental reaction on the other has been extracted to form Table III.

TABLE III

DURATION OF MARIJUANA USE IN RELATION TO DURATION OF
MENTAL REACTION[a]

	Duration of marijuana use		
Duration of mental reaction	Once, 1 cigarette, 1 day, or a few days (no. of subjects)	Short time, some time, months, 7 months, or 1 year (no. of subjects)[b]	Prolonged over 1 year (no. of subjects)[b]
0–2 days	5	0	0
2–5 days	2	2 (3)	1 (2)
5–10 days	2	0	1 (2)
Over 10 days	1	6 (5)	9 (7)
Total number of subjects	10	8	11
Maximum duration[c]	3 weeks	7 months	13 months

[a] Data from Bromberg (1939).
[b] The figures not enclosed in parentheses take account of readmissions to hospital. If only the first admission is considered, the appropriate figures are given in parentheses.
[c] The longest duration of mental reaction in each of the three groups.

The simplest interpretation of this analysis is that duration of mental reaction is positively correlated with duration of marijuana use. It has been suggested that many reactions in inexperienced users are "panic" reactions requiring only reassurance (Becker, 1967; Weil, 1970); although this concept needs closer examination, if adopted it could account for part of the picture. It has also been suggested that, where prolonged psychotic or mental disorder arises after marijuana use, the drug has only revealed an underlying psychopathology. This interpretation, while it requires substantiation, could be applied to the prolonged reactions after moderate or prolonged use. Perhaps the most interesting features, not explicable in these ways, are the two remaining characteristics of the table: that single exposure or few exposures are only rarely associated with prolonged mental aftereffect and that, if sustained use produces a reaction, it is prolonged. The theory that the drug, its metabolites, or their effects have a cumulative effect accounts for the whole picture in an economical way, without ad hoc hypotheses, and is, of course, supported by the recent biochemical evidence of persistence of cannabinoids in the body. The question obviously needs controlled investigation, particularly to disentangle cumulation of chemical substance from cumulation of effects. But it is clear from these and other reports in which time relationships are cited (e.g., Chopra and Chopra, 1957; Asuni, 1964; Keeler *et al.*, 1968; Talbott and Teague, 1969; Grossman, 1969; Colbach and Crowe, 1970; Weil, 1970; Kolansky and Moore, 1971) that it is a sound working rule that recovery from the mental effects of cannabis after single doses is a matter of hours or a day or two but that it takes longer the more prolonged the previous exposure, possibly weeks or months.

E. Cannabis and Dependence Liability

The discussion of this question has been distorted by an almost exclusive comparison between cannabis and the opiates, even though it would be at least as relevant to make the comparison with cocaine, barbiturates, amphetamines, or LSD. In fact, each of the drugs should be considered in its own right, and the primary issue is whether, as a result of drug taking, drug-seeking behavior of significant intensity is established. Once established, the question arises of the forces involved and the extent to which they are specific to the drug. Mere habit or social factors hardly constitute such specific elements. But the establishment of a *drug-seeking behavior*, the production of *tolerance* (which can lead to increased rate of use of the drug), and the production of *withdrawal symptoms* are important to identify and characterize. It should be noted that, although dramatic withdrawal symptoms, such as the diarrhea and cramps of opiate withdrawal, epileptic fits with barbiturates, or delirium tremens with alcohol, have received considerable attention, other withdrawal symptoms of a milder kind can also be very important, particularly if they continue for a long time after withdrawal; insomnia after opiate or barbiturate withdrawal is an example. Fear of the more acute symptoms could help to deter the drug user from giving up drug use, but lesser, long-lasting symptoms such as depression, anxiety, or insomnia could be important reasons for relapse. The latter, of course, shade into psychological factors and, as one would expect, the whole question is deeply complicated by social and cultural elements. It could be said, too, that the distinction often drawn between physical and psychological dependence is largely operational; a good many investigators would expect that in due course physical correlates for the psychological phenomena will be identified.

One point affecting patterns of withdrawal reponse arises directly from the pharmacology of cannabis. It is known that both THC and its metabolites have a relatively long lifetime in the body (Lemberger et al., 1970, 1971, 1972), and the overt effects of a single dose can be prolonged. This means that even when cessation of drug taking occurs, the actual withdrawal from brain and tissues can never be rapid, and any abstinence syndrome is likely to be attenuated by a gradual "weaning-off" originating in the pharmaco-kinetics of the drug. The situation is illustrated by comparing the pattern of opiate withdrawal symptoms after merely ceasing to give some long-acting opiate with the results of giving nalorphine to produce a rapid functional withdrawal.

It is clear that cannabis can induce a drug-seeking behavior or compulsion, as judged by a recognized difficulty in "kicking the habit," a conscious psychic dependence, or a persistence in its use despite recognized disadvantages or harm (Skliar, 1934; Marcovitz and Myers, 1944; Fraser, 1949; Chopra and Chopra, 1957; Chapple, 1966; McGlothlin and West, 1968; Yardley, 1968; Tylden, 1968b; Milman, 1969; Grossman, 1969; Scher, 1970; Mirin et al., 1971; Kolansky and Moore, 1971). In addition, Deneau and Kaymakçalan (1971; Kaymakçalan, 1972) have been able to induce self-injection of THC in two of six rhesus monkeys and in a third after an intervening period on cocaine. Ames' (1958, p. 984) account perhaps points to one way in which the compulsion arises. Two of her ten subjects found the cannabis experience extraordinarily delightful. One subject reported that "it is such a lovely, drifting, voluptuous sensation," and from the other subject, as the experience was ending, "I've got such a let down feeling—it is like coming out of a golden dream." These two subjects were the only ones who felt they would gladly take the drug again. But the compulsion is evidently established only by regular use, and there is general agreement that occasional use can be given up without difficulty.

The question of tolerance is complex. The ready development of tolerance in animals had already been discussed. For man, the older literature (see Walton, 1938) clearly indicates that the dose required to produce a given effect does not rise with repetition when dosage is low or occasional but that with heavy habitual users appreciable tolerance can develop, although never to the degree possible with the opiates. The position was obscured, however, by the report from Weil et al. (1968) that eight chronic users became "high" on a dose that did not produce "highs" in nine naive individuals, together with their extensive discussion of the phenomena and their phrase "a unique example of 'reverse tolerance'." It should be noted, however, that the conditions of double-blind trial were applied only to the naive subjects, and "the chronic users were tested with the drug on their first visit to the laboratory with no practice and were informed that they were to receive high doses of marihuana." Any comparison between the responses of the two groups was therefore invalidated by the difference in set and setting. It is striking that there is, in fact, so far as work on man is concerned, little but anecdotal evidence in support of the concept of increased sensitivity to cannabis with repetition of dose. The most suggestive finding is by Meyer *et al.* (1971) who reported in a controlled study of six heavy and six casual users that while the casual users showed the greater impairment in perceptual and performance tests, the heavy users rated themselves 30 minutes after smoking as higher, on the average by about one point on a five-point subjective rating scale. By the end of the experiment, however, the heavy users were less high. This conjunction in heavy users of diminished effect judged by functional tests and increased but briefer effect judged by subjective rating of the high raises the difficult question of how to control satisfactorily the standards used in the self-rating procedure and the role of learned interpretation of physiological cues. The article by Kiplinger *et al.* (1971) is interesting in this respect. They used seven naive and eight experienced subjects; twelve out of the fifteen correctly identified a dose of 6.25 μg/kg THC by inhalation as differing from placebo, which implies that at least four out of the seven naive subjects were able to recognize so low a dose of drug. Renault *et al.* (1971) found no difference between naive and experienced subjects with regard to effect on heart rate.

One would, in fact, expect to find, under suitable conditions, some augmentation of effect with repetition of dose, since, as pointed out by Gill *et al.* (1970), this would occur with any fat-soluble substance liable to accumulate and is familiar with the barbiturates. As discussed in Chapter 5, Carlini's work suggests that it occurs in animals, but the conditions of its appearance depend on dose and on the distribution and fate of the drug in the body. In contrast, there is some definite evidence for tolerance in man. First, the doses taken by habitual users in the East (see World Health Organization, 1971) or by soldiers in Vietnam, compared with those found experimentally to produce the characteristic effects, are so much larger, sometimes by a factor of 100, that it is necessary to assume that tolerance occurs, doubtless varying with the individual. Second, tolerance has been observed in some experimental studies (Mayor's Committee on Marihuana, 1944; Williams *et al.*, 1946; Meyer *et al.*, 1971). Third, users may report that the drug becomes less effective with continued use (e.g., Chapple, 1966; Scher, 1970). The only definite estimate of degree of tolerance available is that in the Mayor's report. With a standardized marijuana extract at two dose levels, they obtained evidence by a variety of tests showing that users were 2½–3 times less sensitive than nonusers to cannabis given orally. Users were also less sensitive to smoked marijuana. Figure 1 of Chapter 6, constructed from their data, shows the contrasting time courses of oral and smoked cannabis rather elegantly and also reveals the interesting point that the rate of onset and decline of effect is the same for user and nonuser for equieffective doses. There is preliminary evidence (Lemberger *et al.*, 1971) that THC disappears from the blood more quickly in users than in the naive, and this could be relevant to tolerance. However, the position is complicated; induction of enzymes forming an active metabolite could (as Mechoulam, 1970, suggested) lead to sensitization, but only if the enzymes that mediate further metabolism and inactivation were not also induced. For practical purposes, the best judgment at present seems to be that habitual substantial use can produce some tolerance, perhaps to a degree comparable with that to alcohol and barbiturates, but that as regards dependence liability such changes are far less significant than for the opiates.

There is also evidence for an abstinence syndrome. Skliar (1934) gave a brief account of a range of symptoms. Marcovitz and Myers (1944), in their study of cannabis addicts in the army, noted headaches, restlessness, jerking movements of shoulders, arms, head, and trunk, anxiety, suicidal fantasies, and suicidal attempts. Fraser (1949), with Indian ganja smokers, observed irritability, outbursts of excitement, violence, and psychotic behavior. Bensusan (1971) noted anxiety, restlessness, cramps, sweating, and aches. Tylden (1967) reported apathy and bad temper, together with depression over the loss of self-confidence and the fantasy that the drug produced. In Grossman's (1969) third case, the pleasurable "high" was followed more or less regularly by mild depression and agitation for 1–2 days. Headache, irritability, and depression for 1–2 days seem to be normal aftereffects of heavy use (Chapple, 1966; Ames, 1958; McGlothlin and West, 1968; Scher, 1970). It is also evident that there is nothing comparable to the acute opiate abstinence syndrome (Gaskill, 1945; Williams *et al.*, 1946; Chopra and Chopra, 1957). Williams *et al.*, however, found abstinence symptoms after pyrahexyl withdrawal. There was little effect for the first 2 days, but then most patients became restless, slept poorly, had poor appetitites, reported "hot flashes," and sweated more. One patient developed a panic reaction on the second and third days, which was relieved by pyrahexyl. It is often said that no abstinence syndrome is produced in animals. Chopra and Chopra (1957), however, produced irritability and a mild syndrome in cats and albino rats (although few details are given). Further, more recently, Deneau and Kaymakçalan (1971; Kaymakçalan, 1972) have observed a withdrawal syndrome in self-injecting monkeys, consisting of depression, irritability, tremors, and yawning—a picture fully compatible with the clinical reports.

There seems, therefore, some analogy between cannabis on the one hand and alcohol and barbiturates on the other. With casual doses of any of these, there is little dependence liability, but with habitual use of substantial doses compulsion and possibly some tolerance arise, together with abstinence syndromes sharing a number of common features. The point does not appear to have been fully tested, but one would predict that any of these three drugs (or similar drugs) would relieve the abstinence syndrome from any other of them. In fact cross-tolerance between cannabis and alcohol has been found in animals (Newman *et al.*, 1972); pyrahexyl was found by Thompson and Proctor (1953) to relieve postalcoholic symptoms; Jones and Stone (1970) noted a resistance by heavy marijuana users to large doses of alcohol; and Dundee (1956) and Scott (1953) reported a remarkable resistance by the chronic hashish user to barbiturates used for induction of anesthesia. These cross-tolerances do not extend to LSD or mescaline. With opiates there is a curious limited interaction. Cannabis has its normal potency in a morphine-tolerant animal (Isbell and Jasinski, 1969; McMillan *et al.*, 1971), but morphine has reduced analgesic action in a cannabis-tolerant animal (Deneau and Kaymakçalan, 1971). Further, cannabis, like the barbiturates, has been used for the relief of the opiate abstinence syndrome in man (Allentuck and Bowman, 1942), but pyrahexyl was found to be ineffective for the purpose (Himmelsbach, 1944).

II. Toxicity in Man

Cannabis is so insoluble in water that, unless it is given intravenously, it is difficult to achieve a lethal dose in the circulation, and in fact only a few fatal incidents have been recorded, most of them with little detail (see Walton, 1938). The most detailed study is a recent one (Heyndrickx *et al.*, 1969) in which a young man was found dead, no medical cause of death being discoverable at postmortem, with a water pipe and a large amount of cannabis herb and resin in his possession. Body fluids were negative for morphine and other narcotics, barbiturates, amphetamines, benzodiazepines, phenothiazines, and alcohol; carboxyhemoglobin was also negative. But cannabinol was identified in the urine by thin-layer chromatography. The cause of this death, therefore, is as well attested as most heroin deaths. In assessing the case, it must be remembered that cannabis toxicity is cumulative in animals and that in man cannabis can produce postural hypotension and a considerable tachycardia; fatal hypotension or ventricular tachycardia in a subject already heavily exposed to cannabis are by no means unreasonable postulates. Such cases, however, must be expected to be very rare, unless intravenous use develops.

Nonfatal cases of collapse have also been recorded (Walton, 1938; Lewis, 1968; Gourvés et al., 1971). Fowler (1943), after taking a pharmacological dose of tincture orally, felt dizzy and lost consciousness for 3 hours; consciousness returned in waves, and in 2 more hours he was able to stagger about, and vomited. Time sense was disordered for 2–3 days. Such cases are always difficult to interpret, but the hypotensive action of cannabis in an exaggerated form seems a likely contributing factor.

A number of reactions to intravenous injection of crude aqueous extracts have been reported (Henderson and Pugsley, 1968; King and Cowen, 1969; Gary and Keylon, 1970; Lundberg et al., 1971). Symptoms included chills, vomiting, fever, shock, tachycardia, headache, weakness, abdominal pain, blurred or double vision, pulmonary signs, liver and splenic enlargement, jaundice, anuria or oliguria, and a massive drop in white cells; in only one case was there loss of consciousness, for 4 hours. A good deal of these could be attributed to embolic, foreign body reactions, but reports of this sort are uncommon, despite the injection of extraordinary crude preparations from barbiturate capsules, paregoric and the like, and three of the authors concluded that the cannabis contributed specifically to the reaction.

Intravenous injection in the drug addict is, of course, known to produce a wide variety of pathological results, including bacterial, malarial, fungal, and viral infections, largely due to use of dirty syringes (Louria et al., 1967). The case of endophthalmitis described by Sugar et al. (1971) in a patient using many drugs including marijuana is probably of this kind, the fungal organism (Aspergillus) probably having entered the eye from the blood. In interpreting ocular damage, however, one may note that the drug user may in fact come to inject (or be injected) though the cornea (Elkington et al., 1972). There is no evidence that marijuana has any specific effect of its own on the eye, apart from the conjunctival reddening and a fall in intraocular pressure.

A striking, but so far unique, report of severe atherosclerosis in young Muslims in North Africa has come from Sterne and Ducastaing (1960). They were struck by the incidence of this condition, particularly against a general background of much less hypertensive and vascular disease in Muslims as compared with European or Jewish Moroccans. In their 29 cases, the condition, which was restricted to males aged 25–35, presented itself as intermittent claudication during the cold months, and then progressed to gangrene. The patients were of the poorer classes, but it was not believed that this accounted for the phenomenon; the possibilities of Buerger's disease and the arterial sequelae of typhus were excluded. The atheromatous lesions were indistinguishable by arteriography and histology from the arteriosclerosis of old age. One of their patients reported exacerbation on three occasions after heavy cannabis consumption. Twenty of the 29 were found to be generally heavy cannabis users, taking an average of 15 pipes of cannabis a day. In a series of nonarteriosclerotic patients only 6% were cannabis users. There was no diabetes. A leukocytosis linked to secondary infection was seen in 13 cases; some anemia was common; blood platelets were normal in four cases examined. Blood cholesterol was normal. The only effective treatment was unilateral adrenalectomy. Unfortunately no information was given as to duration of cannabis use.

Hughes *et al.* (1970) describe a case in which diabetic coma followed ingestion of marijuana in a patient previously thought not to be diabetic. The case was complex, since the patient had been a user of LSD and marijuana since the age of 18 and was under treatment with substantial doses of chlorpromazine for an acute paranoid schizophrenic reaction. The authors suggest that the nausea and vomiting induced by marijuana may have precipitated a failure of glucose regulation. It is possible that marijuana contributed more directly (see discussion on p. 234), but there is no information as to the effects of marijuana when chlorpromazine is being taken.

The evidence from animals regarding teratogenicity, reviewed in Chapter 5, has shown that in three species of animals (rats, hamsters, rabbits) injection of cannabis into the mother produces fetal deformities, including limb defects. The effect was shown in two species to be dose related, and the dose in the rat (4 mg/kg of resin) is comparable with the human dose, particularly if dose is related to metabolic rate rather than weight. In addition, in all three species, and in mice, fetal resorption occurred. In women, three cases have been reported in which cannabis was used during pregnancy. In one (Hecht *et al.*, 1968) the mother, who had had two induced abortions, was using both LSD and cannabis but gave up the LSD when she realized that she was pregnant. The infant lacked a right hand. The mother's chromosomes were normal, but permission was refused to study those of the infant, and the father had committed suicide. In the case of Carakushansky *et al.* (1969), LSD and cannabis were believed to have been taken in pregnancy; the infant had deficits of left and right hands, webbing of the right foot, and talipes of the left foot; the infant's chromosomes were normal. Gelehrter (1970) reported a case, again with both LSD and cannabis use, with exostrophy of the bladder. Since almost all LSD users have taken cannabis, the abnormalities reported in association with LSD need to be borne in mind (Blanc *et al.*, 1971). It is obvious that although experimentally cannabis produces thalidomide type of deformities in animals and there have been the cases of phocomelia described above, no major rise in incidence of deformity corresponding to the rise in cannabis use has been seen. It may be that the human female does not react as do animals, that few women take cannabis during pregnancy (male use predominates in any case), or that the cases are missed in the overall incidence of around 1% abnormalities in all births. There is a fourth possibility, that in humans the equivalent of fetal resorption takes place. There is some evidence for this in Tylden's (1971) finding, in a group of 6: drug-using women, that while fertility of amphetamine users was higher than in a control group, it was reduced in cannabis users. In the light of the animal data, a full epidemiological investigation of the matter is needed.

A second line of approach is the study of chromosomal aberrations. I must be stressed, as Gilmour et al. (1971) pointed out, that chromosomal changes in somatic cells, found after leukocyte culture, provide no reliable basis for inferences about meiotic chromosome effects or transmission to progeny, nor do they indicate any clinical significance for the host. Further more, no case has been reported of initiation of a clone of cells bearing such abnormalities in drug users. With this caveat in mind one may note that while in the cases described above no chromosomal abnormalities were seen, Gilmour et al. found, in a careful study, that chromosomal aberration wa three to four times control level in a group of heavy marijuana users (taking it more than 10 times per month, often daily), but, as is now normal, the subjects had also taken other drugs. A similar finding was made with heroin users and amphetamine users and in a group receiving substantial doses of phenothiazines. The authors suggest, therefore, that the aberration may be associated with some factor common to drug-using individuals rather than with a specific drug effect.

An important study is that by Campbell et al. (1971), who found evidence for cerebral atrophy in a series of 10 subjects, aged 18–28, who had all smoked cannabis heavily for years, some since the age of 14–15. The first four patients had been referred for neurological investigation of headache, memory loss, or behavior change. Air encephalographic examination showed no signs of brain tumor but revealed enlarged cerebral ventricles, indicating loss of brain substance. Of the remaining patients five were referred by a drug addiction clinic, and one was a case of drug overdose. To estimate the normal ventricular size for the age group, 13 cases were found in the records, matched for age but not for sex, who had presented neurological symptoms but proved to have no obvious neurological disease. References to criticisms made, a rejoinder, and the report of finding normal ventricular size in a heavy amphetamine user may be found in Campbell et al. (1972). The work clearly needs confirmation, but in view of the cumulative tendency of cannabis toxicity, the persistence of mental effect when exposure is prolonged and the serious implications for adolescent development, it is necessary to take the findings seriously. Unfortunately, air encephalography is not a technique that should be practiced without a clear medical reason, and there is no other way at present of testing the point directly.

One further neurological complication has been reported, by Keeler and Reifler (1967). The patient was an epileptic, who had responded to phenytoin and phenobarbital, had stopped taking the drugs, and had been free of grand mal seizures for 6 months. He then took marijuana seven times in a 3-week period, during which he had three grand mal convulsions; these occurred neither during the drug reaction nor immediately thereafter. The report is interesting in view of the curious relationship between cannabis and convulsant phenomena.

The limited evidence as to the irritant effects of cannabis smoke on the respiratory tract, the carcinogenicity of the tar on mouse skin, and the effects on liver were discussed in Chapter 5. The Le Dain Commission (1972) report may also be consulted for its brief accounts of unpublished work.

Attention should be drawn to the possibility of major interactions between cannabis and other drugs. This could arise not only because of an interference, particularly by cannabidiol, with microsomal activity (Paton and Pertwee, 1972), which could modify the effect of any microsomally metabolized drug, but also by competition with protein-binding sites: THC binds to lipoproteins, and the 7-OH metabolite to albumin (Wahlqvist *et al.*, 1970; Widman *et al.*, 1971).

III. Therapeutic Potential of Cannabinoids

The medical uses of cannabis have been explored relatively seriously for over a century, and reference to its use over preceding centuries are not hard to find. However, caution is needed in assessing the published reports. Until relatively recently there were few effective drugs available, so that the merest hint of beneficial action was seized upon; clinical trials were nonexistent. A good corrective is to compare the accounts of other substances also used at that time with their modern assessment. The therapeutic revolution beginning in the 1930's has made older work largely of antiquarian interest. Even in the earlier background, despite initial claims for effectiveness as an anesthetic or for treating tetanus, chorea, neuralgia, rheumatism, epilepsy, melancholy, or as a uterine stimulant, cannabis did not establish itself but remained a drug of interest primarily for its psychic action. One can surmise that the reason for its clinical lack of success was the same as the difficulty with it now—the diversity of its actions. Today its use has been proposed as an analgesic antidepressant, hypnotic, hypotensive, diuretic, or antibiotic, for treating glaucoma, as a psychiatric aid, or in treatment of withdrawal symptoms. For each of these uses there are more potent modern drugs. It is of greater significance that its modern rivals are also more specific; even though cannabis or THC has some particular action, its "therapeutic" use also entails the production of tachycardia (one of the most sensitive and reliable signs of THC action), conjunctivitis, psychic changes, liability to dysphoria or depression as well as to euphoria, excitement preceding sedation, and liability to "vegetative" disturbances. Its fat solubility and pharmacokinetic properties, too, present difficulties for sustained use, although if its toxicity were acceptable, methods could be devised for dealing with these, as with other drugs involving cumulation and tolerance.

Even if no clear opening for the direct clinical exploitation of cannabis and THC themselves is yet established, it remains true that THC presents a novel chemical structure and is a drug that in a low dose produces a fascinating range of actions. The catalytic effect for medicinal chemistry and pharmacology of understanding the chemical structure of a drug is illustrated by the history of the sulfonamides, penicillin, and tubocurarine; an understanding at the cellular level of the psychic effects of THC would surely throw light on many other psychopharmacological problems.

References

Agurell, S. (1970). *In* "The Botany and Chemistry of Cannabis" (C. R. B. Joyce and S. H. Curry, eds.), pp. 175–191. Churchill, London.
Allentuck, S., and Bowman, K. M. (1942). *Amer. J. Psychiat.* **99**, 248.
Ames, F. (1958). *J. Ment. Sci.* **104**, 972.
Asuni, T. (1964). *Bull. Narcotics* **16**, 17.
Baker, A. A., and Lucas, E. G. (1969). *Lancet* **1**, 148.
Baker-Bates, E. T. (1935). *Lancet* **1**, 811.
Becker, H. S. (1967). *J. Health Soc. Behav.* **8**, 163.
Benabud, A. (1957). *Bull. Narcotics* **9**, 1.
Bensusan, A. D. (1971). *Brit. Med. J.* **3**, 112.
Bewley, T. H. (1967). *Brit. Med. J.* **3**, 603.
Bey, D. R., and Zecchinelli, V. A. (1971). *Mil. Med.* **136**, 448.
Bialos, D. S. (1970). *Amer. J. Psychiat.* **127**, 819.
Blanc, W. A., Mattison, D. R., Kane, R., and Chauhan, P. (1971). *Lancet* **2**, 158.
Blum, R. H., and associates. (1969). "Students and Drugs." Jossey-Bars Publ., San Francisco, California.
Blumienfeld, J. (1971). *Mil. Med.* **136**, 39.
Boroffka, A. (1966). *East Afr. Med. J.* **43**, 377.
Brill, N. Q., Crumpton, E., and Grayson, H. M. (1971). *Arch. Gen. Psychiat.* **24**, 163.
Bromberg, W. (1939). *J. Amer. Med. Ass.* **113**, 4.
Campbell, A. M. G., Evans, M., Thomson, J. L. G., and Williams, M. J. (1971). *Lancet* **2**, 1219.
Campbell, A. M. G., Evans, M., Thomson, J. L. G., and Williams, M. J. (1972). *Lancet* **1**, 202.
Campbell, D. R. (1971). *Can. Psychiat. Ass. J.* **16**, 161.
Carakushansky, G., Neu, R. L., and Gardner, L. I. (1969). *Lancet* **1**, 150.
Chapple, P. A. (1966). *Brit. J. Addict.* **61**, 269.
Charen, S., and Perelman, L. (1946). *Amer. J. Psychiat.* **102**, 674.
Chopra, G. S. (1971). *Bull. Narcotics* **23**, 15.
Chopra, I. C., and Chopra, R. W. (1957). *Bull. Narcotics* **9**, 4.
Christozov, C. (1965). *Maroc. Med.* **44**, 630 and 866.

Colbach, E. M., and Crowe, R. R. (1970). *Mil. Med.* **135**, 571.
Curtis, H. C., and Wolfe, J. R. (1939). *J. Kans. Med. Soc.* **40**, 515.
Dally, P. (1967). *Brit. Med. J.* **1**, 367.
Defer, B., and Diehl, M.-L. (1968). *Ann. Med. Psychol.* **2**, 260.
Deneau, G. A., and Kaymakçalan, S. (1971). *Pharmacologist* **13**, 246.
Dundee, J. W. (1956). "Thiopentone and Other Thiobarbiturates." Livingstone, Edinburgh.
Elkington, A., Glasspool, M. G., and Collin, J. R. O. (1972). *Brit. Med. J.* **2**, 766.
Fowler, W. C. (1943). *Lancet* **1**, 368.
Fraser, J. D. (1949). *Lancet* **2**, 747.
Gary, N. E., and Keylon, V. (1970). *J. Amer. Med. Ass.* **211**, 501.
Gaskill, H. S. (1945). *Amer. J. Psychiat.* **102**, 202.
Gelehrter, D. (1970). *J. Pediat.* **77**, 1065.
George, H. R. (1970). *Brit. J. Addict.* **65**, 119.
Gill, E. W., Paton, W. D. M., and Pertwee, R. G. (1970). *Nature (London)* **228**, 134.
Gilmour, D. G., Bloom, A. D., Lele, K. P., Robbins, E. S., and Maximilian, C. (1971). *Arch. Gen. Psychiat.* **24**, 268.
Gourvés, J., Viallard, C., Leluan, D., Girard, J.-P., and Aury, R. (1971). *Presse Med.* **79**, 1389.
Grossman, W. (1969). *Ann. Intern. Med.* **70**, 529.
Hecht, F., Beals, R.-K., Lees, M. H., Jolly, J., and Roberts, P. (1968). *Lancet* **2**, 1087.
Hekimian, L. J., and Gershon, S. (1968). *J. Amer. Med. Ass.* **205**, 125.
Henderson, A. H., and Pugsley, D. J. (1968). *Brit. Med. J.* **3**, 229.
Henderson, D., and Gillespie, R. D. (1962). "Textbook of Psychiatry." Oxford Univ. Press, London and New York.
Heyndrickx, A., Scheiris, C., and Schepens, P. (1969). *J. Pharm. Belg.* **24**, 371.
Himmelsbach, C. K. (1944). *S. Med. J.* **37**, 26.
Hughes, J. E., Steahly, L. P., and Bier, M. M. (1970). *J. Amer. Med. Ass.* **214**, 1113.
Isbell, H., and Jasinski, D. R. (1969). *Psychopharmacologia* **14**, 115.
Jones, R. T., and Stone, G. C. (1970). *Psychopharmacologia* **18**, 108.
Jørgensen, F. (1968). *Acta Psychiat. Scand., Suppl.* **203**, 205.
Kaplan, H. S. (1971). *N. Y. State J. Med.* **71**, 433.
Kaymakçalan, S. (1972). *In* "Cannabis and its Derivatives: Pharmacology and Experimental Psychology" (W. D. M. Paton and J. Crown, eds.), p. 142. Oxford Univ. Press, London and New York.
Keeler, M. H. (1967). *Amer. J. Psychiat.* **124**, 674.
Keeler, M. H. (1968). *Amer. J. Psychiat.* **125**, 386.
Keeler, M. H., and Reifler, C. B. (1967). *Dis. Nerv. Syst.* **28**, 474.
Keeler, M. H., Reifler, C. B., and Liptzin, M. B. (1968). *Amer. J. Psychiat.* **125**, 384.
Keup, W. (1969). *Science* **163**, 1144.
King, A. B., and Cowen, D. L. (1969). *J. Amer. Med. Ass.* **210**, 724.
Kiplinger, G. F., Manno, J. E., Rodda, B. E., and Forney, R. B. (1971). *Clin. Pharmacol. Ther.* **12**, 650.
Klee, G. D. (1969). *Psychiat. Quart.* **43**, 719.
Kolansky, H., and Moore, W. T. (1971). *J. Amer. Med. Ass.* **216**, 486.
Kornhaber, A. (1971). *J. Amer. Med. Ass.* **215**, 1988.
Le Dain Commission. (1972). "A Report of the Commission of Inquiry into the Non-Medical Use of Drugs." Information Canada, Ottawa.
Lemberger, L., Silberstein, S. D., Axelrod, J., and Kopin, I. J. (1970). *Science* **170**, 1320.
Lemberger, L., Tamarkin, N. R., Axelrod, J., and Kopin, I. J. (1971). *Science* **173**, 72.

Lemberger, L. Crabtree, R. E., and Rowe, H. M. (1972). *Science* **177**, 62.

Lewis, A. (1968). *In* "Cannabis: A Report by the Advisory Committee on Drug Dependence," p. 40. HM Stationery Office, London.

Louria, D. B., Hensle, T., and Rose, J. (1967). *Ann. Intern. Med.* **67**, 1.

Lundberg, G. D., Adelson, J., and Prosnitz, E. H. (1971). *J. Amer. Med. Ass.* **215**, 121.

McGlothlin, W. H., and West, L. J. (1968). *Amer. J. Psychiat.* **125**, 370.

McMillan, D. E., Dewey, W. L., and Harris, L. S. (1971). *Ann. N. Y. Acad. Sci.* **191**, 83.

Marcovitz, E., and Myers, H. J. (1944). *War Med.* **6**, 382.

Mayor's Committee on Marihuana. (1944). "The Marihuana Problem in the City of New York." Jaques Cattell Press, Lancaster, Pennsylvania.

Mechoulam, R. (1970). *Science* **168**, 1159.

Meyer, R. E., Pillard, R. C., Shapiro, L. M., and Mirin, S. M. (1971). *Amer. J. Psychiat.* **128**, 90.

Milman, D. H. (1969). *J. Pediat.* **74**, 283.

Mirin, S. M., Shapiro, L. M., Meyer, R. E., Pillard, R. C., and Fisher, S. (1971). *Amer. J. Psychiat.* **127**, 1134.

Moskowitz, D. (1971). *Mil. Med.* **136**, 754.

Newman, L. M., Lutz, M. P., Gould, M. H., and Domino, E. F. (1972). *Science* **125**, 1022.

Paton, W. D. M., and Pertwee, R. G. (1972). *Brit. J. Pharmacol.* **44**, 250.

Paton, W. D. M., Pertwee, R. G., and Temple, D. (1972). *In* "Cannabis and its Derivatives: Pharmacology and Experimental Psychology" (W. D. M. Paton and J. Crown, eds.), p. 50. Oxford Univ. Press, London and New York.

Perna, D. (1969). *J. Amer. Med. Ass.* **209**, 1085.

Renault, P. F., Schuster, C. R., Heinrich, R., and Freeman, D. X. (1971). *Science* **174**, 589.

Scher, J. (1970). *J. Amer. Med. Ass.* **214**, 1120.

Scott, L. T. (1953). *Lancet* **2**, 835.

Siler, J. F., Sheep, W. L., Bates, L. B., Clark, G. F., Cook, G. W., and Smith, W. A. S. (1933). *Mil. Surg.* **73**, 269.

Skliar, N. (1934). *Allg. Z. Psychiat. Ihre Grenzgeb.* **102**, 304.

Smith, D. E., and Mehl, C. (1970). *Clin. Toxicol.* **3**, 101.

Spencer, D. J. (1970). *West Indian Med. J.* **19**, 228.

Sterne, J., and Ducastaing, C. (1960). *Arch. Mal. Coeur Vaiss.* **53**, 143.

Sugar, S. H., Mandell, G. H., and Shalev, J. (1971). *Amer. J. Ophthalmol.* **71**, 1055.

Talbott, J. A., and Teague, J. W. (1969). *J. Amer. Med. Ass.* **210**, 299.

Thompson, L. J., and Proctor, R. C. (1953). *N.C. Med. J.* **14**, 520.

Thurlow, H. J. (1971). *Can. Psychiat. Ass. J.* **16**, 181.

Toker, E. (1966). *Amer. J. Psychiat.* **123**, 55.

Tylden, E. (1967). *Brit. Med. J.* **3**, 335.

Tylden, E. (1968a). *Brit. Med. J.* **1**, 704.

Tylden, E. (1968b). *Newcastle Med. J.* **30**, 184.

Tylden, E. (1970). *Brit. Med. J.* **3**, 158.

Tylden, E. (1971). Unpublished observation.

Ungerleider, J. T., Fischer, D. D., Goldsmith, R. S., Fuller, M., and Forgy, E. (1968). *Amer. J. Psychiat.* **125**, 325.

Wahlqvist, M., Nilsson, I. M., Sandberg, F., Agurell, S., and Grandstrand, B. (1970). *Biochem. Pharmacol.* **19**, 2579.

Walton, R. P. (1938). "Marihuana: America's new Drug Problem." Lippincott, Philadelphia, Pennsylvania.

Weil, A. T. (1970). *N. Engl. J. Med.* **282**, 997.

Weil, A. T., Zinberg, N. E., and Nelsen, J. M. (1968). *Science* **162**, 1234.

West, L. J. (1970). *Ann. Intern. Med.* **73**, 459.

Widman, M., Nilsson, I. M., Nilsson, J. L. G., Sandberg, F., Agurell, S., and Grandstrand, B. (1971). *Acta Pharm. Suecica* **8**, 706.

Williams, E. G., Himmelsbach, C. K., Wikler, A., Ruble, D. C., and Lloyd, B. J. (1946). *Pub. Health Rep.* **61**, 1059.

World Health Organization. (1971). *World Health Organ., Tech. Rep. Ser.* **478**.

Yardley, D. C. M. (1968). *In* "Adolescent Drug Dependence" (C. W. M. Wilson, ed.), p. 181. Pergamon, Oxford.

APPENDIX*

Formulas of Known Natural Cannabinoids and Metabolites and Some Synthetic Cannabinoids

Raphael Mechoulam

I. Known Cannabinoids in Cannabis

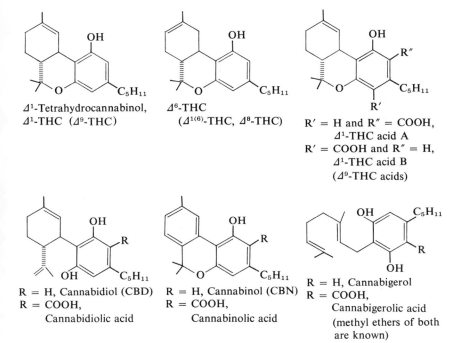

Δ¹-Tetrahydrocannabinol, Δ¹-THC (Δ⁹-THC)

Δ⁶-THC (Δ¹⁽⁶⁾-THC, Δ⁸-THC)

R′ = H and R″ = COOH, Δ¹-THC acid A
R′ = COOH and R″ = H, Δ¹-THC acid B (Δ⁹-THC acids)

R = H, Cannabidiol (CBD)
R = COOH, Cannabidiolic acid

R = H, Cannabinol (CBN)
R = COOH, Cannabinolic acid

R = H, Cannabigerol
R = COOH, Cannabigerolic acid (methyl ethers of both are known)

* The names in parentheses indicate additional names or abbreviations used for the same compound.

367

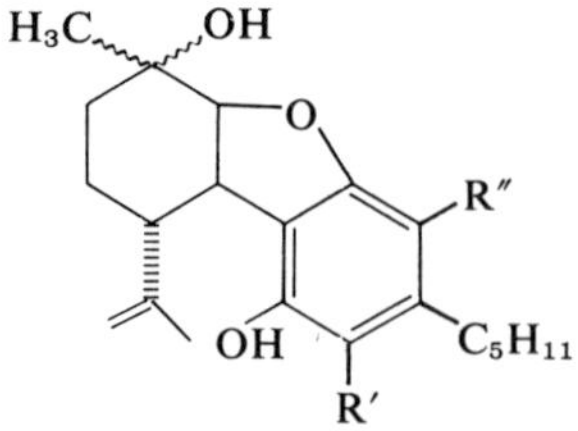

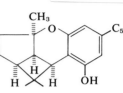

R' = COOH and R" = H,
  Cannabielsoic acid A
R' = H and R" = COOH,
  Cannabielsoic acid B

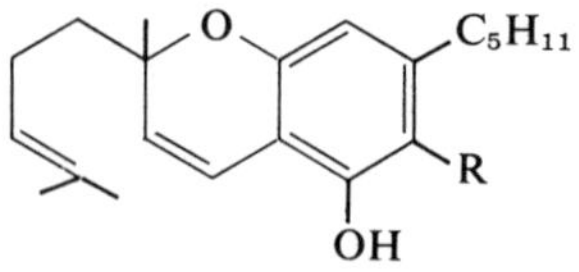

R = H, Cannabichromene
R = COOH,
  Cannabichromenic acid

Cannabicyclol

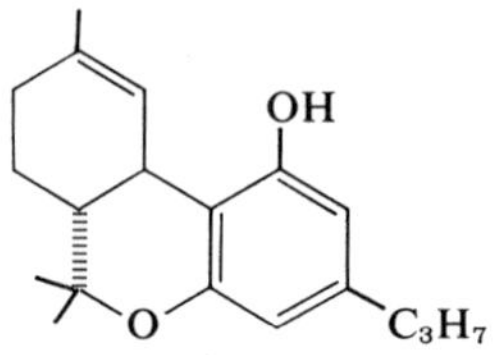

Δ^1-Tetrahydrocannabivarol
(tetrahydrocannabidivarol,
tetrahydrocannabivarin,
propyl-THC)

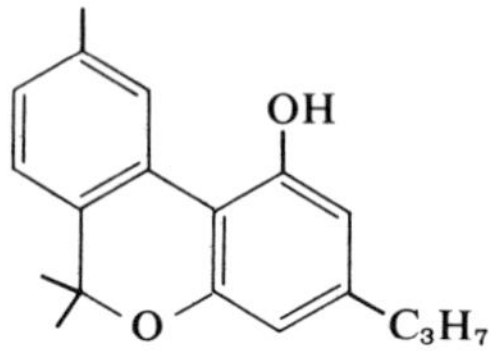

Cannabivarol
(cannabidivarol,
cannabivarin,
propyl cannabinol)

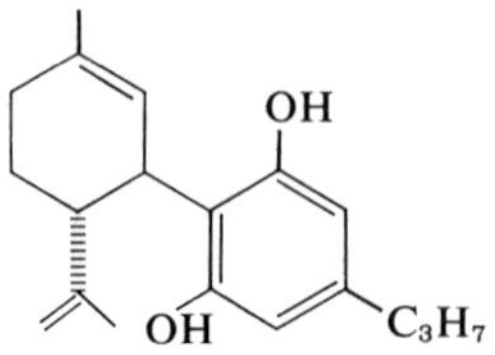

Cannabidivarol
(cannabidivarin,
propyl cannabidiol)

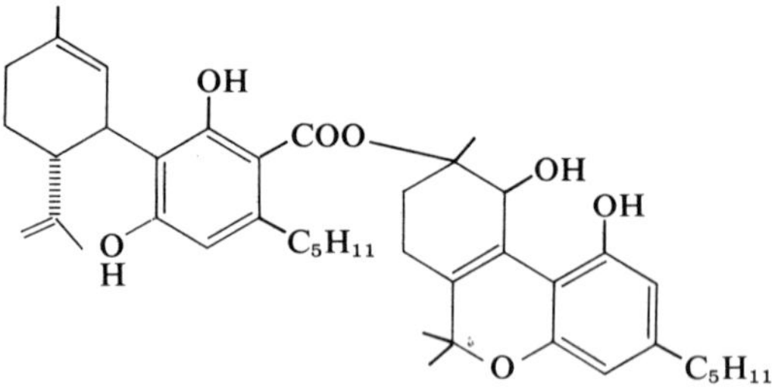

Cannabitriol ester of cannabidiolic acid

Additional known cannabinoids in cannabis are described in the addendum
to Chapter 1.

II. Some THC Metabolites

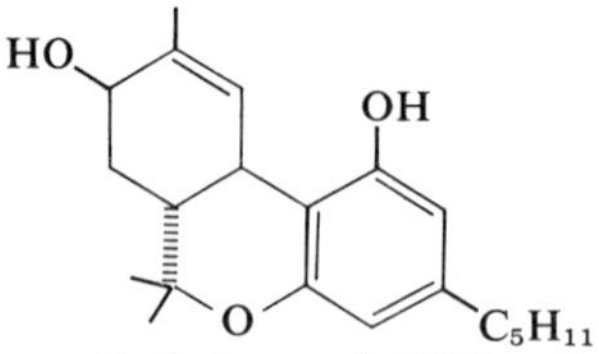

6β-Hydroxy-Δ^1-THC
(8β-hydroxy-Δ^9-THC)

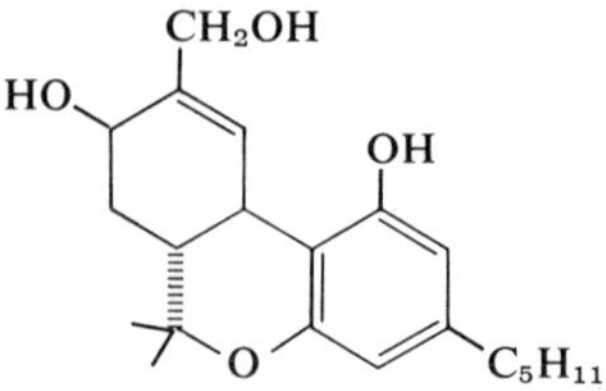

6β,7-Dihydroxy-Δ^1-THC
(8β,11-dihydroxy-Δ^9-THC)

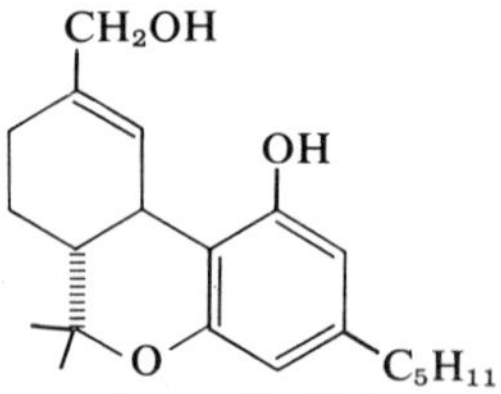

7-Hydroxy-Δ^1-THC
(11-hydroxy-Δ^9-THC)

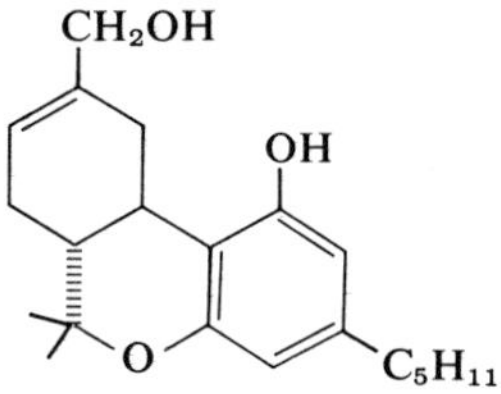

7-Hydroxy-Δ^6-THC
(11-hydroxy-Δ^8-THC)

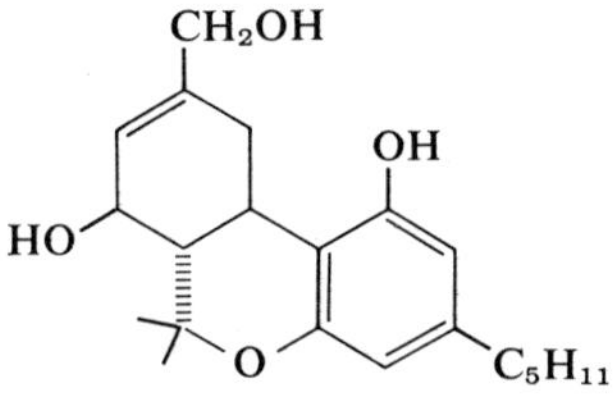

5,7-Dihydroxy-Δ^8-THC
(7,11-dihydroxy-Δ^8-THC)

Additional metabolites are described in the addenda to Chapters 1 and 4.

III. Some Widely Tested Synthetic Cannabinoids

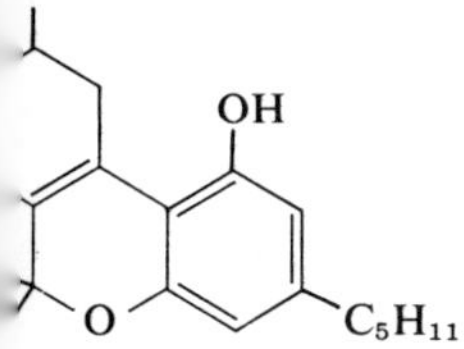

Δ^3-THC
($\Delta^{6a,10a}$-THC)

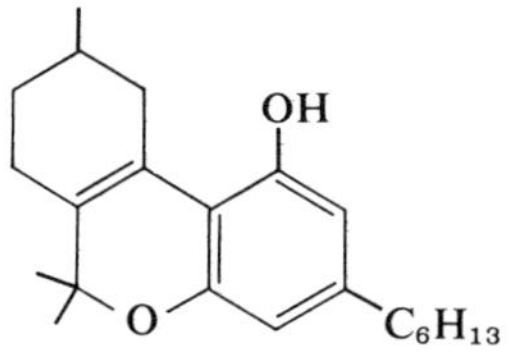

Hexyl homolog of Δ^3-THC
(synhexyl, pyrahexyl,
parahexyl)

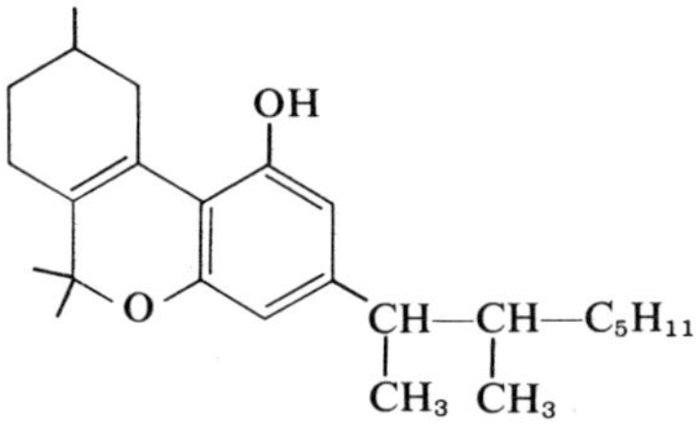

1″,2″-Dimethylheptyl
homolog of Δ^3-THC
(DMHP)

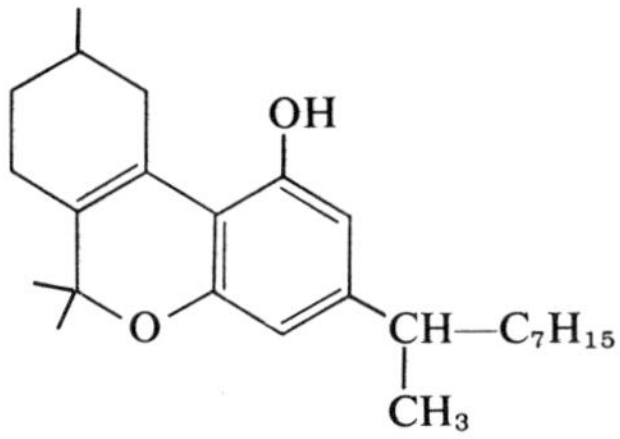

1″-Methyloctyl homolog
of Δ^3-THC (MOP)

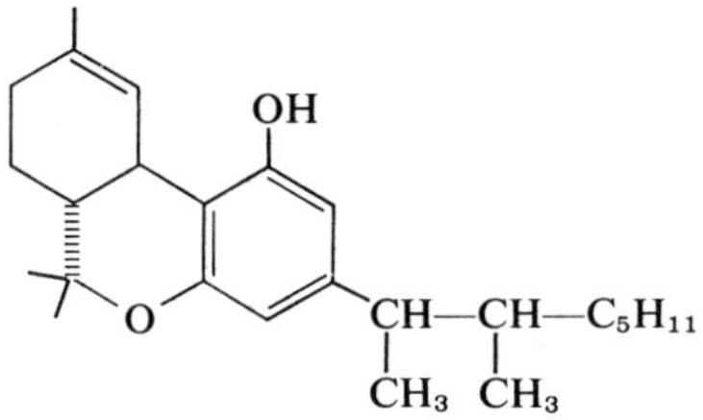

1″,2″-Dimethylheptyl homolog
of Δ^1-THC

Author Index

Numbers in italics refer to the pages on which the complete references are listed.

A

Aaron, H. S., 107, 108, *130*

Abel, E. L., 104, *130*, *133*, 211, 216, 224, 254, *260*, *264*, 277, *282*, 302, 303, 324, *330*

Abou-Chaar, C. I., 12, *86*

Adams, R., 3, 8, 9, 17, 21, 28, 32, 35, 37, 38, 41, 43, 61, 80. 81, *82*, 101, 108, 109, 110, 111, 112, 113, 124, 129, *130*, 140, *156*, 222, *263*, 324, *330*

Adelson, J., 358, *364*

Aguar, O., 88, *98*

Aguiar, M. B., 211, 213, 215, *264*

Agurell, S., 12, 46, 56, 57, 59, 69, 70, 71, *82*, *86*, *87*, 96, *98*, *99*, 117, *132*, 152, 153, *156*, *158*, 168, 170, 171, 173, 174, 175, 176, 177, 178, 179, 180, *182*, *183*, 185, 188, *189*, *190*, 242, 243, 244, 245, 246, 248, *260*, *263*, *264*, *265*, 268, 270, *282*, 288, *330*, 352, 361, *362*, *364*, *365*

Akasu, M., 146, *157*

Akermark, B., 59, 76, *86*

Aldrich, C. K., 293, *330*

Alencar, J. W., 211, 213, 215, *264*

Allen, D. O., 275, 276, *284*

Allentuck, S., 108, *130*, 291, 292, 293, 295, 296, 297, 306, 310, 311, 313, 314, 315, 317, 318, 319, 321, 322, 323, 324, 325, *330*, 339, 357, *362*

Alles, G. A., 8, 11, *84*, 128, *130*, 196, 201, 202, 226, *260*, *262*

Allinger, N. L., 19, 20, 22, 78, *82*

Ames, F., 222, *260*, 292, 294, 295, 296, 297, 299, 301, 305, 306, 307, 308, 309, 310, 311, 313, 314, 315, 317, 320, 321, 322, 323, 324, 325, *330*, 354, 356, *362*

An, R., 276, *283*

Anderson, J. E., 265, *285*

Anderson, S. M., 153, *158*

Anderssen, J. M., 243, *260*

Anker, R. M., 125, *130*, 172, *182*

Aplin, R. T., 22, *83*

Apter, J. T., 219, *260*

Aramaki, H., 11, *87*, 144, *156*, 194, *265*

Archer, R. A., 19, 20, 22, 78, *82*, 97, *99*

Arnold, D. O., 288, *332*

Asuni, T., 339, 353, *362*

Aury, R., 358, *363*

Avico, U., 141, *158*

Avison, A. W. D., 109, 113, 114, *130*, 200, 201, 202, 220, 237, *260*

Axelrod, J., 149, 153, *157*, 176, 180, 181, *183*, 185, *189*, 243, 244, 245, 249, 250, *262*, 352, 354, 356, *363*

Aycock, B. F., 109, 110, *130*

Azuma, T., 11, *87*, 194, *265*

B

Bader, H., 125, *131*

Baeckström, P., 107, *131*

Bailey, K., 90, 97, *98*

Bailey, P. T., 211, 254, *260*, 265, 266, *285*

371

Baker, A. A., 297, *330*, 340, *362*
Baker, B. R., 21, 32, *82*, 101, 108, *130*
Baker-Bates, E. T., 292, 295, 296, 306, 308, 310, 311, 314, 315, 316, 317, 318, 319, 320, 321, 322, 323, *330*, 338, *362*
Baratella, J. R. S., 196, 203, 204, 216, *264*
Baratella, M. R., 103, *133*
Bargellini, G., 15, *82*
Barnes, P. R., 267, 268, 272, 280, *282*, *285*
Barratt, E., 268, 272, *282*, *285*
Barratt, E. S., 267, 280, *285*
Barros, G. G., 12, *87*, 196, 201, 202, 203, *264*
Barry, H., 97, *99*, 102, 104, *132*, 222, 224, 225, 227, 228, 234, *260*, *262*, *264*, 266, 273, 274, 275, *283*, *285*
Bates, L. B., 338, *364*
Baum, M., 211, *262*
Baur, E., 7, *83*
Bawd, W., 150, *156*
Beals, R.-K., 359, *363*
Beam, W., 142, *156*
Becker, H. S., 289, 310, 312, *330*, 352, *362*
Begley, M. J., 24, *82*
Bein, H. J., 227, *263*
Bembry, T. H., 8, *86*
Benabud, A., 339, *362*
Bennett, I. F., 69, 70, 71, *85*, 106, *132*, 289, 290, 295, 307, 319, 322, 325, *331*
Bensusan, A. D., 356, *362*
Ben-Zvi, Z., 10, 13, 17, 27, 54, 56, 57, 59, 65, 68, 74, 82, *82*, *83*, *85*, 91, 92, 93, 94, 95, 96, 97, *99*, 102, 106, 115, 117, 124, 125, 127, *131*, *132*, 135, *136*, 144, 149, 154, *158*, 174, 178, 179, *182*, 205, 242, 249, 251, *260*, *263*, 268, *282*, *284*
Bercht, C. A. L., 11, 83, 88, *99*, 252, *260*
Bergel, F., 7, 8, 15, *83*, *87*, 110, *131*
Berger, H. J., 226, 227, 252, *265*, 278, *282*, *283*
Bergner, K. G., 6, *85*
Bergström, H., 327, *330*
Berkoff, C. E., 51, *83*
Bernstein, K., 327, *330*
Bersohn, I., 325, *331*
Betts, T. J., 144, 148, *156*
Bewley, T. H., 339, 349, *362*
Bey, D. R., 341, *362*
Bhagwat, A. W., 103, *131*, 196, 201, 208, 209, 216, 222, 226, 228, 230, 231, 232, 233, 235, *260*

Bialos, D. S., 341, 349, *362*
Bicher, H. I., 103, *131*, 217, 220, 221, 232, 237, *260*
Biel, J. H., 125, *131*
Bieniek, D., 3, 10, 17, 47, *87*, 91, *99*, 103, 104, 108, 128, 129, *131*, 183, 189, *189*, 201, 203, 205, 210, 251, *261*, 266, *282*, *284*
Bier, M. M., 359, *363*
Billings, D. K., 265, *283*
Bino, T., 279, *282*
Black, M. B., 215, 254, 256, *260*
Blanc, W. A., 359, *362*
Blatt, A. H., 3, *83*, 138, 142, *156*
Bloom, A. D., 360, *363*
Blum, R. H., 347, *362*
Blumienfeld, J., 341, 349, *362*
Bockstahler, T. E., 41, *82*
Boegli, G., 117, *131*, 213, 214, 230, 243, 248, 249, 251, 252, *261*, 269, *282*
Boff, E., 102, 104, 106, *132*, 205, 206, 208, 224, 226, 237, 258, *264*
Bohlig, J. F., 5, *83*
Bolas, T., 15, *83*
Borgen, L. A., 240, 241, *260*, *263*, 272, *282*, *284*
Borger, W., 146, *156*
Boroffka, A., 339, *362*
Bose, B. C., 103, *131*, 196, 201, 208, 209, 216, 222, 226, 228, 230, 231, 232, 233, 235, *260*
Bouquet, J., 11, 12, 69, *83*, 293, 296, 305, 306, 307, 308, *330*
Bowman, K. M., 108, *130*, 291, 292, 293, 295, 296, 297, 306, 310, 311, 313, 314, 315, 317, 318, 319, 321, 322, 323, 324, 325, *330*, 339, 357, *362*
Boyd, D. B., 19, 20, 22, 78, *82*
Boyd, E. S., 104, *131*, 211, 218, 219, 222, 224, 228, 230, 231, 232, 233, 238, 239, *260*, *261*
Bradbury, T., 5, *86*
Braude, M. C., 98, *99*, 271, 272, 274, *282*, *285*
Braun, P., 22, 28, 35, 40, 48, 56, *86*, 102, 115, 124, *132*, 154, *158*, 183, 189, *190*, 205, *263*
Brawley, P., 329, *330*
Breimer, D. D., 3, 17, 19, 21, *87*, 88, *99*
Brill, N. Q., 325, *331*, 349, *362*

Brine, D. R., 56, *87*, 117, *131*, *133*, 149, 152, *158*, 174, 176, 178, *183*, 185, *190*, 213, 214, 230, 242, 243, 248, 249, 251, 252, *261*, *264*, 269, *282*

Brine, G. A., 56, *87*, 117, *133*, 149, 152, *158*, 174, 176, 178, *184*, 242, 243, *264*

Bromberg, W., 291, 292, 294, 295, 296, 297, 301, 305, 306, 308, 309, 310, 311, 312, 313, 315, 316, 317, 319, 321, 323, *330*, 339, 342, 346, 352, *362*

Brown, D. J., 278, *285*

Brown, H., 266, 267, *282*

Brown, P., 91, *99*

Brown, S. A., 56, *86*

Brown, W. R., 69, *86*

Bruni, R. J., 154, *156*, 178, *182*

Buckley, J. P., 275, 276, *282*, *283*

Budzikiewicz, H., 22, *83*

Bueno, O. F. A., 265, 266, *282*

Bullock, F. J., 154, *156*, 178, *182*

Burstein, S. H., 56, 57, *82*, *83*, 96, *99*, 117, *131*, 152, 153, 154, *156*, 162, *164*, 168, 169, 171, 174, 175, 176, 177, 178, 179, 181, *182*, 184, 185, 186, *189*, 242, 243, 249, *260*, 268, 269, 279, *282*

Butler, W. P., 143, *156*

Buxbaum, D. M., 214, 220, 221, *260*, 274, 275, *282*

Byrom, P., 150, *156*

C

Caddy, B., 144, 146, *156*

Cahn, R. S., 5, 7, 8, 13, 15, 16, 31, *83*

Cain, C. K., 21, 32, 61, *82*, 109, 113, *130*

Caldwell, B. V., 154, 155, *156*, *158*

Caldwell, D. F., 289, 292, 293, 307, 308, *330*

Campbell, A. M. G., 320, *330*, 360, *362*

Campbell, C., 278, *284*

Campbell, D. H., 163, *164*

Campbell, D. R., 320, *330*, 341, *362*

Carakushansky, G., 359, *362*

Carder, B., 266, *282*

Cardillo, B., 89, *99*

Cardillo, G., 51, 54, *83*

Cardon, P. V., 185, *190*, 326, *331*

Carlin, R. B., 38, 41, 43, *82*

Carlini, E. A., 103, 104, 108, 128, 129, *131*, *132*, *133*, 196, 201, 202, 203, 204, 205, 210, 211, 213, 214, 222, 224, 235, 238, 239, 251, 254, 255, 256, *260*, *261*, *264*, 265, 266, 267, 274, *282*, *283*, *284*

Carlini, G. R. S., 235, *260*

Case, E. M., 327, *330*

Casparis, P., 7, *83*

Cavasino, A., 320, *331*

Cavero, I., 275, 276, *282*, *283*

Chan, P., 277, *284*

Chapple, P. A., 309, 311, 313, 315, 316, 317, *330*, 354, 355, 356, *362*

Charen, S., 339, 346, *362*

Chari-Bitron, A., 279, *282*

Chaud Sob, J., 220, 221, *261*

Chauhan, P., 359, *362*

Chazan, J.-B., 37, *83*

Chen, K. H., 109, *130*

Chenoweth, M. B., 247, *261*

Chopra, G. S., 337, 354, 356, *362*

Chopra, I. C., 208, 209, 225, 253, *261*, 292, 293, 294, 295, 296, 308, 309, 310, 311, 312, 313, 315, 316, 321, 322, 323, 324, 325, *330*, 339, 353, 354, 356, *362*

Chopra, R. W., 208, 209, 225, 253, *261*, 292, 293, 294, 295, 296, 308, 309, 310, 311, 312, 313, 315, 316, 321, 322, 323, 324, 325, *330*, 339, 353, *362*

Christensen, H. D., 56, *87*, 117, *131*, *133*, 149, 152, *158*, 174, 176, 178, *183*, 213, 214, 230, 242, 243, 248, 249, 251, 252, *261*, *264*, 269, *282*

Christiansen, J., 163, *164*, 180, *182*, 243, *261*

Christison, R., 294, *330*

Christozov, C., 339, *362*

Cirrani, E. S., 141, *158*

Clare, G., 320, *333*

Clark, G. F., 338, *364*

Clark, J. H., 8, 17, 21, 28, 32, 80, 81, *82*

Clark, L. D., 289, 292, 293, 298, 299, 302, 303, 305, 306, 307, 313, 317, 318, 319, 324, *330*

Clarke, D. G., 24, *82*

Claussen, U., 4, 10, 12, 23, 24, 26, 35, 37, 39, 43, 68, 69, 70, 71, *83*, *84*, *85*, *87*, 103, 104, 106, 108, 116, 117, 127, 128, 129, *131*, *132*, *133*, 146, 148, *156*, 196, 201, 203, 205, 206, 210, 251, 254, 255, *261*, *262*, *264*, 292, 293, 296, 297, 299, 308, 319, 321, 322, 325, *331*

Cochran, D. W., 97, *99*

Cohen, A. B., 23, *331*

Cohen, G. M., 265, 279, *282, 285*
Cohn, R. A., 267, 268, 280, *282, 285*
Coker, A.-A. O., 276, *285*
Colasanti, B., 272, *282*
Colbach, E. M., 341, 342, 347, 353, *363*
Collin, J. R. O., 358, *363*
Combes, G., 91, *99*
Conner, A. Z., 61, *87*
Conney, A. H., 175, 181, *182*
Conrad, D. G., 265, *282*
Constantinidis, J., 273, *282*
Cook, A. H., 125, *130*, 172, *182*
Cook, G. W., 338, *364*
Cortez, L., Jr., 220, 221, *261*
Cosmides, G. J., 175, *182*
Costa, E., 184, *190*, 268, 269, *284*
Coutselinis, A. S., 69, 71, *83*
Covello, M., 11, *83*
Cowen, D. L., 358, *363*
Crabtree, R. E., 185, *190*, 354, *364*
Craik, F. I. M., 302, *330*
Crancer, A. J., 289, 319, 328, *330*
Crawford, H. J., 313, *332*
Cricchio, R., 51, 54, *83*
Crim, D., 13, *86*
Crombie, L., 24, 41, 51, 52, 53, 54, 63, 75, *82, 83*
Crowe, R. R., 341, 342, 347, 353, *363*
Crown, J., 288, *332*
Crumpton, E., 349, *362*
Curry, A. S., 196, 197, *261*
Curry, S. H., 4, 56, *84*
Curtis, H. C., 339, *363*
Czerkis, M., 7, *83*

D

Dagirmanjian, R., 219, 222, 224, 228, 230, 231, 232, 233, 238, 239, *261*
Dahi, M. A. Y., 234, 235, *261*
Dahlen, P., 102, 104, 106, *132*, 205, 206, 208, 224, 226, 237, 258, *264*
Dahmen, J., 268, 270, *282*
Dally, P., 339, *363*
Daly, D. D., 316, *330*
Dalzell, B. C., 98, *99*, 269, 271, 276, *285*
Dalzell, H. C., 92, 97, *99*, 269, 271, 276, *285*
Dandliker, W. B., 196, 201, 202, *260*
Davis, J. M., 278, *285*
Davis, J. P., 221, *261*
Davis, K. H., 11, *83*, 141, 146, *156*

Davis, O. L., 220, 235, 237, *261*
Davis, T. W. M., 141, 146, *157*
Davis, W. M., 98, *99*, 210, 218, 240, 254, *260, 263*, 266, 272, 273, 279, 280, *282, 284*
Davy, H., 327, *330*
de Carolis, A. S., 103, *132*
Decourtive, E., 5, *83*
de Farias, R. C., 230, 232, *261*, 290, 293, 295, 305, 306, 308, 309, 310, 311, 313, 314, 315, 316, 317, 321, 322, 323, 324, *330*
de Faubert-Maunder, M. J., 144, *157*
Defer, B., 340, *363*
De Kloet, W. A., 6, *86*, 138, *158*
de la Mare, W., 309, *330*
Delay, J. C., 289, 319, 328, *330*
Delisle Burns, B., 327, *332*
Demarco, P. V., 19, 20, 22, 78, *82*
Demuth, M., 92, *99*
Deneau, G. A., 274, 275, 277, 279, *282, 283*, 354, 356, 357, *363*
Dennis, B., 274, 275, *282*
Denny, J. J. 4, *87*, 288, *333*
Derment, W., 313, *332*
de Ropp, R. S., 9, *83*, 141, 146, *157*
Dever, J. L., 107, *131*
Dewey, W. L., 98, *99*, 104, 126, *131*, 208, 209, 213, 220, 221, 224, 225, 229, 231, 232, 233, 237, 238, 248, 250, 254, 257, *261, 263*, 268, 271, 274, 275, 276, 278, 279, *282, 285*, 357, *364*
De Zeeuw, R. A., 3, 17, 19, 21, *87*, 88, *99*
Diehl, M.-L., 340, *363*
Dille, J. M., 289, 319, 328, *330*
Dingell, J. V., 153, *157*, 173, 178, *183*, 246, 247, *262*, 268, 269, 270, *283*
Di Simone, L., 160, *165*
Dixit, B. N., 227, *264*, 273, *285*
Dixon, W. E., 198, 208, 209, 230, 231, 232, 234, *261*
Djerassi, C., 22, *83*
Dlugosch, E., 39, 43, *85*
Domino, E. F., 133, *136*, 160, *164*, 215, 222, 223, 231, 232, 254, 256, *260, 262*, 265, 267, *284*, 289, 292, 293, 307, 308, 319, 321, 322, *330, 331*, 357, *364*
Doorenbos, N. J., 12, 71, *84*, 141, 142, 147, 148, *157*
Dornbush, R., 320, *333*

Dorsky, A. M., 153, *157*, 183, 189, *190*
Drew, W. G., 265, 266, *283*, 303, *332*
Drewes, H. R., 56, 57, *84*, 104, 117, *131*, 152, *157*, 174, 177, 178, *182*, 242, 249, *261*
Ducastainq, C., 358, *364*
Dundee, J. W., 357, *363*
Dunstan, W. R., 7, *83*
Duquénois, P., 103, *131*, 142, *157*, 204, 216, *261*
Dziak, J., 276, *282*

E

Easterfield, T. H., 5, 6, 7, 8, 13, *87*, 115, *133*, 139, *158*
Eckhardt, G., 201, 208, 210, 225, 226, 231, 234, *263*
Edery, H., 10, 59, *82*, *83*, *85*, 91, 93, 94, 95, 96, 97, *99*, 102, 103, 104, 106, 115, 116, 117, 124, 125, 127, 128, *130*, *131*, *132*, 135, *136*, 140, *158*, 205, 206, 208, 209, 210, 211, 213, 214, 216, 222, 224, 248, 250, 251, 252, *262*, *263*, 268, *282*, *284*
Efron, D. H., 211, 214, 220, 221, 226, 227, *260*, *264*
Egdahl, R. H., 225, *261*
El-Dakhakhny, M., 56, *86*
Elkington, A., 358, *363*
Ellington, A. C., 238, 240, *264*
Elliot, H. W., 6, *85*, 138, *157*, 277, *283*
Elmounaj, D., 88, *99*
Elsmore, T. F., 265, 266, 271, *282*, *283*, *284*
El-Yousef, M. K., 278, *285*
Englert, L. F., 49, *84*, 153, *157*, 168, 178, *182*, *183*, 185, *189*, 206, 241, 246, 247, 248, 249, *262*, *263*, 270, 273, 276, *283*
Erley, D. S., 247, *261*
Eschenmoser, A., 28, 35, 47, 48, 55, *86*
Estabrook, R. W., 175, *182*
Estevez, V., 185, *189*, 270, *283*
Evans, M., 320, *330*, 360, *362*
Ewing, J. A., 297, *331*
Extel, R. J., 273, *285*

F

Fahrenholtz, K. E., 44, 46, 48, *83*, 94, *99*, 171, *182*
Fairbairn, J. W., 88, 89, 98, *99*, 141, *157*
Farenholtz, K. E., 124, *131*
Farmilo, C. G., 138, 139, 141, 146, *157*

Farnsworth, N. R., 97, *99*, 266, *283*
Fehlhaber, H. W., 10, 24, *87*
Feigen, G. A., 8, 11, *84*, 128, *130*, 196, 201, 202, 226, *260*, *262*
Feldstein, S., 320, *333*
Fenimore, D. C., 193, 249, *261*
Fentiman, A. F., 56, 57, *84*, 104, 117, *131*, 152, *157*, 174, 177, 178, *182*, 242, *261*
Ferguson, C. P., 107, 108, *130*
Fernandes, N. S., 103, *132*, 201, 203, 213, 214, *264*
Ferraro, D. P., 265, *283*
Fetterman, P. S., 12, 71, *84*, 141, 142, 147, 148, *157*
Fink, B. R., 241, *261*
Fink, M., 320, *333*
Finley, T. W., 231, *331*
Fish, F., 144, 146, *156*
Fisher, D. D., 312, *333*, 340, *364*
Fisher, S., 274, 275, *282*, 346, 348, 349, 354, *364*
Fiske, H. L., 163, *164*
Fitchie, G. E., 266, 273, 276, *283*
Fletcher, G. V., 266, *283*
Fochtman, F. W., 143, *157*
Foltz, R. L., 56, 57, *84*, 104, 117, *131*, 152, *157*, 174, 177, 178, *182*, 242, 249, *261*
Ford, R. D., 215, 235, 254, *261*, 265, 266, 267, 279, *283*, *284*
Forgy, E., 312, *333*, 340, *364*
Forli-Forti, G., 15, *82*
Forney, R. B., 11, 13, 69, 70, 71, 72, *85*, *86*, *87*, 103, 106, *131*, *132*, 141, 154, *157*, 210, 213, 221, 222, 228, 229, 230, 231, 235, 237, 244, *261*, *262*, *264*, 275, 276, 278, *284*, *285*, 289, 290, 291, 295, 307, 311, 317, 318, 319, 321, 322, 325, 328, *330*, *331*, 355, *363*
Forrest, J. S., 162, *164*, 185, *190*, 268, *283*
Fouts, J. R., 175, *182*
Fowler, W. C., 358, *363*
Fraenkel, S., 7, *84*, 103, *131*, 198, 208, *261*
Francis, E. E. H., 15, *83*
Frank, M., 321, *330*
Frankenheim, J. M., 104, *132*, 205, 215, 224, 254, 256, *261*, *263*, 265, 267, 279, *283*, *284*
Frankfurt, S., 6, *86*
Fraser, J. D., 354, 356, *363*
Freeman, A. E., 277, *285*

Freedman, A. M., 320, *333*
Freedman, D. X., 213, 223, 226, 227, *262*, 322, *332*, 355, *364*
Freudenthal, R. I., 56, *87*, 117, *131*, *133*, 149, 152, *158*, 174, 175, 178, *183*, 213, 214, 230, 242, 243, 248, 249, 251, 252, *261*, *264*, 269, *282*, *283*
Fried, P. A., 266, *285*
Fritchie, G. E., 49, *84*, 153, *157*, 168, 178, *182*, *183*, 206, 241, 246, 247, 248, 249, *262*, *263*
Fuijita, M., 146, 148, *157*
Fujita, T., 26, 68, *86*
Fulginiti, S., 265, *284*
Fuller, M., 312, *333*, 340, *364*
Fulton, C. C., 159, *164*

G

Galanter, I. M., 185, *190*, 308, 326, *330*, *331*
Gallager, D. W., 274, *283*
Gamage, J. R., 4, *84*, 288, *330*
Gaoni, Y., 2, 4, 10, 17, 19, 21, 22, 23, 24, 25, 26, 28, 31, 35, 38, 39, 40, 44, 48, 50, 51, 53, 56, 60, 61, 63, 72, 74, 77, 78, 81, *83*, *84*, 91, *99*, 102, 115, 117, 124, 127, 128, *131*, *132*, 139, 140, 141, 142, 143, 144, 145, 147, 149, 150, 151, 154, *157*, *158*, 183, 189, *190*, 205, 258, *263*
Garattini, S., 103, 104, *131*, 196, 210, 211, 213, 222, 226, 227, 228, *261*
Gardner, L. I., 104, *131*, 211, *260*
Gardner, L. J., 241, *263*, 359, *362*
Garriott, J. C., 103, *131*, 141, *157*, 213, 221, 222, 223, 228, 237, *261*
Gary, N. E., 358, *363*
Gaskill, H. S., 294, 295, 297, 308, 310, 311, 312, 313, 315, 316, 317, 319, 322, 323, 324, *330*, 339, 356, *363*
Gastinel, J. B., 5, *84*
Gau, W., 183, 184, *189*
Gayer, H., 103, *131*, 200, 209, 210, 213, *261*
Geber, W. F., 210, 216, 224, 238, *261*
Gelehrter, D., 359, *363*
Genest, K., 138, *157*
George, H. R., 341, *363*
Gershon, S., 340, 351, *363*
Ghamrawy, M. A., 142, *157*
Ghosh, B., 211, 254, *260*, 265, 266, *284*, *285*
Ghosh, R., 32, 33, 35, 37, *84*, 101, 128, *131*, 274, *284*

Gidley, J. T., 117, *131*, 213, 214, 230, 243, 248, 249, 251, 252, *261*, 268, *282*
Gill, E. W., 3, 6, 13, 21, 49, *84*, 103, 116, 117, *131*, 138, *157*, 183, 184, *189*, 193, 194, 214, 221, 223, 229, 230, 231, 232, 233, 234, 237, 251, 252, 254, *261*, 270, 275, 276, 281, *283*, 352, 355, *363*
Gillespie, H. K., 104, 106, 109, *131*, 289, 291, 292, 294, 295, 296, 297, 299, 302, 305, 306, 307, 308, 309, 310, 311, 312, 313, 314, 315, 316, 317, 318, 319, 321, 322, 323, 324, 325, 328, *331*, *332*, *333*
Gillespie, R. D., 348, *363*
Gillette, J. R., 175, *182*
Gilmour, D. G., 360, *363*
Girard, J.-P., 358, *363*
Glasspool, M. G., 358, *363*
Glick, S. D., 265, 267, *285*
Goldberg, M. E., 265, *285*
Goldman, J., 196, 211, *260*
Goldsmith, R. S., 312, *333*, 340, *364*
Goldstone, S., 299, *330*
Golhke, R., 247, *261*
Gonzalez, S. C., 265, 266, *282*, *283*
Goodall, A., 216, *262*
Goodman, L. S., 196, 221, *263*
Goodwin, D. W., 288, *331*
Gorodetzky, C. W., 71, *84*, 106, 108, 116, 117, 127, *132*, 206, *262*, 292, 293, 296, 297, 299, 308, 321, 322, 324, *331*
Gould, M. H., 265, 267, *284*, 357, *364*
Gourvés, J., 358, *363*
Graff, H., 297, *331*
Granchelli, F. E., 104, 126, *131*, *132*, 208, 209, 213, 220, 221, 231, 248, *261*
Grandstrand, B., 245, *264*, 361, *364*, *365*
Grant, J. D., 164, *164*
Grayeck, T. L., 53, *84*
Grayson, H. M., 349, *362*
Greb, W., 91, *99*
Green, D. E., 162, 163, *164*, 185, *190*, 268, *283*
Greene, M. L., 189, *189*
Griffin, E. D., Jr., 231, 232, 237, 238, *261*
Grilly, D. M., 265, *283*
Grlić, Lj., 3, 12, *84*, 138, 141, 142, 143, 146, 149, 150, *157*, 200, *262*
Gross, S. J., 163, 164, *164*
Grossman, W., 295, 297, 308, 311, 314, 316, 317, *331*, 340, 344, 353, 354, 356, *363*

Grumpert, J., 316, *331*
Grunfeld, Y., 10, 59, *83*, *85*, 93, 94, 95, 96, 97, *99*, 102, 103, 104, 106, 115, 116, 117, 124, 125, 127, 128, *131*, *132*, 135, *140*, 205, 206, 208, 209, 210, 211, 213, 214, 216, 222, 224, 248, 250, 251, 252, *262*, *263*, 268, *284*
Guerrero, O., 12, *84*, 142, 147, 148, *157*
Gurny, O., 93, 94, *99*, 184, 186, 187, 189, *189*, *190*, 268, *283*, *284*
Gustaffson, B., 268, 270, *282*
Guze, S. B., 288, *331*

H

Haag, M., 10, 26, *85*
Haagen-Smit, A. J., 8, 11, *84*, 196, 201, 202, 226, *260*, *262*
Hackel, E., 43, *85*
Hadley, K., 89, *99*
Haefliger, W., 28, 35, 47, 48, 55, *86*, 107, *132*
Haffner, G., 9, 25, 28, 68, *86*, 115, 117, *133*
Haine, S. E., 69, 70, 71, *85*, 106, *132*, 289, 290, 295, 307, 319, 322, 325, *331*
Haldane, J. B. S., 327, *330*
Halikos, J. A., 288, *331*
Hamaoui, A., 265, 266, *282*
Handa, K. L., 11, *86*, 139, 140, *158*
Handrick, G. R., 49, *86*, 97, *99*
Haney, A., 89, *99*
Hansotia, P., 316, *331*
Harbison, R. D., 268, 269, 271, 272, *283*, *284*
Hardman, H. F., 133, *136*, 222, 223, 231, 232, *262*, 275, 276, *283*, *284*
Harfenist, M., 110, *130*
Harger, R. N., 275, 276, *284*
Harris, L. S., 98, *99*, 104, 126, *131*, *132*, 205, 208, 209, 213, 214, 215, 220, 221, 224, 225, 226, 231, 232, 235, 238, 248, 254, 256, *261*, *263*, 265, 267, 271, 274, 275, 276, 278, 279, *282*, *284*, *285*, 357, *364*
Harris, R. A., 265, 267, 279, *284*
Harris, R. T., 265, *283*
Hay, M., 6, *84*
Haykin, M. D., 289, 319, 328, *330*
Hecht, F., 359, *363*
Hefner, M. A., 265, *285*
Hegnauer, R., 11, *84*
Heinrich, R., 322, *332*, 355, *364*
Hekimian, L. J., 340, 351, *363*

Henderson, A. H., 358, *363*
Henderson, D., 348, *363*
Henriksson, B. G., 211, *262*, 265, *283*
Henry, T. A., 7, *83*
Hensle, T., 358, *364*
Hepler, R. S., 322, *331*
Herring, B. S., 104, *133*, 265, 267, *283*, *285*
Heyndrickx, A., 357, *363*
Himmelsbach, C. K., 109, *133*, 216, *265*, 293, 298, 302, 306, 308, 310, 311, 313, 315, 316, 317, 318, 320, 321, 322, 323, 324, 325, *333*, 339, 355, 356, 357, *363*, 365
Hively, R. L., 11, 13, 22, 61, 75, *84*, 116, *138*
Ho, B. T., 49, *84*, 153, *157*, 168, 178, *182*, *183*, 185, *189*, 206, 241, 246, 247, 248, 249, *262*, *263*, 270, 273, 276, *283*
Ho, D. H. W., 276, *283*
Hochman, J. S., 325, *330*
Hockman, C. H., 209, 210, 218, 226, *262*
Hoffman, N. E., 159, *164*
Hoffmann, F. W., 11, 13, 22, *84*, 116, *131*
Hofmann, A., 184, 186, *190*
Holden, K. G., 56, *86*
Hollister, L. E., 104, 106, 109, *131*, 163, *164*, 288, 289, 290, 291, 292, 294, 295, 296, 297, 299, 302, 305, 306, 307, 308, 309, 310, 311, 312, 313, 314, 315, 316, 317, 318, 319, 320, 321, 322, 323, 324, 325, 328, *331*, *332*, *333*
Holloway, P. J., 144, 148, *156*
Holtzman, D., 213, 223, 226, 227, *262*
Hooper, D., 69, *84*
Hoops, J. F., 125, *131*
Horák, M., 25, 68, *85*
Hoshino, K., 196, 201, 202, 204, 214, 222, 264
Hosko, M. J., 275, 276, *283*
Howes, J. F., 98, *99*, 104, 126, *131*, 208, 209, 213, 220, 221, 229, 231, 232, 233, 248, 250, 254, 257, *261*, 269, 271, 276, *285*
Hsia, J. C., 155, *157*
Hudson, J. B., 150, *156*
Hughes, F. W., 103, *131*, 141, *157*, 213, 221, 222, 228, 237, *261*
Hughes, G. A., 38, 39, 41, 43, *84*
Hughes, J. E., 359, *363*
Hughes, R., 293, 298, 299, 302, 303, 305, 306, 307, 313, 317, 318, 319, 324, *330*
Hume, D. M., 225, *261*

Hunt, M., 8, 17, 28, 80, 81, *82*
Hutchinson, E. D., 104, *131*
Hutchinson, E. D., 211, *260*
⠒⠕⠊⠂⠄⠄ ⠄⠄⠄

I

Icke, R. N., 128, *130*, 196, 201, *260*
Idänpään-Heikkilä, J., 49, *84*, 153, *157*, 168, 178, *182*, *183*, 206, 241, 246, 247, 248, 249, *262*, *263*
Irwin, S., 210, *262*
Isbell, H., 71, *84*, 106, 108, 110, 116, 117, 127, *131*, *132*, 206, *262*, 292, 293, 296, 297, 299, 308, 319, 321, 322, 325, *331*, 357, *363*
Ishikawa, Y., 6, 11, *86*, 138, 139, *158*

J

Jacob, A., 11, 17, *84*
Jacobson, G. M., 178, *182*
Jaffe, J. H., 211, 213, 223, 226, 227, *262*
Jaffe, P. G., 211, *262*
Jahns, E., 5, *84*
Jain, N., 13, *86*
Jain, N. C., 11, 72, *87*
Jakubovič, A., 274, 281, *283*
James, W., 300, *331*
Jandhyala, B. S., 275, 276, *282*, *283*
Janowsky, D. S., 278, *285*
Jansson, I., 279, *284*
Järbe, T., 211, *262*, 265, *283*
Jarvik, M. E., 265, 267, *285*
Jasinski, D. R., 71, *84*, 106, 108, 116, 117, 127, *132*, 206, *262*, 292, 293, 296, 297, 299, 308, 319, 321, 322, 325, *331*, 357, *363*
Jasper, H., 328, *332*
Jelinek, C., 109, *130*, 140, *156*
Jen, T. Y., 38, 39, 41, 43, *84*
Jenkins, J., 271, 275, 276, 279, *282*
Joachimoglu, G., 103, *132*, 168, 172, 173, 178, *183*, 210, 213, 214, 237, *262*
Johansson, U-B., 268, 270, *282*
Johnson, K. M., 266, 273, *283*
Johnson, S., 322, *331*
Johnson, W. S., 67, *84*
Jolly, J., 359, *363*
Jones, G., 183, 184, *189*, 193, *261*, *262*, 270, 275, 276, 278, 281, *283*, 326, *331*

Jones, R. T., 290, 298, 299, 307, 308, 310, 311, 312, 323, 324, 328, *331*, 357, *363*
Jørgensen, F., 340, *363*
Joyce, C. R. B., 4, 56, *84*
Jurd, L., 90, *99*

K

Kabelik, J., 9, 11, *84*, 115, 117, *132*, 220, 221, 235, 237, *262*
Kaegi, H. H., 153, *157*, 183, 189, *190*
Kalant, H., 209, 210, 218, 226, *262*
Kane, R., 359, *362*
Kane, V. V., 24, 41, 53, 54, *84*, *86*
Kanter, S. L., 163, *164*, 325, *331*
Kaplan, H. S., 308, 312, *331*, 341, 343, *363*
Karlsen, J., 11, *83*
Karniol, I. G., 265, 266, *283*
Katz, M. M., 222, *264*, 293, 295, 296, 297, 299, 302, 306, 307, 310, 311, 312, 313, 321, 322, 323, *333*
Kaymakçalan, S., 274, 275, 277, 279, *282*, *283*, 354, 356, 357, *363*
Keeler, M. H., 292, 293, 295, 296, 297, 308, 309, 311, 312, *331*, 340, 342, 349, 353, 360, *363*
Keith, E. S., 12, 71, *84*, 141, 142, 147, 148, *157*
Keller, J. H., 103, *133*, 198, *264*
Keller, J. K., 126, *132*
Kennedy, G. W., 5, *85*
Kennedy, J. S., 104, 126, *131*, *132*, 208, 209, 213, 220, 221, 224, 229, 231, 232, 233, 247, 248, 250, 254, 256, 257, *261*, *262*, *263*, 269, 271, 274, 275, 276, *282*, *283*
Kenny, A. F., 273, *285*
Kersons, L., 274, 275, *282*
Kessaris, J., 274, 275, *282*
Keup, W., 340, *363*
Kew, M. C., 325, *331*
Keylon, V., 358, *363*
Khazan, N., 218, *263*, 272, *282*
Kiburis, J., 70, *85*, 168, 172, 173, 178, *183*, 196, *263*
Kierstead, R. W., 44, 46, 48, *83*, 93, 94, *99*, 171, *182*, 184, 185, 186, 187, 189, *189*, *190*, 268, *283*, *284*
Kilbey, M. M., 266, 273, *283*
Kilsheimer, G. S., 276, *284*
Kimura, M., 89, *99*
King, A. B., 358, *363*

King, L. J., 11, *87*, 141, 154, *157*, 213, 222, 228, 244, *261*, *262*
King, S., 241, *263*
King, W. T., 266, 280, *282*
Kiplinger, G. F., 69, 70, 71, *85*, 106, *132*, 289, 290, 291, 295, 303, 307, 311, 317, 318, 319, 321, 322, 325, 327, *331*, *332*, 355, *363*
Kitazawa, R., 6, *86*
Klausner, H. A., 153, *157*, 173, 178, *183*, 246, 247, *262*, 268, 269, 270, *283*
Klee, G. D., 295, 297, 312, 321, *331*, 340, *363*
Klein, F. K., 6, *85*, 138, *157*, 277, *283*
Kochi, H., 44, *85*
Koepfli, J. B., 8, 11, *84*, 196, 226, *262*
Kolansky, H., 341, 346, 353, 354, *363*
Kolšek, J., 146, *157*
Kopin, I. J., 149, 153, *157*, 176, 180, 181, *183*, 185, *189*, 243, 244, 245, 249, 250, *262*, 352, 354, 356, *363*
Kornhaber, A., 341, 346, *363*
Korte, F., 3, 4, 9, 10, 11, 12, 18, 23, 24, 26, 35, 36, 37, 39, 43, 47, 68, 69, 70, 71, 75, *83*, *84*, *85*, 87, 91, *99*, 103, 104, 106, 108, 116, 117, 127, 128, 129, *131*, *132*, *133*, 144, 145, 146, 148, 151, *156*, *157*, 183, 189, *189*, 196, 201, 203, 205, 205, 210, 251, 254, *261*, *262*, *264*, 266, *282*, *284*, 292, 293, 296, 297, 299, 308, 319, 321, 322, 325, *331*
Kralik, P. M., 153, *157*, 246, *262*
Kramer, C., 196, 210, 211, 224, *260*
Krantz, J. C., 278, *283*
Krejčí, Z., 9, 11, 25, 68, *84*, *85*, 115, 117, *132*, 220, 221, 235, 237, *262*
Kubena, R. K., 97, *99*, 102, 103, 104, *132*, 222, 224, 225, 228, 234, *260*, *262*, 266, 275, 276, *282*, *283*, *285*
Küppers, F. J. E. M., 11, *83*
Kupfer, D., 175, 176, 181, *182*, 269, 279, *282*, *284*
Kuriyama, E., 146, 148, *157*
Kutscheid, B. B., 89, *99*

L
Laddu, A. R., 275, *284*
Ladman, A. J., 231, *331*
Lagerlund, I., 59, 76, *86*
Lahiri, P. K., 275, *284*

Lander, N., 92, *99*
Lapa, A. J., 12, *87*, 196, 201, 202, 203, 219, *262*, *264*
Lawrence, D. K., 270, 276, 281, *283*
Layman, J. M., 228, 233, 247, 252, *262*
Leaf, G., 35, 37, *85*, 109, 110, *132*, 258, *262*
Leander, K., 57, 69, 70, 71, *82*, *87*, 168, 175, 177, *183*, 188, *189*, *190*, 242, *265*, 268, 270, *282*
Leclercq, J., 211, 213, 214, *264*
Lees, M. H., 359, *363*
Leighty, E. G., 56, 57, *84*, 104, 117, *131*, 152, *157*, 174, 177, 178, *182*, 242, 249, *261*
Lele, K. P., 360, *363*
Leluan, D., 358, *363*
Lemberger, L., 149, 153, *157*, 176, 180, 181, *183*, 189, *189*, 243, 244, 245, 249, 250, *262*, 308, 326, *330*, *331*, 352, 354, 356, *363*, *364*
Lemmich, J., 56, *86*
Lenard, K., 35, 40, 61, *87*, 114, *133*
Leonard, B. E., 274, 277, *284*
Lerman, H., 230, *262*
Lerner, M., 71, *85*, 148, 151, *157*, 194, *262*
Lerner, P., 146, 148, *157*, 194, *262*
Leuchtenberger, C., 277, *284*
Leuchtenberger, R., 277, *284*
Levi, L., 11, *86*, 139, 140, *158*
Levine, J., 9, 31, 72, *85*, *87*, 115, *133*, 141, *158*, 196, *265*
Levy, S., 10, 24, *87*, 91, 95, 96, 97, *99*, 135, *136*
Lewis, A., 358, *364*
Liautaud, R., 103, *132*
Lieberman, S., 178, *182*
Liebman, A. A., 153, *157*, 183, 184, *190*
Liebmann, J. A., 88, 89, 98, *99*, 141, *157*
Lighter, D. A., 22, *83*
Linker, A., 311, *333*
Lipparini, F., 103, *132*, 209, 210, 217, 222, 224, 251, 252, 254, 257, *262*
Lipton, M., 185, *190*
Liptzin, M. B., 292, 295, *331*, 340, 342, 349, 353, *363*
Livne, A., 279, *285*
Lloyd, B. J., 109, *133*, 293, 298, 302, 306, 308, 310, 311, 313, 315, 316, 317, 318, 320, 321, 322, 323, 324, 325, *333*, 339, 355, 356, *365*

Loev, B., 114, *133*

Loewe, S., 9, 35, 37, 72, 75, *82*, *87*, 101, 103, 108, 109, 110, 111, 112, 113, 115, 116, 117, 124, 127, 129, *130*, *132*, *133*, 140, 141, *156*, *158*, 196, 198, 200, 201, 202, 203, 204, 208, 209, 210, 213, 214, 216, 221, 222, 225, 226, 228, 230, 231, 232, 235, 236, 237, 241, 251, 252, 253, 258, *262*, *263*, *265*

Lomax, P., 164, *164*, 210, 223, 225, 254, *263*, 278, *284*

Longo, V. G., 103, *132*, 209, 210, 217, 222, 224, 251, 252, 254, 257, *262*

Louria, D. B., 358, *364*

Lousberg, R. J. J. Ch., 11, 88, *83*, *99*

Louzada, N. L., 220, 221, *261*

Lovell, R. A., 213, 223, 226, 227, *262*

Loy, P. R., 193, *261*

Lucas, E. G., 297, *330*, 340, *362*

Lundberg, G. D., 358, *364*

Lurie, M., 44, 46, 48, *83*, 171, *182*

Lusuardi, W., 92, *99*

Luthra, Y. K., 274, *285*

Lutz, M. P., 265, 267, *284*, 357, *364*

Lynch, W. C., 265, *283*

Lys, P., 68, *85*

M

McCarthy, T. J., 159, *164*

Macdonald, A. D., 108, 109, 110, 111, 112, 113, 114, 124, 129, *131*, *132*, 201, *264*

McDonough, J. H., 271, *284*

McGlothlin, W. H., 288, *332*, 346, 354, 356, *364*

McGreer, P. L., 274, 281, *283*

Machata, G., 144, *157*

McIsaac, W. M., 49, *84*, 153, *157*, 168, 178, *182*, *183*, 185, *189*, 206, 241, 246, 247, 248, 249, *262*, *263*, 270, 273, 276, *283*

Mackay, B., 276, *283*

MacKenzie, S., Jr., 110, *130*

McLendon, D. M., 265, 266, 273, *283*

McMillan, D. E., 104, *132*, 205, 215, 224, 235, 254, 256, *261*, *263*, 265, 266, 267, 279, *283*, *284*, 357, *364*

McPhee, W. D., 61, *82*, 124, 129, *130*

Magus, R. D., 226, 235, *263*

Mahoney, J. M., 279, *284*

Maître, L., 227, *263*, 274, *284*

Malareck, D. H., 153, *157*, 183, 189, *190*

Malingré, T. M., 88, *99*

Mandell, G. H., 358, *364*

Mann, P. E. G., 231, *331*

Mannering, G. J., 175, *182*, 279, *282*

Manners, G., 90, *99*

Manning, F. J., 265, 266, 271, *284*

Manno, B. R., 276, *284*

Manno, J. E., 11, 13, 69, 70, 71, 72, *85*, *86*, *87*, 106, *132*, 276, *284*, 289, 290, 291, 295, 307, 311, 317, 318, 319, 321, 322, 325, 327, *331*, 355, *363*

Mantilla-Plata, B., 268, 269, 271, 272, *283*, *284*

Marcovitz, E., 293, 309, 310, 312, 313, 314, 315, 321, 331, 339, 354, 356, *364*

Marderosian, A. H. D., 97, *99*

Marshall, C. R., 6, 7, 69, 71, *85*, 198, *263*

Martin, J., 269, *283*

Martin, J. P., 316, *331*

Martin, L. F., 103, *133*, 139, *157*, 198, *264*

Martin, N. H., 11, 59, *83*, *87*, 141, 146, *156*

Martin, P. A., 241, *263*

Martinez, J. L., 272, 276, *284*

Märtz, R. M. W., 265, 266, 267, 275, 276, *282*, *284*

Marx, H., 201, 208, 210, 225, 226, 231, 234, *263*

Masur, J., 196, 211, 218, 224, 238, 239, *260*, *263*, 265, 266, 267, *282*, *284*

Matchett, J. R., 9, 72, *87*, 115, *133*, 141, *158*, 196, *265*

Matičič, M., 146, *157*

Matsudo, V. K. R., 266, *283*

Matsui, M., 44, *85*

Matsumboto, K., 97, *99*

Matsuo, Y., 23, *87*

Mattison, D. R., 359, *362*

Maximilian, C., 360, *363*

May, A. V., 143, 144, *158*

Maynard, D. E., 93, 94, *99*, 184, 185, 186, 187, *189*, *190*, 268, *283*, *284*

Mechoulam, R., 2, 4, 10, 13, 17, 19, 20, 22, 23, 24, 25, 26, 27, 28, 29, 31, 35, 38, 39, 40, 44, 48, 50, 51, 53, 54, 55, 56, 57, 59, 60, 61, 63, 65, 68, 72, 74, 75, 77, 78, 81, *82*, *83*, *84*, *85*, *86*, 89, 91, 92, 93, 94, 95, 96, 97, *99*, 102, 103, 106, 115, 116, 117, 124, 125, 127, 128, *131*, *132*, *133*, 135, *136*, 139, 140, 141, 142, 143, 144, 145, 147, 149, 150, 151, 152, 153, 154, *156*,

157, *158*, 168, 169, 171, 174, 175, 177, 178, 179, *182*, 183, 184, *190*, 194, 205, 206, 217, 220, 221, 232, 237, 242, 243, 248, 249, 250, 251, 252, 258, *260*, *263*, 268, *282*, *284*, 356, *364*

Mehl, C., 338, 341, 345, *364*

Melges, F. T., 289, 297, 299, 302, 305, 306, 308, 309, 310, 311, 317, *332*, *333*

Menezes, F., 56, *83*, 152, 153, *156*, 174, 175, 177, 178, 179, *182*, 242, 243, *260*

Meresz, O., 139, 141, *158*

Meritt, D. A., 104, *131*, 211, 218, 219, *260*

Merkus, F. W. H. M., 3, 17, 21, *85*, 88, *99*, 145, 146, *158*

Merlini, L., 51, 54, 89, *83*, *99*

Merriam, P. E., 289, 292, 293, 307, 308, *330*

Merz, K. W., 6, *85*

Messiha, F. S., 226, 227, 252, *265*

Meyer, R. E., 346, 348, 349, 354, 355, *364*

Mikeš, F., 69, 70, 71, *85*, 184, 186, *190*, 194, *263*

Miller, K. W., 257, *263*

Miller, L. L., 265, 266, *283*, 303, *332*

Milman, D. H., 340, 354, *364*

Milton, A. S., 228, 233, 247, 252, *262*

Milzoff, J. R., 275, 276, *284*

Miras, C. J., 69, 70, 71, *83*, *85*, 168, 172, 173, 178, *183*, 196, 200, 213, 214, 222, 224, 225, 228, 230, 231, 232, 234, 238, 246, 248, *262*, *263*, 273, *282*

Mirin, S. M., 346, 348, 349, 354, 355, *364*

Montero, J. L., 91, *99*

Moore, F., 163, *164*, 325, *331*

Moore, L. A., 4, *85*

Moore, W. T., 341, 346, 353, 354, *363*

Moreton, J. E., 98, *99*, 210, 218, 254, *263*, 266, 273, 279, 280, *282*, *284*

Mørkholdt Andersen, J., 154, *158*, 163, *164*, *165*

Morrison, A. L., 109, 113, 114, *130*, *131*, 200, 201, 202, 220, 237, *260*

Mosher, W. A., 11, 13, 22, 84, 116, *131*

Moskowitz, D., 350, *364*

Mulder, D. W., 316, *330*

Mummenhoff, P., 37, *83*

Munch, J. C., 198, 208, 209, 210, 226, 253, *263*

Munson, P. L., 225, *263*

Murphy, H. B. M., 288, *332*

Murthy, S. N. S., 97, *99*

Myers, H. B., 254, *263*

Myers, H. J., 292, 309,' 310, 312, 313, 314, 315, 321, *331*, 339, 354, 356, *364*

Myers, S. A., 289, 292, 293, 307, 308, 312, *330*

N

Nahas, G. G., 288, *332*

Nakazawa, K., 184, *190*, 268, 269, *284*, 289, 292, 293, 298, 299, 302, 303, 305, 306, 307, 313, 317, 318, 319, 324, *330*

Neel, M. A., 278, *285*

Negm, H., 142, *157*

Neide da Silva, T. N., 103, *133*, 196, 203, 204, 216, *264*

Neide Hyppolito, 103, *133*, 194, 196, 201, 202, *264*

Nelsen, J. M., 104, 106, *133*, 289, 290, 293, 295, 297, 298, 307, 310, 314, 316, 319, 321, 322, 325, *333*, 354, *365*

Nelson, D. F., 143, 144, *158*

Nelson, D. H., 225, *261*

Neto, J. P., 266, 274, *284*

Neu, R. L., 241, *263*, 359, 362

Neumeyer, J. L., 4, *85*

Newby, V. E., 231, 232, 237, 238, *261*

Newman, L. M., 265, 267, *284*, 357, *364*

Nielsen, B. E., 56, *86*

Nielsen, E., 154, *158*, 163, *164*, *165*, 243, *260*

Nigam, I. C., 11, *86*, 139, 140, *158*

Nigam, M. C., 11, *86*, 139, 140, *158*

Nilsson, I. M., 12, 46, 56, 57, 59, 76, 86, *86*, *87*, 96, *99*, 117, *132*, 152, 153, *156*, 168, 170, 171, 173, 174, 175, 176, 177, 178, 179, 180, *182*, *183*, 184, 188, *189*, *190*, 242, 243, 244, 245, 246, 248, *260*, *263*, *264*, *265*, 268, 270, *282*, 361, *364*, *365*

Nilsson, J. L. G., 46, 56, 57, 59, 76, *86*, *87*, 96, *99*, 117, *132*, 152, *158*, 168, 170, 171, 174, 175, 176, 177, 180, *183*, 184, 188, *189*, *190*, 242, 248, *263*, *265*, 268, 270, *282*, 288, *330*, 361, *365*

Nilsson, L., 268, *282*

Nishioka, I., 11, 13, 23, 26, 31, 68, 69, 70, 72, 77, *86*, *87*, 194, *264*, *265*

Noble, E., 325, *331*

Nordqvist, M., 268, 270, *282*

Norton, S., 104, *132*

O

Obata, Y., 6, 11, *86*, 138, 139, *158*
Ohloff, G., 28, 35, 47, 48, 55, *86*
Ohlsson, A., 12, 56, *86*, 117, *132*, 152, 153, *156*, *158*, 173, 174, 175, 176, 177, 178, 179, 180, *182*, *183*, 184, *189*, 242, 243, 244, 245, 246, 248, *260*, *263*, 270, *282*
Okamoto, K., 89, *99*, 277, *284*
Olofsson, K., 12, *86*
Olson, J., 266, *282*
Olsson, J. E., 222, *264*, 293, 295, 296, 297, 299, 302, 306, 307, 310, 311, 312, 313, 321, 322, 323, *333*
O'Rourke, T., 271, 275, 276, 279, *282*
Orrenius, S., 279, *284*
Orsingher, O. A., 265, *284*
Osadchuk, M., 141, *157*
Oskoui, M., 275, 276, *284*
O'Shaughnessy, W. B., 192, *263*
Otis, L. S., 185, *190*, 268, *283*
Ourisson, G., 37, *83*

P

Pace, H. B., 240, 241, *263*, 266, 272, 280, *282*, *284*
Page, T. F., 56, 57, *84*, 104, 117, *131*, 152, *157*, 174, 177, 178, *182*, 242, 249, *261*
Paris, M., 88, *99*
Pal, B., 274, *284*
Parker, C. S., 292, 294, 295, 297, 306, 310, 312, 313, 315, 317, 322, 323, 325, *332*
Parker, C. W., 155, *158*
Parker, J. M., 163, *164*
Parkes, M. W., 109, 113, 114, *130*, 200, 201, 202, 220, 237, *260*
Pars, H. G., 98, *99*, 104, 117, 126, 128, *131*, *132*, 208, 209, 213, 220, 221, 231, 248, *261*, 269, 271, 276, *285*
Pascall, D. C. S., 32, *84*
Paton, W. D. M., 6, 13, 21, *84*, 103, 116, 117, *131*, 138, *157*, 193, 194, 195, 214, 221, 223, 224, 229, 230, 231, 232, 233, 234, 237, 238, 239, 251, 252, 254, 256, 257, *262*, *263*, *264*, 269, 270, 271, 276, 277, 278, 281, *283*, *284*, 288, *332*, 352, 355, 361, *363*, *364*
Patterson, D. A., 146, *158*, 196, 197, *261*
Pease, D. C., 21, 32, *82*
Penfield, W., 328, *332*
Peng, T.-C., 224, 225, *261*

Perelman, L., 339, 346, *362*
Perez-Reyes, M., 189, *190*
Perhach, J. L., Jr., 224, 225, 234, *260*, *262*
Perna, D., 340, *364*
Peron, F. G., 155, *158*
Perrie, R. G., 209, 210, 218, 226, *262*
Persaud, T. V. N., 238, 240, *264*
Personne, J., 5, *86*
Persyko, I., 311, *332*
Pertwee, R. G., 6, 13, 21, *84*, 103, 116, 117, *131*, 138, *157*, 184, *189*, 193, 194, 195, 204, 214, 221, 223, 224, 229, 230, 231, 232, 233, 234, 237, 238, 239, 251, 252, 254, 256, *262*, *263*, *264*, 269, 270, 271, 276, 277, 278, 281, *283*, *284*, 352, 355, 361, *363*, *364*
Petcoff, D. G., 69, *86*
Peterson, D. W., 265, 279, *282*, *285*, *331*
Petrzilka, T., 28, 35, 47, 48, 55, *86*, 92, *99*, 107, *132*
Pfeiffer, C. C., 219, *260*
Phillips, R. N., 13, *86*, 235, 237, *264*, 278, *285*
Pillard, R. C., 288, *332*, 346, 348, 349, 354, 355, *364*
Pirch, J. H., 267, 268, 272, 280, *282*, *285*
Pitcher, R. G., 93, 94, *99*, 184, 185, 186, 187, 189, *189*, 268, *283*, *284*
Pitt, C. G., 11, 56, 59, *83*, *87*, 117, *131*, *133*, *141*, 146, 149, 152, *156*, *158*, 168, 170, 171, 174, 176, 178, *183*, 213, 214, 230, 242, 243, 248, 249, 250, 252, *264*, 269, *282*
Pivik, R. T., 313, *332*
Podolsky, S., 325, *332*
Polaczek, E., 88, *99*
Pond, D. A., 291, 293, 294, 295, 296, 298, 306, 307, 308, 309, 310, 312, 313, 314, 316, 317, 318, 319, 324, *332*
Ponsford, R., 24, 41, 52, 53, 54, 63, 75, *83*
Poole, J., 196, 215, 223, *264*
Porath, G., 59, *82*, 106, 117, 124, 127, *131*, 268, *282*
Porter, C. D., 235, *264*, 325, *332*
Pos, R., 329, *330*
Potvin, R. J., 266, *285*
Powell, G., 8, *86*
Powers, H. O., 241, *263*
Pradhan, S. N., 211, 254, *260*, 265, 266, *285*
Prado Seabra, A., 211, 213, 214, *264*

Prater, A. N., 8, 11, *84*, 196, 226, *262*
Preble, M., 321, *332*
Prendergast, T. J., 321, *332*
Preobraschensky, B., 5, *86*
Price, P. J., 277, *285*
Proctor, R. C., 318, 321, *332*, 357, *364*
Prosnitz, E. H., 358, *364*
Prychodko, W., 223, *264*
Pugsley, D. J., 358, *363*
Puttick, A. J., 97, *99*

Q

Quimby, M. W., 12, 71, *84*, 141, 142, 147, 148, *157*

R

Rafaelson, O. J., 180, *182*, 243, *261*, 328, *332*
Ramachandran, S., 11, *87*
Ramsay, C. H., 268, 270, *282*
Ramsay, H. H., 221, *261*
Raphaelsen, O. J., 163, *164*
Rapoport, H., 6, 56, *85*, *86*, 138, *157*, 277, *283*
Raventos, J., 220, 235, 237, *261*
Raz, A., 279, *285*
Razdan, R. K., 41, 49, 53, 54, 63, 65, *84*, *86*, 92, 97, 98, *99*, 104, 117, 126, 128, *131*, *132*, 150, *158*, 208, 209, 213, 220, 221, 231, 248, *261*, 269, 271, 276, *285*
Reavis, W. M., 231, 232, 237, 238, *261*
Reifler, C. B., 292, 295, *331*, 340, 342, 349, 353, 360, *363*
Renault, P. F., 322, *332*, 355, *364*
Repič, R., 146, *157*
Ribi, E., 69, *86*
Richards, A. B., 103, *131*, 213, 221, 222, 228, 237, *261*
Richards, R. K., 104, 106, 109, *131*, 291, 292, 294, 295, 296, 297, 299, 302, 305, 306, 308, 310, 311, 313, 314, 315, 316, 317, 318, 319, 321, 322, 323, 324, 325, *331*
Rinderknecht, H., 110, *131*
Robbins, E. S., 360, *363*
Roberts, P., 359, *363*
Robertson, A., 5, *86*
Robertson, D. N., 247, *261*
Robichaud, R. C., 265, *285*

Robiquet, E., 5, *86*
Robson, J. G., 327, *332*
Rodda, B. E., 71, *85*, 219, 307, 311, 317, 318, 319, 321, 322, *331*, 355, *363*
Rose, J., 358, *364*
Rose, S. D., 162, *164*
Rosenblatt, J. E., 278, *285*
Rosenfeld, J., 96, *99*, 162, *164*, 184, 186, 189, *189*, 268, *282*
Rosenfeld, R., 117, *131*, 213, 214, 230, 243, 248, 249, 250, *261*, 268, 269, *282*
Rosenkranz, H., 98, *99*, 266, 274, *285*
Rosenthaler, L., 69, *86*
Roth, W. T., 308, 326, *330*
Rouse, B. A., 297, *331*
Rowan, P. K., 288, *332*
Rowe, H. M., 185, *190*, 354, *364*
Ruble, D. C., 109, *133*, 216, *265*, 293, 298, 302, 306, 308, 310, 311, 313, 315, 316, 317, 318, 320, 321, 322, 323, 324, 325, *333*, 339, 355, 356, *365*
Rushton, R., 210, *264*
Russell, P. B., 108, 109, 110, 111, 112, 113, 114, 124, 129, *132*, 201, *264*
Ryrfeldt, A., 268, 270, *282*

S

Saifi, A. Q., 103, *131*, 196, 201, 208, 209, 216, 222, 226, 228, 230, 231, 232, 233, 235, *260*
Salemink, C. A., 6, 11, *83*, *86*, 88, *99*, 138, *158*, 252, *260*
Saller, C., 271, *284*
Salmon, M., 8, *86*
Salustiano, J., 196, 201, 202, 204, 214, 222, *264*
Salzman, C., 222, *264*, 293, 295, 296, 297, 299, 302, 306, 307, 310, 311, 312, 313, 321, 322, 323, *333*
Sampaio, C. A. M., 196, 219, *262*, *264*
Sampaio, M. R. P., 103, *132*, 201, 202, 213, *264*
Samrah, H., 88, *99*
Sandberg, F., 12, 56, *86*, 117, *132*, 152, 153, 156, *158*, 173, 174, 175, 176, 177, 178, 179, 180, *182*, *183*, 242, 243, 244, 245, 246, 248, *260*, *263*, *264*, 268, 270, *282*, 361, *364*, *365*
Sanders-Busk, E., 214, 220, 221, *260*, 274, *283*

Šantový, F., 9, 11, 18, 25, 63, 68, *84, 85, 86,* 115, 117, *132,* 220, 221, 235, 237, *262*

Santos, M., 103, 104, 108, 128, 129, *131,* 201, 202, 203, 205, 210, 213, 214, 251, *261, 264*

Sato, T., 69, 70, *86,* 194, *264*

Sanders, D. R., 189, *189*

Savory, 5, *86*

Schaeppi, U. H., 272, 276, *284*

Scheckel, C. L., 102, 104, 106, *132,* 205, 206, 208, 224, 226, 237, 258, *264*

Scheiris, C., 357, *363*

Schell, F. M., 97, *99*

Schepens, P., 357, *363*

Scher, J., 311, 313, *332,* 346, 354, 355, 356, *364*

Schiff, B. B., 104, *130,* 211, 224, 254, *260*

Schigehiro, M., 146, *157*

Schildkraut, J. J., 211, 226, 227, *264*

Schlesinger, S., 5, *86*

Scholtz, W. S., 289, 307, 319, 321, 327, *331*

Schou, J., 154, *158,* 163, *164, 165,* 243, *260*

Schramm, L. C., 210, 216, 224, 238, *261*

Schultz, O. E., 3, 8, 25, 28, 68, *86,* 115, 117, *133*

Schultze, E., 6, *86*

Schurr, A., 279, *285*

Schuster, C. R., 322, *332,* 355, *364*

Schwartz, W. E., 56, 57, *84,* 104, 117, *131,* 152, *157,* 174, 177, 178, *182,* 242, 249, *261*

Scott, K. G., 235, *264,* 325, *332*

Scott, L. T., 357, *364*

Scotti de Carolis, A., 209, 210, 217, 222, 224, 251, 252, 254, 257, *262*

Seevers, M. H., 133, *136,* 222, 223, 231, 232, *262*

Segal, M., 273, *285*

Segelman, A. B., 97, *99,* 266, *283*

Servi, S., 89, *99*

Shagoury, R. A., 4, *85*

Shalev, J., 358, *364*

Shani, A., 10, 13, 27, 54, 55, 56, 65, 68, 75, 76, *83, 85, 86,* 91, 94, 96, 97, *99,* 102, 106, 115, 116, 117, 124, 127, *131, 133,* 135, *136,* 140, *149,* 205, 206, 250, 251, 252, *263*

Shapiro, L. M., 346, 348, 349, 354, 355, *364*

Sheehan, J. C., 98, *99,* 269, 271, 276, *285*

Sheep, W. L., 338, *364*

Sherwood, S. L., 320, *331*

Shimomura, H., 146, 148, *157*

Shoyama, Y., 11, 13, 23, 26, 31, 68, 69, 70, 72, 77, *86, 87,* 194, *264, 268*

Shvo, Y., 17, 22, 35, 38, 40, 61, 77, *85, 87*

Siebold, L., 5, *86*

Siegel, R. K., 104, *133,* 196, 215, 223, *264*

Sieper, H., 9, 10, 11, 12, 24, 35, 36, 43, 75, *85,* 144, 145, 146, 151, *157*

Siew, S., 325, *331*

Sikemeier, C., 28, 35, 47, 48, 55, *86,* 107, *132*

Silberstein, S. D., 149, 153, *157,* 176, 180, *183,* 243, 244, 245, *262,* 352, 354, *363*

Siler, J. F., 338, *364*

Silva, M. T. A., 104, *133,* 196, 254, 255, *264*

Sim, V., 108, 110, *133*

Simic, S., 88, 89, 98, *99,* 141, *157*

Simonsen, J. L., 11, *86,* 139, *158*

Simos, S., 70, *85,* 196, *263*

Singer, A. J., 288, *332*

Skinner, G. C., 162, *164*

Skinner, R. F., 164, *165*

Skliar, N., 338, 354, 356, *364*

Smart, T., 102, 104, 106, *132,* 205, 206, 208, 224, 226, 237, 258, *264*

Smith, C. M., 35, 37, *82,* 111, 112, 124, 129, *130*

Smith, D. E., 338, 341, 345, *364*

Smith, D. M., 139, *157*

Smith, E. B., 257, *263*

Smith, H., 5, 38, 39, 41, 43, *84, 86*

Smith, K., 189, *189*

Smith, T., 5, *86*

Smith, W. A. S., 338, *364*

So, B., 277, *284*

Sodetz, F. J., 265, 271, *282, 284*

Sofia, R. D., 227, 228, *264,* 273, 274, 275, *285*

Solomon, T. A., 273, *285*

Soueif, M. I., 292, 297, 302, 305, 306, 309, 310, 311, 312, 313, 316, 317, *332*

Souza, J. A., 103, *133,* 194, 196, 201, 202, *264*

Spahn, G. J., 277, *285*

Sparber, S. B., 265, *285*

Staehelin, M., 227, *263*

Spaulding, T. C., 278, *285*

Spector, S., 155, *158*

Steentoft, A., 243, *260*

Spencer, D. J., 341, *364*
Sperling, F., 276, *285*
Spivey, W. T. N., 5, 6, 7, 8, 13, *87*, 115, *133*, 139, *159*
Sprague, R. A., 274, *285*
Stadnicki, S. W., 272, 276, *284*
Steahly, L. P., 359, *363*
Steck, W., 56, *86*
Steentoft, A., 154, *158*, 163, *164*, *165*
Steinberg, H., 210, *264*, 304, 305, 327, *332*
Sterne, J., 358, *364*
Stevens, H. M., 146, *158*
Stevens, K., 90, *99*
Stone, C. J., 275, 276, *284*
Stone, G. C., 290, 298, 299, 307, 310, 311, 312, 323, 324, 328, *331*, 357, *363*
Strain, S. M., 69, *86*
Strojny, E. J., 38, *87*
Strömberg, L. E., 160, *165*
Suqar, S. H., 358, *364*
Suk, W. A., 277, *285*
Sulser, F., 274, *283*
Summerfield, A., 304, 305, 327, *332*
Sundström, G., 107, *131*
Suter, C. M., 107, *133*
Svendsen, A. B., 11, *83*

T
Talbott, J. A., 292, 295, 297, 302, 305, 306, 308, 311, 312, 314, 315, 316, 318, 319, 321, *332*, 340, 343, 353, *364*
Tamarkin, N. R., 153, *157*, 180, 181, *183*, 352, 354, 356, *363*
Tangary, M. R., 103, *133*, 196, 203, 204, 216, *264*
Tart, C. T., 288, 313, *332*
Tayleur-Stockings, G., 291, 292, 293, 294, 295, 305, 306, 309, 310, 311, 313, 314, 316, 317, 319, 321, 322, 324, 325, *332*
Taylor, D., 273, *283*
Taylor, E. C., 35, 38, 40, 61, *87*, 114, *133*
Teague, J. W., 292, 295, 297, 302, 305, 306, 308, 311, 312, 314, 315, 316, 318, 319, 321, *332*, 340, 343, 353, *364*
Temple, D. M., 224, 234, *264*, 270, 271, 276, 277, 281, *284*, 352, *364*
Tennant, F. S., 321, *332*
Testino, L., 117, *131*, 213, 214, 230, 243, 248, 249, 251, 252, *261*, 269, *282*
Theiner, M., 97, *99*, 266, *283*

Theobald, C. W., 111, 112, *130*
Thompson, G. R., 98, *99*, 266, 274, *285*
Thompson, L. J., 318, 321, *332*, 357, *364*
Thompson, W. R., 126, *132*
Thomson, J. L. G., 320, *330*, 360, *362*
Thurlow, H. J., 341, 346, *364*
Timmons, M. L., 168, 170, 171, 174, *183*, 185, *190*
Timo-Laria, C., 219, *262*
Tinklenberg, J. R., 289, 297, 299, 302, 305, 306, 308, 309, 310, 311, 317, *332*, *333*
Tinson, C., 210, *264*
Tira, S., 9, 35, *85*
Todd, A. R., 3, 5, 8, 11, 17, 29, 32, 33, 35, 37, *84*, *85*, *86*, *87*, 101, 103, 108, 109, 110, 111, 112, 113, 114, 115, 116, 124, 128, 129, *131*, *132*, 139, 140, *158*, 201, 258, *262*, *264*
Toffoli, F., 141, *158*
Toker, E., 339, *364*
Tomiyasu, N., 144, *156*
Torres, D. M., 162, *164*
Truitt, E. B., 56, 57, *84*, 104, 117, *131*, 152, 153, *157*, *158*, 174, 177, 178, *182*, 228, 242, 248, *261*, 264
Tscheepe, 4, *87*
Tsukamato, H., 144, *156*
Turk, R. F., 11, 13, 72, *86*, *87*, 235, 237, 254, *263*, *264*, 268, *282*
Turnbull, J. H., 150, *156*
Turner, C. E., 89, *99*, 148, *157*
Tursch, B. M., 211, 213, 214, *264*
Tylden, E., 312, 316, 321, 324, *333*, 339, 340, 346, 349, 354, 356, 360, *364*
Tyminski, I. J., 19, 20, 22, 78, *82*

U
Ungerleider, J. T., 312, *333*, 340, *364*
Upton, A., 316, *331*

V
Valente, L., 5, *87*
Valle, J. R., 12, *87*, 103, *133*, 194, 196, 201, 203, 204, 213, 216, 219, 222, *262*, *264*
van Ginneken, C. A. M., 3, 17, 19, 21, 88, *87*, *99*
van Rossum, J. M., 3, 17, 19, 21, 88, *87*, *99*
Van Zyl, J. D., 159, *164*
Varconi, H., 74, 78, 80, *87*, 91, 93, 94, *99*, 135, *136*, 268, *284*

Vaughan, T. B., 308, 326, *330*
Veen, E., 6, *86*, 138, *158*
Ventry, P., 321, *332*
Verner, D., 90, 97, *98*
Viallard, C., 358, *363*
Vieira, F. J. A., 211, 213, 214, *264*
Vignolo, G., 5, *87*
Vijayvorgiya, R., 196, 216, 231, 233, *260*
Vögele, K., 15, *83*
Volavka, J., 320, *333*
Vollner, L., 3, 10, 19, 47, *87*
von Spulak, F., 10, 23, 24, 71, *83, 84, 87*, 106, 108, 116, 117, 127, *132*, 206, *262*, 292, 293, 296, 297, 308, 319, 321, 322, 325, *331*
Vree, T. B., 3, 17, 19, 21, *87*, 88, *99*

W

Waddell, W. J., 247, *262*, 269, *283*
Wagner, R., 7, *83*
Wahlqvist, M., 56, *86*, 117, *132*, 152, *158*, 174, 176, 177, 178, *183*, 242, 245, 248, *263, 264*, 361, *364*
Wall, M. E., 11, 56, 59, *83, 87*, 117, *131, 133*, 141, 146, 149, 152, 153, *156, 158*, 168, 170, 171, 172, 174, 175, 176, 177, 178, 180, *183*, 184, 185, *190*, 213, 214, 230, 242, 243, 248, 249, 251, 252, *261, 264*, 269, *282, 283*
Wallace, J. E., 289, 319, 328, *330*
Waller, C. W., 4, 12, *84, 87*, 142, 147, 148, *157*, 288, *333*
Walpole, A. L., 220, 235, 237, *261*
Walter, J. L., 56, 57 *84*, 104, 117, *131*, 152, *157*, 174, 177, 178, *182*, 242, 249, *261*
Walters, G. C., 104, *133*, 216, *264*, 265, 267, *285*
Walton, R. P., 4, 8, 69, *86, 87*, 103, *133*, 198, 199, 208, 209, 210, 216, 219, 225, 226, *264*, 354, 357, 358, *364*
Waser, P. G., 69, 70, 71, *85*, 184, 185, *190*, 194, *263*
Waskow, I. E., 222, *264*, 293, 295, 296, 297, 299, 303, 306, 307, 310, 311, 312, 313, 321, 322, 323, *333*
Waters, W., 265, *283*
Watson, J., 274, *282*
Watanabe, A. M., 185, *190*, 326, *331*
Wawra, C. Z., 8, 11, *84*, 196, 226, *262*

Wearn, R. B., 21, 33, 61, *82*
Webster, C. D., 104, *133*, 265, 267, *285*
Weetall, H. H., 163, *164*
Weil, A. T., 104, 106, *133*, 289, 290, 293, 295, 296, 297, 298, 306, 307, 310, 311, 314, 316, 319, 321, 322, 325, *333*, 341, 345, 349, 351, 352, 353, 354, *365*
Weiss, J. L., 185, *190*, 326, *331*
Welch, A. S., 226, 227, 252, *265*
Welch, B. L., 226, 227, 252, *265*, 278, *283*
Weingartner, H., 308, 326, *330*
Weinhardt, K. K., 92, *99*
Welt, P. J. L., 327, *332*
Wenkert, E., 97, *99*
Werner, E., 154, *156*, 178, *182*
West, L. J., 314, *333*, 346, 354, 356, *364*, *365*
Weston, A. W., 107, *133*
Whiting, D. A., 24, *82*
Widman, M., 57, *87*, 168, 175, 177, *183*, 184, 188, *189, 190*, 242, *265*, 268, 270, *282*, 361, *365*
Wijisbeek, J., 88, *99*
Wikler, A., 109, *133*, 216, *265*, 266, *283*, 293, 298, 302, 306, 308, 310, 311, 313, 315, 316, 317, 318, 320, 321, 322, 323, 324, 325, *333*, 339, 355, 356, *365*
Wilcox, H. G., 269, *283*
Wildes, J. W., 11, 59, *83, 87*, 141, 146, *156*
Wilkinson, S., 32, 33, 35, 37, *84, 85*, 101, 108, 109, 110, 111, 112, 113, 114, 124, 128, 129, *131, 132*, 201, 258, *262, 264*
Williams, E. G., 109, *133*, 216, *265*, 293, 298, 302, 306, 308, 310, 311, 313, 315, 316, 317, 318, 320, 321, 322, 323, 324, 325, *333*, 339, 355, 356, *365*
Williams, M. J., 320, *330*
Williamson, E., 56, *83*, 152, 153, *156*, 174, 175, 177, 178, 179, *182*, 242, 243, *260*
Willinsky, M. D., 104, *133*, 142, 145, 146, 148, 153, *158*, 160, *165*, 265, 267, *285*
Wilson, C. W. M., 311, *333*
Wilson, W. D. C., 146, *156*
Winek, C. L., 143, *157*
Winternitz, F., 91, *99*
Witte, A. H., 3, 17, 19, 21, *87*, *99*
Wittstruck, T., 96, *99*, 162, *164*, 184, 186, 189, *189*, 268, *282*
Wolfe, J. R., 339, *363*
Wolff, H., 21, *82*, 109, *130*, 140, *156*

Wollner, H. J., 9, 72, *87*, 115, *133*, 141, *158*, 196, *265*
Wong, R., 164, *164*
Wood, T. B., 5, 6, 7, 8, 13, *87*, 115, *133*, 139, *158*
Woods, J. H., 215, 254, 256, *260*
Woods, L. A., 222, 223, 231, *262*
Woolfe, G., 108, 109, 110, 111, 112, 113, 124, 129, *131*, *132*, 201, *264*
Work, T. S., 8, *87*
Worm, K., 154, *158*, 163, *164*, *165*, 243, *260*
Wright, D. C., 35, 37, *84*, 101, *131*
Wrigley, F., 292, 294, 295, 297, 306, 310, 312, 313, 316, 317, 322, 323, 325, *332*
Würsch, M. S., 185, *190*, 268, *283*
Wyatt, R. J., 185, *190*, 308, 326, *330*, *331*

Y
Yagen, B., 10, 25, 50, 54, 63, 65, *85*, *87*
Yagnitinsky, B., 10, 13, 27, 51, 54, 56, 63, 65, 68, 72, 75, *83*, *85*, 102, 115, 117, *132*, 149, 154, *158*, 205, *263*

Yamaguchi, A., 69, 70, *86*, 194, *264*
Yamauchi, T., 11, 13, 23, 26, 31, 68, 69, 70, 72, 77, *86*, *87*, 194, *264*, *265*
Yang, R. K., 159, *164*
Yardley, D. C. M., 354, *365*
Yonce, L. R., 231, 232, 237, 238, *261*
Yoshimura, H., 144, *156*

Z
Zaks, A., 320, *333*
Zarcore, V., 313, *332*
Zecchinelli, V. A., 341, *362*
Zeffert, J. T., 194, *262*
Zemler, H., 91, 95, 96, 97, *99*, 135, *136*, 143, *158*
Zerkin, E. L., 4, *84*, 288, *330*
Zimmerberg, B., 265, 267, *285*
Zinberg, N. E., 104, 106, *133*, 289, 290, 293, 295, 297, 298, 306, 307, 310, 314, 316, 319, 321, 322, 325, *333*, 354, *365*
Zitko, B. A., 63, 65, *86*, 97, 98, *99*, 269, 271, 276, *285*
Zubyk, W. J., 61, *87*

Subject Index*

A

Abstinence syndrome, for cannabis, 356
3-Acetamido-4-cyanotoluene, in cannabinol synthesis, 32
6β-Acetoxy-1-hydroxyhexahydrocannabinol acetate, synthesis of, 59
6β-Acetoxy-Δ⁷-tetrahydrocannabinol, *58*
   synthesis of, 57
6′-Acetoxy-Δ⁶-tetrahydrocannabinol acetate, *122*
   inactivity of, 122
7-Acetoxy-Δ⁶-tetrahydrocannabinol acetate
   synthesis of, 57
   as synthetic intermediate, 58
Acetyl cannabidiol, *77*
   from cannabidiol esters, 76–77
Acetyl cannabidiol acetate, *77*
   from cannabidiol esters, 76–77
Acetyl cannabinol
   dealkylation of, 16
   early research on, 7
   in isolation of cannabinol, 8
4′-Acetyl-Δ⁶-tetrahydrocannabinol, *121*
   inactivity of, 121
Acuity, cannabis effects on, 292–293
Adrenocorticotropic hormone (ACTH), cannabinoid effects on activity of, 225, 257–258
Adsorption chromatography
   in cannabinoid determination, 144
   for cannabinoid extraction, 141

Aggression
   cannabinoid effects on, 104, 106, 266–267
      in man, 311–312
   test, for cannabinoids, 103, 214
Alcohol
   as cannabinoid solvent, 193
   cannabis effects compared to, 314, 323, 328, 357
   cannabis synergism with, 307, 325
Alcohols A and B, in cannabis oil, 140
Alkaloids
   active cannabis principle and, 5–6
   in cannabis, 6, 88, 277
      determination, 138
   early research on, 4
5-Alkylresorcinols, in Δ³-THC synthesis, 107
Amines, in brain, *see* Brain amines
Aminopyrine, THC inhibition of, metabolism of, 269
Amotivational syndrome, from cannabis, 312–314, 346–350
Amphetamine(s)
   cannabinoid comparison to, 212, 215, 267, 349, 351
   cannabinoid interaction with, 221–222, 253, 259, 278
Analgesia
   from cannabinoids, 220, 253, 274–275
   effects on man, 294–295
4-Androstene-3,17-dione as glc internal standard, 148

*Pages in italics show chemical structures.

389

Anemia, from cannabis, 325–326
Anesthetics, cannabis action compared to, 327
Animals, cannabis pharmacology in, 191–285
Anisidine salt, *see* Fast Blue Salt B
Antibiotics, cannabinoids as, 115, 117, 235
Anticonvulsant action, of cannabinoids, 272–273
Antidepressant, synhexyl as, 101
Antidiuretic hormone, cannabinoid effects on activity of, 234, 257
Antidotes, for psychotomimetic cannabinoids, tests for, 106
Aphrodisiac, cannabis as, 314–315
Appetite, cannabinoid effects on, 205–207, 211, 224, 324, 325
Archimedes spiral test, in marijuana studies, 292
Aryl hydrocarbon hydroxylase, induction by marijuana, 277
Ascaris, cannabinoid effects on, 216
Ataxia, cannabis effects on, in man, 317–319
Ataxia test
    for cannabinoid activity, 101, 197, 198–200, 205, 208–209, 253
    of Δ^3-THC derivatives, 108–114
Atherosclerosis, cannabis use and, 358–359
ATPase activity, effect of THC on, 279
Atropinelike action, of cannabinoids, 6, 253
Atropinelike substances, cannabinoid comparison with, 259, 267
Auditory perception, cannabis effects on, 293–294
Autonomic nervous system
    cannabinoid effects on, 231–232, 275
    in man, 320–324
Azacannabinoids
    psychomimetic studies on, 125–126
    synthesis of, 91
Aza-Δ^3-tetrahydrocannabinol, *125*
    inactivity of, 125
Azobenzoic acid derivatives, of cannabinoids, 163

B

Balfourdine, synthesis of, 56

Barbiturates
    cannabinoid comparison to, 215, 267, 357
    cannabinoid effects on activity of, 197, 228–230, 257, 258
Bamberger reaction, in cannabinoid synthesis, 32
Beam colorimetric test, for cannabinoids, 17, 74, 142–143, 144, 159, 197
Behavior, cannabinoid effects on, 106, 197, 205–208, 253, 265–268
Benactyzine, cannabinoid comparison to, 215
α-Bergamotene, in cannabis oil, 140
Bhang, majoun preparation from, 193
Bibliographies, on cannabis, 4, 88
Bile
    cannabinoid analysis of, 154
    metabolite excretion by, 175, 184, 186, 244, 257, 268, 325
Bioassay, of cannabis activity, 197–205
Biogenesis, of cannabinoids, 29–31
Biological fluids, cannabinoid detection in, 153–156, 162–164
Blood
    cannabinoid determination in, 164
    cannabinoid metabolites in, 246, 247
    as cannabinoid solvent, 193
    THC binding by, 269
Blood pressure, cannabinoid effects on, 231, 232, 275–276, 322–323
Blood sugar, cannabinoid effects on, 234, 325
Body weight, cannabinoid effects on, 224
Bovine serum albumin, in radioimmunoassay of THC, 155
Bradycardia, from cannabinoids, 231, 275, 322
Brain
    atrophy of, from cannabis use, 360
    cannabinoid effects on metabolism of, 235, 280
    cannabinoid metabolites in, 270
    isotope studies, 178, 246, 247–248
Brain amines, cannabinoid interaction with, 226–228, 273–274
Breath, of cannabis users, colorimetric test for, 159
Bulbocapnine, cannabinoid comparison to, 203, 204
Butallylonal, *see* Pernocton

C

Caffeine
  cannabinoid comparison to, 212, 267
  cannabinoid interaction with, 278
Camphene, in cannabis oil, 140
Cannabamines, in marijuana, 6
Cannabichromene, *23, 26, 30, 51, 53, 368*
  analogs of, syntheses and reactions, 91
  biosynthesis of, 30
  from cannabichromenic acid, 26
  from cannibigerol dehydrogenation, 74
  in cannabis material, isolation of, 142
  cyclization of, 63, 65
  gas-liquid chromatography of, 147
  infrared spectroscopy of, 151
  isolation of, 10
  pharmacological activity, 116, 117
  photochemical reaction of, 75
  as racemic compound, 24, 28, 31
  structure studies on, 23–24
  synthesis of, 51–54
  tetracyclic ether, *51*
    synthesis, 52
  thin-layer chromatography of, 145
  uv spectroscopy of, 149
Cannabichromene acetate, cyclization of, 63, 65
Cannabichromenic acid, *26, 30, 368*
  biosynthesis of, 30
  optical inactivity of, 30
  structure studies on, 26
  thermal reactions of, 68
Cannabicyclol, *25, 31, 66, 368*
  biosynthesis of, 30, 31
  from cannabichromene, 75
  gas-liquid chromatography of, 147
  isolation of, 10
  optical inactivity of, 28, 31
  pharmacological activity of, 116, 117, 130, 250
  stability of, 63
  structure studies on, 24
  synthesis of, 51–54
  thin-layer chromatography of, 145
  uv spectroscopy of, 149
Cannabidiol, 3, *17, 29,* 30, 47, *68, 74, 76, 78, 81, 90, 188, 367*
  absence from dagga, 89
  air oxidation of, 74
  aromatic carboxylation of, 81

biosynthesis of, 29, 30, 31
from cannabidiol diacetate, 76
from cannabidiolic acid decarboxylation, 68
in cannabinol samples, 7
in cannabis, 29
  variations, 89, 141, 142, 197
chemobotany of, 12, 13
cis-isomer of, 47
cleavage of, 80–81
colorimetric test for, 144
configuration of, 28
cyclization of, 61–63, 194
from dimeric cannabinoid, 24–25
dimethyl ether, 43, *44, 127*
  psychomimetic activity, 127
gas-liquid chromatography of, 146, 147, 149, 160, 161, 163
effects on liver, 195
hydrogenation of, 77–78
inactivity of, 115, 116–117
infrared spectroscopy of, 151
as interferent in THC metabolism, 326
irradiation effects on, 75
isolation of, 8, 9, 10, 11
metabolism and metabolites of, 184, *188*
pharmacology of, 117, 203, 228, 229, 233, 249, 250, 252, 253, 269, 270, 277, 278, 279
photochemical reactions of, 75–76
propyl analog of, *see* Cannabidivarin
smoking effects on, 70, 71
stability of, 73
structure studies on, 17–19, 25, 38
synthesis of, 38–50, 55, 90, 91
Δ^1-THC from, 39–40
from Δ^1-THC, in smoking, 69–70
thermal reactions of, 69
thin-layer chromatography of, 145, 146, 163
toxicity of, 236–237
in urine, 163
uv spectroscopy of, 149
Cannabidiol acetate, irradiation of, 76–77
Cannabidiol bisdinitrobenzoate, *78*
  epoxidation of, 77–78
  in isolation of cannabidiol, 8
Cannabidiol diacetate, *77*
  irradiation of, 76–77

Cannabidiolic acid, *25, 30, 55, 68, 148,* 367
  as antibiotic, 115, 117, 235
  biosynthesis of, 30
  in cannabis, 29
    isolation, 88
  chemobotany of, 12
  colorimetric test for, 144
  configuration of, 28, 29
  gas-liquid chromatography of, 147–148
  in hemp, 69
  infrared spectroscopy of, 151
  isolation of, 8, 9
  methyl ester, isolation of, 10
  pharmacological activity of 115, 117, 235, 251
  photochemical reaction of, 75
  structure studies on, 25
  synthesis of, 54, 55
  thermal reactions of, 68, 69
  thin-layer chromatography of, 88
Cannabidiorcol, occurrence of, 88
Cannabidivarol, 3, *368*
  isolation of, 10, 17
  structure studies on, 17–19
  synthesis of, 38–50
Cannabidivarin, *see* Cannabidivarol
Cannabielsoic acid A, *28, 31, 368*
  biosynthesis of, 31
  from cannabidiolic acid, 75
  configuration of, 28
Cannabielsoic acid B, *368*
  structure studies on, 28
Cannabielsoic acids, *56, 368*
  biosynthesis of, 30
  inactivity of, 116, 117
  structure studies on, 27–28.
  synthesis of, 55–56
  thermal reactions of, 68
Cannabigerol, *23, 26, 30, 50, 67, 367*
  as antibiotic, 117
  biosynthesis of, 29, 30
  cannabichromene from, 23, 51
  from cannabigerolic acid, 26
  cannabigerolic acid from, 54
  in cannabis material
    variations, 142
  colorimetric test for, 144
  cyclization of, 65, 67
  dehydrogenation of, 74
  gas-liquid chromatography of, 147

infrared spectroscopy of, 151
isolation of, 10, 29
monomethyl ether, isolation and structure of, 23
pharmacological activity of, 116, 117
structure studies on, 22–23
synthesis of, 50–51
thin-layer chromatography of, 145
uv spectroscopy of, 149
Cannabigerolic acid, *26, 367*
  biosynthesis of, 30
  colorimetric test for, 144
  ethyl ester, synthesis, 51, 54, 55
  isolation of, 29
  methyl ether, 26
    chemobotany, 13
    isolation, 10
  structure studies on, 26
  synthesis of, 54
"Cannabin," discovery of, 5
Cannabinin, in cannabis, 6
Cannabinoid acids
  decarboxylation of, in smoking, 194
  inactivity of, 116, 117
  reduction of, 82
  synthesis of, 54–56
Cannabinoid esters, reduction of, 82
Cannabinoid(s)
  absolute configuration of, 28–29
  acids, decarboxylation of, 68
  analytical chemistry of, 140–165
    quantitative, 145–146
  antidotes to, tests for, 106
  behavior effects of, 205–208
  in bile, 154
  in biological fluids, detection, 153–156
  biogenesis of, 29–31
  in *Cannabis sativa* and preparations
    chemobotany, 11–13
    variations in, 88–89, 141–142
  chemistry of, 1–99
  colorimetric tests for, 142–144, 159
  comparison with other drugs, 267–268
  cumulative effects of, 253–257
  definition of, 2
  dehydrogenations of, 70, 71–74
    by chloranil, 72–73
  determination of, 137–165
  dimeric, 24–25
  double bond additions to, 77–80

extraction and isolation of, 8–11, 140–141, 162
fat solubility of, 193
in feces, 154
fluorescence assay of, 154, 162–163
formulas of, 2, 367–369
gas-liquid chromatography of, 146–150, 159–160, 161
hypothalamic action of, 222–225
immunofluorescent assay of, 163–164
infrared spectroscopy of, 150, 151
isomerizations of, 60–67
literature on, 3–4, 88, 288
metabolism of, 172–181, 241–250, 268–271
  in dog, 175, 178
  in man, 180–181
  in monkey, 175, 178
  in rabbit, 175, 178, 184
  in rat, 172–174, 184
metabolites of, 174–181
  extraction, 152
  pharmacological effects, 248–250
  radiolabeled, in plasma, 149
  structure, 56–60
  syntheses, 56–60, 92–97
as monoterpenoids, 2–3
naturally occurring, 8–31
  isolation and identification, 88
  pharmacological activity, 115–117
neurological effects of, 216–221
nomenclature of, 2
NMR-C-13, spectra of, 97
NMR spectra of, 17–28
numbering systems of, 2
oxidation of, 71–74
paper chromatography of, 146
pharmaceutical preparations of, 98
pharmacological activity of, 103–106, 115–117, 191–285, 287–333
photochemical reactions of, 75–77
n-propyl analogs of, 3
radiolabeled
  list of, 168, 183
  preparation, 168–172, 189
reactions of, 60–82
solvents for, 138
stability of, 97–98, 103, 150–152, 160–162
structure-activity relationships of, 101–136
syntheses of, 31–60, 89–91

teratogenicity of, 238–241
therapeutic potential of, 361–362
thermal reactions of, 67–71
thin-layer chromatography of, 144–146, 163
tolerance to, 253–257, 267
toxicity of, 235–241, 271–272
  lethal dosages, 239
in urine, 154, 162–163
uv spectroscopy of, 149–150
Cannabinol, *14, 17, 26, 31,* 73, *177, 367*
biosynthesis of, 30, 31
from cannabinolic acid, 26
in cannabis plant material, variations, 89, 141, 142, 197
from dimeric cannabinoid, 24–25
early research on, 6–7
extraction of, 152
gas-liquid chromatography of, 146, 147, 149, 152–153, 160, 161
from 7-hydroxy-*Δ⁶*-THC, 179
infrared spectroscopy of, 151
isolation of, 8, 9, 10
isomers of, synthesis, 32, 33
in marijuana, 151
metabolites of, 243, 244
  gas-liquid chromatography, 153
  isotope studies, 175, 177
pharmacology of, 115, 116, 203, 227–228, 249–252, 277, 278, 279
as possible natural product, 31
propyl analog of, *see* Cannabivarol
radiolabeled, 168
stability of, 72, 151
structure studies on, 7, 13–17
synthesis of, 31–37
from *Δ¹*-THC, in smoking, 69–70
  by dehydrogenation, 72–73, 97
  as metabolite, 184
  on storage, 151, 152
thin-layer chromatography of, 145, 146, 153, 163
toxicity of, 236–237
in urine, 163
uv spectroscopy of, 149–150
Cannabinol acetate, *16*
  in cannabinol structure studies, 16
Cannabinolactone, 14
  in cannabinol structure studies, 15
Cannabinolactonic acid, *14*

in cannabinol structure studies, 15
Cannabinolic acid, *26, 31, 367*
    biosynthesis of, 31
    formation in storage, 72
    methyl ester, isolation of, 10
    as possible natural cannabinoid, 31
    structure studies on, 26
    from *Δ¹*-THC acid A, 77
Cannabiorcol, *88*
    occurrence of, 88
Cannabipinol, 24
Cannabis, *see also* Cannabinoids; Charas;
    Hashish; Hemp; Marijuana
    alkaloids in, 138
    analytical chemistry of, 137–165
    bioassay of, 197–205
    colorimetric tests for, 142–144, 159
    deterioration changes in, 71–72
    dependence liability and, 353–357
    effects on man, 287–333
        clinical aspects, 335–365
        duration of use, 351–353
        as model psychosis, 350–351
    essential oils of, 139–140
    "extract" of, 195
    extraction of, 138, 141
    "fingerprinting" by THC content, 196, 197
    interaction with other drugs, 361
    intravenous usage, 358
    in multiple drug usage patterns, 349
    pharmacology of, 191–285
    psychiatric problems and, 335–357
    preparations of
        common types, 195–197
        physical and chemical properties, 192–195
        variations, 288–289
    psychopathological phenomena from,
        338–350
    temporal pattern of effects of, 326
    "tincture" of, 195, 204
    waxes in, 138–139
Cannabis indica
    cannabinoid isolation from, 8
    early chemical research on, 6
Cannabis sativa
    bibliographies on, 4, 88
    C₂₁ compounds of, *see* Cannabinoids
    cannabinoids in
    chemobotany, 11–13

    isolation, 8–11
    variations in, 88–89
    chemical research on, historical aspects,
        4
    chemical literature on, 3–4
    essential oils of, 139–140
    male and female plants, cannabinoid
        content, 11, 12–13
    storage changes in, 97–98
Cannabitriol, 10
    isolation of, 11
Cannabivarin, *see* Cannabivarol
    isolation of, 17
    thin-layer chromatography of, 145
Cannabol, isolation of, 11
"Cannin," isolation of, 8, 11
n-Caproic acid, from cannabinol oxidation,
    16
Carbachol, in cannabinoid studies, 276
Carbomethoxy-*Δ⁶*-tetrahydrocannabinols,
    120, 121
    inactivity of, 120, 121
Carbon-14, as cannabinoid label, 153, 162,
    168
Carbon dioxide, ¹⁴C-labeled, use in bio-
    synthesis of labeled metabolites, 168
7-Carboxy-*Δ¹*-tetrahydrocannabinols, as
    urinary metabolite, 162
Carcinogen(s)
    cannabinoids as, 277
    marijuana tar as, 235, 361
Cardiovascular system, cannabinoid effects
    on, 231–232, 275–276, 322–324
Carene oxide, *50*
    in THC synthesis, 49
Caryophyllene and oxide, in cannabis oil,
    139, 140
Case histories, of psychopathological phe-
    nomena from cannabis, 338–350
Catalepsy, from cannabis use, 317–319
    (*see also* Mouse ring catalepsy test)
Cataleptoid test, for cannabinoid activity,
    103
Catecholamines, cannabinoid interaction
    with, 227–228
Cell pathology, from cannabinoids, 277
Charas
    cannabinoid isolation from, 9
    early chemical research on, 6, 7
    stability of, 68–69, 72

Chemobotany, of cannabinoids in *Cannabis sativa*, 11–13
Chlordizepoxide, cannabinoid comparison to, 267
1-Chlorohexahydrocannabinol methyl ether, *60*
  dehydrochlorination of, 59–60
p-Chlorophenylalanine, in studies of cannabinoid effects, 266–267
Chlorophyll, from cannabis, 138, 139
Chlorpromazine, cannabinoid comparison to, 203, 215, 219, 267, 326
Cholestane, as glc internal standard, 148, 160
Cholesterol, Δ^1-THC similarity to, 281
Choline, in cannabis, 5, 6, 138
Cholinergic synapses, cannabinoid effects on, 232–234
Chromatography, *see also* individual types
  of cannabinoids, 9–11
Chromosomes
  aberration of, cannabis use and, 360
  mitotic inhibition in, by cannabis, 241
Cigarettes, placebo-type, 290
Cinchona, 5
Citral, *42*
  cyclization of, 51–52
  in THC synthesis, 39, 41, 42
Citrylidene cannabis, *51, 53*
  synthesis of, 52, 53
Citrylidene malonic acid, *52*
  from citral cyclization, 51–52
Cocaine, 4
  cannabinoid comparison with, 259
Colorimetric tests, for cannabinoids, 142–144, 159
Colors, cannabis effects on perception of, 291–292
Columbianetine, synthesis of, 56
Column chromatography, of cannabinoids, 9–11
Conditioned avoidance response, THC effect on, 104, 211, 215–216
Configuration, of cannabinoids, 28–29
Conjunctiva redness, as cannabinoid symptom, 104
Contrast of images, cannabis effects on, 292
Convulsants, cannabinoid interaction with, 221–222

Corn silk cigarettes, as placebo for marijuana studies, 290, 320
Corneal areflexia test
  for cannabinoid activity, 101, 103, 197, 199, 200–203, 210, 253
  of Δ^3-THC derivatives, 108–113
Corticosteroids, cannabinoid effects on activity of, 224–225
Corticotropin releasing factor (CRF), cannabinoid effects on, 225
Cortisol, in plasma, cannabis effects on, 325
Coumarin
  deoxybruceol from, 52
  in Δ^6 THC synthesis, 38
Countercurrent distribution, of cannabinoids, 10–11
Cryptophenol, in cannabis, 7
Cumulative effects, of cannabis, 253–257, 314
Curcumene, in cannabis oil, 140
Cyclizations, of cannabinoids, 60–67
3′-Cyclohexylcannabidiol, *76*
  from cannabidiol irradiation, 75–76
p-Cymene
  from cannabidiol cleavage, 17, 80–81
  in cannabis oil, 139, 140
Cytochrome P-450, in THC metabolism, 175

D

Dagga
  cannabidiol absence from, 89
  effects on perception, 292, 294
DDQ, in dehydrogenation of cannabigerol, 51
Death, fear of, from cannabis, 311–312
Decarboxylation, of cannabinoid acids, 67–71, 148
Dehydrogenations, of cannabinoids, 71–74, 97
Deoxybruceol, *52*
  synthesis of, 52
Dependence liability, from cannabis, 353–357
Depersonalization, sensation of from cannabis, 308–309
Depressants, cannabinoids as, 253
Depth perception, cannabis effects on, 292

Desmethylimipramine, as THC inhibitor, 269
Detachment, from cannabis use, 312–314
Diabetic coma, from cannabis, 359
Di-*o*-anisidine tetrazolium chloride, *see* Fast Blue Salt B
Diazepines, cannabis use with, 349
Dibromo cannabicyclol, x-ray analysis of, 24
2,6-Dichloroquinone-N-chloroimine, in fluorescence assay of THC, 154
Dicyclohexylcarbodiimide (DCC), *98*
  in THC ester preparation, 98
Diels-Alder reaction, in THC synthesis, 38, 41, 43–44, 97
Diethyl α-acetoglutarate, *45*
  in THC synthesis, 45
Dihydrocannabidiol
  cleavage of, 80–81
8-Dihydrocannabidiol, *76*
  from cannabidiol irradiation, 75–76
Dihydroolivetol, in cannabinol synthesis, 33
Dihydroxyhexahydrocannabinol, *123*
  psychomimetic activity of, 123
Dihydroxyhexahydrocannabinol acetate, *58*
  synthesis of, 57
5,7-Dihydroxy-Δ^6-tetrahydrocannabinols, *369*
  extraction and chromatography of, 152
  pharmacology of, 249
  as Δ^6-THC metabolites, 174, 175, 243
6,7-Dihydroxy-Δ^1-tetrahydrocannabinol
  extraction and chromatography of, 152–153
  pharmacology of, 249
  as THC metabolite, 180, 184, 243, 248
  uv spectroscopy of, 149
1-Dimethylaminonaphthalene 5-sulfonate, cannabinoid derivatives of, 163
5-(1′,2′-Dimethylheptyl) resorcinol, synthesis of, 107
1″,2″-Dimethylheptyl-Δ^1-tetrahydrocannabinol, *120, 369*
  psychotomimetic activity of, 120, 124
Diphenylhydantoin, cannabinoid synergism with, 221
Diuresis, cannabinoid effects on, 234
DMHP, *see* Δ^3-Tetrahydrocannabinol, dimethylheptyl homolog
Dog ataxia test, *see* Ataxia test

Dogs
  cannabinoid effects on, 208–209
  toxicity, 237, 238
  THC metabolism in, 175, 178, 184–185
DOPA, in studies of cannabinoid pharmacology, 267, 274
Dopamine
  cannabinoid comparison to, 227
  cannabinoid effects on activity of, 273–274
Double bonds, of cannabinoids, additions to, 77–80
Dreaming, cannabis effects on, 296
Drugs, cannabinoid interaction with, 278
"Drunken" feeling, from cannabis, 314
Duquénois colorimetric test, for cannabinoids, 142, 143–144
Duquénois reagent, 143
Dysphoria, from cannabis, 311–312

E

Earthworms, cannabinoid toxicity to, 204, 216
n-Eicosane, as glc internal standard, 148
Electroencephalographic studies
  of cannabinoids, 216–219, 253, 272–273, 280
  in man, 320
Electron spin resonance spectroscopy, of THC, 155–156
Emotions, cannabis effects on, 310–312
Endocrine action, of cannabinoids, 222–225
Environment indifference, as cannabinoid symptom, 104, 106
Epilepsy, cannabis and, 328–329, 360–361
Epinephrine, potentiation by cannabinoids, 127
1,2-Epoxyhexahydrocannabinol
  psychomimetic activity of, 133
  as THC metabolite, 93, 268
  synthesis of, 93
Epoxyhexahydrocannabinol acetate *58*
  synthesis of, 57
Erythrocytes, cannabinoid effects on, 235, 279
Essential oils, of cannabis, 5–6, 139–140
Estradiol, THC inhibition of, conjugation of, 269
Estrogen, in cannabinoid imminofluorescent assay, 163

Ethanol, cannabinoid comparison with, 235
Ether sleeping time, cannabinoid interaction with, 278
1-Ethoxyhexahydrocannabinol, *127*
  inactivity of, 127
8-Ethoxy*iso*hexahydrocannabinol, *128*
  inactivity of, 128
Ethoxycarbonyl olivetol, *55*
  in cannabigerolic acid ester synthesis, 54–55
Ethoxyhexahydrocannabinols, from cannabidiol cyclization, 62
Ethyl 5-methylcyclohexanone 2-carboxylate, in cannabinol synthesis, 34, 36
4-Ethyl-*Δ¹*-tetrahydrocannabinol, *122*
  psychotomimetic activity of, 122
Ethyl-*Δ⁶*-tetrahydrocannabinols, *121, 122*
  pychotomimetic activity of, 121, 122
4'-Ethyl-*Δ⁶*-tetrahydrocannabinol, *121*
  psychomimetic activity of, 121
Eugenol, in cannabis oil, 139
Euphoria, from cannabis, 104, 106, 310–311
Extract of cannabis, 5–7, 195
Extraction, of cannabinoids, 140–141, 162
Eyes
  cannabis effects on, 106, 321–322, 358
  on pupil, 321–322

F

Fantasies, from cannabis, 296
β-Farnesene, in cannabis oil, 139, 140
Fast Blue Salt B, as cannabis colorimetric reagent, 144–145, 146, 154, 159
Fat, cannabinoid metabolite deposition in, 270
Fat solubility, of cannabinoids, 193, 257
Fearfulness, from cannabinoids, 205
Feces
  cannabinoid analysis of, 154
  metabolite excretion in, 173, 175, 184, 243, 244, 268
Fetus, cannabis effects on, 240–241, 272
Fish
  cannabinoid effects on, 266
  (*See also* Ichthyotoxicity test)
Fighting behavior test, for cannabinoid activity, 103, 211–212
Fighting fish, cannabinoid effects on, 266, 267

"Fingerprinting" of cannabis, by cannabinoid content, 196
Flashback, from cannabis, 342, 349–350
Fluorescence assay
  of cannabinoids, 162–163
  of *Δ¹*-THC, 154
Friedel-Crafts reaction, reversed, in cannabinoid reactions, 81
Frogs, cannabinoid effects on, 216
Furfural colorimetric test, for cannabis, 159

G

Gas chromatography
  of cannabinoid acids, 71
  of cannabinoids, 21, 146–150
  isolation using, 88
  mass spectrometry with, 164
Gastrointestinal system, cannabinoid effects on, 232–234, 275–276, 324–326
Gayer's rabbit areflexia test, *see* Cornea areflexia test
"Gelastic epilepsy," from Kuru, 316
Geraniol, 90
  cannabigerol from, 23
  in THC synthesis, 38, 91
Gerbil digging activity test, for cannabinoid activity, 104, 216
Geraniol phosphate, as cannabinoid precursor, 29
Geranyl pyrophosphate, *30*
  as cannabinoid precursor, 30
Ghamrawy colorimetric test, for cannabinoids, 142, 143
Ghee, in preparation of majoun, 193
β-Glucuronidase, in studies of THC metabolism, 179, 180, 184
Glycerol, as cannabinoid solvent, 193
Glyceryl trinitrate, 324
Glycols, as cannabinoid solvents, 236
Goldfish, cannabinoid toxicity to, 204
Guaiacol, in cannabis oil, 139
Guinea pigs, cannabis effects on, 216
  toxicity, 236, 237
Gum arabic, as cannabinoid solvent, 193

H

Hallucinations
  as cannabinoid symptom, 104, 106

in man, 296–297
in monkeys, 205–206
Hamsters, cannabis effects on, 216
Hangover, from cannabis, 314
Hashish
    acute toxicity of, 236–237
    "artificial," chemical studies on, 70
    cannabinoid isolation from, 8, 10, 17, 21,
        38
    yields, 142
    deterioration changes in, 71–72
    early chemical research on, 2, 4, 7
    effects, on disinterest, 316
    extraction of, 138, 141
    gas-liquid chromatography of, 147
    iso-THC absence in, 76
    posture peculiarities from, 104
    production of, 68–69
    smoking of, *see* Smoking, of cannabis
    solvent extraction of, 139
    storage changes in, 68–69
    THC content of, 196
    THC acids in, 70
    Δ^1-THC isolation from, 115–116
    thin-layer chromatography of, 145
"Hashish sole," definition of, 69
"Hashishin," early research on, 5
Headache, from cannabis use, 323–324
Heart rate change, as cannabinoid symptom,
    106, 231 275, 322
Helminths, cannabinoid toxicity to, 204
Hemolysis, cannabinoid effects on, 279
Hexahydrocannabinols, *80, 123*
    formation of, 80
    psychomimetic activities of, 123, 125
Hemp
    analgesia from, 220
    cannabidiolic acid in, 69
    cannabinoid isolation from, 9, 11, 12–13,
        26
    early research on, 5, 6
    essential oil components in, 139
    placebo cigarettes from, 290
Hexobarbitone, cannabinoid effects on
    activity of, 229, 269
Histamine, 324
β-Humulene, in cannabis oil, 140
Hunger, *see* Appetite
Hydrazo derivatives, of cannabinoids,
    163–163

8-Hydroxycannabigerol, *30, 31*
    biosynthesis of, 29, 30
    as possible cannabinoid precursor, 31,
        40–41
7-Hydroxycannabinol, *59, 177*
    as cannabinol metabolite, 59, 177
    synthesis of, 57
6-Hydroxyhexahydrocannabinols, *80*
    formation of, 80
7-Hydroxylase, in cannabinoid metabolism,
    181
Hydroxyolivetols, in metabolite synthesis,
    94
Hydroxyquinones, from cannabinoids, in
    Beam test, 144
Hydroxy-Δ^6-tetrahydrocannabinols, *122*
    psychotomimetic activity of, 122
1″-Hydroxy-Δ^6-tetrahydrocannabinol, *95*
    extraction and chromatography of, 152
    inactivity of, 95, 97
    synthesis of, 94–95
    as Δ^6-THC metabolite, 94
2α-Hydroxy-Δ^6-tetrahydrocannabinol,
    psychotomimetic activity of, 125
3″-Hydroxy-Δ^6-tetrahydrocannabinol
    synthesis of, 94–95
    as Δ^6-THC metabolite, 94
5-Hydroxy-Δ^6-tetrahydrocannabinols, 185
    structure-activity studies on, 133
6α-Hydroxy-Δ^7-tetrahydro cannabinol, *124*
    psychomimetic activity of, 124
6β-Hydroxy-Δ^1-tetrahydrocannabinol, *123*
    368
    synthesis of, 59
    psychomimitic activity of, 59, 116, 117,
        123, 131
6β-Hydroxy-Δ^7-tetrahydrocannabinol, *123*
    psychomimetic activity of, 123
7-Hydroxy-Δ^1-tetrahydrocannabinol, *58,
    368*
    binding to albumin, 361
    extraction and chromatography of, 148,
        149
    gas chromatography of, 164
    as major Δ^1-THC metabolite, 174, 175,
        178, 181, 184, 185, 189, 243, 248, 268,
        271
    psychotomimetic activity of, 116, 117,
        248–250
    structure of, 56

synthesis of, 56, 57, 92
UV spectroscopy of, 149
7-Hydroxy-Δ^6-tetrahydrocannabinol, 58, 179, 368
 instability of, 57
 as major Δ^6-THC metabolite, 174, 178–180
 metabolite of, 96
 pharmacology of, 228, 248, 279
 psychotomimetic activity of, 116, 117
 structure of, 56
 synthesis of, 59, 92–93, 96
 in urine test, 243
7-Hydroxy-Δ^1-tetrahydrocannabinol diacetate, as THC metabolite, 184, 185
5-Hydroxytryptamine, cannabinoid interaction with, 226–228, 273–274, 277, 325
Hyperactivity, involuntary from cannabis, 317
Hypotension, 231–232, 275–276, 322
Hypothalamic action, of cannabinoids, 222–225
Hypothermia
 from cannabinoids, 205, 215, 222–224, 253, 275, 277, 323
 in man, 323

I

Ichthyotoxicity test, for cannabinoid activity, 103, 197, 204
Imagery, cannabis effects on, 296
Immunoassay, of cannabinoids, 154–155
Immunofluorescent assay, of cannabinoids in biological fluids, 163–164
Infrared spectroscopy, of cannabinoids, 150, 151
Insight, feelings of, from cannabis, 309
Intraocular pressure, reduction by marijuana, 322
Iodine, in cannabinoid test, 144
Isocannabichromene, 77
 formation of, 77
Isomerizations, of cannabinoids, 60–67
Isopiperitenone, in cannabidiol synthesis, 90
4-Isopropylisophthalic acid, *15*
 in cannabinol structure studies, 15
4-Isopropyl-*m*-toluic acid 15
 in cannibinol structure studies, 15

J

Juglone, positive Beam test from, 143

K

6-Keto-Δ^1-tetrahydrocannabinol, as THC metabolite, 185
5-Keto-Δ^6-tetrahydrocannabinol, psychotomimetic activity of, 133
5-Keto-Δ^6-tetrahydrocannabinol acetate, *75*
 from Δ^6-THC acetate, 74–75
Kidneys, cannabis effects on, 325
Kolbe-Schmidt reaction, in cannabinoid acid synthesis, 54
Kura, epidemic laughter with, 316

L

Labor pains, cannabis effects on, 294
Laughter, from cannabis use, 106, 314–315
Learning, cannabinoid effects on, 205, 266
Leptazol, cannabinoid antagonism of, 221
Light-headedness, from cannabis, 314
Limonene, in cannabis oil, 139, 140
Linalool and oxide, in cannabis oil, 140
Lipophilicity, of cannabis, 257
Liver
 cannabidiol effects on, 195
 cannabis effects on, 325, 361
 THC metabolites in, 186–188, 242–243
LSD, 336, 357
 activity of, THC levels and, 70
 cannabinoid comparison to, 203, 204, 212, 215, 327
 flashback from, 349–350
 psychotic effects of, 351
 teratogenic effects of cannabis and, 359
Lucas reagent, in THC synthesis, 45
Lungs, THC delivered to, by smoking, 71

M

Majoun, preparation of, 192–193
Man
 cannabis effects on, 287–365
 THC metabolism in, 180–181, 185, 189
"Manicured" marijuana, preparation of, 141

Marijuana
  acid cannabinoids in, 147
  alkaloids in, 6
  analytical chemistry of, 138
  cannabinoids in
    extraction and isolation, 8, 9, 11, 141
    for placebo cigarettes, 290
    variations, 89, 141
    yield, 142
  cannabinol in, 151
  early chemical research on, 2
  effects of, 313
    on autonomic nervous system, 322
    on memory, 303–304
  effects of, related to duration of use, 351–353
  essential oils in, 139
  extraction of, 138
  gas-liquid chromatography of, 159–160
  "manicured," 141
  noncannabinoid components in determination, 138–140
  odor of, 139
  production of THC changes in, 68–69
  smoking of, *see* Smoking, of cannabis
  teratogenicity of, 238, 240–241, 359–360
  THC acids in, 70
  UV spectroscopy of, 149
Markovnikoff addition, in cannabinoid reactions, 76
Marmesine, synthesis of, 56
Mass spectrometry
  in cannabinoid isolation, 88
  of cannabinoid metabolites, combined with gas chromatography, 164
  of cannabinoids, 19, 21–22, 24, 27
Maternal effects, of cannabinoids, 272
Memory
  cannabinoid effects on, 266, 289
  in man, 301–305
Menthane carboxylic acid, from cannabidiol degradation, 17, 18
Menthadienol
  in cannabinoid acid synthesis, 55
  in metabolite synthesis, 94
  in Δ^6-THC synthesis, 90
  for radiolabeling, 172
Menthatriene, as cannabinoid precursor, 29
Menthol, 17, *18*

  in cannabinoid structure studies, 29
Meprobamate, cannabinoid comparison to, 215
Mescaline, cannabinoid comparison to, 212, 267
Metabolism
  of cannabinoids, 167–190, 241–250, 268–271
  cannabis effects on, 324–326
Methadone, as glc internal standard, 148
Methamphetamine, cannabinoid effects on activity of, 222
1-Methoxydihydro cannabidiol, *76*
  from cannabidiol, 75–76
Methylisopropylbenzenes, in cannabis oil, 139
Methyl stearate, as glc internal standard, 148
Methyl-Δ^6-tetrahydrocannabinols, *121*, *122*
  psychomimetic activity, 121, 122
4'-Methyl-Δ^6-tetrahydrocannabinol, *82*
Mice
  cannabinoid effects on, 213–215
  toxicity, 236–237, 239
Microsomes, cannabinoid effects on, 279
Mitochondria, cannabinoid effects on, 279
Minnows, cannabinoid toxicity to, 204, 216
Monkeys
  cannabinoid effects on, 205–208, 356
  pharmalocological tests of, 102–106, 141
  toxicity, 236
  THC's metabolism in, 175, 178, 185
Monoterpenoids
  cannabinoids as, 2–3
  numbering for, 3
Mood, cannabis effects on, 310–312
MOP, *see* Δ^3-Tetrahydrocannabinol, methyloctyl homolog
Morphine, 4
  cannabinoid comparison to, 203, 220, 221, 225, 258, 276, 324
Morpholino esters, of THC, preparation, 98
Motor activity
  cannabis effects on
    in animals, 106
    in man, 316–317
Motor activity test, for cannabinoid activity, 103–104
Mouse gross behavior test, for cannabinoid activity, 104

Mouse ring catalepsy test, for cannabinoid activity, 197, 204, 205, 253
Murine leukemia virus, in studies of cannabinoid carcinogenicity, 277
Muscarinic action, of cannabinoids, 6, 253
Muscle strength loss, as cannabinoid symptom, 106
Musical ability, cannabis effects on, 293–294
Myrcene, in cannabis oil, 139, 140

N

NADPH, in cannabinoid metabolism, 243
Narcotics, cannabinoid comparison to, 215
Nausea, from cannabis, 324
Nerol, *50*, 90
    cannabigerol from, 23, 50
Neurological effects, of cannabinoids, 216–221
Nicotine, cannabis and, 5
Nitrocannabinolactone, 14
    in cannabinol structure studies, 14, 15
Nitrogen bases, in cannabis, 11
p-Nitrophenol, THC inhibition of, 269
6-Nitro-*m*-toluic acid, 16
    from cannabinol acetate oxidation, 16
Nitrous oxide, cannabis action compared to, 327
n-Nonecosane, in cannabis, 139
Noradrenaline
    cannabinoid comparison to, 227–228, 277
    cannabinoid effects on, 273–274
Norepinephrine, potentiation by cannabinoids, 127
Normetanephrine, cannabinoid effects on, 273
Norton's sheet, in monkey test monitoring, 104
Nortriptyline, as THC inhibitor, 269
Nuclear magnetic resonance spectra, of cannabinoids, 17–28, 97

O

Odor, of marijuana, essential oils' role, 139
Olive oil, as cannabinoid solvent, 193
Olivetol, *18*, 24, *30*, *50*
    from cannabidiol cleavage, 17, 80–81
    in cannabinoid syntheses, 89–91
    in cannabinol synthesis, 32–34, 37
    in cannabigerol synthesis, 50, 52
    as cannabinoid precursor, 29, 30
    synthesis of, 107
    in THC synthesis, 38–40
    for radiolabeling, 171, 172, 189
Olivetolcarboxylic acid, as cannabinoid precursor, 29
Olivetolic acid, *30*
    as cannabinoid precursor, 29, 30
Olivetyl pinene, *49*, *75*
    photochemical reaction of, 75
    in THC synthesis, 48–49
Operant condition techniques, 104, 211, 215, 216
Opiates, cannabinoid comparison with, 267, 326
Opium, 5
Orcinol
    in cannabinol synthesis, 35, 37
    isoprenoid derivatives of, 90–91
Organs, cannabinoid distribution in, 178, 246
Ouabain, cannabinoid comparison with, 235
Oxidations, of cannabinoids, 57–60, 71–74, 98
Oxoolivetol, in metabolite synthesis, 94
Oxycannabin, *see* Nitrocannabinolactone
Oxygen combustion, of radiolabeled cannabinoids, 153
Oxygenase, hepatic, in THC metabolism, 175

P

Pain, cannabis effects on, 294–295
Paper chromatography, of cannabinoids, 9, 146
Paranoia, from cannabis use, 311–312
Patterns, cannabis effects on perception of, 292
Pentobarbitone, cannabinoids compared to, 225, 229
Perception
    cannabis effects on, 205, 291–297
    auditory perception, 293–294
    time perception, 297–301
    visual perception, 291–293
Performance impairment, as cannabinoid symptom, 106

Pernocton, cannabinoid effects on activity, of, 228, 229
Pharmaceutical preparations, cannabinoids in, 98
Pharmacology of cannabis, 201–241, 272–281
in cats, 209–210
in dogs, 208–209, 267
in man, 287–365
in mice, 213–215, 256
in monkeys, 205–208, 265
in pigeons, 215, 265, 267
in rabbits, 210
in rats, 210–212, 265–267
temporal aspects of, 326
β-Phellandrene, in cannabis oil, 139, 140
Phenitrone, cannabinoid interaction with, 278
Phenobarbitone, effects on cannabinoid metabolism, 271
Phenolics, in cannabis, 11
Phenothiazines, cannabis use with, 349
Phenytoin, cannabinoid comparison to, 259
Photochemical reactions, of cannabinoids, 75–77
Photo-Fries rearrangement, of cannabidiol esters, 76
Physostigmine, cannabinoid comparison with, 267, 278
Pigeons
cannabinoid effects on, 215
toxicity, 237
in tests of cannabinoid activity, 104, 256
tolerance to cannabinoids of, 256, 258
Pinene(s)
in cannabis oil, 140
derivative of, in THC synthesis, 48
Pipe smoking, of cannabis chemistry of, 71
Piperidine,
in cannabis, 6, 138
oil, 139
Piperidinobutyric acid esters, of THC, preparation, 98
Placebo cigarettes, preparation of, 290
Placebo reaction, in cannabis studies, 289–291
Plasma
cannabinoid analysis of, 154–155
THC metabolites in, 180–181, 245–246

Polyethylene glycol, as cannabinoid solvent, 193
Posture peculiarities, as cannabinoid symptoms, 104
Promethazine, cannabinoid comparison to, 203
Propyl cannabidiol, *see* Cannabidivarol
Propyl cannabinoids, 3
occurrence and isolation of, 88
Propyl cannabinol, *see* Cannabivarol
Pseudoptosis
as cannabinoid symptom, 104, 106.
in man, 321
Psychiatric problems, cannabis and, 335–357
Psychotomimetic effects
of cannabis
factors influencing, 288–289 in man, 287–333
Pulse rate, cannabis effects on, 322
Pupil, cannabis effects on, 321–322
Pulegol, *35*
in cannabinol synthesis, 35
Pulegone, *36*
in cannabinol synthesis, 35–37
PVP, as cannabinoid solvent, 193
Pyrans, cannabinoids as, 2
Pyrahexyl (Synhexyl), *369*
as antidepressant, 101
gastrointestinal effects of, 324
metabolism of, 242
pharmacology of, 109, 201, 204, 215, 216, 220, 221, 224, 228, 233, 235, 323
psychotomimetic effects of, 293, 306, 311–323
as standard, 196, 198
tolerance to, 254
toxicity of, 236–237
withdrawal symptoms of, 356
Pyran moiety, importance in cannabis activity, 116

R

Rabbit corneal areflexia test, *see* Corneal areflexia test
Rabbits
cannabinoid effects on, 210
toxicity, 237
THC metabolism in, 174, 175, 178–180, 184, 257

Radioimmune method, of cannabinoid analysis, 154–155
Radiolabeling
of tetrahydrocannabinols, 167–190
with carbon-14, 168–169
in metabolism studies, 168–172, 189, 269–270
Rat, THC's metabolism in, 172–174, 175, 178, 184
Rat gross behavior test, for cannabinoid activity, 104
Rats
cannabinoid effects on, 210–212, 265
toxicity, 236, 237, 239
Red blood cells, *see* Erythrocytes
Red oil, as early standard cannabis preparation, 195–196
Reflexes, cannabis effects on, 317–319
Reproduction, cannabinoid effects on, 234
Reserpine, cannabinoid comparison to, 203, 204, 215, 227
Resin (cannabis)
in hashish, 289
stability of, 194
Resorcinol, positive Duquénois test by, 144
Respiration, cannabinoid effects on, 230–231, 253, 275–276
Rhesus monkeys. (*See also* Monkeys)
in cannabinoid activity tests, 104, 205–206
Robinson annelation, in THC synthesis, 46
Rosmarinus officinalis, positive Beam test from, 143
Rotarod performance test, for cannabinoid activity, 104
Rubidium-86 cannabinoid effects on transport of, 235, 325–326

S

Sabinene hydrate, in cannabis oil, 140
Salvia officinalis, positive Beam test from, 143
Schizophrenia, cannabis activity and, 329, 351
Scintillation spectroscopy, or radiolabeled cannabinoids, 153
Scopolamine, synergistic action with marijuana, 297
Scratching, from cannabinoids, 225–226
α-Selinine, in cannabis oil, 139, 140

Sensory deprivation, cannabis action and, 329
Sensory thresholds, cannabinoid effects on, 205
Serum albumin, as cannabinoid solvent, 193
Sesame oil, as cannabinoid solvent, 193
Sesquiterpene, in charas, 6
Sexual feeling, cannabis effects on, 314–315
Shapes, cannabis effects on perception of, 292
Significance (personal), changes of, from cannabis, 309
SKF-525-A
cannabinoid comparison to, 175, 228, 243, 251, 269, 270, 271, 275, 278
effects on THC metabolism, 269–270
Sleep
cannabinoid effects on, 218, 272–273
in man, 312–314
Sleepy state
as cannabinoid symptom, 106
in man, 312–314
Slow movements, as cannabinoid symptom, 106
Smell, cannabis effects on, 294
Smoke (marijuana)
in cannabis users
breath test for cannabinoids in, 159
Δ^1-THC in, 149, 194
cigarette smoke compared to, 277
from marijuana, gas-liquid chromatography of, 160–162
odor of, 139
Smoking, of cannabis
chemistry of, 25, 67–71, 194–195
metabolic studies, 184
Social pharmacology
of cannabinoids, in mice, 215
Solvents, for cannabinoids, 138, 193
Somesthetic sensations, from cannabis, 295–296
Speech, cannabis effects on, 316–317
Spin-label immunoassay, of THC's, 155–156
Spinal reflexes, cannabinoid effects on, 219–220
Squirrel monkeys. (*See also* Monkeys)
in cannabinoid activity tests, 104, 205
cannabinoid toxicity to, 237
Steroids, cannabinoid interaction with, 281

Sticklebacks, cannabinoid toxicity to, 204, 216
Stork-Eschenmoser cyclization scheme, in cannabinoid cyclization, 67
Straub tail, in mouse, from cannabinoids, 214, 258
Structure-activity relationships
 of cannabinoids, 101–136
 groups active in, 129–130
 natural compounds, 115–117
 pyran moiety importance, 116
 Δ^3-THC derivatives, 107–114
Strychnine, 4
 cannabinoid potentiation of, 221–222
Sugars, in cannabis, 11
Sy-Bi, pharmacology of, 203
Sympathomimetic amines, cannabinoid comparison, 267
Synthesis, of cannabinoids, 31–60
Sweating, cannabis effects on, 323
Synhexyl, *see* Pyrahexyl

T

Tadpoles, cannabinoid toxicity to, 204, 216
Tachycardia, 275, 322, 358, 361
Tar
 from marijuana, carcinogenicity, 235, 361
 in tobacco cigarettes, 235
Taste, cannabis effects on, 294
Temperature sensations, cannabis effects on, 294
Temperature
 of body (*see also* Hypothermia)
 cannabis effects on, 323
Teratogens, cannabinoids as, 238–241, 252, 253, 272
 in man, 359–360
Terpene, in charas, 6
Terpenoid allylic alcohols, olivetol condensation with, 89–90
Terpenoids
 in cannabis, 11
 early research on, 4
Terpenophenolics, cannabinoids as, 2
Terpinenes in cannabis oil, 140
Terpinen-4-ol, in cannabis oil, 140
α-Terpineol, in cannabis oil, 140
Tetanocannabin, in cannabis, 6

Tetrahydrocannabidiol, *18, 78*
 from cannabidiol hydrogenation, 17, 18, 77
Δ^8-*iso*-Tetrahydrocannabidiol, from cannabidiol cyclization, 61–62
Tetrahydrocannabidivarol, 3
 pharmacology of, 251, 252, 253
Tetrahydrocannabinol(s) (THC)
 binding to lipoproteins, 361
 blood binding of, 269
 formulas for, 3
 gas chromatography/mass spectrometry assay of, 164
 heterocyclic analogs of, SAR studies on, 125
 immunofluorescent assay of, 163–164
 intake, in addiction, 348
 iso-compounds, psychotomimetic activity of, 127–129
 isolation of, 8–11
 metabolites of, 95–97
  excretion, 153
  structure-activity studies, 133–136
 morpholino- and piperidinobutyric acid esters of, 98
 numbering system for, 2
 psychotomimetic activity of, 115, 149, 302–303, 311, 319
 radiolabeling of, 167–190
  list of, 168
  preparation, 168–172, 189
 stability of, 194
 synthesis of, 33
 therapeutic potential of, 361–362
 unnatural isomers of, synthesis, 46
 in urine, detection, 154
Δ^1-Tetrahydrocannabinol (Δ^1-THC), *3, 19, 30, 81, 102,* 118, 154, *169, 170, 171, 176, 186, 367*
 acetate, psychomimetic activity of, 119
 biosynthesis of, 30
 blood binding of, 269
 ^{14}C-labeled, synthesis, 46
 from cannabidiol cyclization, 61–63, 194
 from cannabidiol irradiation, 75–76
 from cannabinoid acids, in smoking, 194
 cannabinol from, 31, 150–152
  in smoking, 69–70, 194
 in cannabis plant material
  variations, 88–89, 141, 142

in cannabis preparations, 195, 196, 197
charge distributions of, 20
chemical name for, 3
chemobotany of, 12, 13
cis-isomer of
  formation of, 63
  inactivity of, 118, 119, 130
  isomerization of, 63
  stability of, 72–73
configuration of, 28
conformation of, 19–21
dehydrogenation of, 72, 97
derivatives of, psychotomimetic activity,
  118–129
dimethylheptyl homolog of, *369*
1″,2″-dimethylpentyl homolog of, *120*
  psychomimetic activity, 120
early research on, 4
effects on reflexes, 319
electron spin resonance spectroscopy of,
  155–156
epoxide of, as metabolite, 185, 268
ethyl-derivative of, *122*
  psychomimetic activity, 122
excretion of, 154
extraction of, 152
fetal effects of, 241, 272
fluorescence assay of, 154
gas-liquid chromatography of, 146, 147,
  149, 159–160, 161
  mass spectrometry with, 164
gastrointestinal effects of, 324
hexyl homolog of, *120*
  psychomimetic activity, 120
immunoassay of, 154–155
infrared spectroscopy of, 151
isolation of, 10
isomerization of, 70, 169–170
isomers of, psychomimetic studies on,
  118, 119
lipophilicity of, 257, 281
as marijuana active principle, 102, 116,
  117, 140, 193
metabolic effects of, 325
metabolism and metabolites of, 56–60,
  93–94, 172–181, *176*, 184–189, *186*,
  242–250, 268–271
kinetics of, distribution of, 244–248
methyl ether of
  inactivity, 119

1″-methylpentyl homolog of, *120*
  psychomimetic activity, 120
γ-morpholinobutyric acid ester of, 269
NMR studies on, 97
optical rotation of, 9
oxidation of, 7, 74, 150–151, 194
pharmacology of, 201–241, 272–281
  ED$_{50}$ dose levels, 203
in plasma
  after smoking, 149
  determination, 154
propyl analog of, *see* Tetrahydrocannabivarol
psychotomimetic activity of, 102, 103,
  116, 117
  cigarette levels and, 70–71
  derivatives, 118–129
  list of symptoms, 106
  threshold effective dose, 106
radiolabeled, 153–154, 168, 181, 189
  by biosynthesis, 168–169
  with carbon-14, 171–172, 189
  in metabolism studies, 56, 172–181,
    183–189, 245–246, 269–270
  positions labeled, 168, 183
  with tritium, 169–171
reaction with DNP-isocyanate, 81
reproduction effects from, 240–241
smoking effects on, 70–71
stability of, 97–98, 150–152, 194
storage effects on, 68, 72, 97
  protection against, 152
structure studies on, 19–21
synthesis of, 61–63, 91
in thermal chemistry of marijuana, 69
thin-layer chromatography of, 145, 146,
  152, 153, 163
tolerance to, 254–257
toxicity of, 235–241, 271–272
trans-isomer of
  formation, 65
  isomerization, 60–61
in urine, 163
  determination, 154, 163, 164
  extraction, 162
uv spectroscopy of, 149, 150
Δ$^{1(7)}$-Tetrahydrocannabinol, in metabolite
  synthesis, 92
Δ^2-Tetrahydrocannabinol, *9*
  isolation of, 8–9

Δ³-Tetrahydrocannabinol (Δ³-THC), *34,*
102, 107, 108, 119, 195, *369*
as biological standard for THC, 34
dehydrogenation of, 72
derivatives of
side-chain changes, 108–114
structure-activity relationships, 107
dimethyl carbamate, psychomimetic activity, 133, 136
dimethylheptyl derivative (DMHP), *369*
acetate, bioactivity, 108, 110, 111
psychomimetic activity, 108, 114, 130,
133
pharmacology, 215, 218–219, 221, 222
223, 224, 228, 230, 231, 233, 238
tolerance to, 254
dimethylhexyl derivative, pharmacological activity, 108
hexyl analog (Synhexyl), as antidepressant, 101–102
isomers, pharmacological activity, 258
methyl homolog of, inactivity, 133,
136
1-methyloctyl homolog (MOP), *369*
pharmacology, 200, 209, 219, 221, 224,
228, 230, 231, 238
psychomimetic activity, 133
pharmacology of, 101, 201–203, 204, 213,
222, 228, 322
n-propyl homolog, pharmacology, 203,
204
psychomimetic activity of, 101, 119, 124,
130
stability of, 21
as standard, 195–196, 198
sulfur homolog of, *126*
psychomimetic activity, 126, 127
synthesis of, 34–38, 107
toxicity of, 236–237
as unnatural product, 38
Δ⁴-iso-Tetrahydrocannabinol, from cannabidiol cyclization, 62
Δ⁴⁽⁸⁾-iso-Tetrahydrocannabinol, *23*
from cannabidiol cyclization, 62
from cannabichromene cyclization, 63, 65
NMR studies on, 97
Δ⁵-Tetrahydrocannabinol, *119*
inactivity of, 119, 130
Δ⁶-Tetrahydrocannabinol, *19, 47, 74, 79,*
118, 154, *169,* 171, *177,* 367

acetate, activity of, 119
6-acetoxy derivatives of, *122*
inactivity, 122
acetyl derivative of, *121*
inactivity, 121
from cannabidiol irradiation, 75
in cannabinol samples, 7
in cannabis plant material
variations in, 89
yield, 142
carbomethoxy derivatives of, 120, 121
inactivity, 120, 121
chemobotany of, 13
configuration of, 28
dehydrogenation of, 72
derivatives
psychomimetic activity, 102, 118–129
SAR studies, 124–126
1″,2″-dimethylheptyl homolog of, *120*
psychomimetic activity, 120, 124
1″,2″-dimethylpentyl homolog of, *120*
psychomimetic activity, 120
ethyl derivatives of, *121, 122*
psychomimetic activity, 121, 122
extraction of, 152
fetal effects of, 241
gas-liquid chromatography of, 146
C-glucosidation of, 97
hexyl homolog of, *119*
pharmacology, 206
psychomimetic activity, 119, 124
hydroboration of, 80
hydrogenation of, 78
hydroxy derivatives of, *122,* 268
psychotomimetic activity, 122
infrared spectroscopy of, 151
isolation of, 11, 21–22
from isomerization of Δ¹-THC, 61
isomers, pharmacology, 118, 258
metabolism and metabolites of, 56–60,
93, 94–95, 172–181, *177,* 185, *187,* 243,
268
methyl derivatives of, *121, 122*
psychomimetic activity, 121, 122
methyl ether, inactivity of, 119
1″-methylpentyl homolog of, *119*
psychomimetic activity, 119
NMR studies on, 97
optical rotation of, 9
oxidation of, 74

Δ^6-Tetrahydrocannabinol—*continued*
pharmacology of, 201, 205, 206, 208, 216, 217–218, 222, 226, 229, 231, 232, 248, 277
photolability of double bond in, 76
psychotomimetic activity of, 115, 116, 117
SAR studies, 124–125
standard dosage, 106
quinone, *121*
psychomimetic activity, 121
radiolabeled, 153, 181, 189
with carbon-14, 171–172, 189
positions labeled, 168, 183
synthesis, 172
with tritium, 169–171
stability of, 63, 72–73, 97, 151
stereochemistry of, 22
synthesis of, 38–50, 90, 91, 115
from Δ^1-THC isomerization, 70
tolerance to, 254
toxicity of, 236–237, 271
trans-isomer, formation, 65
uv spectroscopy of, 149
Δ^6-3,4-*cis*-Tetrahydrocannabinol, NMR studies on, 97
Δ^7-Tetrahydrocannabinol
inactivity of, 119, 130
pharmacology of, 249
Δ^9-Tetrahydrocannabinol, *3*
Δ^1-Tetrahydrocannabinol acetate, *59, 79, 93*
cis-isomer, formation of, 63
epoxidation of, 78–79
hydroboration of, 79–80
as metabolite precursor, 59, 93
Δ^6-Tetrahydrocannabinol acetate, *94*
epoxidation of, 78
as metabolite precursor, 94
oxidation of, 74–75
reaction with osmium tetroxide, 80
Δ^8-*cis*-iso-Tetrahydrocannabinol, *76*
formation of, 63
from cannabidiol irradiation, 75–76
Δ^3-Tetrahydrocannabinol menthoxyacetate, formation and properties of, 35
Δ^1-Tetrahydrocannabinolic acid A, *27, 28, 30, 54, 148, 367*
biosynthesis of, 30
cannabinolic acid from, 31
gas-liquid chromatography of, 147–148
inactivity of, 116

isolation of, 10, 11
photochemical conversion to cannabinolic acid, 77
structure studies on, 26–27
storage effects on, 68
thermal reactions of, 68
uv spectrosopy of, 149
Δ^1-Tetrahydrocannabinolic acid B, *27, 28, 367*
chemobotany of, 13
gas-liquid chromatography of, 147–148
inactivity of, 116, 117
isolation of, 10
reactions of, 65
structure studies on, 26–27
Tetrahydrocannabolic acids, *367*
in cannabis evaluation, 88
in cannabis plant material, 149
variations in, 89
chemobotany of, 12
configuration of, 28
gas-liquid chromatography of, 147–148
inactivity of, 251
thermal reactions of, 68
in marijuana and hashish, 70, 147
thin-layer chromatography of, 88, 145, 163
Tetrahydrocannabinol-7-oic acids, as THC metabolites, synthesis and structures of, 96–97
Δ^1-Tetrahydrocannabinol-7-oic acids, hydroxylated, lack of psychobiological activity, 97
in urine, determination, 164
Δ^6-Tetrahydrocannabinol-7-oic acid, *96*
absence of psychobiological activity in, 97
synthesis of, 96
Δ^6-Tetrahydrocannabinol-5-ol
as Δ^6-THC metabolite, 93
psychobiological activity, 94
synthesis of, 93
Δ^1-Tetrahydrocannabinol-6-one
as THC metabolite, 93
synthesis of, 93
Δ^6-Tetrahydrocannabinol-5-one
as Δ^6-THC metabolite, 93
psychobiological activity, 94
synthesis of, 93
Δ^1-Tetrahydrocannabiorcol, occurrence of, 88

Tetrahydrocannabitriol ester of cannabidiolic acid, 24–25, *25*, *368*
.configuration, 28
isolation, 10–11
Tetrahydrocannabivarin, 3
Tetrahydrocannabivarol
in cannabis preparations, 195
chemobotany of, 13
isolation of, 21
pharmacological activity of, 116, 117
synthesis of, 49
Δ^6-Tetrahydrocannabolic acid, methyl ester, *82*
reduction of, 82
Δ^6-Tetrahydrocannabinolic acid, methyl ether, *96*
synthesis of, 96
Tetrahydrodibenzofuran, *75*
from olivetyl pinene, 75
THC, *see* Tetrahydrocannabinols
Thermal reactions, of cannabinoids, 67–71
Thin-layer chromatography
cannabidiolic and THC acids, isolation by, 88
of cannabinoids, 144–146, 152–153, 163
radiolabeled, 153
in urine, 154, 163
"Thinker position"
from cannabinoids, in monkeys, 206
Thiopentone, cannabinoid comparison to, 203
Thirst, cannabinoid effects on, 205
Thought processes, cannabis effects on, 305–308
Thyroid hormones, cannabinoid effects on activity of, 224–225, 253
Thyrotropin-releasing factor (TRF), cannabinoid effects on, 225
Time, cannabinoid effect on concept of, 266, 297–301
Tincture of cannabis, 195
Tobacco, from cigarettes, as cannabis test interferent, 145, 159
Tolerance, to cannabinoids, 253–257, 267, 353, 354–355
p-Toluenesulfonic acid
in isomerization of Δ^1-THC, 169, 171
in tlc of urinary cannabinoids, 154
m-Toluic acid, *14*
from cannabinol, 15

Toxicity
of cannabinoids, 235–241, 271–272
acute toxicity, 235–238, 271
chronic toxicity, 238, 271–272
lethal dosages, 239
to man, 357–361
Tremor, from cannabis use, 317–319
Trifluoroacetyl esters, of cannabinoids, for glc, 159
Trigeminal stimulation, effect of THC on, 219–220
Trigonelline, in cannabis, 6, 138
Trimellitic acid, *15*
in cannabinol structure studies, 15
Trimethylsilylacetamide, use in glc of cannabinoids, 146, 159
Trinitrocannabinol, *14*
in cannabinol structure studies, 13–15
early research on, 7
Tritium, as cannabinoid label, 153, 169–171
Tween 80
as cannabinoid solvent, 193–194

U

Ultraviolet spectroscopy, of cannabinoids, 149–150
Unreality, sensations of, from cannabis, 308–309
Urine
cannabinoids in
determination, 154, 162–163, 164, 243
extraction, 162
metabolite excretion in, 173–174, 178–180, 184, 185, 243, 244, 250

V

Vagal stimulation, cannabinoid effects on, 276
Vanillin, in Duquénois-Negm reagent, 143
Vasodilatation, genital, from cannabis, 315
Vasomotor depression, from cannabinoids, 253
Verbenol, *49*
in THC syntheses, 48–49, 91
for radiolabeling, 189
Visceral effects, of cannabis, 324–326
Visual perception, cannabis effects on, 291–293, 296–297

Vomiting, from cannabinoids, 225–226, 253, 324

W

"Wavelike" action, of cannabis, 289
Waxes, in cannabis, 138–139

Withdrawal symptoms, of cannabis, 253, 279–280, 353, 356
Wittig reaction, in THC synthesis, 43
Wolf-Kischner reagent, in olivetol synthesis, 107
Wolf-Kischner reduction, in cannabinoid reactions, 78